ROYAL HITTITE INSTRUCTIONS

AND RELATED ADMINISTRATIVE TEXTS

Society of Biblical Literature

Writings from the Ancient World

Theodore J. Lewis, General Editor

Associate Editors

Billie Jean Collins
Daniel Fleming
Martti Nissinen
William Schniedewind
Mark S. Smith
Emily Teeter
Terry Wilfong

Number 31
Royal Hittite Instructions and Related Administrative Texts

ROYAL HITTITE INSTRUCTIONS
AND RELATED ADMINISTRATIVE TEXTS

by Jared L. Miller

Edited by Mauro Giorgieri

Society of Biblical Literature
Atlanta

ROYAL HITTITE INSTRUCTIONS AND RELATED ADMINISTRATIVE TEXTS

Library of Congress Cataloging-in-Publication Data

Royal Hittite instructions and related administrative texts / edited by Jared L. Miller.
pages cm. — (Writings from the ancient world / Society of Biblical Literature ; Number 33)
Includes bibliographical references and index.
ISBN 978-1-58983-769-0 (hardcover binding : alk. paper) — ISBN 978-1-58983-656-3 (paper binding : alk. paper) — ISBN 978-1-58983-657-0 (electronic format)
1. Hittites—Rites and ceremonies—Sources. 2. Hittites—Kings and rulers—Sources. 3. Oaths—Middle East. 4. Hittite language—Texts. 5. Inscriptions, Hittite. I. Miller, Jared L., author, editor.
DS66.R69 2013
939'.3—dc23
2013004122

Printed on acid-free, recycled paper conforming to ANSI/NISO Z39.48-1992 (R1997) and ISO 9706:1994 standards for paper permanence.

Contents

Series Editor's Foreword ix

Acknowledgments xi

Hittite Kings and Approximate Dates B.C.E. xii

Notes on Transliterations xiii

Signs and Conventions xv

Abbreviations xvii

Introduction

Hittite Instructions and Oath Impositions (and Related Administrative Texts) 1

Defining the Genre(s) 1

Defining the Corpus 9

A Brief History of Research 13

Origins and Development of the Obligation and Oath Texts 15

Envisioning the Setting 23

Terminology and Formulae 27

Notes on Literary Form, Style, and Structure 32

The Instructions as a Source for Hittite History, Religion, Society, and Thought 43

The Tablets and Their Scribes and Archives 55

Ancient Near Eastern Parallels 65

Chapter 1: Old Kingdom Sources

1. A Royal Reprimand of the Dignitaries (*CTH* 272) 73
2. Instructions and Oath Imposition for Royal Servants concerning the Purity of the King (*CTH* 265) 78
3. Protocol for the Palace Gatekeeper (*CTH* 263) 88
4. Protocol for the Royal Body Guard (*CTH* 262) 98
5. Royal Decree on Social and Economic Matters (*CTH* 269) 122
6. An Akkadian Fragment Mentioning an Oath (*CTH* 275) 126

CHAPTER 2: SOURCES FROM THE REIGNS OF TUDḪALIYA I AND ARNUWANDA I
7. Instructions for Military Officers and Frontier Post Governors (*CTH* 261.II) 129
8. Tudḫaliya I's Decree on Penal and Administrative Reform (*CTH* 258.1) 134
9. Tudḫaliya I's Decree on Judicial Reform (*CTH* 258.2) 140
10. Tudḫaliya I?'s Instructions and Oath Imposition for All the Men (*CTH* 259) 144
11. Instructions and Oath Impositions for the Successions of Tudḫaliya I and Tudḫaliya III (*CTH* 271) 154
12. Instructions and Oath Imposition for Princes, Lords, and Military Officers (*CTH* 251) 168
13. Instructions of Arnuwanda I for the Mayor (of Ḫattusa) (*CTH* 257) 182
14. Loyalty Oath of Town Commanders to Arnuwanda I, Ašmunikkal, and Tudḫaliya (*CTH* 260) 194
15. Instructions and Oath Imposition(s) of Arnuwanda I (*CTH* 275) 206
16. Decree of Queen Ašmunikkal concerning the "Royal Funerary Structure" (*CTH* 252) 208
17. Instructions of Arnuwanda I for the Frontier Post Governors (*CTH* 261.I) 212
18. Instructions and Oath Imposition for Military Commanders (*CTH* 268) 238
19. Āsḫapāla's Oath Regarding an Obligation to Supply Troops (*CTH* 270) 242
20. Instructions for Priests and Temple Personnel (*CTH* 264) 244

CHAPTER 3: EMPIRE PERIOD SOURCES
21. Instructions for Supervisors (*CTH* 266) 267
22. Instructions of Suppiluliuma I for the Military and a Corresponding Oath (*CTH* 253) 270
23. Oath of the Men of Ḫattusa to Ḫattusili III and Pudu-Ḫepa (*CTH* 254) 274
24. Instructions for Priests and Diviners (*CTH* 275) 276
25. Instructions for the UKU.UŠ-Troops (*CTH* 267) 280
26. Tudḫaliya IV's Instructions and Loyalty Oath Imposition for Lords, Princes, and Courtiers (*CTH* 255.1) 282
27. Tudḫaliya IV's Instructions and Oath Imposition for Courtiers (*CTH* 255.2) 294

28. Suppiluliu/ama II's Instructions and Oath Imposition for the Men of Ḫattusa (*CTH* 256) 308

Sources 315
Notes 323
References 415
Index of Divine Names 447
Index of Personal Names 448
Index of Geographical Names 450

Series Editor's Foreword

Writings from the Ancient World is designed to provide up-to-date, readable English translations of writings recovered from the ancient Near East.

The series is intended to serve the interests of general readers, students, and educators who wish to explore the ancient Near Eastern roots of Western civilization or to compare these earliest written expressions of human thought and activity with writings from other parts of the world. It should also be useful to scholars in the humanities or social sciences who need clear, reliable translations of ancient Near Eastern materials for comparative purposes. Specialists in particular areas of the ancient Near East who need access to texts in the scripts and languages of other areas will also find these translations helpful. Given the wide range of materials translated in the series, different volumes will appeal to different interests. However, these translations make available to all readers of English the world's earliest traditions as well as valuable sources of information on daily life, history, religion, and the like in the preclassical world.

The translators of the various volumes in this series are specialists in the particular languages and have based their work on the original sources and the most recent research. In their translations they attempt to convey as much as possible of the original texts in fluent, current English. In the introductions, notes, glossaries, maps, and chronological tables, they aim to provide the essential information for an appreciation of these ancient documents.

The ancient Near East reached from Egypt to Iran and, for the purposes of our volumes, ranged in time from the invention of writing (by 3000 B.C.E.) to the conquests of Alexander the Great (ca. 330 B.C.E.). The cultures represented within these limits include especially Egyptian, Sumerian, Babylonian, Assyrian, Hittite, Ugaritic, Aramean, Phoenician, and Israelite. It is hoped that Writings from the Ancient World will eventually produce translations from most of the many different genres attested in these cultures: letters (official and private), myths, diplomatic documents, hymns, law collections, monumental inscriptions, tales, and administrative records, to mention but a few.

Significant funding was made available by the Society of Biblical Literature for the preparation of this volume. In addition, those involved in preparing this volume have received financial and clerical assistance from their respective institutions. Were it not for these expressions of confidence in our work, the arduous tasks of preparation, translation, editing, and publication could not have been accomplished or even undertaken. It is the hope of all who have worked with the Writings from the Ancient World series that our translations will open up new horizons and deepen the humanity of all who read these volumes.

Theodore J. Lewis
The Johns Hopkins University

ACKNOWLEDGMENTS

I would like first of all to thank Mauro Giorgieri, whose thorough reading of the manuscript and countless comments, suggestions and corrections were simply invaluable. My appreciation is also due to all those scholars who have worked on these texts before me, whose efforts made possible any further progress made in these pages. I would also like to thank Billie Jean Collins for originally suggesting that I treat the Instructions for the Writings from the Ancient World series and her tireless and patient aid during the production process, as well as Ted Lewis for his constant support as the volume developed.

I would further like to express my appreciation to Gernot Wilhelm and the rest of the team of the section "Hethitische Forschungen" at the Akademie der Wissenschaften und der Literatur in Mainz, i.e., Silvin Košak, Gerfrid Müller, Francesco Fuscagni and Gabriella Stivala, for making available the wonderful resources of the Portal, and above all the *Konkordanz*, which have revolutionized the field of Hittitology. Those who have selflessly contributed various invaluable materials to the Portal should also be recognized and thanked, i.e. Natalia Bolatti Guzzo, Paola Dardano, Rita Francia, Detlev Groddek, Massimiliano Marazzi, Jana Součková and Marie-Claude Trémouille.

I would also like to thank my colleagues Birgit Christiansen, Elena Devecchi, Amir Gilan, Federico Giusfredi, Joost Hazenbos, Alwin Kloekhorst, Elisabeth Rieken and Andrej Sidel'tsev for valuable discussions and suggestions on various matters relating to the texts presented here. Special thanks go to Itamar Singer for reading a final draft copy and for his many insightful comments and corrections. Rukiye Akdoğan deserves particular appreciation for her constant willingness to check tablets and take photos in the museum in Ankara. Chiara Cognetti has earned my appreciation for her diligent cross-checking and proofing, as has Sophie Cohen for her carefully creating the indices.

Sincere thanks are due as well to Walther Sallaberger, who has created and maintained an environment at the Institut für Assyriologie and Hethitologie at the LMU München that is so conducive to quality work and research.

Hittite Kings and Approximate Dates B.C.E.

As the Hittites employed no calendrical system in their textual sources, Hittite chronology is heavily dependent on the Assyrian, Egyptian and Babylonian chronologies, which themselves contain their own uncertainties, and all dates provided here are therefore (sometimes rather rough) approximations only. The dates assume (1) a fall of Babylon around 1545 (see, e.g., Boese 2008: 209 and n. 28); (2) that no Ḫattusili II is to be placed among the predecessors of Suppiluliuma I; (3) that only two Tudḫaliyas (I and III$^{!}$) reigned before Suppiluliuma I, whereby Tudḫaliya III nevertheless retains his conventional numbering; (4) that evidence is presently insufficient for placing Kantuzili (father of Tudḫaliya I), Tudḫaliya the Younger (son of Tudḫaliya III and brother of Suppiluliuma I), or Kuruntiya (son of Muwattalli II and king of Tarḫuntassa) among the Hittite kings, though all three are very real possibilities. For recent summaries of the chronological situation see Beckman 2000; Bryce 2005: 375–82; Pruzsinszky 2009. For periodization, see p. xvi.

Ḫuzziya	
Labarna	
Ḫattusili I	ca. 1590s–1560s
Mursili I	ca. 1560s–1540s
Ḫantili I	
Zidanta I	
Ammuna	
Ḫuzziya I	
Telipinu	ca. 1480s–1460s
Alluwamna	
Ḫantili II	
Taḫurwaili	
Zidanza II	
Ḫuzziya II	
Muwattalli I	
Tudḫaliya I	ca. 1420s–1390s
Arnuwanda I	ca. 1390s–1370s
Tudḫaliya III	ca. 1370s–1350s
Suppiluliuma I	ca. 1355–1330
Arnuwanda II	ca. 1330
Mursili II	ca. 1330–1300
Muwattalli II	ca. 1300–1280
Mursili III / Urḫi-Teššub	ca. 1280–1273
Ḫattusili III	ca. 1273–1245
Tudḫaliya IV	ca. 1245–1210
Arnuwanda III	ca. 1210–1208
Suppiluliu/ama II	ca. 1208–1190

Notes on Transliterations

1. Since Hittite is a Subject-Object-Verb language, while English employs a Subject-Verb-Object order, and since Hittite places most pronouns at the beginning of the sentence, it is often difficult or impossible to keep all the elements of the English translation in the same line as the Hittite source if one provides a line-for-line translation, unless one violently manipulates the English syntax, as Beckman (1983), e.g., decided to do with his translations of the birth rituals. For the same reasons, if one employs normal English syntax but chooses nevertheless to insert superscripted line numbers into the translation, as has been done in the present volume, it is impossible to insert each and every line number without discrepancies. The translations here are thus provided with a line number if and when the Hittite and English syntax allows.
2. The basis of the transliterations in this volume is, when available, photographs of the original tablets, and failing these, then the published hand copies. When it was possible to arrive at a better reading on the basis of the photographs vis-à-vis a published hand copy, it has not always been noted, so that there will occasionally be discrepancies between the transliterations and the hand copies.
3. As Streck (2006: 228–33) has shown, the combinations /t+š/, /d+š/ and /ṭ+š/ yield affricates in Akkadian. Cases such as É-*ZU* (*bīt+šu*) are therefore transliterated with the signs of the Z-series (e.g., É-*ZU*) rather than with those of the S-series (e.g., É-*SÚ*), as is traditional.
4. An AḪ sign whose vowel cannot be determined is transliterated *Vḫ*.
5. The present volume treats ^{URU}*ḪA.AT.TI* and ^{URU}*ḪAT.TI* as logographic writings, which seems quite certain to be the case, and also assumes that "Ḫattusa" and, for KUR ^{URU}*ḪA.AT.TI*/*ḪAT.TI*, "Land of Ḫattusa," would in general be the appropriate reading, as this seems also to at least generally have been the case, though not certain in every instance (see Starke 1996: 153 and n. 54; Weeden 2011: 244–50).

6. Only substantial variants in duplicate mss. are noted, either in footnotes or, if warranted, by placing them side by side (No. 2, §§13″–14″; No. 14, §§1–21, 23′, 26′; No. 17, §§11, 16, 27, 54–55).

Signs and Conventions

ut-ni	Lower case italics in the transcriptions represent phonetically spelled words.
KUR	Small capitals represent logograms derived from the Sumerian language.
MA-AT	Small capitals in italics separated by hyphens represent logograms derived from the Akkadian language.
ḪA.AT.TI	Small capitals in italics separated by periods represent logographically written (generally Anatolian) words, usually proper names. This represents a slight innovation vis-à-vis common conventions, allowing the necessary distinction between logographically and phonetically written PNs, GNs, and DNs, while avoiding using the same convention, i.e., small caps in italics separated by hyphens, for what are in fact two distinct categories, namely, logographic writings derived from Akkadian words and logographic writings of Anatolian words.
URU	Determinatives and the plural markers ḪI.A and MEŠ are superscripted, whereby the determinatives DINGIR, MUNUS and DIŠ/I are abbreviated ^{d}, ^{f}, and ^{m}, respectively.
AN	Full-sized capitals represent the sign itself (as opposed to any of its readings) and/or signs that can be read but not interpreted, e.g., if it is uncertain whether an AN should be read DINGIR, *an* or ^{d}.
⊀, ⊀⊀	A so-called *Glossenkeil*, i.e., a single or a double wedge used by the scribe to indicate, generally, a word of foreign, most often Luwian, origin.
x	Illegible sign/traces.
< >	Scribal omission; enclosed sign to be inserted.
{ }	Errant scribal insertion; enclosed sign to be ignored.
* *	Indicate signs written over an erasure or over other sign traces.
?	Reading/restoration of sign uncertain.
(?)	Reading/restoration of word/phrase uncertain.

!	Nonstandard or errant sign, to be read as given in ensuing parentheses. The exclamation and question marks are sometimes used together when a sign should seemingly be read as given, but the traces do not seem to be amenable to the suggestion.
′	Accompanies line numbering that does not begin with the tablet's or column's original first line.
″	Accompanies line numbering following a further gap (or gaps) of uncertain length.
[ ]	Indicate break in text; signs partially enclosed are partially preserved.
⸤ ⸥, ⸢ ⸣	Half brackets indicate damaged but readable signs, the upper brackets suggesting the damage is more on the upper, the lower more on the lower portion of the sign
[x x]	Break of approximately x signs.
[...]	Length of break indeterminate or not provided.
( )	1. In transcriptions, parentheses enclose a) signs restored from a duplicate when placed within square brackets, and b) the sign actually present on the tablet when an alternative reading, indicated with an exclamation mark, is preferred instead. 2. In translations, they enclose elements necessary for a sensible English translation, but not employed or required by the source language.
~	Signals "uncertain/possible hyphen" in transliteration.
italic	An English word in italics in the translations indicates an uncertain interpretation.
+	Indicates a direct join between two tablet fragments.
++	Indicates direct joins among three or more tablet fragments.
(+)	Indicates that fragments are assumed to belong to the same tablet but do not join directly.
//	Indicates duplicate texts.
ā, ē, ī, ū	Plene writings of Hittite words when rendered in transcription are provided with the macron, which is thus intended to indicated no more than the graphic plene writing.

ABBREVIATIONS

GENERAL

abl.	ablative
Akk.	Akkadian
acc.	accusative
act.	active
comm.	(genus) commune
dem.	demonstrative
d.l.	dative-locative
DN	divine name
dupl.	duplicate
eras.	erasure
fut.	future
gen.	genitive
GN	geographical name
Hitt.	Hittite
imp.	imperative
indic.	indicative
inf.	infinitive
instr.	instrumental
lit.	literally/literature
LNH	Late New Hittite
loc.	locative
MB	Middle Babylonian
med.-pass.	medio-passive
MH	Middle Hittite
ms./mss.	manuscript/manuscripts
nom.	nominative
neut.	(genus) neutrum
NH	New Hittite

OB	Old Babylonian
obv.	obverse
OH	Old Hittite
pl.	plural
PN	personal name
poss.	possessive
pres.	present
pret.	preterite
pron.	pronoun
refl.	reflexive
rev.	reverse
RN	royal name
sg.	singular
Sum.	Sumerian
tant.	tantum

The use of the abbreviations OH, MH, NH, and LNH can be confusing not only to nonspecialists, but even to Hittitologists, first because they can refer either to historical periods or to paleographical dating of mss., and second, because both the periodization of Hittite history and views on the particulars of paleographical dating vary from school to school, sometimes even from scholar to scholar. In the current volume, OH, MH, and NH are used in the historical sense to refer to the periods from Labarna and Ḫattusili I to Telipinu, from Alluwamna to Tudḫaliya III, and from Suppiluliuma I to Suppiluliu/ama II, respectively, while OH, MH, NH and LNH refer, when relating to paleography, to the periods, respectively, from the beginning of Hittite cuneiform writing to the immediate predecessors of Tudḫaliya I, from ca. Tudḫaliya I to ca. Suppiluliuma I, from ca. Suppiluliuma I to ca. Ḫattusili III, and from ca. Ḫattusili III to Suppiluliu/ama II.

BIBLIOGRAPHICAL

AASOR 16	*One Hundred New Selected Nuzi Texts.* Transliterated by R. H. Pfeiffer, with translations and commentary by E. A. Speiser. Annual of the American Schools of Oriental Research 16. New Haven, 1936
ABoT	Ankara Arkeoloji Müzesinde Bulunan Boğazköy Tabletleri
AfO	*Archiv für Orientforschung*
AHw	*Akkadisches Handwörterbuch*
AJNES	*Aramazd. Armenian Journal of Near Eastern Studies*
AnSt	*Anatolian Studies. Journal of the British Institute of Archaeology at Ankara*

AOAT	Alter Orient und Altes Testament
AoF	*Altorientalische Forschungen*
AOS	American Oriental Series
ArAn	*Archivum Anatolicum*
ARM	Archives Royales de Mari
ArOr	*Archív Orientální*
AS	Assyriological Studies
AuOr	*Aula Orientalis. Revista de estudios del Próximo Oriente Antiguo*
Belleten	*Türk Tarih Kurumu Belleten*
BiOr	*Bibliotheca Orientalis*
BMECCJ	*Bulletin of the Middle Eastern Culture Center in Japan*
Bo	Inventory numbers of the tablets and fragments excavated at Boğazköy / Ḫattusa between 1906–1912
BoSt	Boghazköi-Studien
CAD	*The Assyrian Dictionary of the Oriental Institute of the University of Chicago*. Chicago, 1956–
CANE	*Civilizations of the Ancient Near East*. Edited by Jack M. Sasson. New York, 1995.
CHD	*The Hittite Dictionary of the Oriental Institute of the University of Chicago*. Chicago, 1980–
CLL	*Cuneiform Luvian Lexicon*
CM	Cuneiform Monographs
CTH	*Catalogue des textes hittites*; supplements in *RHA* 30 (1972) 94–133 and *RHA* 33 (1975) 68–71
DBH	Dresdner Beiträge zur Hethitologie
DMOA	Documenta et Monumenta Orientis Antiqui
EDHIL	Kloekhorst, Alwin. *Etymological Dictionary of the Hittite Inherited Lexicon*. Leiden, 2008.
Eothen	Collana di studi sulle civiltà dell'Oriente antico
FHL	Fragments hittites du Louvre
GrHL	Hoffner, Harry A., Jr. and H. Craig Melchert. *A Grammar of the Hittite Language*. Winona Lake, IN, 2008
HANE/M	History of the Ancient Near East / Monographs
HBM	*Hethitische Briefe aus Maşat-Höyük*. Ankara, 1991
HdO	Handbuch der Orientalistik
HED	Jaan Puhvel. *Hittite Etymological Dictionary*. Berlin, 1984–
HEG	Tischler, Johann. *Hethitisches etymologisches Glossar*. Innsbruck, 1977–
HHw	Tischler, J. *Hethitisches Handwörterbuch* (2nd ed.).

	Innsbruck, 2008
HS	*Historische Sprachforschung*
HSS	Harvard Semitic Studies
HT	*Hittite Texts in the Cuneiform Character from the Tablets in the British Museum*
*HW*²	Friedrich, J. and A. Kammenhuber. *Hethitisches Wörterbuch* (2nd ed.). Heidelberg, 1975
HZL	Rüster, C. and E. Neu *Hethitisches Zeichenlexikon: Inventar und Interpretation der Keilschriftzeichen aus den Boğazköy-Texten.* StBoT Beifheft 2. Wiesbaden, 1989
IBoT	İstanbul Arkeoloji Müzelerinde bulunan Boğazköy Tabletleri(nden Seçme Metinler)
IBS	Innsbrucker Beiträge zur Sprachwissenschaft
IF	*Indogermanische Forschungen*
IL	*Incontri Linguistici. Rivista delle Università degli Studi di Trieste e di Udine*
IstMitt	*Istanbuler Mitteilungen*
JAC	*Journal of Ancient Civilizations*
JANER	*Journal of Ancient Near Eastern Religions*
JAOS	*Journal of the American Oriental Society*
JCS	*Journal of Cuneiform Studies*
JEOL	*Jaarbericht van het Vooraziatisch-Egyptisch Gezelschap "Ex Oriente Lux"*
JESHO	*Journal of the Economic and Social History of the Orient*
JNES	*Journal of Near Eastern Studies*
KASKAL	*KASKAL: Rivista di Storia, Ambiente e Culture del Vicino Oriente Antico*
KBo	Keilschrifttexte aus Boghazköi
Konkordanz	Konkordanz der hethitischen Keilschrifttafeln: http://www.hethport.uni-wuerzburg.de/hetkonk/
KUB	Keilschrifturkunden aus Boghazköi
LAPO	Littératures anciennes du Proche-Orient
MAOG	*Mitteilungen der Altorientalischen Gesellschaft*
MDOG	*Mitteilungen der Deutschen Orient-Gesellschaft zu Berlin*
MesCiv	Mesopotamian Civilizations
MesZL	*Mesopotamisches Zeichenlexikon*
MIO	*Mitteilungen des Instituts für Orientforschung*
MSS	*Münchener Studien zur Sprachwissenschaft*
NABU	*Nouvelles Assyriologiques Brèves et Utilitaires*
OBO	Orbis Biblicus et Orientalis

OLZ	*Orientalistische Literaturzeitung*
OrNS	*Orientalia Nova Series*
PIHANS	Publication de l'Institut Historique et Archéologique Néerlandais de Stamboul
RAnt	*Res Antique*
RGTC	Répertoire Géographique des Textes Cunéiformes
RHA	*Revue hittite et asianique*
RlA	*Reallexikon der Assyriologie*
RO	*Rocznik orientalistyczny*
SCCNH	Studies on the Civilization and Culture of Nuzi and the Hurrians
SMEA	*Studi Micenei ed Egeo-Anatolici*
StAs	Studia Asiana
StBoT	Studien zu den Boğazköy-Texten
StBoT Beih.	Studien zu den Boğazköy-Texten Beiheft
StMed	Studia Mediterranea
THeth	Texte der Hethiter
TUAT	Texte aus der Umwelt des Alten Testaments
TUAT Erg.	Texte aus der Umwelt des Alten Testaments, Ergänzungslieferung
TUATNF	Texte aus der Umwelt des Alten Testaments, Neue Folge
UF	*Ugarit-Forschungen*
VO	*Vicino Oriente*
VSNF	Vorderasiatische Schriftdenkmäler der Staatlichen Museen zu Berlin, Neue Folge
WAW	Writings from the Ancient World
WdO	*Die Welt des Orients*
WZKM	*Wiener Zeitschrift für die Kunde des Morgenlandes*
Xenia	Konstanzer Althistorische Vorträge und Forschungen
ZA	*Zeitschrift für Assyriologie und vorderasiatische Archäologie*
ZABR	*Zeitschrift für Altorientalische und Biblische Rechtsgeschichte*
ZvS	*Zeitschrift für vergleichende Sprachforschung*

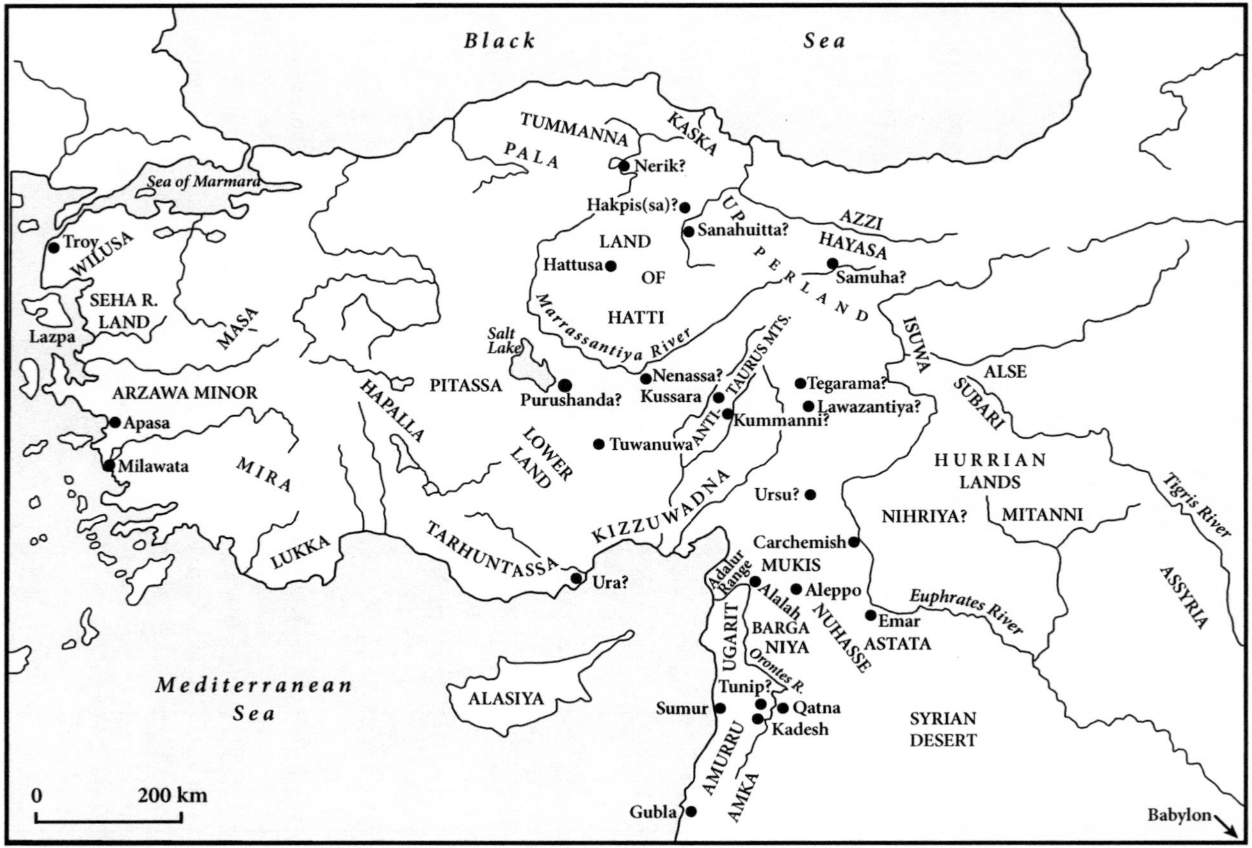
Black Sea
TUMMANNA
KASKA
PALA
Nerik?
Sea of Marmara
Hakpis(sa)?
UPPER LAND
AZZI
Sanahuitta?
HAYASA
Troy
WILUSA
LAND OF HATTI
Hattusa
Samuha?
SEHA R. LAND
MASA
Lazpa
Marrassantiya River
Salt Lake
ISUWA
TAURUS MTS.
ANTI-
ALSE
PITASSA
Nenassa?
Tegarama?
HAPALLA
Purushanda?
Kussara
Lawazantiya?
SUBARI
ARZAWA MINOR
Kummanni?
Apasa
LOWER LAND
Tuwanuwa
HURRIAN LANDS
Milawata
MIRA
Ursu?
Tigris River
NIHRIYA?
MITANNI
TARHUNTASSA
KIZZUWADNA
Carchemish
LUKKA
MUKIS
Adalur Range
Aleppo
ASSYRIA
Ura?
Alalah
Euphrates River
NUHASSE
Emar
BARGA
NIYA
ASTATA
UGARIT
Orontes R.
ALASIYA
Mediterranean Sea
Tunip?
Sumur
Qatna
Kadesh
SYRIAN DESERT
AMURRU
AMKA
0
200 km
Gubla
Babylon

Introduction

The texts presented in this volume were composed in the Hittite language (except for No. 6) and written with the Hittite variant of the Mesopotamian cuneiform script, which was impressed upon clay tablets. They were all found, as far as can be determined, among the remains of the archives of Ḫattusa, the capital of the Hittite Empire (ca. 1600–1190 B.C.E.), located next to the modern village of Boğazkale (formerly Boğazköy), ca. 135 km east of Ankara.[1] These archives are nearly exclusively royal collections, thus reflecting royal interests and perspectives, and this is the case with the texts of the present volume as well. The common denominator among the Hittite instructions and oath impositions (and related administrative texts) presented here, which represent a rather diverse array of genres and typologies, is their role in defining and regulating the relationships between the royal institution and its subordinate personnel along with the duties and responsibilities of the latter. They are thus, in the broadest sense, administrative and normative compositions. Among these, those that can be seen as "obligation and oath" compositions form the core category both numerically and thematically, while a number of decrees and protocols have been included as well.

Hittite Instructions and Oath Impositions (and Related Administrative Texts)

Defining the Genre(s)

In its most essential form the Hittite "instruction" composition—the label by which they are most commonly known—consists of the royal prescription of a set of obligations or instructions (Hitt. *isḫiul-*) addressed to a professional class or classes within the internal state administration. Instructions in this distilled form, however, are rare; those that are labeled merely "instructions" in this volume are for the most part actually fragmentary sections of the much longer compositions that they represent (Nos. 7, 13, 17, 21, 24, 25) and presumably would have contained, or at least referred to, the other constitutive element of the genre as well, that is, the oath (Hitt. *lingai*). Most of the other documents often referred to as "instructions" and treated in this volume in fact include an oath imposition or oath prescription (or several) as well (Nos. 6[?], 10–12, 15.1, 18, 22, 26–28), or at least refer to one (No. 2, §8″). The oath of these texts, likewise prescribed by the king, would have been sworn by the subordinate(s) before the gods, who served as witnesses and guarantors to what was thus a unilateral contractual agreement. There seems to be no evidence in any of the compositions at hand suggesting that the king would have sworn a corresponding oath, though he seems to have, at least in some cases, sworn one or in some way to have been bound by one when concluding vassal treaties (Altman 2003; cf. Christiansen and Devecchi 2013, §A.4).[2]

The terms *isḫiul-*, "bond, obligation," and *lingai-*, "oath," are central to defining the genre. The first, *isḫiul-*, is derived from the verb *isḫai-/isḫiya-*, "to bind," and thus literally means "bond." It can be translated depending on context as "instruction," "obligation," "contract," or "treaty."[3] The second term, *lingai-*, "oath; curse," is likewise a deverbal substantive, from *link-*, "to swear."[4]

This combination, the prescription of obligations (*isḫiul-*) paired with the imposition or prescription of an oath (*lingai*), constitutes what the Hittites seemed to have regarded as a textual category, what one might call an "obligation and oath" genre; and it is this dual structure that distinguishes these "obligation and oath" documents from, for example, epistolary texts authored by the king, which often contain instructions in a style and pertaining to matters quite similar to what one might find in the "instructions," or from edicts, which are composed of similar normative, prescriptive statements, but are not connected with an oath or any other response on the part of the subordinate.[5]

"Instruction" seems therefore not to have been a textual category for the Hittites, but is a genre created by modern researchers into which more or less similar texts have been grouped. Naturally, this does not invalidate this Hittitological category, which can indeed be useful, but merely dates it. Those compositions that modern researchers refer to as such form part of a genre that Hittite scribes would have seen as obligation and oath texts and which, in fact, they labeled either as "obligation" (*isḫiul-*) or "oath" (*lingai-*) texts or, on occasion, both (e.g., No. 15.1).[6] Further, these terms were not used only for the texts concerning internal administration treated in this volume, but also for what are today regarded as state and vassal treaties. While differences can be observed between the texts we term "instructions" and those we label "treaties," which are therefore valid and useful modern categories, Hittite scribes referred to both with the same terms, *isḫiul-* and/or *lingai-*.[7] Both together, two sides of the same coin, constitute an obligation and oath composition. As noted elsewhere (Miller 2011b: 2),

> The Hittites apparently did not develop a category, or employ a word, for the summation of the two elements *isḫiul-* and *lingai-*. They refer to the combined "contract" or "treaty" always as the "obligation/bond" (*isḫiul-*), the "oath" (*lingai-*), or both. From this fact, however, one cannot necessarily deduce that these were two separate genres. Text categorization depends on the usage of words and concepts, not merely on the number of terms extant. One could contrast, e.g., Hittite usage of the designations SISKUR/SÍSKUR and $EZEN_4$, which can in fact be correlated not only with nearly exclusively discrete phenomena, but also with largely discrete textual categories. This is decidedly not the case with the distribution of *isḫiul-* and *lingai-*, which, though obviously referring to two different real-world phenomena, do not correlate well with distinct textual genres.

Upon reflection the Hittites' categorization of "instructions" and "treaties" together is more reasonable and coherent than it might seem at first glance, for the essence of all such "treaties," "contracts," and "instructions" was the sovereign's imposition of the obligations (the *isḫiul-*) upon the subordinate party, that is, the defining of its role and responsibilities within the state administrative structure, and the subordinate's requisite swearing of an oath to uphold those stipulations before the gods (the *lingai-*).[8] Naturally, this pattern could just as well apply, for example, to a Syrian or western Anatolian vassal king swearing allegiance to his Hittite sovereign as to civil servants in Ḫattusa promising to carry out their duties as the king expected them to do. That the Hittites indeed grouped "treaties" and "instructions/oaths" together is further illustrated by the fact that not only treaties such as that concluded between Tudḫaliya IV of Ḫatti and Kuruntiya of Tarḫuntassa were inscribed on tablets of metal, in this case bronze (Otten 1988), and placed in the temples of selected deities, so was at least No. 14 in the present volume, a Loyalty Oath of Town Commanders to Arnuwanda I, Ašmunikkal and Tudḫaliya (3.A, §2′), and one suspects that this was regularly or at least often the case (see Watanabe 1989).

Moreover, Giorgieri (2005: 323) has recently emphasized the Loyalty Oaths' "formale und strukturelle Ähnlichkeiten mit den eidlichen Abmachungen, die die Hethiter mit anatolischen Volksstämmen trafen wie etwa die sogenannten 'Kaškäer-Verträge' oder der 'Išmiriga-Vertrag,'" as well as with the "Treaty" with the Ḫabiru (*CTH* 27; Otten 1957; Giorgieri 1995: 69–89; Bemporad 2009) and the Loyalty Oath Imposition of Ḫattusili III (*CTH* 85.2; Giorgieri 1995: 268–73; Singer 2001b: 399–403). The "Treaty" with the Ḫabiru indeed contains all the elements of the typical obligation and oath composition:

it addresses the oath takers in the 2nd pl., sometimes employing a 3rd-person impersonal; some portions show the 1st pl., indicating what the oath takers were to enunciate; one section even slips into the 1st sg.; and it includes curses upon those that would break the oath. Moreover, the Ḫabiru seem likely to have constituted units associated with the Hittite military, and thus an entity within the state, not a foreign entity with which a "treaty" would have been ratified, as was the case with the Kaska. In the Loyalty Oath Imposition of Ḫattusili III, this sovereign requires all Ḫattusa to swear an oath to his own descendents rather than those of Mursili III / Urḫi-Teššub, whom he had deposed, as well as to Ulmi-Teššub / (Kuruntiya) in his role as king of the secundogeniture in Tarḫuntassa. The fragmentary text breaks off with a list of divine witnesses and either an oath imposition or the reciting of the oath in the 1st pl., now lost in the breaks.

Those compositions that land in the category obligation and oath are thus not just instructive or didactic texts, but are simultaneously legally binding administrative documents or contracts, which come into force upon the subordinate's swearing of an oath in front of its divine witnesses. In his treatment of the Hittite state treaties, which appeared already eighty years ago, Korošec (1931: 29) described these relationships clearly and concisely when he wrote, "*Išḫiul* ist der vom Großkönig aufgestellte Vertragsinhalt, der durch die nachfolgende Beeidigung (h. *lingaiš*) seitens des Vasallen zum rechtsverbindlichen Vertrag wird."[9] Indeed, this description is valid for essentially all the *isḫiul-* and *lingai-* texts, not just the treaties, which were the focus of Korošec's study. Those texts generally called "instructions" may sometimes emphasize more the obligations that the subordinates were to fulfill; the vassal treaties in addition emphasize in a "historical prologue" the relationship that has obtained between lord and servant; while the "military oaths" are concerned above all with the oath that the soldiers are to swear along with the rites and curse formulae connected with them. Nonetheless, all these compositions, which belong to such seemingly widely disparate categories to the modern reader, would have belonged to the same category, an obligation and oath genre, for the Hittite.

This approach to the "instructions" and "oaths," which is in fact the more traditional view, runs somewhat against the grain of some more recent research, which has tended to separate the "instructions" and the "(loyalty) oaths" into two separate genres (e.g., Pecchioli Daddi 2005b), even concluding that the Hittite scribes themselves maintained such a distinction and that they are therefore emic textual genres (p. 600). However, that Hittite scribes did not use the terms *isḫiul-* and *lingai-* to designate two distinct textual categories is shown, inter alia, by Pecchioli Daddi's (2002a: 266) own statement concerning Tudḫaliya I[?]'s Instructions and Oath Imposition for All the Men (No. 10), "which is called *išḫiul*" by its scribe in its colophon, "but, in reality, contains an imposition of oath," along with, one might add, a series of obligations. No. 9 could also be mentioned in this context, since its preserved paragraphs are most closely related to No. 8, suggesting that it should be categorized as an edict or decree, despite it being placed in the oath category by its colophon.

Giorgieri (2005: 323) has similarly emphasized the loyalty oaths' "große Abweichungen gegenüber den technischen, fast ausschließlich auf die mittelhethitische Zeit zurückgehenden, sogenannten 'Instruktionen' oder 'Dienstanweisungen,' die Aufgaben und dienstliche Verpflichtungen verschiedener Beamtengruppen systematisch und detailliert festlegen," and pleads for the "Ansatz einer besonderen Textgattung ... Beamten- und Bevölkerungseiden," which he characterizes as loyalty oaths (323–34). Presumably realizing that much speaks against such a segregation, Giorgieri (326, n. 17) wrote in the same paper that "alle Beamten- und Bevölkerungseide—darunter auch die Eide von Volksstämmen wie jene der Kaškäer—sowie die 'Vasallenverträge' ... als eine einzige Textform zu verstehen (sind)."

Starke (1995b: 75), on a similar tack to Pecchioli Daddi's, has asserted concerning Tudḫaliya IV's Instructions and Oath Imposition for Courtiers (No. 27) that "eigentlich schon ein allgemeiner Vergleich mit der *BĒL MADGALTI*-Instruktion (läßt) erkennen, daß sie mit dieser Textgattung nichts gemein haben," and that in Tudḫaliya's text, in contrast to the Instructions of Arnuwanda I for the Frontier Post Governors (No. 17, i.e., the *BĒL MADGALTI*-Instruction), "von dienstlichen Obliegenheiten der Prinzen, Herren und $^{LÚ.MEŠ}$SAG keine Rede (ist)." That this latter assertion is not entirely correct can be seen in Starke's following comments, where he writes, after pointing out that Tudḫaliya in the incipit imposes an oath upon the addressees (p. 76):

> Mit diesen Worten ist zugleich der Inhalt des Textes umrissen; denn die nachfolgenden Absätze bzw. Paragraphen spezifizieren—wie übrigens auch die Paragraphen des anderen, nicht in seinem Anfang erhaltenen Textes für Prinzen, Herren und $^{LÚ.MEŠ}$SAG!—lediglich die einzelnen Verpflichtungen, die sich aus der Loyalitätserklärung zugunsten des Königs und seiner Nachkommenschaft ergeben.

In other words, while in the incipit Tudḫaliya IV specifies the occasion on which the text was composed, namely, his coronation, and dictates (a perhaps abbreviated version of) the oath that his addressees are subsequently to recite, the remainder of the composition consists of the duties and obligations (Starke's *Verpflichtungen*) thereby incumbent upon the subordinates, that is, instructions, even if these pertain, as must be granted, largely to issues of loyalty to the sovereign.[10] Asserting that the obligations in this case are derivative from the loyalty oath does little to change the fact that the composition consists of both obligations and oath.

Since I have expressed elsewhere my reservations about this artificial, etic division of the compositions at issue into two separate genres (Miller 2011a: 1–8; see also Beckman 1999: 2; Devecchi 2012), I can limit the discussion here to a few brief comments. First, both "instruction" and "oath" texts contain instructions or commands directed to the subordinates in question, the difference being primarily the precise nature or nuance of the obligations. Even the paradigmatic Oath of Āsḫapāla (No. 19), for example, contains not only the oath spoken by the subordinates, but also more or less detailed obligations, in this case the exact number of military units, and from which towns, are to be sent to Ḫattusa to serve the state, and further, how Āsḫapāla and his comrades are to react to enemy movements. This oath was thus sworn in relation to a set of specific obligations. In fact an "instruction" or "obligation" is a logical prerequisite to an oath, as the oath taker must express his acquiescence to some stipulation, even if this consists, for example, (almost) entirely of personal loyalty to the king and his descendents (Miller 2011b: 1–2 and n. 1). The converse would not necessarily be the case, but in practice, hardly an instruction text (or treaty) is entirely devoid of some reference to oath and/or divine sanction. Second, and most importantly, Hittite usage of the terms *isḫiul-* and *lingai-* when used to categorize a composition does not correspond to the categories that we would like to see as "instructions" and "oaths." Hittite scribes use them almost interchangeably when applying them to texts of the type at hand (Miller 2011b: 3–8).

Having emphasized the unity of the obligation and oath genre, it must be recalled that the texts treated in the present volume are quite heterogeneous in nature, since some few belong to other genres entirely and since the style and structure of even those that clearly do belong to the genre vary considerably. In the compositions presented here, then, (at least) the following eight text elements can be distinguished. Most occur together with others in a single document, while only some few texts contain only one of these elements, so that only rarely do these eight categories also constitute textual genres. The titles given to the various compositions are an attempt to extract the most fundamental, constitutive one to two elements and are generally drawn from these eight categories.

1. **Instructions**: These texts and text passages are the most abundant and thus the most varied in the corpus. They are often spoken by the superior—usually, but not always, the king—to his subordinates in the 2nd sg. or 2nd pl., but are nearly as often styled in an impersonal 3rd sg. or pl., either in the imp. or the (pres.-)fut., the latter

often carrying the force of the imp. (Thus one occasionally will see a verb translated as an imperative, though the Hittite verb is formally a pres.-fut.) They may, sometimes seemingly randomly, switch from the 2nd to the 3rd person (e.g., Nos. 17, §§21–22; 24, §§1′–2′) or from sg. to pl., a feature that is not uncommon in other Hittite text genres as well, such as Annals. They are directed to specific persons or groups of persons, occupations or classes. They are usually a mixture of prescriptive and prohibitive clauses. Occasionally positive, but more often negative, consequences are added, including blessings and imprecations, often with reference to the oath deities, sometimes of an entirely secular, penal nature (e.g., No. 8, §§11″–12″). A variety of secondary devices is found within this category, including historical examples in narrative form (e.g., No. 2, §§13″–15″) and rationalization (e.g., No. 2, §6″).

2. **Oath Impositions or Prescriptions**: These texts or text passages are as a rule addressed by the superior—generally the king—in the 2nd sg. or pl. to the subordinate. Like the instructions or directives, they detail acceptable and inacceptable behavior, but strongly emphasize the latter and repeatedly stipulate what behavior is to be placed under oath (e.g., No. 27, §§5′, 9″–17″, 20″–21″, 23″–28″, 30″–35″) and often refer to the catastrophic consequences of breaking the oath or contain an imprecation concerning what the oath deities should do to the transgressor (e.g., Nos. 18, §8″; 26, §9″–11″; 27, §22″). They tend to focus on loyalty to the king and the royal family. The oath to be articulated by the subordinates may be cited explicitly (e.g., No. 2, §8″; No. 27, §1), but usually it is only referred to. Oettinger (1976: 82) fittingly called such texts *Eidesvorschriften*.
3. **Oath**: These texts or text passages are styled as spoken by the subordinate or subordinates in the 1st sg. or pl. (e.g., Nos. 14 and 19). They are generally addressed to the king, queen, and heir apparent and are spoken before the summoned oath deities (e.g., Nos. 22.2, §§2′–3′; 23). They often include a detailed repetition of the instructions and directives to which the subordinate is expressing his acquiescence (e.g., Nos. 14 and 19). It is conceivable that the so-called Military Oaths (*CTH* 427, 493; Oettinger 1976; Collins 1997: 165–68), which consist of ritual actions and accompanying conditional curses as well as the occasional expression of agreement on the part of the soldiers or subordinates, illustrate how one should envision the actual oath-swearing ceremony or rites.

4. **Protocols**: These are represented essentially by Nos. 3 and 4. They simply prescribe the proper protocol or procedures in the given setting for the given officials. They are distinguished from the other compositions by their 3rd person indic. rather than imp. narrative style and the lack of any reference to an oath or to punishment. They are not styled as the word of the king and presumably did not carry the same authority.
5. **Edict or Decree**: These texts or passages consist of an authoritative statement or statements carrying the force of law (e.g., No. 16).[11] They are for the most part composed in an impersonal 3rd person, but exceptions are hardly rare, especially in No. 5, dubbed here a Royal Decree on Social and Economic Matters, which one might even want to classify as an instruction.
6. **Reform**: These passages employ a formulation akin to "Something was x, but now it shall be y" (e.g., No. 5) or are presented more generally as a corrective vis-à-vis an earlier state of affairs (No. 8). They are closely related to the edicts or decrees and might be considered a subcategory thereof.
7. **Reprimand**: These texts or text passages merely accuse the subordinate(s) of failing to fulfill existing obligations and reprimand him/them for it. As far as is preserved, No. 1 consists entirely of a royal (i.e., princely) reprimand.
8. **Summoning of or address to the oath deities**: These passages are spoken to the deities, either impersonally in the 3rd pl. (No. 28, §9′) or directly in the 2nd pl. (e.g., No. 28, §§1–3). They most often constitute simple invitations to be present (e.g., No. 18, §10″) but may extend to rather lengthy addresses (No. 28, §§1–3).

The greater part of the texts presented in this volume can thus be categorized as "Instructions and Oath Impositions" (Nos. 2, 10–12, 15, 18, 26–28) along with some seven further compositions classified here as "Instructions" (Nos. 7, 13, 17, 20–21, 24, 25), though, as noted, these latter might well belong to the "Instruction and Oath Imposition" category, too, even if the available fragments preserve only instructions. Of these, only Nos. 13, 17, and perhaps 20 even raise a suspicion of perhaps having included no oath imposition at all. None of the four admittedly rather fragmentary versions of No. 13 makes any mention of an oath, even though No. 13.1–2 seem likely to preserve beginning and end of the composition; and although No. 13.2 is apparently not finished with the single tablet preserved, it makes no reference whatsoever to any oath in its otherwise extensively preserved or restorable text. No. 15.1, though so poorly preserved, is considered an "Instruction and Oath" due to its explicit mention of both in §1, while No. 15.2 is more tentatively placed in the same category due to the formulation "obligation of purity" (§1) and the assumption that those who would have allotted an evil death in §2 would have been the oath gods. The nearly fully preserved No. 20 prescribes drinking ordeals (§§18′–19′) aimed at discovering thieves, but these cannot simply be equated with the imposition of an oath connected with a text's instructions (see Giorgieri 2002: 319–20; cf. Marazzi 2010: 202–4, 207–8). Thus, the possibility must be granted that these might be merely "Instructions," even if there are no fully preserved instruction texts that can unequivocally be shown to be exclusively "Instructions" and not "Instructions and Oath Impositions."[12] No. 22 has also been classified as an "Instruction and Oath" text on the highly tentative assumption that Nos. 22.1 and 22.2 belong together. Nos. 5, 8, 9, and 16 are classified as "Decrees," though tentatively, due to their state of preservation. Nos. 14, 19, and 23 are considered to be "Oaths" or "Loyalty Oaths." Nos. 3 and 4 are categorized as "Protocols." Finally, No. 1 is classified as a "Royal Reprimand," though comparison with other compositions (cf. Marazzi 2007) might suggest that those portions that are no longer preserved might have contained a royal decree or instructions. No. 6 is too fragmentary for reliable attribution to a genre.

Defining the Corpus

The definition of the corpus presented in the current volume and the criteria according to which compositions were included or excluded are rather complex and, it must be admitted, not absolutely rigid and consistent, partly due to the nature of the textual material, partly due to the disparity between Hittite and modern categories, as noted above, and partly resulting from modern research history and convention. In initial discussions with Billie Jean Collins, who first suggested the possibility of preparing such an anthology, and Ted Lewis, the General Editor of the Writings from the Ancient World series, the volume was originally envisioned as a repository of the "Hittite Instructions," without it being entirely clear to any of us what a disparate group of texts was in fact generally ascribed to the "instructions" and how challenging it would be to formulate criteria according to which a sensible selection of texts could be chosen and for which a suitable overarching book concept and title could be found. It also became clear once work on the volume commenced in earnest that the characterization and categorization of many of the well-known texts initially assumed to belong to the genre were neither necessarily self-evident nor fully and convincingly established by the secondary literature. While the efforts along these lines encased in this volume will surely not render further discussion superfluous, it is hoped that they will make a positive contribution in this direction.

In the end a rather pragmatic approach combined with a few novel considerations on the characterization and categorization of the texts has determined what has been included and what has been excluded. Essentially all of those texts generally referred to as "instructions" in the Hittitological literature, and which are sufficiently preserved, have been included, though some in fact emphasize primarily or almost exclusively the oath that so often accompanied them, and though others could well be regarded as royal decrees to which no oath would have been sworn, and still others constitute protocols rather than instructions. The categorization presented by E. Laroche in his *Catalogue des textes hittites*, where Nos. 251–275 are placed under the heading *Instructions et protocoles*, despite their heterogeneity (Giorgieri 2005: 322–23), remains influential here as well, even if one might reassess some of his assignments today. Just as one could legitimately question the inclusion of this or that text, one could also protest the exclusion of others. It is largely Laroche's placement of Āsḫapāla's Oath (No. 19) among his *Instructions et protocoles* (*CTH* 270), for instance, that accounts for its inclusion in the present volume, while most of the other comparable oaths, such as the Loyalty Oath of a Scribe (*CTH* 124; Laroche 1953: 71–75; Giorgieri 1995: 278–80; Glocker 2009),[13] the Oath of the SA.GAZ- or *ḫabiru*-troops (*CTH* 27; Giorgieri 1995: 69–89; Bemporad 2009)[14] or Ḫattusili III's Loyalty Oath Imposition (*CTH* 85.2; Giorgieri 1995: 268–73; Singer 2001b: 399–403), have been excluded. Similarly, Laroche's placement of the Decree of Queen Ašmunikkal Concerning the "Royal Funerary Structure" (No. 16) at *CTH* 252 has influenced the decision to include it here, while other edicts and decrees have been omitted (*CTH* 5, 19, 44, 57, 63, 64, 86–90).

Further, the volume includes what are often classified as Loyalty Oaths, partly due to Laroche's categorization, to some degree due to some partially new—or rehabilitated—insights. First, as discussed above, the distinction between "instructions" or "obligations" (Hitt. *isḫiul-*) and the "oath" (*lingai-*) was found to be a largely unsatisfactory basis on which to divide Hittite compositions into genres, since Hittite scribes seem for the most part not to have segregated them. Second, most of the texts sometimes referred to as Loyalty Oaths are not oaths per se, but impositions or prescriptions of oaths (Nos. 10–12, 18). They are prescribed by the king and consist for the most part of sometimes detailed portrayals of hypothetical and real situations along with the subordinates' expected behavior and often, in contrast, prohibited potential behavior. Thus, they are essentially "instruction" texts, even if these instructions or directives pertain primarily, though not exclusively, to modes of behavior relating to the royal family rather than concrete tasks and duties. These Oath Impositions should be distinguished from the actual oaths, sworn by the subordinates themselves in the 1st person, "promissory oaths" in Giorgieri's (2005: 324) terminology (Nos. 14, 19, 23). Third, while several of the compositions generally referred to as instruction texts can be subsumed under a genre "obligation and oath," others, despite close parallels as far as their delegation of duties is concerned, clearly must be kept separate from them, for example, No. 3, a Protocol for the Palace Gatekeeper, and No. 4, a Protocol for the Royal Body Guard. These two compositions share a narrative-like 3rd person indic. pres.-fut. style throughout and are devoid of imperatives or address in the 2nd person. It appears, therefore, that they do not constitute directives issued by the king or other royal authority to which the subordinates in question would at some point have sworn an oath. Neither composition includes any reference to oath deities, curses for breaking an oath or anything akin to punishment either secular or divine. They seem rather to comprise something more like instruction manuals, stage directions or protocols, perhaps compiled by those responsible for organizing the texts' respective routines.

As noted, those texts known to modern researchers as state and vassal treaties were placed by the Hittites essentially in the same category as the obligation and oath texts. Fortunately, there is a relatively simple way to distinguish between the two, a distinction, again, that is largely modern. Those texts dealing with internal, domestic administration, that is, within the Hittite heartland up to and including the frontier posts, are included within the present volume, while those concerning external Hittite administration, that is, the state and vassal treaties, are excluded. Thus, texts such as the MH Indictment of Mita of Paḫḫuwa (*CTH* 146; Beckman 1999: 160–66), which in its latter paragraphs contains passages evincing close parallels to some of the instructions; Arnuwanda I's Treaty with or Royal Decree for the Elders of Ura (*CTH* 144; de Martino 1996: 73–79), which shows certain similarities to some of the Oath Impositions; Ḫattusili III's Treaty with or Royal Decree for the People of Tiliura (*CTH* 89; von Schuler 1965a: 145–51; González Salazar 1994); and other more or less analogous texts (*CTH* 46, 47, 65, 93–95, 100, 107, 108, 115) have been neglected, as they apparently pertain to foreign or subject entities.

That Hittite and Hittitological categories often do not correspond precisely represented quite a challenge when deciding which texts to include and which to ignore for the present volume. The compositions known as the Military Oaths, for example, are clearly closely related to texts such as No. 14 (Loyalty Oath of Town Commanders to Arnuwanda I, Ašmunikkal, and Tudḫaliya) and No. 27 (Tudḫaliya IV's Instructions and Oath Imposition for Courtiers).

The latter's primary manuscript is summarized in its colophon with the phrase, "When they bring the army to (swear) an oath" (KBo 6.34++ iv 18–19; Oettinger 1976: 14–15; Collins 1997: 165; Christiansen 2008), suggesting that its Hittite scribe saw it as belonging to the obligation and oath genre. Indeed, one might reasonably assume that just such rites and oath-taking ceremonies would have constituted a common response to those compositions that preserve primarily the instructions issued by the king.[15] Since the focus of the Military Oaths is the ritual procedures accompanying the taking of the oath, however, Laroche, not entirely without justification, included them among the rituals (*CTH* 427, 493). A representative passage from these texts, in which a ritual expert performs the rites and articulates the imprecations while the soldiers express their consent, reads as follows (KBo 6.34++ i 47′–ii 4; Oettinger 1976: 8–9; Collins 1997: 165):

> Then he places wax and sheep fat in their hands, and he casts it into the flame, and he says, "Just as this wax melts and the sheep fat separates, may he who breaks the oath and deceives the [king of] Ḫattusa melt like the wax, and may he be separated like the sheep fat!" And they say, "So be it!"

Finally, it should perhaps be noted explicitly that this volume does not include didactic or wisdom literature, though the term "instructions" could in other contexts easily allow one to suspect that it might. The Sumerian Instructions of Šuruppak, for example, have received the same modern label as the texts treated here, though this composition consists largely of pithy, didactic proverbs concerning moral and ethical matters and thus can be considered wisdom literature. The Hittite instructions are in this sense certainly not didactic, as a rule, though some of the obligations imposed do relate to issues of morality and ethics. In fact, the Hittite archives contain hardly a text that could be considered wisdom literature per se, concerning which Hutter (2009) has recently provided an overview. Perhaps the closest parallels would be the Hurrian parables found together with the Song of Release (Neu 1996; Wilhelm 2001; Haas 2006: 177–92), the so-called Palace Anecdotes (Dardano 1997; 2011; Klinger 2001a: 61–64; Gilan 2007) or the Decree of Pimpira (*CTH* 24; Cammarosano 2006), with its ethical and didactic instructions for the young king Mursili I.[16]

The texts of this volume are presented for all intents and purposes in chronological order, as far as can be established. The texts from what can be seen as the zenith of the instruction genre, those of the reigns of Tudḫaliya I and his successor Arnuwanda I, occupy the central part of the volume, chapter 2, while earlier comparanda and the first examples of the genre comprise chapter 1, and the latest texts, those from the Empire period beginning with Suppiluliuma I, form chapter 3.

A Brief History of Research

The very first Hittite instruction fragment published in hand copy was HT 28, by L. W. King, which appeared in 1920. It was soon followed by the more substantial KBo 5.11, by B. Hrozný, in 1921. The instructions then had to wait until the thirteenth volume of KUB, by H. Ehelolf, which appeared in 1925, to see their first more significant publication, a volume that contained nearly twenty tablets and fragments, including some of the best preserved and most important texts to this day. Further larger groups appeared in KUB 26 (1933) and 31 (1939) and, following the war, in KUB 36 (1955) and 40 (1968). The last significant collection of fragments appeared in 2006 in KBo 50. To date some twenty fragments identified as belonging to the instructions are yet to be published. These have, however, been incorporated into the present volume on the basis of photo evidence available at the Vorderasiatisches Museum in Berlin and the Akademie der Wissenschaften und der Literatur in Mainz.

Though various instruction texts had been sporadically quoted in previous research literature, it was the publication of KUB 13 that allowed Friedrich in 1928/29 to present an edition of the better preserved cols. ii–iii of the Instructions and Oath Imposition for Royal Servants Concerning the Purity of the King (No. 2 in the present volume). The first full edition of a Hittite instruction text, that addressed to the Priests and Temple Personnel (No. 20), was published by Sturtevant in 1934. By the time of Friedrich's and Sturtevant's publications, Hittite was already quite well understood, and their translations provide generally high quality and accurate representations of the documents, even if advances since that time have allowed numerous improvements and corrections. Editions of further major texts were published by Alp in 1947 (No. 7) and von Schuler in 1956 (Nos. 10, 14), while in 1950 Goetze published translations or partial translations of three other important texts (Nos. 2, 17, 20).

Though dedicated primarily to the state and vassal treaties, Korošec's work from 1931 often referred to instruction texts as well and thus formed the first major attempt to evaluate what is called here the obligation and oath compositions in their legal and diplomatic contexts. The next major milestone is constituted by von Schuler's *Hethitische Dienstanweisungen* from 1957, in which several of the major instruction texts known at that time (Nos. 17, 26, 27) were treated with transliteration, translation, and concise commentary. His succinct introductory *Bemerkungen* (pp. 1–7) show that the instructions and oaths, as well as their relationship to the treaties, were already well understood as a genre by this time.

The following decade saw less activity in the area of the instructions, with Jakob-Rost's (1966) edition of the Protocol for the Royal Body Guard (No. 4), published in hand copy already in 1954, the only major advance. In the 1970s, in contrast, appeared a number of studies and text editions (del Monte 1975a; 1975b; Marazzi 1979; Oettinger 1976; Otten 1974; 1979; Pecchioli Daddi 1975; 1979; Rizzi Mellini 1979), which both increased the number of major compositions available in a full edition and allowed a fuller exploitation of the instructions and oaths for their wealth of information concerning Hittite state administration, society, and culture as well as the reassessment of some assumptions that had been made on a narrower textual foundation. This went hand in hand with the growing understanding of ductus and other aspects of paleography, which allowed Hittite texts to be roughly dated independently of their content.

The 1980s saw Süel's (1985) edition of the Instructions for Priests and Temple Personnel and Houwink ten Cate's (1983) discussion of the instruction genre, in which many translations of passages appeared as well, along with Imparati's (1982) investigation of internal Hittite administrative structure, which references instructions and oaths extensively. The following decade witnessed the fundamentally important study by Giorgieri (1995) on the entire corpus of Hittite oath compositions and Güterbock and van den Hout's (1991) new edition of the Instructions for the Royal Body Guard, which placed the text on a significantly more robust philological foundation. Other important studies included Košak's (1990) edition of the Instructions and Oath Imposition for Military Commanders (No. 18) and Westbrook's and Woodard's (1990) edition of Tudḫaliya I's Decree on Penal and Administrative Reform (No. 8), while updated translations of three important compositions (Nos. 4, 17, 20) were presented to a wider audience in an anthology of ancient Near Eastern texts (McMahon 1997).

Finally, the first decade of the new millennium saw again a series of instructions translated in a volume for a wider audience (Klinger 2001a) as well as Pecchioli Daddi's (2003a) new edition of the Instructions of Arnuwanda I for the Frontier Post Governors (No. 17), while a third full edition of the Instructions for Priests and Temple Personnel appeared (Taggar-Cohen 2006). Pecchioli Daddi (2005b) and Mora (2008) also presented updated classifications and brief assessments of all instructions, oaths and edicts, which they refer to as "politico-administrative" and/or "political-juridical" texts, as well as a more thorough review of the MH instructions in particular (Pecchioli Daddi 2005a), while d'Alfonso (2006a; 2008) contributed to further elucidating their nature and placing them within their cultural milieu. At the same time, Giorgieri (2001, 2002, 2005, 2008), who had written his dissertation on the loyalty oaths (1995), published a number of highly insightful studies illuminating various aspects of the instructions and oath texts. Most recently, Christiansen (2008) has completed her dissertation containing a systematic and exhaustive examination of curse and oath formulas in the Hittite political-historical documentation.

Origins and Development of the Obligation and Oath Texts

Several hypotheses and schema, differing rather substantially in some respects, have been put forth by various scholars to account for the attested stages and diverging forms witnessed in the texts at hand.

Origins and Old Hittite Compositions

Von Schuler (1957: 2–3) proposed that the obligation and oath texts would have been derived from the state treaties, but advances in the dating of texts subsequently showed that the instructions, initially thought all to have been NH documents, also reached deep into the MH period, invalidating his hypothesis. Von Schuler (1976–1980: 117) later placed the OH edicts and decrees along with No. 1, a Royal Reprimand of the Dignitaries, at the beginning of the development of the instructions, which would thus have evolved "aus konkreten Anweisungen des Königs."

Among more recent scholars Pecchioli Daddi (e.g., 2005b: 600–601; 2002a: 262) has linked the origins of the obligation and oath genre with texts such as the Palace Anecdotes[17] and the Royal Reprimand of the Dignitaries (No. 1), both of which belong to the oldest phase of Hittite text creation, labeling them "proto-*isḫiul*." She sees in No. 2, the Instructions and Oath Imposition for Royal Servants Concerning the Purity of the King, which she dates to Arnuwanda I, the developmental link between them (2005a: 284). I have suggested (Miller 2011b; see also Gilan 2007: 299–300; Christiansen 2008: 259–63; Cammarosano 2006: 10–12; Klinger 2005a: 358) that the designation "proto-*isḫiul*" overemphasizes to some degree the similarities among them, and that these two early Hittite compositions (the Palace Anecdotes and the Royal Reprimand of the Dignitaries) and similar texts can perhaps be compared with the later instructions at most with regard to their didactic aspects. The Palace Anecdotes, for instance, composed in a narrative style in the 3rd person, show no signs of a contractual nature or divine sanction, and the terms *isḫiul*- and *lingai-* are not to be found in them, nor is a command or prohibition ever encountered. The Royal Reprimand of the Dignitaries (No. 1) is indeed styled as the words of the crown prince, who addresses and reprimands his subordinates in the 2nd person, thus echoing the instructions,[18] but there is, again, no hint of any contractual elements or divine witnesses that one sees in the obligation and oath compositions. In fact, no actual instructions are given; only accusations, reprimands, and warnings are to be found, at least as far as is preserved. Further, if the dating of No. 2 (Instructions and Oath Imposition for Royal Servants Concerning the Purity of the King) to the OH period is correct, as argued here (see introduction to No. 2), then the concept of "proto-*isḫiul*" loses all validity in any case, as there would already be at least one proper obligation and oath composition extant from the earliest phases of the Old Kingdom (see similarly Klinger 2005a: 358; Cammarosano 2006: 11).

A further text that can be profitably compared to many of the instructions is the Telipinu Edict (Hoffmann 1984; van den Hout 1997: 194–98; Liverani 2004: 27–52); indeed, the instructions share more in common with it than with the Palace Anecdotes or the Royal Reprimand of the Dignitaries discussed above. At least a significant portion of the Telipinu Edict is addressed, beginning with §30, to the nobles of the land in the 2nd pl. Further sections (§§35–40), formulated in the 2nd and 3rd pl., detail specific duties that those responsible for the administration of the land are to concern themselves with, for example, instructions concerning the fortification of cities, water supplies, and grain storage. And after relating a moralistic anecdote §39 ends with the curse "Whoever does it, may they allot him an evil fate!," recalling the same curse in Nos. 2 and 15.2 here, whereby it is surely the (oath) gods who are called upon in this passage to fulfill the curse should it become necessary, even if no oath or oath gods are explicitly mentioned in the preserved text. A number of the texts of this volume, though primarily those not belonging to the core of the obligation and oath genre (e.g., Nos. 6?; 11, *passim*; 12, §§33″–34″), also recall previous dynastic strife as a warning against repeating history, echoing a, if not the, principal theme of the Telipinu Edict. Still, the composition's most common designation as the Edict of Telipinu is surely appropriate nonetheless,[19] as it lacks the contractual character of the obligation and oath genre, and accordingly, some of its closest parallels to text passages found in the present volume are seen in those judged to be edicts or decrees. The Telipinu Edict's last sections (§§49–50), for example, regulate legal matters, recalling No. 8, §§4′–6′ (Tudḫaliya I's Decree on Penal and Administrative Reform), especially in their attempts to establish a balance between retribution and reimbursement for bloodshed. Several parallels along similar lines can be found in the Testament of Ḫattusili I (Goedegebuure 2006b).

The didactic anecdotes that are found in numerous, above all older, texts are sometimes discussed as if they were, at least at their core, based on real historical episodes, and this may well be true in some cases.[20] Still, some evidence might speak against such an assumption, though neither can this counterevidence be seen as decisive. The Instructions and Oath Imposition for Royal Servants Concerning the Purity of the King (No. 2), for example, which belongs to the earliest stratum of the genre and likely to the oldest stage of text production from the Hittite capital, contains a story in many ways similar to those in the Palace Anecdotes and other OH compositions.[21] Here one reads in the main manuscript (No. 2, KUB 13.3 iii 21–31 [§§13″–14″]):

> Furthermore, you who are water carriers, you must be very careful concerning the water, and you must always filter the water with a sieve. One time I, the king, in the city of Sanḫuitta, found a hair in the washbasin, and (my), the king's, ire was raised, and I became enraged at the water carriers (and said): "This is disgusting!" Arnili (responded) so: "Zuliya was the overseer!" And the king (continued) thus: "Zuliya shall go through the river(ordeal)! If he is (shown to be) innocent, then let him purify his soul. But if he is (shown to be) guilty, then he will die." So, Zuliya went through the river(ordeal), and he was (shown to be) guilty. And they "dealt with" him in the city of Suresta.

Intriguingly, a small fragment duplicating this passage, after an essentially identical introduction, tells a very different tale (KBo 50.282+Bo 4410; deviations from main ms. in bold):

> Arnili (responded) so: "Z[uliya] was [the oversee]r!" And the king (continued) thus: "[Zuliya] shall go [through] the river(ordeal)! If he is (shown to be) inno[cent], then **[may] you(sg.) [b]e innocent as well**. [But] if he is (shown to be) gui[lty], **[then] you(sg.) shall go too!" And when they went**, Zuliya was (shown to be) guilty, **[and] the othe[r was also guilty]**, [so that] they ["de]alt with" **[the]m** in [...] the city of Surista.

Thus, one is perhaps entitled to wonder if it might be the redactional history that has changed the anecdote in such a basic way or if the stories were simply made up for their didactic merit.

While the OH Palace Anecdotes, the Royal Reprimand of the Dignitaries and the Telipinu Edict provide interesting and instructive comparanda, it seems likely, as noted, that No. 2, the Instructions and Oath Imposition for Royal Servants Concerning the Purity of the King, should be dated to the OH period as well, and thus, that the obligation and oath genre in all its essential aspects was extant already from the earliest phases of Hittite documentation.[22] One may therefore assume that the practice of the sovereign dictating instructions and his subordinates swearing to fulfill them was extant already by the time writing was (re)introduced into Anatolia.

THE ZENITH OF THE GENRE UNDER TUDḪALIYA I AND ARNUWANDA I

Approximately half of the compositions treated in this volume can be dated with greater or lesser certainty to the reigns of just two kings, Tudḫaliya I and his successor Arnuwanda I, and it is from this period that the full depth and breadth of forms of the genre first become available. It is therefore unsurprising that the beginning and early development of the genre has been sought in this period, though views on the derivation and/or bifurcation of the obligation and oath genre during the MH period vary significantly.

Oettinger (1976: 83–84), for example, maintained that

> der Erste Militärische Eid (sich) als Prototyp der Instruktionstexte (erweist), denn er besteht nur aus Treueverpflichtungen mit Eid und Fluchformeln.... Das völlige Fehlen konkreter Verpflichtungen läßt sich bei der Vereidigung von Truppenführern aus deren jeweils wechselnden Aufgaben erklären. Es zeigt gleichzeitig, daß dieses ursprüngliche Vereidigungsritual allein die Treueverpflichtung selbst zum Ziel hatte; von diesem Stadium sind auch die frühen Instruktionen noch nicht weit entfernt.

Further, based on the observation that the treaties with groups of chieftains belong almost exclusively to the MH corpus, while the treaties from the Empire period are all with vassal kings, Oettinger (1976: 84) suggests a similar development for the loyalty oaths and early treaties, concluding that

> sich aus dem gleichen Vereidigungs- und Fluchformular sowohl die Vereidigungen für Gruppen von "Beamten" entwickelten als auch die für benachbarte Häuptlinge. In beiden Bereichen traten dann im Laufe der Entwicklung die Fluchformeln gegenüber den Sachbestimmungen zurück.

The suggestion that the instructions would have developed from the military oaths because the latter consist only of loyalty obligations with oath and curse formulae, however, is simply not compelling. There is no rule that stipulates or tendency that suggests that more complex obligation and oath type compositions should develop from simpler oath and curse formulae. Moreover, since No. 2 can be attributed to the OH period, or is at least significantly older than the Military Oaths—though both are available only in later mss.—it is clear that the obligation and oath genre was extant with all its essential elements already in the OH period, or at least before the Military Oaths, and that the instruction genre did not develop from them.

Neither, it seems, did the "Vereidigungen für Gruppen von 'Beamten'" or "die für benachbarte Häuptlinge" develop from the military oaths. While it is correct that the grandiose and extended curse formulae of the earlier compositions are largely abandoned in the later texts in favor of shorter, more concise formulations, it is likely that texts such as the "Treaty" with the Ḫabiru and the Kizzuwatnean Treaties between Telipinu and Isputaḫsu, between Taḫurwaili and Eḫeya and between Pa/illiya and Zidanza II, some of which show evidence for oath taking despite their extremely fragmentary state of preservation, all preceded the military oaths, as did No. 2, noted above, so that it is difficult to maintain the placement of the military oaths at the beginning of the development of any genre. It seems more likely that the military oaths should be seen as part and parcel of the obligation and oath genre, these particular texts preserving above all the rites and ceremonies accompanying the oath taking, which went hand in hand with the receiving of the instructions.

More recently Pecchioli Daddi has suggested that up through the reign of Tudḫaliya I the instructions "show elements of both *išḫiul* and *lingai-*" (2002a: 266), while beginning with the rule of Arnuwanda I the *isḫiul-* and *lingai-* documents became "autonomous textual categories" (267). Referring to *CTH* 259 and 251 (Nos. 10 and 12 here) she speaks further of an "adjustment phase testified by documents that contain elements typical of both genres" (2005b: 608) and of a "double typological definition 'tablet of bond and oath' in the heading (KUB 26.10, by Arnuwanda I) or in the colophon (KUB 31.102)." Pecchioli Daddi (2002a: 261; 2005b: 607; cf. also Giorgieri 2005: 325 and n. 15, 326, n. 17) has also suggested that the developments in the instruction compositions from the era of Tudḫaliya I and Arnuwanda I signal an innovative administrative structure that would have replaced the Old Kingdom "family management" style regime.

Rather than assuming, however, that the obligation and oath genre underwent a process of mitosis at the end of the reign of Tudḫaliya I, the *isḫiul-* and *lingai-* elements splitting into two autonomous genres by the reign of Arnuwanda I, it seems more fitting to describe a single obligation and oath genre as often tending in the MH period to strongly emphasize practical and concrete obligations (*isḫiul-*), while in its later phases it highlights above all loyalty to the king and his family through stressing the oath and by raising the issue of loyalty to the status of principal obligation, to the nearly total exclusion of other instructions. Thus, only if one assumes that *isḫiul-* and *lingai-* represent "autonomous textual typologies" is one forced to presuppose, unnecessarily, a "phase testified by documents that contain elements typical of both genres …

and the double typological definition 'tablet of bond and oath.'" Indeed, such an "adjustment phase" would, of course, be no different than the documents from before this phase that Pecchioli Daddi describes as showing "elements of both *išḫiul* and *lingai-*." Moreover, these "mixed" compositions from the assumed "adjustment phase" are not outliers among otherwise "autonomous textual typologies," but rather the norm, which in fact demonstrate that the *isḫiul-* and *lingai-* texts belonged, as far as the Hittites were concerned, to one and the same textual category (Giorgieri 2005: 326, n. 17; Christiansen 2008: 259; Miller 2011a: 1–8; 2011b: 193–96). The obligation and oath texts could sway from strongly emphasizing the obligations to highlighting above all the oath and loyalty as the chief obligation incumbent upon its addressees depending on the specific circumstances for which any given text was composed, but the genre as such remained essentially unchanged, entirely capable of containing both elements throughout its history.

Further, Giorgieri (2005: 324) has noted along similar lines that "erst ab der mittelhethitischen Zeit (spielt) der Eid eine entscheidende Rolle bei der politischen Organisation und Verwaltung des hethitischen Staates."[23] Giorgieri (2005: 323, n. 5; citing Starke 1995b: 81, n. 36 and Pecchioli Daddi 2002a: 267–68) has also correctly observed that "die Textgattung der Instruktionen," by which he intends those texts that strongly emphasize the detailed administrative duties of its addressees and de-emphasize or even omit the oaths, "(sich) als ein Spezifikum der mittelhethitischen Zeit erweist." In light of the attribution of No. 2 to the Old Kingdom suggested above, however, Giorgieri's observations must be slightly modified as well. The oath seems already before the MH period to have played a significant role in Hittite administration, as did detailed, technical instructions. Taken together with the OH Loyalty Oath of the Ḫabiru (*CTH* 27), as well as such OH or early MH treaties as Telipinu's with Isputaḫsu, Taḫurwaili's with Eḫeya, and Zidanza II's with Pa/illiya,[24] it appears that the oath, and the loyalty oath in particular, will have played at least some role in the internal and external administration of the OH and early MH periods as well, and that the augmented availability of texts from the reigns of Tudḫaliya I and Arnuwanda I might reflect at least in part rather an increase in the use of writing and/or issues of preservation. Either way, it remains the case, as Giorgieri emphasizes, that detailed technical instructions such as those found in Nos. 2, 13, 17, and 20 are no longer witnessed after the MH period,[25] be it due to circumstances of preservation or to actual changes in the usage of the genre. In the NH "obligation and loyalty oath" texts the "obligations" consist almost exclusively of correct and loyal behavior to the king and his descendents.

Finally, the assertion that the reigns of Tudḫaliya I and Arnuwanda I witnessed a significant change in state and administrative structures is still in need of clear support, though neither should the hypothesis be excluded *a priori*.[26] Issues of archaeological preservation and recovery as well as an increase in the scope of writing practices during this period could have played a role in the well-attested surge in available textual material, too, and even the available documentation might speak against the greater part of this scheme. Since I have outlined elsewhere what elements of this hypothesis do not seem convincing (Miller 2011a: 8–10; see also Christiansen 2008: §5.3.1), there is no need to belabor the point now, and a few succinct notes should suffice. Briefly, it seems more likely that the instruction texts as witnessed during the reigns of Tudḫaliya I and Arnuwanda I constitute an attempt to validate and/or institutionalize state and monarchical structures and administrative modes that already existed rather than significant innovation. Most of the offices and institutions witnessed in the instructions are already found in OH texts, for example; and as noted, text No. 2 seems to show that the full-fledged obligation and oath genre was extant already during the Old Kingdom. Moreover, other genres, such as the rituals, for example, enjoy a similarly significant rapid growth in textual production during the late MH period, and one need not imagine major changes in the prevalence or practice of magic and ritual in order to explain this increase (Miller 2010: 180–81). One is more likely simply seeing the results of a more extensive implementation of writing in the context of administration. Neither does one see a replacement of the nepotistic nature of the "familial" administration, as Giorgieri (2008: 352 and n. 11) has made quite clear. That said, one significant change in administrative practice that is perhaps not to be explained in this manner is the dramatic retreat of the Land Grant (Riemschneider 1958; Imparati 1974; Rüster and Wilhelm 2012), an important text genre and administrative tool attested primarily from the period of Telipinu—or perhaps his immediate predecessor at the earliest (Wilhelm 2005)—through the reign of Muwattalli I, and only sporadically thereafter, with one attestation each from the reigns of Arnuwanda I, Ḫattusili III, and Tudḫaliya IV.[27]

On the more concrete level of redactional history, I sought to show in a recent paper (Miller 2011b) that the earliest preserved manuscript of the Instructions of Arnuwanda I for the Frontier Post Governors (No. 17), a MH manuscript, provides evidence for the hypothesis that the earliest text of this composition may have been composed entirely in a 3rd person impersonal style. Based on this forerunner, in contrast, the later versions were composed largely in the 2nd person, addressed directly to the Frontier Post Governors, perhaps while they were gathered in Ḫattusa in order to receive their instructions and swear an oath upon them (see also below, under "Envisioning the Setting").

A valuable clue in one ms. of this text (No. 17) demonstrates that at least some of the texts in question indeed experienced a degree of redactional history, though certainly not to the same extent evident, for example, in many ritual (Miller 2004; Christiansen 2006) and festival texts. In No. 17, §40′, ms. D, unfortunately only fragmentarily preserved, one finds "The troops [of?] the po[st ...] which are up in the town, ...," while in ms. B a much more precise formulation is seen, "Also the troops of Kasiya, the troops of Ḫimmuwa, the troops of Tagaram[a] and the troops of Isuwa (which are) there, you shall by all (means) keep an eye on them." The text of B thus further specifies the general directives found in D, so that the latter appears almost like a version intended for a particular governor.

The Empire Period

Starke (1995b: 73) suggested, first, that the late loyalty oaths represent "lediglich eine bedingte ... oder unbedingte Loyalitätserklärung," and second, that they therefore are to be expected "nur in ganz besonderen politischen Situationen." This particular situation he then sees in the irregular succession of Ḫattusili III following the reign of Urḫi-Teššub / Mursili III and that of Ḫattusili's son Tudḫaliya IV. Recently, however, Giorgieri (2005: 329–38) and Koch (2008: 35–37) have shown clearly that Starke's conclusion, according to which the loyalty oaths arise only with the irregular successions following Urḫi-Teššub, cannot be sustained. Loyalty oaths and oath impositions containing all the essential elements of the texts of Tudḫaliya IV are known from earlier documents (cf. Nos. 2, 10–12, 14, 18, 22), elements that constitute a fundamental part of the earlier treaties as well. Further, loyalty oaths are associated in texts such as No. 10, Tudḫaliya I?'s Instructions and Oath Imposition for All the Men, with administrative directives that have little or nothing to do with questions of succession (Giorgieri 2005: 335). Koch (2008: 37) is thus justified in concluding that "an einem direkten Zusammenhang zwischen dem Aufkommen der Treueidgattung und der Situation der nicht regulären Thronfolge im Hethiterreich nicht festzuhalten ist, dass es hethitische Treueide vielmehr zeitlich vor und sachlich unabhängig von der nicht regulären Thronfolge von Ḫattusilis III. und Tutḫalija gab."

Pecchioli Daddi (2002a: 267), in contrast, has asserted that "in (the) internal political sphere, the *išḫiul* type texts were no longer composed after the MH period, while the *lingai-* texts were written until the late imperial period." Since I have recently commented on these issues elsewhere (Miller 2011a: 8–10; 2011b: 195–99; cf. also above), I can again limit my remarks here to a few brief notes. It is certainly the case that there is a decided shift away from the detailed instructions regarding practical matters of administration as seen in a composition such as No. 17, the Instructions of Arnuwanda I for the Frontier

Post Governors, and toward a single-minded emphasis on the issue of loyalty to the king in the obligation and oath texts of Tudḫaliya IV and Suppiluliu/ama II. Nonetheless, these latter texts can best be ascribed to the genre "obligation and oath," as shown, *inter alia*, by the repeated attestation—though, admittedly, often in fragmentary and thus obscure context—of both terms in Suppiluliu/ama II's Instructions and Oath Imposition for the Men of Ḫattusa (No. 28 i 16, 18, 26, iii 15′, iv 9′, 15′, 17′: *lingai-/MAMIT*; iii 9′, 24′, 30′, iv 10′: *isḫiul-*). Supporting this conclusion is the observation (e.g., d'Alfonso 2006b: 316–19) that many of the loyalty clauses in Tudḫaliya IV's treaty with Šaušgamuwa of Amurru closely parallel some from his Instructions and Loyalty Oaths for Lords, Princes and Courtiers (No. 26) as well as those for Courtiers (No. 27). This treaty with Šaušgamuwa is without doubt to be ascribed to the obligation and oath genre, and the fact that the loyalty clauses in question are found in it as well demonstrate that they need not be detached from the obligation and oath genre.

In sum, compositions that can be ascribed to an obligation and oath genre thread their way through the entire fabric of Hittite history, from the Old Kingdom to the very last kings of the Empire. They shift, according to the needs of the moment, from emphasizing the one to accentuating the other of the two core elements, the "obligations" and the "oath," but remain firmly within the genre. The most striking poles on the continuum are the highly detailed and technical nature of a significant portion of the texts from the reigns of Tudḫaliya I and Arnuwanda I vis-à-vis the nearly exclusive emphasis on loyal behavior toward the king and his family as the "obligation" in the texts of the NH period. There was thus in this sense no fundamental development in the genre throughout its attested chronological range, those changes that can and have been observed relating more to style, emphasis, context, and various other "cosmetic" matters.

Envisioning the Setting

The sphere in which the texts presented in this volume were created and had their impact is overwhelmingly the royal court of the Hittite imperial capital, Ḫattusa, the only significant or partial exceptions being No. 19 (Āsḫapāla's Oath Regarding an Obligation to Supply Troops) and No. 20 (Instructions for Priests and Temple Personnel). As far as can be determined, Nos. 1–4, 8 (in part), 10–13, 15–16, 18, 21–22, and 25–28 all define and regulate the duties and responsibilities of the innermost circle of officials and administrators beneath the king and the royal family in the capital. No. 5, a Royal Decree on Social and Economic Matters, would seem perhaps to constitute a broader social and economic reform, though its fragmentary state prevents any dogmatic conclusions, and the 2nd pl. forms in §§3′–4′, 8″–10″ might perhaps suggest that even this text was addressed to a more limited audience in the king's surroundings. A number of texts are directed at least in part toward officials who might not have been stationed (permanently) in Ḫattusa itself, but would have been directly answerable to the king and thus well within the tightest of royal circles (e.g., Nos. 1, 7, 10, 14, 17, 21). Similarly, some relate to military officers of various rank that might, at any point in time, have been stationed far and wide throughout the empire, but were of course immediately responsible to the king (Nos. 7, 10, 12, 18, 22, 25). As has been noted (e.g., Giorgieri 2005: 332; del Monte 1975a: 140), the occasional reference to "all of Ḫattusa," "all the men of Ḫattusa" or "the whole populace of Ḫattusa" as the persons upon whom the obligations and oath are incumbent relates in fact to those men belonging to the administration of the state, not to the entire population, as the terms would suggest in modern parlance.

Nos. 19 and 20, as noted, are to some degree exceptional in this sense. In No. 19 Āsḫapāla and his men do swear their allegiance to Ḫattusa and promise to provide troops "[for] His Majesty,"[28] but these are to remain in the provinces, and the oath takers are to report enemy movement to the provincial governor, so that the sphere reflected in this text seems to be at least one step removed from the royal court in Ḫattusa. No. 20 is an exception insofar as its addressees, though employed in the temple(s) of Ḫattusa (see §4′, 45′; §6′, 15; §8′, 41″, 43″; §11′, 21, 27; §13′, 50), are encouraged to express their fidelity not to the king and his family, not even in his role as chief priest of the land, but to the gods directly. They seem to be deemed rather servants of the gods than servants of the king and the state, as anachronistic as such a distinction between secular and religious might sound. No. 24, the fragmentary Instructions for Priests and Diviners, strikes one as quite similar to No. 20 in this sense, except for the interesting command (§2′, 8′–9′), "And the daily bread which *I*, My Majesty, *b*[*ring*] for the deity you priests must prepare as follows: …" (cf. No. 24, n. 20). No comparable statement is found in No. 20 (except perhaps for two fragmentary references to the palace in §1′, 11′–12′), suggesting perhaps that the instructions of No. 24 might have been envisioned for priests and diviners that stood directly in the service of the king in his duties as chief priest, while those of No. 20 were directed toward personnel in a temple or temples that may have functioned largely, or at least somewhat more, autonomously. Naturally, the fragmentary state of No. 24 prevents placing much faith in such a tentative hypothesis.

Among the important points that must be emphasized concerning the setting in which these compositions were created and served their purpose is that they are thoroughly prescriptive rather than descriptive texts. That is to say, one is glimpsing in them not necessarily what the daily reality would have been, but rather royal expectations of what daily reality should have been. They are thus quintessentially normative compositions (d'Alfonso 2006b, 2008). Naturally, these royal expectations will have been filtered through royal (and presumably scribal) experience of daily reality, and in many or most cases will likely have been composed by the king in consultation with the various subordinates at issue, and they therefore provide a certain refracted reality, but one must guard against confusing potentially idealistic royal prescriptions with concrete reality or descriptive documentation. That said, some of the texts of this volume certainly do relate to concrete historical persons and known historical episodes. The military officer Zardummani, for example, who appears as an oath taker along with other officers in No. 14 (3.A i 15′), a Loyalty Oath of Town Commanders to Arnuwanda I, Ašmunikkal, and Tudḫaliya, is likely to be the same person as that known from a number of other MH documents. He is the addressee of several letters from the Great King and his military commanders found at Maşat Höyük, the MH outpost Tapikka (HBM 34, 60, 68; see Marizza 2007: 168–69; Hoffner 2009: 160–61, 211); and he may well be the same person as the Zardummani who appears in the treaty of Arnuwanda I for the city of Ismerigga (KUB 23.68 rev. 20).

The instructions are presumably not to be regarded as "einen genauen und vollständigen Katalog von Anweisungen" (Pecchioli Daddi 2005a: 280), as Christiansen (2008: 480) has convincingly countered. Perhaps more likely is Pecchioli Daddi's (2005a: 280) assumption that their "Abfassung *aus dem Bedürfnis* (erwuchs), allumfassende und zeitlich unbegrenzt gültige offizielle Richtlinien festzusetzen" (emphasis mine). That such a need might have been felt, however, does not allow the conclusion that the texts would in fact have succeeded in functioning as such. Even the most detailed and well-preserved instructions and protocols (e.g., Nos. 4, 13, 17, 20) would naturally not even approximate a catalogue of everything that the various officials in question must have been responsible for doing. No. 20, the Instructions for Priests and Temple Personnel, for example, is rather concerned with preventing the gods from being offended and forbids more behaviors than it commands. It seeks rather to convince and motivate, to dissuade and warn, less to catalogue.

In a previous paper (Miller 2011b: 197–202) I tried to show how some evidence might suggest that at least some of the instructions would in fact have been read out to the subordinates to whom they were addressed, or that they were at least composed with such a scenario in mind. Among the hints that would seem to suggest such is a passage in the Instructions of Arnuwanda I for the Frontier Post Governors (No. 17, §31′, 26′–28′), were one reads, "But in whatever town the governor of the post drives back to, he shall count the *ritualists*, the priests, the anointed ones, and the mother-deity priestesses, and he shall speak to them thus: …." This passage has been translated quite differently in various treatments. McMahon (1997: 223b), for example, translates "In a city through which the margrave drives"; Pecchioli Daddi (2003a: 135) suggests "Per quanto riguarda la città in cui il 'signore della postazione' si reca nel suo giro di ispezione"; the *Chicago Hittite Dictionary* has thus far translated the passage four times, each time significantly differently: "To what city the governor of a border province drives" (*CHD* L–N, 226b); "… in any town to which he drives again" (*CHD* P, 266b); "to whatever city the governor of the border province drives in turn" (*CHD* Š, 144b); and "Whatever city a district commander visits on his rounds" (*CHD* Š, 191b; cf. also Goetze 1950: 210). Some of these are somewhat free translations; some ignore the preverb *āppa* or interpret it differently. Behind them all, it seems, lurks the conception of the frontier post governor travelling from one town in his province to another. If one imagines a scenario, in contrast, in which the frontier post governors would have been gathered at Ḫattusa, perhaps to hear the instructions of this very text read aloud to them, then one can translate the sentence in the grammatically and semantically most obvious manner, that is, "But in whatever[29] town the governor of the post drives back to, …."

Similar is the passage at the beginning of §40′, 29–30, where instead of *āppa pennai* the parallel locution *āppa arti* is found, which yields the translation, "In the city to which you return you shall call out the whole population." In both cases the most sensible translation is also the simplest, if one assumes that the scenario envisioned by the composition involves the frontier post governor journeying from Ḫattusa back to his province. Further passages, which were not discussed in the paper mentioned above, would seem to support this interpretation as well, such as No. 21, §3′, l. 16′ (Instructions for Supervisors): "Should [you] at some point re[turn] to the city, then you shall call out the craftsmen (and) the elders, [and] you shall speak to them as follows: …"; No. 27, §§23″–24″ (Tudḫaliya IV's Instructions and Oath Imposition for Courtiers), where those courtiers "who were here promptly" in order to swear the oath are contrasted with those who "were not here now" and who must therefore "swear the oath as one";[30] and No. 7, §3′ (Instructions for Military Officers and Frontier Post Governors), where the king speaks of "coming back" to Ḫattusa to venerate the gods, suggesting at least that the scribe saw the king in Ḫattusa in his mind's eye while composing the text.

It thus seems that the connection between the texts and the situations that they relate is in general quite close. At a minimum one can assume that at least some of the texts were envisioned and composed with the subordinates as a bodily present audience in mind. Still, the compositions presented here have as a whole only begun to be subjected to questions touching on the relationship between text and practice, their *Sitz im Leben* and their redactional histories, so that much further progress in these areas is to be expected.

TERMINOLOGY AND FORMULAE

As will have become clear in the discussion thus far, the text corpus presented in this volume is rather more heterogeneous than corpora normally collected in such an anthology. Still, it may be a useful exercise to try to eke from them a selection of the principal terminology and formulary and to attempt to identify some literary and structural patterns.

CURSE FORMULAE

Among the most commonly recurring formulae are those containing oaths and curses, naturally found primarily in those texts that can be classified as "oaths" (Nos. 14, 19, 23) or "instructions and oath impositions" (Nos. 2, 10–12, 18, 22, 26–28). Among the most essential and recent literature pertaining to oaths and curses in the present context are Oettinger 1976: esp. 71–94; Giorgieri 1995: 52–54; 2005: 328–29; Hagenbuchner-Dresel 2010a, 2010b; and Feder 2010; while Christiansen (2008) has provided the first systematic and exhaustive examination of all blessing, curse, and oath formulae in the Hittite political-historical documentation. Some of the most common formulae from the texts in the present volume are the following, whereby, in an attempt to retain some semblance of order among the formulae from texts of varying genres, the Nos. from the **Instruction and Oath** texts appear in bold and those from the ***Instructions*** in bold italics, while those from the Oaths are double underlined and those of the **Decrees** are bold underlined:

"then that matter shall be placed under oath for you(pl.)" (**No. 26**, §2′, i 10′: *nu-uš-ma-aš a-pa-a-aš me-m*[(*i*)]-*aš* GAM *NI-ÌŠ* DINGIR-*LÌ* GAR-*ru*; similarly, **No. 18**, §5′ obv. 27′; **No. 27**, §9″, i 61′; **No. 28**, §13″, iii 15′; "for him": **No. 26**, §3′, i 18′, §4′, i 26′, §5′, i 32′, §6′, i 35′, §7′, i 39′–40′, §12″, ii 36′, §19″, iii 31; **No. 27**, §14″, ii 47′, §15″, ii 53′; "for us": No. 19, §4, 19–21; reduced versions in **No. 12**, §5′, i 20′; No. 19, §1, 2–3; **No. 26**, §1′, i 3′, §3′, i 21′, §13″, iii 2, §14″, iii 6, §15″, iii 12, §16″, iii 20, §17″, iii 23, §18″, iii 28, §20″, iii 35, §22″, iv 2, §26″, iv 42, §27″, iv 50, §30″, left edge 5; **No. 27**, §10″, B ii 2′, §11″, ii 8′,

§12″, ii 20′, §13″, ii 42′, §16″, ii 58′, §17″, ii 63′–64′, §20″, iii 31, §21″, iii 36, §23″, iii 52, §24″, iii 57, §25″, iii 66, §26″, iv 2, §27″, iv 6, §28″, iv 10, §30″, iv 28, §31″, iv 37, §32″, iv 41, §33″, iv 45, §34″, iv 48; **No. 28**, §17″, iv 9′, §18″, iv 15′; reduced to *ŠA-PAL*/GAM *ME/A-ME-TU₄/TI*: **No. 26**, §23″, iv 15, §24″, iv 32, §25″, iv 37; cf. also **No. 11.B₁**, §4′, 11′);

"[(then)] let [(these oa)t]h gods grab him, and let them [destr]oy him along with his wife and his sons!" (**No. 12**, §8′, i 39′–40′: [(*na*)]-*an* [(*ke-e NI-I*)*Š* DI]NGIR^MEŠ *ap-pa-an-du* ⌜*na*⌝-*an QA-DU* DAM-*ŠU* DUMU^MEŠ-*ŠU* [*ḫar-ni-in*]-*kán-du*; cf. similarly in **No. 12**, §1′, i 2′, §2′, i 6′, §4′, i 13′–14′, §6′, i 26′–27′, §10′, i 49′–50′, §12′, i 60′–61′, §13′, i 69′–70′, §14′, i 75′–76′, §16″, ii 5′–6′, §18″, ii 20′, §32″, iv 6–7, §36″, iv 31?, §38″, iv 45′?, §43″, iv 73′–74′; No. 16, B rev. 18′?; cf. also No. 14, §27″, 6′–7′, §28″);

"to him and his descendents they (the deities) will allot an evil fate" (**No. 2**, §9″, iii 8: *nu-uš-ši QA-DU₄* NUMUN-*ŠU* ḪUL-*lu* ÚŠ-*an pí-ia-an-zi*; cf. similarly in **No. 2**, §7″, ii 19′, §17″, iv 6′–7′; ***No. 15.2***, §2, i 6; 2nd pl. in **No. 2**, §12″, iii 19–20);[31]

"then may these gods completely destroy him!" (**No. 26**, §10″, ii 22′: *na-an-kán ku-u-uš* DINGIR^MEŠ *ar-ḫa ḫar-ni-in-kán-du*; similarly in **No. 26**, §9″, ii 11′, §11″, ii 28′; **No. 28**, §16″, iii 32′);

"then may these oath deities destroy you!" (**No. 27**, §22″, iii 44: *nu-ut-ták-kán ku-u-uš* DINGIR^MEŠ *ḫar-ni-in-kán-du*);

"[…] you^(sg.) will perish along with your!(text "his") wife (and) your!(text "his") sons" (**No. 2**, §2′, i 9′: […] *QA-DU* DAM-*KU*!(ŠU) DUMU^MEŠ-*KU*!(ŠU) *ḫar-ak-ti*; 2nd pl. in ***No. 20***, §18′, iv 54–55);

"He along with his descendants will be completely destroyed" (***No. 20***, §13′, iii 51–52: *na-aš QA-DU* NUMUN-*ŠU ḫar-ak-zi-pát*; similarly in ***No. 20***, §13′, iii 53);

"then may you, o deity, continually haunt us, along with our wives and our sons" (***No. 20***, §19′, iv 76–77: *nu-wa-an-na-aš zi-ik* DINGIR-*LU₄ tu-el* ZI-*aš* ⸗*zu-u-wa še-er QA-DU* DAM^MEŠ-*NI* DUMU^MEŠ-*NI pár-ḫi-iš-ke*; cf. also **No. 11.A₂**, §1″ rev.? 5′, §2″ rev.? 10′, cf. **No. 11.A₁**, §3′, 8′; **No. 11.B₁**, §3′, 10′);

"then may (these) oat[h deities …] utterly destroy you [alon]g with your wives (and) your sons, [and let them] eradi[cate] your names and your seed from the [dark ea]rth" (**No. 18**, §8″, rev. 8′–10′: *nu-uš-ma-aš-kán NI-I*[*Š* DINGIR^MEŠ …] [*QA-D*]*U* DAM^MEŠ-*KU-NU* DUMU^MEŠ-*KU-NU ar-ḫa ḫar-ni-in-kán-du* [*nu-kán da-an-*

ku-wa-az] [*ta-g*]*a-an-zi-pa-az* ŠUM^MEŠ^-⌜*KU*⌝-*NU* NUMUN-⌞*KU-NU*⌟-*ia ar-ḫa ḫar-*[*ni-in-kán-du*]);

"But let [these] oath deities destroy whoever does not obey the wor[d]s of this tablet!" (**No. 10**, §25″, iv 5′–6′: *ku-i-ša ke-e-el tup-pí-ia-aš ud-*⌜*da-a*⌝-[*ar*] ⌜*Ú-UL*⌝ *pa-aḫ-ša-r*[*i na-an ke-e*] *NI-ÌŠ* DINGIR^MEŠ^ *ḫar-ni-in-kán-*{**du**}*du*);

"Any and every *kukupalatar* shall be placed under oath!" (**No. 27**, §35″, iv 52–53: *ku-it im-ma ku-it* ⩤*ku-ku-pa-la-tar* GAM *NI-ÌŠ* DINGIR-*LÌ* GAR-*ru*);

"may you, o gods, pour out his soul like water!" (**No. 2**, §8″, iii 1–2: ⌜*nu-wa*⌝-*kán a-pé-e-el* ZI-*an* DINGIR^MEŠ^ *ú-wi*$_5$*-te-na-aš i-wa-ar ar-ḫa la-a-aḫ-ḫu-wa-tén*);

"th[en] may [the oath deities] not [re]lease you!" (**No. 18**, §9″, 15′–16′: *n*[*u-uš-ma-aš NI-IŠ* DINGIR^MEŠ^] [EGI]R-*an le-e tar-na-an-zi* [...]);

"you, my god, my lord, shall [*tor*(*ment*)] him! May he seize his household below (and) above!" (*No. 20*, §6′, i 65′–66′: ⌞*nu*⌟-*wa-ra-an-kán* DINGIR-*LÌ* EN-*ia* EGIR-*an* [*ki-ia-*(*aḫ-ḫu-ut*)] *nu-wa-za-kán a-pé-e-el* ⌜É⌝-*er* GAM-*an ša-ra-a e-ep-du*).

REPETITION OF THE OATH

An important, if only occasionally recurring, formula pertains to the requirement that the subjects repeat the oath taken:[32]

"you^(pl.)^ shall swear an oath to the person of the king month for month" (**No. 2**, §8″, 25′–26′: LUGAL-*wa-aš* ZI-*ni še-er* ITU-*mi* ITU-*mi li-in-ki-iš-ke-tén*);

"[And] month for month we will [swe]ar this oath to the person of Suppiluliuma [and to] Tadu-Ḫepa, the Queen, and to the sons of the king, [the grandsons of the king], (and) thereafter also to (his) descendents" (**No. 22.2**, §2′ i 8′–11′: [*nu ka*]-⌞*a*⌟-*ša* ITU-*mi* ITU-*mi A-NA* SAG.DU ^m^*ŠU.UP.PÍ.LU.LI.U.MA* [LUGAL.GAL *Ù A-NA*] ⌞^f^⌟*TÁ.DU.ḪÉ.PA* MUNUS.LUGAL *Ù A-NA* DUMU^!MEŠ!^ LUGAL [DUMU.DUMU^MEŠ^ LUGAL^(?)^ *k*]*at-ta ḫa-aš-ša ḫa-an-za-***aš***-ša* [*še-er li-in-k*]*i-iš-ke-u-wa-ni*; similarly No. 14, 3.A, i 16′–21′ and 1 i 24–29; cf. also No. 23, §2).

DEATH SENTENCES

Unsurprisingly, a death sentence was one of the most commonly prescribed punishments for infractions, a subject which has recently been treated by de Martino and Devecchi (2012) for the Hittite documentation in general:

“It is a capit[al] offense for him(/them/you)” (***No. 20***, §6′, ii 16: *na-at-ši* SAG.DU-*aš ag-ga-t*[*ar*]; similarly **No. 2**, §1′, i 3′, §13″, iii 31; cf. ***No.*** *7*, §7″, ii 17′?; ***No. 20***, §5′, i 57′–58′, §8′, ii 45″, 49″–50″, §14′, iii 83; with *wastul* instead of *aggatar*: ***No. 20***, §10′, iii 16, §17′, iv 33, §18′, iv 46, §19′, iv 66);

“Let them(/him) die!” (**No. 11.A**$_3$, §1′, 5′: *na-⸢at⸣ ak-kán-*tu**; similarly **No. 11.A**$_4$, §1′, 5′?; **No. 12**, §6′, i 25′, §26″, iii 9′, §27″, iii 11″–12′; **No. 16**, obv. 12; ***No. 20***, §5′, i 59′, §8′, ii 50″, §10′, iii 20, §14′, iii 83; cf. **No. 2**, §4′, i 18′?).

A General Admonition

Typical of several texts of the genre is the following admonition:

“You must be very careful/vigilant/reverent,” often strengthened with *mekki* and/or *marri* (**No. 2**, §13″, iii 22: *nu-uš-ma-aš ... na-aḫ-ḫa-an-te-eš e-eš-tén*; similarly in **No. 2**, §15″, iii 36–37; ***No. 13.1–2***, §1, i 2–3, §12″, iii 27′, §14″, iv 7′–8′; ***No. 13.4***, §10″ iv 8′; ***No. 20***, §3′, i 38′, §7′, ii 24″, §8′, ii 29″, §12′, iii 43, §13′, iii 44, §14′, iii 56–57; with *paḫḫs*(*nu*)- instead of *naḫḫ*-: No. 3, §6, i 23–24; ***No. 20***, §10′, ii 73″–74″, §13′, iii 54).

Seeing, Hearing, Knowing; Reporting, Revealing, and Apprehending vs. Concealing

A further important set of phrases involves the seeing (*au(s)-/u(wa)-*), hearing (*istamass-*) or knowing (*sakk-*) about and reporting (*mema-*) of someone or something evil, revealing it or denouncing (*tekku(s)snu-*, *ḫanti tiya-*) the suspect, occasionally preceded by a phrase for apprehending (*ep-*) vs. concealing something (*sanna-*) or someone (*munnai-*) from the king or his administration,[33] often connected with a phrase concerning whether the matter becomes known (*isduwa-*):

“and (if) you know about it” (**No. 27**, §20″, iii 27: *zi-ik-ma-at ša-ak-ti*; similarly **No. 26**, §5′, i 30′, §24″, iv 25; fragmentary: **No. 10**, §6″, iv 4′);

“(if) a colleague sees him [*by chan*]*ce* and he does [not] denounce him” (**No. 27**, §33″, iv 43–45: LÚ*a-ra-aš-ma-an-kán* [EGIR-*an*]-*da a-uš-zi na-an-kán ḫa-an-ti-i* [Ú-UL] *ti-ia-zi*; similarly **No. 26**, §30″, left edge 3–4; **No. 27**, §28″, iv 7–10, §32″, iv 38–39);

“Or if he sees some malevolence of his, and he conceals it” (**No. 27**, §26″, iv 1–2: [*n*]*a-aš-ma a-⸢pé⸣-el ku-⸢it⸣-ki* GÙB-*tar ⸢a-uš-zi⸣ na-at mu-un-na-a-zi*);

"If you(pl.) conceal it, though, ..." (**No. 2**, §12″, iii 18: *ták-ku ša-a-na-at-te-e-ni-ma*; similarly ***No. 20***, §16′, iv 19; with 3rd sg.: ***No. 20***, §14′, iii 82; **No. 27**, §32″, iv 41; similarly, with *munna-*: No. 8, §11″, iii 13′–14′; fragmentary: **No. 2**, §2′, i 8′);

"his commander and his *clan* chief must not conceal him" (**No. 10**, §7″, i 4: LÚDUGUD-*ŠU-ma-an* UGULA *LI-IM-ia le-e mu-un-na-iz-zi*; similarly, 3rd sg., with *sanna-*: **No. 27**, §32″, iv 40; and 2nd sg.: **No. 27**, §29″, iv 14, §30″, iv 23);

"whoever seizes him, but conceals him, ..." (***No. 20***, §8′, ii 48″: *ku-iš-ma-an e-ep-zi na-an mu-un-na-a-iz-zi*; similarly **No. 12**, §6′, i 25′, §13′, i 69′; fragmentary: **No. 22.1**, §3′, iv 12′–13′; **No. 11.A**$_6$, §2′, 7′);

"But afterwards it becomes known" (**No. 2**, §9″, iii 7–8: EGIR-*pé-ez-zi-ia-ma-at iš-tu-wa-a-ri*; similarly **No. 2**, §12″, iii 18–19; ***No. 20***, §14′, iii 82, §16′, iv 21, §17′, iv 30, §18′, iv 45–46; without *appezziya*(*n*): ***No. 20***, §19′, iv 66; negated: ***No. 20***, §17′, iv 31, §18′, iv 46–47, §19′, iv 68; cf. No. 8, §11″, iii 17′–18′);

"or (if) someone hears from someone some evil matter" (No. 14.2, §22′, ii 3–4: *i-da-a-lu-*un* me-mi-an ku-iš-ki ku-e-da-ni-ik-ki an-da iš-ta-ma-aš-zi*; similarly, 1st pl.: No. 19, §3, 11);

"or (if) you hear of it, but you do not report it to My Majesty imm[edi]ately" (**No. 18**, §5′, obv. 24′–25′: *na-aš-ma-at šu-me-eš-ma*[ ] [*i*]*š-ta-ma-aš-ta-ni na-at ma-a-an A-NA* dUTU-*ŠI ḫu-*[*u-da*]*-a-ak Ú-*UL me*-ma-at-te-ni*; similarly **No. 26**, §23″, iv 5–7, §24″, iv 25–32, §27″, iv 44–45, **No. 27**, §16″, ii 55′–57′; fragmentary **No. 27**, §12″, ii 18; **No. 10**, §7″, i 2);

"And if you hear from anyone about evil concerning My Majesty, then you must not conceal it" (**No. 27**, §24″, iii 54–57: *nu-kán ma-a-an ŠA* dUTU-*ŠI ku-e-da-ni-ik-ki* ḪUL-*lu an-da iš-da*$_4$*-ma-aš-te-ni na-at le-e mu-*˻*un-na*˼*-it-te-ni*);

"but he does not divulge (it) over this oath" (**No. 26**, §5′, i 30′–31′: *ke-e-da-ni-ma-za-kán* ˻*A-NA*˼ *NI-ÌŠ* DINGIR-*LÌ pa-ri-ia-an Ú-UL me-ma-i*);

"He who hears this, and conceals it, and does not report it in the palace" (**No. 26**, §4′, i 25′–26′: *na-*˹*at ku*˺*-iš iš-ta-ma-aš-zi na-at mu-un-na-iz-zi* [*na-a*]*t I-NA* É.GAL-*LÌ UL me-ma-i*; similarly **No. 26**, §6′, i 33′–34′, §9″, ii 9′, §26″, iv 41–42, §30″, left edge 4–5, **No. 27**, §23″, iii 47–49, 50–52; fragmentary: **No. 26**, §22″, iv 1–2; cf. **No. 2**, §11″, iii 15, §15″, iii 42; No. 4, §10, 58);

"but he does not [reve]al/[denou]nce him" (**No. 12**, §6′, i 25′: [*te-ek-ku-uš*]*-nu-uz-zi-ma-an Ú-UL*; in 2nd pl.: **No. 18**, §8″, rev. 5′–6′; in 1st pl.: No. 14.1, §23′, ii 5; similarly **No. 26**, §15″, iii 11; fragmentary: **No. 22.1**, §3′, iv 13′; **No. 27**, §14″, ii 46′);

"if y[ou] do not seize him immediately" (**No. 18**, §8″, rev. 7′: *[šu-me-š]a-an ma-a-an ḫu-u-da-a-ak* Ú-UL *e-ep-t[e-ni]*; similarly, 3rd sg.: **No. 12**, §14′, i 75′; 1st pl.: No. 14.1, §23′, ii 10; fragmentary: **No. 11.A**$_6$, §2′, 6′; **No. 12**, §14′, i 73′, §39″, iv 51′; **No. 16**, rev. 13′; ***No. 17***, §61″, iv 9′; **No. 28**, §18″, iv 11′);

"he must se[ize] him and rev[eal]/deno[unce] him" (**No. 12**, §13′, i 68′: *na-an e-e[p-du na-a]n te-⌜ek⌝-ku-u[š-nu-ud]-du*);

"he must seize him, and he must send him to the palace" (**No. 10**, §7″ i 2: *na-an e-ep-du na-an* I-NA É.GAL-LÌ *up-pa-ú*; similarly ***No. 17***, §16a, i 18′–21′, §16b$_2$, i 29′; similarly, 2nd pl.: **No. 10**, §12″, i 27; **No. 18**, §4′, obv. 19′);

"he must reveal [(him)] in the [(palace)] immediately" (**No. 10**, §7″, i 5: I-NA [(É.GAL-LÌ-*ia-an*) *ḫu*]-*u-da-a-ak te-ek-ku-uš-ša-nu-ud-du*; similarly **No. 10**, §6″, iv 5′).

Protecting and Supporting

Another ubiquitous demand or expectation is to protect or support (*paḫs-*) the king (**No. 12**, §13′, 63′?; **No. 18**, §3′, 12′; **No. 26**, §3′, 18′; **No. 27**, §1, 3–4, §2, 8, §3, 26–27) or his heir(s) (**No. 11.A**$_1$, §4′, 13′; **No. 26**, §3′, 19′; **No. 27**, §1, 4–5, §2, 8, 15–16, §3, 24–25, 26–27), occasionally his trusted officials (**No. 11.A**$_2$, §4′, 20′), or simply some matter pertaining to the king (**No. 12**, §12′, 59′–61′); cf. also fragmentary **No. 12**, §15′, 80′; No. 14, §23′, 27–28; ***No. 15.1***, §3′, 4′; **No. 18**, §2′, 5′; **No. 27**, §6′, 9′. It must be noted in this context that *paḫs-* is also commonly used with regard to things that must be guarded or maintained, such as the doorbolt of the city gate (*No.* ***13.1–2***, §5′, 3′–4′), a town (***No. 17***, §11a, 34, §12, 35–36, §15, 8′), or a temple (***No. 20***, §10′, 14, 17, §11′, 26).

Notes on Literary Form, Style, and Structure

The literary forms evinced in the texts presented in this volume vary considerably, even among those that can be attributed to a single genre, and one could certainly categorize them in a number of different ways. D'Alfonso (2006a; 2008: 348–50), for example, has identified six general types of formulations in the edicts, instructions, and oaths.[34] The present section highlights a selection of the most common and pertinent elements of the texts' literary forms and styles. The discussion here is ordered from the most to the least common "genre" and within each genre from the earliest to the latest composition.

THE "INSTRUCTIONS AND OATH IMPOSITIONS"

No. 2, the Instructions and Oath Imposition for Royal Servants Concerning the Purity of the King, which would seem to stem from the OH period, already shows all the essential elements of the "classical" Instruction and Oath Imposition compositions from the time of Tudḫaliya I and Arnuwanda I, though at the same time it preserves a number of the literary elements familiar from other OH compositions. For the most part it is styled as the direct speech of the king, in the 1st person, addressing his subordinates in the 2nd pl.[35] and issuing instructions in the imp. There are numerous conditional statements, the protasis generally setting out the undesirable behavior of the subordinate(s), the apodosis indicating its punishment and/or ill effects. These conditional statements are phrased sometimes in an impersonal 3rd sg., sometimes in the 2nd pl., and sudden shifts from one to the other in the same paragraph or even the same sentence are found. Likewise, the curses or evil consequences of the apodoses are usually phrased in an impersonal 3rd sg., but sometimes in the 2nd pl. In contrast to the later compositions, the style of No. 2 is more personal, direct and expressive, and it includes at least one illustrative anecdote (§§13″–14″), as found so often in other OH texts. As far as is preserved, the composition seems to follow no overall structure—unless the classes of servants found in or at the beginnings of §§5″, 8″, 9″, 10″, 13″, 20″, and perhaps 21″ are to be understood as lending it such—but rather to consist of a series of more or less related injunctions and instructions in no intrinsic order.

No. 10, Tudḫaliya I?'s Instructions and Oath Imposition for All the Men, shows an uncommon structure (cf. Nos. 22.2, 23), in that it begins with a reference to the oath to be sworn to the royal family, immediately after which the gods called to witness are listed. As Giorgieri (2005: 327) has noted, the list of divine witnesses is thus found at the beginning in this text,[36] in the middle in Nos. 14 and 28 and at the end in Nos. 12 and 18, strengthening the impression that the genre was never strictly standardized. Though the initial reference to the swearing of the oath (§1′), of which only a few fragmentary traces remain, could conceivably have been formulated either in the 1st person, that is, spoken by the subordinates themselves, or in the 2nd or 3rd person, as imposed by the king upon his subordinates, the closest parallels (cf. Nos. 22.2, 23) would seem to suggest the former. Nevertheless, the composition is styled for the most part as the words of the king spoken to his subordinates, whom he addresses in the 2nd pl. imp., though the 3rd impersonal is often employed as well, especially in the protases of conditional clauses. (The fragmentary context of what would seem to be a 1st sg. in §2″ allows no further commentary.) It favors "When ..., you must ..." and "If ..., then you must" constructions, inserting simple imperative admonitions only occasionally (e.g., end of §12″). In contrast to No. 26, for example, this text does not reference the oath at the end of nearly every paragraph, contenting itself with a single mention at the end (§25″). It specifically references its own words as preserved on the tablet in §25″.

The highly fragmentary texts of No. 11, Instructions and Oath Impositions for the Successions of Tudḫaliya I and Tudḫaliya III, are unique in their specific attempts to regulate the behavior of various branches of the royal family and possible pretendents to the throne toward one another as well as in their tendency to name them by name. Like the Telipinu Edict, they clearly constitute attempts to prevent or arrest potentially violent interdynastic struggles, and above all, to protect the particular person who had succeeded in mounting the throne. In No. 11.A the sons of Ḫimuili and/or the sons of Kantuzzili are addressed in the 2nd pl. (No. 11.A_1, §4′), as are the "Men of Ḫattusa" (No. 11.A_1, §5′). Sometimes the addressee is spoken to in the 2nd sg. (No. 11.A_1, §3′), but at no time is it clear who specifically is being addressed in the 2nd sg. The fragments attest several conditional statements detailing undesirable behavior in the protasis and the punishment in the apodosis as well as several passages that seem to refer to concrete historical events (e.g., 11.A_2, §2′). A single 1st pl. is attested (11.A_6, §2′), but its context is unclear. The fragments of No. 11.B, in contrast, speak of those involved mostly in the 3rd pl. (but cf. 11.B_2, §2′), nearly as often referring to a person in the 3rd sg., at one point to a certain Ḫattusili (11.B_1, §3′, 9′). Some passages are styled in the 1st pl. (11.B_1, §4′, B_2, §3′), but their fragmentary contexts allow no further comment. The fragments of 11.C at no point unequivocally address anyone in the 2nd person (unclear in 11.C_2, §§3′, 4″). They always speak of persons in the 3rd pl. and sg. No. 11.C_1 occasionally speaks in the 1st pl., while 11.C_2 is styled both in the 1st sg. and pl. At no point do these fragments seem to issue concrete instructions, but rather to implore concerning abstract attitudes and modes of behavior.

No. 12, the Instructions and Oath Imposition for Princes, Lords and Military Officers, is characterized by nearly every paragraph ending with a curse referring to "these oath deities," always directed against an impersonal 3rd sg. object. It is styled as the words of the king speaking in the 1st person. The first seven preserved paragraphs are formulated largely in the impersonal, only occasionally reverting to the 2nd pl. In contrast §§8′ to 15′ are dominated by the 2nd pl., while beginning with §16″ the remainder of the composition employs only the 3rd person, usually impersonally, except perhaps for one exception in §20″ in unclear context.[37] The 1st pl. forms toward the end of §15′, in fragmentary context (cf. also §37″), are presumably a quote of what the addresses are expected to say in support of the king during a campaign. In §8′ is seen a short anecdote reminiscent of those common in the OH texts, while in §§33″–34″ are seen fragmentary references to dynastic quarrels, recalling the fragments of No. 11. The last two paragraphs call the gods to witness and list them, at least partially. As noted above, the list of divinities is found at the beginning in No. 10, in the middle in Nos. 14 and 28, and at the end in this text and No. 18. In its conditional statements, this composition tends to favor formulations with indefinite pronouns (e.g., §6′), that is, "He who/Whoever does …," after which the curse is pronounced. It occasionally includes concise attempts at providing rationale for its commands (§9′, 43′–44′) as well as statements that could potentially be uttered by unworthy subordinates, which are to be avoided (e.g., §10′, 47′–49′). It issues for the most part general admonitions concerning loyal and energetic service, but becomes slightly more specific at several points, addressing such topics as the proper provisioning of the military (§9′) or the harboring of fugitives (§6′).

As far as preserved, Nos. 15.1 and 15.2, two fragmentary Instructions and Oath Imposition(s) of Arnuwanda I, are styled as the words of the king, introduced with *UMMA*,[38] speaking to his subordinates in the 2nd pl. and sg. or employing the 3rd impersonal.

No. 18, the Instructions and Oath Imposition for Military Commanders, lists the deities who are to witness the oath at the end, as does No. 12, in contrast to No. 10, where they are found at the beginning, and Nos. 14 and 28, where they are placed in the middle, highlighting the disparate structures employed in drafting these compositions (cf. comments sub Nos. 10, 12, 14, 28). The text employs the 2nd pl. to the exclusion of the sg., though it occasionally uses the impersonal 3rd person. It emphasizes throughout personal loyalty to the person of the king, who speaks generally in the 1st sg. Most paragraphs consist of protasis and apodosis. Some contain a hypothetical situation in the protasis and the expected behavior in the apodosis (e.g., §4′), some rather a series of negative behaviors in the protasis and the actions being placed under oath in the apodosis (e.g., §5′). The text may well have concluded with an oath spoken in the 1st pl., judging from the largely preserved *k*]*āsa* of rev. 17′. Similarly to No. 12, it issues primarily general admonitions concerning loyal and energetic service, only occasionally becoming slightly more specific.

What little is preserved of No. 22.1 contains instructions and/or an oath imposition, partly in the 2nd pl., partly in the 2nd sg. It is presumably styled as the words of the king. The phrases "the […] of the king (and) queen are many" (§2′) and "ev[il] to the king's […] and of his descendents" (§3′) would seem to suggest that loyalty to the king and his family is the principal theme. It includes a rare reference within the body of the text to a named king (§2′, 7′). Since the first fragment (No. 22.1) seems to contain instructions and perhaps an oath imposition, while the second (No. 22.2) appears to consist of an oath expressed in the 1st pl. (§2′, 8′), this might conceivably be a unique case of the obligations/instructions being recorded on one tablet and its corresponding oath on another, though this remains highly tentative.

No. 26, Tudḫaliya IV's Instructions and Loyalty Oath Imposition for Lords, Princes and Courtiers, completes every paragraph with the phrase "may that (misdeed) be placed under oath," with minor variations, except for §§9″–11″, which end with "may these (oath) gods destroy him," with minor variants. (The latter shows also that the composition most likely would have included a list of divine witnesses as well.) In this regularity it compares well with No. 12. It employs the 2nd pl. throughout except in §§10″ and 17″, where the 2nd sg. appears when addressing the subordinates. Otherwise, it portrays a series of potential situations in the 3rd impersonal. (The fragmentary context of the 1st pl. in §28″ allows no further commentary.) Nearly the entire composition is styled as a conditional protasis, or series thereof, often linked with "or," with the conditional lexeme occurring only occasionally, the apodosis consisting of the phrase "(then) may that (misdeed) be placed under oath." As far as can be ascertained, the composition is divided into several sections, each addressed specifically to a class of officials, beginning with the field commanders (§2′), then the lords who command the frontier posts (§10″), followed by the lords and princes (§14″), and finally, the courtiers (§21″). A further feature of the composition is the sometimes detailed definitions of various family statuses, relating above all to those who might represent a threat to the throne, along with incessant demands for unequivocal loyalty to the current king and his descendants. It often cites potential treasonous statements or excuses for treasonous behavior (§§3′, 4′, 9″, 12″, 15″, 16″, 20″, 27″, 28″?) as examples of words not to be spoken or tolerated. Paragraphs 10″–12″, 32′, apart from their standard references to the oath gods, seem to depart from the content and style of the rest of the paragraphs to some degree, and might constitute an insertion, perhaps indicating some degree of redactional history.

No. 27, Tudḫaliya IV's Instructions and Oath Imposition for Courtiers, introduced by *UMMA* (cf. n. 38), begins with the unique statement that the author had become king, requiring the oath imposition, which is then cited in the 1st pl. as if placed in the mouths of the subordinates. It then switches back to the 1st sg. address of the king, who speaks to his subordinates mostly in the 2nd pl., often in the imp., occasionally in the 2nd sg. The characteristics noted for No. 26 apply for the most part to this text as well, and the two could conceivably belong to a single composition. Reference to the oath swearing is made in §§23″–24″, the contents of which seem to suggest that the manuscript at hand was composed for the occasion of a second oath-taking session, at which a first group of subordinates who had already sworn upon the document were present a second time as well. As was the case with No. 10, this composition specifically references its own words as preserved on the tablet in §35″. Most paragraphs end with the statement that the described behavior will be placed under oath, but not all, as in No. 26.

No. 28, Suppiluliu/ama II's Instructions and Oath Imposition for the Men of Ḫattusa, shows perhaps the most intriguing structure of all. Its first paragraph constitutes the introduction of a plea, a prayer, formulated in the 1st sg. as the words of Suppiluliu/ama II, the last-known king of Ḫattusa, replete with genealogy, addressed to the gods of the land, an abbreviated list of which appears in the first lines. At least the following paragraph continues as an address to the gods. The text thereafter becomes too fragmentary to be certain, but it would seem to continue in the same vein before breaking off entirely. Most of col. ii consists of the list of deities called to witness the oath, then ends with the call (§9′, 32′), "Let them observe! [Let them] lis[ten]!" Just before the text breaks off again the author turns to the "men of Ḫattu[sa]" in the 2nd pl. imp. As noted, the list of divine witnesses is thus found in the middle of this text and in No. 14, at the beginning of No. 10, and at the end in Nos. 12 and 18. The instructions portion of this composition, dealing with obligations related to the cult of the ancestors, is then fragmentarily preserved after the loss of the remainder of col. ii and the first half of col. iii. These are interlaced with curses and mentions of the divine oath, in which manner the text continues in the poorly preserved paragraphs of col. iv as well, whereby a 1st pl. "we will be [*ru*]*ined*" is found toward the end of the last paragraph (§18″), unfortunately too poorly preserved to allow one to ascertain whether the subordinates are speaking or whether the author is quoting what some person had said or should say. As with most of the other obligation and oath texts, the instruction portion is styled as a series of conditional statements, partly in an impersonal 3rd person and partly in the 2nd pl.

The "Instructions"

No. 7, the Instructions for Military Officers and Frontier Post Governors, of which only four paragraphs can be meaningfully reconstructed, is spoken largely in the impersonal 3rd person, slipping at one point into the 2nd pl. imp. In one passage (§2′) the speaker, the Great King, reserves for himself the right to decide which army contingents are to be left as an occupying force and which are to be given leave rather than opting for a negative formulation forbidding his military commanders from making such decisions. The king switches between referring to himself in the 3rd person and formulating his sentences in the 1st sg. Only one paragraph contains a conditional statement, while the rest employ the 2nd and 3rd imp.

Nos. 13.1–2 are introduced with *UMMA* (cf. n. 38) and are styled as the direct address of the Great King Arnuwanda I to the Mayor of Ḫattusa in the 2nd sg., only occasionally in the impersonal 3rd sg. (e.g., 13.1, §§10″–11″). Nos. 13.3 and 13.4, lacking incipits and colophons, likewise address the mayor in the 2nd sg. These are thus the only text(s) in the corpus directed to a single individual rather than a class of subordinates. In addition to employing paragraph dividers, the text(s) divide various topics by means of "Moreover" (*anda=ma*) and are thus thematically rather well-structured compositions. They consist partly of simple 2nd sg. imperatives directed to the mayor, while much of the text lays out the basic rules, regulations and procedures that must have structured a normal day's activities in Ḫattusa, formulated mostly in the 3rd sg. and pl. imp. and pertaining to various officials of the city. Its complete exclusion of any reference to an oath, divine punishment or the like—the ends of 13.1–2, §§10″ and 11″ being the only hints at retribution of any sort—leaves open the possibility that the composition would have been an instruction text only. It is often very concrete and specific, regulating matters as specific as the number of guards that are to be posted at which structures (13.1–2, §2), when and what the herald is to cry out (13.1–2, §11″), not using workers employed by the palace for one's personal projects (13.3, §5′), the plastering of particular walls of particular building complexes (13.4, §5′) and the scraping of the city's sewage pools (13.4, §11″).

No. 17, the Instructions of Arnuwanda I for the Frontier Post Governors, is introduced via *UMMA* as the words of the king (cf. n. 38), though 1st sg. forms do not occur, even when My/His Majesty is referenced, suggesting that it might well be employed as a literary device to lend royal authority to the text rather than indicating a directly dictated composition.[39] As detailed elsewhere (Miller 2011b) the first twenty-one paragraphs are composed in the 3rd sg. and pl., even when referring to the governor of the post, employing mostly the imp. Beginning with §22 the governor is sometimes addressed in the 2nd sg., sometimes in the 3rd person, often switching within a single paragraph or even a single sentence, whereby there are significant differences among manuscripts of varying dates. Much of the text is concerned with property and personnel for which the governors would be responsible, referring to them with an impersonal 3rd passive. Many of its instructions are detailed and precise, including specific figures and dimensions for architectural structures and even, for example, for firewood. For an outline of its structure see the introduction to the text there. As is the case with No. 13, the composition as preserved makes no reference to an oath or divine punishment, and though it does not appear to be finished with the single extant tablet, it can be seen as a candidate for an unalloyed instruction text without an oath element.

No. 20, the Instructions for Priests and Temple Personnel, anonymously addresses the subordinates in the 2nd pl. for the most part, but also frequently switches to the impersonal 3rd sg. or pl. More than any other composition this text tends to offer, in addition to its threats, a sometimes extensive rationale for the instructions and injunctions it gives (e.g., §§2′–3′), and further, often attempts to anticipate the reasoning and self-justification that the subordinates might use to circumvent regulations, and then, to counter these arguments. Similarly, it seems to want to cover any and all potential ways in which a regulation might be abrogated, anticipating up to eight possibilities (e.g., §7′). It makes extensive use of lengthy protases consisting of long series of eventualities, followed by apodoses declaring such behaviors as criminal offenses to the gods. It thus sometimes evinces an almost conversational or persuasional style, as if it were giving advice as much as imposing obligations, possibly to be explained by the temple personnel being regarded not as servants of the issuing authority, perhaps the palace, but of the gods.

No. 21, Instructions for Supervisors, is styled partly in the 3rd impersonal, partly as a 2nd sg. imp. address. It lays out rather specific regulations in §2′, while §3′ commands a unique questioning of the inhabitants of the addressees' revier, formulating a series of probing questions.

No. 24, Instructions for Priests and Diviners, addresses its audience in the 2nd pl. imp., but resorts to a 3rd impersonal for substantial passages. It regulates rather specific duties of its addressees.

No. 25, Instructions for the UKU.UŠ-troops, addresses the subordinates in the 2nd pl. imp. and is styled as the words of the king speaking in the 1st person. It regulates rather specific and concrete matters.

The "Decrees"

No. 5, a Royal Decree on Social and Economic Matters, is formulated in the 2nd pl. for the most part, but includes sections in an impersonal 3rd person (§§1′–2′), unfortunately too fragmentary to determine their exact nature. §§3′–4′ prescribe economic reforms with the formula "earlier you(pl.) did X, but now you(pl.) will do Y." In the ensuing futilely fragmentary paragraphs the speaker refers repeatedly to his father, presumably the king, seemingly in the context of a reform concerning scales and weights.

No. 8, Tudḫaliya I's Decree on Penal and Administrative Reform, is introduced with *UMMA* as the words of the king (cf. n. 38). It and No. 27 are the only texts in the corpus to begin with an historical allusion, however brief, as the occasion for the issuing of the text. The historical event in the present text includes the complaints of the men of Ḫattusa, presented as a direct quote, about the king's absence from the capital due to military campaigns, which had led to chaotic circumstances. As the text breaks off at this point, the transition from this introductory passage to the ensuing decree is unfortunately lost. After the break the following section is styled in the impersonal 3rd person pres.-fut., suggesting that it should be seen as a decree or an edict. The remainder of the composition, however, switches among an impersonal 3rd person and the 2nd pl. (§§10″, 13″) or sg. (§§11″, 13″), with a 1st sg. in unclear context (§13″, iv 3′).[40] It seems, then, that the composition overall is to be seen as a reply to the very "men of Ḫattusa" who prompted the response in the first place. As preserved it contains no reference to oaths, curses, or divine witnesses, only some quarter of the text at the most being extant.

The two preserved paragraphs of No. 9, Tudḫaliya I's Decree on Judicial Reform, are formulated in an impersonal 3rd person. Both paragraphs seem to consist of long protases detailing problematic actions, followed by consequences in the apodoses, formulated partly as imperatives, partly in the pres.-fut. As it is labeled an oath in its colophon, it likely would have included sections containing other forms of address as well.

No. 16, the Decree of Queen Ašmunikkal concerning the "Royal Funerary Structure," following *UMMA* (cf. n. 38) and a single "we" in the long introductory clause, is formulated entirely in the impersonal 3rd person. It thus reads like a code of laws or regulations in contrast to the other texts of the volume. It is the only text in the collection without paragraph dividers, at least as far as is preserved.

The "Oaths" or "Loyalty Oaths"

No. 14, the Loyalty Oath of Town Commanders to Arnuwanda I, Ašmunikkal, and Tudḫaliya, is styled as the words of an oath spoken by these commanders in the 1st pl. pres.-fut., relating to the royal trio in the 3rd person. It is introduced with the *UMMA ... -MA* formula adopted from Mesopotamian letters (cf. n. 48), after which the names and origins of the numerous oath takers are listed. What the oath takers then swear to do and not to do echoes clearly the oath prescriptions found in the 2nd pl. in other related texts, so that it can be assumed that the text was written for the oath takers by the king and his scribes. Indeed, this is done rather crudely and mechanically on occasion, such as in §22′, 7–8, where the speakers are made to swear "or (if) we support so[(me)] enemy of ours," as if there was some great likelihood that these persons would support their own enemies. Naturally, the intent is that they are not to support an enemy of the royal family, to which "of ours" would have referred in the mind of the composing scribe. Also included in the "oath" in the first pl. are explanatory notes such as the fact that the oath tablets were fashioned as bronze tablets and placed before specific deities of specific towns (3.A §2′, 24′–28′), which one would not expect to be part of an oath per se. The section detailing acceptable and inacceptable behavior (§§22′–23′) consists of one long series of conditional clauses in a protasis. The apodosis is lost, but would presumably have asked "a[(ll)] the gods of Ḫattusa" (end of §23′), who are then listed beginning in §24′, to punish the oath breaker. After a gap, §25″ and the first part of §26″, in contrast, are formulated in the impersonal 3rd sg. and pl. and may perhaps constitute a section of the composition not spoken by the subordinates, but by the issuing authority. The latter part of §26″, then, resumes the 1st pl. statement of the troops. As Giorgieri (2005: 327) has noted, the list of divinities is found in the middle of this text (§24′) and No. 28, at the beginning of No. 10, and at the end in Nos. 12 and 18.

No. 19, Āsḫapāla's Oath Regarding an Obligation to Supply Troops, is in many respects an outlier among the texts of this volume. It is spoken in the 1st pl. pres.-fut., introduced by *UMMA* (cf. n. 26), and promises merely to support Ḫattusa instead of the enemy, to supply a small number of troops for the king, and to report enemy plans to the provincial governor. The text seems to be introduced by some third person, however, who either quotes what Āsḫapāla and his men had said or formulates an oath for them, writing that it "[shall be] pl[aced und]er o[ath] for them" (§1). The letter-like physical format of the tablet, its brevity, and its lack of divine witnesses and curses might suggest that the document represents a memorandum or draft of sorts, which at some later juncture would have been worked into a full loyalty oath or obligation and loyalty oath composition. Despite its format, it does not appear to be a letter per se, as it lacks an addressee and a sender.

No. 22.2, §2′ constitutes the remains of an oath in the 1st pl. It states the intention of swearing to the royal family every month, and continues with an invocation to the gods at the end of the paragraph, followed by a list of divine witnesses (§3′). Since its opening paragraphs show affinities to Nos. 10, 14, and 23 (see No. 22.2, n. 13), that is, to both Instruction and Oath Imposition as well as Oath compositions, it is difficult to establish unequivocally if this fragment should be considered as an oath imposition in which the oath as it is to be enunciated by the subordinates in the 1st pl. is included (cf. also No. 27) or as a text consisting entirely of an oath.

No. 23, labeled here an Oath of the Men of Ḫattusa to Ḫattusili III and Pudu-Ḫepa, could just as well have been an obligation and oath composition like No. 22.1 or a loyalty oath in the 1st pl., like Nos. 14 and 22.2, as it is uncertain whether it was spoken in the 1st pl. or otherwise.

The "Protocols"

No. 3, a Protocol for the Palace Gatekeeper, begins nonchalantly with the start of the gatekeeper's workday, "When he reaches the door bolt of the palace, …." It continues throughout with a prescription, always in the 3rd sg. or pl. pres.-fut., never using the imp., of his routine and that of the personnel with whom his day is concerned. §§3–5 constitute a uniquely formatted list of the occupational titles with which he is to address the court personnel, with the Hattian terms in the left column, the Hittite or Sumerian writings in the right. As is the case with No. 4, it includes no 2nd-person address and no commands and makes no mention of oaths, curses, or punishment. It is thus presumably not of directly royal origin, but may perhaps have been composed by some official responsible for the activities reflected in the text.

No. 4, the Protocol for the Royal Body Guard, belongs to a different category than the obligation and oath genre defined above, though labeled an "obligation; instruction" (*isḫiul-*) in its colophon. Like No. 3 it includes no 2nd-person address and no commands and makes no mention of oaths, curses, or punishment. Rather, it simply prescribes the protocol of the royal bodyguard as if it were a set of stage directions, generally in the 3rd sg. or pl. pres.-fut., occasionally using the prohibitive. It refers to the king in the 3rd person as well. Even the occasional passage that one would like to translate in the imp. is actually formulated in the pres.-fut., such as the last sentence of §10. It sounds more like the words of a clerk than a king, and one might speculate that it could have been drawn up by the scribe of whoever was responsible for the guard, perhaps the chief of the royal bodyguard, the GAL *MEŠEDI*. It includes a number of conditional clauses, providing for some of the various contingencies of daily life, but is otherwise a straightforward protocol. For an outline of the structure of the composition and a discussion of the additions and corrections, see the introduction to the text.

The "Royal Reprimand"

No. 1 is in many ways an outlier among the texts of the present volume. Though it addresses its audience in the 2nd pl., it formulates no instructions or commands and there is no mention of oaths or divine sanction. One suspects, however, that at some point in the now-lost portions of the text the tone would have switched to that of a decree or perhaps a set of instructions. As it stands it contains only reprimands composed in various styles, including rhetorical questions that border on the sarcastic. The speaker is presented as a prince, a son of the king and a supporter of his policies, rebuking his listeners for not following them as they should. It includes two paragraphs (§§3′–4′) devoted to what seems to be an anecdote-like aside that appears to touch on the activities in which the audience is involved.

THE INSTRUCTIONS AS A SOURCE FOR HITTITE HISTORY, RELIGION, SOCIETY, AND THOUGHT

The present section can naturally only briefly highlight a very limited selection of cultural characteristics witnessed in the corpus. It should be emphasized again that mining these compositions for clues on Hittite society must be done without losing track of the fact that they essentially present a normative view of the way things should be, and this, as a rule, from the viewpoint of the king.

THE KING AND THE STATE

As in most other text genres from Ḫattusa, the texts of the present volume illustrate ubiquitously how the Hittite king was the sovereign over every aspect of his realm, uniting what today is viewed as executive, military, judicial, and religious power. The first two paragraphs of No. 8, Tudḫaliya I's Decree on Penal and Administrative Reform, constitute one clear example among many:

> Thus (speaks) the Sovereign,[41] Tudḫaliya, Great King: Once I destroyed Āssuwa, I [ca]me back to Ḫattusa, and I provided for the deities, so that all the men of Ḫattusa began to revere me, and they spoke thus: "You, Your Majesty, our [L]ord, you are a *campaigner*, and so you have not been able to render judgment concerning law cases, and [...] evil persons have utterly destroyed [...]. [...]-s, land holdings and *sarikuwa*-troops [...] he/it has become [*awf*]*ul*."

Here Tudḫaliya follows up his military successes against Āssuwa in western Anatolia by fulfilling his duties as chief priest to the Hittite pantheon (cf. similarly in No. 7, §§2′–3′). His attention to military matters, however, had caused him to neglect rendering judicial decisions, which had led to an anarchic situation in the capital.

That the king was the final instance regarding any conceivable question in his realm is seen in the repeated demand for important law cases, decisions, and evildoers to be brought directly to His Majesty (e.g., No. 7, §6″, 5′–6′, §7″, 16′–17′: fugitives; No. 10, §12″, 27: disparager of the king; No. 10, §14″, 36–37, No. 17, §38′, 23–24: law case beyond authority of a judge; No. 17, §16, end: refuser of military duty; No. 17, §34′, 43′: record of cult paraphernalia; No. 17, §55a′, 23′–24′: robber of the palace servants; No. 14, §23′, 11–12: writer of an evil matter; cf. also No. 8, §10″, 9′–10′ and No. 20, §8′, 49″ for bringing an offender "to the king's gate").

In No. 10, §16″, Tudḫaliya I?'s Instructions and Oath Imposition for All the Men, one sees that the signing of a treaty with a bordering land was the prerogative of the king alone and was not allowed the provincial governors.

Text No. 2 (Instructions and Oath Imposition for Royal Servants Concerning the Purity of the King) constitutes a clear example of the import attached to the purity of the king in Hittite society; indeed in Hittite thought the purity and well-being of the king were directly correlated with the well-being of the Land of Ḫattusa itself. The concept of purity (*parkui-*, *suppi-*; see Wilhelm 1999; Christiansen 2013) can doubtless be considered one of the fundamentally constitutive and pervasive conceptions of Hittite society, as demonstrated not only by the great attention paid to preserving the king's purity in texts such as No. 2, but also, for example, by the large corpus of purification rituals designed to restore purity if lost for any reason (Collins 2007: 178–90).

A further prominent feature of especially early Hittite society is the assembly, which apparently maintained some significant degree of power alongside and vis-à-vis royalty, a subject which Beckman (1982) has treated in depth. Collins (2007: 40) defines the assembly (*panku-*; also *tuliya-*) as "an ad hoc judicial body composed of members of the state bureaucracy whose role was to witness and enforce agreements and royal proclamations and to try criminal offenders of particularly high status." The situation of No. 1, §5′ (A Royal Reprimand of the Dignitaries) suggests its potential involvement in an investigation into the illegitimate activities of high officials.

The texts of this volume also constitute one of the richest sources for the reconstruction of the various offices of the state administrative structure. The great number of professional titles was catalogued by Pecchioli Daddi (1982), while Beal (1992) treated all military categories and Imparati (1999) has provided a recent overview of Hittite state structures.

Some light on how the general populace, as it seems, could access and appeal to the king is found in No. 4, §§29–36, the Protocol for the Royal Body Guard, where it appears that the king would stop during his journeys to outlying towns in order to receive petitioners and review their law cases. Executive decisions or decrees concerning economic matters can be glimpsed in the unfortunately badly fragmentary No. 5, §§3′–5′, a Royal Decree on Social and Economic Matters, where prices for basic commodities such as beer, wine, and textiles are set and, apparently, a reform of weights and scales is set out. For the most part, however, the texts reveal little concerning the lives of ordinary inhabitants of Ḫattusa and Ḫatti.

Law and Justice

Obviously, the king was not omnipresent and did not judge all law cases personally. He would have functioned analogously to a supreme court, judging only the most intractable, potentially important cases, presumably often involving members of the upper strata of society, for the most part in the capital. Other law cases were handled by the governors and magistrates representing the central administration and by community elders (e.g., No. 10, §14″; No. 17, §§37′–40′). If such law cases exceeded the capacity or authority of the local administration, they were to be directed to the king himself (e.g., No. 17, §38′, 23–24). Recent summaries of law and judicial procedure have been provided by Haase (2003) and Archi (2008).

In Text No. 1, evidence both for hierarchical power structures in Hittite society that had led to great differences in wealth and status and to oppression of the lower by the upper stratum on the one hand, as well as for an explicit and passionate moral stance opposing such oppression on the other can be seen. Here a royal prince is seen angrily rebuking officials of his own administration for their unjust treatment of the poor and their cronyism with the rich. It is precisely such ethically zealous passages that have prompted a number of researchers of the ancient Near East to draw special attention to this feature of Hittite society, as, for example, Archi has done with his paper entitled *L'humanité des Hittites* (1979),[42] in which Text No. 1 plays a central role alongside the Decree of Pimpira (*CTH* 24; Cammarosano 2006), with its strongly ethical and didactic instructions to a young king. Several passages that forbid various behaviors and formulate severe punishments for infractions are at pains to stress that both the highest and the lowest classes of persons will be brought to justice equally. In No. 9, §1, for example, one reads "And if … (a man) *impedes* the king (in his judicial duties)—be he a royal body guard, a palace servant or a *clan* chief (or) a dignitary—they shall drive him away. He shall pay the *appropriate* compensation from his estate" (cf. similarly in No. 12, §§6′, 26″–27″). And in the following paragraph one finds an even more broadly encompassing statement, "be he a great lord, be he the lowli[est …] man, he shall surely die" (No. 9, §2; cf. fragmentary No. 12, §§28″–29″).

Remarkably, some Hittite officials are even instructed to seek out the craftsmen and elders in the towns in which they are responsible and inquire of them whether the guards of the city gates, the men of the royal households and other persons are corrupt, even directing them to ask if "they take wine for themselves" while pouring "water [*for you*]" (No. 21, §3′). At least a couple further passages in No. 13.3 (§4′, 19′; §5′) seem to aim at preventing corruption, but are too fragmentary to allow certainty. A number of passages warn against oppression of lower classes or subordinates (No. 1, *passim*; No. 13.1–2, §14″; No. 28, §13″?).

In No. 4, §§29–40 one finds a protocol concerning how petitioners are to be granted an audience with the king during a journey from town to town, and there seems to be no indication that these petitioners were only to be allowed access if they belonged to a certain class. It therefore seems, at least theoretically, that any person in the Hittite realm could directly petition the highest authority in the land. In several passages of a number of texts those responsible for adjudicating law cases are warned not to "make a superior case inferior" or to "make an inferior case superior" (No. 10, §14″, 34–35; No. 17, §39′; cf. No. 9, §1, 3–4). They are also instructed essentially to excuse themselves from law cases in which they may have a personal interest: "He (the governor of the post) shall not, however, do it for a lord, nor shall he do it for a brother, his sister or his friend" (No. 17, §39′). They are explicitly directed to take up law cases pending for servants and for women without kin (No. 17, §40′), that is, the weakest and most vulnerable of the lowest classes of society. Taking bribes is occasionally explicitly forbidden (No. 12, §5′, 20′; No. 17, §39′).

This scattered but nevertheless striking evidence suggesting a strong sense of social justice stands in stark contrast to passages in these compositions and elsewhere, in which, for example, various punishments are said to be reserved for different classes of persons. As mentioned below, a thieving servant could be blinded, while a thieving free man was not.

The very first lines of No. 2, among many others, mention the common practice of condemning offenders to death; far more poorly attested in the Hittite texts are cases where such sentences are actually carried out (de Martino and Devecchi 2012; Haase 2003: 651). While executions are generally noted simply with words for "to kill," more specific attestations mention decapitation, throat slitting, hanging, and burning at the stake. At least some executions were carried out at a city gate (Miller 2011c). Offenses deemed worthy of death included crimes against the king or state, acts compromising especially the purity of the king or the gods, sorcery, rape, adultery, certain cases of bestiality, and homicide (de Martino and Devecchi 2012). The type of punishment for at least some matters of sexual impropriety was considered better left to local tradition, as seen in No. 17, §37′, where either execution or banishment is allowed for.

Death in the Hittite world could be meted out not only by terrestrial authorities, however; in Hittite thought the gods and goddesses were equally, or more so, to be feared. A passage more illustrative of this fact than §6″ of No. 2 can hardly be hoped for: "[If] someone causes [impur]ity, someone [rais]es the ire of the king, and you say as follows: '[The king] won't see us!' On the contrary, the *king's* gods are already watching you! They will turn you into a goat, and they will drive you into the mountains; or they will turn you into a *gaggapa*-animal, and they will drive you to the cliff!" The gods were assumed to be relentless in seeking out and punishing those who would transgress.

Naturally, death was not the only punishment that could be inflicted by men and gods upon the guilty. The texts of this corpus are highly informative concerning a myriad of further more or less gruesome penalties that could be imposed as well. Importantly one finds here that collective punishment is generally considered to be the acceptable norm. Wives, sons, and further descendents are to be destroyed along with their wayward men (e.g., No. 2, §§7″, 9″; No. 12, §§6′, 8′, 14′; No. 20, §13′), and the gods could avenge themselves upon not only the sinner, his wife, his sons and his descendents, but also his family, his servants and even his cattle, sheep and grain (No. 20, §2′, 32′–§3′, 38′).[43] One passage (No. 20, §13′) even calls for all those present in a temple that is destroyed in a disaster caused by neglect to be annihilated along with their families and descendents.

The blinding of a servant was apparently an acceptable and sufficient punishment if he was caught stealing, as he was in this case not to be handed over to the injured party (e.g., No. 8, §5′; cf. also No. 14, §23′ and n. 277). A free man caught stealing, however, was not to be blinded, but was allowed to pay compensation (e.g., No. 8, §6′). In No. 17, §37′, 15′–16′ is seen a type of punishment known as *sakuwai-*, the nature of which remains unclear (also No. 8, §10″, 11′, §11″, 18′; cf. No. 17, n. 423), for anyone who would allow a person banished for sexual crimes to return to the community. One intriguing passage (No. 20, §11′, 31–34) relates that if a guard is not executed for neglecting to sleep up at the temple he could instead be forced to carry water from a spring into the temple three times in the nude, which probably suggests that nakedness must have been a grave humiliation in the Hittite mind rather than a relatively light punishment.

Other punishments are more akin to talion, such as a member of the temple personnel found to have cheated the temple of some amount of grain having his own grain taken and added to the temple supplies (No. 20, §16′, 23–24) or having to replace an ox consumed rather than presented to the gods (No. 20, §17′, 31).[44] Compensation for bloodshed is also mentioned (No. 8, §5′), which is said to "redeem" (SAG.DU-*ZU* *wa-aš-ta*) the murderer and disallow his being turned over to the injured party.

Religious Beliefs and Behavior

The nearly fully preserved Instructions for Priests and Temple Personnel (No. 20) provides an unparalleled wealth of information on religious thought, practice, and, intriguingly, even on potential religious misdeeds and heterodox conceptions or behavior. Especially regarding the latter one must remain cautious, though, since these are not objectively observed transgressions and explicitly formulated thoughts, but rather an attempt at proactively heading off offenses that the writer anticipates might occur. Nevertheless, all the potential crimes mentioned are quite believable, and one can surely assume that these warnings reflect for the most part real occurrences and real thought processes. The text is so uncommonly revealing because it provides not only instructions on how mundane tasks are to be properly fulfilled and seeks not only to enforce compliance through threats and promises of reward, but also attempts to provide convincing reasoning, based naturally on the prevailing worldview in which it is set, as to *why* they should be performed as such; further, it occasionally attempts to counter what it foresees as potential excuses that the temple personnel might come up with in order to justify impious behavior.

Unsurprisingly, the purity of the addressees, that is, the priests and temple officials, is a chief concern for the author of the text, as their impurity could, in the minds of the Hittites, lead to the aggravation and even the departure of the gods, upon whom the well-being of the land was believed to depend. Among the most illuminating attempts at convincing the personnel of the importance and the appropriateness of the duties demanded of them is the extended metaphor in No. 20, §2′, in which the relationship of a human servant to his/her divine master is explicitly likened to that between a human servant and his/her earthly master:

> Is the mind of man and (that) of the gods somehow different? No! (And) in regard to this very (matter)? No! The mind is indeed one and the same. When a servant stands up before his master, he is washed and he wears pure (clothes), and he gives him (something) to eat or he gives him (something) to drink. And since he, his master, eats (and) drinks, he is of a tranquil mind, and he is therefore attached to him. If, however, he is ever *neglected*, is he not *perturbed*? And is the spirit of a deity somehow different?

That the mind or spirit of man and the mind or spirit of the gods are essentially alike is a statement whose value for our understanding of Hittite theological views can hardly be overestimated.

Perhaps one of the most difficult facts for modern observers to keep in mind while considering ancient societies, including the Hittite, is that practically any and every important decision was made in what was considered to be consultation with the gods, that is, with reference to omens and oracles (Collins 2007: 166–69; Haas 2008; Taracha 2009: 144–49),[45] and these find reflection in the texts of this corpus as well. The river ordeal mentioned in No. 2, §§7″ and 13″–14″ is one type found here (see No. 2, n. 57). The drinking ordeal in No. 20, §§18′–19′ would have functioned similarly. No. 10, §11″ shows that a decision that the king had to make concerning what military forces were to remain behind in an occupied land could be based upon oracular inquiry, as could decisions about whether or not to ratify a peace agreement with foreign lands (No. 10, §16″). The threatened oracle inquiry in No. 20, §15′ seems intended to determine the guilt or innocence of the parties involved and/or to determine the punishment to be meted out to the guilty. Bird omen experts are found in the royal court in No. 3, §22″, unfortunately with no further intelligible context.

Several of the instruction and oath texts preserve lists of the gods invoked to witness the oaths (No. 10, §2′; No. 12, §§42″–43″; No. 14, §24′; No. 18, §10″; No. 22.2, §3′, No. 28, §§6′–9′; cf. also No. 14.3, §2′, 24′–32′ and No. 28, §1), and these lists, found similarly in the treaties, have long played an important part in reconstructing the Hittite pantheon or panthea. Giorgieri (1995: 47–52) has studied the lists in these oaths in particular.

Man and Society

Despite their overwhelmingly royal perspective, several texts, first and foremost the Instructions of Arnuwanda I for the Frontier Post Governors (No. 17), unintentionally provide a limited degree of insight into the daily lives of the village and town inhabitants of provincial Ḫatti, or at least those that potentially would have been exposed to some threat. One finds that the populace of the town, along with its domestic animals, would have spent the night within the fortified town walls and its locked and guarded gates, which were only opened again the following morning (No. 17, §§7–9). If an enemy force—the Kaska peoples is presumably intended—was sighted, the town would have been closed up until the danger had passed (§15). The town and this routine was regulated and guarded by a state military organization. Such towns were the seat of a royal residence (§§27′–29′) with all the accompanying structures and their maintenance.

This and other texts also provide important attestations for the Hittite conception of the essential nature and composition of the human being, above all in its partition of a person into a material (Hitt. *tuekka*, often expressed with Sum. NÍ.TE) and an immaterial (Heth. *istanzan(a)-*, Sum. ZI) component, akin to the physical body and the *anima* or "soul," respectively.[46] This fundamental dualism was also projected onto the divine world, as seen, for example, in No. 20, §2′. The sphere in which the Hittite *istanzan(a)-* was thought to function overlaps only partially with that familiar to those versed in the Christian and classical Roman and Greek traditions.[47] Not only one's volition, will (No. 4, §6; No. 10, §§16″–17″), and loyalty (No. 10, §12″) lay in the realm of the *istanzan(a)-*, rage as well was thought to be a function of the *istanzan(a)-*, as shown in No. 2, §13″. Depending on the context it can also be translated "will," "heart" or "mind." The most thorough study of the Hittite attestations of heart, mind, and soul remains Kammenhuber's exhaustive papers (1964, 1965).[48]

WRITING

The texts of the corpus—even apart from their colophons (see below) and their status as textual artifacts in their own right—also provide a significant number of revealing references to the functions, modi, and media of writing in the upper levels of Hittite society. In No. 1, §6′, the author, the crown prince, refers to a tablet[49] upon which his father, the king, had written to the dignitaries, reprimanding them for their unethical actions. As argued in the introduction to the text and above, this composition is to be dated to the Hittite Old Kingdom, perhaps even to the reign of Mursili I, demonstrating the usage of the medium already at this point.[50] In No. 10, §25″, unfortunately in fragmentary context, the words of the tablet refer to themselves, emphasizing that its addressees must obey the words "of this tablet" and that the oath deities are to destroy whoever does not obey the words "of this tablet." Words are thus no longer understood only as what a person enunciates, but also as that which is recorded on a written medium, whereby writing fulfils one of its primary functions, preserving for long periods of time words that otherwise may be forgotten, disputed or manipulated. Presumably it is in this context that the equally fragmentary mentions of the "obligation(s) of purity" in No. 15.2, §1 are to be seen, where the words of the obligation (*isḫiul-*) no longer refer merely to the statements uttered by the king, but also, in their most authoritative and indelible avatar, to the written words of the tablet. Paradoxically, a passage in No. 27, §35″ seems almost to seek to work against this conception, as here the king advises his courtiers against attempting to adhere strictly to the "letter of the law" at the expense of the "spirit of the law" when he warns them against claiming, "On this tablet these words are not to be found, so it shall be permissible for me." In No. 11.C_1, §4′, one sees what is likely a reference to a land grant, one of the most important and well-attested legal and administrative instruments of the late OH and MH periods (Riemschneider 1958; Rüster and Wilhelm 2012). Here estates are said to have been given to Pariyawatra, Kantuzili, and Tulpi-Teššub, progeny of Arnuwanda I and Ašmunikkal, grants that were "recorded for [the]m on a tablet."

The instructions refer, however, not only to clay tablets, but also to the other primary writing medium extant at the time in Anatolia, to wooden writing boards, presumably to be understood either as a wooden diptych whose inner surface(s) were covered with wax into which the characters were impressed or as wooden panels onto which one wrote with some type of ink. Researchers have long argued for either Luwian hieroglyphics or for cuneiform as the form of writing employed on wooden writing boards among the Hittites (Symington 1991; Marazzi 2000; Herbordt 2005: 36–39; Mora 2007; 2010b: 96–97; Hoffner 2009: 6–10; Waal 2011; 2012), but no conclusive evidence has yet become available. In No. 17, §38′, the governor of a frontier post is instructed to judge law cases well, whereby a person bringing "a sealed writing board from a clay tablet" is mentioned, a phrasing that has caused some discussion (cf., e.g., Symington 1991: 119; *CHD* Š, 16b–17a). If in fact this passage indicates that an archival judicial document preserved as a clay tablet could be copied onto a wooden writing board, which might then be sealed and subsequently presented to an official responsible for adjudicating such law cases, it would represent an enlightening passage indeed. Alas, too little information is provided by the terse passage to allow more secure conclusions. A further interesting reference is found in the same text, No. 17, §54a′, where the provincial governor is warned against the possibility of someone misappropriating the grain stores and then destroying the wooden writing boards, presumably in an attempt to disguise from the administration the fact that the amount of grain remaining no longer matched that found in the administrative records. As discussed more extensively elsewhere (Miller 2011b), this detail is found only in the later NH copy, not in the MH original, which might potentially have repercussions for our understanding of the development of the usage of wooden writing boards in Ḫattusa. Moreover, the passage would seem to have implications regarding the oft-noted lack of administrative and economic documents at Ḫattusa, and might support those who have suggested that such records would have been written on precisely such wooden writing boards, which naturally have not survived. No less revealing is the passage in No. 20, §8′, in which is described how a member of the temple personnel, who are otherwise forbidden to own silver or gold, is to have a valuable royal gift documented as follows, so as to avert suspicion: The gift was to be (a) designated as a royal present; (b) weighed and registered; (c) the occasion of its presentation was to be recorded; and (d) the names of those who had witnessed the presentation were to be appended to it; (e) the temple employee was to sell it in the presence of the nobility; the sale, too, was then (i) to be recorded on a wooden writing board, which was (ii) to be "pre-sealed" (*peran siyandu*), pending the return of the king to the city, at which time the seller was (iii) to present the tablet in the palace (iv) for it to be sealed officially. One wonders, of course, why the king would present a gift to a temple functionary that s/he would just have to register and sell, the sale of which s/he had to have notarized by the king, and thus, just how real the envisioned scenario would have been. On the other hand, bureaucracy in any culture often has its own perception of what is to be regarded as sensible, so that such a cumbersome procedure cannot be ruled out *a priori*. The passage does seem to suggest, at a minimum, that certain commodities were kept at least to some degree under state control, and that sealing and documentation by means of wooden writing boards played some role in the policing mechanisms employed to maintain that control. Reference to a scribe of wooden writing boards is found also in the fragmentary passage in No. 24, §5."

The writing of letters between the king and his officials and military officers is mentioned in passing on numerous occasions (No. 10, §§11″, 25; 15″, 1′; 16″, 8′; No. 18, §5′), while correspondence among officials is found as well (No. 14, §23′, 8–10). In the face of such common references to letter writing among Hittite administrators, as well as its archaeological attestation at sites such as Maşat Höyük / Tapikka, it remains a mystery why comparatively little correspondence has been recovered at Ḫattusa. Clearly the royal letter archives of the Hittite kings have not yet been found.

Political History

As far as the present texts' contribution to political history is concerned, the earliest would seem to be the dreadfully fragmentary No. 6, which mentions Zitanza, Muttall[i], and Ḫumm[ili?] in the context of oath taking, names that have understandably been equated with the Hittite kings Zidanza—generally called the II, in order to distinguish him from the similarly named Zidanta of the Old Kingdom—and Muwattalli I as well as the latter's officer and eventual murderer, Ḫimuili, the latter two of which were involved in bloody dynastic feuds before the reign of Tudḫaliya I. Unfortunately, the fragment here surrenders nothing that is not known from other documents.

Among the most important texts historically are those subsumed under No. 11, since these, despite their particularly fragmentary condition, help fill in an epoch that has remained equally spotty, notwithstanding the significant new evidence touching on the period discovered in recent years.[51] The composition(s) of No. 11.A, much in the spirit of Telipinu's Edict, seems to attempt to quiet the bloodshed that saw the assassinations of the kings Ḫuzziya II and Muwattalli I, in the wake of which Tudḫaliya I, son of Kantuzzili, gained the throne, bringing calm to the royal court again for some three generations, until Suppiluliuma I's murder of Tudḫaliya the Younger. At least some passages of these fragments address directly the sons of Ḫimuili and Kantuzzili, two men who are known to have participated in the disposal of Muwattalli I, who himself had played a role in and benefited from the murder of his predecessor, Ḫuzziya II. Those addressed are forbidden to continue the bloodshed and to remain loyal to the current occupant of the throne. Other passages address Ḫattusa in general with similar demands. The murder of [Muw]attalli is mentioned, as is the apprehension that Muwā, Muwattalli's chief bodyguard and the nemesis of Kantuzzili and Ḫimuili, would kill the queen, who is also tellingly called "your(pl.) mother," but who remains aggravatingly unidentified.[52]

The even more fragmentary texts of No. 11.B reflect a similar situation in which members of the royal family and the nobility are required to swear allegiance to a new king, but to which new king cannot be reliably derived from the preserved text, despite repeated claims to the contrary (see introduction to No. 11.B). The fragments of No. 11.C are again similarly conceived and relate to the situation surrounding the installation of Tudḫaliya III as king two generations later, while his predecessor, Arnuwanda I, and his queen, Ašmunikkal, at least according to some, were still alive and in office. The further mention of the princes Tulpi-Teššub, Pariyawatra, and Kantuzili, as well as the princesses Mušu-Ḫep[a] and, apparently, Lalantiwasḫa has led to much discussion of the prosopography of the MH royal family (Marizza 2007).

In a short anecdotal passage, No. 12, §34″, also refers to Mūwattalli's murder of Ḫuzziya, mentioning the important fact that the father of the speaker, presumably Kantuzzili, had been bound to him by oath, whereby it can only be assumed that "to him" refers to the murdered king Ḫuzziya, thus providing a justification for Kantuzzili's subsequent participation in the murder of Mūwattalli. As Oettinger has noted (1976: 82), §§33″–34″ remind one of Telipinu's description in his Edict of the royal strife preceding his own age.

The opening lines of No. 8 are of course important for their reference to Tudḫaliya I's destruction of Āssuwa, apparently a confederacy of sorts in western Anatolia, a campaign or campaigns detailed in his extremely fragmentary annals (Carruba 1977; 2008). For a narrative summary, including discussion of the entities Wilusiya and Taruisa, often equated with Ilios and Troy, one can refer to Bryce (2005: 123–27, 357–71). Other references in three texts to the Kaskaeans (Nos. 4, §37; 10, §17″; 26, §10″) assist the historian in understanding the relationship between Ḫatti and this group of apparently seminomadic clans, which lived roughly in the mountainous Pontic region north of the Hittite core lands and with which the Hittites maintained an intermittent struggle for centuries (see most recently Klinger 2002, 2005a).

No. 14 (1, §21, 26–27; 3, §2′, 18′–19′, 31′–32′, §29″) provides several clear references to Arnuwanda, his wife Ašmunikkal, and to "Tudḫaliya, son of the king, crown prince," a welcome anchor for a period that vexes historians to this day. No. 17, §40′, instructs its addressees to keep an eye on the troops of Kasiya, Ḫimmuwa, Tagarama, and Isuwa, which has relevance for the question of the extent of the Hittite Empire toward the east during this period in which Isuwa was an important buffer state between Ḫatti and Mittani. No. 22.2, §2′, provides an attestation of Suppiluliuma I together with the queen (mother), Tadu-Ḫepa, while No. 23 attests Ḫattusili III and Pudu-Ḫepa.

No. 26 is important for its illustration of the perpetual fear in which Tudḫaliya IV seems to have lived due to the numerous progeny of the former kings Mursili II, Muwattalli II, and his own father Ḫattusili III (§3′), while No. 27 (§2) adds Suppiluliuma I to the list. It was surely the norm, however, not an exception, that the reigning king would have lived alongside numerous branches of the royal line descended from younger sons of former queens and secondary wives. It is known, of course, that Kuruntiya, a son of Muwattalli and king of the secondogeniture in Tarḫuntassa, in fact posed a menace at some point, even taking the title Great King at some juncture, and that Karkamiš, which was also ruled by descendants of former Hittite kings, outlived the dynasty at Ḫattusa by at least some length of time. Moreover, Tudḫaliya's parents, Ḫattusili III and Pudu-Ḫepa, who themselves usurped the throne upon sidelining Ḫattusili's nephew Urḫi-Teššub, son of Ḫattusili's brother, Muwattalli II, are known to have been pathologically paranoid in their concern about their son successfully inheriting the kingdom, so that their angst may well have rubbed off on him as well. No. 26 also shows (§10″) that the lands of Azzi in the east, the Kaska lands in the north and the Lukka lands in the southeast were all considered territories external to the Hittite Empire at this point. The colophon in No. 27 provides the potentially important information that these instructions and loyalty-oath prescriptions were drawn up for the courtiers in the city of Ūssa, which seems to have been an important city in Tarḫuntassa, the very secondogeniture in which Tudḫaliya's cousin, Kuruntiya, ruled as king. In what context was Tudḫaliya IV imposing an oath upon his innermost circle of administrators within the land of his viceroy, who, it should be mentioned, as the second son of Muwattalli and brother of Urḫi-Teššub, whom Tudḫaliya's father, Ḫattusili had driven from the throne of the empire, could be said to have had a stronger claim to the throne than did Tudḫaliya himself? Was Ḫattusa's, and thus Tudḫaliya's, control over the appanage states of Tarḫuntassa (and Karkamiš) tighter than is normally assumed? Or was this oath imposed at some point when Tudḫaliya had driven Kuruntiya from his throne and assumed full control himself? At present, the answers to these questions are not known (see recently Bryce 2007; Freu 2005).

Finally, No. 28 provides in its incipit and colophon an attestation of the genealogy of Suppiluliu/ama II, the last-known king of the Hittite Empire.

The Tablets and Their Scribes and Archives

The poor quality and lack of recording of Winckler's and Makridi's clumsy digging in Ḫattusa between 1906 and 1912, from which most of the larger and more complete tablets stem, prevent the modern researcher from being able to make firm conclusions about the provenience of most tablets and text genres, including most of those of the present volume. Still, the distribution of those fragments for which a findspot is known from later excavations may perhaps be significant.

- All tablets and fragments from Text Nos. 2, 3, 5, 10, 14, 17, 18, 20, 26, and 27 for which a findspot is known were found in the Temple I complex. Some of the tablet fragments constituting Nos. 12 and 13 were found in the Temple I complex, but not all. Further fragments from Texts 1 and 8 were found in secondary contexts in the Lower City and might conceivably have originally been stored in the Temple I complex, but this can no longer be ascertained with any confidence.
- All tablets and fragments from Nos. 11, 19, and 21 for which a findspot is known were found in Building A of the royal palace on the Büyükkale. Some of the tablet fragments constituting Nos. 12 and 13 were found in Building A, but not all.
- Only Text No. 13 includes a tablet fragment known to have been found in the so-called House on the Slope. A further fragment from Text No. 8 was found in secondary context near the House on the Slope, but cannot with certainty be associated with it.

A large, perhaps even significant, majority of the texts of the present volume are thus seen to have originally been stored in the archives of the Temple I complex. If one were to ignore for the moment Text No. 8, which is to be seen rather as a decree than an obligation and oath text, and No. 19, which may well be a tablet that functioned almost like a letter sent to the royal administration, then the distribution leans even more decidedly toward the Temple I complex. Still, tablets and fragments of some compositions that should probably be considered to belong to the core of the obligation and oath genre, such as No. 12 and perhaps Nos. 13 and 21, were found in Büyükkale A and the House on the Slope, so that one cannot assert that all such texts were stored in the Temple I complex; and even assuming that they would have been stored in the Temple I complex as a rule is a risky proposition, since the archives of the Temple I complex constitute the largest collection of tablets and fragments overall, so that it cannot be considered unexpected that a majority of the texts were found in them, and since a ratio of 14 to 7,[53] while obviously tendential, is not based on a sample size that inspires confidence.

If this tendency were to prove significant nonetheless, one might speculate on its relevance. While most of the fragments of the pre-NH compositions (mostly in NH copies) of this volume stem from the Temple I complex (Nos. 2, 3, 5, 10, 12, 13, 14, 17), a significant number of the pre-NH originals, too, were found in the Temple I complex (Nos. 10, 17, 18); fragments of pre-NH originals of Nos. 11, 12, and 19 come from the Büyükkale. The distribution thus does not seem to be strongly correlated with the fact that in general Büyükkale A's archives include a disproportionate number of pre-NH manuscripts compared to the other archives of Ḫattusa. Alternatively, the tendency might be connected with the fact that the obligation and oath texts were conceived as documents that were to be kept in the temple, where the gods as witnesses could keep an eye on them. Against this would militate the fact that none of the tablets in question would seem to represent an "original"—certainly none is inscribed on a metal tablet (cf. above)—that might have been placed in front of the deities themselves, as were the treaties. Rather, it seems that they would likely have been stored in archival rooms of the administrative complex constructed around the temple.

As van den Hout has demonstrated in a series of recent papers (2006, 2008, 2009b), most of the texts of the present volume belong to those categories of texts that were copied and recopied throughout the centuries (Nos. 2, 3, 5, 8, 10, 12–14, 16, 17, 20, 22, 24, 26, 27). Why exactly such texts were copied decades or even centuries after they were originally composed, whether for a perceived concrete relevance or more for archival or educational purposes, can for the moment only be speculated upon.

As much of the information available for this section is preserved in the incipits and colophons, they are assembled here for ease of reference, and followed by a brief discussion:

No. 3. Protocol for the Palace Gatekeeper (*CTH* 263)

Incipit

(1)*ma-a-an I-NA* É.GAL-*LÌ za-ak-ki-ti-i ar-ta-ri nu-*⸢*za* ^{LÚ}Ì.DU$_8$⸣ (2) ^{GIŠ}TUKUL^{MEŠ} EGIR-*an ki-iš-ša-an kap-pu-u-e-zi* ^{LÚ}Ì.DU$_8$-*kán* (3)*IŠ-TU* KÁ.GAL *kat-ta ti-i-e-zi nu na-a-ši-*[*l*]*i ki-iš-ša-an* (4)*te-ez-zi ḫa-lu-ga-aš ḫa-lu-ga-aš*

(1)When he reaches the door-bolt in the palace, the gatekeeper (2)tallies the trades(men) as follows: (3–4)The gatekeeper steps down from the main gate, and he speaks as follows in Hittite: "An announcement! An announcement!"

Colophon A

(26′)DUB.1.KAM *še-er še-e-šu-wa-aš QA-TI* [Š]U ^{m}*SAK.KA.PÍ* (27′)DUMU ^{m}*U*!(NU).*ZA* DUMU.DUMU-*ŠÚ ŠÁ* *m**MA.U.I.RI* (28′)*PA-NI* ^{m}*AN.GUL.LI IŠ-ṬUR*

(26′)Tablet One of Sleeping up Above; finished. The [ha]nd of Sakkapi, (27′)son of Uza, grandson of Mauiri, (28′)wrote it in the presence of Angulli.

Colophon B

(11′)[DU]B.1.KAM *še-er še-e-šu-u-wa-aš QA-T*[*I*] (12′) ^{m}GIŠ.GI-PÌRIG-*iš A-NA PA-NI* ^{m}⸢*A*?⸣.[*NU.WA.AN.ZA*(?)] (13′)*TUP-PU* ^{URU}*ḪA.*[*AT-TI IŠ-ṬUR*]

(11′)[Tabl]et One of Sleeping up Above; finish[ed]. (12′)GIŠ.GI-PÌRIG [...] in the presence of A[nuwanza(?)] (13′)[wrote] (this) tablet of Ḫa[ttusa].

No. 4. Protocol for the Royal Body Guard (*CTH* 262)

Colophon

(53)DUB.1.KAM *ŠA* ^{LÚ}*ME-ŠE-DI iš-ḫi-ú-l*[*a-a*]*š Ú-UL* ⸢*QA*⸣*-TI*

(53)Tablet One of the Oblig[ati]ons of the Bodyguard: not finished.

No. 8. Tudḫaliya I's Decree on Penal and Administrative Reform (*CTH* 258.1)

Introductory lines

§1 (1)*UM-MA TA.BA.AR.NA* ^{m}*TU.UD.ḪA.LI.*⸢*IA* LUGAL⸣.GAL (2)*ma-a-an* ^{URU}*A.AŠ.ŠU.WA ḫar-ni-in-k*[*u-u*]*n*(3)*a-ap-pa-ma* ^{URU}*Ḫa-at-tu-ši*[*ú-wa*]*-nu-un*(4)*nu-kán* DINGIR^{MEŠ}

aš-ša-nu-nu-un [*n*]*u-mu* LÚ^MEŠ URU^*ḪA.AT.TI* ^(5)*ḫu-u-ma-an-za a-ru-ú-e-eš-ke-*˻*u*˼*-*[*w*]*a-an da-a-iš nu kiš-an me-mi-er*

§2 ^(6) ^dUTU-*ŠI-wa an-ze-el* [*B*]*E-LÍ-NI* ^LÚ*la-aḫ-ḫi-ia-la-aš* ^(7)˻*zi*˼*-ik nu-wa-aš-ša-a*[*n*] *ḫa-an-né-eš-na-an-ni* ^(8)[*ḫ*]*a-an-nu-wa-an-zi Ú-UL tar-ra-at-ta* ^(9)[x]x-*aš-ša-wa-*˻*kán*˼ *i-da-la-u-i-eš* UN^MEŠ-*ši-iš* ^(10)[…]x-NI *ar-ḫa ḫar-ni-in-ke-er* ^(11)[…]x˻^ḪI.A˼ *ú-pa-a-ti*^ḪI.A *Ù* ^LÚ.MEŠ*ša-ri-ku-wa-aš* ^(12)[… *i-da-l*]*a*^?*-u-e-eš-ta*

§1 ^(1)Thus (speaks) the Sovereign, Tudḫaliya, Great King: ^(2)Once I destroyed Āssuwa, ^(3)I [ca]me back to Ḫattusa, ^(4–5)and I provided for the deities, so that all the men of Ḫattusa began to revere me, and they spoke thus:

§2 ^(6) "You, Your Majesty, our [L]ord, you are a *campaigner*, so you have not been able to render judgment concerning law cases, ^(9–10)and […] evil persons have utterly destroyed […]. ^(11)[…]-s, land holdings and *sarikuwa*-troops ^(12)[…] he/it has become [*awf*]*ul*."

Colophon

^(9′)[ ] *QA-TI* ^(10′)ŠU ^m*A.LI.*˻*IḪ*˼*.ḪI.*˻*NI*˼ DUMU ^mAN.ŠUR-LÚ DUMU.DUMU-*ŠÚ ŠA* ^mGIŠ.KIRI$_6$.NU ^(11′)GÁB.ZU.ZU [*Š*]*A* ^m*ZU.WA.A* EN GIŠ.KIN-*TI*

^(9′)Finished. ^(10′)Hand of Aliḫḫini, son of AN.ŠUR-LÚ, grandson of GIŠ.KIRI$_6$.NU, ^(11′)apprentice of Zuwā, chief of the *labor bureau*.

No. 9. Tudḫaliya I's Decree on Judicial Reform (*CTH* 258.2)

Colophon

^(1′)DUB.2.KAM ^m*TU.UD.ḪA.LI.*⌈*IA* LUGAL.GAL⌉[ ] ^(2′)*ŠA MA-***ME-TI* x x* *QA-TI*

^(3′)*ki-i TUP-PU ar-ḫa ḫar-ra-***an* {AŠ} *e***-eš-*[*ta*] ^(4′)*na-at A-NA PA-NI* ^m*MA.AḪ.ḪU.ZI* ^(5′)*Ù A-NA* ^m*ḪAL.WA*-LÚ ^(6′)*ú-uk* ^m*Du-da-aš* ^(7′)EGIR-*pa ne-wa-aḫ-ḫu-un*

^(1′)Second Tablet (*of*) Tudḫaliya, Great King, [ ] of the Oath; finished.

^(3′)This tablet wa[s] damaged, ^(4′)and I, Duda, renewed it in the presence of Maḫḫuzi and Ḫalwa-ziti.

No. 10. Tudḫaliya I?'s Instructions and Oath Imposition for All the Men (*CTH* 259)

Incipit

§1′ (1′)[…]x x x[…] (2′)[… KU]R URU*ḪA.AT-TI* […] (3′)[…] *A-NA* SAG.DU [mRN LUGAL.GAL] (4′)[x x x] x [fRN MUNUS.LUGAL.G]AL *Ù* [*A-NA* mRN] (5′)[*kat-ta ḫa-aš-ša*] ⌜*ḫa-an-za-aš*⌝*-ša še-er* [*link-* …] (6′)[*nu ka-a-š*]*a*(?) *k*[*e*]-⌜*e-da*⌝*-ni li-in-ki-*[*ia* …]

§1′ (2′)[… La]nd of Ḫattusa […] (3′)[…] to the person [of RN, Great King] (4′)[… to RN, Gre]at [Queen], and [to RN …] (5′)(and) [thereafter progeny] and descendents [… swear] upon, (6′)[and *here*]*by* to [t]his oath […]

Colophon

(7′)DUB.2.KAM *QA-TI ŠA* m*DU.UT.ḪA.LI.IA iš-ḫi-ú-la* (8′)UNMEŠ*-an-na-aš ḫu-u-ma-an-da-aš*

Tablet Two, finished, of the Obligations of Tudḫaliya, (8′)for All the Men.

No. 13. Instructions of Arnuwanda I for the Mayor (of Ḫattusa) (*CTH* 257)

Incipit

(1)[*U*(*M-MA TA.BA.AR.NA*)] m*AR.NU.WA.AN.DA* LUGAL.GAL (2)[LU(GAL KUR URU*ḪA.AT.TI*)] *zi-ik-za* LÚ*ḪA-ZA-AN-NU* (3)[*ḫ*(*a-li-ia-aš ud-da-n*)]*i-i me-ek-ki na-aḫ-ḫa-an-za *e-eš** (4)[*n*(*u* URU*Ḫa*)*-a*(*t-tu-ši ḫ*)]*a-a-li* SIG$_5$*-in uš-kán-du*

(1)[T(hus says the Sovereign)], Arnuwanda, Great King, (2)[Ki(ng of the Land of Ḫattusa)]: You, Mayor, (3)must be extremely vigilant in the [(matte)]r [(of the) g(uard)! (4)An(d in Ḫattusa)] they must keep the guard well.

Colophon Tablet 1

(12′)[…] (eras.) (13′)[…] (eras.)-**NI** (14′)[… DUB.1.KAM LÚ*Ḫ*]*A-ZA-AN-NI iš-ḫi-ú-la-aš* (15′)[…] *QA-TI*

[Tablet One] of the Obligation(s) for the Mayor; […] finished.

Colophon Tablet 2

(1′)[…]DUB.2.KAM [ ]x x […] (2′)[…]LÚ*ḪA-ZA-AN-NI iš-ḫi-ú-la-a*[*š*]

Tablet Two […] Obligation(s) for the Mayor; […]

No. 14. Loyalty Oath of Town Commanders to Arnuwanda I, Ašmunikkal, and Tudḫaliya (*CTH* 260)

Incipit

(1)[*U*]*M-*˹*MA* UGULA LÚ˺MEŠ [*L*]*I-IM* LÚ.MEŠDUGUD *ŠA* ÉRINMEŠ KUR URU*KI.*˹*IN*˺*.NA.RA*

(1)[T]hus (say) the [C]lan Chiefs (and) the Commanders of the Troops of Kinnara:

No. 15. Instructions and Oath Imposition(s) of Arnuwanda I (*CTH* 275)

Incipit 15.1

(1)*UM-MA TA.BA.AR.NA* m*AR.N*[*U.WA.AN.DA* …] (2)*ka-a-ša tu-uk A-NA* EN x[…] (3)*iš-ḫi-u-la-aš li-in-ki-aš-š*[*a* …] (4)*nu-ut-ta ki-i iš-ḫi-ú-ul*[…]

(1)Thus (says) the Sovereign, Arn[uwanda …] (2)hereby […] you(sg.) to the lord (of) […] (3)of the obligation(s) an[d] of the oath […] (4)and […] these obligations to you(sg.).

Incipit 15.2

(1)˹*UM*˺*-MA T*[*A.B*]*A.AR.NA* m*A*[*R.NU.WA.AN.DA* …] (2)*ki-i~iš-*˹*ša*˺*-aš at-ta-aš-ma-aš* x[…] (3)*ku-it pár-ku-e-an-na-aš iš-ḫi-*⸤*ú*⸥*-*[*ul* …] (4)*nu ke-e-*˹*el*˺ *tup-pí-ia-aš pár-ku-i*[*a-an-na-aš iš-ḫi-ú-ul* …]

(1)Thus (says) the S[ove]reign, A[rnuwanda …] (2)this […] of the mouth of my father […] (3)which obligat[ion] of purity […] (4)and [… obligation of] purity of this tablet […]

NO. 16. DECREE OF QUEEN AŠMUNIKKAL CONCERNING THE "ROYAL FUNERARY STRUCTURE" (*CTH* 252)

Incipit

(1)*UM-MA* ^{f}*AŠ.MU*-^{d}NIN.GAL MUNUS.LUGAL.GAL É.NA$_4$-*aš ku-it i-ia-u-e-en* (2)*nu A-NA* É.NA$_4$-*ni ku-i-e-eš* URU$^{ḪI.A}$ *pí-ia-an-te-eš* LÚ^{MEŠ} *BE-EL QA-TI ku-i-e-eš pí-an-te-eš* (3) $^{LÚ.MEŠ}$APIN.LÁ $^{LÚ.MEŠ}$SIPAD.*GU$_4$* $^{LÚ.MEŠ}$SIPAD.UDU *ku-i-e-eš pí-ia-an-te-eš* (4) $^{LÚ.MEŠ}$*ša-ri-wa-za-kán ku-i-e-eš da-an-te-eš na-at QA-DU* É^{MEŠ}-*ŠU-NU* URU$^{ḪI.A}$-*ŠU-NU* (5)*A-NA* É.NA$_4$ *pí-ia-an-te-eš* $^{LÚ.MEŠ}$*ḫi-lam-mi-e-eš-ša ku-i-e-eš ka-ru-ú* (6)*A-NA* É.NA$_4$ *pí-ia-an-te-eš na-at-kán ša-aḫ-ḫa-na-za lu-zi-ia-za a-ra-u-e-eš a-ša-an-du*

(1)Thus (speaks) Ašmunikkal, Great Queen: The royal funerary structure that we created, (2)the towns that have been given to the royal funerary structure, the craftsmen that have been given, (3)the ploughmen, cowherds, and shepherds that have been given, (4)those who were taken from the *sari(ku)wa*-troops and along with their homes and their towns (5)given to the royal funerary structure, and the *ḫilammi*-cult personnel that had already (6)been given to the royal funerary structure, they shall be exempt from the *saḫḫan* and *luzzi*-levies.

NO. 17. INSTRUCTIONS OF ARNUWANDA I FOR THE FRONTIER POST GOVERNORS (*CTH* 261.I)

Incipit

(1)[(*UM-MA* ^{d}U)TU-*ŠI* ^{m}*AR.NU.WA*].*AN.DA* LUGAL.⌜GAL⌝ (2)[*ma-a-an*(?) *a-ú-ri-ia-aš* EN^{M}]^{EŠ} *ḫa-an-te-ez-zi-uš a-ú-ri-*⸤*uš*⸥ (3)[… (x-*aš-kán-z*)*i nu-uš-ma-a*]*š iš-ḫi-ú-ul* (4)[(*ki-iš-ša-an*) …] *e-eš-tu*

(1)[(Thus) says His (Maj)esty, Arnuw]anda, Great King: (2)[When(?) (fron)tier post (governor)]s [(continually) …] the frontier posts, [thei]r duty shall be [(as follows)]:

Colophon

(10′)DUB.1.KAM *iš-ḫi-ú-la-aš* [… *Ú-UL QA-TI*]

(10′)Tablet One of the Obligations [… . Not finished.]

No. 19. Āsḫapāla's Oath regarding an Obligation to Supply Troops (*CTH* 270)

Incipit

(1)[*U*]*M-MA* ^{m}*A.AŠ.ḪA.PA.A.LA na*[*m-ma-ia* ÉRIN^{MEŠ}] (2)[*ku-i*]*-e-eš kat-ti-iš-ši l*[*i-in-ki-ia-aš-ma-ša-at*] (3)[*kat-t*]*a-an ki-iš-ša-an k*[*i-it-ta-ru*]

(1)[T]hus (speak) Āsḫapāla, [and] fu[rther, th]ose [troops] that are with him; thus [shall it be] pl[aced] for them [und]er o[ath]:

No. 20. Instructions for Priests and Temple Personnel (*CTH* 264)

Colophon

(78)DUB.1.KAM *ŠA* LÚ^{MEŠ} É DINGIR-*LÌ ḫu-u-ma-an-da-aš* (79)*ŠA* EN^{MEŠ} TU$_7$ DINGIR^{MEŠ} LÚ^{MEŠ} APIN.LÁ DINGIR^{MEŠ} (80)*Ù ŠA* $^{\text{LÚ.MEŠ}}$SIPAD.GU$_4$ DINGIR-*LÌ* $^{\text{LÚ.MEŠ}}$SIPAD.UDU DINGIR-*LÌ* (81)*iš-ḫi-ú-la-aš QA-TI*

(78)Tablet One of Obligations for All the Temple Personnel, the Kitchen Personnel of the Deities, the Ploughmen of the Deities and for the Cowherds of the Deity (and) the Shepherds of the Deity. Finished.

No. 23. Oath of the Men of Ḫattusa to Ḫattusili III and Pudu-Ḫepa (*CTH* 254)

Incipit

§1 (i 1)[… ^{m}*ḪA.AT.TU.ŠI.L*]*I* LUGAL.GAL LUGAL KUR *ḪA.AT.TI* (2)[…]x DUMU^{MEŠ}. LUGAL (3)[…]x ÉRIN^{MEŠ} ANŠE.KUR.RA^{MEŠ} (4)[…]*UN?*^{MEŠ}*-uš* $^{\text{LÚ.MEŠ}}$MÁŠDA (5)[… *ḫu-u-ma-a*]*n-za ku-iš-kán INA* KUR ^{URU}*ḪAT.TI an-da* ˻*e-eš-zi?*˼

§2 (i 6)[*nu ka-a-ša* ITU-*mi* ITU-*mi*] *A-NA* SAG.DU ^{m}*ḪA.AT.TU.ŠI.LI!* (7)[LUGAL.GAL *Ù A-NA* SAG.DU ^{f}*PU.DU.ḪE*]*.PA* MUNUS.LUGAL.GAL (erasure) (8)[*Ù A-NA* DUMU^{MEŠ}*-ŠU-NU* DUMU.DUMU^{MEŠ}*-ŠU-NU kat*]*-*˻*ta*˼ *ḫa-aš-ša ḫa-an-za-aš-ša še-er* (9)[*li-in-ku-u-e-ni nu ka-a-ša ke-e-da-ni*] ˻*li-in-ga-i*˼ (10)[*LI-IM* DINGIR^{MEŠ} *tu-li-ia ḫal-zi-ia-an-te-eš nu uš-kán-d*]*u iš-ta-ma-*[*aš-kán-du*]

§1 (1)[… Ḫattusil]i, Great King, King of the Land of Ḫattusa, (2)[…] sons of the king, (3)[…] troops, chariotry, (4)[…] *men* (and) peasants (5)[enti]re […], he who is in the Land of Ḫattusa.

§2 (6)[Hereby do we swear, month for month], to the person of Ḫattusili, [Great King, and to the person of Pudu-Ḫe]pa, Great Queen, [and to their sons and grandsons, (and) there]after to further generations, [and hereby are the thousand gods called to assembly for this] oath, [so that they m]ay [see, that they may] hear.

No. 27. Tudḫaliya IV's Instructions and Oath Imposition for Courtiers (*CTH* 255.2)

Incipit

(1)[*U*]*M-MA* ^{m}*TU.UD.ḪA.*⸢*LI*⸣*.IA* ⸢LUGAL⸣.GAL LUGAL-*ez-zi-aḫ-ḫa-at-wa* (2)[*nu*]*-wa šu-um-me-eš*$_{15}$ LÚ^{MEŠ} SAG *A-NA* SAG.DU ^{d}UTU-*ŠI* (3)[*še*]*-er kiš-an li-in-ik-*<*tén*> ^{d}UTU-*ŠI-*⸤*wa AŠ-ŠUM*⸥ EN-*UT-TI* (4)[*p*]*a-aḫ-šu-u-e-ni kat-ta-ma-wa* DUMU^{MEŠ} ^{d}UTU-*ŠI* (5)*ḫa-aš-ša ḫa-an-za-aš-ša AŠ-ŠUM* EN-*UT-TI pa-aḫ-šu-u-e-ni*

(1)[T]hus (speaks) Tudḫaliya, Great King: I have become king, (2)[so] you courtiers <must> swear an oath [up]on the person of My Majesty as follows: "We will [p]rotect His Majesty with regard to the lordship, and thereafter we will protect the sons of His Majesty (and his) sons and grandsons with regard to the lordship."

Colophon

(54)DUB.1-*PU ŠA MA-ME-TI* (55)*I-NA* ^{URU}*U.UŠ.ŠA* (56)*ŠA* LÚ^{MEŠ} SAG

(54)Tablet One of the Oath; (55)in the City of Ūssa, (56)for the Courtiers.

No. 28. Suppiluliu/ama II's Instructions and Oath Imposition for the Men of Ḫattusa (*CTH* 256)

Incipit

(1)[… ^{d}10 ^{URU}*Z*]*I.IP.*PA*.LA.A*[*N.DA*] (2)[… ^{d}10 ^{URU}*NE*]*.RI.IK.KA*$_4$ (3)[… ^{d}*T*]*A.RU.UP.PA.ŠA.NI* (4)[… ḪUR].SAG^{MEŠ} I$_7$^{MEŠ} *ŠA* KUR ^{URU}[GN] (5)[… ^{m}*Šu-up-pí-lu-li-i*]*a-ma-aš* LUGAL.GAL LUGAL KUR ^{URU}KÙ.BABBAR (6)[UR.SAG DUMU ^{m}*TU.UD.ḪA.LI.IA* LUGAL.GAL LUG]AL KUR ^{URU}KÙ.BABBAR UR.SAG (7)[DUMU.DUMU-*ŠU ŠA* ^{mGIŠ}GIDRU.DINGIR-*LÌ* LUGAL.GAL UR].SAG ŠA!.BAL.BAL ^{m}*ŠU.UP.PÍ.LU.*[*LI.U.MA*] (8)[LUGAL.GAL UR.SAG … *ar-k*]*u-wa-ar i-ia-at*

(1)[… Storm God of Z]ippala[nda], (2)[… Storm God of Ne]rikka, (3)[… T]aruppasani, (4)[… moun]tains, rivers of the Land of […],(5)[… Suppiluli]ama,

Great King, King of the Land of Ḫattusa, (6)[Hero, Son of Tudḫaliya, Great King, Ki]ng of the Land of Ḫattusa, Hero, (7)[Grandson of Ḫattusili, Great King, He]ro, Descendant of Suppilu[liuma], (8)[Great King, Hero], made a [pl]ea.

Colophon

(16′)[DUB.1.KAM] *UL* [*Q*]*A-TI* (17′)[*li-in*]*-ki-ia-aš* (18′)[*ŠA* ᵐ*Š*]*U.UP.PÍ.*[*LU.L*]*I.U.MA* (19′)[DUMU ᵐ*TU.U*]*D.ḪA.LI.IA*

(16′)[Tablet One], not [fi]nished, (17′)of the [Oa]th (18′)[of S]uppiluliuma, (19′)[Son of Tu]dḫaliya.

The incipits of most of the compositions style the text as the quoted speech, generally of the king or queen (Nos. 8, 13, 15.1–2, 16, 17, 27), in three cases of the person(s) taking the oath (Nos. 14, 19, 23). One seems to be styled in the incipit as a prayer, that is, is addressed to the gods (No. 28), and the following paragraphs indeed seem to speak to the gods concerning the matter of the oath to follow. While most of the four partially preserved paragraphs of its col. ii enumerate the deities called to witness the imposition of the oath, the prayer to the gods ends before the text breaks off, continuing after the break by addressing the men of Ḫattusa, dealing primarily with the status of and obligations to the towns or communities dedicated to the presumably royal ancestors. In keeping with its status as a protocol rather than an obligation and oath text, No. 3 begins with a 3rd sg. pres. indic. narrative, essentially without any introductory attribution, and thus not with an incipit per se. No. 10 represents an outlier of sorts, as its incipit may well have styled the composition as an oath spoken in the 1st person by the subordinates enunciating it, though the remainder of the text following the divine list of §2′ is unquestionably placed in the mouth of the king speaking to his servants.

The colophons are quite heterogeneous. The most common type categorizes the composition as "the obligation(s) of …," whereby the regens can be either the official or class of officials upon which the obligations were imposed (Nos. 4, 13, 20) or, seemingly, the issuing king (No. 10, with n. 82). No. 17 will have been of this sort as well, but the regens is lost. Three colophons label the text as an oath, whereby one (No. 9) would seem to attribute the tablet to the issuing king, though not marked in the gen., while the "oath" is explicitly marked as gen. No 27 is a tablet "of the oath," to which is appended the place in which the oath was imposed and for whom it was intended, that is, the courtiers. No. 28 would seem to be styled as the "oath of RN," whereby "oath imposed by RN" is naturally to be understood. No. 3, in keeping with its nature as a protocol, does not relate the composition to an obligation or oath, but simply provides a title from the content of the text. No. 8 provides no information on the composition other than the fact that it was "[ ] finished."

Only the colophons of Nos. 3.A, 3.B, 8, and 9 contain further notes concerning the responsible scribes and their activities and affiliations. The scribe of No. 3.B, ^{m}GIŠ.GI-PÌRIG, is known only from this entry, and if ^{m}⌜*A*$^{?}$⌝.[*NU.WA.AN.ZA*] is indeed to be restored thereafter, it would date the tablet probably to the reign of Ḫattusili III or that of Tudḫaliya IV (Gordin 2008). For thoughts on the meaning of the locution *TUPPU* ^{URU}*ḪA.AT.TI* found therein, see Torri 2011. No. 3.A would have been a product of a generation or two later, toward the very end of the Empire period, since its scribe, Sakkapi, who also provides his genealogy, wrote it under the supervision of Angulli, who in turn had been a subordinate of Anuwanza (Gordin 2008). The scribe of No. 8, Aliḫḫini, can be dated through the genealogy he provides to the very end of the Empire period as well (Gordin 2008). The scribe Duda of No. 9 is otherwise unknown, but his supervisors Maḫḫuzi and Ḫalwa-ziti are well known as MAGNUS.SCRIBA from a number of seal impressions from Nişantepe and as the scribe of the Bronze Tablet containing the treaty between Tudḫaliya IV of Ḫatti and Kuruntiya of Tarḫuntassa, respectively (Gordin 2008).

Finally, some very rough calculations made on the back of a napkin, so to speak, suggest that significantly less than 20 percent of the original tablet collection represented by the tablets and fragments presented in this volume is currently extant.[54] In other words, the minimum number of original tablets that must have been present in the archives of Ḫattusa to account for the tablets and fragments utilized for the current volume is around seventy. The tablets and fragments listed under Sources, however, if puzzled altogether, would produce only around 20 percent of those seventy tablets. The actual numbers, of course, would likely have been much bleaker. One can perhaps assume that at most only some 10 percent of the original text of the instructions is preserved today.

Ancient Near Eastern Parallels

The term "instructions" has been used with regard to ancient Near Eastern texts rather broadly. Oppenheim's *Glass and Glassmaking in Ancient Mesopotamia* (Oppenheim et al. 1970), for example, was subtitled *An Edition of the Cuneiform Texts which Contain Instructions for Glassmakers*, as the texts treated in it consist of detailed instruction manuals concerning the production of glass in all its facets. The hippiatric texts from Ugarit (C. Cohen 1997), Assyria (Ebeling 1951), and Ḫattusa (Kammenhuber 1961; Starke 1995a) are in this sense similarly conceived care and training manuals, even if those from Ugarit and Aššur are composed in the 2nd sg. pres.-fut., those from Ḫattusa in the 3rd sg. and pl. pres.-fut., a stylistic contrast well known from the ritual literature from these lands as well. Though this type of instruction manual is quite different from what is intended when one refers to the Hittite instructions, there are passages in the latter that are somewhat similar in their prescription of rather meticulous directives, such as the building instructions in No. 17, §§19–25′, the Instructions of Arnuwanda I for the Frontier Post Governors.

The Sumerian Instructions of Šuruppak (Alster 1974; 2005: 31–220; Black et al. 1998; Römer 1990) is perhaps the most recognizable composition of the well-attested genre of instruction literature from Mesopotamia. These are styled as the advice of a wise old father, Šuruppak, to his son, Ziudsura, largely on practical matters ranging from agriculture to interpersonal and social relations. Similarly conceived Akkadian compositions, though much less-well preserved, are extant as well, such as those known as the Councels of Wisdom and the Councels of a Pessimist from Lambert's edition (1960: 96–111; cf. von Soden 1990). The Instructions of Šūpê-amēlī or Dialog between Šūpê-amēlī and His Son (Dietrich and Keydana 1991; Seminara 2000; Foster 2005: 416–21; Sallaberger 2010; Y. Cohen 2013), known from Ugarit, Emar, and Ḫattusa, belongs to the same general genre and are obviously more relevant for the regions peripheral to Mesopotamia. The so-called Farmer's Instructions (Civil 1994) likewise contain the advice of a father for his son, but are restricted to agricultural matters. The compositions in the present volume offer almost nothing analogous to such wisdom literature. Even the occasional anecdote (e.g., No. 2, §§13″–15″; No. 12, §8′) designed to reinforce the practical, normative, and ethical nature of a given instruction or directive is structured and styled very differently than the verses of these literary compositions from Mesopotamia.

Egyptian sources provide numerous parallels to these didactic wisdom texts from Mesopotamia.[55] Into this category fall, for example, the Instructions of the Vizier Ptahhotep (Wilson 1969: 412–14; Lichtheim 1973: 61–80; Parkinson 1999: 246–72; Hagen 2012), the Instructions for King Meri-ka-re (Wilson 1969: 414–18; Parkinson 1999: 212–34), The Instructions of Prince Hardjedef (Wilson 1969: 419–20; Lichtheim 1973: 58–59), The Instructions of Ani (Wilson 1969: 420–21; Quack 1994) and the Instructions of Amen-em-opet (Wilson 1969: 421–25; Lichtheim 1973: 146–49). More similar in some ways to some of the Hittite instructions or protocols is the composition known as the Duties of the Vizier (Wilson 1969: 212–14; van der Boorn 1988). Its first lines read as follows:

> Instruction for the session of the governor of the city, the vizier of the Southern City and of the Residence in the bureau of the vizier: As for every act of the official, the vizier, when hearing (cases) in the bureau of the vizier, has to sit on the *pḥdw*-chair, the reed-covered dais on the ground, the vestment on him, a leather cushion under his back, a leather cushion under his feet, the [...] on him, the *ʿb3*-scepter beside him, the forty leather rods spread out in front of him, the great ones of the ten of Upper Egypt in two rows in front of him, the chamberlain on his right-hand side, the curator of the access on his left-hand side, the scribes of the vizier beside him. While one stands rigid fixedly facing the one opposite to him amongst everyone (present at the session), one has to be heard after the other without allowing the low (ranking official) to be heard before the high (ranking official). If (however) the high (ranking official) says: "No one beside me is to be heard," (then) he shall be arrested by the messengers of the vizier. (van der Boorn 1988: 12–13)

On the one hand these lines recall the prescription of the protocol for allowing petitioners to access the king specifically (No. 4, §§29–36), while on the other one is reminded above all of the protocols (Nos. 3 and 4) in general. Instructions issuing from a king and addressed to a class of subordinates upon which the servants are to take an oath, however, is a genre apparently not known from Egypt.

Somewhat closer parallels are found among the edicts and instructions from Nuzi from the fourteenth century (Müller 1968, 1971), above all the Instructions for the Mayor (1968: 195–202; Jankowska 1969: 273–76; Zaccagnini 1979: 17–24; Maidman 2010: 30–33). Of interest is the fact that the document preserving the Instructions for the Mayor was not issued by the royal palace, but by one of the mayors of a town of Arrapḫe named Tašuḫḫe, who for whatever reason felt the need to record the directives that he had received from the king. Whether the king had issued his instructions in writing or orally can probably not be determined for certain.

> (1–2)[The king] issued a directive [as follows] for the mayor of the town of Tašuḫḫe. (3–5)Each and every mayor shall guard any borderland of his town up to its limit. (5–7)The mayor must guard (any) abandoned *dimtu*-structure, being in the hinterland of his town. (8–9)No robbery may be committed within the borderland of his town. (9–10)No enemy may kill or plunder. (10–14)And if in its borderland any robbery should be committed or any enemy plunder or kill, then the mayor bears the responsibility. (15–19)If any Arrapḫean fugitive flees from the borderland of that town and reaches another land, then the mayor bears any and all responsibility. (20–24)The mayor bears responsibility for (any) abandoned *dimtu*-structure in the borderland of that town. (25–30)And the governor shall give tablets individually to each of the *dimtu*-structure owners and he shall issue the directive as follows: (31–38)"If anyone leaves that *dimtu*-structure for

> purposes(?) of robbery (or) if any enemy kills or plunders, then the *dimtu*-structure owner has committed an offense, and I shall take the *dimtu*-structure (from him). (39–44)You shall approach me and tell me. And that man [shall not] evade (this) proclamation. … (45–47)And if anyone evades [the proclamation], [you] seize him and have him come to the <government> house." (48)Seal of Mušteya. (HSS 15.1; trans. based on Maidman 2010: 33–34)

Also providing significant parallels is the Decree for the Palace Personnel (AASOR 16, no. 51; Müller 1968: 7–10; Roth 1995: 195–96), which is worth mentioning first and foremost because of its provision requiring it to be read out to the palace personnel every three or four years, recalling the similar provisions in No. 2, §8″, 25′–26′; No. 22.2, §2′; No. 23, §2?; No. 14.1, §21; No. 14.3.A, §2′. Still, this edict concerns only a single issue, an injunction against any of the palace personnel allowing a daughter to become destitute or a prostitute without the permission of the king, and is therefore hardly to be classified with the Hittite instructions, despite specific similarities.

Among the edicts and instructions from Nuzi the Instructions for the Mayor provide the closest parallel to the Hittite instructions in that they seem to articulate duties and obligations that are to remain in force indefinitely for an entire class of royal subordinates. This is not, or is not necessarily, the case with the other edicts from Nuzi discussed by Müller, though they are all termed *ṭēmu*, "instruction, order," in the texts in question. The Instructions to Tarmi-Tilla (Müller 1968: 265–67; Jankowska 1981; Fadhil 1983: 70), for example, are issued to a single named individual and concern a discrete, specific event. The same can be said of the Instructions to Agip-taššenni (Müller 1968: 292–94; Jankowska 1969: 276), which is also interesting for the fact that the tablet on which the order is preserved is sealed with the seal of Agip-taššenni, suggesting perhaps that his official acquiescence to the command received was required of him by the palace. Further instructions for the Officials of the City of Atakkal (Müller 1968: 261–62) and for Subordinate Officials (263–64) are unfortunately too fragmentary for further discussion.

Similar instructions and prohibitions from the Middle Assyrian period can be found in the so-called Harem Edicts or Palace Decrees (Roth 1995: 195–212; Weidner 1954–56), dating from the fourteenth to the eleventh centuries. These are issued in the name of a particular king for a specific set of subordinates, the palace personnel, and are composed in the 3rd sg. pres., as are many of the Hittite instructions. They show no hint of any requirement for the palace personnel to take an oath upon the instructions given (Zaccagnini 1990: 65), and the punishments enumerated for failure to fulfill the obligations are entirely secular. A typical passage reads as follows:

> Tukultī-apil-Ešarra, king of the universe, king of Assyria, son of Aššur-rēša-iši, himself also king of Assyria, issued a decree for the court attendants: ... If a court attendant wishes to speak with a palace woman, he shall approach no closer to her than seven paces. Whoever violates this decree, and the palace commander hears of it and does not impose a punishment upon him, the palace commander shall be held responsible for a punishable offense. Even if the officials of the palace commander do not carefully inspect the entire palace area, and do not inform him of any punishable offenses—later, should the king hear of a punishable offense, they shall impose punishments upon the palace commander. (Roth 1995: 206–7)

Perhaps the closest parallels from the ancient Near East to Nos. 14, 19, 22, and 23 are the loyalty oaths from Mari, known only since the late 1980s and early 1990s (Durand 1988: 13–15; 1991; Charpin 2010).[56] These fascinating texts from the mid-eighteenth century are formulated in the 1st person sg. and are addressed to a specific king, Zimrī-Līm. They enumerate in quite some detail what the oath taker will and will not do in the fulfillment of his duties. Known thus far are an Oath of the Diviner, an Oath of the Quartermaster, an Oath of a Subordinate, an Oath of Governor Sûmu-ḫadû, an Oath of Karana, an Oath of the Bedouin and an Oath of a High Official.[57] Some preserve, and all may perhaps have contained, as do the Hittite compositions, self imprecations such as "May the gods destroy all the descendents of my name and my progeny!" (Charpin 2010: 66 and nn. 32–33). From the Diviner's Oath, for example, we read:

> (1–6)When making an oracular inquiry for Zimrī-Līm, my lord, (or) when doing a ritual procedure, as many as I see occur, or when making an oracular inquiry for a commoner, (or) when doing a ritual procedure, as many as I see occur: I will indeed tell Zimrī-Līm, my lord, about every single evil or unfavorable sign that I see; I will not hide (them). (7–10)An evil and unfavorable sign that I see occur when making an oracular inquiry for Zimrī-Līm, my lord, whether in an *izbu* or in an *izmu*, I will not tell (it) to any person at all. (11–16) And the guarded matter than Zimrī-Līm, my lord, tells me in order to do an oracular inquiry, or, he tells my diviner colleague, and I hear, or even (if) I see the sign when my diviner colleague is doing an oracular inquiry, that matter I will indeed guard. ... (22–30)And the one who plans an evil rebellion against the life of Zimrī-Līm, my lord, who orders me to do an oracular inquiry, or who orders my diviner colleague (to do one) and I hear, or even (if) I see my diviner colleague at a time of making an oracle inquiry, I will not hide him. On that very day I will indeed tell Zimrī-Līm, my lord. I will indeed send a message. I will not hide him; I will not forgive him. (ARM 26/1, 1; trans. based on Lenzi 2008: 42–43)

Interesting, among other things, for its reference to the enthronization of Zimrī-Līm (cf. No. 27, §1) in its first line is the Oath of the Quartermaster:

> Depuis l'intronisation de mon Seigneur Zimri-Lim, argent, or, pierre fine, bœuf, âne, esclave mâle of femelle, étoffe, couverture, fourniture de luxe de qualité qui peut exister et qu'il est loisible qu'un humain quelconque prenne, je jure que je ne l'ai pas pris ni n'ai dit à quelqu'un de le prendre, peu ou prou, ni ne l'ai vendu, ni ne l'ai mis en dépôt pour ma succession, ni ne l'ai donné à quelque humain que ce soit en contre-don ou en cadeau. (A.3696, 1–9; Durand 1991: 17–18)

Also worth mentioning, though from a much later period, are the Neo-Assyrian Loyalty Oaths (Akk. *adê*; Parpola and Watanabe 1988; Parpola 2011), probably the best known of the sources discussed here, due to their oft-assumed relevance for the concept of the covenant in Hebrew scriptures (Christiansen and Devecchi 2013).[58] In fact, alongside the obvious differences, these Loyalty Oaths provide some of the closest typological parallels to those compositions labeled in the present volume Instructions and Oath Impositions (Nos. 2, 10–12, 15, 18, 22, 26–28).[59] The primary aim of the nearly completely recovered composition of Aššur-aḫḫe-iddina (Esarhhadon: 681–669 B.C.E.; Parpola and Watanabe 1988, No. 6) was to assure the succession of his son, Aššur-bāni-apli (Ashurbanipal: 668–627 B.C.E.), to the throne of Assyria by means of imposing a loyalty oath upon the various rulers and officials of his empire. Following a preamble stating this purpose (§1), the divine witnesses are evoked (§2) and the subjects are commanded to swear by them (§3). The following lengthy and detailed paragraphs (§§4–36) define the loyal behavior that is expected. These are followed by the punishments, illustrated in sometimes graphic and gruesome detail, to be inflicted upon the disloyal subject by a daunting list of deities (§§37–56). The following paragraph (§57), significantly, changes to the 1st person pl. and would thus constitute the words with which the subjects were to have responded to the oath imposition. The composition concludes (§§58–106) with a vast list of psychopathologically creative curses against the potential oath breaker, two of my personal favorites being,

> just as a sna[ke] and a mongoose do not enter the same hole to lie there together but think only of cutting each other's throats, so may you and your women not enter the same room to lie down in the same bed, (but) think only of cutting each other's throats, (§71)

and,

> just as (this) bug stinks, just so may your breath stink before god and king (and) mankind (§87).

The literature on these documents is vast. A good overview is provided, in addition to Parpola and Watanabe 1988, by Parpola (2003, 2011).

The question naturally arises whether any of these traditions, especially those spatially and chronologically near to the Hittite setting in question, might have influenced the Hittite corpus of instructions presented in this volume. The question can certainly not be approached without reference to the Hittite state and vassal treaties, which the Hittites classified together with the instructions. In brief, it would seem that there is little or no influence in the Hittite treaties and instructions that can be clearly traced directly to previous traditions.[60] The Hittite instructions are likely an indigenous Anatolian development and seem to show little or no dependence on Syrian or Mesopotamian analogues.[61] This appraisal, however, has not been the opinion of all who have posed the question.

Weidner (1954–56: 258), for example, held the view that the Hittite instructions must have been dependent on the Middle Assyrian Palace Edicts, though, unfortunately, he does not specify which Hittite compositions are intended: "Die hethitischen Vorschriften und ein assyrisches Edikt aus der Zeit Tiglatpilesers I. (unten Nr. 21) sind nun inhaltlich so nahe verwandt, dass man sich nicht gut eine völlig unabhängige Entstehung vorstellen kann." The paragraph in question, his No. 21, is that quoted above in Roth's translation.

Similarly, von Schuler (1957: 6) concluded, "die juristische Terminologie und die Benennung der Instruktion sind aus babylonischen Vorbildern entwickelt. Anders steht es mit dem Instruktionsformular. Dafür finden sich nur assyrische Gegenbilder." In contrast to Weidner's more general statement, von Schuler (p. 5) presents four passages from the Assyrian Oath texts that he feels provide "einzelne Wendungen, für die sich in den hethitischen ‚Eiden' gewisse Entsprechungen finden.... Es ist dabei augenfällig, daß das, was innerhalb des assyrischen Textes als leidlich konkretes Gebot angesehen werden kann, innerhalb der hethitischen „Eide" eine blasse, mehrfach wiederkehrende Formel ist." To these he compares six passages from Tudḫaliya IV's Instructions and Loyalty Oath Imposition for Lords, Princes, and Courtiers (No. 26).

More recently, Wilhelm (1988: 364) has suggested that the preamble type found in the Tudḫaliya-Sunaššura, Telipinu-Isputaḫsu, and Zidanza-Pilliya treaties "sicherlich auf eine nordsyrische Tradition zurück (geht), die wir bisher nur mit dem ins 17. Jh. v. Chr. datierenden Vertrag AT *1 fassen können." It would seem to be this claim that is followed by Klinger (2005a: 358), though not referenced specifically, when he claims that "die Ausbildung des Staatsvertrages als Textform in seiner Frühphase (war) erheblich von fremden Schultraditionen abhängig."

It is, of course, notoriously difficult to reach definitive conclusions on whether similar text passages from adjacent cultures point toward lateral borrowing, vertical inheritance from a common source, or independent development conditioned by biologically similar groups of peoples coming to grips with similar situations in similar environments.[62] Though one would certainly not want to exclude *a priori* the possibility that the Hittites might have borrowed some elements of their obligation and oath compositions from neighboring cultures, the similarities and parallels mentioned thus far in the literature as suggesting such borrowing are quite general and vague, leading one to suspect that they might be found not only in Hittite and Mesopotamian sources, but in other, unrelated cultures as well, which would suggest, in turn, that they may just as well have arisen independently. Weidner's considerations certainly do not suffice, as he expresses only a vague impression, without even comparing specific passages. Neither do von Schuler's quoted passages convince, as they observe merely that protecting the king, reporting sedition, and seeking no other overlord are common to both corpora, hardly elements that one would be hard pressed to find elsewhere in entirely unrelated cultures. Nor would Wilhelm's observation appear to be sufficient to demonstrate borrowing from Syria, for as he himself notes (1988: 364), in AT *1 "ist der einleitende Temporalsatz jedoch noch nicht Präambel, sondern Einleitung des historischen Rückblicks und läßt sich damit zwangslos aus der Gattung der Königsinschrift ableiten." It seems, then, that the Hittite instructions are likely an indigenous Anatolian development that owes little or nothing to Syrian or Mesopotamian analogues.

Chapter One
Old Kingdom Sources

No. 1
A Royal Reprimand of the Dignitaries (*CTH* 272)

This text is preserved by a single-columned tablet broken in the middle, so that the upper half of the obv. and the lower half of the rev. are lost; hence, only approximately the middle half of the composition is extant. It was found in the Lower City in secondary context.

Though nothing in the text allows one to date this OH original specifically, it is clear from numerous paleographical, morphological, syntactical, and thematic details that it belongs among the earliest of the texts presented in this volume, and some have seen in it a forerunner to the instructions of the MH period (e.g., von Schuler 1976–80: 117; Pecchioli Daddi 2005b: 600–601; cf. Gilan 2009: 134). It may well date to the time of Ḫattusili I and Mursili I (Marazzi 2007: 439, 499; Cammarosano 2006: 12, n. 15; Archi 2010: 43; cf. Gilan 2009: 132).[1]

Though Marazzi (2007: 493, 499; cf. Mora 2008: 303–4) classifies this text as a royal edict—and though the no-longer-preserved portion of the tablet might have contained such—there is in fact no decree or edict found in the text. As preserved it includes only a first section of censure (§2′), followed by an illustrative anecdote (§§3′–4′), then three further paragraphs of reprimand (§§5′–7′). It may well be the case that this portrayal of a deplorable situation was intended to form the background to a corrective royal decree, but if so, it is no longer preserved. In any case, it is one of the very few texts in the corpus not issued by the king (or queen; No. 16), but by a prince, who refers to his father as the one whose "word" he is seeking to uphold (§§1′, 2′, 5′, 7′), a favorite theme in texts from the time of Ḫattusili I and Mursili I (Archi 1979: 44 and n. 25).

The text is unique in several formal and contextual ways. As Kloekhorst (2010: 203–4) has noted, the distribution of the writing of dental stops with the

DA and TA signs is very regular in the Hittite corpus, except in two texts, KBo 6.2+ and the present one. Boley (1992: 9) has observed in addition that there is not a single local particle in the entire text, which is rare and quite striking. And Mora and Giorgieri (2004: 194) have pointed out that only in this text (ll. 16′, 21′) and in KUB 23.102 i 16′ (largely restored) does one find in the Hittite texts the OB form *abī*, "my father," as opposed to MB *abū(y)a*. These facts might, hypothetically, place the composition of the text in a phase of early Hittite history in which writing conventions had not yet been standardized as they were subsequently, observations that are of potential relevance for the current debate

---

TRANSLITERATION

(somewhat more than the upper half of the obv. is lost)

§1′ (obv. 1′)⸢*A-BI*⸣-*I*[*A* ...] (2′)*da-ru-up-pé-*⸢*e*⸣*-t*[*e*?*-ni*?[2]

§2′ (3′)*šu-me-eš* LÚ^{MEŠ} ^{GIŠ}TUKUL *ta-me-eš-kat*[3]*-te-ni* ⸢*a-pé-e-ia*? *kat*?*-ta*⸣*-a*[*n*? ...][4] (4′)*da-me-eš-ke-wa-an da-a-er ki-iš-ša-an* **A-WA-A-AT** *A-BI-*⸢*IA*⸣ (5′)*pa-aḫ-ša-nu-ut-te-en ták-ku šu-me-eš na-at-ta ša-ak-te-e-ni* (6′)*ka-a-ni* ^{LÚ}ŠU.GI-*eš-ša* NU.GÁL *nu-uš-ma-aš me-ma-i A-WA-AT A-BI-IA*

§3′ (7′)^{m}*TA.A.AŠ*[5] ^{LÚ}KUŠ$_7$[6] ^{URU}*KU.Ú.LU.UP.PA ŠU-Ú-UT* ^{m}*ŠAR.KA* (8′)^{m}*NU.UN.NU* ^{m}*MU.Ú.WA* ^{m}*ḪUR.ME.EL* ^{m}*KU.U.UK.KU* ^{m}*ZU.Ú.RU* (9′)5 $^{\text{LÚ.MEŠ}}$*NA-ŠI ṢÍ-DI-TI*$_4$*-ŠU* 1 UDU 1 TÚG 1 ^{TÚG}*ḫi-iš-ta-ni* (10′)3 *KA-BAL-LU*$_4$ 3 *pu-uš-ša-le-eš* 3 *TA-PAL* ^{KUŠ}E.SIR (11′)1 *zi-pát-ta-an-ni* Ì.ŠAḪ DÙG.GA 5 GA.KIN.AG 5 *EM-ṢÚ* (12′)6 *PA* ZÍD.DA ZÍZ *A-NA* NINDA.KASKAL *da-aš-ke-ez-zi*

§4′ (13′)*ki-ma ḫé-en-ku-wa-aš-ša-aš* 50 NINDA$^{\text{ḪI.A}}$ 10$^{\text{TA.ÀM}}$ É-*az*[7] (14′)1 LÚ 1 MUNUS *kat-ti-iš-ši i-e-en-ta Ù* 1 *ka-pu-nu* A.ŠÀ (15′)*pa-ra-a da-a-aš*

§5′ (edge 16′)*ma-a-an A-BI tu-li-ia-*{*aš*}[8] *ḫal-za-i nu-uš-ma-aš* (17′)*gul-la-ak-ku-wa-an ša-aḫ-zi na-at-ta* (rev. 18′) $^{\text{LÚ.MEŠ}}$*NA-ŠI ṢÍ-DI-TI*$_4$*-KU-NU-Ú ka-a-ša-at-ta-wa* (19′) $^{\text{LÚ.MEŠ}}$*NA-ŠI ṢÍ-DI-TI*$_4$*-KU-NU da-me-eš-kat-te-ni* (20′)*ta* LUGAL-*i kar-di-mi-ia-at-tu-uš pé-eš*$_{15}$*-kat-te-ni*

§6′ (21′)*zi-ik-ka-*{*wa*} ^{GIŠ}TUKUL *a-pa-aš-ša* ^{GIŠ}TUKUL *ma-a-an-ša-ma-aš A-BI* (22′)*pár-na-aš-ma tar-na-i nu-uš-ma-aš ma-a-an-ḫa-an-da ḫa-at-ri-ìš-ke-ez-zi* (23′)*na-at-ta-ša-ma-aš* LÚ^{MEŠ} DUGUD-*aš tup-pí ḫa-az-zi-an ḫar-zi* (24′)*ka-a-ša-at-ta-wa ut-ni-ia pa-it-te-ni nu ŠA* ^{LÚ}MÁŠDA (25′)*e-eš-ḫar-še-et na-at-ta ša-an-ḫi-iš-kat-te-ni*

among Hittitologists concerning when the Hittites began writing in their own language, Hittite, as opposed to Akkadian, a topic that van den Hout (2006, 2008, 2009a, 2009b; cf. Archi 2010) above all has addressed of late.

Among this text's remarkable features is its harangue against exploiting the poor while enjoying the life of the rich. In this and in other aspects it shows similarities to the so-called Decree of Pimpira, likely datable to Mursili I as well (Archi 1979; Košak 1988a: 200–201; Cammarosano 2006). Its strong stance against oppressors and its use of anecdotes as examples also recall the Palace Anecdotes (Dardano 1997; Gilan 2007).

TRANSLATION

(somewhat more than the upper half of the obv. is lost)

§1′ (1′)[… m]y father […] (2′)[yo]u[9] have assembled […]

§2′ (3′–5′)You constantly oppress the *land tenants*,[10] and *afterwards* they began to oppress […]. Thus you have preserved my father's word? If you do not know (his word), (6′)are there no old men here either? He[11] can tell you the word of my father.

§3′ (7′–12′)Tās, a chariot driver of the city of Kūluppa, normally takes that belonging to Sarka, (i.e.,) Nunnu, Mūwa, Ḫurmel, Kūkku, (and) Zūru, his 5 pack bearers, (along with) 1 sheep, 1 garment, 1 *ḫistani*-garment, 3 (pairs of) *boots*, 3 *pussali*, 3 pairs of shoes, 1 *zipattani*-measure of good lard, 5 (portions of) cheese, 5 (portions of) sourdough,[12] (and) 6 measures of emmer wheat as provisions for the journey.

§4′ (13′)This, however, is his provision: 50 bread (loaves), 10 each;[13] (14′–15′)1 man (and) 1 woman travel from home with him. And he selected 1 *kapunu*-area of farmland.[14]

§5′ (edge 16′–17′)When my father calls together the assembly he will investigate among you for corruption,[15] not (among) your pack bearers (saying):[16] "You constantly oppress your own[17] pack bearers, (20′)and you repeatedly cause the king aggravation."

§6′ (21′–22′)So, you(sg.) are a *land tenant*[18] and he, too, is a *land tenant*.[19] When my father allows you (to go) back home, as[20] he writes you regularly, (23′)has he not written you dignitaries a tablet[21] (in which is written): (24′–25′)"You yourselves go into the province(s), but you do not avenge the blood of the poor,[22]

§7′ (26′) LÚ.MEŠ*NA-ŠI ṢÍ-DI-TI*$_4$*-ŠU na-at-ta pu-nu-uš-te-ni* (27′)*ta* LÚ*ḫa-ap-pí-na-an-da-aš i-iš-te-e-ni* (28′)*pár-na-aš-ša pa-i-ši e-ez-ši e-uk-ši pí-ia-na-az-zi-at-ta*[23] (29′) LÚ*a-ši-wa-an-da-na ši-e-et*[24] *da-a-at-ti* (30′)*DI-IN-ŠU na-at-ta pu-nu-uš-ši nu ki-iš-ša-an* (31′)*A-WA-A-AT A-BI-IA ar-ḫa-a-an ḫar-te-ni-i*[25] (32′)*ki-nu-un* ˹*ka-a*˺*-aš ki-iš-ša-an i-iš-ša-i* LÚ.MEŠ*NA-ŠI ṢÍ-*˹*DI-TI*$_4$˺*-ŠU* (33′)[ ] x[…]-˹*uš*?˺ *i-iš-te-ni-i*

(somewhat more than the lower half of the rev. is lost)

§7′ (26′) “you do not question his pack bearers, (27′)and you are accustomed to do (the will) of a rich man.” (28′)You(sg.) go to his home, you(sg.) eat, you(sg.) drink, and he rewards you(sg.), (29′)but …, you(sg.) *exploit* the poor man. (30′)You(sg.) do not investigate his case. And in this way (31′)you have *completed/limited* my father’s word? (32′–33′)Now this will occur as follows: Do you make/do […] his pack bearers?

(somewhat more than the lower half of the rev. is lost)

No. 2
Instructions and Oath Imposition for Royal Servants concerning the Purity of the King (*CTH* 265)

This composition is preserved on one primary tablet (A) and one small fragment (B), which duplicates several lines of A iii. Of the main ms. only about the bottom half of col. ii and the upper half of col. iii as well as fragmentary portions of i and iv are preserved, so that at most only about a quarter of the composition is extant today. The smaller fragment comes from the Temple I complex, while no find spot is known for the main ms. No incipit or colophon is preserved. Both mss. are clearly NH copies, but many details of morphology, orthography and vocabulary show that these tablets were copied from significantly older texts, probably even from the OH period. The placement of a principal narrative in the city of Sanaḫuitta (§§13″–14″) recalls the importance of this city during the Old Kingdom period (Miller 2009a),[26] and the story reminds one of the typical OH style anecdotes. A more exact dating is somewhat speculative, unless one wants to relate it to the misdeeds of Sinaḫḫuwa and Ubariya mentioned toward the end of §9 in the Testament of Ḫattusili I (Goedegebuure 2006b), which must be regarded as rather tenuous.[27]

Based on these and related clues Pecchioli Daddi (2004: 451 and n. 5, 457–58; 2005b: 609) assigns the text to the early reign of Arnuwanda I, but several indications would seem to point rather to an OH date of composition.[28] Pecchioli Daddi (2004: 458) seems to derive her dating in large part from her typological scheme, in which this text would provide the "main link between the Middle Hittite *išḫiul* texts, defined as a specific typology by this sovereign (i.e., Arnuwanda I), and the ancient Hittite proto-*išḫiul*, issued by Muršili I to regulate the activities of palace functionaries." In this instance, however, theoretical and classificatory considerations seem to have been forced upon the documents, slightly abusing the evidence in order to fit it to the theoretical construct rather than the other way around.[29] Her conclusion also tends to assume *a priori* a more or less linear evolution of the genre, which would allow the various compositions to be aligned neatly along a continuum, which is not necessarily the case.

The style and structure of the text bear some resemblance to those of a number of other compositions, some of which have been included in the present volume (Nos. 1, 11, 12), some of which lie outside its purview, such as the Palace Anecdotes (Dardano 1997; Gilan 2009: 137–44). On the other hand, this composition seems to witness the basic characteristics of the classic "instruction and oath" texts from the MH period, and may therefore constitute the earliest of the genre. It is suggested here that the composition should be dated significantly earlier than Tudḫaliya I and Arnuwanda I, perhaps, to the period before Telipinu, and that the hypothesis according to which the instruction genre in its most recognizable form was developed only as late as the reign of Arnuwanda I should be abandoned (see Introduction).

In this text the king speaks directly to his servants, the primary emphasis being the kitchen personnel, mostly in the 2nd pl., occasionally in the 2nd sg. (§2′). An oath imposition or prescription is found in §8″, but no oath spoken in the first person is preserved. Pecchioli Daddi (2004: 454; 2005b: 603) and Mazoyer (2007: 253) have rightly emphasized that the entire preserved text is devoted to the all-important purity of the king.[30]

The first, very poorly preserved paragraphs (§§1′–4′, 5″) seem to detail specific dos and don'ts along with corresponding punishment, that is, death and destruction. Paragraph 6″ would seem to continue this pattern, whereby the first example of an attempt to anticipate the potential excuses, self-justification and mitigating circumstances that the personnel might resort to, followed by profilactic counterargument(s), is seen, a feature found repeatedly, for example, in the Instructions for Priests and Temple Personnel (No. 20). Paragraphs 7″–8″ are addressed to the kitchen personnel, enumerated specifically in §8″, whereby the close connection between royal instructions and prohibitions on the one hand and oath taking on the other is seen, as the personnel are to swear an oath to the king every month by pouring out a cup of water and imploring the gods to pour out their own souls likewise should they cause the king any impurity. Paragraphs 9″–12″ are addressed to the leatherworkers who supply the royal footwear and coach, the key regulation being that leather for both is to be taken only from the royal kitchen. Of interest is the stipulation (§11″) according to which abrogation of the regulation will not be punished if it is reported voluntarily to the king, since such products, even if not fit for the king, might do just fine as gifts for a foreigner or a servant. In §§13″–14″ the king turns to his water carriers, who are reminded always to filter his water with a sieve, whereby an anecdote is employed to illustrate the gravity of the matter. The anecdote is extremely interesting, not only for its vividness and touch of dark humor, but also thanks to the fact that it is at precisely this portion of the text where ms. B sets in, offering a substantially alternative outcome (Miller 2011b: 196–97; Marazzi 2010: 208–10): whereas in the main manuscript a certain Arnili, perhaps the accused water carrier, is able to shift the blame to his overseer, Zuliya, who is therefore forced to undergo the river ordeal, thereby found guilty and summarily dispatched, in manuscript B, the outcome of Zuliya's river ordeal is applied to Arnili as well, and they are both eliminated. In §15″, then, the lesson illustrated in the previous paragraphs is repeated as the text breaks off. The remaining §§16″–25″ are too fragmentary to summarize in detail, but seem to continue a similar pattern.

TRANSLITERATION

(first ca. three-quarters of col. i missing entirely)

§1′ (A i 1′)[…]x-⌜te⌝-e-ni (2′)[…] (empty) (3′)[…] x [SA]G?.DU-aš ak-ka4-tar

§2′ (4′)[… I]Š?-TU É.GÚ.È.A (5′)[…]-ḫu-ut (6′)[…]x-aš wa-aš-da-nu-zi (7′)[… LÚta-pa-an(?)-d]a-ni-li-iš (8′)[…]x mu-un-na-a-ši-ma (9′)[…] QA-DU DAM-KU!(ŠU) DUMUMEŠ-KU!(ŠU) ḫar-ak-ti

§3′ (10′)[…]MEŠ IN-BI (11′)[…-(i)]a/⌜e⌝-eš-ḫi TU7 ŠU-it le-e (12′)[…-w]a?-al-li la-aḫ-ḫu-u-wa-i (13′)[…] a-ri-i (14′)[…] uš-kat-te-e-ni (15′)[…]x-zi

§4′ (16′)[… B]I? ŠU-⌜an?⌝ ku-iš-ki (17′)[…-i]š? ⌜ša?⌝-li-ik-zi (18′)[…] a-ki

(first ca. one-half of col. ii missing entirely)

§5″ (ii 1′)[… -t]e?-n[i?…] (2′)[…]x-⌜la⌝-aš L[Ú … LÚNINDA].DÙ.DÙ […] (3′)[… -(i)]a-mi-iš LÚ⌜E⌝-[PIŠ GA] LÚki-ip-li-ia-l[a-aš] (4′)[… -la-a]š LÚtap-pa-a-⌜la⌝-[aš LÚš]e-e-ša-la-a-aš LÚuš-ḫa-a-⌜la?-aš?⌝ (5′)[… LÚta-pa-an-d]a-a-ni-li-iš LÚḫar-ši-ia-la-aš (6′)[…]x-aš

§6″ (7′)[ma-a-an pa-ap-ra]-⸤a⸥-tar ku-iš-ki i-ia-zi LUGAL-aš ZI-an ku-iš-ki (8′) [kar-tim-mi-i]a-nu-⸤zi⸥ šu-me-e-eš-ša ki-iš-ša-an te-e-te-ni (9′)[LUGAL-uš-wa-a]n-na-aš ⸤Ú-UL⸥ a-uš-zi (10′)⌜LUGAL⌝[31]-aš-ma-aš-ma-aš DINGIRMEŠ-⸤uš⸥ ka-ru-ú ⸤uš⸥-kán-zi (11′)nu-uš-ma-aš UZ6[32]-an ⸤i⸥-ia-an-zi nu-uš-ma-aš-kán ḪUR.SAG-an pár-ḫa-an-zi (12′)ga-ag-ga-pa-an-ma-aš-[m]a-aš i-ia-an-zi (13′)nu-uš-ma-aš-kán NA4⸤pé⸥-e-ru-ni pár-ḫa-an-zi

§7″ (14′)ku-wa-pí UD-at *LUGAL!*-wa-aš ⸤ZI⸥-za iš-ḫi-iz-zi-ia-zi (15′)šu-me-eš-ša ENMEŠ TU7 ḫu-u-ma-an-du-uš ḫal-zi-iḫ-ḫi (16′)nu-uš-ma-aš I7-i ma-a-ni-ia-⌜aḫ⌝-mi nu ku-iš pár-ku-e-eš-zi (17′)na-aš LUGAL-aš ÌR-iš ku-iš pa-ap-ri-iš-zi-ma (18′)na-an-za-an LUGAL-uš Ú-UL ⸤i⸥-la-a-li-ia-mi (19′)QA-DU4 DAM-ŠU-ši DUMUMEŠ-ŠU Ḫ[U]L-lu ḫi-in-kán pé-e-an-⸤zi⸥

§8″ (20′)an-da-ma šu-me-e-eš BE-LUMEŠ TU7[33] ḫu-u-ma-an-te-eš (21′) LÚSAGI.A LÚ GIŠBANŠUR LÚMUḪALDIM LÚNINDA.DÙ.DÙ (22′) LÚda-a-wa-la-la-aš LÚwa-al-aḫ-ḫi-ia-la-aš LÚZABAR.DAB (23′) LÚpa-ša-an-da-la-aš LÚE-PIŠ GA LÚki-ip-li-ia-la-aš (24′) LÚšur-ra-la-aš LÚtap-pa-a-la-aš LÚḫar-ši-ia-la-aš (25′) LÚzu-up-pa-a-la-aš LUGAL-wa-aš ZI-ni še-er ITU-mi ITU-mi (26′)li-in-ki-iš-ke-tén DUG.GIR4-aš GAL-in ú-wi5[34]-te-ni-it (27′)šu-u-ni-iš-tén na-an-kán dUTU-i me-na-aḫ-ḫa-an-da (28′)ar-ḫa la-aḫ-⌜ḫu-tén⌝ nu ki-iš-ša-an te-e-tén

TRANSLATION

(first ca. three-quarters of col. i missing entirely)

§1′ (1′)[…] you[35] do (2′)[…] (empty) (3′)[… it is a cap]ital offense.

§2′ (4′)[… o]ut of the clothes closet (5′)[…] you(sg.) shall (6′)[…] he sins/makes sinful (7′)[… *tapan*]*danili*(?)-man (8′)[…] but you(sg.) conceal (9′)[…] you(sg.) will perish along with your!(text "his") wife (and) your!(text "his") sons.

§3′ (10′)[…] fruit (11′)[… shall] not […] *soup* with the hand (12′)[…] s/he pours (13′)[…] s/he/it stands/steps/arrives (14′–15′)[…] you see/look […]

§4′ (16′)[…] whoever (17′)[…] *he touches/approaches* (18′)[…] he will die […]

(first ca. one-half of col. ii missing entirely)

§5″ (1′)[… *y*]*ou d*[*o* …] (2′)[… bak]er (3′)[… dair]yman, *kipli*(*ja*)-ma[ker] (4′)[…] *tappa*-maker, fruit-keeper, *usḫa*-maker (5′–6′)[… *tapand*]*ānli*-man, thickbread-maker […][36]

§6″ (7′–8′)[If] someone causes [impur]ity, someone [rais]es the ire of the king, and you say as follows: (9′)"[The king] won't see us!" (10′)On the contrary, the *king's* gods are already watching you! (11′)They will turn you into a goat, and they will drive you into the mountains; (12′)or they will turn you into a *gaggapa*-animal, (13′)and they will drive you to the cliff!

§7″ (14′)On a day when (my) temper gets the best of (me), the king, (15′)and I call all of you kitchen personnel, (16′)and I put you through the river(ordeal), then he who is (thereby shown to be) innocent, (17′)he is a servant of the king, while he who is (shown to be) guilty, (18′)I, the king, will have no need of him. (19′)They (i.e. the gods) will allot him an evil fate, together with his wife (and) his sons.

§8″ (20′)Furthermore, all you kitchen personnel—(21′)the cupbearer, the table servant, the chef, the baker, (22′)the *tawal*-beer brewer, the *walḫi*-drink maker, the bronze dish bearer, (23′)the *taster*, the dairyman, the *kipli*(*ja*)-maker, (24′)the *surra*-maker, the *tappa*-maker, the thickbread maker, (25′–28′)the *zuppa*-vessel man—you shall swear an oath to the person of the king month for month. You shall fill a ceramic cup with water, and you shall pour it out before the Sun Deity, and you shall speak as follows:

(29′)ku-iš-wa pa-ap-ra-tar i-ia-zi nu-wa LUGAL-i *x* (30′)ḫar-ra-⸤an⸥ wa-a-tar pa-a-i *x x* (rev. iii 1)⸢nu-wa⸣-kán a-pé-e-el ZI-an DINGIR^{MEŠ} ú-wi$_5$-te-na-aš (2)i-wa-ar ar-ḫa la-a-aḫ-ḫu-wa-tén

§9″ (3)an-da-ma-za šu-me-e-eš ku-i-e-eš $^{\text{LÚ.MEŠ}}$E-PIŠ ^{KUŠ}E.SIR (4)nu LUGAL-aš ^{KUŠ}E.SIR ku-i-e-eš an-ni-iš-kat-te-e-ni (5)nu KUŠ.GU$_4$ ŠA É ^{LÚ}MUḪALDIM da-a-aš-ka$_4$-te-en (6)da$_4$-ma-i-in-ma[37] le-e da-a-aš-ka$_4$-te-e-ni (7)ku-iš da$_4$-ma-i-in-ma da-a-i EGIR-pé-ez-zi-ia-ma-at (8)iš-tu-wa-a-ri nu-uš-ši QA-DU$_4$ NUMUN-ŠU ḪUL-lu ÚŠ-an pí-ia-an-zi

§10″ (9)an-da-ma-za šu-me-eš ku-i-e-eš $^{\text{LÚ.MEŠ}}$AŠGAB ŠA É ^{LÚ}tar-ši-pa-a-li-ia-aš[38] (10)ŠA É ^{LÚ}tup-pa-a-aš Ù ^{LÚ}UGULA 10 ^{LÚ}tar-ši-pa-a-la-aš (11)LUGAL-wa-aš ^{GIŠ}GIGIR$^{\text{ḪI.A}}$ ti-ia-u-wa-aš ku-i-e-eš an-ni-eš-kat-te-e-ni (12)nu KUŠ.GU$_4$ KUŠ.MÁŠ[39] ŠA É ^{LÚ}MUḪALDIM[40] ta-aš-kat-tén (13)ta-ma-a-i-ma le-e da-at-te-ni

§11″ (14)ma-a-an-ma ta-ma-a-i-ma da-at-te-e-ni (15)LUGAL-i-ma-at te-et-te-en nu-uš-ma-ša-at Ú-UL wa-aš-túl (16)LUGAL-ša-at ^{LÚ}a-ra-a-aḫ-zé-e-ni-ma up-pa-aḫ-ḫi (17)[n]a-aš-ma-at A-NA ÌR pé-eḫ-ḫi

§12″ (18)ták-ku ša-a-na-at-te-e-ni-ma ap-pé-ez-zi-ia-an-ma-at (19)iš-tu-wa-a-ri nu-uš-ma-aš QA-DU$_4$ DAM^{MEŠ}-KU-NU (20)DUMU^{MEŠ}-*KU-NU x* i-da-a-lu ḫi-in-kán pí-ia-an-zi

§13″ (21)an-da-ma-aš-ma-aš šu-me-eš ku-i-e-eš $^{\text{LÚ.MEŠ}}$A ŠA KUŠ.LÁ (22)nu-uš-ma-aš ú-wi$_5$-te-na-aš na-aḫ-ḫa-an-te-eš e-eš-tén (23)nu ú-wi$_5$-ta-ar ^{GIŠ}še-ša-ru-li-it še-ša-ri-iš-ke-tén (24)ka-ru-ú-ša-an LUGAL-uš I-NA ^{URU}ŠA.NA.ḪU.IT.TA (25)ŠÀ ^{URUDU}ÁB×A te-e-da-na-an ú-e-mi-ia-nu-un (26)nu LUGAL-aš ZI-an-za iš-ḫi-iz-zi-ta nu-kán A-NA $^{\text{LÚ.MEŠ}}$A ŠA KUŠ.LÁ (27)kar-tim-mi-ia-nu-un …

(A iii 27)… ki-i-wa gul-la-ku-wa-an UM-MA ^{m}AR.NI.LI (28) ^{m}Zu-li-ia-aš-wa pa-ra-a ú-wa-an-za e-eš-ta (29) UM-MA LUGAL-MA ^{m}Zu-li-ia-aš-wa ḫa-pa-a pa-id-du (30)ma-a-an-na-aš pár-ku-e-eš-zi nu-za ZI-ŠU pár-ku-nu-ud-du [ ] (31)ma-a-an-na-aš pa-ap-ra-aš-zi-ma nu-wa-ra-aš a-k[u]

(B, 1′)[…]x ⸢TA⸣ x[[41]…] (2′)[…-u]n-wa ki-i x[[42]…] (3′)[… UM-MA] ^{m}AR.NI.LI ^{m}Z[u-li-ia-aš-wa] (4′)[pa-ra-a ú-wa-an-z]a e-eš-ta UM-MA LUGAL-M[A[43] ^{m}Zu-li-ia-aš-wa] (5′)[A-NA] ⸢^{d}I$_7$⸣ pa-id-du ma-a-na-aš pár-k[u-e-eš-zi] (6′)[e-e]š$^{(?)}$ zi-ik-ka$_4$ pár-ku-iš ma-a-na-aš pa-a[p-ra-aš-zi-ma] (7′)[nu z]i-ik-ka$_4$ i-it ma-a-ne pa-a-e[r …]

(29′–30′)"He who causes impurity and gives the king impure water, (iii 1–2) may you, o gods,[44] pour out his soul like water!"

§9″ (3)Furthermore, you who are shoemakers (4)and who make the king's shoes: (5)You shall always take cowhide from the kitchen, (6)you shall take no other; (7)he who does take another, though, and afterwards (8)it becomes known, to him and his descendents they will allot an evil fate.

§10″ (9)Furthermore, you who are leather workers of the *coachmen*-facility, (10) of the warehouse and (of) the overseer of 10 *coachmen*, (11)(i.e.) you who produce the step-coach of the king; (12)you shall always take cowhide (and) ram's hide from the kitchen. (13)You shall take no other.[45]

§11″ (14)If, however, you do take another, (15)but you report it to the king,[46] then it is no offense on your part. (16)I, the king, will send it to a foreigner, instead, (17)or I will give it to a servant.

§12″ (18–20)If you conceal (it), though, and afterwards it becomes known, then they will allot you together with your wives (and) your sons an evil fate.

§13″ (21)Furthermore, you who are water carriers, (22)you must be very careful concerning the water, (23)and you must always filter the water with a sieve. (24)One time I, the king, in the city of Sanaḫuitta, (25)found a hair in the washbasin,[47] (26)and (my), the king's, ire was raised, and I became enraged at the water carriers (and I said):

(A iii 27) "This is disgusting!" Arnili (responded) so: (28)"Zuliya was the overseer[48]!" (29)And the king (continued) thus: "Zuliya shall go through the river (ordeal)![49] (30)If he is (shown to be) innocent, then "let him purify his soul." (31)But if he is (shown to be) guilty, then he will die."

(B, 1′–2′)[…] "this […"] (3′)Arnili (responded) [so]: "Z[uliya] (4′) was [the oversee]r!" And the king (continued) thus: "[Zuliya] (5′)shall go [through] the river (ordeal)! If he is (shown to be) inno[cent], (6′) then **[may] you(sg.) [b]e innocent as well**. [But] if he is (shown to be) gui[lty], (7′)**[then] you(sg.) shall go too!" And when they went,**

§14″	(32)nu ^{m}Zu-li-ia-aš ḫa-pa-a pa-it na-aš pa-a[p-ri-it] (33)nu ^{m}Zu-li-ia-an I-NA ^{URU}ŠU.RE.EŠ.T[A] (34)ti-it-ta-nu-e-er na-an LUGAL-uš x[50][…] (35)na-aš ak-ta […]	(8′)[nu] ˻^{m}˼Zu-li-ia-aš pa-ap-ri-it a-pa-a-[aš-ša pa-ap-ri-it] (9′)[nu-u]š I-NA ^{URU}ŠU.RI.IŠ.TA [I-N]A? x[…] (10′)[ti-i]t-ta-nu-er ˻nu-uš˼ LUGAL-uš[…] (11′)[… z]i?-i[k?-ka$_4$$^{(?)}$ x] ˻GE˼ E[N …]

§15″ (36)ki-nu-un-ma-aš-ma-aš šu-me-e-eš LÚ^{M}[^{EŠ}A ŠA KUŠ.LÁ$^{(?)}$] (37)ú-wi$_5$-te-na-aš na-aḫ-ḫa-an-te-eš [e-eš-tén nu ú-wi$_5$-ta-ar] (38) ^{GIŠ}še-ša-ru-li-it še-ša-r[i-iš-ke-tén ma-a-an-ma …] (39)ú-wi$_5$-te-na-aš pa-ap-r[a-tar ku-it-ki …] (40)na-aš-ma-kán te-e-d[a-na-an …] (41)ú-e-mi-ia-tén ˻nu˼[…] (42) te-e-˻tén˼[51] […] (43)˻ták-ku˼[…]

(remaining ca. one-third of col. iii and first 2 to 3 lines of col. iv missing)

§16″ (iv 1′)[…]x-⸢ša⸣ ma-a-an ^{LÚ}MUḪALDIM (2′)[… ḫu-u-m]a-an-du-uš (3′)[… šu]-me-e-ša EGIR-pa (4′)[…] (empty)

§17″ (5′)[… pa-a]p-re-eš-zi-ma (6′)[… nu-uš-š]i QA-DU DAM-ŠÚ DUMU^{MEŠ}-ŠÚ (7′) [ḪUL-lu ÚŠ-an pí-ia-an-zi] (empty)

§18″ (8′)[… EGIR-p]a pa-a-i-mi (9′)[… ^{LÚ}A]GRIG[52] TUR LUGAL-wa-aš (10′)[… -a]t?-za ŠIM na-an-né-eš-ši[53] (11′)[… ḫa-a]n?-da-a-an

§19″ (12′)[… ^{UD}]$^{U?}$i-ia-an-da-*an-še*[54] (13′)[… k]a-ag-ga-pa-an (14′)[…]x NINDA-an ZÍZ-aš (15′)[… ku-uš]-ku-šu[55]-ul-li ḫu-u-ma-an (16′)[…]-ik nu ku-it-ta pa-ra-a (17′)[…] (empty)

§20″ (18′)[… ḫu-u-m]a-an-te-eš pé-ra-an ŠA *x* (19′)[…] ^{LÚ}MUḪALDIM ^{LÚ}MU-RI-DI ^{LÚ}ta-wa-*la-<la>-aš* (20′)[… ^{LÚ}pa-aš]-ša-an-da-la-aš ^{LÚ}NINDA.DÙ.DÙ (21′)[… ^{LÚ}]ki-ip-li-ia-la-aš ^{LÚ}šu-u-ra-la-aš (22′)[…]-ḫa-na-la-aš ^{LÚ}ḫar-ši-ia-la-aš (23′)[…]x-u-uš-ši-it mar-ki-iš-ke-u-wa-an da-a-i (24′)[… t]i?-ia-at-te-ni nu-za TU$_7^{HI.A}$ (25′)[…]x ^{GIŠ}AD.KID ki-i mar-ak-te-ni im-ma (26′)[…]x-te-ni

§21″ (27′)[…]ḪI ÉRIN^{MEŠ} mar-nu-wa-an BA.BA.ZA ZÍD.DA (28′)[…]x x še-*er ta*-ma-i ŠUM-an ḫal-za-it-ti (29′)[…]x pa-a-i ku-it-ki (30′)[… -t]e-ni (31′)[…] (empty)

§22″ (32′)[… ḫu]-˻u?-ma?˼-an[56] mar-ak-te-ni (33′)[…]x-wa-ra-˻at˼ (34′)[… p]u-ug-ga-nu-ut-te-ni[57] (35′)[…] SAG.GÉME.ÌR-an (36′)[…] (empty)

§23″ (37′)[…]Ú-UL (erasure) (38′)[… n]a-aḫ-ḫa-a-an e-eš-ta (39′)[…]x ḫa-an-da-an mar-ak (40′)[…] (empty)

§14″	(32)So, Zuliya went through the river (ordeal), and he was (shown to be) gui[lty]. (33–34)And they "dealt with"[58] him in the city of Surest[a], and the king […] him, (35)and he died.	(8′)Zuliya was (shown to be) guilty, **[and] he, [too, was guilty]**, (9′–10′)[so that] they ["de]alt with" **[the]m** *in* […] the city of Surista, (11′)and the king […] **them**. […][59]

§15″ (36)Now, then, you [water carrie]rs (37–39)[must be] very careful concerning the water! [You must] fil[ter] the [water] with a sieve. [But if … any] impu[rity] in the water […] (40)or a ha[ir …] (41)you have found, and […] (42)you must report (it). (43)If […]

(remaining ca. one-third of col. iii and first 2 to 3 lines of col. iv missing)

§16″ (1′)[…] If the chef (2′)[… a]ll (3′–4′)[…] but [y]ou again/back […]

§17″ (5′)[…] but he will be [imp]ure/[gui]lty (6′–7′)[… then they will allot hi]m together with his wife (and) his sons [an evil fate].

§18″ (8′)[…] I will give [bac]k (9′–10′)[…] the king's subordinate [ad]ministrator […] (11′)[…] is [arr]anged/[cor]rect.

§19″ (12′)[…] *a sheep to him* (13′)[… *k*]*aggapa*-animal (14′)[…] bread, grain (15′)[… mor]tar, all (16′–17′)[…] and from each […]

§20″ (18′)[… al]l before (19′)[…] a chef, a *butcher*,[60] the *tawal*-beer brewer (20′)[… the *pas*]*sanda*-maker, the baker (21′)[…] the *kipli(ya)*-maker, the *sura*-maker (22′)[… the …]-*ḫanala*-maker, the thickbread-maker (23′)[…] he begins to divide/slaughter (24′)[…] you *stand*, and soups (25′)[…] wickerwork, these you divide/slaughter (26′)[…] you do […]

§21″ (27′)[…] troops, *marnuwan*-beer, porridge, flour (28′)[…] you(sg.) call another name (29′)[…] he gives/goes, whichever (30′–31′)[…] you do […]

§22″ (32′)[…] you divide/slaughter all (33′)[…] "it/they (34′)[…] you cause (someone) to be despised (35′–36′)[…] a female servant […][61]

§23″ (37′)[…] not (38′)[…] was very reverent (39′–40′)[… you(sg.) must] divide/slaughter *correctly*! […]

§24″ (41′)[…] *pé-eḫ-ḫi* (42′)[…]-*aš nu* LUGAL-*uš* (43′)[…] (empty)

§25″ (44′)[… *p*]*í*[?]-*ia-mi* (45′)[…]x x x

(remaining ca. one-third of col. iv missing entirely)

§24″ (41′)[…] I give (42′–43′)[…] and the king […]

§25″ (44′–45′)[…] I go […]

(remaining ca. one-third of col. iv missing entirely)

No. 3
Protocol for the Palace Gatekeeper (*CTH* 263)

This composition is for numerous reasons one of the most intriguing and at the same time one of the most neglected pieces of the corpus. Its main manuscript (A), the provenience of which is unfortunately unknown, is a rare example of a tablet not only the obv. and rev. of which are each divided into two columns, at least some of the resulting columns are also partly subdivided into two columns.[62] The lines of text are also unusually strongly tilted upwards to the right, especially in rev. iv, where the slant reaches nearly 20°.[63] Only for manuscript C is an approximate findspot known, the Temple I complex. All told, only about one quarter of the original composition is preserved.

Though the main manuscript and its two small duplicates (B and C)[64] are all NH copies, numerous morphological features indicate clearly that these are copies of an earlier, perhaps late OH or early MH composition, even if it is, admittedly, difficult to ascertain its dating more precisely (Klinger 1996: 201). It thus provides otherwise extremely scant information about the linguistic landscape of the Hittite capital during this period, as the text is often quite specific about language. The first paragraph relates that the gatekeeper is to call out from the main gate, and this in Hittite.[65] His "announcement" then consists of calling out the job titles of those who sleep up in the palace, and these he calls out in Hattian (cf. also §§20″, 23″).[66] Presumably because not all these titles would have been current to the palace scribes, these Hattian terms are provided in the text with Hittite translation and/or their Sumerian logographic equivalent. It is of course quite interesting for the question of the *Sitz im Leben* of the instructions, or at least of this composition, that essentially a bilingual word list follows at this point. That is to say, the composition switches from the narrative/prescriptive level, on which the gatekeeper is said to call out these occupational titles in the Hattian language, to a presumably purely textual level, likely intended primarily for the scribal community. On this level one finds not what the gatekeeper presumably would have called out in Hattian, but a bilingual word list for administrative purposes (see Klinger 1996: 202–7; Beal 1988: 284–85; for Hattian terms in general O. Soysal 2004).

The linguistic diversity of the palace court is thereby not exhausted however; as soon as the gatekeeper is finished with the names of these workers, he calls to those who tend the fire, and to these he is supposed to speak in Luwian.[67] What he is to say to the tenders, however, is written out in Hittite, not in Luwian (Otten 1953b: 12, n. 4). The final paragraph (§36″) even seems to employ the Hattian language as a security check of sorts, much like the famous shibboleth episode from Judg 12:5–6. The gatekeeper must ask a cleaner going up to the palace for identification, and the cleaner is to respond with the Hattian word *tāḫaya*, meaning "cleaner." If not, that is, presumably if the gatekeeper receives a proper answer in Hittite, his own language, then the man is suspect of not being a cleaner, but the servant of some man and a possible security threat, so he is to be arrested. Yakubovich (2009: 264–65) understands these observations as indicating "that the potential readers of the instruction were expected to be Hittite and Luvian bilinguals and to have no difficulties with translating this utterance back into Luvian." Most or at least many residents of Ḫattusa would thus have been speakers of Hittite and Luwian, but not of Hattian, which, though still preserved, for example, in some occupational titles, was no longer familiar to persons such as the gatekeeper and the scribe, so that translations were provided. Such linguistic hints are found in similar contexts as well in §§12a and 57 of No. 4, the Protocol for the Royal Body Guard, to which it shows numerous other parallels, too.

The Protocol for the Palace Gatekeeper, though fully preserved at its beginning and end, includes no incipit or any proper introduction or conclusion; and it ends as abruptly as it begins. The title attached to the composition by its scribe in the colophon is "Sleeping Up Above," which at first seems somewhat puzzling. In fact, however, this text is specifically a protocol pertaining to waking up those palace servants and workers who sleep up in the palace complex and beginning the morning's routine in an organized and secure manner (§§2, 35″).

The gatekeeper, upon reaching the palace gate and calling out the occupational titles of the employees who sleep up in the palace (§§1–5), then encourages those who tend the fire to be careful (§6), at which point the text, while mentioning further palace personnel (§7), becomes too fragmentary for a coherent assessment of its contents (§§8′–21″). Of interest in the following, only slightly better preserved, paragraphs is the mention of bird-omen experts, who apparently were assumed to have been present during the morning routine, along with certain military classes and runners (§§22″–23″). The ensuing sections are again largely lost (§§24″–31″), the next notable statement being that some personnel are not to stand up for a series of certain persons, while for the daughters of the king they are indeed to stand up (§32″). The following paragraph (§33″) remains somewhat mysterious. Presumably the royal bodyguard had also spent the night on the palace grounds, but why he is to drink as he drinks day to day is unclear. In §§34″–35″ the windows of the upper floors are closed, as is the door to the stairway leading up to them and the roof. This is done by a palace servant who is preceeded by a deaf man, probably because this man is to close the windows to rooms inhabited by some of the royal family itself and the door leading to this area, and one can be certain that a deaf man will not overhear anything said in confidence. Finally, at the end of §35″

the palace servants are to give their bed rolls to the cleaners, and in the final paragraph (§36″) is mentioned how the gatekeeper is supposed to subject any cleaner coming up to the palace to a shibboleth test, as noted above.

The entire text is composed in the 3rd sg. pres., thus in a simple prescriptive narrative referring to the duties of the gatekeeper (cf. Pecchioli Daddi 2005b: 607). As discussed more fully in the introduction to No. 4, this is unique

---

TRANSLITERATION

§1 (A i 1–4) $^{(1)}$*ma-a-an I-NA* É.GAL-*LÌ za-ak-ki-ti-i ar-ta-ri nu-*⸢*za* ^{LÚ}Ì.DU$_8$⸣ $^{(2)}$ ^{GIŠ}TUKUL^{MEŠ} EGIR-*an ki-iš-ša-an kap-pu-u-e-zi* ^{LÚ}Ì.DU$_8$-*kán* $^{(3)}$*IŠ-TU* KÁ.GAL *kat-ta ti-i-e-zi nu na-a-ši-*[*l*]*i ki-iš-ša-an* $^{(4)}$*te-ez-zi ḫa-lu-ga-aš ḫa-lu-ga-aš*

§2 (A i 5–7; C, 1′–3′)

$^{(5)}$ *nu I-NA* É.GAL-*LÌ ku-i-e-eš še-er* *še-e-ša-an-* [ ] *zi*
$^{(6)}$ *na-at pa-ra-a ti-i-an-zi* ^{LÚ}Ì.DU$_8$-*ma-aš-kán ḫa-*[*at-ti*]-⸤*li*⸥
$^{(7)}$ *lam-ni-it ḫal-zi-iš-* *ša-*[ ] *-i*

§3 (A i 8–11; C, 4′–6′)

$^{(8)}$ ^{LÚ}*wi$_i$-in-du-uk-ka$_4$-ra-* *am* ^{LÚ}SAGI-[ ] *aš*
$^{(9)}$ ^{LÚ}*zu-u-lu-u-we$_e$-* *e* LÚ ^{GIŠ}BANŠUR-[ ] *aš*
$^{(10)}$ ^{LÚ}*ḫa-an-ti-ip-šu-wa$_a$-* *a* ^{LÚ}MUḪALDIM-[ ] *aš*
$^{(11)}$ ^{LÚ}*pár-ši-e-* *el* ^{LÚ}ALAM.ZU$_9$ [ ]

§4 (A i 12–15)

$^{(12)}$ ^{LÚ}*ša-aḫ-ta-ri-i-* *il* ^{LÚ}GALA~ [ ][68]
$^{(13)}$ ⸤^{LÚ}*du*$^?$-*ú*$^?$-*e*⸥- *el*[69] ^{LÚ}*zi-li-pu-ri-ia-tal-la* [ ]-*aš*[70]
$^{(14)}$ ^{LÚ}*ḫa-ag-ga-*⸢*zu-e*⸣-[ ] *el* ^{LÚ}*a*$^!$-*ku-ut*$^!$-*tar-ra-* [*aš*]
$^{(15)}$ ^{LÚ}*da-a-gul-ru-na-*⸢*a*$^?$⸣-[ ] *il* LÚ ^{GIŠ}ZA.LAM.BAR~ [ ]

§5 (A i 16–20)

$^{(16)}$ ⸢^{LÚ}⸣*ta-a-ni-ša-* *wa* LÚ ^{GIŠ}GIDRU~ [
$^{(17)}$ ^{LÚ}*tu-uš-ḫa-wa$_a$-du-un ta-*⸢*a-ni-ša-ú-e*⸣ ^{LÚ}GAD.TAR~ [
$^{(18)}$ ^{LÚ}*lu-u-i-iz-zi-i-* *il* ^{LÚ}KAŠ$_4$.E~ [
$^{(19)}$ ^{LÚ}*ki-i-lu-* *uḫ* ^{LÚ}NÍ.ZU$^?$ ^{LÚ}KAŠ$_4$.E~ [
$^{(20)}$ ^{LÚ}*du-ud-du-uš-*⸢*ḫi*⸣*-ia-* *al* ^{LÚ}*du-ud-du-uš-ḫi-ia-al-la-a*[*š*$^?$

§6 (A i 21–24)

$^{(21)}$*nam-ma-az* LÚ^{MEŠ} *pa-aḫ-ḫu-e-na-aš* EGIR-*an kap-pu-u-ez-z*[*i*]
$^{(22)}$*na-at pa-ra-a ti-ia-an-* *zi* *nu* ^{LÚ}Ì.DU$_8$ *lu-ú-i-li ki-iš-š*[*a-an*]

to these two compositions, closely linking them functionally and stylistically, perhaps also chronologically.

Klinger (1996: 206) has suggested that some elements in the composition make it likely that this procedure or protocol was in fact practiced, and this is presumably correct at least for the OH period from which this composition (as well as No. 4) stems. Whether this was still the case by the time of the NH copies seems less likely, though not impossible.

TRANSLATION

§1 (1)When he reaches the door bolt in the palace, the gatekeeper (2)tallies the trades(men) as follows: (3–4)The gatekeeper steps down from the main gate, and he speaks as follows in Hittite: "An announcement! An announcement!"

§2 (5)And those who sleep up in the palace (6–7)step forth. The gatekeeper, then, calls them by (trade)name in Ha[tti]an:

§3	(8)*windukkaram*	wine-cup bearer
	(9)*zūlūwē*	table server
	(10)*ḫantipšuwā*	chef
	(11)*paršiēl*	entertainer
§4	(12)*šaḫtarīl*	cult singer
	(13)*dūēl*(?)	priest of the god Zilipuri
	(14)*ḫaggazuēl*	(cultic) drinker
	(15)*dāgulrunāil*	tent man
§5	(16)*tānišawa*	scepter-bearer
	(17)*tušḫawadun tānišaue*	tailor(?)
	(18)*lūīzzīl*	runner
	(19)*kīluḫ*	sentry-runner
	(20)*duddušḫiyal*	*duddusḫiyalla-*

§6 (21)Further, he keeps track of the men who tend the fire. (22–24)They step forth, and the gatekeeper says in Luwian as follo[ws]: "Come![71]

(23)*te-ez-zi ú-wa-at pa-aḫ-ḫu-ni-*	*it*	{*te-ez-zi ú-wa-at* IZI-*it*}[72] <*me-ek-ki*> *mar-*[*ri*]
(24)*pa-aḫ-ḫa-aš-nu-wa-an*		LUGAL-*it pa-*aḫ*-ša-nu-wa-an e-e*[*š-tén*]

§7 (A i 25–27)

(25)[*ma-aḫ-ḫ*]*a-an-ma a-ap-pa-i nu ku-iš*	GIŠ*za-ak-ki-ti-i ti-i-e-e*[*z-zi*?]
(26)[x x x DUM]UMEŠ É.GAL *ma-a-*˻*na*˼*-aš*	*ku-iš im-ma ku-iš* DU[MUMEŠ É.GAL
(27)[ ]˻*I*?-*NA*?˼ x[	]˻*ma-aḫ-ḫa-an A-NA*˼[

(gap of up to ca. 30 lines)

§8′ (A i 1′)[…]-*an ŠUM-ŠU ḫal-za-a-i*

§9′ (A i 2′)[… LÚ*zi-l*]*i-pu-u-ri-ia-tal-la-aš* (3′)[…]-*wa*

§10′ (A i 4′)[… *ḫal-za-a*]-*i*

§11′ (A i 5′)[…]x-*wa*

(gap of up to ca. 30 lines)

§12″ (A ii 1′)EGIR-[…] (2′) GIŠGIDRU[…] (3′)ŠA[

§13″ (A ii 4′) LÚx[…] (5′)*te-*x[…] (6′)*aš*/LÚ~*t*[*a-*…] (7′)*ši-*[…]

§14″ (A ii 8′)EGI[R-…]

§15″ (A ii 9′) LÚ*ḫ*[*a*?-…] (10′)*te-*[…]

(short gap)[73]

§16″ (A ii 1″)[… *k*]*i*?-˹*iš-ša*?*-an*˺

§17″ (A ii 2″)[…] (3″)[…]x-*wa*

§18″ (A ii 4″)[… *ŠUM-Š*]*U*? *ḫal-za-a-i* (5″)[…]-*zi*

§19″ (A ii 6″)[…LÚ*du-ud-du-uš*]-*ḫi-ia-al-la-wa* (7″)[…]-**wa**

§20″ (A ii 8″)[…]*ḫa-at-ti-i-li* (9″)[*ki-iš-ša-an te-ez*]-*zi*

§21″ (A ii 10″)[…]*ki-iš-ša-an me-ma-i* (11″)[…]-*wa-ra-aš e*?(EŠ)-*eš-zi*[74]

§22″ (A ii 12″)[…]˹1?˺ KÙ?(ZU/GÍN).BABBAR *wa-al-aḫ-zi* (13″)[…]x~E A GIŠ*za-ak-ki-ti ku-iš ar-ta-ri* (14″)[…]x LÚÌ.DU8-*ša* LÚMEŠ IGI.DÙ (15″)[… *n*]*a*?-*at ú-ba-a-ti* LÚDUGUD-*ia-kán ŠUM-ŠU ḫal-za-a-i* (16″)[… -*z*]*i kat-ti-iš-ši-wa-aš-ši* 10-*an-za*

B[e] <extre>me[ly] careful with the fire (and) careful regarding the king!"

§7 (25)[As so]on as he is finished, though, he who stand[s] by the door-bolt (26)[…] the palace [per]sonnel. If any one of the [palace] pers[onnel] (27)[…] *in* […] when to […]

(gap of up to ca. 30 lines)

§8′ (1′)[…] he calls his name,

§9′ (2′–3′)[…] priest of the god [Zil]ipuri

§10′ (4′)[… he call]s,

§11′ (5′)[…]

(gap of up to ca. 30 lines)

§12″ (1′)[…] back/behind […] (2′–3′)scepter […]

§13″ (4′–7′)[…]-man […]

§14″ (8′)[…] bac[k]/behin[d …]

§15″ (9′)[…] the *ḫ*[*a*…]-man […] (10′)sa[ys …]

(short gap)

§16″ (1″)[… *as*] *follows*:

§17″ (2″–3″)[…]

§18″ (4″–5″)[…] he calls hi[s name …]

§19″ (6″–7″)[… *duddus*]*ḫiyalla*-man […]

§20″ (8″–9″)[… he speak]s in Hattian [as follows]:

§21″ (10″)[…] he speaks thus: (11″)"He/It *is* […]."

§22″ (12″)[…] he strikes 1 (*piece of*) *silver* (13″)[…] he who stands by the door-bolt (14″)[…] the gatekeeper, though, […] the bird omen experts (15″)[… *an*]*d* they are an *upati*-military unit,[75] and the dignitary calls his name (16″)[…] with him a group of 10 (persons?)[76]

§23″ (A ii 17″)[… L]ÚKAŠ$_4$.E LÚ*du-ud-d*[*u-u*]*š-*˻*ḫi*˼*-ia-al-la-aš* (18″)[… *iš-ta-ma-aš-š*]*a*?*-an-z*[*i*] (19″)[… *ḫa-a*]*t*?*-ti-i-*[*li*] (20″)[*ki-iš-ša-an te-ez-zi*]

(gap of up to ca. 25 lines)

§24″ (A ii 1″)*na-*[…] (2″)É UD[…] (3″) LÚÌ.DU$_8$[…] (4″) LÚ*šar-*˻*me*˼*-i*[*a-*…] (5″) *ḫal-za-a-*˻*i*˼[…] (6″)x x x[…]

(gap of ca. one-half to three-quarters of a col.)

§25″ (A iii 2′)[…] *ma-a-an-*˹*ši*?/*wa*?˺ x[ ]x x x-*ia* (3′)[…]-*up*~*pí-in kat-ta ti-an-zi* (4′)[…]x *pí-an-zi nu-uš-ma-aš a-da-an-*˹*zi*˺ (5′)[…]

§26″ (A iii 6′)[…]x-*ša-*˹*at*?˺ ˹*še*?˺*-e-ša-an-zi* (7′)[…]x *ar-ḫa* {*ar-ḫa*} ˻*šar*˼*-ra-*˻*an*˼*-zi* (8′)[…-*z*]*i ma-a-an-kán* ˻DUMU É.GAL˼ (9′)[…] *nu-za* LÚÚ.ḪÚB (10′) […]x *uš-*˻*ke*˼*-ez-zi* (11′)[…]x *ni-ni-ik-zi*

§27″ (A iii 12′)[…]x *uš-kán-zi* (13′)[… G]IŠ?*ḫu-up-pár-ri*(?) (14′)[…]x-*ni*~*pu-u-un-na-aš-ši* (15′)[…]

§28″ (A iii 16′)[…]x-*a* (17′)[…]x-*zi*

(short gap)

§29″ (A iii 1″)*ma-*[…] (2″)*ti-a*[*n-*…] (3″)*an-d*[*a* …] (4″)*nu-za* x[…] (5″)*nu* GIŠ*z*[*a-ak-ki-*…] (6″)*pa-ra-*˹*a*˺[…]

§30″ (A iii 7″)*na-aš-t*[*a* …] (8″)*na-aš* d3077*-aš*[…] (9″)*ku-i-*[*e-eš* …] (10″)*ti-e*[*n-*…] (11″)*pé-ra-*[*an* …] (12″)*ḫa-a*[*n-*…]

(gap of ca. one-half col. length)

§31″ (A iv 1′)*na-*x[…] (2′)*šu-ú-*[…] (3′)LUGAL-*uš*~x[…]

§32″ (A iv 4′)*nu* GIŠIG *an-da* x x[[78]…] (5′)*nu-za* LÚMEŠ *ME-ŠE-DI* É˹*ḫi-i*˺-x[…] (6′)*ku-iš* ˻*ú*?˼*-ez-zi na-at Ú-UL š*[*a-ra*]*-*˹*a ti-an-zi ma-a*˺*-a*[*n* …] (7′)*pa-ra-a* ˻*ú*?˼*-wa-an-zi na-at Ú-UL* ˹*ša*˺*-ra-a ti-*˻*an*˼*-zi ma-*˻*a*˼*-a*[*n*] (8′)DUMU.MUNUSMEŠ LUGAL-˹*ma*?˺ *pa-ra-a ú-wa-an-zi na-*[*a*]*t ša-ra-*[*a t*]*i-an-z*[*i*]

§33″ (A iv 9′)*ma-aḫ-ḫa-an-ma ḫa-li-in-du-wa ta-ra-an-zi nu* LÚ*ME-ŠE-DI A-N*[*A* …] (10′)*ḫal-za-a-i ka-a-az-zu-e nu ša-aš-ta-an ša-ra-a da-a-i* (11′)*na-an-kán kat-ta pé-e-da-i nu* ˻*ḫa*˼*-li-in-du-wa-aš ma-aḫ-ḫa-a*[*n*] (12′)UD-*at* UD-*at ak-ku-*˻*uš-ke*˼*-ez-zi na-aš QA-TAM-MA e-ku-z*[*i*]

§34″ (A iv 13′–17′; B iv 1′–2′) (13′)*n*[*a-aš*]*-ta* DUMU É.GAL *šu-uḫ-*˻*ḫa*˼ *ša-ra-a pa-iz-zi pé-ra-an-ma-aš-ši* [LÚÚ.ḪÚB][79] (14′)*ḫu-ia-an-za nu* LÚÚ.[Ḫ]ÚB GIŠABḪI.A *an-da iš-ta-a-pí nu* DUMU [É.GAL] (15′) GIŠ*za-ak-*˻*ki-in*˼ [*p*]*é-eš-*

§23″ (17″)[…] the runner, the *duddusḫiyalla*-man (18″)[…] they [*hea*]*r* (19″–20″)[… he speaks in Ha]ttian [as follows]:

(gap of up to ca. 25 lines)

§24″ (1″)And […] (2″)*white* building […] (3″)gatekeeper […] (4″)a *sarme*[*ya*]-man […] (5″)he calls […]

(gap of ca. one-half to three-quarters of a col.)

§25″ (2′)[…], if […] to him (3′)[…] they step down (4′–5′)[…] they give, and they eat *for them*.

§26″ (6′)[…] they sleep. (7′)[…] they split/divide up. (8′)[…] If a palace servant (9′)[…], and a deaf man (10′)[…] he watches (11′)[…] he lifts.

§27″ (12′–15′)[…] they watch […]

§28″ (traces)

(short gap)

§29″ (1″–2″)I[f? … they] stan[d …] (3″)in […], (4″)and […], (5″)and the do[orbolt …] (6″)forth […]

§30″ (7″)And […] (8″)and he […] the Moon God […], (9″)they wh[o …] (10″)sta[nd …] (11″–12″)befo[re …]

(gap of ca. one-half col. length)

§31″ (1′–2′)[…] and […] (3′)the king […]

§32″ (4′)And […] in the door […], (5′)and the royal body guards the […] *cour*[*tyard*, …] (6′)he who comes, they do not stand up. If […] (7′)they come out, they do not stand up. If […] (8′)the daughters of the king come out, though, they stand up.

§33″ (9′)But when they say "to the palace complex" (*ḫalinduwa*), the royal bodyguard (10′)calls out *kāzzue*[80] to […], and he picks up the bed (11′–12′)and he carries it down. And just like he drinks in the palace complex day to day, so he drinks.

§34″ (13′)Then a palace servant goes up to the roof, but before him [a deaf man] (14′)leads. Then the deaf man pulls the windows shut, and the [palace] servant (15′)throws the door-bolt closed, and he co[mes] down. (16′)Then the

ši-ia-az-zi na-aš-kán kat-ta ú-e[*z-zi*] (16′)*nu* ^{LÚ}Ú.ḪÚB ˹SAG˺.[D]U ^{GIŠ}KUN$_5$ *an-da iš-ta-a-pí nu* DUMU É.G[(AL)] (17′) ^{GIŠ}*za-ak-ki-in pé-*˻*eš-ši*˼*-ia-az-zi*

§35″ (A iv 18′–21′; B iv 3′–6′) (18′)*ma-aḫ-ḫa-an-ma* SIG$_5$-*ri na-aš-t*[(*a* ^{LÚ})]˻ŠU˼.I[81] *iš-tar-ni-ia-aš* KÁ.GAL-*T*[*I*?] (19′)*kat-ta ti-i-e-ez-zi nu ḫal-za-*˹*a-i*˺ [(*mi*)]-˻*iš*˼-*ša-a mi-iš-ša-a nu m*[*a-aḫ-ḫa-an*] (20′)ÌR[82](TI)^{MEŠ} LÚ^{MEŠ} *BE-LU-TÌ iš-ta-ma-aš-ša-a*[(*n-z*)]*i nu ša-aš-du-uš š*[*a-ra-a*] (21′)*da-an-zi na-aš A-NA* $^{LÚ.MEŠ}$ŠU.I *pí-an-zi*

§36″ (A iv 22′–25′; B iv 7′–10′) (22′) ^{LÚ}Ì.DU$_8$-*ma-kán A-NA* KÁ.GAL-*TÌ an-da ar-ta-ri na-aš-t*[*a* ...] (23′)*ma-aḫ-ḫa-an* ^{LÚ}ŠU.I *ša-ra-a pa-iz-zi nu* ^{LÚ}Ì.DU$_8$ *ḫal-za-*[(*a-i*)] (24′)*zi-ik-za ku-iš* ^{LÚ}ŠU.I-*ma ki-iš-ša-an te-ez-zi ta-a-ḫ*[*a-ia*] (25′)*ku-i-ša ta-a-ḫa-ia-ma Ú-UL te-ez-zi na-aš* ÌR! ˹LÚ[83] *na-an ap-pa-an*˺-[*du*]

COLOPHON A

(A iv 26′)DUB.1.KAM *še-er še-e-šu-wa-aš QA-TI* [Š]U ^{m}*SAK.KA.PÍ* (27′)DUMU ^{m}*U*!(NU).*ZA*[84] DUMU.DUMU-*ŠÚ ŠÁ* *m* *MA.U.I.RI* (28′)*PA-NI* ^{m}*AN.GUL.LI IŠ-ṬUR*

COLOPHON B

(B iv 11′)[DU]B.1.KAM *še-er še-e-šu-u-wa-aš QA-T*[*I*] (12′) ^{m}GIŠ.GI-PÌRIG-*iš A-NA PA-NI* ^{m}˹*A*?˺.[*NU.WA.AN.ZA*(?)] (13′)*TUP-PU* ^{URU}*ḪA*.[*AT.TI IŠ-ṬUR*]

deaf man pulls the top of the staircase closed, and the pal[(ace)] servant (17′)throws the door-bolt closed.

§35″ (18′–19′)As soon as it's alright, then, the cleaner steps down to the inner gate, and he cries out "[(T)]ake! Take!" (*miššā miššā*).[85] And w[hen] (20′–21′)the servants of the men of governance hear (it), they take u[p] the(ir) beds and give them to the cleaners.

§36″ (22′)The gatekeeper, though, stands at the gate, and […]. (23′)When the cleaner goes up, the gatekeeper cri[(es)] out (24′)"Who are you?" Then the cleaner says this: "The clea[ner] (*tāḫ*[*aya*])." (25′)He who does not say *tāḫaya*, though, he's a man's servant, and they [must] grab him.[86]

COLOPHON A

(26′)Tablet One of Sleeping up Above;[87] finished. The [ha]nd of Sakkapi, (27′)son of Uza, grandson of Mauiri, (28′)wrote it in the presence of Angulli.

COLOPHON B

(11′)[Tabl]et One of Sleeping up Above; finish[ed]. (12′)GIŠ.GI-PÌRIG […] in the presence of A[nuwanza(?)] (13′)[wrote] (this) tablet of Ḫa[ttusa].

No. 4
Protocol for the Royal Body Guard (*CTH* 262)

This text is of great interest, among many other reasons, due to the nature of the tablet and its writing. Unlike most of the other instructions, this composition is preserved on a single ms. only, and, fortunately, on a nearly completely preserved tablet, the provenience of which is not known. It is a MH tablet,[88] which apparently was not subsequently copied, as far as we know, whether this indicates that its content was no longer applicable or simply that it was not used for scribal training. It is the first tablet of a set of unknown length, and the original composition is thus slightly less than half preserved at best.

Its other most striking feature is the many additions and/or corrections placed above, between and below the originally inscribed lines as well as around the edges and onto the opposing surface of the tablet, generally in a very small, less-carefully and less-deeply impressed script, apparently added after the entire body of the text was written, which often renders their reading rather difficult. In most cases it is clear where the addition or correction was meant to be incorporated within the text, but there are a couple of significant exceptions. Above all the order in which the additions at the end of the first and third paragraphs of the first column along with that which runs between the lines of the third column into the blank area beneath the colophon of column four has been variously interpreted. The present treatment deviates from the standard edition published by Güterbock and van den Hout (1991), a thorough explanation for which has appeared elsewhere (Miller 2011a). An attempt has been made to give the reader some sense of this situation by placing the additions and corrections in a smaller and/or superscript font.

The Royal Body Guard ($^{\text{LÚ.MEŠ}}$*MEŠEDI*) were "spear carrying guardsmen who formed the innermost ring of protection around the king" (Beal 1992: 212–24), and the present text is by far the most detailed source of information about them and their duties (p. 224). The first paragraphs (§§1–5) relate to their precise deployment in the courtyard of the royal palace, presumably in Ḫattusa.[89] The entirety of §§6–8 regulate visiting the latrine while on duty, followed by the proper procedure for a bodyguard when exiting the gate of the palace complex (§§9–11).

At this point the focus turns to the procedures for accompanying the king when he travels by coach to another town (§§12–59). Whereas Güterbock and van den Hout (1991: 2) assumed that the king returns to Ḫattusa beginning in §42, arriving in §§44–49, it seems rather to be the case that it is not a return to Ḫattusa that is at issue here, but the arrival at whatever town is being visited. This is suggested first and foremost by the optional locution in §48, "If there are two gat[ehouses], they may come up to the lower gate, but they may not come up to the upper gate." This would be difficult to explain if it related to Ḫattusa, as the scribe would have known perfectly well if there were two gatehouses at Ḫattusa or not. Thus, it must refer to an unspecified fortified city being visited by the king and his entourage. Other hints would seem to support this interpretation. In §49 it is detailed who is to bow before the king as he alights from his carriage. If the chief of the bodyguard is present, he does it; if (only) some other lord is present, then he assumes the duty; and if no important lord at all is there, then whatever bodyguard happens to be standing there is entrusted with the task. No important lord at all present in Ḫattusa? Surely this is the situation being imagined by the scribe at some provincial backwater, not the imperial capital (cf. No. 13, 1–2, §7′). Thus, if the return of the king to Ḫattusa was described in this composition, it must have been related in a subsequent, no longer extant, tablet.

In any case, §§12–26 relate the preparations for and the departure from Ḫattusa, whereby the additions in ll. 69–72 allow for the possibility that the departing journey begins in some other town in which the normal procedure, conceived for departing from Ḫattusa, must be adjusted to less monumental architecture. Of interest is reference to calling for a cleaner in Hattian, which clearly echos §36″ of No. 3. The disposition of the entourage during the journey is then described in detail (§§13–26), whereby the scribe was faced with the same difficulty that any author faces when attempting to describe multi-faceted events through time: in order to remain coherent one must first describe the actions of some portion of the events, then back up and describe another set, as many times as is necessary. In this way, the scribe begins describing one set of details with "As soon as the king goes out" at the beginning of §12a, finishing in §17. With §18 he begins describing the duties of other persons, and again we read "the king comes out," which of course refers to the same event.

In §§27–28, then, is detailed how the entourage is to deal with various threats along the way. At this point (§§29–36) is discussed how petitioners are to be dealt with, and from the total lack of reference to any architectural term, it might well be assumed that the author envisions petitioners approaching the convoy along the road. Paragraphs 37–39 continue with the arrangement of the entourage for the continuation of the journey, in particular in case the king "calls some foreign troops, either hostile Kaskean troops, or Kummaḫean troops, or whatever troops," which is not entirely transparent. In §§40–41 the scribe backs up again, beginning once more with the conclusion of the hearing of the petitioners, and describes the arrangement of the entourage.

With §42 begins the description of the convoy's arrival at its destination, whereby the latter portion of §42 and the beginning of §43 represent a slight diversion in order to relate how the entourage is to organize itself in case the king gives order to turn around. In §§44–48 the description of the arrival at the town is resumed. The king's dismounting from his carriage and entrance to his residence as well as the entourage's corresponding arrangement is recounted in §§49–53. Finally, the somewhat fragmentary §§54–59 describe the proper protocol once dinner at the town of destination is served, whereby at one point (§57) the gold-spearman calls out to the spearmen in Luwian, which, again, echoes No. 3, §6. In outline form, the structure of the texts is as follows:

1. Protocol for deploying in the royal courtyard (§1–§11)
    a. Arrival and disposition (§1–§5)
        i. Arrival of the bodyguards in the courtyard (§1)
            1. Initial description of arrival (§1, 1–6)
            2. Addition of procedure regarding the gate (§1, 7–8)
        ii. Disposition of the bodyguards in the courtyard (§2)
            1. Description of basic disposition with 12 bodyguards (§2, 9–11)
            2. Description of alternative disposition if 12 are not available (§2, 11–15)
        iii. Disposition of the gold-spear men in the courtyard (§3)
            1. Original description of disposition (§3, 16–19)
            2. Subsequently added further procedures (§3, 19–21h)
                a. Procedure in case there is insufficient *reed* (§3, 19–21a)
                b. Further, fragmentary procedures (§3, 21a–21h)
        iv. Procedure when chief and commander of ten of bodyguard arrive (§4)
        v. Procedure for the arrival of bodyguards *of* the staff (§5)
            1. Procedure if the king [...] (§5, 29–30)
            2. Alternatives (§5, 30–32)
    b. Regulations during the watch (§6–§11)
        i. Procedure for a guard who needs to use the toilet (§6–§8)
            1. Procedure if he must urinate (§6–§7)
            2. Procedure if he must *defecate* (§8)
                a. Proper procedure for obtaining permission (§8, 43–45)
                b. Consequences of going without permission (§8, 45–47)
        ii. Procedures for leaving the courtyard (§9–§11)
            1. Procedure for bodyguard exiting the gatehouse (§9)
            2. Ensuring that a bodyguard does not exit the gatehouse with a spear (§10)
            3. Exiting through main vs. postern gates (§11)

a. Bodyguards and palace personnel use postern (§11, 60–61)
b. Authorized bodyguards, lords and chiefs use main gate (§11, 61–63)

2. Protocol for a journey of the king (§12a–§59)
   a. Preparations for appearance of the king (§12a–§17)
      i. Opening of the gate (§12a, 64–68)
         1. They call for a cleaner (§12a, 64–66)
         2. The gates are opened (§12a, 66–68)
         3. The gate is cleaned (§12a, 69)
      ii. Preparation of the king's chariot (§12a, 69–§12b, 72)
         1. Normal disposition (§12a, 69–70)
         2. Disposition for leaving less monumental town (§12a, 70–§12b, 72)
         3. Duties of the bodyguard who holds the step-stool (§12b, 72–74)
      iii. Disposition of the king's travelling entourage (§13–§17)
   b. Protocol for king's appearance and mounting the carriage (§18–§19)
   c. Procedure for passing through the gate (§20)
   d. Disposition for the march (§21–§26)
   e. Procedures for eventualities during the march (§27–§41)
      i. Crowd control measures (§27)
      ii. Responsibility for security breaches caused by livestock (§28)
      iii. Handling of petitioners along the way (§29–§40)
         1. Protocol for normal cases (§29–§35)
         2. Protocol for case in which bodyguard/palace servant is involved (§36)
         3. Situation in which king calls foreign troops (§37–§39)
         4. Procedure for finishing session for petitioners (§40)
   f. Procedure for resuming the journey (§41)
   g. Protocol for arrival at town of destination (§42–§59)
      i. Procedure in case the king turns his carriage (§42, 63–§43)
      ii. Protocol for king's arrival at royal residence (§44–§49)
         1. Procedure for passing through the main gate (§44–§46)
         2. Procedure for reaching the residence (§47–§48)
         3. Procedure for receiving the king into the residence (§49)
      iii. Disposition once the king enters the palace (§50–§53)
      iv. Feeding the guards and palace personnel (§54–§55)
      v. Further fragmentary procedures (§56–§59)

Košak (1990: 85), in his edition of No. 18, suggested that it might be the continuation of the present text, which according to its colophon has not come to an end with the extant tablet, but this must be deemed quite unlikely. Though the identity of the addressees of No. 18 remains unclear and could conceivably be the royal bodyguard, as Košak suggests, the bodyguards in the present text are never addressed in the second person, nor does the king speak in the 1st person, as is the case with No. 18. This text employs 3rd indic. pres.-fut. verb forms throughout, while No. 18 is replete with imperatives. See also Giorgieri (2005: 327 and n. 23).

This narrative style, in fact, is otherwise found only in No. 3, the Protocol for the Palace Gatekeeper. It therefore may be the case that these two texts do not constitute directives issued by the king or other royal authority to which the subordinates in question would at some point have to swear an oath. In fact, neither composition includes any reference to oath deities, curses for breaking an oath, or anything of the sort. It might be suggested that these texts comprise

---

TRANSLITERATION

§1 (i 1)[…]x x x x[…-(*i*)]*a-an-*⸢*zi*⸣ (2)[…]x x-⸢*an*?-*zi*? $^{\text{LÚ.MEŠ}}$⸣*ME-ŠE*-⸢*DU*⸣-*T*[*I*?][90]-[*m*]*a*? [… *ša/pa-r*]*a-a* (3)[… -*an-z*]*i na*-⸢*at*?⸣ $^{\text{LÚ.MEŠ}}$⸢Ì.DU$_8$⸣-*aš* $^{\text{LÚ.MEŠ}}$KISAL.⸤LUḪ⸥-*aš* ⸢*pé-ra*⸣-*a*[*n* x x x-*a*]*n*?-*zi*[91] (4)[*na-a*]*t-kán an-da pa*-⸢*a*⸣-*an-zi na*-⸤*at-ša-an*⸥ ^{É}⸢*ḫi-i-la*⸣-*aš* ⸢KÁ⸣-[*aš*] ⸤*ti-en*⸥-*zi* (5)[I]GI$^{\text{ḪI.A}}$-*ŠU-ma-at-kán pa-ra-a ne-i*[*a-an-t*]*e-eš*[92] *nu-za*-⸤*kán* ^{É}⸥*ḫa-l*[*e-en-t*]*u-wa-aš* (6)1 ^{É}*ḫi-i-la-an* EGIR-*pa ta-me-eš*-⸢*ša-an-zi*⸣ *na-aš-ta ša-an-ḫa-an* x[[93] … -*z*]*i*? *x x x x* 94 (7)*x x x x x x x x x x x[95] *kar*?-*pa*?-*an*?-*zi*? x x x x x x x x $^{\text{LÚ?.MEŠ?}}$*ME-ŠE**-*DI pé-ra-an* [x x x x]-*zi* (8)**na-at* x x-*ni*?-*it*? *kar-pa-an-zi* ^{É}*ga*?-*aš-ga*?*-*aš-te-pa-aš*[96] [^{UR}]^{UDU}*za*-⸢*ak-ki-in Ú*?-*UL kar-pa*⸣-*an-zi na-aš-t*[*a* $^{\text{LÚ.MEŠ}}$*ME-ŠE-D*]*I* $^{\text{LÚ.MEŠ}}$Ì.DU$_8$ (8b) $^{\text{LÚ.MEŠ}}$KISAL.LUḪ *pa-ra-a ú*?-*wa-an-zi*

§2 (9)*nu-za* $^{\text{LÚ.MEŠ}}$*ME-ŠE-DI ŠA* ^{LÚ}*ME-ŠE-DI* ^{É}*ḫi-i-li pé-e-ta-an ap-pa-an-zi* (10)*nu* ^{É}*ḫa-le-en-tu-u-wa-za ku-iš an-dur-za ku-uz-za nu* 12 $^{\text{LÚ.MEŠ}}$*ME-ŠE-DI* (11)*a-ra-an-ta* ^{GIŠ}ŠUKUR$^{\text{ḪI.A}}$-*ia ḫar-kán-zi ma-a-an* 12 $^{\text{LÚ.MEŠ}}$*ME-ŠE-DI-ma* (12)*ša*-⸤*ra*⸥-*a Ú-UL ar-ta na-aš-šu* KASKAL-*an ku-iš-ki pé-e-ia-an-za* (13)*na-aš-ma I-NA* É-*ŠU ku-iš-ki tar-na-an-za* ^{GIŠ}ŠUKUR$^{\text{ḪI.A}}$-*ma ma-ak-ke-eš-zi* (14)*nu-kán ku-e* ^{GIŠ}ŠUKUR$^{\text{ḪI.A}}$ *a-aš-zi na-at-kán pa-ra-a pé-e-da-an-zi* (15)*na-at IT-TI* $^{\text{LÚ.MEŠ}}$Ì.DU$_8$ *ti-an-zi*

§3 (16)*a-aš-ka-az-ma ku-iš ku-uz-za nu-uš-ša-an* LÚ^{MEŠ} ŠUKUR KÙ.SIG$_{17}$ *an-da a-ra*-⸢*an-ta*⸣[97] (17)1 ^{LÚ}*ME-ŠE-DI-ma ke-e-ez IŠ-TU* ^{LÚ}*ME-ŠE-DI ku-ut-ta-az* KÁ-*aš ma-an-ni-ku-wa-an* (18)*ar-ta ke-e-ez-ma IŠ-TU* LÚ^{MEŠ} ŠUKUR

rather something more akin to instruction manuals, stage scripts or protocols, perhaps compiled by those responsible for organizing the respective routines, that is, possibly the chief of the bodyguards in the present case, perhaps whatever official was responsible for the palace guards in the case of No. 3. In this sense, these two texts would be functionally and stylistically more closely related to those ritual texts composed in a 3rd-person prescriptive style (Miller 2004: 469–506). They might constitute a handbook of sorts, perhaps a reference work as well, for those responsible for organizing these important duties, just as the ritual texts likely served as manuals for the scribes and/or ritual experts who would have referenced them.

These striking parallels might suggest that the two compositions should be dated similarly as well. Since it was deemed likely (see No. 3, Introduction) that the Protocol for the Palace Gatekeeper is to be dated to the late OH or early MH period, perhaps this Protocol for the Royal Body Guard should be placed in the same period.

Translation

§1 (1)[…] they do […] (2)[…] they do […]. The bodyguards, [*tho*]*ugh*, […] [u]p/[for]th, (3)and they […] before the gatekeepers (and) the forecourt-cleaners. (4)[Then] they go in, and they stand at the gate of the courtyard. (5–6)Their [e]yes are tu[rn]ed forwards, so that they cover one courtyard of the pa[la]ce, and [*th*]*ey* [*keep*] *watch*.[98] […] (7)*they lift up* […] bodyguards (be)fore […], (8)and they lift it up *with* […]; they do not lift the doorbolt of the gate. And the [body-gua]rds, the gatekeepers (and) the forecourt-cleaners come out.

§2 (9)Then the bodyguards take (their) place in the courtyard of the bodyguard; (10–11)and 12 bodyguards stand by the inside wall in the direction of the palace, and they hold spears. If, however, 12 bodyguards (12)are not available—either someone has been sent on a journey (13)or someone is at home on leave—and there are too many spears, (14)then they carry away the spears that are left, (15)and they place them with the gatekeepers.

§3 (16)Gold-spear men, though, stand by the wall in the direction of the gate; (17–19)(i.e.), one bodyguard stands to one side near the gate in the direction of the wall of the bodyguard, whereas one gold-spear man stands to

KÙ.SIG$_{17}$ *ku-ut-ta-az* 1 LÚ ˻ŠUKUR KÙ.SIG$_{17}$˼*-ma* {1? ZA?}[99] (19)KÁ*-aš ma-an-ni-in-ku-wa-an ar-ta nu* UD*-az ḫa-a-li uš-kán-zi ma-⸢a⸣-an an-dur-za ku-iš-⸢ki⸣* (20)⸢URUDU*za⸣-ak-ke-eš Ú-UL kar-pa-an-za na-aš-ma* É.NA4KIŠIB *ku-it-ki ḫa-aš-ša-an-zi nu* GI *wa-ak-aš-ši-zi na-aš-ta ma-a-an* GI (21) 100 *˻ap˼-pé-ez-zi-iš* DUMU É.GAL *pa-ra?-a ú-ez-zi na-an-ši* LÚ ŠUKUR ⸢KÙ.SIG$_{17}$⸣ *Ú-UL pa!-a-i! na-aš-ta ku-wa-pí pa-ra?-a* GAL*-i[š?]* DUMU ⸢É.GAL *ú-ez?-zi⸣ na-⸢aš?-šu?⸣* (21a)UGULA 10 *na-aš-ma* *NIMGIR.ÉRIN*MEŠ *M[E-Š]E-⸢DI⸣ ú?-ez-⸢zi?⸣ nu* GI *a-⸢pé⸣-e-da-ni pí-an-zi ma-a-na-aš-t[a]* x x[…] (21b)*p[a-r]a?-a ⸢ú?⸣-ez-⸢zi?⸣ nu ú?-ez-zi na?-aš?-šu?* LÚ*ME-ŠE-DI* **na-aš?-ma?** LÚ ŠU[KUR? KÙ.SIG$_{17}$? …] (21c)[… LÚ]*ME-⸢ŠE-DI⸣-ma* É*ḫi-i-li* UGULA 10 ŠUKUR KÙ.SIG$_{17}$*-pát du-ud-du-uš-ke-ez-zi* (21d)*ma-a-an i-da-a-lu ku-iš ar-ta na-*[…] x […] x[…] […] (21e)*nu-uš* UGULA 10 ŠUKUR KÙ.SIG$_{17}$*-pát du-ud-[du-uš-ke]-ez-zi na-*x[…]x KI[…] x 1 DUMU [É.GAL] (21–22)*ma-a-an* LÚ*ME-ŠE-DI-ma* [… *a*]*-ra-aš a-ri m[e]-ma-⸢i⸣* [*m*]*a?-⸢a?⸣-n[a-* …]x (21g)*˻ne-e?-a?˼-[ri? n]a-˻aš-za˼-kán* [… *k*]*u-ut-ti an-da* EGIR*-pa* *A? x x*[…]x x[…] (21h)⸢*na-at?*⸣ […] *me-ma-i*[…] […]

§4 (22)*ma-a-aḫ-ḫa-an-na-kán* GAL *ME-ŠE-DI* UGULA 10 *ME-ŠE-DI-ia ša-ra-a ú-wa-an-zi nu* ⸢GAL⸣ *ME-ŠE-DI* (23)*ku-it* GIŠGIDRU *ḫar-zi na-aš ma-a-aḫ-ḫa-an A-NA* dLAMMA GIŠŠUKUR[101] *UŠ-KÉ-EN ˻nu˼ ku-iš* (24) LÚ*ME-ŠE-DI* GAL *nu-uš-ši-kán* GIŠGIDRU *ar-ḫa da-a-i na-˻an-ša-an˼ iš-ta-⸢na⸣-a-ni* EGIR*-pa* (25)*da-a-i* UGULA 10 *ME-ŠE-DI-ma ku-in* GIŠGIDRU*-an ḫar-zi na-˻an˼ [pa-ra-a*(?)][102] *˻A-NA˼* ⸢LÚ⸣*ME-ŠE-DI pa-a-i* (26)*na-an-š[i]* LÚ*ME-ŠE-DI ḫar-z[i* …]

§5 (27)[LÚ.MEŠ*M*]*E-Š[E-D]U-⸢TI⸣-ma*[103] GIŠGIDRUḪI.A *˻ḫu-u˼-ma-an-te-eš-p[át?* x x x x x]*-zi*[104] *˻na˼-at-kán* (28)[*ša-r*]*a-a ku-wa-pí ú-˻wa-an˼-z[i nu* GI]Š˻GIDRUḪI.A˼[105] [x x x x *A-NA* LÚ]˻Ì˼.DU$_8$ *pí-an-zi* (29)[*m*]*a-⸢a-an⸣* LUGAL*-uš-ma* [… *nu-z*]*a* DUMU É.GAL LÚ*ME-ŠE-DI* (30)LÚ ŠUKUR KÙ.SIG$_{17}$ *pa-⸢ra⸣-[a pí-i-e-ez-zi* … L]UGAL*-uš-ma lam-ni-ez-zi* (31)*na-an-za pa-ra-a pí-i-⸢e⸣-e[z-zi* …] ⸢*ma*⸣*-a-an* LÚ*-LU*$_4$ *na-an-za* (32)ZI*-˻it˼ pa-ra-a Ú-UL pí-i-⸢e⸣-[ez-zi* …]

§6 (33) LÚ*ME-ŠE-DI-ia-kán* ZI*-it a-aš-⸢ka⸣ [pa-ra-a Ú-UL pa-iz-z]i*[106] ⸢*ma*⸣*-a-na-an-za-kán* (34)*še-e-ḫu-na-an-za-pát ta-ma-a-aš-zi na-a[š A-NA]* L[Ú].M[EŠ*M*]*E-ŠE-DU-˻TI˼ ḫu-u-ma-an-da-a-aš* (35)EGIR*-an ḫu-wa-a-i nu-uš-ši ku-iš* LÚ*M[E-Š]E-⸢DI⸣ pé-ra-aš-ši-it ar-ta-ri* (36)*nu-uš-ši te-ez-zi* DUG*kal-ti-ia-wa kat-⸢ta⸣-an pa-i-mi a-pa-⸢a⸣-ša pa-ra-a da-me-ta-ni* (37) LÚ*ME-ŠE-DI te-ez-zi a-pa-ša pa-ra-a* LÚ*tar-ri-ia-na-al-li te-ez-zi* (38) LÚ*tar-ri-ia-na-al-li-iš-ma* LÚ*du-ia-na-al-li te-ez-zi*

§7 (39) LÚ*du-ia-na-al-li-˻iš˼-ma A-NA* UGULA 10 *˻ME-ŠE-DI˼ te-ez-zi* ⸢*ma-a-an*⸣ ˻GAL *ME˼-[ŠE]-˻DI-ia˼* (40)*ḫa-an-da-it-ta-ri ŠA* LÚ*ME-ŠE-DI-aš* ⸢É⸣[*ḫi-i*]*-⸢li⸣ e-eš-zi na-a[t]-k[án*[107] U]GU[LA 10 *ME-ŠE-D*]*I* (41)*A-NA* GAL *ME-ŠE-DI-ia ar-*

the (other) side near the gate in the direction of the wall of the gold-spear men, and they keep watch by day. If inside (20–21)some doorbolt has not been lifted, or if they open some storehouse and there is not enough *reed*,[108] then if a low-ranking palace servant comes out (*for*) *reed*,[109] the gold-spear man does not give it to him, so that when a high-ranking palace servant comes out—(21a)either a commander-of-10, a military herald or a b[ody]guard comes—they (can) give him *reed*. If [...] (21b)comes o[u]t, whereupon either a bodyguard or a [gold-spe]ar man [...]. (21c)In the guard's court, though, the aforesaid commander-of-10 of the gold-spear *excuses* (them).[110] (21d)If someone stands badly, then [...]. (21e)And the aforesaid commander-of-10 of the gold-spear *ex*[*cus*]*es* them. And [... a palace] servant. (21f)If a bodyguard, though, [... one co]lleague tells the (other) colleague; i[f ...] (21g)he tur[ns], he [...] to the wall again [...] (21h)and he says it.

§4 (22–23)And when the chief of the bodyguard and the commander-of-10 of the bodyguard come up, since the chief of the bodyguard holds a staff, as soon as he prostrates himself to the tutelary deity of the spear,[111] then whatever (24–25)bodyguard of rank (is there) takes the staff from him, and he places it behind the altar. The staff that the commander-of-10 of the bodyguard holds, however, he hands it [*over*] to a bodyguard, (26)and the bodyguard holds it for h[im].

§5 (27–28)All the bod[ygu]ards *of* the staffs, though, [...], and when they come [u]p, they give the [st]affs [... to the ga]tekeeper. (29–30)[Wh]en the king [...], though, [then he sends] ou[t] a palace servant, a bodyguard (or) a gold-spear man. [... the k]ing designates [...], though, (31–32)and he sen[ds] him out, [...]. If [...] a man, he does not send him out on his own volition.[112]

§6 (33)And a bodyguard [does not (just) go] outside on his own volition. If (34–37)he really has to pee, then he will run after the whole [bo]dyguard, and he will tell the b[od]yguard who stands before him, "I have to go down to the toilet," then that one passes it on to another bodyguard, then that one passes it on to a man of third rank, (38)then the man of third rank tells a man of second rank,

§7 (39)then the man of second rank tells the commander-of-10 of the bodyguard. If the chief of the bod[yg]uard (40)is also present, (i.e.) he is in the [cou]rt of the bodyguard, then the [co]mman[der-of-10 of the bodygua]rd

nu-uz-zi DUG⸢*kal-ti*⸣*-ia-wa-ra-aš kat-*˻*ta*˼*-an p*[*a-i*]*z-*⸢*zi*⸣ (42)*nu* GAL *ME-ŠE-DI te-ez-zi pa-id-du-wa-ra-aš*

§8 (43)*ma-a-an-za-kán ga-ma-ar-šu-wa-an-za-ma ku-in ta-ma-aš-*˻*zi*˼ *nu a-ra-aš a-*⸢*ri te*⸣*-ez-zi* (44)*nu-uš-ša-an a-pa-at-ta A-NA* GAL *ME-ŠE-DI a-ri še-*⸢*e*⸣*-ḫu-na-wa-ra-aš pa-iz-zi* (45)*nu* GAL *ME-ŠE-DI te-ez-zi pa-*⸢*id*⸣*-du-wa-ra-aš* LÚ*ME-ŠE-D*[*I-m*]*a ku-iš še-ḫu-na pa-iz-zi* (46) dUTU-*ŠI-ša-an-za kap-pu-u-ez-zi nu-uš-ša-an še-*⸢*e-ḫu*⸣*-na-aš-ša ut-*˻*tar*˼ *I-NA* É.GAL-*LÌ a-*˻*ri*˼ (47)ZI-*it-ma-aš-kán pa-ra-a Ú-UL pa-iz-zi*

§9 (48) LÚ*ME-ŠE-*⸢*DI*⸣*-ma* É*ḫi-lam-ni* ⸢*an-da*⸣ *in-na-ra-*˻*a Ú-UL*˼ *ti-i-e-ez-zi* ⸢*ma*⸣*-a-na-aš in-na-ra-ma* (49)*ti-i-e-*⸢*ez-zi*⸣ *nu-uš-ši-kán* LÚÌ.DU8 *ka*[*r-di-mi*]*-ia-it-ta na-aš-šu-wa-kán* ⸢*ša*⸣*-ra-a i-it* (50)*na-aš-ma-wa-kán kat-ta-ma i-it ma-a-an-k*[*án* L]Ú*ME-ŠE-DI-ma* É*ḫi-lam-na-*⸢*az pa-ra*⸣*-a pa-iz-zi* (51)*na-aš-*⸢*ta* É*ḫi*⸣*-lam-mar iš-tar-na ar-ḫa* GIŠŠU[KUR-*p*]*át ḫar-zi lu-uš-ta-ni-ia-ma-aš a-ri nu* GIŠ*ŠUKUR* (52)*IT-TI* ⸢LÚ⸣Ì.DU8 *da-a-i a-pa-ša-kán ka*[*t-t*]*a pa-iz-zi*

§10 (53)*ma-a-an-*⸢*kán*⸣ LÚ*ME-ŠE-DI-ma ar-ḫa mi-ir-*⸢*zi*⸣ *na-aš-ta* GIŠŠUKUR *lu-uš-ta-ni-ia-az kat-ta pé-da-i* (54)*na-an* ⸢LÚÌ⸣.DU8 *wa-aš-du-li e-ep-zi nu-uš-ši-kán* KUŠE.SIR *ar-ḫa la-a-i ma-a-an* LÚ*ME-ŠE-DI-ma* (55)⸢LÚ⸣Ì.DU8 ⸢*ap*⸣*-pa-la-a-iz-zi na-aš-ta* GIŠŠUKUR *kat-ta pé-e-da-i* LÚÌ.DU8*-ma-an Ú-UL* *a**-uš-zi* (56)*nu* LÚ*ME-ŠE-*⸢*DI*⸣ LÚÌ.DU8 *wa-aš-du-li e-*⸢*ep*⸣*-zi* GIŠŠUKUR*-wa Ú-UL ku-it a-uš-ta* (57)*ma-a-an-wa-*[*ká*]*n* ⸢*ša*⸣*-ra-a-ma ku-iš an-tu-u-wa-aḫ-ḫa-aš ḫa-an-da-a-iz-zi nu-wa-ra-an ku-wa-pí a-ut-ti* (58)*na-an* ⸢*A-NA* É⸣.GAL-*LÌ tar-kum-mi-ia-an-*⸢*zi*⸣ *nu* LÚÌ.DU8 *pu-nu-uš-ša-an-zi nu* GIŠŠUKURḪI.A (59) *a-pa-aš* ˻*na-aḫ-ša*˼*-ra-az uš-ke-ez-zi*

§11 (60) LÚ.MEŠ*ME-ŠE-DU-*⸢*TI*⸣*-ma-kán* DUMU⸢MEŠ É⸣.GAL-*TÌ* G[A]L-*ia-az* KÁ.GAL-*az kat-ta Ú-UL pa-iš-kán-da* (61)*na-at-kán lu-uš-da-ni-ia-az kat-ta pa-iš-*[*kán-d*]*a nu* 1 LÚ*ME-ŠE-DI ku-iš šar-kán-ti-in* (62)*ú-i-da-a-iz-zi* UGULA DUMUMEŠ.KIN-**za** *ku-in pa-r*[*a-a pí*]*-i-e-eš-ke-ez-zi nu-kán* *GAL*[113]*-ia-az kat-ta* (63)⸢*a-pa*⸣*-aš pa-iš-ke-et-ta BE-LU-TÌ-ia-kán* UGULA *LI-*˻*IM*˼*-TI-ia* GAL-*ia-*⸢*az*⸣ *kat-ta pa-iš-kán-ta*

§12a (64) *˻*ma-a-aḫ*˼*-ḫa-an-ma** LUGAL-*uš a-ra-aḫ-za pa-iz-zi na-aš-ta* 1 ˻DUMU É˼.GAL ⸢É⸣*ḫa-le-en-tu-u-az* (65)*pa-ra-a* ˻*ú*˼*-ez-zi nu ḫa-at-ti-i-li ta-ḫa-ia ḫal-*˻*za*˼*-i ta-ḫa-*˻*ia*˼*-an-ma-za ḫa-*⸢*at-ti*⸣*-li* (66) LÚŠU.I *ḫal-zi-iš-ša-an-zi* **nu** LÚ*ME-ŠE-DI* LÚ GIŠŠUKUR KÙ.SIG17 LÚÌ.DU8*-ia* (67) É*ka-a-aš-ka-a-aš-ti-pa pa-a-an-zi nu* GAL-*ia-az* KÁ.GAL-*az* URUDU*za-*˻*ak*˼*-ki-in kar-pa-*˻*an-zi*˼ (68)*nu* GIŠIG-*TÌ* EGIR-*pa ḫa-aš-ša-an-zi na?*-x x LÚ? ŠUKUR KÙ.SIG17 x x ŠI? NI? IŠ? *za?-ak?* x x[ ]x-*a?-i?* LÚŠU.I-*ma* GIŠ*ga-la-a-*⸢*ma*⸣ *ḫ*[*ar-z*]*i na-aš-ta* (69)KÁ-*uš ar-ḫa wa-ar-ši* ∡[114] LÚ.[M]EŠ*ša-a-la-aš-ḫe-eš* GIŠ*ḫu-*lu-ga-an*-ni-i*[*n w*]*a-aḫ-*

(41)conveys it to the chief of the bodyguard, (asking), “May he [g]o down to the toilet?” (42)And the chief of the bodyguard will say, “He may go.”

§8 (43)If, however, anyone’s *bowels are troubling* him,[115] then one colleague tells another colleague, (44)so that this, too, reaches the chief of the bodyguard (thus): “May he go pee?” (45)Then the chief of the bodyguard will say, “He may go.” Whatever bodygua[rd] goes to pee (without asking), [th]ough, (46)His Majesty will take note of, so that the pissing affair will reach the palace; (47)he does not (just) go on his own volition.[116]

§9 (48)A bodyguard, though, does not (just) barge into the gatehouse. If he does (just) (49)barge in, the gatekeeper will be fu[rio]us with him (and say): “Either you go up (50)or you go down!” When a bodyguard does go out of the gatehouse, though, (51–52)he keeps only a sp[ear] out through the gatehouse, but upon reaching the postern he deposits the spear with the gatekeeper, and then he goes d[ow]n.

§10 (53)If a bodyguard does run off, though, and he carries a spear down out of the postern, (54)and the gatekeeper catches him in (his) delinquency, then he “unfastens his shoe.” If, however, the bodyguard (55)tricks the gatekeeper, and he carries down a spear, but the gatekeeper does not see him, (56)then the bodyguard will catch the gatekeeper in (his) delinquency, (saying): “Since you did not see the spear, (57)if some man *manages* (*to go*) up, will you ever notice him?” (58–59)And they will report him to the palace, and they will question the gatekeeper. That (gatekeeper) will observe the spears with vigilance.[117]

§11 (60)The bodyguards (and) the palace servants, though, do not go down out of the main gate, (61–63)th[ey] go down out of the postern gate. A bodyguard who brings a petitioner,[118] (i.e.) the one whom the chief of the messengers di[sp]atches, he goes down out of the main (gate), and the lords and the *clan* chief[119] go down out of the main (gate).

§12a (64–66)As soon as the king goes out, though, then one palace servant will come out of the palace, and he cries “*taḫaya*” in Hattian—in Hattian they say “*taḫaya*” for “cleaner.”[120] Then a bodyguard, a gold-spear man and a gatekeeper (67)go to the gatehouse, and they lift the doorbolt from the main gate, (68)and they reopen the door. *And* [...] the gold-spear man [...]. The cleaner, though, h[a]s a *broom*, and (69)he cleans out the gate. The grooms turn the carriage[121] around, but the bodyguards (70)stand to the right alongside the *passageway*.[122] If, however, in some town standing to the [rig]ht

nu-an-⸢*zi* LÚ.MEŠ*ME-ŠE-DI-ma*⸣ (70) É*ar-ki-ú-i ta-pu-uš-za* ZAG-*za ti-en-zi ma-a-an ku-e-da-ni-*⸢*ma*!⸣ URU-*r*[*i* ZA]G-*az ti-ia-u-an-*⸤*zi*⸥

§12b (71)*⸢*Ú*?*-UL*?⸣ *tar*?*-ḫa*⸣*-an*[123] *na-at* GÙB-*la-za ti-e*[*n*]*-zi uk-tu-u-*⸤*ri-ma*⸥*-aš-*⸤*ma-aš*⸥ *ti-*⸢*ia*⸣*-u-wa-a*[*r* ZAG?*-a*]*z*?*-pát* [É]⸤*ar-ki-ú-i*⸥* (72)*⸤*ta*⸥*-pu-uš-za* {ZAG-*az ti-en-zi*}*[124] *nu* LÚ*ME-ŠE-DI ku-iš* GIŠG[U.Z]A GIŠ*ḫu-lu-ga-an-*⸢*ni* GIŠ?UMBIN? *ḫar*?*-zi*?⸣ (73)*na-aš-ta an-da-ia Ú-*⸢*UL*⸣ *ku-in-ki tar-*na*-i pa-ra-a-ia-kán Ú-UL ku-in-*⸢*ki tar-na*⸣*-*[*i*] (74)*n*[*a-a*]*t-kán pa-ra-a ŠA* LÚ*M*[*E-Š*]*E-DI* É*ḫi-i-la-az ú-iš-kán-da-ri*

§13 (75)[…]x ⸢LÚ.MEŠ*zi*⸣*-in-zi-*⸤*ni-ú*⸥*-i-le-e-eš a-ra-an-ta* ⸢GIŠTUKUL?ḪI.A⸣ x x x[…] (76)[…]*-zi BE-EL* ÉRINMEŠ*-aš-ma-aš kat-ta-an ar-ta* ⸢GIŠGIDRU⸣*-ia* x[…] (77) […]x[125] *nam-ma ḫi-*⸤*lam-mi*⸥*-li ú-e-eš-ša-an-ta na-at*[…]

§14 (78)[EGIR-*pa-m*]*a-kán iš-tar-*[*na*] ⸢1 IKU⸣ *nu* 2 ⸢LÚ⸣ x x x[…]x[…] (79)[…]x x-⸤*ia ḫar-kán-zi nu-uš-ma*⸥*-aš* x x[…] (80)[…]x x x x x x x x x x x x x x[…]

§15 (ii 1)⸢EGIR⸣*-pa-*⸢*ma*⸣*-kán nam-ma* ⸢*iš*⸣*-ta*[*r-na* …] (2)⸤2?⸥ LÚ.MEŠ*LI-IM ṢE-RI a-ra-*⸢*an*⸣*-*[*ta nu-uš-ma-aš* …] (3)NIMGIR.ÉRINMEŠ*-ia kat-ti-iš-mi a-ra-an-*⸢*ta*⸣[…] (4)*pé-ra-an ḫu-ia-an-te-eš* […]

§16 (5)EGIR*-pa-ma-kán nam-ma iš-tar-na* 1 IKU *n*[*u* …] (6)*a-ra-an-ta* GIŠŠUKURḪI.A*-ia ḫar-kán-zi nu-uš-m*[*a-aš* …] (7)NIMGIR.ÉRINMEŠ*-ia kat-ti-*{*mi*}*-iš-mi a-ra-an-ta* GIŠ<GIDRU>ḪI.A *ḫa*[*r-kán-zi*] (8)*na-at* LUGAL*-i pé-ra-an ḫu-ia-an-te-eš* […]

§17 (9)⸤2?⸥ LÚMEŠ ŠUKUR.DUGUD*-ma-kán* LUGAL*-i me-na-aḫ-ḫa-an-da* ZAG*-az a-ra-*[*an-ta*] (10)[GIŠŠ]UKURḪI.A *Ú-UL ḫar-kán-zi nu-uš-ma-aš* LÚ ŠUKUR KÙ.SIG$_{17}$ *ka*[*t-ti-iš-mi ar-ta*] (11)[GIŠŠUK]UR KÙ.SIG$_{17}$ GAR.RA*-ia ḫar-zi ŠA* GIŠŠUKUR*-ma* DUMU É.GAL […] (12) GIŠ⸢*IŠ-TU*⸣*-UḪ-ḪU* GIŠ*ḫu-lu-ga-an-na-aš-ša* GIŠ*mu-kar ḫar-zi* ⸢*na*?*-aš*?⸣ [LUGAL*-i*] (13)*pé-ra-an ḫu-ia-an-za na-aš pa-iz-zi* GIŠ*ḫu-lu-ga-an-ni* ⸢GÙB⸣*-l*[*a-az*][126] (14) GIŠUMBIN ⸤*kat*⸥*-ta-an ti-ia-az-zi*

§18 (15)LÚ*ME-ŠE-DI-ma* GIŠGU.ZA *ti-it-ta-nu-zi* LUGAL*-uš-kán pa-ra-a* ⸢*ú*?*-iz*?*-zi*?⸣[ ] (16)GAL DUMUMEŠ É.GAL*-ma-an QA-AZ-ZU ḫar-zi* LUGAL*-uš-ša-an* GIŠ⸢*ḫu-lu*⸣*-g*[*a-an-ni*] (17)*e-ša* LÚMEŠ ŠUKUR.DUGUD*-ma ḫi-in-kán-ta nam-ma-at pít-*⸢*ti*[127]*-an-zi*⸣[ ] (18)*na-at pé-ra-an ḫu-ia-an-zi na-at-za* (ca. 5 signs erased) ⸤LÚ?[128] ŠUKUR⸥[ ] (19)*kat-ta-an i-ia-an-ni-an-zi*

§19 (20)LÚ ŠUKUR KÙ.SIG$_{17}$*-ma-aš-ma-aš ku-iš kat-ta-an ar-*⸢*ta*⸣*-at* ⸢*ti*?*-ia*?*-az*?*-zi*?⸣ (21)*ŠA* GIŠŠUKUR DUMU É.GAL*-ma* GIŠ**IŠ**-⸤*TU*⸥*-UḪ-ḪA A-NA* GAL DUMU⸢MEŠ É.GAL *pa-a-i*⸣ (22)GAL DUMUMEŠ É.GAL*-ma-at* LUGAL*-i* ⸤*pa*⸥*-a-*⸤*i*⸥ *nu* GIŠ*ḫu-lu-ga-an-ni-*⸢*ia pé-ra-an*⸣ (23)GAL LÚ.MEŠ*ša-a-la-aš-ḫa-*⸢*aš ḫu*⸣*-ia-*⸢*an*⸣*-za* GIŠGIDRU*-ia ḫar-*⸢*zi*⸣ *ma-a-*⸢*aḫ-ḫa-an-ma*⸣*-*[*ká*]*n*? (24) GIŠ*ḫu-lu-ga-an-ni-iš*

§12b (71–72)*is not possible*, then they stand on the left; but normally only standing t[o the right] alongside the *passageway* (is appropriate) for them. And the bodyguard who holds the *ste[p-stoo]l*[129] at the carriage *wheel* (73)lets no one in and lets no one out; (74)th[en] they come out from the courtyard of the bo[dy]guard.

§13 (75)[…] *zinzinwili*-officials take their place. […] *weapons* […]. (76)A troop commander takes his place next to them, and […] a staff. […] (77)[…] are, moreover, dressed as gate-men, and they […].

§14 (78)[Thereafter, tho]ugh, (there is) 10 m.[130] betwe[en] (them), and 2 […] -men (79–80)have/hold, and [… with] them. […]

§15 (1)Thereafter (there is), moreover, […] betw[een] (them). (2)Two *rural clansmen* take (their) places, [and … them, …] (3)and military heralds take their places with them. […] (4)they walk ahead of […].

§16 (5)Thereafter (there is), moreover, 10 m. between (them), a[nd …] (6)take (their) places, and they hold spears; and […] (7)and military heralds take their places with them. [They h]old s<taff>s, (8)and they walk ahead of the king.

§17 (9)*Two* heavy-spear men,[131] though, ta[ke] their places opposite the king to the right; (10)they do not hold [s]pears. A gold-spear man [takes his place bet]ween them, (11)and he holds a gold-plated [spe]ar. A palace servant of the spear, however, holds […] (12–14)a whip and the *mukar*-equipment[132] of the carriage. He runs before the [king], whereby he takes his place to the left of the carriage next to the wheel.

§18 (15)The bodyguard, though, sets up the *step-stool*, the king *comes* out, (16–17)while the chief of the palace personal holds his hand and the king sits in the carri[age]. The heavy-spear men bow, then they run (18–19)so they can run ahead. And they march next to the […] spear-man.

§19 (20)The gold-spear man who stood next to them, though, *takes his place*; (21)the palace servant of the spear, however, gives the whip to the chief of the palace servants, (22–23)the chief of the palace servants, in turn, gives it to the king. The chief of the grooms runs ahead of the carriage, and he holds a staff. But when (24–25)the carriage moves out, the chief of the pa-ra-a i-ia-an-na-i GAL DUMU^{MEŠ} ⸢É.GAL-ma EGIR$^{?}$⸣-[an$^{?}$] $^{(25)}$ḫi-in-ga-ri nu LUGAL E[GI]R-pa A-NA GAL ME-ŠE-⸢DI⸣ ḫi-ik-zi

§20 $^{(26)}$ ^{LÚ}ME-ŠE-DI-ma ku-iš ^{GI}[^{Š}G]U.ZA [ḫ]ar$^{?}$-⸤zi⸥ na-aš ^{GIŠ}ḫu-lu-ga-an-ni ^{GIŠ}⸢UMBIN GÙB⸣-l[a-az] $^{(27)}$ŠA ^{GIŠ}ŠUKUR DUMU ⸤É⸥.[GAL kat-t]a-an i-ia-an-na-i ma-a-aḫ-ḫa-⸢an-ma-aš kat⸣-t[a] $^{(28)}$ ^{É}ka-a-aš-⸢ka⸣-t[e-p]a a-ri na-aš ^{GIŠ}ú-i-du-ú-li-ia EGIR-an [ti-i]a-zi $^{(29)}$nu-⸤uš⸥-ši-kán ma-a-aḫ-[ḫa-a]n $^{LÚ.MEŠ}$ME-ŠE-DI DUMU^{MEŠ} É.GAL-ia ḫa-an-da-a-an-ta[133] $^{(30)}$nu ^{GIŠ}GU.ZA A-NA L[Ú ^{GIŠ}GU].ZA {*pa-ra-a*} pa-ra-a pa-a-i a-pa-ša-az ^{GIŠ}ŠUKUR $^{(31)}$⸤da⸥-a-i na-aš-kán A-N[A L]$^{Ú.MEŠ}$ME-ŠE-DI an-⸤da i-ia-an-na⸥-i

§21 $^{(32)}$ $^{LÚ.⸢MEŠ⸣}$ME-ŠE-DI-ma ku-w[a-p]í i-ia-an-ta ⸤nu⸥ 2 $^{LÚ.MEŠ}$ME-ŠE-⸢DI⸣ pé-⸤ra-an⸥ ḫu-⸤ia-an-te⸥-[eš] $^{(33)}$ ^{GIŠ}ŠUKUR$^{ḪI.A}$-ia ḫar-ká[n]-*zi* na-at-kán ⸢ḫa⸣-an-da-a-an-te-eš ⸢GÙB-la⸣-[az] ⸢DUMU É.GAL⸣ $^{(34)}$⸤i-ia⸥-at-ta nu ^{GI}[^{Š}ka]l-mu-uš ḫar-⸢zi⸣ na-aš-ta a-pa-aš-ša ⸢A-NA 2 $^{LÚ⸣.M}$[^{EŠ}ME-ŠE-D]I $^{(35)}$ [ḫa-a]n-da-a-an-za ⸤na⸥-a[t-k]án 3-e-eš ták-⸤ša⸥-an ⸤ḫa⸥-an-da-a-an-te-eš ⸤EGIR$^{?}$-pa$^{?}$-ma$^{?}$-aš$^{?}$⸥-[ma-aš][134] $^{(36)}$ $^{⸢LÚ⸣.M}$[^{EŠ}ME]-ŠE-DI DUMU ⸤É$^{?}$⸥.[GAL-T]I[135] 3 ša-a⸣-ri-i-e-eš i-ia-an-ta $^{(37)}$ŠA $^{LÚ.MEŠ}$ME-⸢ŠE-DI 2⸣ ša-a-ri-i-e-eš ŠA DUMU^{MEŠ} É.GAL-ia ⸤1 ša⸥-a-ri-⸤ia⸥-aš $^{(38)}$A-NA ^{GIŠ}ḫu-⸢lu⸣-ga-an-ni-ma-at EGIR-pa 1 IKU ⸢i-ia⸣-an-ta

§22 $^{(39)}$1 ⸢DUMU⸣ É.GAL-ma pa-iz-zi nu-uš-ši ^{LÚ}ŠÀ.TAM $^{GIŠ⸢}$BAN ḫu⸣-it-ti-an ⸢an⸣-d[a-m]a-⸢at-kán⸣ $^{(40)}$ ^{KUŠ}pár-du-ug-⸤ga⸥-an-ni tar-na-an 1 ^{KUŠ}É.MÁ.URU$_5$.URU-ši É?/ŠA? LÚ? RI? x136 IŠ-TU ⸢$^{GI?}$GAG.Ú.TAG.GA⸣ $^{(41)}$⸢šu⸣-u-un-ta-an pa-a-i na-aš EGIR-an-da pa-iz-zi ⸤na⸥-aš-kán ⸢$^{LÚ⸣.MEŠ}$ME-⸤ŠE-DU-TÌ⸥ $^{(42)}$DUMU^{MEŠ} É.⸤GAL⸥-ia a-wa-an ar-ḫa pa-iz-zi na-aš pa-iz-zi $^{(43)}$ŠA![137] ⸢^{GIŠ}ḫu⸣-lu-ga-an-ni ^{GIŠ}UMBIN GÙB-la-az ti-ia-az-zi

§23 $^{(44)}$EGIR-pa-ma-kán iš-tar-na 1 IKU nu LÚ ŠUKUR KÙ.SIG$_{17}$ ^{GIŠ}ŠUKUR K[Ù.SI]G$_{17}$ G[AR.R]A ḫ[ar$^{?}$-z]i $^{(45)}$ ^{LÚ}A.ZU-ia ^{GI}[^{Š}m]u-ú-kar ḫar-zi na-at ták-ša-an i-ia-⸤an-ta⸥ $^{(46)}$nu ^{LÚ}A.ZU ⸤ḫu-uk⸥-ki-iš-ke-ez-zi

§24 $^{(47)}$⸢EGIR⸣-pa-ma-kán iš-tar-na 1 IKU nu 2 LÚ^{MEŠ} ŠUKUR (ca. 3 signs erased) ⸢i-ia-an-ta-ri⸣ $^{(48)}$ma-a-na-at $^{LÚ.⸢MEŠ⸣}$DUGUD-TÌ ma-a-na-at pé-ra-an ti-in-te$_9$-eš $^{LÚ.⸢MEŠ}$SIG$_5$-TÌ⸣ $^{(49)}$ ^{TÚG}NÍG.⸢LÁM⸣$^{ḪI.A}$-⸢ma⸣-aš-ma-aš ^{KUŠ}E.SIR SIG$_5$-TÌ ḫi-lam-mi-li ú-⸢e-eš-ša-an-ta⸣ $^{(50)}$ *GAL LÚ^{MEŠ} ŠUKUR*[138]-ia-aš-ma-aš NIMGIR.ÉRIN^{MEŠ}-ia kat-ti-iš-mi i-ia-an-⸤ta ^{GIŠ}GIDRU$^{ḪI.A}$ ḫar-kán-zi⸥

§25 $^{(51)}$ *⸢EGIR-pa-ma-kán⸣* nam-ma iš-tar-na 1 IKU {*nu nam-ma*} 2 $^{LÚ.MEŠ}$L[I-I]M ṢE-RI ⸢kat$^{?}$-ta$^{?}$⸣ $^{(52)}$i-ia-an-ta ^{GIŠ}ŠUKUR$^{ḪI.A}$ ḫar-kán-zi ma-a-na-at $^{LÚ.MEŠ}$DUGUD-TÌ ma-a-na-at $^{(53)}$pé-ra-an ti-ia-an-te-eš $^{LÚ.MEŠ}$SIG$_5$-TÌ ^{TÚG}NÍG.LÁM$^{ḪI.A}$-ma-aš-ma-aš ^{KUŠ}E.SIR SIG$_5$-TÌ ḫi-lam-me-li ⸢ú-e⸣-eš-ša-an-ta $^{(54)}$UGULA LI-IM ṢE-RI-ia-aš-ma-aš NIMGIR.ÉRIN^{MEŠ}-ia kat-ti-iš-mi-{ia} i-ia-an-ta $^{(55)}$ ^{GIŠ}GIDRU$^{ḪI.A}$ ḫar-kán-zi

palace servants bows behi[nd] (it), thus turning the king b[ac]k over to the chief of the bodyguard.

§20 (26–28)The bodyguard who [ho]lds the *ste*[*p-sto*]*ol*, then, marches [to] the left of the wheel of the carriage [nex]t to the pal[ace] servant of the spear. But as soon as he arrives down at the gateh[ous]e, he [ste]ps behind the *chariot-box*. (29)And as so[on] as the bodyguards and the palace servants are aligned with him, (30–31)then he hands the *step-stool* over to the [*step-st*]*ool* man. He takes a spear for himself, and he marches along with the bodyguards.

§21 (32)W[he]n the bodyguards march, though, two bodyguards run ahead; (33–35)they also hold spears, and they are aligned. [To] the left marches a palace servant, and he holds a *l*[*it*]*uus*; and he too is [ali]gned with the two [bodyguar]ds, so that the three of them are aligned together. *Behind t*[*hem*], *though*, (36)march the [bod]yguards and the pa[lac]e servants in three rows: (37)two rows of bodyguards and one row of palace servants. (38)But they march 10 m. behind the carriage.

§22 (39–42)One palace servant goes (along), then, and the administrator gives him a strung bow—it is, however, inserted into a bow case—(and) one quiver [...] full of arrows; then he goes back, and he walks *around*[139] the bodyguards and the palace servants, whereupon (43)he takes his place to the left of the wheel of the carriage.

§23 (44)Behind (them), with 10 m. in between, the gold-spear man h[ol]ds a g[ol]d-pl[at]ed spear, (45)and the medicine man holds a [*m*]*ukar*-instrument. They march together, (46)and the medicine man incantates.

§24 (47)Behind (them), with 10 m. in between, two spear-men march; (48–49) be they dignitaries or be they infantry officers, they wear good uniforms (and) shoes like gate-men. (50)Also the chief of the spear-men and the military herald march with them; they hold staffs.

§25 (51–50)Farther behind (them), with 10 m. in between, two *rural c*[*la*]*nsmen* march *with* (them); they hold spears; be they dignitaries or be they (53) infantry officers, they wear good uniforms (and) shoes like gate-men. (54) Also the chief of the *rural clansmen* and the military herald march with them; (55)they hold staffs.

§26 (56)EGIR-*pa-ma-kán nam-ma iš-tar-na* 1 IKU *nu nam-ma* 2 LÚ.MEŠ*LI-IM ṢE-RI* (57)*i-ia-an-ta* GIŠŠUKURḪI.A *ḫar-kán-zi* TÚGNÍG.LÁMḪI.A-*ma-aš-*<*ma-aš*> KUŠE.SIR SÍG-*TÌ ḫi-lam-mi-li* (58)*ú-e-eš-ša-an-ta* UGULA *LI-IM ṢE-RI-ia-aš-ma-aš* NIMGIR.ÉRINMEŠ *kat-ti-iš-mi i-ia-an-ta* (59) GIŠ<GIDRU>ḪI.A *ḫar-kán-zi*

§27 (60)*ŠA* ⌜*LI-IM*⌝ *ṢE-RI-ma ku-iš* ⌜ÉRINMEŠ⌝-*az nu ták-šu-la-a-an ta-pu-ú-ša* (61)⸤*iš-ga-ra*⸥*-a-an ḫar-zi* GÙB-*la-aš* GÙB-*la-az iš-ka-ra-a-an ḫar-zi n*[*a*?-*a*]*t*? (62)⸤ZAG-*ša* ZAG⸥-*az iš-ka-ra-a-an ḫar-zi ar-ḫa-ma-aš* 3 IKU ⌜*i-ia-at-ta*⌝ (63)⸤*ma-a-an*⸥*-ši*[140] *pé-ra-an-ma ku-wa-pí* KASKAL-*iš ḫa-at-ku-uš na-aš an-da* ⌜*pa-iz-zi*⌝

§28 (64) ⌜*nam-ma*⌝ *ma-a-an ḫa-an-te-ez-zi-aš ku-iš ku-it tar-na-i* (65)*na-aš-šu* ⌜ANŠE.KUR.RAḪI⌝.A *na-aš-ma ta-at-ra-an-ta-an* GU₄ *na-at* ⌜*ḫa*⌝*-an-te-*⌜*ez*⌝*-zi-aš* (66) ⌜*wa*⌝*-aš-túl* ⌜*ma*⌝*-a-*⌜*an ap*⌝*-pé-ez-*⌜*zi*⌝*-aš-ma ku-iš ku-it tar-na-i* (67)*n*[*a-a*]*t* ⌜*ap-pé*⌝*-ez-*⌜*zi*⌝*-*[*aš*] *wa-aš-túl*

§29 (68)[*ma-a-a*]*n* [*šar*]-⌜*kán-ti*⌝*-*[*i*]*n-ma ú-wa-*⌜*da-an-zi*⌝ *nu* ⌜LÚ?MEŠ? ŠUKUR?ḪI?⌝.[A?] ⌜*ku-e*⌝ (69)[…]x x ⌜GIŠ⌝ŠUKURḪI.A *na-an ḫu-u-*⌜*ma*⌝*-*[*an*~…]*-*⌜*a*?⌝*-an* (70)[…]*t*[*i-i*]*t-*⌜*ta-nu*⌝*-wa-an-*⌜*zi nu*?⌝ x x[…]x x ⌜*ma*?*-a-an*⌝ (71) […]⸤*kar*?*-pa-an-zi* LÚ?⸥ x[…] (72)[…]x x x x[…]x x x (73)[…]x x x[…] (74)[…]x x[…] (75)[…] x […]

§30 (iii 1)[LÚ*ME*]-⌜*ŠE-DI ku*⌝*-iš šar-kán-*⌜*du*⌝*-uš* [*ú-i-da-a-iz-zi* …][141] (2)*na-aš A-NA* LÚ ŠUKUR KÙ.SIG₁₇ EGIR-⌜*an*?⌝ [*ti-i-e-ez-zi ma-a-aḫ-ḫa-an-ma*] (3) LUGAL-*uš DI-NA₇ ú-e-ek-zi na-at* LÚ*ME-ŠE-D*[*I* …][142] (4)*na-at-kán A-NA* GAL *ME-ŠE-DI ki-iš-ša-ri-i d*[*a*?*-a-i* …] (5)*DI-NU na-at A-NA* GAL *ME-ŠE-DI* **me**-*ma-i* GAL *ME-ŠE-DI-ma*[…]

§31 (6)*nam-ma* GAL *ME-ŠE-DI pa-iz-zi* EGIR-*an-na-aš-ši* 2 LÚ.⌜MEŠ⌝*BE-L*[*U-TI pa-a-an-zi*] (7)*ma-a-an* GAL LÚ.MEŠKUŠ₇ *na-aš-ma* UGULA 10 *na-at A-NA* GAL *ME-ŠE-*⌜*DI*⌝ [EGIR-*an*] (8)*a-ra-an-ta a-ra-aḫ-zé-ia-az* 1-*aš ḫar-zi ma-a-na-aš* ⌜LÚ*ME*⌝*-*[*ŠE-DI ma-a-na-aš*] (9)*BE-LU ku-iš-ki nu šar-kán-ti-i-uš ku-iš* LÚ*ME-ŠE-DI ú-*⌜*i-da-a*⌝*-iz-z*[*i*] (10)*na-aš* EGIR-*pa-pát píd-da-a-i na-aš pa-iz-zi A-NA* LÚ ŠUKUR KÙ.SIG₁₇ (11)*ti-i-e-ez-zi na-aš-ta nam-ma* 1 *DI-NA₇ pa-ra-a* ⌜*kar*⌝*-pa-an-zi*

§32 (12)*IŠ-TU* DUMUMEŠ É.GAL-*TÌ-ma* GAL DUMUMEŠ É.GAL *ar-ta* EGIR-*an-na-aš-ši* (13)2 DUMUMEŠ É.GAL *a-ra-an-ta na-at* 3-*e-eš ma-a-aḫ-ḫa-an-ma šar-kán-ti-in* (14)*ar-ḫa tar-na-an-zi nu-za* GAL *ME-ŠE-DI pé-e-ta-an-pát ḫar-zi* 2 *BE-LU-TI-ma-aš-ši* (15)*ku-i-e-eš* EGIR-*an a-ra-an-ta* *ma-a-*⸤*na*?*-at*?⸥ LÚ?ŠUKUR?⸥ *ma-*[*a-na-at* LÚ]*ME-ŠE-DI* [143]*na-at* EGIR-*pa pa-a-an-zi nu* EGIR-*pa* (16) LÚ.MEŠ*ME-ŠE-DI ú-e-mi-an-zi a-ra-aḫ-zi-ia-az ku-iš* LÚ*ME-ŠE-DI ḫar-zi* (17)*ma-a-aḫ-ḫa-an-ma šar-kán-ti-in ta-ma-in ú-wa-te-ez-zi*

§26 (56)Farther behind (them), with 10 m. in between, two further *rural clansmen* (57–58)march; they hold spears; they wear good uniforms (and) shoes like gate-men. Also the chief of the rural *clansmen* and the military herald march with them; (59)they hold s<taff>s.

§27 (60–62)The troops of the *rural clansmen*, though, keep the *peaceful (onlookers) pushed* to the side: (he) of the left keeps (them) *pushed* to the left; *a*[*nd*] (he) of the right keeps [*th*]*em pushed* to the right. He marches 30 m. away (from the procession); (63)if the road ahead is at some point too narrow for him, then he walks (closer) in.[144]

§28 (64)Further, if one of the forward men allows something in (to the procession), (65)either horses or aggressive cattle, then it is the forward man's (66)fault; if, however, one of the rear men allows something in (to the procession), (67)th[en i]t is the rear man's fault.

§29 (68)[Whe]n they bring a [pet]itioner, though, the *spear-men* who (69)[…] spears, and al[l …] him. (70)[…] they have [… t]ake (his) place, and […] if (71–75)[…] they lift. […]-man […].

§30 (1)The [bod]yguard who [brings] the petitioners […], (2)and he [takes his place] behind the gold-spear man. [Then as soon as] (3)the king requests the law case, the bodygua[rd …] it (4)and p[laces] it in the chief of the bodyguard's hand. […] (5)law case, and he tells it to the chief of the bodyguard, but the chief of the bodyguard […].

§31 (6)Then the chief of the bodyguard goes, and two lor[ds walk] behind him; (7–8)be it a commander of charioteers or a commander-of-10, they stand [behind] the chief of the bodyguard. One (man) holds the outside, be he a bod[yguard, or be he] (9)some lord. Then the guard who brings in the petitioners (10–11)runs right back, whereupon he takes his place by the gold-spear man, and they bring forth a further law case.[145]

§32 (12)The chief of the palace servants, though, stands with the palace servants, and behind him (13–14)stand two palace servants, so that there are three. As soon as they release a petitioner, though, the chief of the bodyguard holds that place, while the two lords (15–17)who stand behind him—be they *spear-men* o[r be they] bodyguards—they go back and join the bodyguards again. But as soon as the bodyguard who holds the outside brings another petitioner,

§33 (18)nu A-NA GAL ME-ŠE-DI ku-i-e-eš 2 BE-LU-TI EGIR-an a-ra-an-ta na-at šar-kán-ti (19)an-dur-za ta-pu-ša i-ia-an-ta a-ra-aḫ-za-ma-az ku-iš LÚME-ŠE-DI ḫar-zi (20)na-aš-ta ma-a-aḫ-ḫa-an šar-kán-ti-in A-NA LÚ.MEŠME-ŠE-DU-TÌ ḫa-an-da-a-an-zi (21)a-pa-ša-kán šar-kán-ti-in {*EGIR-an ar-ḫa*} EGIR-an ar-ḫa pa-iz-zi (22)˹na˺-aš šar-˹kán˺-ti-i a-ra-aḫ-za ZAG-az i-ia-an-na-i

§34 (23)ma-a-an DUMU É.GAL-ma EGIR-an-da me-[mi]-an ú-da-i na-aš GÙB-la-az-pát (24)IŠ-TU DUMUMEŠ É.GAL EGIR-an-da ú-ez-zi EGIR-pa-ma-aš ku-wa-pí ú-ez-zi (25)na-aš a-ap-pa-ia-pát a-pu-u-un KASKAL-an ú-ez-zi A-NA LÚ.MEŠME-ŠE-DU-TI-ma-aš-kán (26)pé-ra-˹an˺ ar-ḫa ú-ez-zi

§35 (27) LÚME-˹ŠE-DU˺-ia ku-iš EGIR-an-da pa-iz-zi na-aš ZAG-az IŠ-˹TU˺ LÚME-ŠE-DI (28)EGIR-an-˻da˼ pa-iz-zi EGIR-pa-ia-aš ZAG-az ˻a˼-pu-u-un-pát KASKAL-an pa-iz-zi (29) LÚ.MEŠME-˻ŠE˼-DU-TI-ma-aš-kán pé-ra-an ar-ḫa Ú-˻UL˼ pa-iz-zi na-aš IŠ-TU (30)DUMU É.[G]AL pa-iz-zi

§36 (31)ma-˻a˼-[a]n šar-kán-ti-iš-ma ar-ta A-NA LÚME-ŠE-DI-ma na-aš-ma A-NA DUMU É.GAL (32)[DI]-NU na-aš-kán ˹šar˺-kán-ti-in pé-ra-an ar-ḫa Ú-UL pa-iz-zi (33)˹EGIR˺-an ar-ḫa-aš-kán pa-iz-zi nu-za a-ra-aḫ-za ku-iš ḫar-zi (34) na-aš pa-iz-zi a-pé-e-da-ni kat-ta-an ti-ia-az-zi

§37 (35) ˹ma˺-a-˹an˺ a-ra-aḫ-ze-na-an-ma ku-in-ki ÉRINMEŠ-an na-aš-šu ÉRINMEŠ URUKA4.A.AŠ.GA ku-u-ru-ra-aš (36)na-aš-ma ÉRINMEŠ URUKUM.MA.ḪA ku-i-na-an im-ma ku-in ÉRINMEŠ LUGAL-*uš* ḫal-za-a-*i* (37)nu LÚ.MEŠME-ŠE-DU-TÌ EGIR-an-da ḫu-u-ma-an-te-eš pa-a-an-zi *ma*-a-[an-š]a-ma-aš (38) GIŠŠUKURḪI.A-ma te-pa-u-e-eš-zi na-aš-ta A-NA LÚMEŠ ŠUKURḪI.A GIŠŠU[KURḪI.A] (39)˻ar˼-ḫa ta-an-zi na-at EGIR-an-da pa-a-an-zi na-at-za ḫu-u-la-li-˹ia-u˺-wa-ar (40)ḫal-˻zi-iš˼-ša-an-zi

§38 (41)˻GIŠ˼GIDRUḪI.A-u-wa-an-te-eš-ma-at EGIR-an-da Ú-UL pa-a-an-zi Ú-UL-aš-ma-aš a-˻a˼-r[a] (42)[LÚ].MEŠME-ŠE-DU-TI-ma-kán ku-i-e-eš a-aš-ša-an-zi nu ma-a-an GIŠŠUKUR ku-iš (43)˻Ú˼-UL ḫar-˻zi˼ nu-za GIŠGIDRUḪI.A ku-it ta-an-zi na-at-kán ŠA GIŠkal-mu-ša-aš (44)D[UMU] ˻É˼.[GAL] Ú-UL ḫa-an-da-˻a˼-[it]-t[a-r]i pa-ra-a da-ma-a-e-eš 2 DUMU É.GAL (45)ti-˹en˺-zi ˹nu-uš˺-ši-˹kán˺ a-pé-e ḫa-a[n-da-a-a]n-zi LÚ.MEŠME-ŠE-DI-ma ku-i-e-eš (46) GIŠGIDRUḪI.A ḫar-kán-zi na-at-ša-ma-aš[146] [EGIR-an i-ia-a]n-ta

§39 (47) ˹ma˺-a-an LÚḪA-ZA-AN-NU-ma na-aš-ma UGULA NIMGIR.ÉRINME[Š ḫa-an-da-it-t]a-ri nu-uš-ma-aš-kán (48)a-pé-e ḫa-an-da-a-an-zi a-pé-e-da-aš a-a-r[a ma-a-an-kán GI]Šḫu-lu-˻ga-an-ni-ma˼ (49)EGIR-an-da pa-a-an-zi na-at GIŠGIDRU-u-wa-an-t[e-e]š ˹EGIR-an-da˺ Ú-UL pa-˻a˼-[an-zi] (50) GIŠŠUKURḪI.A-za ta-an-zi

§33 (18–19)then the two lords who stand behind the chief of the bodyguard march inside alongside the petitioner. The bodyguard who holds the outside, however, (20)as soon as they align the petitioner with the bodyguards, (21)he goes out behind the petitioner, (22)then he marches outside to the right of the petitioner.

§34 (23–24)After that, though, if a palace servant brings a me[ss]age, he comes specifically from the left, from behind the palace servants. But when he comes back, (25–26)he also comes back that same way, but he comes out in front of the bodyguards.

§35 (27–28)And the bodyguard who walks behind walks behind with a bodyguard to the right, and he goes back that very way on the right; (29–30)he does not walk out in front of the bodyguards, though; he walks with the palace servant.

§36 (31–32)However, if the petitioner is standing (there), but the [la]w case relates to the bodyguard or the palace servant,[147] he does not go out in front of the petitioner, (33)he goes out behind,[148] whereupon he who holds the outside (34)thereupon takes that place next to him.

§37 (35–36)But if the king calls some foreign troops, either hostile Kāskean troops, or Kummaḫean troops or whatever troops, (37–40)then all the bodyguards walk behind. But i[f] there are too few spears for them, then they take spe[ars] from the spear-men and they walk behind. That's called "encircling."[149]

§38 (41)As staff bearers, though, they do not walk behind; it is not rig[ht] for them. (42–46)But if someone (among) the bodyguards that remain has no spear—since they take (only) staffs—he does not li[ne u]p with the pa[lace serva]nt of the *lituus*.[150] Two other palace servants step forth, and they li[ne] up with him. The bodyguards who hold staffs, though, they [*march behind*] them.

§39 (47–49)But if the mayor or the chief of the military heralds is [prese]nt, then they line up with them. For them it is alright. [If] they walk behind the carriage, though, they do not wa[lk] behind as staff bearers, (50)they take spears.

§40 (51)ma-a-an šar-kán-te-eš-ma zi-in-na-an-ta-ri nu ap-pé-ez-zi-an ku-⌜in⌝ (52)šar-kán-ti-in pé-ḫu-ta-an-zi na-aš ma-a-aḫ-ḫa-an pé-ra-an ar-ḫa pa-iz-zi (53)nu LÚME-ŠE-DI ku-iš šar-kán-ti-uš ú-i-da-a-iz-zi nu A-NA GAL ME-ŠE-DI *na[151]-aš-⌜ma⌝* A-˻NA GAL?? DUMU?MEŠ? É?˼.[GAL] ⌜na?-aš?-ma?⌝ [A?-N]A? ku⌝-iš ⌜LÚ⌝ME-ŠE-D[I a]n-dur-za ḫar-zi nu a-pé-˻e˼-[d]a-ni te-ez-zi (54)ḫu-u-la-li-it-ta-at-wa GAL ME-ŠE-DI-ma na-aš-ma UGULA 10 ME-ŠE-DI na-aš-ma ⌜NIMGIR⌝.ÉRIN⌜MEŠ⌝ LUGAL-i te-ez-zi ta-ru-up-ta-at-wa

§41 (55)nu LUGAL-uš ma-a-an GIŠGIGIR ú-e-ek-zi LÚME-ŠE-DI-ma GIŠGU.ZA pé-e-da-i (56)na-at da-a-i nu-za LUGAL-uš GIŠGIGIR e-ep-zi kar-šu-wa-ša ku-iš LÚME-ŠE-˻DU˼ (57)nu GIŠGIDRU ḫar-zi nu ZAG-an ANŠE.KUR.RA ZAG-az ki-iš-ša-ra-az ZABARšu-u-ur-⌜zi⌝ (58)e-⌜ep⌝-zi GÙB-la-az-ma GIŠka-a-pu-úr ḫar-zi GIŠGIDRU-za-an an-da ḫar-zi (59)nu GIŠGIGIR me-na-aḫ-ḫa-an-da ta-me-eš-ša-an ḫar-zi na-˻at˼ Ú-UL ak-kur-ri-ia-i

§42 (60) LÚ.MEŠME-ŠE-DI-ma ku-e GIŠŠUKURḪI.A ḫar-kán-zi na-at A-NA LÚša-la-aš-ḫa ⌜GIŠŠUKUR?ḪI?⌝.[A?] (61)pí-an-zi ma-a-aḫ-ḫa-an GIŠḫu-lu-ga-an-ni-iš pár-na-aš-ša pa-iz-zi LÚša-la-aš-ḫa-aš-⌜ma⌝ (62) GIŠŠUKURḪI.A A-NA LÚÌ.DU8 pa-a-i ⌜na⌝-at-kán Éḫi-lam-ni ša-ra-a pé-e-da-⌜i⌝ (63)ma-a-an GIŠḫu-lu-ga-a-an-na-za-ma ne-e-a-ri nu 1 LÚME-ŠE-DI IŠ-TU GIŠ⌜ŠUKUR⌝ (64)A-NA LÚ.MEŠME-ŠE-DU-TÌ A-NA DUMUMEŠ É.GAL-ia iš-ki-da-a-aḫ-ḫi nu URUNI.ŠI.LI ki-iš-ša-an t[e-e]z-[zi] (65)ta-pu-ú-ša

§43 (66)nu LÚ.MEŠME-ŠE-DU-TI DUMUMEŠ É.GAL-ia EGIR-an ar-ḫa pít-ti-ia-an-zi (67) LÚ.MEŠša-a-la-aš-ḫi-iš-ma-aš-ša-an GÙB-li A-NA ANŠE.GÌR.NUN.NA še-er ar-ḫa x[…] (68)na-aš-ta GIŠḫu-lu-ga-an-ni-in EGIR-pa ne-ia-an-zi GIŠŠUKURḪI.A-ma [ma-a-aḫ-ḫa-an(?)] (69)ŠA LÚMEŠ ŠUKUR *Ù ŠA* LÚ.MEŠLI-IM ṢE-RI ú-e-eḫ-zi nu ḫa-a[n?-te-ez-zi] (70)ap-pé-ez-zi ki-ša-ri […]

§44 (71)nu GIŠḫu-lu-ka-a-an-na-az Éḫa-le-tu-u-wa-aš pa-iz-zi nu [ma-a-aḫ-ḫa-an] (72)KÁ.GAL-aš ma-an-ni-in-ku-wa-aḫ-ḫi nu LÚ.MEŠALAM.ZU9-TÌ LÚ[ki-i-ta-aš-ša] (73)ŠA LÚMEŠ ŠUKUR A-NA GIŠŠUKURḪI.A *ḫa-an-te-ez-zi EGIR!?-an x* [ḫu-ia-an-te-eš] (74)na-aš-ta ma-a-aḫ-ḫa-an LÚ.MEŠALAM.ZU9 KÁ.GAL-aš an-da [a-ra-an-zi] (75)nu a-ḫa-a ḫal-zi-ia-an-zi LÚki-i-ta-aš-ma Ú-UL [ḫal-za-a-i ...]

§45 (76)ma-a-aḫ-ḫa-an-ma-kán GIŠḫu-lu-ga-an-˻ni-ia˼~[…] (77)pa-ra-a ap-pa-an-zi nu LÚ.MEŠ˻ALAM˼.Z[U9 LÚki-i-ta-aš-ša a-ḫa-a ...] (78)ḫal-zi-˻an˼-[zi ...]

§46 (iv 1)[LÚMEŠ UR]UḪA.AḪ.ḪA-ma ⌜EGIR⌝-an ḫu-ia-an-te-eš ŠA ⌜LÚMEŠ ŠUKUR⌝-ma-aš-<ma-aš> GIŠŠUK[URḪI.A] (2)[LÚMEŠ Š]UKUR KÙ.SIG17-ia[152] pé-ra-an KI.MIN ḫu-ia-an-te-eš LÚMEŠ URUḪA.⌜AḪ⌝.ḪA-ma EGIR-an[ ] (3)[i-ia-a]n-ta nu

§40 (51–52)When the petitioners are finished, though, as soon as the last petitioner that they lead (in) walks out front, (53)then the bodyguard who brings the petitioners says to the chief of the bodyguard or to the *chief of the pa*[*lace*] *personal or* [*t*]*o* the bodyguard who holds the inside, to him he says, (54)"It's *wrapped up*."[153] The chief of the bodyguard, or the commander of 10 bodyguards or the military herald says to the king, "It's *finished*."[154]

§41 (55)Then, when the king requests the chariot, a guard brings the *step-stool* (56)and sets it (up), and the king takes the chariot. And the bodyguard who is the *farrier*[155] (57–58)holds a staff, and he grasps the horse on the right by the *bit* with the right hand, while with the left he holds the *stave*; he *restrains* it with the staff,[156] (59)and he holds the chariot *tight before (him)*, so that it does not *lurch*.

§42 (60–62)The bodyguards who hold spears, though, they give them, the *spears*, to the groom. As soon as the carriage *passes* the residence, too,[157] then the groom gives the spears to the gatekeeper, and he carries them up to the gatehouse. (63–64)If he (the king) turns around with the carriage, though, then one bodyguard signals the (other) bodyguards and the palace servants with (his) spear, and he s[ays] in Hittite, (65) "To the side!"

§43 (66)Then the bodyguards and the palace servants run out behind. (67)The grooms, though, [...] to the mule out over on the left, (68)and they turn back the carriage. But [*when*] the spears (69)of the spear-men and of the *rural clansmen* turn around, the fi[rst] (70)becomes the last.

§44 (71)Then he (the king) goes to the palace by carriage, and [as soon as] (72) he nears the main gate, the entertainers [and the chant]er (73)[run] behind the spears of the spear-men. (74)And as soon as the entertainers [arrive] in the main gate, (75)they cry out "*hail*!"; but the chanter [does] not [cry out].

§45 (76–78)As soon as they take out [...] out [o]f the carriage,[158] though, the entertainers [and the chanter] cry out ["*hail*!"]

§46 (1)The Ḫaḫḫe[ans], then, are the rear-runners, while the spear-men *with* spe[ars][159] (2–4)and the gold-spear [men] are *accordingly*[160] fore-runners before th<em>. The Ḫaḫḫeans, though, [mar]ch behind, and they sing.

SÌR-*RU ma-a-aḫ-ḫa-an-ma-aš-ta* LÚ.MEŠALAM.ZU9 ⸢É⸣*ḫi-lam-*⸢*na-aš*⸣ (4)[KÁ.GA]L-*aš an-da a-ra-an-zi nu a-ḫa-a ḫal-zi-an-zi* LÚ*ki-i-ta-aš-ma* (5)[*nam*]-*ma Ú-UL ḫal-za-a-i ma-a-aḫ-ḫa-an-ma* ANŠE.GÌR.NUN.NAḪI.A KÁ.GAL-*aš pa-ra-a* (6)[*kar*?]-*pa-an-zi nu* LÚ.MEŠALAM.ZU9 LÚ*ki-i-ta-aš-ša ḫal-za-a-i nam-ma-*⸢*at*⸣*-kán* (7)[*lu-u*]*š-ta-ni-ia-az kat-ta pa-a-an-zi*

§47 (8)[*nu*?][161] LÚMEŠ ŠUKUR *ma-a-aḫ-ḫa-an* É*ḫi-lam-mar ar-ḫa ták-ša-an ša-a-*⸤*ar*?*-ri*⸥[162] (9)[*nu*?] {**ku-wa-pí**} LÚMEŠ ŠUKUR *ku-i-e-eš* GIŠŠUKURḪI.A? **ti*?*-ia-an-te-eš ku-wa-pí*[163] *pa-a-an*?*-zi*?[164] *a-pé**-*t*[*a*?*-a*]*z*?*-*⸢*pát*?⸣[165] *pa-iz-zi* GAL ŠU[KURḪI.A?] (10)[*kat*?*-t*]*a*?*-an*[166] **ti*?*-ia*?*-zi*[167]* LÚ*ME-ŠE-DI-ma* GIŠGU.⸢ZA⸣ *da-a-i na-aš-kán A-N*[*A* DUMUME]Š ⸢É⸣.[GA]L-*TÌ* (11)[GÙ]B-*la-az a-wa-an ar-ḫa pa-iz-zi na-aš pa-iz-zi* GIŠUM[BI]N GÙB-*la-az* (12) ⸢*i*⸣*-ia-at-ta ma-a-aḫ-ḫa-an-ma* GIŠ*ḫu-lu-*⸤*ga-an-ni*⸥*-in wa-aḫ-nu-*⸢*wa-an*⸣*-zi* (13)*nu* GIŠGU.ZA *ti-it-ta-nu-zi*

§48 (14)LÚMEŠ URU*ḪA.AḪ.ḪA-ma ka-ru-uš-*⸤*ši*⸥*-an-zi* [ ]Š[A?]x x-*ma-kán* [*ŠA*? É?.G]AL-*LÌ*-*{*ma-at*?*-kán*}* KÁ.⸤GAL x⸥ (15)*ša-ra-a Ú-UL ú-wa-an-zi ma-a-an* 2 É*ḫi-l*[*am-mar*][168] *na-at-kán kat-te-ra* (16)KÁ.GAL-*TÌ ša-ra-a ú-wa-an-zi ša-ra-a-*⸢*az-zi-ma*⸣*-at-kán* KÁ.GAL (17)*ša-ra-a Ú-UL ú-wa-an-zi*

§49 (18)*ma-a-***aḫ-ḫa-an-ma-kán** LUGAL-*uš* GIŠ*ḫu-lu-ga-na-az* ⸤*kat-ta*⸥ *ti-i-e-ez-zi nu ma-a-an* (19)GAL *ME-ŠE-DI ar-ta nu* GAL *ME-ŠE-DI* EGIR-*a*[*n*]-*ta UŠ-KÉ-EN nu* *LUGAL-*un** EGIR-*pa* (20)*A-NA* GAL DUMUMEŠ É.GAL *ḫi-ik-zi ma-a-an ta-*⸤*ma*⸥*-iš-***ma** *ku-iš-ki BE-LU* {*LUM*} (21)*ḫa-an-da-a-it-ta ku-iš ḫa-an-te-ez-zi-*[*a*]*n-ni ar-ta nu a-pa-aš UŠ-KÉ-EN* (22)*ma-a-an BE-LU* GAL-*ma Ú-UL ku-iš-ki ḫa-a*[*n*]*-da-a-it-ta-ri nu ku-iš* (23) LÚ*ME-ŠE-DI-ma ar-ta nu a-pa-aš UŠ-*⸤*KÉ-EN*⸥ *ma-a-na-aš-ta* GIŠGIGIR-*za-ma ku-wa-pí an-da pa-iz-zi* (24)*na-aš-ta ma-a-aḫ-ḫa-an* LUGAL-*uš* GIŠGIGIR-*za kat-ta ti-ia-*[*zi* GAL *ME-Š*]*E-DI* LUGAL-⸢*i* EGIR⸣*-an-da IT-TI* LÚ.MEŠ*ME-ŠE-DI UŠ-KÉ-EN-*[*NU*] ⸤*kar*⸥*-šu-wa-ša ku-*⸢*iš*⸣ LÚ*ME-ŠE-DI na-aš ŠA* GIŠGIGIR ZAG-*aš* GIŠUMBIN *me-na-aḫ-ḫa-an-da UŠ-KÉ-EN* ⸤LÚ*KAR*⸥*-TAP-PU-ma* GÙB-*la-aš* GIŠUMBIN *me-na-a*[*ḫ-ḫa-an-da*] *UŠ-KÉ-EN*

§50 (25)LUGAL-*uš-kán* É*ḫa-le-en-tu-u-wa-aš* [*an-da p*]*a-iz-zi* ⸢*na*⸣*-aš-ta* LÚ*ME-ŠE-DI* (26)LÚ ŠUKUR KÙ.SIG17 LÚÌ.DU8 *an-da* ⸤*ú*⸥[169]-[*wa-an-z*]*i* ⸢*nu*⸣*-uš-ša-an* GAL-*az* (27) É*ka-a-aš-ka-aš-te-pa-az ša-ra-*⸤*a*⸥ [*ú-wa-a*]*n-*⸢*zi*⸣ *nu* URUDU*za-ak-ki-in pé-eš-ši-an-zi* (28)LÚ ŠUKUR ⸤KÙ.SIG17⸥ GIŠŠUKUR GAR.RA *ku-it ḫar-zi n*[*a-at* É*ḫ*]*i-i-*⸤*li kat-ta da*⸥*-a-*⸤*i*⸥

§51 (29)*nu* LÚ ŠUKUR KÙ.SIG17 GIŠŠUKUR GAR.RA *k*[*u-it ḫa*]*r-zi na-at* É*ḫi-i-li kat-ta* (30)*da-a-i* LÚ.MEŠ*ME-ŠE-DI ku-wa-pí* **du**-*u*[*n-na-ke-e*]*š-ni* **ti**-*iš-ša-kán-zi*

But as soon as the entertainers arrive in the [gat]e of the gatehouse, they cry out "*hail!*" The chanter, though, (5–6)does not cry out [aga]in. But as soon as they [*dr*]*ag*[170] the mules forth in the main gate, then the entertainers and the chanters cry out. Then they (7)go down out the [po]stern gate.

§47 (8)[*And*] as soon as the spear-men pass through the middle of the gatehouse, (9–12)[*then*] the spear-men who go where the spears are placed, [fr]om right the[re] he goes; the chief of the *sp*[*ears* …] takes his place [*nex*]*t* to […]. But a guard takes the *step-stool*, and he walks *around* the pa[lac]e [servant]s to the [lef]t, whereupon he marches at the left of the wh[ee]l. As soon as they turn the cart around, though, (13)he sets up the *step-stool*.

§48 (14–17)The Ḫaḫḫeans, however, remain silent. […], though, do not (just) come up to the gate [*of the pa*]*lace*. If there are two gat[ehouses], they come up to the lower gate, but they do not come up to the upper gate.

§49 (18) But as soon as the king steps down from the carriage, and if (19–20)the chief of the bodyguard is standing (there), then the chief of the bodyguard bows behind (him), and he turns the king over to the chief of the palace servants. But if some other lord (21)is present who is standing at the front of the line, then it is he who bows. (22)But if no important lord at all is present, then whatever (23)bodyguard is standing there bows. If, however, he (the king) goes into some place by chariot, (24)then as soon as the king step[s] down from the chariot, the [chief of the body]guard along with the bodyguards bow behind the king. The bodyguard who is the *farrier*[171] bows opposite the right wheel of the chariot, while the charioteer bows oppo[site] the left wheel.

§50 (25)The king [g]oes [into] the palace, and a bodyguard, (26–27)a gold-spear man (and) a gatekeeper c[om]e in. They [com]e up through the main gate, and they throw the door-bolt. (28)Since the gold-spear man holds a plated spear, he lays [it] down in the [co]urtyard.[172]

§51 (29–30)And s[ince] the gold-spear man [ho]lds a plated spear, he lays it down in the courtyard, where the bodyguards stand by the inn[er cham]ber.

§52 (31) $^{LÚ.MEŠ}$ME-ŠE-DI-ma ku-e ^{GIŠ}⸤ŠUKUR⸥[$^{ḪI.A}$ ḫar-kán]-zi na-at-kán pa-ra-a ŠA ^{LÚ}ME-ŠE-DI (32) ^{É}ḫi-i-li pa-a-a[n-z]i nu-[za pé-e-ta-an] ap-pa-an-zi na-at a-ra-an-ta-ri (33) ^{GIŠ}ŠUKUR$^{⸢ḪI⸣.A}$-ia ḫa[r-kán-zi kat-ta-ma-at$^{(?)}$] Ú-UL ti-an-zi

§53 (34)ku-⸢in?⸣-ma ^{LÚ}ME-ŠE-DI x[...]*x-iz?/an?-zi? na-aš-kán pa-ra?-a? pa-iz-zi* ^{GIŠ}ŠUKUR-^{ia} ḫar-zi (35)na-*aš?-⸢kán⸣ É?.GAL?-LÍ?-x*[...]x-ma-aš ^{É}lu-uš-*ta*-ni-ia a-ri!(ḪU) nu ^{GIŠ}ŠUKUR (36)⸤IT⸥-TI ^{LÚ}Ì.DU$_8$ É[...]-ma? ⸢KI⸣.MIN

§54 (37)nu ku-it-⸤ma-an⸥ x[...] SIG$_5$-*at-ta* nu ^{LÚ}ḫa-ag-ga-zu-wa-aš-ši-iš (38) IŠ-TU ⸢É⸣ x[...]x 1 ^{UZU}ÚR za-nu-wa-an IŠ-TU É.GA-ia (39)1 NA-MA-AN-⸢DU⸣ [GA.KU$_7$ ...]$^{⸢LÚ⸣.MEŠ}$ME-ŠE-DI-TÌ pa-a-i na-at-za a-ta-an-zi

§55 (40)A-NA DUMU^{MEŠ} É.GAL-⸢ia⸣[... 1 ^{UZU}Ú]R ⸤za-nu-wa-an⸥ 1 ⸤NA-MA-AN-DU GA.*KU$_7$* (41)pí-an-zi na-at-za [a-ta-an-zi ...]

§56 (42)ma-a-aḫ-ḫa-an-ma du-x[...]x[...]*x* (43)ú-ez-zi nu A-⸢NA⸣ L[Ú ...]x x[...]x-an[...] (44)ḫal-za-a-i ú-da-an-[du-wa~ ...]* x x *[...] [...]

§57 (45)LÚ ŠUKUR KÙ.SIG$_{17}$-m[a ...]x ⸢A-NA⸣ LÚ^{MEŠ} ⸢ŠUKUR lu⸣-ú-i-li [...] (46) ki-iš-ša-an ḫal-za-⸢a⸣-[i ...]x [...]

§58 (47)LÚ ŠUKUR-ma-za ^{GIŠ}ŠUK[UR ... ŠUK]UR-ma ⸤ZABAR⸥ kat-ta ne-[...] (48) na-aš É ^{LÚ}MUḪALDIM pa-iz-[zi ...]ki-iš-ša-⸢an te⸣-ez-z[i ...] (49)du-un-na-ki-⸤iš⸥-n[a ...] [...]

§59 (50)nam-ma ^{LÚ}ŠUKU[R ...]x ŠA ^{GIŠ}ŠUKUR-ma[...] (51)[ZA]BAR ša-x[...] LÚ^{M}[$^{EŠ?}$...] (52)[...]É.GAL-LÌ [...]

(ca. 18 empty lines)

COLOPHON

(53)DUB.1.KAM ŠA ^{LÚ}ME-ŠE-DI iš-ḫi-ú-l[a-a]š Ú-UL ⸢QA⸣-TI

§52 (31–32)The bodyguards who [hol]d spear[s], though, go out to the bodyguard's courtyard, they take [their places], and they stand (there). (33)They h[old] spears, [and] they do not put [*them down*].

§53 (34)The bodyguard who *they* […], though, goes out, and he holds a spear, (35–36)and he […] the palace. […] he reaches the postern, though, he […] the spear with the gatekeeper; […], though, ditto.

§54 (37)And while […] is put in order, the *ḫaggazuwassi*-servant (38)[…] from the building […] one cooked limb, and from the dairy (39)he gives one jug of [sweet milk … and … to] the guards, and they eat.

§55 (40–41)They also give the palace servants [… one] cooked [li]mb (and) one jug of sweet milk, and they [eat].

§56 (42)But as soon as […], […] (43)comes, […] to the […]-ma[n …] (44)cries out: "They sh[all] bring […]."

§57 (45–46)The gold-spear man, thou[gh …] call[s] out to the spear-men in Luwian[173] thus: "[…]"

§58 (47)The spear man, though, […] a spe[ar; …] bronze [sp]ear, however, tu[rn …] down/with […], (48)and he goe[s] into the kitchen, and he say[s] thus: "[…] (49)inner chamber […]."

§59 (50)Further, the spear man […] of the spear, though, […] (51)[br]onze […] me[n …] (52)[…] palace […]

(ca. 18 empty lines)

COLOPHON

(53)Tablet One of the Oblig[ati]ons of the Bodyguard: not finished.

No. 5

Royal Decree on Social and Economic Matters (*CTH* 269)

This text is perhaps best characterized as a Royal Edict or Decree Concerning Social and Economic Reform, as Košak (1988a) entitled it in his edition. As it relates its stipulations at least once to previous regulations that are to be superceded (§§3′, 4′), one could also dub it a reform. It shows some similarities to Tudḫaliya I's Penal and Administrative (No. 8) and his Judicial Decrees (No. 9) as well as to the Hittite Laws (Hoffner 1997a). The composition is only very fragmentarily preserved, in one small MH piece (B) and a NH copy (A). Ms. A was found in the Temple I complex.

On the basis of similar prices mentioned here and in the Hittite Laws as well as the speaker's reference to a ruling of "my father" and the mention of corruption and the exploitation of the poor, it has been suggested (Košak 1988a: 202; Beckman 1991: 212) that the composition might date to Mursili I; and while this conclusion is certainly a possibility, it must be regarded as quite tentative in view of the fragmentary state of the text.[174] It seems a dating generally to the OH or earlier MH period is appropriate. Laroche's (*CTH*, p. 180) suggestion that this market reform might be catalogued in the shelf list KUB 30.61 i 5', which reads "Tablet one of the 'Edi[ct]' (*isḫiul*[*as*) of the Market"

Transliteration

§1′ (B, 1′–6′; A i 1′–2′) (1′)[… UR]U⸢*ḪA.AT*⸣.*TI* LÚ.MEŠx[…] (2′)[…]x x LÚZA.LAM.GAR LÚ[…] (3′)[… LÚMAŠK]IM.URUKI LÚ.MEŠ*ḫa-l*[*i*?-*ia-tal-le-eš* …] (4′)[… -(*i*)]*a-ar-mu-ši* LÚ.MEŠx[…] (5′)[…]x LÚ.MEŠÚ.*ḪÚB x* LÚ.M[EŠ …] (6′)[… (*d*)]*a-aš-kán-z*[*i*]

§2′ (A i 3′–6′; B, 7′–10′) (3′)[… UR]U*A-ri-in-na-*[(*aš* LÚ.MEŠ*ḫa-a-p*)*í-e-eš* …] (4′)[…]x LÚMEŠ <(URU)>*ḪAR.ḪA*[(*R.NA* LÚ.ME)Š …] (5′)[…]x x LÚ.MEŠ*mi-na-a*[(*l-le-e-eš ki*)- …] (6′)[ ]x *da-aš-kán-z*[(*i*) …]

§3′ (A i 7′–11′; B, 11′–14′) (7′)⸢*ka-ru*⸣*-ú ŠA* 1 TÚG*a-t*[*u-*(*up-li* 3 GÍN KÙ).BABBAR *ŠI-IM-ŠU*(?)] (8′)⸢*i-ia*⸣*-at-te-en ŠA* 1 TÚG.B[(ÁR 1 GÍN KÙ.BABBAR) *ŠI-IM-ŠU*(?)] (9′)⸢*i-ia*⸣*-at-*⸢*te*⸣*-en ŠA* 1 UDU 1 G[Í(N KÙ.BABBAR *ŠI-I*)*M*?*-ŠU*(?)] (10′)⸢*i-ia-at*⸣*-te-en ŠA* 1 *TA-PAL* KU[Š(E.S)IR x GÍN KÙ.BABBAR *ŠI-IM-ŠU*(?) *i-ia-at-te-en*] (11′)⸤*ki-nu-na* 2⸥ GÍN 1½ GÍN KÙ.B[ABBAR *i-ia-at-te-ni*]

§4′ (A i 12′–14′) (12′)⸢*ŠA*⸣ 3 D[UG K]A.DÙ 1 GÍN KÙ.BABBA[R *ŠI-IM-ŠU*(?)] (13′)⸢*i-ia-at-te-en*⸣ 1 DUG GEŠTIN 1 G[ÍN KÙ.BABBAR *ŠI-IM-ŠU*(?) *i-ia-at-te-en ki-nu-na*] (14′)⸢2 GÍN⸣ 1½ GÍN ⸢KÙ⸣.BABBAR *i-ia-a*[*t-te-ni*]

(Dardano 2006: 53–54), also remains a possibility, though KI.LAM actually never means "market; market price" in any clear case in the Hittite texts, as it does in Mesopotamian compositions (including those from Ḫattusa; *HW*² Ḫ, 586a; cf. Singer 1975: 93–94), but rather "gatehouse." One should perhaps translate the shelf list entry "Tablet one of the obligat[ions]/instruct[ions] concerning the gatehouse," in which case it should probably not be linked with any extant composition.

It is composed throughout, as far as can be ascertained, as the words of the son of the king (§5′) directed to his subjects in the 2nd pl. In §§1′–2′ are mentioned a number of different persons or occupations and actions that they are to take. In §§3′–4′ previously valid prices for various commodities are reformed, apparently with reference to a new exchange rate for silver (see n. 176). Paragraphs 5′–6′ then address the issue of standard scales and weights with regard to a ruling that had been issued by the speaker's father; unfortunately the paragraphs are too fragmentary to establish their exact content. Paragraph 7′ is almost completely lost before a long gap ensues, §8″ is equally fragmentary. Paragraph 9″ mentions a lenient decision of the speaker's father, while §10″ takes up the refrain of corruption and exploitation of the poor so common in OH texts. Paragraph 11″ returns to the matter of scales and weights before the text breaks off entirely.

TRANSLATION

§1′ (1′)[…] Ḫattusa, […]-men, (2′)[…] "tent-man," […]-man, (3′)city [commi]ssioner, *gu*[*ards*, …], (4′)[…]-men, (5′)[…] deaf men […]-men (6′)[…] they will take.

§2′ (3′)[… (the *ḫāpi*-men)] of the [cit]y of Arinna (4′)[…] men of the <(city)> of Ḫarḫa[(rna, the me)n of …], (5′)the *mina*[(*lla*-men) …] (6′)[…] they will take.

§3′ (7′–10′)Earlier for an *at*[(*upli*)]-garment you[175] set [*a price* (of 3 shekels of si)lver]; for a ro[(ugh)] garment you set [*a price* (of 1 shekel of silver)]; for a sheep you set [(*a pr*)*ice*] of 1 sh[(ekel of silver)]; for a pair of leath[er (sh)oes you set *a price* of x shekel of silver]; (11′)now, however, [you will set] (the price at) 2 shekels to 1½ shekels[176] of sil[ver].

§4′ (12′–13′)For 3 j[ugs of lig]ht beer you set [*a price*] of 1 shekel of silver; for a jug of wine [you set *a price*] of 1 sh[ekel of silver; now, however], (14′)[you wil]l set (the price at) 2 shekels to 1½ shekels of silver.

§5′ (A i 15′–17′) (15′)⌞*ke*⌟-*e-ma ud-da-a-ar at-ta-aš-m*[*i-iš* …] (16′)⌜*Ù*⌝ NA$_4$ GIŠ.ÉRIN *ZI-BA-NA* LUGAL-*u*[*š* …] (17′)GIŠ.ÉRIN *ZI-PA-NA Ù* NA$_4$$^{HI.A}$[…]

§6′ (A i 18′–21′) (18′)[*k*]*u-iš-za* É-*er* ^{GIŠ}KIRI$_6$.GEŠTIN x[…] (19′)[*nu*?] GIŠ.ÉRIN *ZI-PA-NA ke-e k*[*i*?- …] (20′)[ ]x-⌞*a*?⌟-*an*-⌞*ki*?⌟ *ku*?-*iš*⌟-*za* É x[…] (21′)[*ḫu*]-⌞*ur-ta-li-ia-zi*⌟ *ta*-[…]

§7′ (A i 22′) […]x x-⌞*ia*⌟-*na*-⌞*az*⌟ x x[…]

(gap of more than 2 columns)

§8″ (A iv 1′–4′) (1′–2′)(traces) (3′)[*š*]*u*?-*me-eš*[…] (4′)*na-aš-t*[*a*? …]

§9″ (A iv 5′–8′) (5′)*at-ta-aš-ma*~[…] (6′)*Ú-UL ku-en-ta*[…] (7′)*šu-me-eš-ša at-ta-aš-ma-aš*[…] (8′)*ḫa-an-nu-an da-a-iš-t*[*e-en* …]

§10″ (A iv 9′–12′) (9′)*ku-iš-za* É-*er* ^{GIŠ}KI[RI$_6$.GEŠTIN …] (10′)*šu-ma-ša ma-aš-ká*[*n* …] (11′)[*k*]*u-iš-ma ma-aš-k*[*án* …] (12′)⌞*nu*⌟ $^{LÚ.MEŠ}$MÁŠD[A …]

§11″ (A iv 13′–14′) (13′)⌞NA$_4$?⌟ GIŠ.ÉRIN *ZI-P*[*A-NA* …] (14′)(traces)

§5′ (15′)This ruling of m[y] father, though, […] (16′)as well as stone (and) scales. The king […] (17′)scales and stones […]

§6′ (18′)He who […] a household, a garden […], (19′)[and/then] scales […] these […]; (20′–21′)he who [… *con*]*fuses* a household […]

§7′ (traces)

(gap of more than 2 columns)

§8″ […] (3′)you […], (4′)and […]

§9″ (5′)My father, though […] (6′)did not kill. […] (7′)You, too, my father's […] (8′)y[ou] shall begin to decide.

§10″ (9′)He who […] a household, a ga[rden …]; (10′)but you […] a brib[e …]; (11′)he who […] a brib[e], though, […] (12′)and poor men […]

§11″ (13′–14′)Stone(s) (and) sca[les …]

No. 6
An Akkadian Fragment Mentioning an Oath (*CTH* 275)

Since this is the only Akkadian-language fragment sometimes referred to in the research literature as an instruction or an oath, it is included here, but it must be recognized that this categorization is far from certain. Why a document concerning internal administration such as that evidenced by the rest of the documents in this volume would be drawn up in Akkadian is difficult to imagine, so that classifying it as a treaty would seem perhaps more likely.

Transliteration

§1′ (1′)˹*ù ag*?-*ga*?˺-[…] (2′)*la-a i-de*$_4$*-šu-n*[*u*~ …] (3′)*ti-de*$_4$*-šu-nu-ti-m*[*a* …][177]

§2′ (4′)*ù ma-mi-ta ša*~*a*[*n*? …] (5′)*e-li* ^{m}*Zi-ta-an-za* x[…] (6′)*ša i-pu-šu ša i*-x[…]

§3′ (7′)*ù šum-ma i-ba-aš-ši*~x[…] (8′)*ù ma-mi-tú ša-a-ši*[…] (9′)*a-na* ^{m}*Mu-ut-ta-al-l*[*i* …]

§4′ (10′)*ù an-na-nu-u*[*m*~ …] (11′)*it-ti* ^{m}*Mu-*[*ut-ta-al-li* …]

§5′ (12′) ^{m}*Ḫu-um-m*[*i-li* …] (13′)*ki-ia*~x[…] (14′)*i-n*[*a* …]

The names Zitanza (5′), Muttalli (9′, 11′) and Ḫummili (12′) have led to suggestions that these might be equated with the MH king Muwattalli I, with either the military officer Zidanza known from the time of Tudḫaliya I or even Muwattalli's second predecessor on the throne, Zidanta II, and with the Ḫimuili who played a role alongside Kantuzzili in the prelude to Tudḫaliya I's reign (e.g., Klengel 1999: 95; Klinger 2000: 10; Marizza 2007: 48). Obviously, while possibilities, these must remain speculative in view of the fragment's state of preservation.

TRANSLATION

§1′ […] (1′)and […] (2′)he does not know the[m …] (3′)you(pl.) know the[m …].

§2′ (4′)And the oath that […] (5′)upon Zitanza […] (6′)that he swore (lit. "made"), which he […]

§3′ (7′)And if it is extant […] (8′)and this oath […] (9′)to Muttall[i …]

§4′ (10′)And her[e …] (11′)with Mu[ttalli …]

§5′ (12′)Ḫumm[ili …] (13′)*thus* […] (14′)in […]

Chapter 2
Sources from the Reigns of Tudḫaliya I and Arnuwanda I

No. 7
Instructions for Military Officers and Frontier Post Governors (*CTH* 261.II)

Laroche placed this text together with No. 17 (*CTH* 261.I), but while similarities are to be found, it is clear that it represents an independent composition (e.g., Kammenhuber 1976: 33, n. 65). Giorgieri (1995: 206–11) regarded it as a parallel to No. 10 (cf., e.g., §§1′–3′ here and No. 10, §9″), though del Monte (1975a: 137) felt that it actually has little in common with that text.

Only a few paragraphs of a single tablet are preserved. The paleography of the fragment is MH, likely a rather early than late MH, so that one suspects that it may be a text of Tudḫaliya I at the latest. As the tablet fragments were discovered during Winckler's and Makridi's poorly documented excavations of Ḫattusa from 1906 to 1911, no provenience is known.

The paragraphs of the first column pertain to preparedness for military campaigns, to the exclusive authority of the Great King to decide what army divisions are to be released and which are to be retained for work duties and to the authority of whoever is designated by the king as commander in his absence. The two paragraphs of the second column deal with the capture and extradition of fugitives.

TRANSLITERATION

(somewhat more than first half of col. i missing)

§1′ (i 1′)[…]x x[…] (2′)[…]x[1]-˹zi?-iš˺ ḫu-u-˹ma-an˺-[za?] x x[…]x[…] (3′)[nu? ku?]-iš ar-ḫa tar-nu-ma-aš ÉRIN^MEŠ-˹az na?-an?˺ ^d˹UTU-ŠI˺ x[…]x[2…]

§2′ (4′)ma-a-an ^dUTU-ŠI-ma ku-wa-pí a-pa-a-ši-la la-aḫ-ḫi-ia-iz!-zi nu [KUR-e(?)] ŠA ^LÚK[ÚR?] (5′)a-pí-ia-ia ḫu-u-da-aš e-eš-tu nu ^LÚKÚR kar-ši za-aḫ-ḫi-ia-ad-du-˹ma˺-at ma!-a!-aḫ-ḫa-an-[ma] (6′) ^LÚKÚR-aš a-ki ku-u-ru-ur ku-iš ḫar-zi nu ku-iš ÉRIN^MEŠ a-ša-an-du-la-<aš>[3] na-aš-kán (7′)an-da a-ša-an-du-la-aš da-a-la-aḫ-ḫi ku-iš ar-ḫa tar-nu-ma-š[a É]RIN^MEŠ-az na-an (8′) ^dUTU-ŠI ar-ḫa tar-na-aḫ-ḫi [ ]

§3′ (9′)[ma]-⸤a⸥-an ^LÚKÚR-ma ku-wa-at-ka za-lu-uk-nu-zi ku-u-ru-ur ku-iš [ḫar-z]i ^dUTU-ŠI-ma (10′)[EGIR]-an A-NA DINGIR^MEŠ-ŠU i-ia-u-wa-an-zi ú-ez-zi na-aš-ma-aš-ši [ku-wa-p]í ⸤a⸥-[aš-šu] (11′)[na-aš] a-pád-da pa-iz-zi *tu*-zi-ia-ma pé-ra-an ma-a-an DU[MU LUGAL na-aš-ma BE-EL GAL] (12′) [ku-in-k]i wa-tar-na-aḫ-ḫi nu ma-a-aḫ-ḫa-an ŠA ^dUTU-ŠI i[š-ḫi-ú-ul a-pé-el-la QA-TAM-MA] (13′)[e-eš-t]u[4] na-an ḫu-u-ma-an-te-eš iš-ta-ma-aš-š[a-an-du[5] …] (14′)[tu-uz-z]i-ia pé-ra-an ku-iš wa-tar-na-aḫ-ḫa-[…] (15′)[ar-ḫa i-d]a-a!-lu-un ku-in-ki me-mi-ia-[an pé-e-ḫu-te-ez-zi …]

§4′ (16′)[… tu-u]z-zi-ia p[é-ra-an …] (17′)[…]x x[…]

(gap of ca. 1 column)

§5″ (ii 1′)[…]x x[… ḫ]a-an-da-a-[…]

§6″ (2′)[^LÚḫ]u-˹ia-an˺-[da-š]a-aš-ma-aš ut-tar ˹a˺-[ú-wa]-r[i-i]a-aš iš-ḫa-a-aš ⸤ḫu⸥-u-ma-an-d[a-aš] (3′)˹iš˺-ḫi-ú-ul i-ia-an e-eš-tu na-aš-ta ˹KUR!?˺-ia[6] an-da wa-t[a]r-na-aḫ-ḫa-an ˹e˺-[eš-tu] (4′)nu ku-iš ^LÚḫu-ia-an-da-an ú-e-mi-iš-ke-ez-zi na-an [a]p-pí-iš-ke-ed-d[u] (5′)na-an a-ú-wa-ri-ia-aš iš-ḫi-i ⸤pa⸥-ra-a ti-it-ta-nu-ud-du a-ú-wa-ri-ia-aš-ma (6′)iš-ḫa-a-aš MA-ḪAR ^dUTU-ŠI up-pí-[i]š?-ke-ed-du nu-za-kán ^LÚḫu-ia-an-da-an (7′)K[UR-e a]n-d[a] ⸤le⸥-e-pát da-a-l[a]-i [ ]

§7″ (8′)[… i-d]a?-⸤a?-lu?⸥~[[7]x x -i]k-kán-za an-tu-wa-aḫ-ḫa-aš KUR-e iš-tar-˹na ar-ḫa˺[ ] (9′)[…]x[8] ú-e-mi-ia-az-z[i-pá]t[9] nu-uš-še-eš-ša-an pu-u-nu-uš-šu-a[n-zi][10] (10′)[…]x SIG₅-in pu-u-nu-uš-d[u] na-aš na-aš-šu ^LÚḫu-ia-an-za (11′)[… -l]i i-ia-at-ta n[a-aš-m]a ŠA É.GAL-LÌ ku-iš-ki (12′)[…]na-at pé-e ḫar-zi k[u?-i]t?[11] ŠA BAD-TU₄ a-aš-šu-u (13′)[… p]é-e ḫar-zi na-aš-ma p[a-la]-aḫ-ša-an[12] da-ia-an ú-e-da-i[z-zi] (14′)[… ^LÚḫ]u?-ia-an-da-an

TRANSLATION

(somewhat more than first half of col. i missing)

§1′ (2′)[…] entire (3′)[… And] I, My Majesty [… th]at contingent that has leave.

§2′ (4′)When His Majesty himself, though, at any time goes on a campaign [*in the land*] of the *e*[*nemy*], (5′)there too, preparedness must obtain, and you(pl.) must fight the enemy unreservedly. (6′)As soon as the enemy has been vanquished, [though], (*if*) some (enemy) retains hostility, then the occupation contingent that (is to be left behind), (7′–8′)I will leave behind for the occupation, while the contingent that (is to have leave), I, My Majesty, will give leave.

§3′ (9′)[I]f an enemy, though, somehow *perseveres*, (if) some (enemy) [retai]ns hostility, My Majesty, however, (10′–12′)comes [bac]k in order to venerate his gods, or he goes [whereve]r it seems b[est] to him, if I commission a pr[ince or som]e [great lord] at the head of the army, then just like the o[rders] of My Majesty, [so, too, should his (orders) likewise] (13′)[b]e (regarded), and all should obey him! (14′)He who […] command before the [arm]y, (15′)[… he carries out] some [e]vil act […]

§4′ (16′–17′)[…] b[efore the ar]my […]

(gap of ca. 1 column)

§5″ (traces)

§6″ (2′–3′)And let the matter of [fu]gi[ti]ves be made an obligation for all the governors of the p[os]ts, and l[et it be] decreed in the land: (4′)He who finds a runaway, he must apprehend him (5′)and surrender him to the governor of the post. The governor of the post, though, (6′–7′)must bring (him) before My Majesty. He must in no case rel[ea]se him [wi]th[in] the l[and].

§7″ (8′)[… *b*]*ad* […] a man within the land […] away (9′)[…] he will [surel]y find, and [… *to*] question him, (10′–11′)[…] he shall question […] thoroughly, and whether the fugitive goes […, o]r someone of the palace, (12′)[…] and he has it/them in his possession, *w*[*hic*]*h* goods of the *lordship*[13] (13′)[…] has in his possession, or he carri[es] a stolen *p*[*al*]*aḫsa*-blanket, (14′)[…-s t]he fugitive, or cattle (and) sheep, (15′)[he shall apprehend him

x[x x]*na-aš-ma* GU_4ḪI.A UDUḪI.A (15′)[*na-an ap-pí-iš-ke-ed-du na-a*]*n a-ú-wa-*[*ri-ia-aš i*]*š-ḫi-i pa-ra-a ti-it-ta-n*[*u-ud-du*] (16′)[*a-ú-wa-ri-ia-aš-ma iš-ḫa-a-aš* MA-ḪAR ᵈUT]U-˻ŠI *up*˼-[*pí-iš-ke-ed-d*]*u ḫu-ia-an-da-an-ma* (17′) [*ku-iš-ki* ...]-˻*iz*?˼*-zi* ŠA SAG.DU-ŠU (18′)[…]x

§8″ (19′)[…]x-*za*[14] KUR-*e iš-tar-na a*[*r-ḫa*] (20′)[…]x

(gap of ca. 1.5 columns)

§9″ (iv 1′)x[…]

§10″ (2′)*ku-i-*[*e-eš* …] (3′)*ma-a-na*-x[…] (4′)*ku-iš-ki k*[*u*?- …] (5′)*an-tu-*[*w*]*a-a*[*ḫ*- …] (6′)˻*nu*˼-x[…]

and he shall] surrender him to the governor of the [po]st. (16′–18′)[The governor of the post, though], m[ust] b[ring] (him) [before] My [Majes] ty. [Whoever …-s] the fugitive, though, […] of his head/a matter of capital […]

§8″ (19′–20′)[…] within the land […] a[way …]

(gap of ca. 1.5 columns)

§9″ (traces)

§10″ (2′)Those w[hich …] (3′)if […] (4′)whoever […] (5′)ma[n …], (6′)and […]

No. 8
Tudḫaliya I's Decree on Penal and Administrative Reform
(*CTH* 258.1)

This decree is known from two larger pieces of one tablet (A) and three smaller fragments, which may belong to a single second tablet (B_{1-3}). As the composition seems to have occupied no more than a single tablet, some one-quarter to one-third of the original text is preserved. No findspot is known for ms. A, while the fragments of B_{1-3} were found in secondary contexts in the lower city and near the *Haus am Hang*. Determining whether the latter thus belong to a single tablet from either the Temple I complex or the *Haus am Hang* on the one hand or if they belong to two tablets, originally stored in the Temple I complex (or elsewhere) and in the *Haus am Hang*, will remain difficult until and unless further joins are made.

This composition is particularly difficult to categorize, as is the following one (No. 9). Its content would seem transparent enough. It deals primarily with reform in the penal code (§§4′–7′), particularly in regard to blood feuds and vigilante justice, as well as the administration and protection of royal property (§§10″–11″). Its introduction, unique among the instructions in its narrative of historical background (but cf. No. 27, §1), seems to identify the problem its paragraphs seek to redress as a lack of law and order, which had resulted from Tudḫaliya's long absence due to military concerns. Its preserved colophon does not provide the text with a title. The following composition (No. 9) seems equally clear in its content, which constitutes a reform of judicial procedure. Significantly, however, No. 9 is regarded in its colophon as an oath, albeit in a syntactically incomplete and thus unclear clause, and parallels with No. 12 suggest that its lost portions might well have contained an oath imposition. It would seem, therefore, that although the preserved text of No. 9 contains only regulatory prescriptions, which could be regarded as constituting a decree or instructions, the assumption is that those officials affected by the ensuing changes would have been expected to swear an oath concerning their commitment to the reforms.

Pecchioli Daddi (2005b: 599) has struck this text from her list of instructions, protocols, and oaths, asserting that it has "no specific recipient." While it could perhaps be the case that it should be regarded as an edict or a decree rather than as an "obligation and oath" text (e.g., Westbrook and Woodard 1990; Marazzi 2007: 496; cf. already Riemschneider 1961: 28), it is not entirely correct that it is directed at no specific recipient. Though most of the composition is formulated impersonally, at least §10″ is addressed specifically to "you men of the city," and the 2nd pers. is employed in §§10″, 11″, and 13″ as well. Further, in light of its "historical prologue," which appears to frame the composition as a response to the complaints of the "men of Ḫattusa," it seems clear enough that these reforms are directed at these officials and administrators of the capital, as indeed are Nos. 10, 12, and 28 (Pecchioli Daddi 2006: 121; cf. Miller 2011a: 4 and n. 10).[15]

In any case, the present text is one of several in this volume (see the introduction, n. 38) that are introduced with *UMMA*, "thus (speaks RN)," placing the words directly in the mouth of the king. Unique among the instructions (but cf. No. 27, §1), the body of the text is preceded by a prologue describing the historical situation that gave rise to the needs being addressed in its directives (§§1–2). Due to his long campaign, during which he claims to have defeated Āssuwa, the legal system had, without its king and "chief justice" at the helm, deteriorated, so that reform was needed. Unfortunately, further details escape us, as the text breaks off at this point. There seems to be no concrete reason to assume that this "historical prologue" should be considered a "literary fiction," as do de Martino and Imparati (1998: 395). It is perfectly conceivable that law and order would have broken down to some degree during an extended absence of its primary judicial authority, and that he was called upon or even challenged to restore order upon his return.

One thing that the authors mentioned thus far seem to agree upon is that Nos. 8 and 9 represent two different compositions. On this point, however, perhaps one should reserve judgment. The fact that No. 9 is categorized as an oath in its colophon while No. 8 is not provided with any such title should not necessarily be seen as excluding the possibility. The choice of a NH copyist to add a colophon including an attribution to a category—or to copy elements of the original colophon, in case it was provided with one—should not obscure the close parallels between the two compositions. Among other similarities, they both deal with legal reform in cases of bloodshed (No. 8, §5′; No. 9, §2) and they both speak of compensation instead of revenge (No. 8, §§5′–7′, 10′; No. 9, §1), topics that are not at all common in the text genres in question.

Though Westbrook and Woodard (1990), followed, e.g., by Jackson (2008: 42), attributed the composition to Tudḫaliya IV (late-thirteenth century), Hittitologists are unanimous in ascribing it to a Tudḫaliya of the MH period, that is, either Tudḫaliya I or III, as shown already by Otten (1979; see also Giorgieri 1995: 132–34; Marazzi 2007: 497, n. 22, 499). Though all mss. are NH copies, that the original composition was pre-NH is demonstrated, *inter alia*, by forms such as *n=e=z=san* in 1.A iii 16′ or the use of *takku* in ii 16 and is supported by numerous other features. Indeed, these elements are surprising for a text of the age of Tudḫaliya I, and one wonders if some portions of the text might even have been copied from the earlier judicial documents that it intends to supercede.[16]

Westbrook and Woodard (1990: 641–42) also concluded that this composition deals at least in part with debt release, based on their understanding of *parā tarna-* (A ii 1, 6, 8, 10, 13, 15, 19, iii 16′), which however, likely refers to the

---

TRANSLITERATION

§1 (A i 1–5) (1)*UM-MA TA.BA.AR.NA* m*TU.UD.ḪA.LI.*˹*IA* LUGAL˺.GAL (2)*ma-a-an* URU*A.AŠ.ŠU.WA ḫar-ni-in-k*[*u-u*]*n* (3)*a-ap-pa-ma* URU*Ḫa-at-tu-ši* [*ú-wa*]*-nu-un* (4)*nu-kán* DINGIRMEŠ *aš-ša-nu-nu-un* [*n*]*u-mu* LÚMEŠ URU*ḪA.AT.TI* (5)*ḫu-u-ma-an-za a-ru-ú-e-eš-ke-*˻*u*˼*-*[*w*]*a-an da-a-iš nu kiš-an me-mi-er*

§2 (A i 6–12) (6) dUTU-*ŠI-wa an-ze-el* [*B*]*E-LÍ-NI* LÚ*la-aḫ-ḫi-ia-la-aš* (7)˻*zi*˼*-ik nu-wa-aš-ša-a*[*n*] *ḫa-an-né-eš-na-an-ni* (8)[*ḫ*]*a-an-nu-wa-an-zi Ú-UL tar-ra-at-ta* (9)[x]x[17]*-aš-ša-wa-*˻*kán*˼ *i-da-la-u-i-eš* UNMEŠ*-ši-iš* (10)[…] x-NI[18] *ar-ḫa ḫar-ni-in-ke-er* (11)[…]x˻ḪI.A˼ *ú-pa-a-ti*ḪI.A *Ù* LÚ.MEŠ*ša-ri-ku-wa-aš* (12)[… *i-da-l*]*a*?*-u*[19]*-e-eš-ta*

§3 (A i 13–17) (13)[… *-a*]*n*?*-*te-eš-ša** (14)[…] (15)[… *-l*]*i-ta* (16)[…]*-mi-iš* (17)[…]x

(remaining ca. three-quarters of col. i missing entirely)

§4′ (A ii 1–2) (1)*na-aš-ta pa-ra-a Ú-UL tar-na-i nu-uš-ši* EGIR*-pa* (2)*PU-UḪ-ŠU a-pé-e-ni-ìš-šu-u-wa-da-an* A.ŠÀ *pa-a-i*

§5′ (A ii 3–15; B_2 ii 1–8) (3)*ma-a-an e-eš-ḫa-na-aš-ša ku-*˻*iš*˼*-ki šar-ni-ik-zi-il* (4)*pí-ia-an ḫar-zi nu-za-ta* SAG.DU*-ZU wa-aš-ta* (5)*na-aš-šu* A.ŠÀ*-LA_{12} na-aš-ma* LÚ.U_{19}.LU (6)*na-aš-ta pa-ra-a Ú-UL ku-iš-ki tar-na-i* (7)*ma-a-na-aš-za QA-DU* DAMMEŠ*-ŠU* DUMUMEŠ*-ŠU da-a-an ḫar-zi* (8)*na-an-ši-iš-ta pa-ra-a* ˻*tar*˼*-na-i ma-a-an ta-i-iz-zi-la-aš-ša* (9)*ku-iš-ki šar-ni-ik-ze-*˻*el*˼ *pí-ia-an ḫar-zi* (10)*nu ma-a-an* A.ŠÀ *na-aš-ta pa-ra-a Ú-UL tar-na-an-zi* (11)*ma-a-an* ÌR*-ma da-ia-at na-an ta-i-az-zi-la-an-ni ḫar-zi* (12){**ḫar-zi**} *na-aš ma-a-an ta-šu-wa-aḫ-ḫa-an-za* (13)*na-an-ši-iš-ta pa-ra-a Ú-UL tar-na-an-zi* (14) *ma-a-*na*-aš Ú-UL ta-šu-wa-aḫ-ḫa-an-za* (15)*na-an-ši-iš-ta pa-ra-a tar-na-an-zi*

§6′ (A ii 16–19; B_1 ii 1′–4′) (16)*ták-ku EL-LA_{12}-ma ku-iš-ki da-i-*ia*-zi* (17)*nu da-i-ia-zi-la-aš šar-ni-ik-ze-el* (18)˻*nu-za*?˼ x x*-iš*? [20] ˻*na-an Ú*˼*-UL ta-šu-wa-aḫ-ḫa-an-zi* (19)[…[21] *pa-ra-a tar*]*-na-an-zi*

handing over of the suspect to one party or another (see n. 21). Thus, the text has nothing to do with a specific or general debt release.

Translation

§1 (1)Thus (speaks) the Sovereign, Tudḫaliya, Great King: (2)Once I destroyed Āssuwa, (3)I [ca]me back to Ḫattusa, (4–5)and I provided for the deities, so that all the men of Ḫattusa began to revere me, and they spoke thus:

§2 (6–8) "You, Your Majesty, our [L]ord, you are a *campaigner*, so you have not been able to render judgment concerning law cases, (9–10)and [...] evil persons have utterly destroyed [...]. (11)[...]-s, land holdings and *sarikuwa*-troops (12)[...] he/it has become [*awf*]*ul*."

§3 (13–17)[...] and [...]-s [...]

(remaining ca. three-quarters of col. i missing entirely)

§4′ (1–2)and he will not hand (him/them) over to (him),[22] and he will give him back just the same amount of land in its stead.

§5′ (3–5)If[23] someone has paid compensation for blood(shed), too — be it a field or personnel — and thereby redeemed himself,[24] (6)then no one will hand (him, i.e., the murderer) over (to the injured party). (7)If he (i.e., the injured party) has taken them[25] (i.e., the items of compensation) together with his (the murderer's) wives (and) his sons, (8–9)then he (i.e., the injured party) will hand it/him/them[26] over to him (i.e., the murderer). If someone has paid compensation for theft, too, (10)and if it (the compensation) is a field, then they will not hand (him, i.e., the thief) over (to the injured party). (11)If a servant, though, has stolen, and he (i.e., the injured party) detains him for larceny, (12)and if he (the thief) has been blinded, (13)then they will not hand him (i.e., the thief) over to him (i.e., the injured party); (14)if he has not been blinded, (15)then they will hand him (i.e., the thief) over to him (i.e., the injured party).[27]

§6′ (16)If, however, some free man steals, (17)and compensation for the theft (is paid), (18)and [...], then they will not blind him. (19)[...] they will [... ha]nd him over.

§7′ (B_1 ii 5′–7′) (5′)[… *-š*]*i*? *na-aš-šu a-ki* (6′)[… *wa-a*]*š*(?)*-ta* (7′)[…]⸤*Ú*⸥*-UL šar-ni-ik-zi*

§8′ (B_1 ii 8′) […]x *wa*-x[…]

(remaining ca. two-thirds of col. ii and the first ca. two-thirds of col. iii missing entirely)

§9″ (A iii 1′–2′) (1′)[…]x (2′)[…]x*-ša-ri*

§10″ (A iii 3′–11′; B_3 iii 1′–7′; B_1 iii 1′–2′) (3′)[(*an-da-ma* LÚ) x] x x [x x x]x[28].GAL?ḪI.A*-TÌ ku-i-e-eš* (4′)⸢*ma-ni-ia*⸣*-aḫ-ḫi-iš-kán-z*[*i nu m*]*a-a-an* LUGAL*-wa-aš* ÉSAG*-an* (5′)*ki-nu-uz-zi na-aš-ma*~[x x]x[29] LÚSIG$_5$ *pé-e-ia-zi* (6′)*na-an ki-nu-ud-du* LÚ[ ]x[30]*-ma* LÚ.MEŠ*ḫa-at-tal-wa-la-aš* (7′) LÚAPIN.LÁ*-aš* LUGAL*-wa-aš* ÉSAG-[*an P*]*A-NI* ZI*-ŠU le-e ku-iš-ki ki-nu-uz-zi* (8′)*ku-iš ki-nu-uz-zi-ma* [*š*]*u-me-eš-ša-an* LÚMEŠ URU*-LÌ e-ep-tén* (9′)*na-an* LUGAL*-wa-aš a-aš-ki* ⸤*ú*⸥*-wa-te-et-tén ma-a-an Ú-UL-ma* (10′)*ú-wa-da-te-e-ni nu* [É]SAG*-an* LÚMEŠ URU*-LÌ šar-ni-in-kán-zi* (11′)*gi-nu-ut-ma-an ku-*⸢*iš*⸣ *na-an ša-ku-wa-an-zi*

§11″ (A iii 12′–18′; B_1 iii 3′–9′) (12′)*ku-iš-za-an ke-e-da-aš* LUGAL*-wa-aš ud-da-na-aš* (13′)*ka-ru-ú-uš-ši-ia-zi na-aš-za na-aš-šu* LÚ*a-ra-ši-iš* (14′)*mu-un-na-a-ši nu-*⸤*uš*⸥*-ši ma-aš-ka-an pa-a-i* (15′)*nu-za-ta*[31] *na-aš-šu* ⸢LÚ⸣*ma-ni-ia-aḫ-ḫa-an-da-aš-ša*[32] LÚḪA.LA*-ŠU* (16′)*pa-ra-a Ú-UL tar-na-i ne-ez-za-an ud-da-ni-i* EGIR*-an* (17′)*ták-ša-an Ú-UL ap-pí-ia-zi*[33] *ap-pé-ez-zi-ia-an-na* (18′)*ut-tar i-ši-ia-aḫ-ta-ri nu-uš* 2*-i-la-pát ša-ku-wa-an-zi*

§12″ (A iii 19′–20′; B_1 iii 10′–12′) (19′)*an-da-ma ma-a-an ḫa-an-na-an* DI-**šar ku***-iš-ki* EGIR*-pa da-a-i* (20′)*nu a-pa-a-at ut-tar* *SIG$_5$**-in pár-ku-wa-an-zi* (B_1 iii 12′) […]x-⸤*an*⸥ x-⸤*eš*?*-ḫa*?⸥-x[…]

(first ca. three-quarters of col. iv missing entirely)

§13″ (A iv 2′–8′) (2′)[…]x-⸢*ta-an*?*-ti*⸣ (3′)[…]*-mi na-an-ta* (4′)[…]x *IŠ-TU* ZI*-KU-NU-ma-aš-ma-aš* (5′)[…]x EN GIŠTUKUL*-ma PA-NI* ZI*-ŠU da-a-i* (6′)[… *n*]*a-*⸢*an*⸣ *ta-šu-wa-aḫ-ḫa-an-zi na-an* (7′)[x x] x x [… *n*]*a-aš-za ku-it ku-it da-a-an ḫar-zi* (8′)[*nu*] *ḫu-u-ma-*⸢*an*⸣[x x]⸢TA⸣ A AN[34] *pé-eš-ke-ez-zi*

COLOPHON

(A iv 9′–11′) (9′)[ ][35] *QA-TI* (10′)ŠU m*A.LI.*⸤*IḪ*⸥*.ḪI.*⸤*NI*⸥ DUMU mAN.ŠUR-LÚ DUMU.DUMU*-ŠÚ ŠA* mGIŠ.KIRI$_6$.NU (11′)GÁB.ZU.ZU [*Š*]*A* m*ZU.WA.A* EN GIŠ.KIN*-TI*

§7′ (5′)[…] or he dies (6′)[…] he [*rede*]*ems* (7′)[…] he will not compensate.

§8′ (traces)

(remaining ca. two-thirds of col. ii and the first ca. two-thirds of col. iii missing entirely)

§9″ (traces)

§10″ (3′–5′)[(Moreover, …-man/men) …] those who administer the […]-s: if he opens the royal grain storage pit, or […] sends an officer, (6′–7′)then he shall open it. A […]-man, the gatekeepers (or) a ploughman, however: no one shall open the royal grain storage pit *on his own accord.* (8′)Whoever does open it, though, you(pl.) men of the city must apprehend him (9′) and you(pl.) must bring him to the king's gate. If you(pl.) do not (10′)bring (him), though, the men of the city will compensate for the grain storage pit, (11′)while they will *sakuwa*-[36] the one who opened it.

§11″ (12′–13′)He[37] who remains inactive in these royal affairs, (i.e.) he or his associate, (14′)(and) you(sg.) conceal (it), then he gives him a bribe, (15′)and he or the associate of the *administrator*[38] (16′)does not hand (him) over, so that following the affair (17′)it is not (al)together finished, and afterwards (18′)the matter is made known, then they will *sakuwa*- the both of them.

§12″ (19′)Moreover, if anyone takes (up) an adjudicated case again, (20′)they will clarify the matter appropriately. […]

(first ca. three-quarters of col. iv missing entirely)

§13″ (3′)[…] I do/will do […], and […] him/it to/for you(sg.) (4′)[…] but […] them of your(pl.) own will (5′)[…], but the chief handworker takes/places […] of his own accord, (6′–7′)[…, the]n they will blind him, and […] him. And whatever he has taken, (8′)he will give all […].

COLOPHON

(9′)Finished. (10′)Hand of Aliḫḫini, son of AN.ŠUR-LÚ,[39] grandson of GIŠ.KIRI$_6$.NU, (11′)apprentice of Zuwā, chief of the *labor bureau*.[40]

No. 9
Tudḫaliya I's Decree on Judicial Reform (*CTH* 258.2)

Some aspects of this text were discussed already in the introduction to No. 8, as the two compositions are closely related. Only the first two paragraphs and the colophon of this single tablet, the second of an originally two-tablet set, are preserved, that is, only about five percent of the original composition. No findspot is known. These two sections appear to address procedural matters in the adjudication of law cases, whereby impeding the king in his judicial duties, if understood correctly (see n. 51), receives particular attention.

Pecchioli Daddi (2005b: 604) and Giorgieri (1995: 122–36) classify this document as an "oath," understandably enough, due to its explicit labeling as such in its colophon. There is, however, as far as is preserved, no mention of any oath. Naturally, lost portions of the composition may have included such; indeed the clear parallel between i 18–23 here and No. 12, §26″ (cf. nn. 49 and 186) suggests that this may well have been the case (Giorgieri 1995: 135 and

---

Transliteration

§1 (i 1)*[ma-a-an-ma-aš-ta*[41] *an-t]u-wa-aḫ-ḫa-aš* LUGAL-*un* **IŠ-TU** *DI*-**NI** *kar-ap-[zi]* (2)[…]x[42] *ŠA* A.ŠÀ *ḫa-an-né-eš-šar* (3)[…]*x x*-*pí?-ma-an*[43] *me-ma-i nu kat-te-ra-an še-er* (4)[… L]ÚMÁŠDA *da$_4$-mi-iš-*ḫa*-iz-zi* (5)[…] x-⸤*na?-ši?*[44] *ú?*⸥-*u!-wa!-e-ni*[45] EGIR-*an ú-e-mi-ia-u-e-ni* (6)[…]-⸢*u-e-ni*⸣ *n[u-u]š-ši-iš-ta šu-up-pa ar-ḫa da-an-zi* (7)*[na-an IŠ]-TU* ⸤LÚ?.MEŠ?⸥x x[46] ⸤*ar*⸥-*ḫa šu-wa-an-zi* (8)⸢*na-aš-ta*⸣ *nam-ma* ⸤É?.GAL? *Ú-UL*⸥ *šar-ra-at-ta-ri* (9)*ma-a-na-an-za ku-wa-pí-ma ap-pé-ez-zi-an* LUGAL-*uš* EGIR-*an kap-pu-u-e-ez-zi* (10)*na-aš A-NA* dUTU-*ŠI a-a-ra e-eš-du ma-a-na!-aš ap-pé-ez-zi-an-na* (11)*na-aš-šu*[47] LÚ*ME-ŠE-DI na-aš-ma* DUMU É.GAL *na-aš-ma* LÚUGULA *LI-IM* LÚDUGUD (12)*na-aš-ta* LUGAL-*un kar-ap-zi na-an ar-ḫa pár-ḫa-an-zi* (13)*KI-NA$_7$*[48] *IŠ-TU* É-*ŠU šar-ni-ik-zi*

§2 (i 14)*ma-a-na-at iš-ḫa-na-a-ša ut-tar an-tu-wa-aḫ-ḫa-aš na-aš-šu BE-EL DI-NI-ŠU* (15)*na-aš-ma-aš-ši kat-ta-wa-na-al-li-iš a-pa-a-ša-kán* LUGAL-*un kar-ap-zi* (16)*na-an-kán A-NA* LUGAL *iš-ši-iš-ši an-da pa-a-i na-aš-ta a-pu-u-un* (17)*an-tu-uḫ-ša-an ku-na-an-zi nu-za *a*-pa-a-aš kat-ta-wa-tar ša-na-aḫ-zi* (18)*nu a-pu-u-un* UN-*an A-NA* LUGAL *in-na-ra-a ku-na-an-na pa-a-i* (19)*ap-pé-ez-zi-an-na ú-e-mi-az-zi nu* ⸤*ni-wa-al*⸥-*la-an* (20)*an-tu-uḫ-ša-an ku-na-an-na pa-iš na-a[t?-ši?]* ⸤*a-a-ra-pát?*⸥[49] [ ]x x[ ] (21)*ud-da-ni-i ḫa-an-da-a*[50]-*an* SAG LUGAL *wa-[…]* (22)*na-aš ma-a-an BE-LU* GAL *na-aš-*

n. 30; del Monte 1975a: 129). The whole of the preserved text is placed in the mouth of the king, except for the quoted words in a mutilated passage or two toward the beginning of §1, which appear to represent the king's anticipation of some officials' reactions or excuses, a common device in the instructions. The main point of the two paragraphs seems to be a distinction between impeding the king in a law case involving property in which a verdict of banishment is given, which results merely in the person guilty of obstruction of justice being banished (from Ḫattusa?) on the one hand, and hindering him in a capital case leading to an execution, which is a capital crime, on the other. From the preserved contents the text would thus clearly be categorized as an edict or decree.

As noted, it is not clear (cf. Pecchioli Daddi 2006: 121 and n. 33) that this text is directed to specific categories of royal employees; it may have been directed to the "men of Ḫattusa," as are other instructions and edicts (cf. Introduction to No. 8). The categories of royal employees mentioned in this text are not addressed directly, but only referred to in the 3rd person.

TRANSLATION

§1 (1)[If, however], a [m]an *imped*[*es*][51] the king from (properly deciding) a law case, (2)[…] a law case of a plot of land (3)[…], "*my*[52] […]," he says, and […] the inferior (one) over (4)[…] he exploits the poor man, (5)"[…] *whereupon* we will *investigate*[53] (6)(and) we will […]," and they take (his) offering meat from him,[54] (7)[then] they will *expel* [*him* fr]om […], (8)so that he no longer sets foot in the *palace*; (9)if, however, the king reassesses him (i.e., his case) at some point, (10–12)then he shall be a legitimate (case) for His Majesty.[55] And if afterwards, too, he *impedes* the king – be he a royal body guard, a palace servant or a *clan* chief (or) a dignitary – they will drive him away. (13)He will pay the *appropriate* compensation from his estate.

§2 (14)If it (i.e., the law case) is a matter of blood(shed), though, (and) a man — either his legal opponent (15)or his avenger — that (man) *impedes* the king, (16–17)(in that) he surrenders him to the king's judgment, and they execute that man, (i.e.) he is seeking vengeance (18)and he deliberately gives that man to the king to be executed, (19)and thereafter he finds (that) (20)he gave an innocent man to be executed — then *i*[*t*] *is in no case permissible* [*for him*]; (21)in (that) matter the person of the king truly […]; (22) be he a great lord, be he the lowli[est …] (23)man, he shall surely die. The *ma-aš ap-pé-e*[*z-zi-aš* …] (23)*an-tu-wa-aḫ-ḫa-aš na-aš a-ku-pát* LUGAL-*uš-za* […] (24)*na-at-ta-at-ši a-a-ra* […]

(remainder of composition, except for colophon, entirely lost)

COLOPHON

(iv 1′)DUB.2.KAM m*TU.UD.ḪA.LI.*˹*IA* LUGAL.GAL˺[ ] (2′)*ŠA MA*-**ME-TI* x x* *QA-TI*

(iv 3′)*ki-i TUP-PU ar-ḫa ḫar-ra-*an* {AŠ} *e*-eš-*[*ta*][56] (4′)*na-at A-NA PA-NI* m*MA.AḪ.ḪU.ZI* (5′)*Ù A-NA* m*ḪAL.WA*-LÚ (6′)*ú-uk* m*Du-da-aš* (7′)EGIR-*pa ne-wa-aḫ-ḫu-un*

king himself […],[57] ⁽²⁴⁾it is not permissible for him.

(remainder of composition, except for colophon, lost)

COLOPHON

⁽¹′⁾Second Tablet (*of*) Tudḫaliya, Great King, ⁽²′⁾[ ] of the Oath; finished.

⁽³′⁾This tablet wa[s] damaged, ⁽⁴′–⁷′⁾and I, Duda, renewed it in the presence of Maḫḫuzi and Ḫalwa-ziti.

No. 10
Tudḫaliya I?'s Instructions and Oath Imposition for All the Men (*CTH* 259)

This composition is preserved by four fragmentary tablets, two larger pieces or joined blocks of fragments (B and C) and two smaller pieces (A and D). It seems that ms. A is likely the only representative of Tablet I, the other three mss. thus belonging to the second of the two-tablet text. Altogether something along the lines of twenty percent of the original composition is preserved. The sequence of the fragmentary passages from C iii // D_1 iii (§§15″–17″), B ii (§§18″–19″), B iii (§§20″–21″) and C iv (§§22″–24″) is quite uncertain. All mss. are thirteenth-century copies except C, which, as Košak (*Konkordanz*) has noted, *pace* Klinger and Neu (1990: 146), is rather older, probably to be dated to the late MH or early NH period. *Pace* Starke (1996: 173, n. 144), ms. B cannot be dated to the end of the fourteenth century, but belongs rather to the second half of the thirteenth. Both C and D_1, the only ms. for which findspots are available, come from the Temple I complex.

While older treatments (e.g., Alp 1947) dated the composition to Tudḫaliya IV, more recent discussions (e.g., del Monte 1975a: 134, 140) have dated it to Tudḫaliya III or Tudḫaliya IV or to Tudḫaliya I or III (Giorgieri 2005: 326–27). In the present treatment it is assumed that Pecchioli Daddi (2005a: 281) is likely correct in dating it to Tudḫaliya I, though a dating to Tudḫaliya III should not at this point be ruled out.

Alp's (1947) edition restored numerous passages after No. 7 (KUB 26.17), though, as emphasized by del Monte (1975a), the two compositions are only somewhat similar, not really parallel or duplicate. Restorations in the present treatment are consequently more reserved. As Giorgieri (2005: 326–29, 343–44) has demonstrated, the structure of this composition is actually quite similar to that of Arnuwanda I's Treaty with the Men of Ismeriga and the much more fragmentary Texts Nos. 22 and 23 (cf. also No. 14).

Giorgieri (2005: 327 and n. 22) has also shown that the title "Militärinstruktionen eines Tutḫalijas" is misleading and has argued that the composition should be regarded as a loyalty oath. In the present treatment it is regarded as a set of instructions and/or directives coupled with the imposition of an oath; it is, however, not itself an oath. Nor are the directives addressed to the military alone, but specifically to lords (§§4″, 12″) and governors of the posts (§4″) responsible for troops and chariotry, primarily, but not only, with regard to military matters. Though §1′ may well have been placed in the mouth of the subordinates in question in the 1st pl. (see n. 60), this cannot at present be verified due to the fragmentary condition of the tablet, and the entire remainder of the text following the list of deities (§2′) is without question spoken by the king and addressed to his subordinates; in this it is similar to No. 27, §1. It is therefore the set of obligations upon which the subordinates likely would have sworn their oath, but is not the oath per se. In the colophon it is labeled with the term *isḫiul-*, "obligation."

The stipulations enumerated consist of a series of instructions and directives regarding appropriate behavior as military leaders and governors. In §3″ the subordinates are seemingly warned against trying to falsely influence the opinion (of the king?) about someone (cf. No. 2, §22″), while §4″ switches to the responsibilities of lords and governors of the posts in charge of troops and chariotry to mobilize immediately and without excuse when called upon to do so. In §7″, and seemingly already in §6″, the governors of the posts are instructed to reveal to the palace immediately any officer assigned to their jurisdiction who might not promptly heed a call to mobilization or who even deserts. Paragraph 8″ concerns willingness to take part in military campaigns and in any work details associated with them, while §9″ clarifies who is to decide who will be released from duty and who is to remain after a campaign is finished. Paragraphs 9″ and 10″ touch on obedience to any prince or great lord whom the king might place in charge in his stead, and §11″ essentially repeats the previous clauses,[58] adding, however, the detail that such decisions will be made by the king on the basis of oracle inquiry. Especially interesting is §12″, in which the subordinates addressed are actually required to contravene the previous instructions to obey whomever is placed in charge of the military in the king's stead and to arrest him if he is deemed to speak against his sovereign. Paragraph 13″ consists of an admonition to maintain the same affection for the king as one would for one's own family and property. In §14″ are found stipulations concerning the proper handling of law cases in the provinces, echoing No. 17, §§37′–38′ and Mursili II's Dictate to Tuppi-Teššub's Syrian Antagonists (*CTH* 63.II; Miller 2007a: 130 and n. 39). After a further gap §16″ stipulates that peace agreements can be made by responsible officials, but that the king must be consulted before any oaths are sworn upon them. The last halfway-intelligible paragraph detailing directives (§17″) discusses captives from the Kaska territories and apparently the question of releasing them on one's own authority. Finally, §25″ invokes the oath deities to destroy whoever would not obey the words of the tablet.

TRANSLITERATION

(gap of probably only a few lines)

§1′ (A i 1′–6′) (1′)[...]x x x[...] (2′)[... KU]R URU*ḪA.AT.TI* [...] (3′)[...] *A-NA* SAG.DU [mRN LUGAL.GAL][59] (4′)[x x x] x [fRN MUNUS.LUGAL.G]AL *Ù* [*A-NA* mRN] (5′)[*kat-ta ḫa-aš-ša*] ⌈*ḫa-an-za-aš*⌉*-ša še-er* [*link-* ...] (6′)[*nu ka-a-š*]*a*(?) *k*[*e*]-⌈*e-da*⌉*-ni li-in-ki-*[*ia*[60] ...]

§2′ (A i 7′–17′) (7′)[dUTU *Š*]*A-ME-E* dUTU URU*A.RI.IN.NA* d[...] (8′)[dIŠ]KUR? URU*ZI.IP.PA.LA.AN.TA* dIŠKU[R ...] (9′)[dIŠK]UR URU*NE.RI.IK* dIŠKUR URU*ḪA*.[...] (10′)[dIŠK]UR URU*ŠA.MU.U.ḪA* dIŠKUR KI.LA[M ...] (11′)[d*Z*]*i-it-ḫa-ri-ia-an* dLAMMA U[RU ...] (12′)[d]⌈É⌉.A[61]*-an* d*Te-li-pí-nu-un* d[...] (13′)[d*A*]*š-ka-še-pa-an* MUNUS.LUGAL*-an* ⌈d⌉[[62] ...] (14′)[d*ḪÉ.BA*]*T*? MUNUS.LUGAL d*IŠTAR ṢÉ-R*[*I* ...] (15′)[...]d*ZA-BA*$_4$*-BA*$_4$ d*IA.A*[*R.RI* ...] (16′)[...]x*-ma-aš* d˻*ḪA*?*.AT*?˼.x[...] (17′)[...]x x x[...]

(ca. three cols. entirely missing)

§2″ (C i 0′) [...]x*-mi*[63]

§3″ (C i 1′–6′) (1′)*na-*⌈*an*⌉ *m*[*a*?*-* ...] (2′)*nu-uš-ša-an wa-*x[...]x (3′)*ar-nu-ut-tén ma-aḫ-ḫ*[*a-an* ...] (4′)SIG$_5$*-ta-an i-da-a-lu* *x*[...] (5′)SIG$_5$*-ta-an le-e me-ma-*x[...] (6′)*a-aš-ši-ia-nu-zi le-e* x[...]x~⌈*ma*?*-kán*?⌉*-*x⌉[...] (7′)*pu-uk-ku-nu-zi le-e* [...]

§4″ (C i 8′–18′) (8′)*an-da-ma-az* LÚ.MEŠ*BE-LU-TÌ ku-i-*⌈*e-eš*⌉ *šu-me-eš* LÚ.MEŠ*BE-EL MAD-GA-LA-TU*$_4$ (9′)ÉRINMEŠ ANŠE.KUR.RAMEŠ *ku-i-e-eš ma-ni-ia-aḫ-ḫi-iš-ke-et-te-ni* (10′)[*nu*] ˻*ma-aḫ-ḫa-an BE*?˼*-*[*LÍ*? ÉRI]NM[EŠ ANŠE.KU]R.RAMEŠ *ni-ni-in-ku-wa-aš me-ḫur ti-i-e-zi* (11′)[... ÉRINMEŠ A]NŠE.KUR.RAMEŠ *ni-ni-in-ku-wa-an-zi* (12′)[...] *Ú-UL MA-ḪAR* dUTU*-ŠI* (13′)[... *me-ma*]-˻*i*˼ ÉRINMEŠ*-wa-mu-uš-ša-an* ANŠE.KUR.R[AMEŠ] (14′)[... ÉRINMEŠ AN]ŠE.KUR.RAMEŠ *ni-ni-ik-tén* (15′)[... *ḫu-u-d*]*a-a-ak ar-nu-ut-tén* (16′)[... *ni-ni-i*]*n-ku-wa-an-zi* (17′)[... *ša-ku*]-˻*wa*˼*-aš-ša-ri-it* (18′)[ZI*-it* ...]

§5″ (C i 19′) (traces)

(gap of up to ca. one-half column)

§6″ (A iv 1′–5′; C ii 1′–3′) (1′)⌈*I*?*-NA*⌉[[64] ...] (2′)*nu-za da-a-*⌈*i*⌉[...] (3′)*na-aš-ma ap-p*[*é-ez-zi-iš* ...] (4′)*ú-wa-te-ez-z*[*i* ... *k*(*u*?*-iš I-DE*)] (5′)*na-an I-NA* É.[GAL*-LÌ te-ek-k*(*u-uš-ša-nu-ud-du*)]

§7″ (B i 1–5; A iv 6′–13′; C ii 4′–12′) (1)[(*A-NA* LÚ*BE-EL MAD-GAL*$_9$*-T*)]*I-*⌈*ma*?⌉*-aš-kán ku-e-da-ni an-da* LÚSIG$_5$ *la-aḫ-ḫi-ma-aš Ú-UL pa-a-an-za* LÚ*BE-EL*

TRANSLATION

(gap of probably only a few lines)

§1′ (2′)[... La]nd of Ḫattusa [...] (3′)[...] to the person [of RN, Great King] (4′)[... to RN, Gre]at [Queen], and [to RN ...] (5′)(and) [thereafter progeny] and descendents [... swear] upon, (6′)[and *here*]*by* to [t]his oath [...]

§2′ (7′)[Sun God of He]aven, Sun Goddess of Arinna, deity [...] (8′)[Sto]rm God of Zippalanta, Sto[rm God ...] (9′)[Stor]m God of Nerik, Storm God of Ḫa-[...] (10′)[Sto]rm God of Samūḫa, Storm God of the Gateh[ouse ...] (11′)[Z]itḫariya, tutelary deity of the ci[ty of ...] (12′)Ea, Telipinu, deity [...] (13′)[A]skasepa the queen, deity [...] (14′)[Ḫeba]t the queen, Ištar of the Battlefie[ld, ...] (15′)[...] Zababa, Iya[rri ...] (16′)[...] *Ḫat*-[...]

(ca. three cols. entirely missing)

§2″ (0′)[...] *I will* [...].

§3″ (1′)And [...] him [...] (2′)and [...] (3′)you[65] must bring; wh[en ...] (4′)good(acc. comm. sg.) (*or*) evil [...] (5′)good(acc. comm. sg.) must not say. [...] (6′–7′)[...] he shall not cause to be favored, [...] *but* he shall not cause to be disfavored.

§4″ (8′–9′)Moreover, those of you lords, those of you governors of the posts who are responsible for troops (and) chariotry: (10′)As soon as the time comes *for a lo*[*rd*] for the mobilizing of the [troo]ps (and) [char]iotry, (11′)[...] to mobilize [troops] (and) [ch]ariotry (12′)[...] not in the presence of My Majesty (13′)[... say]s: "[...] troops and chariot[ry] to me (14′)[...];" you shall mobilize the [troops] (and) [ch]ariotry. (15′)You must bring [... imm]ediately. (16′–18′)[... to mob]ilize [... wh]oleh[eartedly ...]

§5″ (traces)

(gap of up to ca. one-half column)

§6″ (1′)[...] *in* [...] (2′)and he takes/places himself [...] (3′)or an infan[try soldier ...] (4′)he brings [... (he) *w*(*ho* knows) ...], (5′)then [(he shall) rev(eal)] him in the pal[ace].

§7″ (1)However, to whatever [(govern)]or [(of the post)] an officer is assigned who will not go into battle, [(but)] the gove[(rnor) of the] post [... (him)],

MA-AD-G[(*AL*$_9$-*TU*$_4$-*ma-an*)] (2)[x x x x x *ma-aḫ-ḫ*(*a-a*)]*n*[66] *iš-ta-ma-aš-zi na-an e-ep-du na-an I-NA* É.GAL-*LÌ up-pa-ú da-a-i-ma-az* (3)[(*le-e*) *na-an ar-ḫ*]*a le-e tar-na-a-i ma-a-an-kán* ^{LÚ}SIG$_5$ *na-aš-ma ap-pé-ez-zi-iš an-tu-wa-aḫ-ḫa-aš* [ ] (4)[(*la-aḫ-ḫa-az* KASKAL-*az* EG)I]R-*pa ḫu-u-wa-a-i* ^{LÚ}DUGUD-*ŠU-ma-an* UGULA *LI-IM-ia le-e mu-un-na-iz-zi* (5)*I-NA* [(É.GAL-*LÌ-ia-an*) *ḫu*]-*u-da-a-ak te-ek-ku-uš-ša-nu-ud-du*

§8″ (B i 6–9; C ii 13′–20′) (6)*ma-aḫ-ḫa-an-*[*ma tu-uz*]-*zi-iš* ÉRIN^{MEŠ} ANŠE.KUR.RA$^{ḪI.A}$ *an-da a-ri nu ma-a-an* ^{d}UTU-*ŠI la-aḫ-ḫi a-pa-a-ši-la i-ia-at-ta* (7) *nu ŠA* ⸢LÚ?⸣[x x] *ḫu-u-ma-an-da-aš ḫu-u-da-aš e-eš-du nu* ^{LÚ}KÚR *kar-ši za-aḫ-ḫi-ia-ad-du-ma-at ma-a-an* KIN-⸤*ma*⸥ *ku-it-k*[(*i*)] (8)*na-aš-ma ú-*[*e-tum-m*]*ar na-aš-ma ku-iš im-ma* KIN-*az nu-uš-ša-an an-da ar-du-ma-at na-an ša-a-ku-wa-aš-š*[(*a-ri-i*)*t*] (9)⸤ZI-*it*⸥ *an-ni-iš-ke-et-tén na-at ŠA* EGIR!(TUM) UD-*MI pa-aḫ-ḫa-aš-ša-nu-wa-an* KIN *e-eš-*[*d*(*u*)]

§9″ (B i 10–15; C ii 21′–31″; D$_1$ ii 1′–10″) (10)*ma-aḫ-ḫa-an-ma* ^{LÚ}KÚR *a-ki na-aš-ma-kán* KIN *aš-ša-nu-ud-da-a-ri nu ku-iš* ÉRIN^{MEŠ} *a-ša-an-du-la-aš na-an-kán* ^{d}UT[(U-*ŠI*)] (11)*a-ša-an-du-li an-da ta-la-aḫ-ḫi ku-iš ar-ḫa tar-nu-um-ma-aš-ma* ÉRIN^{MEŠ}-*az na-an* ^{d}UTU-*ŠI ar-ḫa tar-n*[*a-aḫ-ḫi*] (12) *ma-a-an* ^{LÚ}KÚR-*ma ku-wa-at-ka*$_4$ *za-lu-ga-nu-zi ku-u-ru-ur ku-iš* {*KI*} *ḫar-zi* ^{d}UTU-*ŠI-ma* EGIR-*pa A-NA* DINGIR^{MEŠ}-[*IA* DÙ-*wa-an-zi*][67] (13)*ú-wa-mi na-aš-ma ku-wa-pí A-NA* ^{d}UTU-*ŠI a-aš-šu nu* ^{d}UTU-*ŠI a-pád-da pa-iz-zi tu-uz-zi-ia-*⸤*ma*⸥ *pé-ra-an ma-a-a*[(*n* DUMU LUGAL)] (14)*na-aš-ma BE-EL* GAL *ku-in-ki wa-a-tar-na-aḫ-mi nu ma-aḫ-ḫa-an ŠA* ^{d}UTU-*ŠI iš-ḫi-ú-ul a-pé-el-la QA-TAM-*<(*MA*)> ⸢*e*?⸣-[*eš-ša-at-tén*][68] (15)[*na-a*]*n tu-uz-zi-iš ḫu-u-ma-an-za iš-ta-ma-aš-ke-ed-du*

§10″ (B i 16–19; C ii 32″–38″; D$_1$ ii 11′–16″) (16)[(*m*)]*a-a-an* ^{d}UTU-*ŠI-ma la-aḫ-ḫi ú-ki-la Ú-UL pa-a-i-mi nu tu-uz-zi-ia ku-in* DUMU LUGAL *na-aš-ma BE-E*[*L* GAL] (17)*wa-a-tar-na-aḫ-mi nu tu-uz-zi-in la-aḫ-ḫi a-pa-a-aš pé-e-ḫu-te-ez-zi nu-uš-ši-kán ku-it* ^{d}UTU-*ŠI* ⸢*ú*?⸣-[*ki-la*[69] *tu-uz-zi-in*] (18)*ki-iš-ša-ri te-eḫ-ḫi na-an tu-uz-zi-iš ḫu-u-ma-an-za iš-ta-ma-aš-ke-ed-du nu ŠA* ^{d}UTU-*ŠI* [(*i*)*š-ḫi-ú-ul ma-aḫ-ḫa-an a-pé-el-la QA-TAM-MA*][70] (19)*iš-ša-at-tén nu ḫu-u-ma-an-za ḫu-u-da ḫar-du nu* ^{LÚ}KÚR *kar-ši za-aḫ-ḫi-ia-ad-du-ma-*[*at*]

§11″ (B i 20–25; C ii 39″–43″) (20)*ma-a-an ú-e-tum-mar-ma ku-it-ki na-aš-ma ku-iš im-ma ku-iš a-ni-ia-az nu-uš-ša-an an-da ar-d*[*u-ma-at*] (21)*na-an ša-ku-wa-aš-ša-ri-it* ZI-*it* KIN-*eš-ke-tén na-at ŠA* EGIR.UD-*MI pa-aḫ-ḫa-aš-nu-an* KIN *e-eš-d*[*u*] (22)*ma-aḫ-ḫa-an-ma* ^{LÚ}KÚR *a-ki na-aš-ma-kán* KIN-*az a-aš-ša-nu-ud-da-a-ri nu tu-uz-zi-iš MA-ḪA*[*R* ^{d}UTU-*ŠI*] (23)*ú-ez-zi na-an* ^{d}UTU-*ŠI ar-ḫa a-ri-ia-mi nu ku-iš ar-ḫa tar-nu-ma-aš na-an* ^{d}UTU-*ŠI ar-*[*ḫa*

(2–3)[... as so(on)] as he hears (about) him, he must seize him, and he must send him to the palace. But [... (not)] take/place himself, [and] he must not let [him g]o. If an officer or an infantry soldier (4)flees [(from a campaign)], his commander and his *clan* chief must not conceal him. (5) He must reveal [(him)] in the [(palace) im]mediately.

§8″ (6)[But] as soon as the [ar]my, (i.e.) the troops and the chariotry, arrive, and if His Majesty himself goes on campaign, (7)then there shall be promptness on the part of all [...]-men, and you must fight the enemy unreservedly. When there is some task, though, (8–9)either cons[truc]tion duty or any task whatsoever, you must show up for it, and you must perform it wholehe[(art)]edly, as it should be a robust, long-lasting achievement.[71]

§9″ (10–11)However, as soon as the enemy has been vanquished or the work has been performed, then the troops that are to remain for the occupation, I, [(My Ma)]jesty, will leave them for the occupation, while whatever troops are to be released, I, My Majesty, [will] relea[se]. (12–14)But when an enemy that retains hostility somehow persists, but I, My Majesty, come back in order [to venerate my] gods, or His Majesty goes wherever His Majesty pleases, and if I place some [(prince)] or great lord in command of the army, then just like the command of My Majesty [you must] ca[rry out] his (command) likew<(ise)>, (15)[and] the whole army must obey [hi]m.

§10″ (16)But if I, My Majesty, do not go on campaign myself, then whatever prince or [great] lord (17–19)I place in command of the army will lead the army on campaign, and since I, My Majesty, *p[ersonally*] place the [army] in his hand, the whole army shall obey him. And [*just like the* (*co*)*mmand*] of My Majesty you shall [likewise] carry out [his as well]. And everyone shall maintain readiness, and you sh[all] fight the enemy unreservedly.

§11″ (20)When there is some construction duty, though, or any task whatsoever, [you mu]st show up for (it), (21)and you must perform it wholeheartedly, as it shou[ld] be a robust, long-lasting achievement. (22–23)However, as soon as the enemy has been vanquished or the work has been performed and the army comes (to appear) befo[re My Majesty], I, My Majesty, will inquire about it by means of an oracle; then, what(ever) (troop) is to be

tar-na-aḫ-ḫi] (24)*ku-iš-ša* ÉRIN^{MEŠ} *a-ša-an-du-la-aš-ma na-an-kán* ^{d}UTU-*ŠI a-ša-an-du-la-an-ni da-a-la-aḫ-ḫi ma-a-a*[*n-ma*] (25)*tu-uz-zi-iš MA-ḪAR* ^{d}UTU-*ŠI Ú-UL ú-ez-zi* **nu** ^{d}UTU-*ŠI tu-u-wa-az ma-aḫ-ḫa-an ḫa-at-ra-a-mi n*[*u*[72] *QA-TAM-MA iš-ša-at-tén*]

§12″ (B i 26–29; D_2, 1′–3′) (26)*ma-a-an-kán a-pa-a-aš-ma* DUMU LUGAL *na-aš-ma BE-LU*$_4$ *tu-uz-zi-ia pé-ra-an ar-ḫa i-da-a-lu ut-tar pé-e-ḫu-te-*[*ez-zi*] (27)*na-aš-ta* ^{d}UTU-*ŠI za-am-mu-ra-a-iz-zi šu-ma-aš-ša-an e-ep-tén na-an MA-ḪAR* ^{d}UTU-*ŠI ú-wa-te-et-tén* (28)*nu ú-wa-mi* ^{d}UTU-*ŠI ut-tar ú-ki-la pu-nu-uš-mi BE-LU*^{MEŠ} *ku-i-e-eš* ÉRIN^{MEŠ} ANŠE.KUR.RA$^{\text{ḪI.A}}$ *a-ú-ri-uš* (29)*ma-a-ni-ia-aḫ-ḫi-iš-ket*$_9$*-te-ni nu-uš-ša-an ša-ku-wa-aš-ša-ri-it* ZI-*it kat-ta-an ti-ia-an ḫar-tén*

§13″ (B i 30–31; D_2, 4′–7′) (30)*nu-za šu-um-me-eš ma-aḫ-ḫa-an tu-ek-ka*$_4$*-aš-ša*[73] *A-NA* DAM^{MEŠ}-*KU-NU* DUMU^{MEŠ}-*KU-NU* É^{MEŠ}-*KU-NU ge-en-zu ḫar-te-ni* (31)LUGAL-*u-wa-aš ša-ak-li-ia ge-en-zu QA-TAM-MA ḫar-tén na-at* SIG$_5$-*in ma-a-ni-ia-aḫ-ḫi-iš-ke-et-tén*

§14″ (B i 32–37) (32)*DI-NA*$_7$$^{\text{ḪI.A}}$ KUR-*TI ku-e ḫa-an-ni*$_5$*-iš-ket*$_9$*-te-e-ni na-at* SIG$_5$-*in ḫa-an-ni-iš-ke-et-tén na-at-za-kán a-pé-e-el* (33)*ŠA* É-*ŠU ŠA* ŠEŠ-*ŠU* DAM-*ŠU ḫa-aš-ša-an-na-aš-ši pa-an-ku-na-aš-ši* ^{LÚ}*ka-e-na-an-ti*[74] ^{LÚ}*a-re-eš-ši* (34)**ŠA** NINDA$^{!}$ [75] KAŠ *ma-a-ni-ia-aḫ-ḫi-ia-at-ti*[76] **le**-*e ku-iš-ki i-ia-zi nu ša-ra-a-az-zi* DI-*šar* (35)*le-e kat-te-er-ra-aḫ-te-e-ni kat-te-er-ra-ma ḫa-an-ne-eš-šar le-e ša-ra-a-az-zi-ia-aḫ-te-ni* (36)*ku-it-ma* DI-*šar šu-me-el Ú-UL tar-aḫ-ḫu-u-wa-aš na-at* LUGAL-*ia*[77] *ŠA*$^{!}$ *BE-LÍ-KU-NU me-na-aḫ-ḫa-an-da* (37)*ú-da-at-tén na-at* LUGAL-*uš a-pa-a-ši-la pu-nu-uš-zi*

(gap of probably less than half a column)

§15″ (C iii 1′–4′; D_1 iii 1′–4′) (1′)[…]x-⌜*aš*?⌝ *Ú-UL ḫa-a*[(*t-ra-a-te-ni*)] (2′)[…]x-*i na-a-i-i*[*š-t*(*e-ni*)] (3′)[… *p*]*u*?-⌜*nu*?-*uš-ket*$_9$⌝*-te-ni na-at* [(x-*pát ku-ni-l*)]*i*? (4′)[… *ḫ*]*a-at-re-eš-ket*$_9$*-te-ni* [ ]

§16″ (C iii 5′–11′; D_1 iii 5′–8′) (5′)[… *k*]*u-it-ki na-aš-ma an-tu-wa-aḫ-ḫa-aš ku-iš-k*[*i*] (6′)[… EGI]R?-*TI ták-šu-la-a-iz-zi nu-uš-ši* ˻*a*˼*-pa-a-aš BE-EL MAD-GAL*$_9$*-TU*$_4$ (7′)[… (x-*da*)] *NI-IŠ* DINGIR-*LÌ* ZI-*it le-e i-e-zi* (8′)[… ^{d}UTU-*ŠI*(?)-*i*]*a-at ḫa-at-ra-a-i-id-du n*[*a-a*]*t-za ma-aḫ-ḫa-an* (9′)[…]x *ar-ḫa a-ri-ia-zi ma-a-an a-ra-aḫ-zé-na-ša* (10′)[…]-*e-ra-an ú-e-ek-zi na-an-ši BE-EL MAD-*˻*GAL*$_9$˼*-TU*$_4$ (11′)[…]x-*i A-NA* ^{d}UTU-*ŠI-ia-an ḫa-at-ra-a-i-id-du*

§17″ (C iii 12′–16′) (12′)[…]x *ku-i-e-eš IŠ-TU* KUR ^{LÚ}KÚR *i-ia-*˻*an*˼*-ta-ri* (13′)[… $^{\text{LÚ.MEŠ}}$*a*]*p-pa-an-du-uš*(?) *IŠ-TU* KUR ^{URU}*GA.AŠ.GA* (14′)[…]˻*I*˼*-NA* KUR ^{LÚ}KÚR ZI-*it* EGIR-*pa* (15′)[… Z]I-*it le-e* […] (16′)[… -*d*]*u na-an* Z[I]-˻*it*˼

released, I, My Majesty, [will release] them, (24)while the troops that are to remain for the occupation, I, My Majesty, will leave them for the occupation. [But] when (25)the army does not appear before My Majesty, th[en you shall proceed as] I, My Majesty, write from afar.

§12″ (26)However, if that prince or great lord in charge of the army speak[s] a malevolent word, (27)and he disparages My Majesty, then you must seize him, and you must bring him before My Majesty, (28–29)and I, My Majesty, will thereupon inquire into the situation myself. You lords in command of the troops, chariotry, (and) (frontier) posts, you must remain loyal with your whole heart.

§13″ (30)And just as you hold dear (your own) persons, your wives, your sons (and) your homes, (31)you shall also feel affection for the imperative of the king, and you must govern them[78] well.

§14″ (32–35)The provincial law cases that you decide, you must decide well. No one shall do it for the *provision* of bread and beer for his (own) estate, for his brother, his wife, his kin, his clan, his in-law, (or) his colleague. You must not make a superior case inferior, neither shall you make an inferior case superior. (36–37)A law case that you cannot manage yourselves, though, you must bring before the king, your lord, and the king himself will investigate it.

(gap of probably less than half a column)

§15″ (1′)[… (you do)] not wri[(te)] (2′)[… (you)] turn to (3′)[…] you [*int*]*errogate*, and […] it [(*for the bett*)]*er*[79] (4′)[…] you write repeatedly.

§16″ (5′)[…] some […] or some man (6′–8′)[… *low ra*]*nk* makes peace, and that frontier post governor […] to/for him, he shall not conclude the oath on his own volition, […] he shall write about it to [*My Majesty*], an[d] as soon as (9′)[…] he investigates [i]t by means of an oracle, if exterior/foreign, though, (10′)[…] he demands/requests, then the governor of the post (11′)[…] him to him […] he shall write about him to My Majesty.

§17″ (12′)[…] those who journey from an enemy land (13′)[… *c*]*aptives* from the Gasga territory (14′)[…] back into the enemy land […] on his own volition (15′)[…] shall not […] on his own [vol]ition (16′)[… he sh]all, and […] him on his own vo[lit]ion. […]

(gap of probably less than half a column)

§18″ (B ii 1′–8′) (1′)x[…] (2′) L[Ú …] (3′)*nu-u*[*š* …] (4′)*a-ra*-[…] (5′)*ku-i*[*š*? …] (6′) DINGIR?-*L*[*A*12 …] (7′) LÚx[…] (8′)*ki-i*[*t*? …]

§19″ (B ii 9′) x[…]

(gap of up to ca. 1 column)

§20″ (B iii 1′–5′) (1′)*n*[*u*? …] (2′)*m*[*a*?- …] (3′) LÚx[…] (4′) LÚx[…] (5′)*A-N*[*A*? …]

§21″ (B iii 6′) AN[…]

(gap of probably less than half a column)

§22″ (C iv 1′–4′) (1′)x[…] (2′)*na*-[…] (3′)*na*-x[…] (4′)*Ú-U*[*L* …]

§23″ (C iv 5′–9′) (5′)*ŠA* […] (6′)*l*[*a*?- …] (7′)˹*Ú*?˺-[*UL*? …] (8′)*Ú*-[*UL*? …] (9′)*ḫa*-[…]

§24″ (C iv 10′) *Ú*-[*UL*? …]

(gap of probably less than half a column)

§25″ (B iv 1′–6′) (1′)x˹ḪI.A-*KU-NU*˺ *x* *ḫ*[*u-u-ma-an*~ …] (2′)*ki-na-a-at-tén nu-k*[*án* …] (3′)*zi-ia-du*[80] *ŠA an-t*[*u-wa-aḫ-ḫa-aš*(?)…] (4′)*ke-e-el tup-pí-aš ud-da-a-ar p*[*a-aḫ-ša-ri* …] (5′)*ku-i-ša ke-e-el tup-pí-ia-aš ud*-˹*da-a*˺-[*ar*] ˹*Ú-UL*˺ *pa-aḫ-ša-r*[*i*[81] *na-an ke-e*] (6′)*NI-ÌŠ* DINGIRMEŠ *ḫar-ni-in-kán*-{*du*} *du*

COLOPHON

(B iv 7′–8′) (7′)DUB.2.KAM *QA-TI ŠA* m*DU.UT.ḪA.LI.IA iš-ḫi-ú-la*[82] (8′)UNMEŠ-*an-na-aš ḫu-u-ma-an-da-aš*

(gap of probably less than half a column)

§18″ (1′)[…] (2′)m[an …], (3′)and […] th[em …] (4′)*arri*[*ve* …] (5′)*he wh*[*o* …] (6′)the deity […] (7′)man […] (8′)*pla*[*ced* …]

§19″ (trace)

(gap of up to ca. 1 column)

§20″ […] (1′–2′)*a*[*nd* …] (3′)man […] (4′)man […] (5′)*t*[*o* …]

§21″ (trace)

(gap of probably less than half a column)

§22″ […] (2′)and […] (3′)and […] (4′)no[t …]

§23″ (5′–6′)Of […] (7′)*n*[*ot* …] (8′–9′)no[t …]

§24″ (10′)No[t …]

(gap of probably less than half a column)

§25″ (1′)[…] your en[tire …] (2′)you must *break apart*/*sort*, and […] he/it must […] (3′)… of a *m*[*an* …] (4′)[he shall] ob[serve] the words of this tablet. […] (5′–6′)But let [these] oath deities destroy whoever does not obey the wor[d]s of this tablet!

COLOPHON

(7′)Tablet Two, finished, of the Obligations of Tudḫaliya, (8′)for All the Men.

No. 11
Instructions and Oath Impositions for the Successions of Tudḫaliya I and Tudḫaliya III (*CTH* 271)

The three compositions grouped together here, despite their very fragmentary state of preservation, have received a great deal of scholarly attention (see Sources), above all due to their historical content relevant to a complex period that otherwise suffers from a dearth of documentation and is therefore ardently debated, namely, the generations preceding Suppiluliuma.

The fragments would seem likely to belong to three, perhaps just two, compositions. All of them were found in or associated with Building A of the royal palace, unlike most of the other instructions; all are MH tablets. The first set (A_{1-7}) appears to constitute a decree or series of directives along with the prescription of an oath, likely for the occasion of the enthronement of Tudḫaliya I, and as such it includes several passages apparently intended to justify his installation in the aftermath of the murder of Muwattalli I at the hands of Ḫimuili and Tudḫaliya's father, Kantuzili. In this it seems to present an analogue to §§32″–35″ of No. 12. The text is styled as presented to the sons of Ḫimuili and Kantuzili in particular (A_1, §§2′, 4′) and to the nobility of Ḫattusa in general (A_1, §5′), while at some points it addresses a single individual in the 2nd sg. (e.g., A_1, §§2′–3′, A_2, §4′), perhaps Tudḫaliya himself. Though it seems more or less likely that all seven pieces (A_{1-7}) belong to a single tablet, *inter alia*, due to their similar scripts, this cannot presently be ascertained for certain. Four of its fragments were found within Rooms 4–5 of Building A on the Büyükkale, two further pieces nearby (see the *Konkordanz*). All seven fragments together would constitute about a tenth of the text of the original tablet.

The second group (B_{1-2}) may in fact belong to the first composition (e.g., Beckman 1982: 441, n. 74), but since it preserves only the PN Ḫattusili, whose historical setting is still disputed, as opposed to those PNs found in A_{1-7}, and because the fragments of ms. B were discovered in Rooms 2 and 3 of Building A, it is kept separate from ms. A in this treatment. Mss. A and B do, however, show a very similar if not identical hand and other shared features, such as the color of their clay, so that they may in the end all belong to a single tablet (Giorgieri 2005: 332 and n. 52). That B_1 and B_2 belong to a single tablet is, in my view, made all but certain, in addition to their similar hands, findspots and content, by the fact that they both preserve five to six horizontal wedges neatly pressed into one of their paragraph dividers, in that following l. 10′ in B_1 and in that following l. 13′ in B_2, a very rare feature.

It should be noted at this point that fragment B_1 has repeatedly been referred to in an effort to substantiate the existence of a MH king Ḫattusili II. I must agree with Klinger (1988: 33–34; cf. now Hawkins 2011: 86, n. 421a.), for example, who shows clearly that the oft-defended link between the PN Ḫattusili and the mention of an anointing for kingship three lines earlier (§3′) is highly tenuous at best, and that any number of alternative possibilities must be taken into account. In fact, the intent would seem either to require the addressees to continue their enmity toward Ḫattusili, perhaps because of hostile acts against the royal family, or to invoke a divine curse upon him.

The third composition (C_{1-2})[83] is similarly conceived, but apparently for the situation surrounding the installation of Tudḫaliya III as king two generations later; according to some, while his predecessor, Arnuwanda I, and his queen, Ašmunikkal, were still alive and in office, thus establishing a coregency.[84] Alone among the compositions presented under No. 11, it is composed at least partly in the 1st pl. (but cf. 1st sg. in C_2, §2″), presumably as the words of the royal pair. Its mention of the royal princes Tulpi-Teššub, Pariyawatra, and Kantuzili (C_1, §§1′, 4′) has led to much discussion of the prosopography of the MH royal family. Though in part discovered right alongside the fragments of ms. A in Rooms 4–5 of Building A in the royal palace, it is clear that these two blocks of directly joining fragments of ms. C do not belong to the first tablet(s), as they show a hand that differs from that of mss. A and B, and because they deal with a different historical setting that does ms. A.

As noted, these texts are in a dismal state of preservation, so that even ordering the fragments in relation to one another is a speculative undertaking. The sequence in the present edition therefore courageously avoids the issue entirely, and within each of the three groups those fragments that preserve somewhat more text are presented first.

Though listed by Laroche among the instructions (*CTH* 271), he dubbed these texts *Protocoles de succession dynastique*; and indeed, though they contain elements comparable to those of some of the instructions, it might be suggested that they bear as much of a resemblance, for example, to the Edict of Telipinu than to any other composition (van den Hout 1997: 194–98), and Giorgieri (2005: 332) has rightly noted their similarities to the loyalty oaths, calling them a "Vereidigungstext," "der die Thronfolge regelte" (p. 333). In this light, the compositions are deemed in the present treatment as instructions or directives coupled with an oath imposition or prescription, upon which an oath would at some point have been sworn by the persons addressed. They all appear to be concerned first and foremost with bringing a period of infighting and political upheaval to an end through assuring the loyalty of the nobility to a single royal individual and his descendants.

A. Instructions and Oath Impositions Dealing with the Installation of Tudḫaliya I (I/II)

Transliteration (A$_1$)

§1′ (A$_1$ r. col. 1′) (1′)⸢DUMU^MEŠ⸣ x[…]

§2′ (A$_1$ r. col. 2′–5′) (2′)*kat-ta-ma zi-*⸢*ik*⸣ DUMU^MEŠ ⸢^m*ḪI.MU.I*⸣.[*LI*[85]…] (3′)*le-e* {*AŠ*} *ku-e-da-ni-ik-ki ták-k*[*a-* …] (4′)*ŠA* ^m*ḪI.MU.I.LI*[86] *A-NA* DUMU.DUMU^ME[^Š …] (5′)*ku-e-da-ni-ik-ki ták-ša-an-zi* ⸤*e*?⸥-[…]

§3′ (A$_1$ r. col. 6′–11′) (6′)*ma-a-an šu-ul-li-ši-ma nu-uk-ká*[*n* …] (7′)*A-NA* DUMU^MEŠ LÚ^MEŠ GAL.GAL *i-da-lu k*[*u*[87]*-* …] (8′)*nu-*⸤*ut*⸥*-ta pár-ḫa-an-ta-ru nu-za-ká*[*n* …] (9′)*nu-uk-kán ki-i ut-tar a-ap-pa-a*[*n* …] (10′) ^m*Ḫi-mu-i-*⸢*li*⸣*-iš* ^m*Kán-tu-*⸢*u-zi*⸣*-l*[*i-iš-ša* …] (11′)*i-da-a-lu ták*-M[A-x]-*zi*[88] [*š*]*u-me-e-ša-aš-š*[*e*[89] …]

§4′ (A$_1$ r. col. 12′–17′) (12′)*šu-me-e-ša* DUMU^ME[^Š ^m*ḪI.M*]*U.I.LI* DUMU^MEŠ ^m*KÁ*[*N.TU.U.ZI.LI* …] (13′)*šu-me-ša a-pu-*⸢*u-un*⸣ *pa-aḫ-ḫa-aš-du-ma-a*[*t* …] (14′) *ku-iš šu-*⸢*ul*⸣*-li-ez-zi-ma iš-tar-n*[*a*? … *i-da-a-lu*] (15′)*ták-ke-eš-*⸢*zi*⸣[90] *na-an ki-i NI-IŠ* DINGIR-*LÌ* x[[91] …] (16′)⸤*nu*⸥*-za-kán BE-LU-UT* É-*ZU ḫu-iš-wa-a-*[*tar* …] (17′)[*n*]*a-aš nam-ma le-e* ÌR LUGAL *šu-ma-a-š*[*a*? …]

§5′ (A$_1$ r. col. 18′–23′) (18′)[*a*]*n-da-ma* LÚ^MEŠ ^URU*ḪA.AT.TI pa-an-ku-uš* ^URU*Ḫa-a*[*t-tu-ša-aš* …] (19′)[*nu*?] ⸢*a*⸣*-pa-at ut-tar a-ru-ma ta-aš-nu-an ḫar-te-e*[*n*$_6$ …] (20′)[*ki*?]-⸤*i*?⸥*-pát* 1-*EN ut-tar na-ak-ki-i e-eš-du* x[…] (21′)[…]x-*ti-an-pát e-eš-du nu ma-aḫ-ḫa-an* I[92][…] (22′)[…]x LUGAL LUGAL-*u-iz-ni ti-it-ti-an-z*[*i*? …] (23′)[… *š*/*n*]*a*?*-an* DUMU LUGAL-*pát* […]

§6′ (A$_1$ r. col. 24′–25′) (24′)[… ^URU*Ḫa-a*]*t-tu-ši i-da-a-lu*[…] (25′)[…]-⸤*lu*?*-u-e-eš-ke*⸥*-e*[*t*? …]

(gap of unknown length)

§1″ (A$_1$ l. col. 1′–6″) (1′-3′)(traces) (4″)[…]x-*an-zi* (5″-6″)(traces)

§2″ (A$_1$ l. col. 7″–13″) (7″)[…] (8″)[… ^m*ḪI.M*]*U.I.LI-ma* (9″)[…]x *na-at-ta-ma* (10″–13″)(traces)

TRANSLATION (A_1)

§1′ […] (1′)sons […]

§2′ (2′)Moreover you(sg.) […] the sons of Ḫimui[li …], (3′)to no one […] *conco*[*ct*[93] …] (4′–5′)to the sons of Ḫimuili […] they *concoct* […] for anyone. […]

§3′ (6′)If you(sg.) become arrogant, though, and […] (7′)evil to the sons of the grandees, (8′)then they shall haunt you(sg.), and […]; (9′)and this matter again/behind […] (10′)Ḫimuili [and] Kantūzil[i …] (11′)evil, but you(pl.) […] to hi[m].

§4′ (12′)But you(pl.), sons of [Ḫim]uili (and) sons of Ka[ntūzili …], (13′)you(pl.) must protect[94] him! […] (14′–15′)He who becomes arrogant, though, amon[g …] he *concocts* [evil …, let] this divine oath […] him! (16′)And the ownership of his estate […] lif[e …], (17′)[a]nd he shall no longer be a servant of the king. You(pl.), *how*[*ever*, …].

§5′ (18′)[Mo]reover, men of Ḫattusa, the whole of Ḫa[ttusa …], (19′)[*and*] you(pl.) shall even reinforce that matter. (20′)[*Thi*]*s* one matter alone shall be of consequence. […] (21′)[…] shall be only […], and as soon as/just like […] (22′)[… *t*]*hey* install *the king*[95] in the kingship […] (23′)[… *an*]*d* […] *him* only a prince.

§6′ (24′)[…] evil [in Ḫa]ttusa […] (25′)[…]s/he always […]-ed. […]

(gap of unknown length)

§1″ (4″–7″)[…] they will […]

§2″ (8″)[… Ḫim]uili, though, (9″–13″)[…] but not […]

TRANSLITERATION (A_2)

§1′ (A_2 obv.? 1′–7′) (1′)[…]x-e-eš nu A-N[A …] (2′)[…]x-te-eš šu-me-e-eš x[…] (3′)[… -t]e-eš šu-me-e-eš nu x x x[…] (4′)[…]-ta ku-iš-ki ti-it-ta-nu-u[t …] (5′)[… NI-I]Š DINGIR-LÌ šar-ra-at-ta nu-u[š~…] (6′)[…]x x A-NA DUMU^{MEŠ} LÚ^{MEŠ} GAL.GAL i[96]-d[a?-lu …] (7′)[…]-an ki-iš-ša-an ša-a-ak~[…]

§2′ (A_2 obv.? 8′–13′) (8′)[… MUNUS].LUGAL AMA-KU-NU ku-en-zi šu-ma-a-š[a~…] (9′)[… p]é-ra-an-na ^{m}Ḫi-mu-i-li-iš ^{m}Kán-t[u-u-zi-li-iš-ša …] (10′)[… ^{m}Mu-w]a-at-ta-al-li-in ˻ku˼-e-né-er nu-x[…] (11′)[…]x a-ap-pa-ma[97] a-pé-da-aš-pát UD$^{!ḪI.A}$-a[š[98] …] (12′)[… ^{m}M]u-wa-a-aš MUNUS.LUGAL AMA-KU-NU ku-en-z[i …] (13′)[…] ku-en-zi[…]

§3′ (A_2 obv.? 14′–19′) (14′)[…]LUGAL-aš MUNUS.LUGAL-aš-ša kat-ta-an ti-i-˻e?˼-[er? …] (15′)[…]ḫu-iš-nu-e-er nu-za LUGAL-uš MUNUS.L[UGAL-aš-ša …] (16′)[…]x IT-TI LÚ^{MEŠ} GAL.GAL kat-ta[…] (17′)[… LUGAL-u/aš] MUNUS.LUGAL-aš-ša ^{m}Ḫi-mu-i-li-in[…] (18′)[… ^{m}Kán-t]u-u-zi-li-ša[99] Ù LÚ^{MEŠ} GAL.GAL[…] (19′)[…]-at […]

§4′ (A_2 obv.? 20′–21′) (20′)[…]˻LÚ^{MEŠ} GAL.GAL˼ pa-aḫ-ši nu-uš~[…] (21′)[… n]u-˻uš˼-ša-˻an˼[…]

(gap of unknown length)

§1″ (A_2 rev.? 1′–5′) (1′)[…]x[…] (2′)[… -i]š-ḫa ku-x[100][…] (3′)[…]x MUNUS.LUGAL-aš x[…] (4′)[…]-iš-ḫa ku-na-an~[…] (5′)[… DINGIR^{MEŠ} pár-ḫ]a-an-da-ru[…]

§2″ (A_2 rev.? 6′–10′) (6′)[… ^{URU}]ḪA.AT.TI pa-an-ga-[u- …] (7′)[…]na-aš-ma-aš-ša-an ḫ[u?- …] (8′)[…]x ut-tar Ú-UL pár-ku-x[…] (9′)[…]x-zi nu ^{m}Ḫi-mu-i-l[i~ …] (10′)[… D]INGIR^{MEŠ} [101] pár-ḫa-an-ta-ru[…]

§3″ (A_2 rev.? 11′–16′) (11′)[…]-ma e-ez-za-an GIŠ-r[u …] (12′)[…]x ˻ti?˼-it-ti-an ˻e˼-[…] (13′)[…]x É.GAL ŠA[…] (14′)[… n]a?-aš-ma-aš-ši […] (15′)[… p]a-it-ti[…] (16′)[… ku]-˻e˼-da-ni-i[k?-ki …]

§4″ (A_2 rev.? 17′) (17′)[…]x[…]

TRANSLITERATION (A_3)

§1′ (A_3 1′–5′) (1′)[… ~n]a?-˹an? A?˺-[…] (2′)[… L]Ú?-an-na ši-˹pa˺-a[n- …] (3′)[… -(i)]a ga-né-eš-ša-an~[…] (4′)[…]~ni/i]n-kán-d[u?] ^{m}Ḫi-mu-i-li~šu-x[…] (5′)[…]x-na na-˹at˺ ak-kán-*tu*[…]

TRANSLATION (A_2)

§1′ (1′)[…]-s, and to […] (2′)[…]-s, you(pl.) […] (3′)[…]-s you are, and […] (4′)[…] whoever arranged/set up […] (5′)[…] he will break the [oa]th, and […] (6′)[…] *ev*[*il*] to the sons (*of*) the grandees […] (7′)[…] know thus […]

§2′ (8′)[…] he will kill the [qu]een, your(pl.) mother, b[ut] you(pl.) […] (9′)[…] and [b]efore […] Ḫimuili [and] Kant[uzzili …] (10′)[…] killed [Muw]attalli, and […] (11′)[…] But thereafter/again in/for those very *days* […] (12′)[… M]uwā will kill the queen, your(pl.) mother. (13′)[…] he will kill.

§3′ (14′)[… *they*] supported the king and queen […] (15′)[…] they let live, and the king [and] the que[en …] (16′)[…] together with the grandees […] (17′)[… the king] and queen […] Ḫimuili(acc.) […], (18′–19′)[…] but [Kant]ūzili and the grandees […]

§4′ (20′)[…] you(sg.) must protect the grandees, and […], (21′)[…] and […]

(gap of unknown length)

§1″ (1′–2′)[…] *ki*[*ll* …] (3′)[…] the queen […] (4′)[…] *to kil*[*l*[102] …] (5′)[…] may [the gods hau]nt […]!

§2″ (6′)[…] Ḫattusa, the whol[e …] (7′)[…] or […] (8′)[…] the matter not pure/legitimate […], (9′)[…] and Ḫimuil[i …] (10′)[…] may the gods haunt […]!

§3″ (11′)[…] but straw (and) woo[d …] (12′)[…] w[as]/w[ere] set/founded […] (13′)[…] palace of […] (14′)[…] or to him/her […] (15′)[…] you(sg.) go/will go […] (16′)[…] to [so]meo[ne] / [so]methi[ng].

§4″ (traces)

TRANSLATION (A_3)

§1′ (1′)[… *an*]*d* […] *him* […] (2′)[…] and a [*m*]*an* […] off[er]/sacrif[ice …] (3′)[…] recognize […] (4′)[…] they sha[ll …] Ḫimuili […], (5′)[…] then let them die!

§2′ (A_3 6′–12′) (6′)[… LUGAL MUNUS.LU]GAL *Ù A-NA* DUMU^MEŠ^-*ŠU-NU i-da-lu tá*[*k-* …] (7′)[…]-*ma-aš-ša-an* GÌR-*an ták-ša-an-zi n*[*a-* …] (8′)[… -*a*]*n*?-*na A-NA* m*Ḫi-mu-i-li na-aš-m*[*a* …] (9′)[…]x-*iz-zi* m*Ḫi-mu-i-li-ša* m*Kán-t*[*u-u-zi-li-iš-ša* …] (10′)[… LU]GAL MUNUS.LUGAL *an-da na-at-ta* […] (11′)[…] x-*an* NU.GÁL *ku-it-ki* m*Ḫi-mu-i-l*[*i*~ …] (12′)[…]-*an-zi* […]

§3′ (A_3 13′) (13′)[…]x[…]x-x-⌞*ia*⌟-*u*-⌞*en*⌟[…]

TRANSLITERATION (A_4)

§1′ (A_4 l. col. 1′–7′) (1′)[…]-*ká*[*n*? m]*Ká*[*n-*? …] (2′)[… -*š*]*i*?-*iš-š*[*i*? …] (3′) […]⌜*A*⌝-*NA* m*Kán-tu-z*[*i-li* …] (4′)[…]x-*te-en*$_6$ *nu ma-a-an* x[…] (5′)[… LÚ*ḫa-an-t*]*i-ti-at-tal-la-aš a-ku* (6′)[…]x-*an-tu* LÚ*ḫa-an-ti-ti-tal-an* (7′)[…] x-*an-zi*

TRANSLITERATION (A_5)

§1′ (A_5 1′–4′) (1′)[*š*]*a*?-*r*[*a*?- …] (2′)*nu-uš*~[…] (3′)*nu* LÚ*ḫa-*⌜*an-ti*⌝-*t*[*i-* …] (4′) LÚ*ḫa-an-ti-ti-a*[*t-tal-la-* …]

§2′ (A_5 5′–10′) (5′)*Ù A-NA* m*Ḫi-mu-*⌞*i*⌟-[*li* …] (6′)*ḫu-u-ma-an-te-et* […] (7′)*i-da-lu ku-e-d*[*a-* …] (8′)*a-ap-pa e-e*[*p*?- …] (9′)*e-eš-zi nu* x[…] (10′)[m*Ḫ*]*i-*⌞*mu-i-li*⌟~[…]

TRANSLITERATION (A_6)

§1′ (A_6 1′) (1′)[…]x ⌜KU⌝ x[…]

§2′ (A_6 2′–8′) (2′)[…]x-⌜*ša-an*⌝ *da-i-ú-en* ⌜*ma*⌝-[…] (3′)[…]x *A-NA* m*Kán-tu-zi-li A-N*[*A* …] (4′)[… *ki*?]-*i-wa* LÚ^MEŠ^-*eš ak-kán-du nu*-x[…] (5′)[…]x *an-tu-wa-aḫ-ḫa-aš pa-iz-zi nu* ⌜m⌝[…] (6′)[…]⌞*e*⌟-*ep-zi na-an ku-uš-du-wa-i*[*z-zi* …] (7′)[… L]Ú*ḫa-an-ti-ti-tal-an mu-un-n*[*a-* …] (8′)[… -*a*]*t-ta-ta*[*r* …]

§3′ (A_6 9′–12′) (9′)[… m*Kán-tu-z*]*i-*⌞*li*⌟ *I-NA* ŠÀ.BI […] (10′)[…]x-*a-an-zi nu* x[…] (11′)[…]x-*ú*~*tar*~*ú*-x[…] (12′)[…]x x[…]

MANUSCRIPT A_7

The 16 lines on one side and 4 on the other are too fragmentary for translation; mentioned are Ka[ntuzili (§1′, 1′), Ka]ntuz[ili (§4′, 14′) and Ḫi]muil[i (§4′, 13′).

§2′ (6′)[…] *con*[*cocts*] evil [for the king, for the que]en and for their sons […] (7′)[…] but they take up a knife an[d …] (8′)[…] to Ḫimuili or […] (9′)[…] s/he […]s, but Ḫimuili [and] Kant[ūzzili …] (10′)[…] not to/by the [ki]ng (and) the queen […] (11′)[…] are/were not, some(thing) […] Ḫimuil[i …] (12′)[…] they do/will do.

§3′ (13′)[…] we did […]

TRANSLATION (A_4)

§1′ […] (3′)[…] to Kantuz[ili …] (4′)[…] you(pl.) shall/you(pl.) did […], and if/when […] (5′)[… acc]user shall die! (6′–7′)[…] let them […]! […] they will […] the accuser.

TRANSLATION (A_5)

§1′ (1′)[…] *u*[*p*]/*ov*[*er*] […] (2′)and […] (3′)and the acc[user …] (4′)the accus[er …]

§2′ (5′)And to/for Ḫimui[li …] (6′)with/by means of all/every […] (7′)evil what[ever …] (8′)back/again *ta*[*ke* …] (9′)is, and […] (10′)[Ḫ]imuili […]

TRANSLATION (A_6)

§1′ (traces)

§2′ (2′)[…] we placed […] (3′)[…] to/for Kantuzili, to/for […] (4′)[… "*the*]*se* men shall die!" And […] (5′)[…] the/a man goes, and [PN …] (6′)[…] seizes, and he scorns him […] (7′–8′)[…] concea[l …] the accuser […]

§3′ (9′)[… Kantuz]ili within […] (10′–12′)[…] they will […], and […]

B. Instructions and Oath Impositions Mentioning a Ḫattusili

Transliteration (B$_1$)

§1′ (B$_1$ 1′–2′) (1′)[… -e]š?-zi nu ú-wa-at t[u-[103]…] (2′)[… -i]n? nu ^{URU}Ḫa-at-tu-ša-aš a-r[a?- …]

§2′ (B$_1$ 3′–4′) (3′)[…] (erasure) […] (4′)[…] (erasure) […]

§3′ (B$_1$ 5′–10′) (5′)[ki-nu]-na[104] ka-a-ša A-NA DUMU^{MEŠ} LUGAL iš-tar-na x[…] (6′)[LUGA]L-u-iz-ni lam-ni-er na-an-za ŠEŠ^{MEŠ}-⸢ŠU DAM?/NIN?⸣$^{\text{ḪI.A}}$-ŠU?/Š[U?-NU …] (7′)[pa]-an-ku-uš-ša LÚ^{MEŠ} ^{URU}ḪA.AT.TI še-ek-kán-⸢du⸣ nu x[[105]…] (8′)[k]u?-i-ta[106] ŠEŠ^{MEŠ}-ŠU $^{\text{LÚ.MEŠ}}$ga-i-na-aš-ši-iš na-a[t-ta …] (9′)[^{m}]Ḫa-at-tu-ši-i-li me-na-aḫ-ḫa-an-da SAG.⸢DU⸣-Z[U? …] (10′)[^{L}]^{Ú}KÚR-ŠU e-eš-du na-an pár-ḫa-[an-da-ru …]

§4′ (B$_1$ 11′–15′) (11′)[an?-d]a[107]-ma li-in-ki-ia kat-ta-an ki-i-ia ut-[tar …] (12′)[ku-i]-˻e˼-eš a-aš-šu-wa-an-te-eš ŠA ZI-ŠU-NU na-at~[…] (13′)[a-aš-š]u-wa-an-te-eš LUGAL-ma-at MUNUS.LUGAL-ri 2-ŠU 3-[ŠU …] (14′)[x]x na-at-ta ḫar-wa-ni ma-an-n[a?- …] (15′)[nu LUGAL] ˻MUNUS.LUGAL ki-i NI-IŠ˼ [DINGIR-LÌ …]

Transliteration (B$_2$)

§1′ (B$_2$ 1′) (1′)[…]x[…]

§2′ (B$_2$ 2′–6′) (2′)[…]x-⸢na⸣-aš ⸢ḫu?⸣-[…] (3′)[… ki-i]š-ša-an tar-te-n[i? …] (4′)[…]x-uš ka-ru-ú x[…] (5′)[… T]U? LUGAL MUNUS.LUGAL […] (6′)[…] a-pí-ia pí-ip-x[…]

§3′ (B$_2$ 7′–11′) (7′)[… -m]a ma-a-an UR-R[A-AM …] (8′)[… LÚ]^{MEŠ} GAL.GAL iš-tar-n[i? …] (9′)[…]x aš-ša-nu-ma-ni[…] (10′)[…]-tu nu-uš-še e-x[…] (11′)[…]x-ŠU A-NA É-ŠU[…]

§4′ (B$_2$ 12′–13′) (12′)[…]le-e i-la-a-l[i- …] (13′)[… k]i-*i* da-aš-ša-u-e-[eš …]

§5′ (B$_2$ 14′–19′) (14′)[…]x ka-a-ša GIBI[L …] (15′)[…]-uš ḫu-u-ma-an-za LÚ[…] (16′)[… $^{\text{LÚ.MEŠ}}$]DUGUD $^{\text{LÚ.MEŠ}}$KUŠ$_7$ KÙ.GI[…] (17′)[… $^{\text{LÚ.MEŠ}}$]ḪA-A-I-ṬU$_4$ LÚ^{MEŠ} ŠA x[[108]…] (18′)[… pa-a]n?-ku-uš ^{URU}Ḫa-at-tu-š[a-aš …] (19′)[… li]-in-kán-te-eš […]

§6′ (B$_2$ 20′–23′) (20′)[… -š]a-an ku-iš LUGAL.G[AL …] (21′)[… ḫ]a-aš-ša ḫa-an-za-aš-š[a …] (22′)[… ku-i]š-ki da-a-i ták-ku[…] (23′)[…]x-˻iš-ši˼ x x x[…]

Translation (B_1)

§1′ (1′)[…] s/he will […], and – *mer*[*cy*! – …], (2′)[…] and […] *of* Ḫattusa […]

§2′ (erased)

§3′ (5′)But [no]w, here among the princes, […] (6′)they designated for [kin]gship, and his brothers (and) *h*[*is*] *sisters/t*[*heir*] *wives*[109] […] (7′)and the [as]sembly, the men of Ḫattusa, shall recognize him! And […] (8′)But [*si*]*nce/*[*wh*]*at* his brothers (*and*) his inlaws *do no*[*t* …] (9′)before the person of Ḫattusīli […] (10′)he shall be his enemy! And [they shall] haunt him!

§4′ (11′)[*Furth*]*er*, also this mat[ter …] under oath; (12′)[wh]ich are good in their view and/no[t …] (13′)are [goo]d. But they […] to/for the king (and) queen twice, thr[ice …] (14′)we will not keep/hold, and if/should […], (15′)[and king] (and) queen this oa[th …]

Translation (B_2)

§1′ (traces)

§2′ […] (3′)[…] you(pl.) say/will say [t]hus: […] (4′)[…] earlier […] (5′)[…] king (and) queen […] (6′)[…] topple there[110] […]

§3′ (7′)[… b]ut if/when in the fut[ure …] (8′)[…] among the [gra]ndees […] (9′)[…] we will supply, […] (10′)[…] shall […]! And to/for him/her […] (11′)[…] his […] to/for his house […]

§4′ (12′)[…] shall not desi[re …] (13′)[… the]se powerful […]

§5′ (14′)[…] here new […] (15′)[…] every man […] (16′)[…] commander[s], golden chariot fighters […] (17′)[…], night watch[men], […]-men […] (18′)[… the *who*]*le* (*of*) Ḫattus[a …] (19′)[…] they are [… swor]n by oath […]

§6′ (20′)[…] he who […] gr[eat] king […] (21′)[… f]urther generations […] (22′)[…wh]oever takes/places, if/when […] (23′)[…] to him/her […]

C. Instructions and Oath Impositions Dealing with the Installation of Tudḫaliya III

Transliteration (C_1)

§1′ (C_1 1′–2′) (1′)[x x x] x ˹AN?˺ x[...] (2′)[x x][111] x ^{m}*Túl-˹pí-*^{d}10˺-[*ub-* ...]

§2′ (C_1 3′–5′) (3′)[^{m}*Du-ut*]-*ḫa-li-ia-an* ŠEŠ[112][...] (4′)[*ma?-a?*][113]-*an* ^{m}*Du-ut-ḫa-li-i*[*a~* ...] (5′)[*nam?-m*]*a?-an-kán* LUGAL-*u-iz-ni iš-ki-˹er˺*[...]

§3′ (C_1 6′–7′) (6′)[KUR ^{URU}]*ḪA.AT.TI-wa ḫu-u-ma-an* Š[A ...]x[114] x x[...] (7′)[^{m}*Du*]-*ut-ḫa-li-ia-aš* LUGAL.GAL UR.S[AG *ma-n*]*i-ia-aḫ-ḫi-˹iš˺-ke-˹ed-du˺* [...]

§4′ (C_1 8′–10′) (8′)[x[115] M]^{EŠ}-*ŠU-ma-wa-aš-ši ku-i-e-eš* [^{m}*Pa*]-*ri-ia-wa-at-ra-aš* ^{m}*Kán-tu-z*[*i-li-iš* ...][116] (9′)[^{m}*Túl-pí*]-˹^{d}˺10-*ub-aš-ša* DUMU.DUMU-*NI nu-wa-*[*aš?-m*]*a?-aš* É$^{ḪI.A}$ *pí-ia-a-an* (erasure) [...][117] (10′)[*nu-wa-aš-ma*]-⌞*ša-at*⌟[118] *tup-pí i-ia-*[*a*]*n-ta* [...]

§5′ (C_1 11′–14′) (11′)[... ^{ḪI}]⌞.^{A}-*TÌ*[119] *ku?*⌟-*e*[120] ^{GIŠ}ŠÚ.A$^{ḪI.A}$ GAL$^{ḪI.A}$-*TÌ nu-wa-ra-at a-pé-e* K[I? ...] (12′)[... -*w*]*a?* LUGAL.GAL *ku-it* UR.SAG *nu-wa-aš-ma-aš BE-EL-ŠU-N*[*U?* ...] (13′)[... *ša-a*]*k-ku nu-wa-ra-aš-za na-aḫ-ḫa-a-an ḫar-du* (erasure) [...] (14′)[... -*t*]*i? da-ma-in* ^{GIŠ}ŠÚ.A-*it le-e ku-in-ki šal-l*[*a-nu-*[121] ...]

§6′ (C_1 15′–16′) (15′)[... *ku*]-˹*e*˺ *šal-la-e-eš a-ša-an-du nu-wa-za a-pé-el*[...] (16′)[...]x-*ia* ⌞*ma*⌟*-ni-ia-aḫ-ḫi-iš-kán-du* [...]

§7′ (C_1 17′–19′) (17′)[...]x-x[122] ⌞*i?*⌟*-e-zi* ^{m}*D*[*u-ut-ḫa-li-ia~* ...] (18′)[... -*i*]*š?*-⌞*ke*⌟*-et*[...] (19′)[...]⌞IT?⌟[...]

Transliteration (C_2)

§1′ (nothing preserved before paragraph divider)

§2′ (C_2 r. col. 1′–4′) (1′)*nu-za am-mu-uk!*(AZ) *ma-aḫ-ḫa-an* ^{f}*Mu-šu-˹ḫé˺-p*[*a~* ...] (2′)*ge-en-zu ḫar-ú-e-ni A-NA* ^{m}*Pa-ri-ia-w*[*a-at-ra~* ...] (3′)*A-NA* DUMU^{MEŠ}-*ŠU* DUMU.MUNUS^{MEŠ}-*ŠU Ù A-NA* ^{m}*Túl-p*[*í-*^{d}10-*ub~* ...] (4′)*kat-ta ḫa-a-aš-ša ḫa-an-za-aš-ša QA-TAM-MA* x[...]

§3′ (C_2 r. col. 5′–8′) (5′)[*n*]*u-*⌞*un*⌟*-na-aš-ša-an* [*k*]*u-it ut-tar* ZI-*ni ú-e-˹mi˺-*[...] (6′)[...]x-⌞*da?/i?~ša-*x[...]*ku-it tu-e-eg-ga-aš-m*[*a* ...] (7′)[...]x[...-*n*]*i? nu-uš-ma-ša-at-kán Ú-U*[*L* ...] (8′)[...]*ḫa-an-di me-mi-iš-ke-u-wa-ni*[...]

TRANSLATION (C_1)

§1′ […] (2′)[…] Tulpi-Tešš[ub …]

§2′ (3′)[Dut]ḫaliya(acc.) […] brother […], (4′)[*i*]*f*/[*whe*]*n* Dutḫaliy[a …]; (5′)[*furth*]*er* they anointed him for kingship (saying):

§3′ (6′)"The entire [land] of Ḫattusa […] (7′)[Du]tḫaliya, Great King, He[ro], shall [go]vern!

§4′ (8′)"His […]s, though, (i.e.,) [Pa]riyawatra, Kantuzi[li …] (9′)and [Tulpi]-Teššub, our grandson, to [*th*]*em* estates have been given, (10′)[and] it has been recorded for [the]m on a tablet.

§5′ (11′)"[…]s which are great thrones, they […] them, (12′)because the great king is a hero, to them their lord […] (13′)he shall [recog]nize and he shall hold them in esteem! (14′)[…] by means of the throne [… shall/will] make no one else greater.

§6′ (15′)"[…] they [wh]o shall be greater, his […] (16′)[…] they shall govern!

§7′ (17′–19′)[…] s/he will do/make […]; D[utḫaliya …]

TRANSLATION (C_2)

§1′ (nothing preserved before paragraph divider)

§2′ (1′)And just as Mušu-Ḫep[a …] to me, (2′)we are well disposed [to …]; to Pariyaw[atra …] (3′)to his sons, to his daughters and to Tulp[i-Teššub …] (4′)and thereafter further generations likewise […]

§3′ (5′)And the matter [w]hich […] find in our hearts […] (6′)[…] which/because of the body, tho[ugh, …], (7′)[…] and […] it not to them/you(pl.) […] (8′)[…] in front of […] we will repeatedly say.

§4′ (C_2 r. col. 9′–10′) (9′)[…]x~*da-an-zi* [*n*]*a-at da-an*-x[...] (10′)[…]*pé-eš-ši-ia-an*[[123]]˹*ú*˺*-e-eš-ša*[...]

§5′ (C_2 r. col. 11′) (11′)[… *i-da-l*]*a-u-i pár-r*[*a-an-da* ...]

(gap of unknown length)

§1″ (C_2 l. col. 1′–2′) (1′)[…]x ˹*i-e*˺*-zi* (2′)[…]-˹*a*?*-na*?˺*-aš ḫi-in-ga-na-aš-ma n*[*a-*]x

§2″ (C_2 l. col. 3′–5′) (3′)[…] ^{f}*LA.LA.AN.TI.WA.AŠ.ḪA A-NA* DUMU^{MEŠ}~Š[A? ...] (4′)[… *a*]*m-mu-uk-za ma-aḫ-ḫa-an* ^{m}*Kán-tu-zi-l*[*i*~ ...] (5′)[…]A DUMU^{MEŠ}-*ia*[124] *ge-en-zu ḫar-mi*

§3″ (C_2 l. col. 6′–7′) (6′)[…]˹f˺*LA.LA.AN.TI.WA.AŠ.ḪA A-NA* DUMU^{MEŠ} DUMU.MUNUS$^{\text{ME[Š]}}$ (7′)[…] *ḫar-wa-ni na-aš-za-kán* DINGIR^{MEŠ}*-aš*

§4″ (C_2 l. col. 8′–10′) (8′)[… *A-NA* G]AL.GEŠTIN *Ù A-NA* ^{f}*LA.LA.AN.TI.W*[*A.AŠ.ḪA* ...] (9′)[… *i-da*]*-lu ut-tar* ZI*-ni ú-*⸤*e*⸥*-*[*m*]*i-ia-*[...] (10′)[…]*-wa-ni nu-uš-ma-š*[*a-* ...]

§4′ (9′)[…] they will […], and it/they […] (10′)[…] is/are disregarded, and we […]

§5′ (11′)[…] ov[er to ev]il […]

(gap of unknown length)

§1″ (1′)[…] s/he will do/make (2′)[…] but of death […]

§2″ (3′)[…] Lalantiwasḫa to the sons […] (4′)[…] like Kantuzil[i …] to me […] (5′)[…] I am well disposed to […] and to the sons.

§3″ (6′)[…] Lalantiwasḫa to the sons (and) daughters […] (7′)we will hold/keep, and […] the gods.

§4″ (8′)[… to the ch]ief vintner and to Lalantiw[asḫa …] (9′)[…] find an [evi]l matter in […] heart […] (10′)[…] we will […], and to them/you(pl.) […]

No. 12
Instructions and Oath Imposition for Princes, Lords, and Military Officers (*CTH* 251)

This composition is preserved on one tablet (A), of which cols. i and iv retain significant amounts of text, and four small fragments of a second tablet (B_{1-4}). If the text is complete with this single tablet, then about one-quarter of the original composition is preserved. Ms. A is a MH version written roughly contemporarily with the text's composition. Its constituent fragments were found in and near Room 5 of Building A of the Royal Palace. Ms. B is a NH copy, some pieces of which were found in front of Storerooms 11–12 of the Temple I complex.

The dating of the composition remains uncertain, the two leading candidates being the reigns of Tudḫaliya I and his successor Arnuwanda I (cf. de Martino 1991: 5 n. 7; Pecchioli Daddi 2002a: 265–66; Forlanini 2005: 231, n. 8, 232, n. 20; Giorgieri 2005: 325, n. 14; O. Soysal 2006: 132; Freu 2007a: 175). Deliberations in this regard pertain primarily to §34″, in which the father of the speaker is said to have been bound to Ḫuzziya II (or perhaps to Muwattalli I) by oath and to have acted in some manner vis-à-vis Muwattalli. This could apply either to (a) the father of Tudḫaliya I, now known to have been named Kantuzzili, who was involved in the murder of Muwattalli I, who had himself colluded in bumping off Ḫuzziya II to become king, or (b) to the father of Arnuwanda I, that is, Tudḫaliya I, who presumably acted alongside his father at the time of the fall of Muwattalli, and who became as the new king the primary beneficiary of the series of skirmishes.

The composition would thus seem to be closely related to the texts of No. 11 (cf. further in Oettinger 1976: 81–82), in that it comprises a series of du-

---

Transliteration

§1′ (A i 1′–2′) (1′)[… *na-an ke-e* *NI-IŠ* DINGIR^{MEŠ}] *ap-*⸢*pa-an-du*⸣ (2′)[*na-an* *QA-DU* DAM-*ŠU* DUMU^{MEŠ}-*ŠU* *ḫar-ni-in-kán*]*-du*

§2′ (A i 3′–6′) (3′)[… *e-e*]*z-za-az-zi* (4′)[… *d*]*a-a-i na-an ku-iš* (5′)[… *-a*]*n-zi na-an ke-e* (6′)[*NI-IŠ* DINGIR^{MEŠ} *ap-pa-an-du na-an* *QA-DU* DAM-*ŠU* DUMU^{M}]^{EŠ}-*ŠU* *ḫar-ni-in-kán-du*

§3′ (A i 7′–9′) (7′)[… *an*]*-tu-uḫ-ša-an š/t/n*[*a-* …] (8′)[…]*$^{d?}$*UTU-*ŠI-ma* x[*š*]*u-me-e-ša-an* (9′)[… *da-a-l*]*i-iš-te-*[*en*$^{(?)}$ …]

ties and obligations imposed upon its addressees by a new and—especially if Tudḫaliya I is its author—politically insecure king. It is spoken not by the oath takers, the addressees, but by the king, and is therefore not a loyalty oath per se, but a series of obligations or instructions upon which the subordinates would at some point have had to swear an oath—an oath referred to at the end of almost every paragraph. Occasionally the obligations imposed are referred to explicitly as "obligation(s)," *isḫiul-* (§§9′, 11′). Oettinger (1976: 82) thus coined the term "Eidesvorschrift," an "oath-directive," which indeed has much to recommend itself. The addressees include at least princes, lords and military personnel (§§6′, 9′, 14′, 27″), perhaps even all the nobility of Ḫattusa (§§12′, 13″), and the directives concern largely, but not exclusively (cf., e.g., §§28″–33″), military duties. Oettinger (1976: 82) has emphasized the numerous parallels, above all in the curse formulae, between this text and the Military Oaths.

The first paragraphs detail responsibilities relating to loyalty in military command and service (§§2′–10′). The following sections (§§11′–15′) deal primarily with personal loyalty to the king and his family and descendents. The ensuing paragraphs are rather fragmentary, but by §26″ the topic seems to have changed to judicial duties, and this seems to continue to §32″, after which the issues of justice thereby raised lead to the issue of the swearing of an oath to "those who were kings" (§33″) and the oaths sworn to the speaker's immediate predecessors (§34″), and then apparently to those sworn to the speaker himself (§§35″–36″). In §§42″–43″ a list of deities are called to witness the oath taking rites. Though no fewer than forty-three paragraphs are at least partially represented, the fragmentary state of almost every paragraph often makes understanding even the gist of their intent a major challenge.

TRANSLATION

§1′ (1′)[…, then] let [these oath deities] grab [him], (2′)[and] let [them destroy him along with his wife and his sons]!

§2′ (3′)[…] he [e]ats (4′)[…] he takes/puts, and he who […] him (5′)[… t]hey […], then [let] these (6′)[oath deities grab] him, [and] let them destroy [him along with his wife and] his [son]s!

§3′ (7′)[… a/the m]an(acc.) […] (8′)[…] but *My Majesty* [… y]ou[125] […] him(acc.) (9′)[…], you sha[ll *le*]*ave alo*[*ne* …]!

§4′ (A i 10′–14′) (10′)[... a]r? [126]-ḫa ú-i-⸢da⸣-a-mi na-at (11′)[... -V]ḫ-ḫi a-pí-ia-ia-at li-in-ga-nu-mi (12′)[... -m]i?-⸢e?⸣-[...]x-aš ku-iš-ša-an A-NA LUGAL-ma (13′)[i-da-a-lu t]ák-*ki*-i[š-zi ...]x[127]-at-ta-ma na-an ke-e (14′) [NI-IŠ DINGIR^{MEŠ}] ap-pa-an-[du na-an QA-DU DAM-Š]U DUMU$^{\text{MEŠ!}}$-ŠU ḫar-ni-in-kán-du

§5′ (A i 15′–20′) (15′)[ma-a-an]-⸢ma⸣-az-kán za-aḫ-⸢ḫi⸣-x[...]x-aš[128] ḫa-an-te-ez-zi-an šar-ḫi-i-e-ed-du (16′)[na-aš-t]a? ku-in KIN?-an LUGAL-u[š? ... ḫ]u-u-ma-an-za nu-un-tar-ri-ed-du (17′)[an?-d]a?-ma ma-a-an ÉRIN^{MEŠ}-an la-[aḫ-ḫa ...]x-iš-kán-ta[129] (18′)[nu] ḫu-u-ma-an-za nu-un-tar-ri-e-e[d-du ... n]i[130]-ni-ik-du-ma-at (19′)ku-ud-da-ni-e-ez-zi-ma le-⸢e⸣[[131] ... a]r-ḫa le-e ku-iš-ki (20′)tar-na-i nu-za ma-aš-ka-an da-a-⸢i⸣ [na-at NI-IŠ DINGIR-LÌ kat-ta-a]n[132] ki-it-ta-ru

§6′ (A i 21′–27′; B_2, 1′–8′) (21′)ku-iš-kán na-ak-ki-ia-az-m[(a l)a-aḫ]-⸢ḫa⸣-[az ḫu-u-wa-a-i(?) n]a-aš-ma-kán ^{d}UTU-ŠI[133] (22′)tu-uz-zi-iš-ša I-NA KUR! ^{L}[^{Ú}KÚR a]n-da m[a?- x x x x x -a]n-te-eš[134] ^{LÚ}KÚR-ma (23′)ka-ru-ú an-da ú-e-mi-an [ḫa]r-kán-zi n[u-kán[135] ku?-i(š? t)]u-⸤uz⸥-zi-az? (24′)ḫu-u-wa-a-i na-aš-ma-an-za *x* [ḫ]a-an-te-ez-zi-[aš-ši-iš ar-ḫa ta]r-na-i[136] {*na*} (25′)⸤na-at⸥ ak-kán-du-pát ku-i-ša-an mu-un-na-i[z-zi te-ek-ku-uš][137]-nu-uz-zi-ma-an Ú-UL (26′)m[(a-a-n)a-aš] ^{LÚ}UGULA LI-IM ma-a-na-aš ^{LÚ}DUGUD-pát nu a-p[u-u-un (ke-e NI)]-IŠ DINGIR^{MEŠ} (27′)[(ap)-p]a-[an-d]u na-an QA-DU DAM-ŠU DUMU^{MEŠ}-ŠU [ḫar-ni-in-kán-d]u

§7′ (A i 28′–33′) (28′)[... -a]z-ta ^{LÚ}ḫu-ia-an-da-an-^{na} ^{d}UTU-ŠI [...] e-eš-tu (29′) [ma-a-a]n[138] ^{d}UTU-ŠI-ma Ú-UL ŠA ^{LÚ}KÚR la-aḫ-[ḫi ...] (30′)[na-a]k-ki-ia la-aḫ-ḫi *x ku-e-da-ni*-ik-k[i ...] (31′)[a]n-[t]u-wa-aḫ-ḫa-aš-ma-kán ḫu-wa-a-i na-aš l[e-e ...] (32′)[ḫ]a-an-te-ez-zi-aš-ši-iš i-e-ez-z[i nu?]-⸢za?⸣ [...]x x[...] (33′)[x-a]n-na na-an QA-TAM-MA [...]

§8′ (A i 34′–40′; B_4, 1′–9′) (34′)[(an-d)]a-ma MU.IM.MA ^{URU}KI.LI.MU.N[A~ ...]-te-en nu-za ^{L}[(^{Ú}x)...][139] (35′)[...]x ap-pé-ez-zi-uš wa-a-t[ar-na-aḫ-t]e-en NINDA.ÉRIN$^{\text{MEŠ.ḪI.A}}$-KU-NU-wa-z[a][140] (36′)[ḫu-u-d]a-⸤a-ak⸥ e-ez-za-te-en KIN-a[n-ma[141] l]e-e a-ni-ia-at-te-n[i [142]...]x[...] (37′)[... ḫu-u-d]a-a-ak tar-na-an-z[i (n)]u-⸢za⸣ a-pé-e-ez-za ud-da-n[a-za[143] š]u-me-en$_6$-⸢za⸣-[an] (38′)[SAG.DU$^{\text{ḪI.A}}$-K]U-NU[144] wa-ag-ga-ri-⸤i-e-et⸥-te-en nu ki-iš-š[a-an] (39′)[... -e]n ki-nu-na-{^{wa}}[145] ku-iš a-p[é-ni]-iš-šu-wa-an ut-tar i-e-e[z-zi (na)]-an (40′)[(ke-e NI-I)Š DI]NGIR^{MEŠ} ap-pa-an-du ⸢na⸣-an QA-DU DAM-ŠU DUMU^{MEŠ}-ŠU [ḫar-ni-in]-kán-du

§9′ (A i 41′–45′; B_3, 1′–5′) (41′)[an-da-m(a Š)]A NINDA.ÉRIN^{MEŠ} ut-tar ki!-⸤it⸥-pa-an-da-la-az iš-ḫi-ú-ul ⸢e-eš-tu⸣ (42′)[(nu ma-a-an É)]RIN^{MEŠ}-an la-aḫ-ḫa

§4′ (10′–11′)[…] I bring [*aw*]*ay*, and I […] it/them, […] and there I have them swear an oath, […], but (12′)whoever *concocts* (13′)[evil] to/for the king, though, […] then l[et] these (14′)[oath deities] grab him, [and] let them destroy [him along with h]is [wife] and his sons!

§5′ (15′)[When …] battle, though, then let […] *attack* the first of the […]. (16′)[And] the *task* that the king […], let everyone make haste! (17′)[*Moreov*]*er*, if they keep […] the troops on cam[paign], (18′)[then] l[et] everyone make haste! You must [m]obilize[146] the […]! (19′–20′)[…], though, should not overpower […], no one should let […] away, and take a bribe. [And] may [it] be placed u[nder oath]!

§6′ (21′)Whoever [*runs*] from a crucial [(ca)mpa]ign, thou[(gh)], whether My Majesty (22′–24′)and the army are […] in e[nemy] land, but they [ha]ve already found the enemy, [*he w*(*ho*)] runs from the army, or [his] first officer [le]ts him [get away], (25′)then they shall surely die! Whoever hide[s] him, rather than [denou]nce him, (26′–27′)whether he's a *clan* chief or even if he's a commander, then let [(these o)]ath gods [(gr)a]b h[im], and let t[hem destroy] him along with his wife and his sons!

§7′ (28′)[…] also the fugitive […] My Majesty […] shall be! (29′)But [i]f My Majesty […] not the campai[gn] of the [en]emy […] (30′)in some [cru]cial campaign […], (31′)but a [m]an flees, then he shall n[ot …] (32′)his superior makes/does, [*and* …], (33′)and […] him likewise.

§8′ (34′–36′)[(Furthe)]rmore, last year you […]-ed the city of Kilimun[a~…], and you com[man]ded the […]-m[en] (and?) the subordinates […] (thus): "Eat your soldiers' bread [imme]diately, [but] do not do the work!"[147] (37′)[…] they release/allow [… imme]diately; then because of that matter, too, yo[u] (38′)[yoursel]ves *fell short*; and thu[s …]; (39′–40′)[…] whoever do[es su]ch a thing now, though, let [(these oa)t]h gods grab him, and let them [destr]oy him along with his wife and his sons!

§9′ (41′)[Moreov(er)], let the matter of the soldiers' bread be a binding obligation from this moment on. (42′–45′)[(When)] they mobilize the army for a

ni-ni-[i]n-kán-zi nu-za-ta LÚUGULA LI-IM LÚDUGUD-⸢ša?⸣ (43′)[…]x[148] NINDA.ÉRINMEŠ-ŠU ZÍD.DA-[Š]U me-na-aḫ-ḫa-an-da a-uš-du ku-iš-za ⸤NINDA.ÉRIN⸥MEŠ-ŠU-ma (44′)[Ú-UL(?) ḫar-z]i[149] nu-za-kán Ú-U[(L)]x-ia-an-na[150] zi-ik-ke-ez-zi la-aḫ-ḫi-ia-u-wa-aš-za (45′)[ut-tar(?)] ⸢Ú⸣-UL im-ma še-e[k-t]e-ni še-ra-aš-ta ku-it-ki šar-ra-an

§10′ (A i 46′–50′; B₁, 1′–6′) (46′)[an?-da?-ma?]-aš-ša-an ku-iš k[u-u-r]u-ri pa-ra-a ga-la-an-kán-za nu ki-iš-ša-an (47′)[im-ma t]e-ez-zi ma-an-wa i-ni ku-u-ru-ur ar-ḫa ḫar-ak-zi nu ⸤ki-iš-ša⸥-an (48′)[(im-ma t)]e-ez-zi (erasure of ca. 12 signs) ma-an-wa i-ni [ku-u-ru-u]r? (49′)[le-(e a)]l-pu-e-eš-zi[151] [nu] ⸤a⸥-pu-u-un ke-e NI-IŠ DINGIRMEŠ ap-pa-an-du n[a-an QA-DU] (50′)[DAM-ŠU] DUMUMEŠ-ŠU ḫar-ni-[(i)]n-kán-du [ ]

§11′ (A i 51′–54′) (51′)[nu-uš-m]a-aš ke-e dUT[U-Š]I ku-e iš-ḫi-ú-ul iš-ḫi-iš-ke-mi du-[ug-ga]-⸢a-ru⸣-[uš-ma-aš][152] (52′)[ku-it] ⸢I⸣-NA QA-TI-KU-NU an-da te-eḫ-ḫu-un na-at-za-kán ḫu-u-ma-[a]n-[pát] (53′)[an-ni-ì]š-ket₉-te-en na-[aš-t]a ŠA *d*UTU-ŠI du-ud-du-mi-ìš-ša[153] ḫ[u?-u-da-ak(?) le-e][154] (54′)[ku-e-d]a-ni-ik-k[i] me-er-zi

§12′ (A i 55′–61′) (55′)[nu-uš-m]a-aš šu-me-⸢en₆⸣-za-an-pát A-NA SAG.DUḪI.A-KU-NU URU!Ḫa-at-t[u-ša-aš] x[ ] (56′)[… d]u-ud-du-uš-⸤ke⸥-mi nu ŠA LÚKÚR ut-tar ḫu-u-ma-an-ti-ia kat-t[a …]x[…] (57′)[…]x ḫu-u-ma-a[n]-ti-ia ḫu-u-da-aš e-eš-tu dUTU-ŠI-iš x[…]x x[…] (58′)[ḫu-u-m]a-an-da-a[n] ⸤ḫu⸥-iš-nu-uš-⸤ke-mi⸥ nu ka-a-ša ⸤zi[155]⸥-[…] (59′)[nu-uš-m]a-aš-kán k[u-i]t ⸤ut-tar I-NA⸥ QA-TI-KU-NU ⸤zi⸥-[ik-ke-mi na-at …] (60′)[pa-aḫ-š]a-ru k[u-i-š]a-⸢at⸣[156] Ú-UL-ma pa-aḫ-ša-ri n[a-an ke-e NI-IŠ DINGIRMEŠ] (61′)[ap-pa]-a[n-du na-a]n QA-DU DAM-ŠU DUMUMEŠ-ŠU ḫar-ni-i[n-kán-du]

§13′ (A i 62′–70′) (62′)[nam?-ma?[157] ma-a]-aḫ-ḫa-an š[u-m]e-en₆-za-an SAG.DUMEŠ-KU-NU ⸤URUḪa-at⸥-[tu-ša~ x x x x]x x[ ][158] (63′)[nu? šu-me-e-eš(?)][159] pa-an-ku-uš URUḪa-at-tu-ša-aš ⸤SAG.DU⸥ d⸤UTU⸥-Š[I pa-aḫ-ḫa-aš-du-ma-a]t(?) (64′)[nu dUTU-Š]I-aš[160] TI-wa-tar i-la-li-iš-ke-et-[te]-e[n …]x[… i-da-a-lu(?) le]-⸢e?⸣ (65′)[ku-iš-k]i(?)[161] ták-ki-iš-zi LUGAL-*uš-ša-an* ku-x[[162] … d]a?-a-i (66′)[…][163] A-NA LUGAL-TÌ iš-ki-ez-zi na-an-za š[u-me-e-eš kat-ta DUMUMEŠ-K]U?-N[U? DUMU.DUMUMEŠ][164]-KU-NU (67′)[še-ek-t]e-en[165] nu-uš-ša-an ku-iš a-pé-e-da-[ni-pát[166] i-da-a-lu tá]k-⸢ki⸣-i[š-zi][167] (68′)[ku-i-ša-a]n iš-ta-ma-aš-zi-ma na-an e-e[p-du na-a]n te-⸢ek⸣-ku-u[š-nu-ud]-du (69′)[ku-i-ša-a]n[168] {x} mu-un-na-iz-zi-ma na-an k[e-e NI-IŠ DING]IRMEŠ ap-pa-an-⸢du⸣ (70′)[na-an QA-D]U DAM-ŠU DUMUMEŠ-ŠU ḫar-ni-in-k[án]-du

campaign, let a *clan* chief and a commander inspect[169] […], its soldiers' bread (and) its flour. He who [*does not have*] his soldiers' bread, though, will no[t] undertake […], either. Do you not even k[no]w the [*matter*] of campaigning? Because of such (matters) transgressions (have occurred)![170]

§10′ (46′–48′)[*Furthermore*], whoever is appeasing regarding the e[nem]y, and [even s]peaks thus: "Maybe this war will be lost," and he [(even s)]peaks thus: "I hope that this [*wa*]*r* (49′–50′)does [no(t e)]scalate!"[171] [Then] let these oath deities grab him, and let them destroy [him along with his wife] and his sons!

§11′ (51′)[And] these obligation(s) that I, My Maj[es]ty, am imposing on [yo]u, [*let them be*] *im*[*portant to you*]! (52′–53′)[That which] I have placed in your hands, [accom]plish every la[st bit of it]! Let also the *benevolence* of My Majesty (54′)in [no wa]y *a*[*bruptly*] diminish!

§12′ (55′)[And to y]ou, to your very persons of Ḫatt[usa …], (56′)[…] I will show benevolence, and the matter of the enemy [… b]y every […] (57′)[…] in/to every […] let there be promptness! I, My Majesty, […] (58′)will let [al]l […] live, and for my part […]. (59′–61′)[And] wh[atev]er matter [I] p[lace] in your hands, may [… defend/preserve it]! H[e wh]o does not protect it, though, [let these oath deities gr]a[b him, and let them] destr[oy h]im along with his wife and his sons!

§13′ (62′)[*Further*, ju]st as you, yourselves, […] Ḫat[tusa], (63′)[so mus]t [*you*], the whole of Ḫattusa, [protect] the person of My Majest[y]! (64′–65′)[And] you mu[st] desire life for [My Majes]ty! [… *no on*]*e concoct* [*evil* …]. […] the king [t]akes, (66′)[and …] anoints for the kingship, you [and thereafter *y*]*ou*[*r* sons and] your [grandsons] (67′–68′)must [recognize] him! And [whoever] learns of anyone [at all] who [*co*]*nco*[*cts* evil] against hi[m], he [must] se[ize] him and deno[un]ce him! (69′)[Whoever] hides [h]im, though, let th[ese oath deit]ies grab him, (70′)[and le]t them destroy [him alo]ng with his wife and his sons!

§14′ (A i 71′–76′) (71′)[nu? šu-me-e-eš(?) k]u-i-e-eš DUMU*MEŠ* LUGAL ma-a-an i-da-a-lu x[x]x x x[…]x (72′)[… šu-me-e]n$_6$-za-an(?) BE-LA$_{12}$[172] GAL ku-in-ki an-da ḫu-i[t-ti-ia-u-wa-an-zi e]-ep-zi (73′)[…]-aš? e-ep-zi na-aš-ma-at A-NA ÉRIN^MEŠ[…] (74′)[…]x-kán na-iš-du-ma-at nu-wa-kán ku-i[n?~…] (75′)[…]x-^zi na-an Ú-UL e-ep-zi na-an k[e-e NI-IŠ DINGIR^MEŠ] (76′)[ap-pa-an-du n]a-an QA-DU DAM-ŠU DUMU^MEŠ-ŠU ḫar-ni-i[n-kán-d]u

§15′ (A i 77′–82′) (77′)[… ap-p]é-ez-⸤zi⸥-aš ḫa-an-te$_9$-ez-zi nu-un-tar-ri-id-du nu-u[š-m]a-aš ^dU[TU?-ŠI?] (78′)[…]x x-⸤pí?⸥-ia-an ḫar-kán-du nu KIN-az a-pé-e-ez a-ni-e[š?-ke-…] (79′)[…]x-an KUR-ia-az ar-ḫa šu-ú-it ki-nu-na (80′)[…]x pa-aḫ-ḫa-aš-du-ma-at nu nu-un-tar-ri-it-ta-⸤ni⸥[173] (81′)[…]-ḫu-e-ni na-aš-ta ú-e-eš-ša ^LÚKÚR-an[174] KUR-⸢e?⸣[ ] (82′)[…]-ni ⸤EGIR?-pa?⸥ e-⸤šu⸥-aš-ta

(gap of only some few lines)

§16″ (A ii 1′–6′) (1′)[…]x x[…] (2′)pé-e-ez-zi *x*[…] (3′)i-da-a-lu le-[e …] (4′)nu-uš-ši na-aš-šu […] (5′)kat-ta-^an KUR-ni ḫar-x[… na-an ke-e NI-IŠ DINGIR^MEŠ ap-pa-an-du] (6′)na-an *x* QA-DU [DAM-ŠU DUMU^MEŠ-ŠU ḫar-ni-in-kán-du]

§17″ (A ii 7′–13′) (7′)an-da-ma ^dUTU-[ŠI …] (8′)ḫa-an-da-an n[u? …] (9′)KUR ^URUḪA.AT.TI ⸢Ù⸣[…] (10′) ^LÚME-ŠE-*DU!* DUMU É.GA[L …] (11′)DUMU^MEŠ ^URUḪA.AT.TI n[u- …] (12′)DUMU-⸤ŠU⸥ da$_4$-mi-iš-ḫa-[…] (13′)na-[… -t/š]a-an […]

§18″ (A ii 14′–20′) (14′)na-x-x[x]šu-up-[pé-eš- …] (15′)na-[…]x[… -V]ḫ-ḫi x[…] (16′)ud-⸢da-ni⸣-[i ...]x[…] (17′)na-at x x[…]x[…] (18′)še-er ⸢ar-ḫa⸣-i[a …] (19′)nu ki-iš-ša-an t[e- …] (20′)na-an ke-e NI-[IŠ DINGIR^MEŠ ap-pa-an-du na-an QA-DU DAM-ŠU DUMU^MEŠ-ŠU ḫar-ni-in-kán-du]

§19″ (A ii 21′–27′) (21′)ma-a-na-at-ša-an[…] (22′)IŠ-TU DINGIR^MEŠ pár-ku-[…] (23′)ḫa-an-na-ri Ú-U[L …] (24′)šu-up-pé-eš-na-aš […] (25′)ma-a-an DINGIR-LU$_4$ x[…] (26′)te-ed-du ku-x[…] (27′)šu-up-pé-eš-n[a-aš …]

§20″ (A ii 28′–31′) (28′)ku-i-ša-t[a …] (29′)ma-a-an x[…] (30′)⸤pé⸥-ra-an[…] (31′)[…]x x[…]

(ca. 6 lines entirely missing)

§21″ (A ii 1″–2″) (1″)na-x[…] (2″)da-a-i ⸢ku⸣-x[…]

§22″ (A ii 3″–9″) (3″)ma-a-na-at A[N …] (4″)na-at QA-TAM-M[A …] (5″)nu-za PA-NI ZI[…] (6″)ku-[x] an-t[u- …] (7″)[ku-i]n-ki[…] (8″)⸤Ú⸥-[UL …] (9″)⸤A?⸥[…]

§14′ (71′)[*And you* w]ho are princes: if […] evil, (72′)[… be]gins [to] dr[aw …] some great lord [*of you*]*rs* into […], (73′)[…] he seizes, or […] it/them to the troops, (74′–76′)[…] you turn […] (saying): "*Whome*[*ver* …]," and he does not seize him, then [let] th[ese oath deities grab him], [an]d [le]t them dest[roy] him along with his wife and his sons!

§15′ (77′–78′)[… the la]st shall hurry *to the fore*, and [*My*] *Maj*[*esty* …] t[o y]ou […] they shall keep/have […], and [… *keep*] *working with/from that task.* (79′)[…] he chased from the land; but now (80′)you must protect […],[175] and/so you will hurry, (81′)"We will […], and we, too, […] the enemy *in* the land (82′)[…] we will *oppose* […]."

(gap of only some few lines)

§16″ (2′–3′)[…] he sends […] shall no[t …] evil, (4′)and to him/it or […] (5′)(in)to the land below/with [… let these oath deities grab him], (6′)and [let them destroy] him along with [his wife and his sons]!

§17″ (7′)Furthermore, [My] Majesty […] (8′)is arranged/proper, *an*[*d* …] (9′)the land of Ḫattusa an[d …] (10′)a royal bodyguard, a palace servant […] (11′) sons of Ḫattusa, an[d …] (12′)afflict his son […] (13′)and […]

§18″ (14′)And puri[ty …] (15′)and I do […] (16′)to/for the matter/word […] (17′) and it/them […] (18′)up away […] (19′)and s[ay] as follows: [" … "], (20′) then [let] these oat[h gods grab] him, [and let them destroy him along with his wife and his sons]!

§19″ (21′)If/When […] it/them, […] (22′)from/through the gods purify […] (23′) he decides/will decide, […] no[t …] (24′)of purity […]. (25′)If/When the deity […] (26′)he shall speak […] (27′)o[f] purity […].

§20″ (28′)And whoever […] yo[u(sg.) …]. (29′)When/If […] (30′–31′)before […]

(ca. 6 lines entirely missing)

§21″ (1″)And […] (2″)takes/places […]

§22″ (3″)If/When […] them/it […], (4″)and […] them/it likewi[se …], (5″)then … before […] (6″)which ma[n …] (7″)whom […] (8″–9″)no[t …]

(ca. 18 lines entirely missing)

§23″ (A ii 1″–5″) (1″)x[…] (2″)[…] (3″)*še-/t[e-* …] (4″)LÚ[…] (5″)x[…]

§24″ (A ii 6″–11″) (6″)AN[…] (7″)*n[a-* …] (8″)LÚ[…] (9″)*nu*[…] (10″)NUMU[N …] (11″)⌞*QA*⌟-*T*[*AM-MA*(?) …]

(gap of ca. 12 lines)

§25″ (A iii 1′–4′) (only traces preserved)

§26″ (A iii 5′–9′) (5′)*k*[*u*?-…]x[…] (6′)*ú-*[*e-mi-ia*[176]*-az-zi nu ni-wa-a*]*l-la-an* x x x[…] (7′)*na-a*[*t*[177] ... *-i*]*a*?*-u-wa-aš*[178] *ud-da-ni-i ḫa-*[*an-da-an* …] (8′) *wa-*x[… *-z*]*i na-aš ma-a-an* BAD GAL *na-*[*aš-ma-aš* …] (9′)*a-pa-*[*a-aš an-tu-uḫ-š*]*a-aš na-aš a-ku-pát* LUGAL*-an-za-kán Ú-*[*UL* …]

§27″ (A iii 10′–13′) (10′)*an-d*[*a-ma*[179] *m*]*a-*⸢*a*⸣*-an* LÚ*-aš a-ú-ri-ia an-da*[…] (11′) *e-e*[*p-zi*] *ma-a-na-aš* BAD GAL *ma-a-na-aš* ÉRINMEŠ*-az nu*[…] (12′)*ak-k*[*i-iš*]*-kán-du-pát* É*-ZU-ma A-NA* É.GAL*-*[*LÌ* …] (13′)*ku-in-n*[*a*?*-m*]*a*?*-aš-ta*[180] dUTU*-ŠI da-a-i na-at-še* A x[…]

§28″ (A iii 14′–22′) (14′)*an-da-*[*m*]*a ma-a-an an-tu-*uḫ-še-eš* ḫa-an-*⌞*ne*⌟*-*[*eš-ni* …] (15′)*ḫu-wa-a*[*p-p*]*í ku-iš-ki ku-e-da-ni na-aš-*x[…] (16′)[*u*]*t*?*-*⌞*tar*?⌟ *na-a*[*š-t*]*a ma-a-an a-pé-e an-tu-u*[*ḫ-še-eš* …] (17′)[*BE-LU*][181] GAL [*na*]*m-ma-aš ḫa-ap-pí-na-an-za* A[…] (18′)[*ku-i-š*]*a-k*[*á*]*n*? *ḫu-wa-ap-pí ku-e-da-*[*ni* …] (19′)[*nu ku-i*]*š p*[*a-a*]*p-re-ez-zi*[182] *na-aš a-k*[*i* …] (20′)[*na-at-š*]*i* ⸢*a*⸣*-a-ra e-eš-tu ma-a-na-*[…] (21′)[*ḫu-wa*]*-a*[*p*]*-pa-aš-ma ku-iš na-aš ma-a-a*[*n* …] (22′)[*ma-a-a*]*n* ⌞*A-NA*⌟ LUGAL *a-aš-šu-wa-an-za n*[*a-* …]

§29″ (A iii 23′–27′) (23′)[…]x [*ap-p*]*é-ez-zi-aš* LÚMÁŠD[A …] (24′)[…]x[… L]Ú⌞MÁŠDA⌟*-pát* x[…] (25′)[…]x[…]x ⌞RI?⌟ x[…] (26′)[…]RI?[…] (27′)[…]*-zi* […]

§30″ (A iii 28′–29′) (28′)[*na-a*]*t/n*?*-ša-a*[*n*? …] (29′)[…]⌞*kat*?*-ta*?⌟*-a*[*n*? …]

(nearly two-thirds of a col. entirely missing)

§31″ (A iv 1) (1)[…]*-ša-an le-e tap*?*-pí*?*-a*[*n*[183] …]

§32″ (A iv 2–7) (2)[…]x EGIR*-an IT-TI* BAD [GAL? …] (3)[…]⌞*a*⌟*-pa-a-aš ŠA* LÚMÁŠDA[…] (4)[…]x*-zi nu* LÚMÁŠDA *l*[*e-e*] (5)[… *a*]*r-ḫa le-e šu-ú-ez-zi* [*nu ku-i*]*š* (6)[… *na-an k*]*e-e NI-IŠ* DINGIRMEŠ *ap-pa-an-d*[*u*] (7)[*na-an QA-DU* DAM*-ŠU* DUMUMEŠ*-ŠU*] *ḫar-ni-in-kán-d*[*u*]

§33″ (A iv 8–13) (8)[… *k*]*u-i-e-eš* LUGALMEŠ *e-šer nu-wa* L[Ú.MEŠMÁŠD]A[184] (9) [… *li-in*]*-ga-nu-uš-ke-er nu da-aš-ša-mu-u*[*š* …]x*-uš*[185] (10)[…] (erasure)

(ca. 18 lines entirely missing)

§§23″–24″ (Too fragmentary for translation.)

(gap of ca. 12 lines)

§25″ (only traces preserved)

§26″ (6′)[… he] fi[nds, and … inno]cent […], (7′)and i[t/th[ey…] in the matter it is se[ttled] (thus): (8′)[…] if he's a great lord o[r if he's …] (9′)th[at ma]n, then he shall surely die. The king […] no[t …] him.[186]

§27″ (10′–11′)Furthe[rmore, i]f a man beg[ins] to […] in a watch(tower) […], be he a grand lord or be he from the army, then […] (12′)they shall surely die. His house, though, […] to the palace, (13′)[*bu*]*t* His Majesty will take/place *eac*[*h one*]; and […] it/them to him.

§28″ (14′)Further[mor]e, if men [… in] a court ca[se …] (15′)someone is mal[evo]lent to someone and/or […] (16′)[*w*]*ord/*[*ma*]*tter*, and if those me[n …] (17′)a grand [lord, fu]rther he is wealthy, […], (18′)but [he who] is malevolent to someo[ne …], (19′)[then he wh]o is found g[ui]lty shall di[e. …], (20′)[and it] shall be allowed [for h]im. If […], (21′)but he who is [male]volent, and if he […], (22′) [i]f it pleases the king, th[en …].

§29″ (23′)[… the *low*]*liest* peasa[nt …] (24′)[…] that very peasant […]

§30″ (only traces preserved)

(nearly two-thirds of a col. entirely missing)

§31″ (1)[…] shall not […].

§32″ (2)[…] behind/after with the [*grand*] lord […] (3)[…] the aforementioned […] of the peasant […] (4)[…] he […]-s, and the peasant shall n[ot …] (5)[…] he shall not chase away, [and he w]ho (6)[…], let these oath deities grab [him], (7)[and] let them destroy [him along with his wife and his sons]!

§33″ (8)[… t]hose who were kings:[187] "P[easan]t[s] (9)[…] they made [swe]ar an oath." And the *important* ones (10)[…] every man(acc.) [of Ḫ]attusa (11) *ku-in-na an-du-uḫ-ša-a*[*n*[188] *ŠA* URU*Ḫ*]*A.AT.TI* (11)[…]x-*az/uk-kán* BE-EL-ŠU *ku-en-zi me-*[[189] …]x-*ma-aš-ši* (12)[…] x [*n*]*u-wa-*⸤*az*⸥ *ŠA* BE-LÍ-ŠU *e-eš-ḫar* x[…]x (13)[…]x ḪA T[A …]xMEŠ-*uš šar-la-a-*[…]

§34″ (A iv 14–20) (14)[… *u*]*t-tar*[190] *A-BI* d⸢UTU⸣-[*ŠI š*]*ar-la-a-it nu-wa-ra-aš-ta*[…] (15)[m*Mu-u-wa-at-t*]*a-al-li-iš* m*Ḫu-uz-zi-an ku-en-*⸤*ta A*⸥-[*BI* dUTU]-*ŠI-ma-aš-ši*[191] (16)[*me-na-aḫ-ḫa-a*]*n-da NI-IŠ* DINGIR-*LÌ-ŠU e-eš-ta nu-wa-aš-ši* [… -*r*]*i*? (17)[… *n*]*u*?-*wa-ra-aš A-NA* m*Mu-u-wa-at-ta-al-li*[…] (18) […]x-*it* URU*Ḫa-at-tu-ša-aš-ma-aš-ši* EGIR-[*an* …] (19)[…]~GAZ[192]-*za-wa-aš-ši* EGIR-*an ar-ḫa wa*-x[…] (20)[…]x-*da* *1*-*EN da-a-le-e-*[…]

§35″ (A iv 21–26) (21)[… URU*Ḫa*]-*at-tu-ša-aš* ⸤*ki-i*⸥ ⸢*ut-tar*⸣ x x[…] (22)[… *ki*]-⸤*i*?⸥ *u*[*t*?-*tar*] *kar-pé-er nu-wa-r*[*a-* …] (23)[…]x DINGIRMEŠ *ḫu-u-ma-an-te-eš* x[…] (24)[…]-*ḫa-an-du nu-wa-*⸤*ra-an* d⸥UTU-**ŠI** LUGAL-⸢*u*⸣-[*i*]*z-z*[*i-ia* …] (25)[… -*wa-r*]*a-aš-kán* LUGAL-*u-i*[*z-zi-ia* …]x-*ki* LÚŠU.GI[…][193] (26) […]x DUMUMEŠ dU[TU-*ŠI* DUMU.DUMUMEŠ] dUTU-*ŠI QA-TAM-M*[*A* …]

§36″ (A iv 27–31) (27)⸢*nu-wa*⸣-[…]AB x[[194]… *ar*]-*ḫa za-am-mu-ra-*⸤*iz*⸥-[*zi* …] (28)*nu-wa-*[x] x *wa-a*[*k-*[195]…]-*e-eš A-NA* dUTU-*Š*[*I* …] (29)*nu~ut*?-x[[196] …] x-*a*[*n* …]x-*ḫa-an-zi* *x *šu**-x[…] (30) URU*Ḫ*[*a-at-tu-š*]*a-a*[*š* … -(*i*)]*a-an* *x* *ti-ia*-x[…] (31)⸤*na*⸥-x[…]x x[…]x-*zi nu a-pu-u-un*[…]

§37″ (A iv 32–34) (32)[…]x-⸢*ni*⸣ *ud-da-ni-*[*i* …]x *te-ek-*[…] (33)[…]x *ma-az-zu-e-n*[*i* …]x x[…] (34)[…]x x[…]

(ca. 10 lines entirely missing but for the occasional indecipherable trace)

§38″ (A iv 44′–45′) (44′)[…]*ŠA*[…] (45′)[…] *ap-p*[*a-*[197] …]

§39″ (A iv 46′–51′) (46′)[… *u*]*d*?-*d*[*a*?-*ni-i* …]x x[…] (47′)[… *a*]*r-ḫa* x[…] (48′)[x x ˈ*i-da-a*]-*lu ut-ta*[*r* …] (49′)[… *a*]*r-ḫa za-am-*[*mu-ra-* …] (50′)[…]-*at-ta A-N*[*A* …] (51′)[… *e*]-*ep-zi na*-x[…]

§40″ (A iv 52′–56′) (52′)[…]*ku-iš ḫa-az-zi* ⸢Ú⸣[…] (53′)[…]*na-aš* LUGAL-*i ú-ed-d*[*u*? …] (54′)[… *k*]*i-iš-ša-an-ma t*[*e-* …] (55′)[…] ⸤*a*⸥-*pé-ni-iš-šu-wa-an*[…] (56′)[…]x-*na-az ḫu-it-*[*ti-* …]

§41″ (A iv 57′–63′) (57′)[…]x *ma-a-an* LUGAL-*uš*[…] (58′)[…]*ku-it me-ḫur nu* A x[…] (59′)[…]xḪI.A-*TI*! LÚ.MEŠDUGUD[…] (60′)[…-*z*]*i ma-a-na-aš-ta t*[*i-*/*n*[*am-* …] (61′)[… Ḫ]I.A-*TI*! LÚ.MEŠDUGUD x[…] (62′)[…]⸢d⸣UTU-*ŠI-iš I-NA* ÉḪI.A[…] (63′)[…]-*ma a-pu-u-uš tar-*⸤*na*⸥-*an-du* […]

§42″ (A iv 64′–67′) (64′)[…]-*wa-u-wa-an-zi-ma-*[*š*]*a-an* x[…] (65′)[…]x *na-aš-*wa*?*-du*-x-*aš iš-ḫ*[*a*?- …] (66′)[…]x DINGIRMEŠ *ḫu-u-da-*[*a*]*n*?-*te-*eš** *t*[*u-* …] (67′)[… *ku-u*]*t-ru-e-ni-i*[*š*] ⸤*a*⸥-*ša-an-*[*du*]

[…] he kills his lord. "But […] to him […], (12)and the blood of his lord […] (13)[…] *elevate* […]."

§34″ (14–16)[Then … *acc*]*laimed* [the ma]tter/[w]ord of the father of [My] Majesty (saying), "[… Mūwatt]alli has killed Ḫuzziya." The f[ather of] My [Majesty], though, was bound [t]o him by oath,[198] (and he said): "[…] to/for him. (17)And he […]-ed to/for Mūwattalli." (18)But Ḫattusa […] behind him […] (saying): (19)"[…] behind him […] away […] (20)[…] leave/left […] a single one."

§35″ (21)[… Ḫ]attusa […] this matter […] (22)[…] they took up [thi]s ma[tter] (saying):[199] (23)"[…] all the gods […] (24)[…] let them […], and […] him, My Majesty, [in] kingship […] (25)[… in] kingship […] old man […] (26)[…] sons of [My] Ma[jesty (and) the grandsons of] My Majesty likewise."

§36″ (27)"And […] he insulted […], (28)and […] to My Majesty […] (29)and they do/will do […] (30)Ḫ[attus]a […], (31)and […], and […] him.

§37″ (32)"[…] to/for the matter […] *rev*[*eal* …] (33–34)we will resist […]"

(ca. 10 lines entirely missing but for the occasional indecipherable trace)

§38″ (Too fragmentary for translation.)

§39″ (46′)[… *in the ma*]*tt*[*er* …] (47′)[… f]orth/a]way […] (48′)[… the evi]l matte[r …] (49′)[…] insult-[…] (50′)[…] to […] (51′)[…] he seizes, and […]

§40″ (52′)[…] he who *pierces*[200] […] (53′)[…] he must come to the king! […] (54′)[…] but s[ay?] as follows: "[…] (55′)[…] as such […] (56′)[…] dr[aw] from […]"

§41″ (57′)[…] if/when the king […] (58′)[…] which/because time, and […] (59′)[…] the dignitaries […] (60′)[…] if/when […] (61′)[…] the dignitaries […] (62′)[…] My Majesty in the building […], (63′)[…] but they must release them! […]

§42″ (64′–65′)[…] but to […] the *hurrying*[201] gods […] (66′–67′)[…] let them be [wit]nesses! […]

§43″ (A iv 68′–74′) (68′)[…]x dLAMMA dU[TU URU*A.R*]*I.IN.*[*NA* …] (69′)[… -*w*]*a-ni-iš du-*[…] (70′)[… *ḫu-u-m*]*a-an-te-eš* x[…] (71′)[…] I₇ḪI.A GAL x[…] (72′)[… *ša*]*r-ra-at-ta*[…] (73′)[… *QA-DU* D]AM-*ŠU* DUMUM[EŠ-*ŠU* …] (74′)[… -*d*]*u*? *na-*[202 …]

§43″ (68′)[…] protective deity, S[un] Goddess [of Ar]in[na …] (69′)[… *witne*]*sses* […] (70′)[… al]l […] (71′–72′)[…] great rivers […] (72′)[… tr]ansgresses […] (73′)[… together with] his wife and [his] son[s…]

No. 13
Instructions of Arnuwanda I for the Mayor (of Ḫattusa)
(*CTH* 257)

The Instructions of Arnuwanda I for the Mayor of Ḫattusa consist in fact of three groups of clearly related fragments, which, however, cannot be attributed to a single composition with absolute certainty. From the first group (13.1–2), generally assumed to represent Tablets 1 and 2 of the composition (but see n. 232), an incipit and two colophons are partially preserved, providing the author and addressee. The other two groups (13.3 and 13.4) are placed together with these Instructions for the Mayor due to the specific mention of the mayor (13.3, §§2′–3′) and the references to various duties "in Ḫattusa" (13.4, §§2′, 10″) or at structures known to be in Ḫattusa (e.g., the *asusa*-gate in 13.4, §5′; see also Sources, nn. 9, 11–12).

No. 13.1 is preserved by two larger blocks of fragments (A and E) along with three smaller fragments or blocks of fragments (B, C, D), while No. 13.2 is represented by one small fragment only, preserving nothing more than a colophon. No. 13.3 is found on one mid-sized (A) and two smallish fragment blocks (B, C), and No. 13.4 is represented by one mid-sized (A) and one small (B) fragment. If one were to assume that 13.1–4 belonged to a single composition of two tablets, then only about one fifth of the original composition at most would be preserved.

Transliteration (13.1–2)

§1 (1.E i 1–12; 1.A i 1!–10! [1′–7′];[203] 1.B i 1–6; 1.D i 1′) (E i 1)[U(M-MA TA.BA.AR.NA)] ^{m}AR.NU.WA.AN.DA LUGAL.GAL (2)[LU(GAL KUR ^{URU}ḪA.AT.TI)] zi-ik-za ^{LÚ}ḪA-ZA-AN-NU (3)[ḫ(a-li-ia-aš ud-da-n)]i-i me-ek-ki na-aḫ-ḫa-an-za *e-eš* (4)[n(u ^{URU}Ḫa)-a(t-tu-ši ḫ)]a-a-li SIG$_5$-in uš-kán-du (5)˻2[204] LÚ˼.^{MEŠ}E[N.NU.UN[205]-k]án ku-i-e-eš ^{URU}KÙ.BABBAR-ši še-er (6)nu ša-ra-a-az-[z]i kat-ti-ir-ri-ia ku-wa-pí (7) ^{URU}Ḫa-at-tu-ši $^{LÚ.MEŠ}$EN.NU.UN BÀD tar-[n]a-an-zi (8) na-an[206]-kán tu-uk A-NA ^{LÚ}ḪA-ZA-AN-NU EGIR-an ar-ḫ[a] (9)le-e tar-˻ni-iš˼-kán-zi DUMU-KA na-aš-ma ÌR-KA (10)ḫa-*ad-da-an*-<da-an> u-i-ia nu-kán $^{LÚ.MEŠ}$EN.NU.UN BÀD (11)BÀD$^{ḪI.A}$-aš ša-˻ra˼-a kap-pu-u-e-eš-na-az (12)a-pa-a-aš tar-ni-iš-ke-ed-du

§2 (1.E i 13–20; 1.A i 11!–24! [8′–21′]; 1.C i 1′–11′; 1.D i 2′–9′)[207] (E i 13)[an-d]a-ma an-˻tu˼-u-ri-ia-aš $^{LÚ.MEŠ}$EN.NU.UN (14)[ki-i]š-˻ša˼-an iš-ga-ri-iš-ke I-NA GIŠ$^{ḪI.A}$ KÙ.BABBAR-[ia] (15)[2 $^{LÚ.MEŠ}$EN.N]U.˻UN˼ a-ra-an-ta-ri pa-ra-

Nos. 13.1–2 are concerned primarily with the security of the city and pertain to the fortifications and the guards who watch them (§§1–2). Special attention is naturally given to the city-gate and its locking and unlocking (§§5′–7′). A second concern is hygiene (§§10″–12″). No. 13.3 relates above all to the administration of various classes of workers. No. 13.4 pertains first to various construction and renovation projects in the city (§§1′–7′), while its remaining paragraphs (§§9″–13″) touch on matters of hygiene and, apparently, horticulture.

Otten's (1964; see also Singer 1998) overview of the duties of the mayor, based largely on the text presented here, remains essentially valid. Since the appearance of his paper, Beal (1992: 437–42; see also Neu 1996: 182) has examined the relationship between the *ḪAZANNU*, generally translated "mayor," and the EN KUR, Hittite *utniyasḫa-*, "provincial governor," while Mora (2004) has discussed the relation of these offices to that of Hieroglyphic Luwian REGIO. DOMINUS and cuneiform LÚUGULA.KALAM.MA.

As is so often the case with the instructions, most of the tablets for which a findspot is known come from the Temple I complex (1.C, 1.E, and 3.B), while 1.A was found in the *Haus am Hang* and 1.D and 2 were found together in Building K of the royal citadel. While the composition is clearly from the MH period, only 4.A shows the MH script. All others are NH copies, 1.A and 1.D being LNH.

TRANSLATION (13.1–2)

§1 (1)[T(hus says the Sovereign)], Arnuwanda, Great King, (2)[Ki(ng of the Land of Ḫattusa)]: You,[208] Mayor, (3)must be extremely vigilant in the [(matte)]r [(of the) g(uard)! (4)An(d in Ḫattusa)] they must keep the guard well. (5)The 2 gu[ards] who are up in Ḫattusa,[209] (6–7)when the guards leave the fortification walls in upper and lower Ḫattusa,[210] (8–12)they shall not turn them back over to you, the Mayor. You shall send your son or a capab<le> servant of yours, and he shall let the fortification guards up onto the fortification walls numerically.

§2 (13–15)[More]over, you shall arrange the interior guards as [fol]lows: [2 gua]rds will stand at the (*fire*)wood [*and*] at the silver (*reserve*);[211] further, (16)2 guards will sta[(nd) at …]; (17–18)[further], 2 gu[ards will stand at]

a-m[(*a*)] (16)[*I-NA* x x x]x 2 LÚ.*MEŠEN.NU*.UN *a-ra-an-t*[(*a-ri*)] (17)[*pa-ra-a-ma I-NA* K]Á[212] *ḫa-ni-ia-aš* 2 LÚ.MEŠE[N.NU.UN] (18)[*a-ra-an-ta-ri p*(*a-ra*)]-⸤*a*⸥-*ma I-NA* É dḪal-[(*ki-aš*)] (C i 3′) … [2 LÚ.MEŠEN.NU.UN *a-ra-an-t*(*a-ri pa-ra-a*)-*m*(*a*)] (4′)[*m*]*e-na-aḫ-ḫa-an-da* [… 2 LÚ.MEŠEN.NU.UN *a-ra-an-ta-r*(*i*)] (5′)[*p*]*a-ra-a-ma I-NA* ⸤É⸥[… 2 LÚ.MEŠEN.NU.UN] (6′)[*a-r*]*a-an-ta-ri pa-*[*ra-a-ma* … 2 LÚ.MEŠE(N.NU.UN) *a-ra-an-ta-ri pa-ra-a-ma*] (7′)[*A/I-N*]*A* d10 URU*ZI.I*[(*P.PA.LA.TA*) 2 LÚ.MEŠEN.NU.UN] (8′)[*a*]*-ra-an-ta-ri pa-r*[*a-a-ma A/I-NA* …] (9′)[2 L]Ú.MEŠEN.NU.UN *a-*[*ra-an-t*(*a-ri*) …] (10′)[ ]*-ša-an* x x[…] (11′)[…]x[-*z*(*i*)]

§3 (1.A i 25!–35! [22′–32′]) (A i 25!)[…] (26!)[… URUḪa-at]-*tu-ši* (27!)[…-*z*]*i*? (28!)[…] (29!)[…]x-*at*?-*ta* (30!)[…]x-*ni* (31!)[…-*n*]*u*? (32!)[…-*t*]*a-az* (33!)[…]-*zi* (34!)[…] (35!)[…]x-*zi*

(remaining ca. half of 1.A col. i and ca. 2 lines at beginning of col. ii missing)

§4′ (1.A ii 1′) (traces)

§5′ (1.A ii 2′–11′; 1.D ii 1′–9′) (A ii 2′)*an-da-m*[*a* …] (3′) URUDU*za-ki-i*[(*a*)- …] (4′)*pa-aḫ-ša-nu-wa-an-z*[(*a*) *e-eš-du* …] (5′)*ku-i-e-eš ŠA* K[Á.GA(LḪI.A URUḪa)-*at-tu-ši* …] (6′)*nu* URUDU*za-ak-ki-i*[(*a*) …] (7′)DUMU-*KA na-aš-ma* Ì[(R-*KA ḫa*)-*ad-da-an-da-an u-i-ia* …] (8′)*nu* GIM-*an* URUDU*za*!(ḪA)-*ak*-[*ki*-[213] …] (9′)*pé-eš-ši-ez-zi na-aš*~[…] (10′)*A-NA* KÁ.GAL *an-da*[…] (11′)*nam-ma še-er* SIG$_5$-*i*[*n* …]

§6′ (1.A ii 12′–17′; 1.D ii 10′–11′) (A ii 12′)GIM-*an-ma* URUDU*za-a*[*k-ki-eš ŠA*(?) KÁ.GAL(?) URUḪa-*at-tu-ša-aš*(?)] (13′)*ḫu-u-ma-an-ta-aš pé-*[*eš-ši-ia-an-te-eš*(?) ...] (14′)*nu za-ak-ki-uš a*[*r-* …] (15′)*ú-da-a-i nu ku-w*[*a*?-*pí*? …] (16′)*še-eš-ti* URUDU*za-ki-*[…] (17′)*kán-kán-te-eš a-ša-*[*an-du* …]

§7′ (1.A ii 18′–28′) (18′)*ma-aḫ-ḫa-an-ma lu-u*[*k-kat-ta ŠA* KÁ.GALḪ]I.A (19′) URUDU*za*!(ḪA)-*ak*!(AḪ)-*ki-uš kar-*[*ap-pa-an-du*]x-*ia*[214] DUMU-*KA* (20′)*na-aš-ma* ÌR-*KA ḫa-*[x] x[215] [x x *Š*]*U*?-*PUR*[216] (21′)*na-aš-ta ma-aḫ-ḫa-an* ⸤*A*⸥-*NA* KÁ.GAL NA4KIŠIB (22′)*ú-e-eḫ-zi*[217] EGIR-*ŠU-ma ku-iš BE-LU* URU*ḪAT.TI* (23′)*na-aš-šu* LÚUGULA *LI-IM na-aš-ma ku-iš im-ma* (24′)*BE-LU ḫa-an-da-i-*it-ta-ri* na-aš-ta* *NA4KIŠIB* (25′)*A-NA* KÁ.GAL **ták-ša-an** *kat-ta ú-wa-an-du* (26′)*nu* KÁ.GAL *QA-TAM-MA ḫé-e-ša-an-du* (27′) URUDU*za-ak-ki-uš-ma* EGIR-*pa I-NA* É-*KA* (28′)*ú-da-an-du* ⸤*na-aš-ta*⸥ **AŠ-RI**-*ŠU* EGIR-*pa i*[*š-tap-pa-an-du*]

§8′ (1.A ii 29′–32′) (29′)*an-*⸤*da*⸥-*ma A-NA* L[ÚMAŠ]KIM.URUKI ⸤*iš*⸥-*ḫi-ú-u*[*l*] (30′)[É]RINMEŠ *ar-nu-wa-*⸤*la*⸥-[*aš*[218] *k*]*u-iš nu-uš-š*[*i*~...]x[…] (31′)*ku-e AŠ-RI*ḪI.A […-*i*]*š-šu-u*[*l*~ …] (32′)⸤*na-at*?-*za*?⸥ x x[…-*z*]*i*? x[…]

the *ḫaniya*-[gat]e; [f(urt)]her, [2 guards will sta(nd)] in/at the temple[219] of Ḫal[(ki; furthe)r, 2 guards will stan(d) o]pposite [...]; (C i 5′–6′)[f]urther, [2 guards] will [st]and at the [...] building; fu[rther, 2 g(uard)s will stand at ...; further], (7′–11′)[2 guards] will stand [b]y the Storm God of Zi[(ppalata)]; fur[ther, 2] guards [(will)] s[tand at ...]

§3 [...] (26! [23′])in [Ḫat]tusa [...]

(remaining ca. half of 1.A col. i and ca. 2 lines at beginning of col. ii missing)

§4′ (traces)

§5′ (2′)Moreov[er, ...] (3′)the doorbo[lt[220] ...] (4′)[must be] protected. (5′)The g[at(es of Ḫa)ttusa] which [...], (6′–7′)and doorbol[t ... you must send] your son or a [(ca)pable] se[(rvant of yours)], (8′–9′)and as soon as [...] throws (shut) the doorbo[lt], then he [...] (10′)to the gate [...]. (11′)Further, on/over [...] good/well.

§6′ (12′–13′)As soon as the door[bolts] *of* all [*the gates of Ḫattusa are*] *th*[*rown shut*], (14′–15′)then [...] brings the doorbolts [...], and *wh*[*ere* ...] (16′)you sleep, the doorbo[lts ...] (17′)[should] be hung up.

§7′ (18′)As soon as it da[wns], though, (19′–20′)[they shall] li[ft open] the doorbolts [of the gate]s. And you shall [se]nd your [...] son or a [...] servant of yours, (21′–22′)and once *he turns to* the seal (of) the gate — after which whatever lord of Ḫattusa[221] (23′)or *clan* chief or whatever (24′–25′)lord at all is present — then they shall examine together the seal of the gate, (26′–28′) and they shall open the gate accordingly. But they must bring the doorbolts back into your house, and [they shall] se[cure] (them) back in their place.

§8′ (29′–30′)Moreover, [wh]atever regulati[on](s) regarding [tr]oops (and) refugees there are for the city [commi]ssioner, (31′–32′)whatever places [...] to hi[m, ...] it/them [...]

(ca. latter half of 1.A ii and first half of 1.A iii lost)

§9″ (1.A iii 1′–6′; 1.D iii 1′) (A iii 1′)*ú-*⌜*e*⌝-[…] (2′)*na-aš-ma* *⌜*wa*?⌝*-x[…] (3′) *na-aš-ma-kán* UN[…] (4′)*ú-e-mi-ia-iz-z*[*i* …] (5′)EGIR-*pa-an da-a-i n*[*a*- …] (6′)*na-at-kán kat-ta p*[*é*-x-x-*a*]*n*?[…]

§10″ (1.A iii 7′–12′; 1.D iii 2′–8′) (A iii 7′) *ma-a-an I-NA* UD.3.KAM *n*[*a-a*]*š-ma I-N*[*A* UD.x.KAM (LÚM)AŠK(M.URU-*LÌ*)] (8′) URU*Ḫa-at-tu-ša-an Ú-UL ú-*⌞*e*⌟-[(*ḫ*)*i-i*(*š-ke-ez-zi*)] (9′)*nu ma-a-an A-NA* LÚ*ḪA-ZA-AN-NI* EGI[R-*pa* (*ku-iš-ki*)] (10′)*me-ma-i ak-kán-za-wa-kán* URU*Ḫa-a*[(*t-t*)*u-ši še-er*] (11′)*ki-it-ta-ri nu* LÚ*ḪA-ZA-AN-NU* LÚ<MA>ŠK[IM.URU] (12′)*wa-aš-du-li e-ep-zi*[ ]

§11″ (1.A iii 13′–25′; 1.D iii 9′–10′) (A iii 13′)*an-da-ma-kán* LÚNIMGIR *ku-iš* URU*Ḫa-at-tu-ši še-*⌜*er*⌝ (14′)*ma-aḫ-ḫa-an* LÚ.MEŠEN.NU.UN *a-ú-ri ḫal-za-a-i* (15′)*na-aš-***ta** *ḫa-an-te-ez-zi ḫa-a-li an-da* **ḫal***-za-a-i* (16′)*pa-aḫ-ḫur-wa ki-iš-***ta***-nu-ut-tén iš-tar-ni-ia-ia-*⌞*kán*⌟ (17′)*ḫa-a-li an-da ḫal-za-a-i pa-ḫur-***wa*{*-wa* x x}* (18′)*pa-aḫ-ša-nu-wa-an e-eš-du nam-ma ŠA* DINGIR-*LÌ* (19′)⌞*ku*⌟*-iš lu-li-iš ku-un-ga-li-ia-aš nu-kán* LÚNIMGIR (20′)*ḫa-le-en-zu še-er ar-ḫa da-aš-ke-ez-zi* (21′)*ma-a-an-ma-kán* LÚ*ḪA-ZA-AN-NU* ⌞*A*⌟*-N*[*A l*]*u-*⌞*li*⌟ *ku-un-ga-li-*⌞*ia*⌟*-*[*aš*] (22′)*ḫa-le-en-zu te-pu an-*[*da* x x -*i*] *a-*⌞*an*?⌟*-zi*[222] (23′)*na-aš-ma-kán* d*Ḫal-ki-i*[*n I-NA lu-li k*]*u*?*-*⌞*iš*⌟*-*[*ki*] (24′)*an-da a-ar-ri n*[*a*-…] (25′)*wa-aš-túl* LÚ*ḪA-ZA-AN-NU*[…]

§12″ (1.A iii 26′–33′) (26′)*an-da-ma-kán tu-*[…] (27′)*me-ek-ki na-aḫ-ḫa-a*[*n-za/te-eš e-eš-du/aš-ša-an-du* …] (28′)*ú-e-da-an-za e-*[*eš-du*…] (29′)*a-ra-aḫ-za-an-ta w*[*a*- …] (30′)*nam-ma pé-e-da-aš*[…] (31′)*nu-kán* UN-*aš an-da*[…] (32′)*pa-iz-zi* UR.GI$_7$*-ia-ká*[*n* …] (33′)*le-e pa-iz-zi za-*[*/ḫ*[*a*- …]

§13″ (1.A iii 34′–38′) (34′)*an-da-ma-kán* ÉRINME[Š …] (35′)KIN *an-ni-iš-k*[*e*- …] (36′)*ḫa-***an-da***-a*[*n~* …] (37′)*na-*x[…] (38′)x[…]

(ca. half a column missing entirely)

§14″ (1.E iv 1′–8′; 1.D iv 1′–2′) (E iv 1′)[…]x ⌜*pa-ra-a*⌝ x[…] (2′)[…]x KIN *ma-ši-wa-an-n*[*a*? …] (3′)[…]x *pé-ra-an kap-pu-wa-i*[*š~* …] (4′)[…-*š*]*a-an-te-eš nu-uš-ma-aš* LÚ.MEŠ[…] (5′)⌜*ar*⌝*-ḫa* ⌜*tar*⌝*-*[*na-an-z*]*i nu-uš-ma-aš a-pu-u-uš* x[…] (6′)*da-aš-kán-z*[*i* x x]x*-ma-kán* **ta***-mi-iš-***ket*$_9$*-t**[*a-ni*] (7′)*nu-za zi-ik* [LÚ*ḪA-Z*]*A-AN-NU A-***WA***-AT* KIN […] (8′)*me-ek-ki na-a*[*ḫ-ḫa-an-z*]*a e-eš*

§15″ (1.E iv 9′–11′; 1.D iv 3′–5′) (9′)*nu zi-ik* LÚ*ḪA-Z*[*A-A*]*N-NU ŠA* URU*ḪA.AT.TI* (10′) *iš-ḫi-ú-ul kiš-an pa-aḫ-ši nu-ut-ták-kán ud-da-na-a*[z] (11′)*le-e ku-iš-ki kar-***ap-zi**

(ca. latter half of 1.A ii and first half of 1.A iii lost)

§9″ (1′)[…] (2′)or […] (3′)or a *man* […] (4′)he finds/meets […] (5′)he places/takes after/behind/back, a[nd …], (6′)and […] it/them below/with.

§10″ (7′–8′)If the [(city co)mmission(er)] does not p[at(rol)] Ḫattusa every 3[223] [o]r […] days, (9′–12′)and if there[after (someone)] says to the mayor, "A corpse is lying [up in] Ḫa[(tt)usa];" then the mayor shall catch the [city] <com>mis[sioner] in his misdeed.

§11″ (13′)Moreover, whatever herald is up in Ḫattusa, (14′)when he calls the guards in the tower,[224] (15′)he calls at the first watch: (16′)"Put out the fire!" And at the middle watch (17′)he calls: "The fire (18′–20′)has to be tended!" Further, the herald shall regularly take the *ḫalenzu*-(water plant) up off whatever *kungali*-pool (there is) for a deity. (21′–22′)But if the mayor […] a bit of *ḫalenzu*-(water plant) (in)to the *kungali*-[po]ol, (23′–24′)or [so]meo[ne] washes grain[225] [in the pool], th[en …] (25′)the failing is the mayor's.

§12″ (26′)Moreover, […] (27′)[must be] extremely careful […] (28′)[shall b]e built […] (29′)around […] (30′)further, to/of the place(s) […] (31′–32′)and a man goes in(to) […]. And a dog […] (33′)shall not go […].

§13″ (A iii 34′)Moreover, troops […] (35′)do the work regular[ly …] (36′)*arran[ge]/proper[ly* …] (37′)and […]

(ca. half a column missing entirely)

§14″ (1′)[…] out/forth […] (2′)[…] work, as many/much as […] (3′)[…] before count […] (4′)[…] they are […], and to/for them […] the men […] (5′–6′)[they l]et out […] and they take these […] to/for them […] (7′–8′)but y[ou(pl.)][226] oppress. So you, [ma]yor, must be extremely car[eful] about the matter of the work!

§15″ (E iv 9′–11′)So you, ma[y]or, must fulfill (your) obligation(s) to Ḫattusa in this way, and let no one deter you from the(se) matters!

Colophon of Tablet 1 (1.E iv 12′–15′; 1.A iv 1′)

(E iv 12′)[…] (erasure) (13′)[…] (erasure) -*NI* (14′)[… DUB.1.KAM ^{LÚ}Ḫ]A-ZA-AN-NI iš-ḫi-ú-la-aš (15′)[…] QA-TI

Colophon of Tablet 2 (2 iv 1′–2′)

(2 iv 1′)[…]DUB.2.KAM[227] [ ]x x[…] (2′)[…]^{LÚ}ḪA-ZA-AN-NI iš-ḫi-ú-la-a[š]

Transliteration (13.3)

§1′ (3.A r. col. 1′–3′) (1′)[…]x$^{⸢ḪI.A⸣}$ x x[…] (2′)[še]-er nu-uš-ša-an ḫu-u-[ma-an~…] (3′)É-ŠU SIG_5-aḫ-ḫi-iš-[…]

§2′ (3.A r. col. 4′–7′) (4′)an-da-ma-at-ta ÉRIN^{MEŠ} KIN ku-i[š? …] (5′)ÉRIN^{MEŠ}-az ku-e-da-ni KIN-ti[…] (6′)⸤^{LÚ}ḪA⸥-ZA-AN-NU ku-e-da-ni-i[a …] (7′)nu-⸢za⸣ $^{LÚ.MEŠ}$DUGUD LÚ^{MEŠ} ÉRIN^{MEŠ} a[r- …]

§3′ (3.A r. col. 8′–11′) (8′)zi-⸤ga!⸥-az ^{LÚ}ḪA-ZA!(A)-AN-NU ŠA ÉRIN^{MEŠ}[…] (9′)⸤$^{LÚ.MEŠ}$A⸥ ŠA ⸤KUŠ⸥[228] le-e ti-it-t[a-nu- …] (10′) $^{LÚ.}$⸤^{MEŠ}SIPAD⸥.GU_4 $^{LÚ.}$⸤^{MEŠ}SIPAD⸥.UDU l[e-e …] (11′)GIŠ-ru ^{GIŠ}⸤zu⸥-up-pa-⸤a-ri⸥ EGIR ANŠ[E …]

§4′ (3.A r. col. 12′–22′) (12′)ma-a-an-⸢za LÚ⸣^{MEŠ} ÉRIN$^{⸢MEŠ⸣}$-ma ku-i-uš~[…] (13′) ^{É}ḫi-li an-da a-ša-an-du […] (14′)na-at LUGAL-wa-aš KIN$^{ḪI!.A!}$ še-er x[…] (15′) ^{LÚ}u-ra-al-la-an-ni le-e x[x t]a-me-⸤e-da⸥-n[i~ …] (16′)le-e pé-$eš_{15}$-ke-ši ma-a-na-an [I?-NA?] É-KA-ma ⸤ku?-wa?-pí?⸥[…] (17′)nu-uš-ši *ku*-it lam-ni-ia-ši [nu-uš-š]i kat-ta-an x[…]x x[…] (18′)nu-ut-ta a-pa-a-at ⸤Ú⸥-NU-UT ḫ[u-u-da]-ak ú-da-a-⸤ú?⸥[…] (uninscribed) (19′)I-NA É-KA-ma-aš [l]e-e iš-t[a-an-t]a-iz-zi ma-⸤an⸥-k[án] ŠA ÉRIN^{MEŠ}-⸤ma⸥ (20′)ku-iš-ki IŠ-⸤TU⸥ KIN ar-ḫa ḫu-[wa-a-i[229] n]u-za-kán UD.1.⸤KAM⸥-ia pa-ra-a le-e (21′)ša-me-nu-uš[230] nu-uš-ši EGIR-an-⸤da⸥ [ḫu-u-da]-⸤a⸥-ak-pát ŠU-PUR na-an EGIR-pa (22′)ú-wa-da-an-du *na-aš*-kán KIN-⸤ti⸥ [le-e wa]-ag-ga-aš-ši-ia-an-za (22a′){*∢na-aš x x*}

§5′ (3.A r. col. 23′–27′) (23′) $^{LÚ.MEŠ}$NAGAR-ia-aš-ša-an ku-i-[e-eš $^{LÚ.MEŠ}$NA]GAR LUGAL-wa-aš KIN$^{ḪI.A}$-aš pé-ra-an (24′)nu ŠA É.GAL-LÌ KIN$^{ḪI.A}$ [x x x]x zi-ga-an-za I-NA É-KA (25′)le-e pé-e-ḫu-te-ši nu-[kán? I-NA] ⸤É?⸥-KA KIN-an le-e (26′)an-ni-iš-kán-zi A-NA [É-ri-an-kán(?) Š]A $^{LÚ.MEŠ}$MÁŠDA-TÌ (27′)le-e pé-$eš_{15}$-ke-ši nu-[kán ... a]n-ni-iš-kán-z[i]

Colophon of Tablet 1

(14′)[Tablet One] of the Obligation(s) for the [M]ayor; (15′)[…][231] finished.

Colophon of Tablet 2

(1′)Tablet Two […] (2′)Obligation(s) for the Mayor; […]

Translation (13.3)

§1′ (1′)[…] (2′)[… u]p/[ab]ove (is/are) […], and al[l …] (3′)set his house right.

§2′ (4′)Moreover, the work that the workforce […] you, (5′)for which work the workforce […], (6′)the mayor, also to which […], (7′)and the dignitaries and the men of the workforce […].

§3′ (8′)And you, mayor, […] of the workforce, (9′)the water carriers shall not pla[ce …] (10′)the cattle herders (and) the shepherds [shall] n[ot …] (11′)wood (and) torch behind […] hors[e …].

§4′ (12′)If/When […] some men of the workforce, though, […] (13′)they should be in the courtyard. (14′)And […] it/them on/concerning the works of the king, […] (15′–16′)for the job of horse trainer […] you shall not give to someone else! If [you …] him *somewhere/ever* [in] your house, though, (17′)because you name/assign (it/them) for/to him, [and] down to/with [hi]m, (18′)then let him bring you that tool im[medi]ately, (19′–22′)but he shall [n]ot li[ng]er in your house. Should someone from the workforce r[un] away from the work, though, you *must not let* even a single day pass. Send (someone) after him [immed]iately, and let them bring him back! He shall [not be an ab]sentee at work!

§5′ (23′)And those carpenters wh[o] are [carp]enters responsible for the king's projects, (24′–27′)and […] the palace projects, you shall not bring it (i.e., the work) into your house, and they should not perform the work [in] your house. Neither shall you give [it] to a poor[*house*], and they […] perform [it].

§6′ (3.A r. col. 28′–31′) (28′)*ŠA* É.GAL-*LÌ-az ú-e-*[x x x x x]x GIBIL *IṢ-BAT*[232] […] (29′)⌞1?⌟ *pí?-ip-pí-aš-ma-aš*[233] GIŠ-*ru* x[x x x x x]x GIŠŠU.ÚR.MÌN […] (30′)[1?] ⌞GIŠ?⌟*ip-pí-ia-an ku-it k*[*u?*- x x x x x x *n*]*a?-at-za ḫu-*⌞*e?*⌟*-eg*⌟*-ga-*[234][…] (31′)[*nu l*]*e?-*⌞*e da*⌟*-aš-*⌞*ke*⌟*-ši da-*[x x x x x x]x-⌞*ke?*⌟*-ši* […]

(gap of unknown length)

§1″ (3.C ii? 1–7; 3.B, 1′–8′) (1)[… *-z*]*a*[235]*-an* LÚ*u-ra-la-an-*⌜*ni le*⌝*-e pí-i-e-ez-z*[*i*] (2)[… (*pa-ra*)*-a* …]*-ma ku-iš* LÚ*ḫu-up-ra-la-an-ni e-ep-z*[*i*] (3)[… *p*(*í-i-e-eš*)*-ke-ed-*(*du*) …*-i*]*š-ša-an* É*ḫi-i-li-ia an-da na-an wa-*[… *i*(*a-an-za-a*)*n* …] (4)[… (*ḫa-an-n*)*a-* … *pa/ša-r*]*a-a* LUGAL*-u-wa-aš* KINḪI.A*-aš pí-i-e-eš-ke-ed-d*[(*u*)] (5)[… *-k*]*i?-ia pé-eš-ke-ed-du ma-a-na-aš* SIG5*-at-t*[(*a-ri-ma*)] (6)[(*na-aš*)*-š*(*i*)*/w*(*a-aš-kán*)] ⌞É⌟*ḫi-i-li an-da le-e mi!?-ia-ḫu-un-t*[(*e-eš-zi*)][236] (7)[… (*ši-i*)]*a-an te-ek-ku-uš-nu-ut* […]

§2″ (3.B, 9′–13′; 3.C ii? 8–15) (9′)[… *-z*]*a/-i*]*a-kán* LÚTIBIRA KIN*-az ar-ḫa* […] (10′)[(*le-e d*)*a-* ... *le*]*-*⌞*e?*⌟ *ku-iš-ki da-a-i na-an-za-an I-NA* x[…] (11′)[… *le*]*-*⌞*e*⌟ *pí-i-e-ez-zi nu ŠA* É-[(*ŠU* KI)N …] (12′)[…]*le-e ku-e-da-ni-ik-ki pa-*[… (⌞*le*⌟*-e a-*⌞*ni-i?-e?*⌟*-zi*)] (3.C ii? 11)[… *-a*]*n?* LÚNAGAR*-ma ku-iš ḫa-*[… *l*(*e?-e?*) …] (12)[… *n*]*u? a-pa-a-aš* LÚNAGAR x[…] (13)[… *a*]*r-ḫa da-a-ú n*[*a-* …] (14)[…]x ÉRINMEŠ A[…] (15)[…]x[…]

TRANSLITERATION (13.4)

§1′ (4.A i? 1′–5′) (1′)x x x*-ma ku-*⌜*it*⌝ x x[237…] (2′)*ku-*⌜*i-e*⌝*-eš nu* GIŠIG*-an-na k*[*i?-* …] (3′)EGIR*-pa ne-u-wa-aḫ-ḫa-an e-eš-tu* […] (4′)*a-ša-an-du nam-ma še-er tu-e-*x[238…] (5′)*nu-ut-ta* EGIR*-an ar-ḫa le-e* x[…]

§2′ (4.A i? 6′–9′) (6′) URU*Ḫa-at-tu-ši-ia-*[*ká*]*n ku-e* ⌜*ku*⌝*-e* x[…] (7′)*ḫu-u-ma-an-da-a-aš* EG[IR*-a*]*n ar-ḫu-u*[*t* …] (8′)⌜*ú*⌝*-e-te-eš-kán-zi na-at* EGIR*-an-*[*da* …] (9′)*ḫu-te-ek-ki-iš-kán-du* ⌜*ú-e*⌝*-te-eš-ká*[*n-du*]

§3′ (4.A i? 10′–12′) (10′)⌜*na*⌝*-at ŠA* EGIR.UD*-MI ú-e-tum-mar e-eš-*[*tu* …] (11′)*ḫu-u-te-ek-ki-iš-kán-du* EGIR*-an-da-m*[*a-at* …] (12′)*ma-ak-nu-uš-kán-*[*du*]

§4′ (4.A i? 13′–15′) (13′)*nam-*⌜*ma*⌝ *ku-in* ⌜*ku-in*⌝ *tal-ḫi-in* x[…] (14′)*tal-*⌜*ḫi-iš-kán?-du?*⌝ x x*-ša-at-ta* x[…] (15′)*nu-*[*za?*] *tal-ḫ*[*i-i*]*a?* ⌜*ḫu-u-ma*⌝*-an-ti-ia QA-*⌜*TAM-MA*⌝ x[…]

§5′ (4.A i? 16′–21′) (16′)⌜*ŠA*⌝[239] É URU[*ḪA*].⌞*LA*⌟*.A*[*B-ká*]*n ku-i-e-*⌜*eš* BÀD⌝*-eš-na-aš*[240] ⌜*a*⌝*-ra-*⌜*aḫ*⌝*-z*[*é-na-aš*] (17′)*nu-uš tal-*⌜*ḫa-u*⌝*-*[*w*]*a-*[*an-z*]*i*[241] *zi-*⌜*in-ni nam-ma*⌝ *IŠ-*⌜*TU* KÁ⌝.GAL*-a*[*z?* …] (18′)[*k*]*u-i-e-eš* x [x x] x *nu a-pu-u-*

§6′ (28′)Of the palace […] *he took* himself new […]. (29′)But 1 (piece of) *pippi*-wood(?), […] cypress, (30′)[1?] (piece of) *ippiya*-wood that […], and swear?/thresh? it/them, (31′)[and] you shall [n]ot take (it/them), you shall […]

(gap of unknown length)

§1″ (1)[…] he shall not send him to/for the job of horse trainer, (2)[… (for)th]. But he who holds […] to/for the job of potter, (3)[… h(e shall se)nd …] in the courtyard, and […] him. (4)He shall send [… u]p/[ou]t to/for the work projects of the king, (5)[…] he shall give. When/If it is auspicio[(us, though)], (6)[… (he)] shall not *grow old* [(*for him*)] in the courtyard! (7) You shall let […] be seen![242]

§2″ (9′–10′)[…] the metal smith [(shall not) …] away from the work, (11′)[… no o]ne [sha]ll place/take […], and he [shall n]ot send him into […], and the [(wor)]k for [(his)] house (12′)[…] shall for/to no one/nothing, [… (he shall not perform) …], (3.C ii? 11)[…] but the carpenter who [… *sh*(*all not*) …] (12)[…, *an*]*d* that carpenter […] (13)[…] he shall take away, an[d …] (14)[…] workers […]

TRANSLATION (13.4)[243]

§1′ (1′)[…] but which/since […] (2′)which are […], and also the door(acc.) […] (3′)shall be renewed […]s (4′)shall be […]; further […] over/on *you*[*r* …], (5′)and shall not […] out behind you.

§2′ (6′)And whichever […]-s in Ḫattusa […], (7′)you shall stand be[hi]nd them all. […] (8′)they continually build, and thereaf[ter …] (9′)they shall *close* […] it/them and th[ey sh]all build.

§3′ (10′)And it sh[all] be a building for the ages […]. (11′–12′)They shall close […], but thereafter they shall increase [… it/them].

§4′ (13′–14′)Further, they shall *plaster* […] whatever *plaster*, and (to) you […], (15′)and […] to all the *pla*[*st*]*er* likewise.

§5′ (16′–18′)You must finish *plaste*[*ring*] the out[er] defense wall of the [Al]ep[po] House. Further, you must also build those […] from the city-gate, and […] (19′)them from the [*a*]*susa*?-city-ga[te][244] in the Aleppo

uš-⸢ša⸣ ú-e-te nu-uš-kán x[…] (19′)[I]Š-TU KÁ.G[AL a?]-⸢šu?-ša?⸣-aš I-NA É URUḪA.LA.AB-⸢ša-an⸣[245] an-[da? …] (20′)[a-r]a-aḫ-zé-⸢na⸣-[aš BÀ]D?MEŠ ḫa-pal-li-ia-an-da na-an[…] (21′)[na-a]t ḫu-u-[ma]-⸢an⸣ zi-in-[ni]

§6′ (4.A i? 22′–24′) (22′)[ ] x x [ ] x [ú]-⸢e⸣-te-eš-ke-ši iš-ki-iš-ke-ma-at n[a- …] (23′)[…] x x x-˻zi ḫu-it˼-ti-ia-an-zi na-aš an-d[a …] (24′)[… -i]š? ḫu-u-ru-te-eš-kán-zi[246] x[…]

§7′ (4.A i? 25′–27′) (25′)[…]x[247] ḫu-it-ti-ia-u-wa-a[n-zi] (26′)[… -a]n-˻zi zi˼-in-ni […] (27′)[…]x x[…]

(nearly 3 columns missing entirely)

§8″ (4.A iv? 1′–2′) (2′)[… l]e-e ⸢ku-iš-ki [248]pa-iš-ket$_9$-ta⸣ […]

§9″ (4.A iv? 3′–7′) (3′)[…]ḫa-aḫ-ra-an-na-aš[249] ŠA GIŠTIRḪI.A GIŠKIRI$_6$.G[EŠTIN?ḪI.A …] (4′)[…] na-aš PÚḪI.A-aš ku-ut-ta-aš EGIR-an ša-ra-a x[…] (5′)[… -i]t-tal-na-ia še-er I-NA ḪUR.⸢SAGTa-a-ḫa⸣[250 …] (6′)[…]-li-ia-ia-ša-an an-da le-e x x[251 …] (7′)[…]x-du-ša-kán[252] an-da le-e pé-eš-ši-iš-x[…]

§10″ (4.A iv? 8′–10′) (8′)[nu][253] ka-ma-ar-šu-wa-aš ud-da-ni-i me-ek-ki na-aḫ-⸢šar⸣-x[…] (9′)[na]m-ma-kán URUḪa-at-tu-ši še-er ḫa-aš-[š]u-uš[254] le-e p[é?-eš-ši-ia-an-zi(?)] (10′)⸢na⸣-aš-ta [ḫ]a-⸢aš⸣-šu-uš kat-ta šal-la-a-i ḫu-uš-ši-li-pá[t[255] pé-eš-ši-ia-an-du(?)]

§11″ (4.A iv? 11′–13′; 4.B iii 1′–2′) (11′)⸢nam-ma⸣ ku-i-e-eš ku-i-e-eš ku-e-lu-wa-né-eš še-er É.x[256][ ] (12′)⸢ku⸣-i-e-eš nam-ma ku-i-e-eš ku-⸢wa⸣-pí nu-uš ḫu-u-ma-an-du-[uš] (13′)wa-na-al-li-iš-kán-du iš-tal-ki-iš-kán-d[u]

§12″ (4.A iv? 14′–17′; 4.B iii 3′–7′) (14′)[nam-m]a?-kán[257] {*kán*} ku-i-e-eš ku-i-e-eš GIŠKIRI$_6$.GEŠTINḪI.A GIŠti-i-e-[(eš-šar)] (15′)[…][258] še-er na-at ḫu-u-ma-an-da wa-aḫ-nu-ma-a[n-da (e-eš-du)] (16′)[… G]IŠti-i-e-eš-šar ḫu-u-ma-an [ḫ]u-u-ur-[…] (17′)x[…]ši-iš-šu-u-ri-ia-u-wa-an-z[(i)]

§13″ (4.A iv? 18′–22′; 4.B iii 8′–10′) (18′)x x[… ḫ]u-u-ma-an-te-eš x[…] (19′) x x[… -a]n-du? a-ra-aḫ-z[é- …] (20′)x x[…]x x x GI[(ŠTIRḪI.A) …] (21′) (traces) (22′)(traces)

§14″ (4.A iv? 23′) (23′)(traces)

House. (20′)The [ou]ter [defence *wa*]*lls* […] are *damaged*, so […] it, [and] (21′)[you must] finish [the]m a[l]l.[259]

§6′ (22′)[…] you must [bu]ild regularly, but you must oil them, a[nd …] (23′)[…] they pull, and […] in/to […] (24′)[…] they repeatedly overturn […]

§7′ (25′)[…] to pull […] (26′–27′)you must finish […-i]ng […]

(nearly 3 columns missing entirely)

§8″ (2′)[…] no one shall continually go.

§9″ (3′)[…] of *harrowing*, of forests (and) viney[ards][260] […] (4′)and up behind the walls of the spring-pools […] (5′)over/on […] in/at Mount Tāḫa […] (6′)shall not […] in/to […] (7′)shall not reje[ct …]

§10″ (8′)[And …] very cautious in the matter of feces. (9′)[Fu]rther, they shall not *t*[*hrow out*] the ashes up in Ḫattusa; (10′)[they must *throw out*] the [a]shes only down in the big pit.

§11″ (11′)Moreover, whatever sewage pools are up (*by*) the […]-building, (12′–13′)and further, whichever ones are anywhere else, they must scrape them all out and smooth them.

§12″ (14′–15′)[*Furthe*]*r*, whatever gardens (and) orch[(ards)][261] there are up above […], they all [(shall be)] enclos[ed]. (16′)[…] all the orchards [*to*] *spri*[*nkle*[262] …] (17′)to irrigate[263] […]

§13″ (18′)[…] all (19′)[…] they must […], outs[ide …] (20′–22′)[(forests) …]

§14″ (23′)(traces)

No. 14
Loyalty Oath of Town Commanders to Arnuwanda I, Ašmunikkal, and Tudḫaliya (*CTH* 260)

This composition represents a proper loyalty oath. It is spoken in the 1st pl. by the Town Commanders (§§1–21) to the king, queen, crown prince, and their descendants (§§21–23′, 26″–27″, 29″) in the presence of the gods (§§21, 24′). The subordinates in question, listed by name, are the Clan Chiefs and Troop Commanders (LÚDUGUD; see n. 266) of several towns specifically (§§1–21) as well as the whole of Ḫatti/Ḫattusa and various classes of military officers generally (§21).

It appears that three versions are extant, one each for the Commanders of the troops of the lands of Kinnara (No. 14.1), Ḫa/urranāssi (14.2) and Kissiya (14.3.A and 3.B_{1-2}), respectively. This is seen most clearly by the juxtaposition of all three toponyms in 1 ii 4, 2 ii 6 and 3.A ii 12 (§23′) as well as the contrast of Kinnara in 1 iii 7′ vs. Ḫa/urranāssi in 2 iii 10′, 15′, 17′ (§26′). Kinnara appears further in 1 i 24, 29 (§21), while Kissiya is found in 3.A i 11′ and 3.B_1 i 3′.[264] Unfortunately, the preservation of the fragments at these points is too poor to allow confidence in further conclusions. None of the towns has been located securely.

Each version apparently began with a listing of the commanders of the troops from the various towns of the respective region (1 i 1–23; 2 i 1–10′(?); 3.A i 1–14, 1′–15′).[265] Then follows the oath takers' statement that they would pledge their allegiance to the royal family and that the oaths, prepared on bronze tablets, would be placed before the appropriate deities (3.A i 16′–31′ // 3.B_1 i 1′–12′). Thereafter come various more detailed stipulations concerning what the oath takers would and would not do (§§22′–23′), which may well be recapitulations of the directives addressed to them by the king, no record of which survives. The next section, almost entirely lost, seems to have preserved a further listing of oath deities (§24′). Also quite fragmentary are the ensuing passages detailing what the oath takers were to do and not to do (§26″). Finally comes a section expressing again that the oath takers' loyalty would be to the royal family and its descendents (§§27″–29″). On the left edge of 14.1 are preserved three further place names, the context of which remains unclear (§30″).

As Klinger and Neu (1990: 146) have stated, 14.1, 2, and 3.A are all NH copies. Since the appearance of their paper, the (likely late) MH ms. 3.B_{1-3} has been published. All tablets and fragments, except perhaps 14.2, for which no findspot is known, were found in the Temple I complex. Taking the three versions as variants of one composition and assuming that it would be finished with a single tablet, only about a quarter of the original composition would be preserved.

The Zardummani found in 3.A i 15′ may well be the same Zar/ldummani known from several other MH documents, including an addressee, along with other military officers, of three MH letters from the Great King found in the excavations of Maşat Höyük (HBM 34, 60, 68; see Marizza 2007: 168–69; Hoffner 2009: 160–61, 211) and perhaps the individual named in the treaty of Arnuwanda with the town of Ismerigga (KUB 23.68 rev. 20). Moreover, the Asḫapala found in 14.1, §10, could well be the Āsḫapāla whose oath is preserved as No. 19. As Giorgieri (2005: 336) and Klinger (2005a: 357) have noted, the text at hand in fact shows a number of similarities to the treaties with the Kaskaeans and that with Ismerigga, including the listing of the personal names of the oath takers at the beginning of the documents.

Of special interest in the light of the discovery of the Bronze Tablet of the treaty between Tudḫaliya IV and Kuruntiya of Tarḫuntassa (Otten 1988) is the mention (3.A i 24′–32′) of a bronze tablet or tablets on which the present composition was apparently inscribed and that were subsequently placed in the temples of the Storm God of Ḫatti, the Sun Goddess of Arinna, and the various gods in the towns of the commanders in question. Watanabe (1989: 266–67) has discussed this passage in the context of all other attested sealings and mentions of sealings of Hittite treaties.

TRANSLITERATION

Text 1 i 1–2	2 i 1–10′	3.A i 1–3
§1 (1)[*U*]*M*-˹*MA* UGULA	§1 (1)[… DUG]UD?-*TÌ ŠA*	§1 (1)[… URU]˹*KI*?˺.*I*[*Š*?.
LÚ˺MEŠ [*L*]*I-IM*	KUR URU*KA.LA.AS.MA*	*ŠI.I*]*A*? (2)[…]x-˹*ša*?˺ [*Š*]*A*?
LÚ.MEŠDUGUD *ŠA* ÉRINMEŠ	(2)[…]x~*ḪU.LI.A.A.***AŠ**	ÉRIN˹MEŠ URU*UN*?˺.*TA*.x[ ]
KUR URU*KI.*˹*IN*˺.*NA.RA*	(3)[…].*IA.RI.IT.TA* (4)[…	(3)[…].*KA.A.AŠ.ŠA*
(2) m*Wa-at-ta-aš-šu-uš*	-*l*]*i*?~*kat-ti-wa* (5)[…-*t*]*i*?	
LÚDUGUD URU*KU.I.IZ.ZA.NA*	(6-10′)(traces)	

TRANSLATION

Text 1	2	3.A
§1 (1)[T]hus (say) the [C]lan Chiefs (and) the Commanders of the Troops of the Land of Kinnara:[266] (2)Wattassu, Commander of Kuīzzana,	§1 (1–5)[…*Comma*]*nder* of the land of Kalasma […]	(1)[…] *Ki*[*ssiy*]*a* (2)[… o]f the troops of Un?ta-[ ]

1 i 3–23

§2 (3) mMa-an-na-an-ni-iš LÚDUGUD URUŠA.A.ŠA.NA

§3 (4) mPa-ab-ba-aš LÚDUGUD URUMA.AL.LI.WA.AT.TA

§4 (5) mḪA.AK.KU LÚDUGUD URU⸤ŠA⸥.IZ.TA.WA

§5 (6) ⸢m⸣NA.A.NI LÚDUGUD URUGA.AG.GA.PA.ḪA

§6 (7) mTU.UT.TU LÚDUGUD URUMA.KAR.WA.ŠI.AN.DA[267]

§7 (8) mPIŠ.ŠA.A LÚDUGUD URU⸤KU⸥.I.IZ.NA

§8 (9) mAT.TA.A LÚDUGUD URUGA.AG.⸤GA⸥.BA.ḪA

§9 (10) mAN.DU.LU LÚDUGUD URUA[R.x.Š/T]A.MA (erasure)

§10 (11) mAŠ.ḪA.PA.LA LÚDUGUD URUŠ[A.A.Š]A.NA

§11 (12) mPA.AB.BA LÚDUGUD URUA[R].ŠA.A.ŠA

§12 (13) m⸤MA⸥.ME.TA[268] LÚDUGUD URU ZI.[W]A?.AŠ?.RA[269]

§13 (14) mŠA.AR.PA LÚDUGUD URUMA.A[L?.L]I?.⸢IT⸣.TA.⸢MA⸣

§14 (15) mNA.A.Ú.I.NI.IA LÚDUGUD URUT/G[A.x].Ú.IA

§15 (16) mPAL.LU.UL.LU LÚDUGUD URUZI.NI.IP~[... m....(I)]A?.RI.*IA* LÚDUGUD URU⸤KI?.PA?.AZ?⸥.ZI.⸢IA⸣

§16 (17) m⸢NA.A⸣.NI LÚDUGUD URUTU.AR.PA.A mx[.A]T?.TA LÚDUGUD ⸢URU⸣TÁK.KI.Š[A]

3.A i 4–14, 1′–14′

(4)[... LÚDUGU]D URUA.TAR.RA.U.WA.AN.NA (5)[... LÚDUGU]*D* URUŠA.AP.PA (6)[...]LÚDUGUD URUḪA/UR.TA.A.NA (7)[... LÚDUGUD] URUTA.ḪA.RA.AM.MA (8)[...LÚDUGUD] URUḪA/UR.ŠU.WA.AN.DA (9)[... LÚDUGU]D URUNi-in-ni-wa-aš [ ] (10)[... LÚDUGU]D URU⸤ZA.A?.AZ?.ZA?⸥[ ] (11)[... .I]A?.AN.NA mḪU.IT.TA.[...] (12)[... UR]U?ḪU.U.ḪU.LI ⸤i?⸥-[...] (13)[...]x-⸤ti⸥-li-ip[...] (14)[...]x x[...]

(perhaps rather small gap)

(1′)[UGULA] LI-⸢IM ŠA ÉRIN?⸣M[EŠ? ...] (2′)[URU]*MA*.AL.LI.*TA.AŠ*.KU.R[I.IA ... LÚDUGUD] (3′)[URUZ]A?/A?.TAR.ZI.IA mḪA.A.AM.MI L[ÚDUGUD ...] (4′)[mT/Š]A.A.TI.I.LI LÚDUGUD URUM[A?. ...] (5′)[mZ]i-ú-i-ni-ia-aš LÚDUGUD URUḪA.R[A. ...] (6′)[mḪ]U.UT.TA-LÚ LÚDUGUD URUI.ḪU.WA.AL.L[I. ...] (7′)[m]x.RI.IA.AŠ.ŠAR.MA LÚDUGUD URUGA.NI.IN.x[...] (8′)[mx]-*ri-ia-aš LÚDUGUD* URUI.ŠAR.Ú.IŠ.ŠA mḪI.IT.TA[L. ...] (9′)[URU]Ú.I.ŠA.AŠ.PU.RA mA.PÁ/ÍT.TI.I LÚDUGUD [URU ...] (10′)[mT/Š]A?.TI.I.IA LÚDUGUD ŠA ÉRINMEŠ URUŠA.x[...] (11′)[A-N]A KUR URUKI.IŠ.ŠI.IA-kán ku-x[...] x x[...] (12′)[UGULA L]I-IM-ŠU-NU-ma-aš-ma-aš m[...] (13′)[ŠU.N]ÍGIN 29 LÚ.MEŠDUGUD ŠA [...] (14′)[x UG]ULA LI-IM-ŠU-NU-ma-aš-ma-[aš ...] (15′)⸢mZA.AR⸣.⸤DU.UM⸥.MA.AN.⸤NI⸥~x[x x]x x[...]

Text 1

§2 (3)Mannanni, Commander of Sāsana,

§3 (4)Pabba, Commander of Malliwatta,

§4 (5)Ḫakku, Commander of Saiztawa,

§5 (6)Nāni, Commander of Gaggapaḫa,

§6 (7)Tuttu, Commander of Makarwasiyanda,

§7 (8)Pissā, Commander of Kuizna,

§8 (9)Attā, Commander of Gaggabaḫa,

§9 (10)Andulu, Commander of A[r-x-s/t]ama,

§10 (11)Asḫapala, Commander of S[ās]ana,

§11 (12)Pabba, Commander of A[rs]āsa,

§12 (13)Mameta, Commander of Zi[w]as?ra,

§13 (14)Sarpa, Commander of Ma[ll?]ittama,

§14 (15)Nāwiniya, Commander of T/Ga-[x]-wiya,

§15 (16)Pallullu, Commander of Zinip-[…], […-i]ariya, Commander of *Kipazziya*,

§16 (17)Nāni, Commander of Tuarpā, [x-a]t?ta, Commander of Takkis[a],

3.A

(4)[PN, Commande]r of Atarrawanna, (5)[PN, Commande]r of Sappa, (6)[PN], Commander of Ḫa/urtāna, (7)[PN, Commander of] Taḫaramma, (8)[PN, Commander of] Ḫa/ursuwanda, (9)[PN, Commande]r of Ninniwa, (10)[PN, Commande]r of *Zāzza*, (11)[… -i]yanna (*and*) Ḫuitta-[…] (12–14)[… *of*] Ḫūḫuli […]

(perhaps rather small gap)

(1′)*Clan* [Chief(s)] of the troop[s … of] (2′)Mallitaskur[iya: PN, Commander of] (3′)[Z?]atarziya, Ḫāmmi, C[ommander of GN], (4′)[T/S]ātīli, Commander of M[a?-…], (5′)[Z]iwiniya, Commander of Ḫar[a-…], (6′)[Ḫ]utta-ziti, Commander of Iḫuwall[i-…], (7′)[x]-riyassarma, Commander of Ganin-[…], (8′)[x]-riya, Commander of Isarwissa; Ḫitta[l-…, Commander of] (9′)Wisaspura, Apa/ittī, Commander of [GN], (10′)[T/S]atīya, Commander of the troops of Sa-[…]. (11′)[T]o/[Fo]r the land of Kissiya […], (12′)and their *Clan* [Chief]s […] them; [PN …], (13′)[alto]gether 29 Commanders of […], (14′)and their *Clan* [Ch]iefs: (15′)Zardummanni […]

§17 (18) ^{m}*TU.U.TU.˹I?˺.LI* ^{LÚ}DUGUD ^{URU}*ZI.I*[*P*?.]x ^{m}*NA.A.NA* ^{LÚ}DUGUD $^{\text{˹URU˺}}$*UK.KU.E.RI.IA*

§18 (19) ^{m}*NI.IN.NA* ^{LÚ}⸤DUGUD⸥ ^{URU}*KA.AZ.ZI.LU.*[x ^{m}]*ZU.LI.IA* {*^{LÚ} x*} (20) ^{LÚ}DUGUD ^{URU}*PU.U*[*K.K*]*I.IŠ.ŠU.WA* ^{m}x[.x].*LU.LU* ^{LÚ}DUGUD ^{URU}⸤*KA*⸥.*KAR.PA*

§19 (21) ^{m}*ZU.Ú.LI.IA* ^{LÚ}DU[GUD ^{URU}*Z*]*I*?.*I*[*T.TI*?.*I*]*Š*?.*ŠA* ^{m}*NA.A.NI* ^{LÚ}DUGUD!(MI) ^{URU}*WA.AŠ.TI.ŠA*

§20 (22) ^{m}*MA.RA.AK.KU.I* ^{LÚ}D[UGUD ^{URU}x.x.x.*Š*]*A* ^{m}*A.PA.AŠ.ŠI.IA* {*^{LÚ}*} (23) ^{LÚ}DUGUD ^{URU}*ḪU.TAR.N*[*A*?~…]

1 i 24–30

§21 (24)*A-NA* ÉRIN^{MEŠ} KUR ^{URU}*KI.I*[*N.NA.RA* x x x]x-⸤*az*?-*zi*⸥-*iš* ⸤LÚ?⸥ 2 *ḫi-*⸤*na*?⸥-*ri*?-*ia-aš* Ú x x[271] (25)*ka-a-ša* KUR ^{URU}*ḪAT.T*[*I* *ḫu-u-ma-an-za* *BE-LU*^{MEŠ} *Š*]*A* [ÉRIN^{M}]^{EŠ} ANŠE.KUR.RA^{MEŠ} (26)ÉRIN^{MEŠ} $^{\text{LÚ.MEŠ}}$*ša-ri-w*[*a-aš* *ḫu-u-ma-an-za* *A-NA* SAG.DU ^{m}*AR.NU.WA.A*]*N.DA* LUGAL.GAL (27)*A-NA* SAG.DU ^{f}*AŠ.M*[*U.NI.KAL* MUNUS.LUGAL.GAL *Ù* *A-NA* SAG.DU ^{m}*TU.UD.Ḫ*]*A.*⸤*LI*⸥.*IA* (28)[DUM]U ⸤LUGAL⸥ *tu-ḫu-kán-ti* [*kat-ta* DUMU^{MEŠ}-*ŠU* DUMU.DUMU^{MEŠ}-*ŠU* *Ù* *A-NA* SAG.DU DUMU^{MEŠ} LUG]AL (29)[*kat-t*]*a* DUMU^{MEŠ}-*ŠU-N*[*U* DUMU.DUMU^{MEŠ}-*ŠU-NU* *še-er* ITU-*mi* ITU-*mi* *li-in-ku-u-wa-ni*] (30)[*ú-e-ša-za* *ka-a-ša* UGULA *LI-IM* ^{LÚ}DUGUD *ŠA* ÉRIN^{M}]^{EŠ} ^{URU}*KI.IN.NA.RA* DINGIR^{MEŠ} *nu-un-na-aš*

3.A i 16′–32′;[270] 3.B$_1$ i 1′–12′

§2′ (16′)*ka-a-ša* KUR ^{URU}*ḪA.AT.TI* *ḫ*[*u-u-ma-a*]*n-za* *BE-LU*^{ME}[^{Š} *ŠA* ÉRIN^{MEŠ} ^{GIŠ}GIGIR][272] (17′)ÉRIN^{MEŠ} GÌR-*PÍ* ÉRIN^{MEŠ} *ša-ri-k*[*u-wa-a*]*š* *ḫu-u-ma-an-za* [*A-NA* SAG.DU] (18′) ^{m}*AR.NU.WA.AN.DA* LUGAL.GAL [*Ù*] *A-NA* SAG.DU [^{f}*AŠ.MU.NI.KAL*] (19′)MUNUS.LUGAL.GAL *Ù* *A-NA* SAG.D[U ^{m}*D*]*U.UT.ḪA.LI.I*[*A* DUMU LUGAL *tu-ḫu-kán-ti*] (20′)*kat-ta* DUMU^{MEŠ}-*ŠU* DUMU.DUMU^{MEŠ}-*Š*[*U*] ⸤*Ù*?⸥ *A-NA* SAG.DU [DUMU^{MEŠ} LUGAL] (21′)*kat-ta* DUMU^{MEŠ}-*ŠU-NU* DUMU.DUMU^{MEŠ}-*ŠU-*˹*NU* *še-er* *ITU-*mi* ITU*˺-*m*[*i* *li-in-k*(*u-u-wa-n*)*i*][273] (22′)*ú-e-ša-za* *ka-a-ša* UGULA *LI-IM* ^{LÚ}[D]UGUD *ŠA* ÉRIN^{M}[^{EŠ} ^{UR}(^{U}*KI.IŠ.Š*)*I.IA*] (23′)*ḫu-u-ma-an-*za QA-DU** DAM^{MEŠ}-*NI* DUMU^{MEŠ}-*NI* *kat-ta* DUMU.DUMU^{M}[(^{EŠ}-*NI*)]

§17 (18)Tūtuili, Commander of Zip-[x]; Nāna, Commander of Ukkueriya

§18(19)Ninna, Commander of Kazzilu; Zuliya, (20)Commander of Pu[kk]issuwa, [...]-lulu, Commander of Kakarpa

§19 (21)Zūliya, Com[mander of *Z*]*it*[*tis*]*sa*; Nāni, Commander of Wastisa

§20 (22)Marakkui, Co[mmander of ...-s]a; Apassiya, (23)Commander of Ḫutarn[a~ ...]

Text 1

§21 (24)To/For/Among the troops of the land of Ki[nnara ...] .... (25) Hereby do we, the [whole] Land of Ḫatt[usa, lords o]f the [troop]s, the chariot forces, (26)the *sariwa*-troops [all together, to the person of Arnuwa]nda, the Great King, (27)to the person of Ašm[uni,kal, the Great Queen, and to the person of Tudḫ]aliya, (28)[So]n of the King (and) Crown Prince, (and) [thereafter his sons, his grandsons and to the persons of the sons of the ki]ng, (and) (29)[thereaft]er to their sons, [their grandsons, month for month swear an oath]. (30) [Hereby, then, have we, the *Clan* Chief, Commander of the troop]s of Kinnara; *gods*, *and* [...] *us* [...]

3.A; 3.B$_1$

§2′ (16′)We, the e[nti]re Land of Ḫattusa, the lords [of the troops, the chariot] troops, (17′)the foot troops, the *sarik*[*uwa*]-troops all together, [to the person of] (18′)Arnuwanda, the Great King, [and] to the person of [Ašmunikkal], (19′)the Great Queen, and to the perso[n of T]udḫaliy[a, Son of the King, Crown Prince], (and) (20′)thereafter his sons, h[is] grandsons and to the person of [the sons of the king], (and) (21′)thereafter their sons (and) their grandsons, month for mon[th, we shall swear]. (22′–23′)Hereby, then, have we, the *Clan* Chief (and) Commander of all the troops of [(Kiss)iya], together with our wives, our sons, (and) hereafter [(our)] grandsons,

(24′)QA-DU KUR-NI li-in-ki-ia-aš TUP-PU ZABAR ḫa-a[(n-ti)] (25′)[i-i]a-u-en na-at I-NA URUḪA.AT.TI A-NA PA-NI ⸤d⸥[(10 URUḪA.AT.TI)] (26′)[NI-I]Š-⸤KU⸥-UN I-NA URUA.RI.IN.NA-ma-at A-NA PA-N[(I)] (27′) [(dUTU URU)]⸤A⸥.RI.IN.NA NI-IŠ-KU-UN I-NA URUḪA/UR.T[A?.274...-ma-at] (28′) [A-NA P(A-NI)] ⸤d⸥I.IA.AR.RI NI-⸤IŠ⸥-KU-UN an-z[e-el ...] (29′)[... n]u-un-na-aš li-˹in-ga˺-ia-aš TU[P-PUḪI.A(I.A DINGIRMEŠ)] (30′)[... -(NI/ni-i)]a? NI-IŠ-KU⸥-UN (eras.) [...] (31′)[... mAR.NU.W]A.⸤AN.DA⸥ LUGAL.[G(AL) ...] (32′) [...mTU.UD.Ḫ(A.LI).IA DUMU LUGAL]

(gap of ca. half a column)

§22′ (3.A ii 1–11; 1 ii 1–3; 2 ii 1–5; 3.B₃ ii 1′–2′) (3.A ii 1)[...]x ˹EGIR˺-an ša-ra-a x[...] (2)[...] na-aš-ma-kán DUMUMEŠ-NI BE-LUMEŠ-[NI ...] (3)[...]x x x IŠ-TU ZI-NI i-da-la-a-wa-[aḫ-...] (4)na-aš-ma-za LUGAL MUNUS.LUGAL *x* DUMUMEŠ LUGAL kat-ta DUMU.DUMUMEŠ LUGAL[ ] (5)AŠ-ŠUM BE-LU-UT-TI-NI ˹Ù˺ AŠ-ŠUM LUGAL-UT-TÌ (6)TI-an-ni-ia IŠ-TU EGIR U₄-MI Ú-UL (7)i-la-a-li-iš-ga-u-e-ni na-aš-ma LÚKÚR-NI ku-e-da-ni-[(ik-ki)] (2 ii 2)EGIR-an ti-ia-u-e-ni na-aš-ma-kán ŠA É.GAL-LÌ-ma (3)i-da-a-lu-*un* me-mi-an ku-iš-ki ku-e-da-ni-ik-ki (4)an-da iš-ta-ma-aš-zi I-NA É.GAL-LÌ-kán *x* (5)ku-iš-ki ku-it-ki za-am-mu-ra-a-iz-zi

§23′ (1 ii 4–29; 2 ii 6–27; 3.A ii 12–26; 3.B₂ ii 1′–9′; 3.B₃ ii 3′–10′)

(1 ii 4)an-za-aš-ša A-NA ÉRINMEŠ URUKI.IN.NA.RA ḫu-u-ma-an-ti-ia [(Ú-UL (5)kat-ta-wa-tar	(2 ii 6)an-za-a-ša-aš A-⸤NA⸥ ÉRINMEŠ URUḪAR.RA.NA.A.AŠ.ŠI (7)ḫu-u-ma-an-te-i!?-e Ú-UL kat-ta-wa-tar	(3.A ii 12)[an-za-a-š]a-aš A-NA ÉRINMEŠ KUR URUKI.IŠ.ŠI.I[A] (13)[ḫu-u-ma-an-ti-ia Ú-UL] kat-ta-wa-tar

na-an Ú-UL ti-ik-ku-uš-nu-um-me-e-ni (1 ii 6)na-aš-ma-kán LÚa-ra-aš LÚa-ri ku-iš-ki (7)ku-ru-ra-aš me-m[(i-a)]n pé-ra-an pé-e-ḫu-te-ez-zi (8)na-aš-ma-an-na-aš-k[(án)] LÚṬE₄-MU-ma ku-iš-ki kat-ta-an ar-ḫa (9)u-i-ia-az-zi n[(u-u)]n-na-aš ḪUL-lu-un me-mi-an (10)ku-in-ki ḫa-at-ra-˹a˺-iz-zi na-an *ep*-pu-u-e-ni *Ú*-[(UL)] (11)na-an ta-šu-wa-aḫ-ḫu-u-e-ni Ú-UL na-an MA-Ḫ[(AR)] ⸤d⸥U[(TU-ŠI)] (12)Ú-UL ú-wa-tu₄-um-me-e-ni na-aš-ma ku-iš [ ] (13)IT-TI BE-LUḪI.A-NI A-NA *KUR URU*ḪA.AT.TI-ia[ ] (14)me-na-aḫ-ḫa-an-da

(24′–28′)together with our land, [ma]de a sepa[(rate)] bronze tablet of the oath, and [we] placed it in Ḫattusa before the [(Storm God of Ḫattusa)], while in Arinna we placed it before the [(Sun Goddess)] of Arinna, [while] in Ḫa/urt[a- …] we placed [it be(fore)] Iyarri. (29′–30′)Our […], and (these) oath tab[let(s)] we placed [… (the gods)], (31′)[… Arnuw]anda, the [Gr(eat)] King […] (32′)[… Tudḫ(ali)ya, Son of the king …]

(gap of ca. half a column)

§22′ (1)[…] up behind/again […] (2)[…] or (if) our sons, [our] lords […] (3)[…] of our own volition [do] evil […]; (4–2 ii 5)or (if) we do not desire the king, the queen, the sons of the king, (and) thereafter the grandsons of the king for our lordship and for the kingship (our) lifelong in the future; or (if) we support so[(me)] enemy of ours; or (if) someone hears from someone any evil matter regarding the palace, someone insults someone in the palace,

§23′

(1 ii 4)and (he) is [(not)] an affront to us, to the entire troop of Kinnara,	(2 ii 6–7)but he is not an affront to us, to the entire troop of Ḫarranāssi,	(3.A ii 12–13)but he is [not] an affront [to us], to [the entire troop] of the land of Kissiya,

(1 ii 5)and we do not denounce him; (6–7)or (if) some colleague expresses a hostile re[(ma)]rk against (another) colleague; (8–10)or (if) someone sends a messenger to us, and he writes to us some evil matter, and we do n[(ot)] seize him, (11–17)and we do not *blind*[275] him, and we do not bring him bef[(ore)] His Ma[(jesty)]; or if we do [not] fight unreservedly he who is hostile against our lords and against the Land of Ḫattusa; o[(r)] he is not an affront to us; further, (if) the life of our lords is not more important than

ku-⌞ru-ur⌟ na-an *ma*-a-⌜an kar-ši⌝ [Ú-UL] (15)za-aḫ-ḫi-ia-u-wa-aš-t[(a n)]a-[(aš-m)]a-an-na-*ša-aš* Ú-UL (16)kat-ta-wa-tar ⌜nam-ma⌝-kán ⌞an-ze⌟-el TI-an-ni (17)Ú-UL *ŠA BE-LU-NI TI-tar ⌞na⌟-ak*-ki-i (18)nam-ma-kán ke-e ud-da-a-ar A-NA DUMU^{MEŠ}-NI DUMU.DUMU^{ME}[(^{Š}-NI)] (19)pé-⌞ra-an Ú⌟-UL ú-e-da-u-e-⌜ni⌝ (20)⌜nam-ma-kán⌝ BE-LU$^{\text{ḪI.A}}$-NI pa-an-q[(a-u-e)] QA-DU DAM^{M}[(^{EŠ}-Š)U-NU] (21)DUMU^{MEŠ}-ŠU-NU DUMU.DUMU^{MEŠ}-ŠU-NU Ú-UL [(a-aš-ši-i)]a-nu-uš-ka$_4$-⌞u⌟-[(e-ni)] (22)nam-ma-an-na-aš DINGIR^{MEŠ} ku-wa-p[(í ši-pa-an-d)]u-u-e-ni[ ] (23)na-aš-ta ḫu-u-da-ak an-d[(a ŠA BE-LU^{MEŠ}-N)]I (24)ki-i-ia li-in-ki-ia-aš [(ud-da-a-ar) Ú-UL …-u-e-(ni)] (25)A-NA DAM^{MEŠ}-NI-at DUMU^{MEŠ}-[(N)I …] (26)nam-ma-*kán* DINGIR^{MEŠ}-*aš*-š[a … Ú-UL] (27)i-la-li-iš-ka$_4$-u-e-n[(i) m(a-a-an) …] (28)Ú-UL pa-aḫ-šu-e-ni […] (29) DINGIR$^{\text{MEŠ URU}}$ḪAT.TI ḫu-u-[(ma)-an-t(e-eš) …]

§24′ (3.B$_2$ ii 10′–14′; 1 ii 30–31) (10′)[(^{d}UTU ^{URU}⌞A.RI⌟.I)N.NA ^{d}10] ^{URU}NE.⌜RI⌝.IK ^{d}LAM[MA …] (11′)[(^{d})10 ^{URU}PÍ.IT.TI.IA.RI.IG].⌞GA⌟ ^{d}LAMMA ^{URU}GA.RA.[AḪ.NA …] (12′)[…]⌞^{d}⌟IŠTAR ṢE-RI x[…] (13′)[… ^{URU}Ša-m]u-u-ḫa-aš ^{d}[…] (14′) (traces)

(gap of somewhat less than 1 column)

§25″ (3.B$_2$ iii 1′–15′) (1′)x[… u]d$^{?}$-da-a-[ar$^{(?)}$…] (2′)ku-i-⌜e⌝-e[š]x-⌜an$^{?}$⌝[ ] x na-at[…] (3′)a-ša-an-du n[u]-za a-aš-⌜šu-li⌝ x[…] (4′)ma-a-an ḫi-in-[g]a-na-aš~⌞ma/ku⌟-w[a~…] (5′)nu-uš-ši LUGAL MU[NUS.L]UGAL LÚ^{MEŠ}[…] (6′)ḫa-an-da-a-an ⌞DI⌟-NA$_7$ ⌜ḫa⌝-[an-na- …] (7′)i-da-a-lu-ma-aš-⌞ši⌟-iš-ša-a[n …] (8′)[tá]k-ki-iš-zi ⌜ma⌝-a-an šar-[…] (9′)[k]ap-pí-la-a[z-m]a-an I~x[…] (10′)ku-iš-ki tar-[na]-i ma-a-an[…] (11′)ŠA BE-LU^{MEŠ}-[NI?]276 ⌞DUMU.DUMU⌟^{ME}[^{Š}-NI$^{?}$ …] (12′)nu-uš-ma-aš x[…] (13′)ḫa-an-da-a-a[n …] (14′)a-aš-ši-i[a- …] (15′)⌞IŠ⌟[…]

(relatively short gap)

§26″ (2 iii 1′–20′; 1 iii 1′–7′) (1′)[…]x x[…] (2′)[…]-⌜ši$^{?}$-wa$^{?}$-ma$^{?}$⌝ Ú-U[L …] (3′)[…]-⌜zi⌝ wa-aš-[tú]l-li-ma [(Ú-U)L] (4′)[…]x ap-pa-an-zi ⌜ḪUL⌝-lu-ma~x[…] (5′)[… ḪUL-(u-wa-a)]*n$^{?}$-ni$^{?}$* EGIR-an le-e […] (6′)[ku-iš-k]i i-⌜e-zi⌝ nu ut-tar an-da ḪUL-u-wa-⌜an⌝-[ni] (7′)x-[x]-⌜al$^{?}$⌝-la$^{?}$-iz-zi na-at-za ^{LÚ}a-ra-aš (8′) ^{LÚ}⌜a⌝-[r]i a-wa-an kat-ta ḪUL-u-wa-an-ni (9′)*le*-⌞e⌟ ku-iš-ki me-ma-i ú-e-ša-kán ku-wa-pí (10′)ÉRIN$^{\text{MEŠ!(ME)}}$ ^{URU}[Ḫ]AR.RA.NA.AŠ.ŠI IŠ-TU ^{URU}$^{\text{DIDLI.ḪI.A}}$-NI (11′)ar-⌞ḫa ú$^{?}$-wa$^{?}$⌟-ú-e-ni nu A-NA LUGAL MUNUS.LUGAL (12′)A-NA ^{m}T[U.UD].⌞ḪA⌟.LI.IA DUMU LUGAL ^{LÚ}tu-*ḫu*-kán-ti (13′) kat-ta A-N[A DUMU^{M}]^{EŠ}-*ŠU DUMU*.DUMU^{MEŠ}-ŠU (14′)Ù A-NA SA[G$^{?}$.DU$^{?}$]$^{\text{MEŠ?}}$ DUMU^{MEŠ} LUGAL kat-ta A-NA DUMU^{MEŠ}-⌜ŠU⌝-NU (15′)še-er A-NA PA-NI [^{d}1]0 ^{URU}ḪAR.RA.NA.AŠ.ŠI (16′)*x ku-it-ma-an ⌜li⌝-[i]n-ku-u*-e-ni

our own live(s); (18–19)further, (if) we do not convey this declaration to our sons (and) [(our)] grandsons; (20–21)further, (if) we do not perpetually [(*cham*)]*pion*[277] our lords in their enti[(rety)], along with [(th)eir] wives, their sons (and) their grandsons; (22)further, whenever we [(sacrifi)]ce for ourselves to the gods, (23–24)(if) [(we) do not] immediately […] also this [(matter)] of the oath [(to ou)]r [(lords)]; (25)[…] it to our wives (and) [(ou)r] sons; (26–29)further, (if) we [do not] desire […] of/for the gods, too; [(if)] we do not protect […], a[(ll)] the gods of Ḫattusa […]:

§24′ (10′)[(The Sun Goddess of Ari)nna, the Storm God] of Nerik, the prote[ctive deity of …] (11′)[the Storm (God) of Pittiyarig]ga, the protective deity of Gara[ḫna …], (12′)[…] Ištar of the Battlefield […], (13′–14′)[… of Sam]ūḫa, the god of […]

(gap of somewhat less than 1 column)

§25″ (1′)[…the m]atte[r …] (2′)they wh[o …], and (3′)they shall be [.… A]nd in goodness […]. (4′–6′)But if […] of death […] and to/for him the king, the q[ue]en, the […] men de[cide …] a proper legal case, (7′–8′)but he [do]es him an evil turn; if […], (9′)but out of [a]nger […] (10′)but someone al[lo]ws/rel[ea]ses him; if […] (11′)of [*our*] lords, [*our*] sons […], (12′)and […] them, (13′)a proper […] (14′–15′)favor[…]

(relatively short gap)

26″ (2′)[…] but no[t …], (3′)but [(no)t] in wro[ngd]oing, (4′–9′)[…] they seize, but evil […], no [on]e shall do […] again [wic(ked)]ly. And he […] the matter wickedly; and no colleague shall wickedly divulge it to (another) colle[ag]ue. We, however, whenever we, (10′–16′)the troops of [Ḫ]arranassi, come out of our towns, and so long as we swear in front of the Sto[rm God] of Ḫarranassi an oath to the king, the queen, to T[ud]ḫaliya, son of the king, crown prince, (and) thereafter, to his [son]s, his grandsons and to the *pe*[*rson*]*s* of the sons of the king, (and) thereafter to their sons,

(1 iii 7′)[*nu ke-e ud-da-a-ar A-NA PA-NI*] ^{d}10 ^{URU}*KI.IN.NA.RA ku-it-*[*ma-an*] (8′)[*me-mi-u-e-ni*]	*nu ke-*e** (2 iii 17′)*ud-da-a-ar A-NA PA-*⌜*NI*⌝ ^{d}10 ^{URU}*ḪAR.RA.NA.AŠ.ŠI* (18′)*ku-it-ma-an me-mi-u-*⌜*e*⌝*-*⸤*ni*⸥

nam-ma la-aḫ-ḫi (2 iii 19′)*QA-TAM-MA pa-a-i-*wa-ni nu* k*[*u-w*]*a-pí tu-uz-zi-iš* (20′)*an-da a-ri-iš-kán-*⸤*zi*⸥

(gap of less than half a column)[278]

§27″ (3.B$_1$ iv 1′–9′) (1′)[…]-⌜*na*⌝*-ia* (2′)[…]x-*ša-at-kán* (3′)[…]⸤*A*⸥*-NA* LUGAL (4′)[MUNUS.LUGAL *A-NA* ^{m}*TU.UD.ḪA.LI.IA* DUMU LUGAL ^{LÚ}*tu*]*-ḫu-kán-ti* (5′)[…]x-⌜*ia-ia/ma*⌝ (6′)[… *QA-DU* DAM^{MEŠ}*-NI*] DUMU^{MEŠ}-⸤*NI*⸥ (7′)[*kat-ta* DUMU.DUMU^{MEŠ}*-NI* …]x-x-*ša*-x-*ni*[…] (8′–9′)(traces)

(relatively short gap)

§28″ (3.B$_2$ iv 1′–7′) (1′–4′)(traces) (5′)[…]x ⌜DUMU⌝.DUMU^{MEŠ}*-ŠU* (6′)[…] GU$_4$⌜$^{ḪI.A}$*-ŠU*⌝ (7′)[…]x ⌜*ḫar*⌝*-ni-in-kán-du*

§29″ (3.B$_2$ iv 8′–15′) (8′)[… *A-N*]*A PA-NI* ^{m}*AR.NU.WA.AN.DA* (9′)[LUGAL.GAL *Ù A-NA PA-NI* ^{f}*AŠ.MU.NI.KAL*] MUNUS.LUGAL.GAL (10′)[*Ù A-NA PA-NI* ^{m}*TU.UD.ḪA.LI.IA* DUMU LUGAL $^{(LÚ)}$*t*]*u-ḫu-kán-ti-in* (11′)[… *-m*]*u*?*-*⸤*uš*?⸥*-kán* (12′)[…] (13′)[… ^{m}*TU.UD.ḪA.LI.IA* DUMU LUGAL $^{(LÚ)}$*tu-ḫ*]*u-kán-ti* (14′)[…]x-*AM*?/*pí*? AMA-*AM* (15′)[…]x ⸤*ŠUM-MI*⸥

(relatively short gap)

§30″ (1 left edge 1–3) (1) ⌜^{URU}*Ši/Me*⌝*-*⌜*ku*?⌝-x[x x] (2) ^{URU}**Ḫi*?**-in*?*-n*[*a*?*-ri*?*-i*]*a-aš* (3) ^{URU}*Ḫu-u-wa-*⌜*ar*?⌝*-*ra*?**-aš*

(1 iii 7′–8′)[and] so lo[ng as we speak these words before] the Storm God of Kinnara,

(2 iii 16′–17′)and so long as we speak these words before the Storm God of Ḫarranassi,

we will further go on campaign likewise, to wh[ere]ver the troops campaign.

(gap of less than half a column)

27″ (2′)[…] it/they (3′)[…] to the king, (4′)[the queen, to Tudḫaliya, son of the king, cr]own prince, (5′)[…] and/but […] (6′)[… along with our wives], our sons, (and) (7′–9′)[thereafter our grandsons …]

(relatively short gap)

§28″ (5′)[…] his grandsons (6′)[…] his cattle (7′)[…] may they destroy!

§29″ (8′)[… be]fore Arnuwanda, (9′)[the Great King, and before Ašmunikkal], the Great Queen, (10′–12′)[and before Tudḫaliya, son of the king, c]rown prince, […] (13′)[… Tudḫaliya, son of the king, cro]wn prince (14′)[…] mother (15′)[…] name […]

(relatively short gap)

§30″ (1)The town of *Si/Meku*-x[x x], (2)the town of *Ḫinn*[*ariy*]*a*, (3)the town of Ḫūwarra.

No. 15

Instructions and Oath Imposition(s) of Arnuwanda I (*CTH* 275)

These two small fragments of Instructions of Arnuwanda I are both NH copies of older originals. No findspots are known. The first seems to be concerned with obligations relating to royal property. Pecchioli Daddi (2002a: 263) has suggested reading EN N[A4KIŠIB in l. 2 and seeing the composition as intended for this "lord of the seal," who would thus be a chief administrator, an appealing hypothesis that can at present be neither confirmed nor refuted.[279]

Transliteration (15.1)

§1 (1 i 1)*UM-MA TA.BA.AR.NA* m*AR.N*[*U.WA.AN.DA* ...] (2)*ka-a-ša tu-uk A-NA* EN x[...] (3)*iš-ḫi-u-la-aš li-in-ki-aš-š*[*a* ...] (4)*nu-ut-ta ki-i iš-ḫi-ú-ul*[...]

§2 (1 i 5)LUGAL-*wa-aš a-aš-ša-u-i nu-za*[...] (6)*nu* LUGAL-*wa-aš e-eš-zi*~IN?[...] (7)*e-eš-zi-ia ku-it nu*-x[...] (8)*nu-za* LUGAL-*wa-aš a-aš-ša-*[*u-i* ...] (9)[*nu*?] LUGAL-*wa-aš pár-na-aš*[...] (10)[*le*]-*e kar-ap-z*[*i*? ...] (11)[*l*]*e-e i-ia-a*[*n-* ...] (12)⸤*Ú*?⸥-*NU-UT* x[...]

(remainder of text lost except for last few lines)

§3′ (1 iv 1′)[*l*]*e*?-*e*~x[...] (2′)⸢*ša*⸣-*ra-a* x[...] (3′)*pé-di* ZAG-⸢*i*?⸣[...] (4′)*pa-aḫ-ša-nu-te-e*[*n* ...] (5′)BE-*an na-at-*[*ta* ...] (6′)*ḫar-ti* [...]

Transliteration (15.2)

§1 (2 iii 1)⸢*UM*⸣-*MA T*[*A.B*]*A.AR.NA* m*A*[*R.NU.WA.AN.DA* ...] (2)*ki-i*~*iš*-⸢*ša*⸣-*aš*[280] *at-ta-aš-ma-aš* x[...] (3)*ku-it pár-ku-e-an-na-aš iš-ḫi*-⸤*ú*⸥-[*ul* ...] (4)*nu ke-e*-⸢*el*⸣ *tup-pí-ia-aš pár-ku-i*[*a-an-na-aš iš-ḫi-ú-ul* ...]

§2 (5)*ku-i-ša-at Ú-UL-ma pa-aḫ-š*[*a-* ...] (6)DUMUMEŠ-*ŠU i-da-a-lu ḫi-in-kán* [*pí-ia-an-zi*]

§3 (7)[*ki-n*]*u*-⸤*na*⸥ *ka-a-ša* m*AR.NU.WA.A*[*N.DA* ...] (8)[...]-*aš* ENMEŠ-*aš ḫu-u-m*[*a-an-da-aš* ...] (9)[...]x-*li* LÚ*mu-li*-[...] (10)[...]x-*aš* LÚ x[...] (11)[...]x ⸤LI⸥[...]

(remainder of text lost except for traces toward end of rev. iv)

The second composition seems to have been concerned with issues of purity (cf. No. 2, n. 30) and was related in some way to a proclamation that Arnuwanda's father had made. What appears to be the beginning of the composition is found at the top of col. iii, causing one to wonder if the text was thus recorded as part of a *Sammeltafel* or if the introduction of the king's words followed, for example, a list of deities (cf. No. 28) and/or a list of persons who were to swear the oath (cf. No. 14), possibilities that must remain purely speculative.

TRANSLATION (15.1)

§1 (1)Thus (says) the Sovereign, Arn[uwanda ...] (2)hereby [...] you(sg.) to the lord (of) [...] (3)of the obligation(s) an[d] of the oath [...] (4)and [...] these obligation(s) to you(sg.).

§2 (5)For the property of the king: And [...] (6)and it belongs to the king. [...] (7)and because/what it is, and [...] (8)and [for] the property of the king [...] (9)[*and*] of the estate of the king [...] (10)he [shall n]ot raise! (11)[... sha]ll not do! [...] (12)utensils [...]

(remainder of text lost except for last few lines)

§3′ (1′)[... *shall n*]*ot* [...] (2′)over [...] (3′)to/at the place, to/at the border [...] (4′)you(pl.) must protect! [...] (5′)If no[t, ...] (6′)you(sg.) will have/keep [...]

TRANSLATION (15.2)

§1 (1)Thus (says) the S[ove]reign, A[rnuwanda ...] (2)this [...] of the mouth of my father [...] (3)which obligat[ion] of purity [...] (4)and [... obligation of] purity of this tablet [...]

§2 (5)He who does not guard it, though, [...] (6)[will allot] his sons an evil death!

§3 (7)[No]w, then, hereby Arnuwa[nda ...] (8–11)[...] of/to al[l] the lords [...] (traces)

(remainder of text lost except for traces toward end of rev. iv)

No. 16
Decree of Queen Ašmunikkal concerning the "Royal Funerary Structure" (*CTH* 252)

This intriguing MH composition, the sole text in this volume issued by a queen, Ašmunikkal, spouse of Arnuwanda I, has long been known from a NH copy (A) preserving approximately the upper third or half of the obv., the rev. of which is not inscribed.[281] The extant portion of the tablet is very nicely preserved and easily readable. More recently a dupl. (B) was identified (Košak 1988b: 312; van den Hout 1990: 426), but despite the fact that nearly the entire tablet was recovered, this likewise NH copy is of limited help in reconstructing the remainder of the composition, since the tablet was badly burned in antiquity and its surface is severely damaged. It thus seems that from about one-fifth to one-third of the composition is preserved, assuming that its entirety was preserved on a single tablet. For neither is a findspot known. No paragraph divisions are preserved in A, while B is one of the rare tablets from Ḫattusa on which every line is followed by a divider. Accordingly, no paragraph numbers are found in the edition presented here, but blocks of content are set apart from each other.

As is the case with many other texts included in this volume, the genre of the present composition can and has been debated. Otten (1974) referred to it as a *Schenkungsurkunde*, a grant, since the occasion on which its instructions were enumerated seems to have been the granting of tax and labor exemptions to a presumably recently created "royal funerary structure" (ll. 1–6), while van den Hout (2002: 82) dubs it an "exemption text." It could in this light just as well be seen as a royal decree, the content of which concerns the exemption of the "royal funerary structure" from specific taxes and duties.[282] In some of

---

Transliteration

(A obv. 1–6) (1)*UM-MA* ^{f}*AŠ.MU*-^{d}NIN.GAL MUNUS.LUGAL.GAL É.NA$_4$-*aš ku-it i-ia-u-e-en* (2)*nu A-NA* É.NA$_4$-*ni ku-i-e-eš* URU$^{\text{ḪI.A}}$ *pí-ia-an-te-eš* LÚ^{MEŠ} *BE-EL QA-TI ku-i-e-eš pí-an-te-eš* (3) $^{\text{LÚ.MEŠ}}$APIN.LÁ $^{\text{LÚ.MEŠ}}$SIPAD.*GU$_4$* $^{\text{LÚ.MEŠ}}$SIPAD.UDU *ku-i-e-eš pí-ia-an-te-eš* (4) $^{\text{LÚ.MEŠ}}$*ša-ri-wa-za-kán ku-i-e-eš da-an-te-eš na-at QA-DU* É^{MEŠ}-*ŠU-NU* URU$^{\text{ḪI.A}}$-*ŠU-NU* (5)*A-NA* É.NA$_4$ *pí-ia-an-te-eš* $^{\text{LÚ.MEŠ}}$*ḫi-lam-mi-e-eš-ša ku-i-e-eš ka-ru-ú* (6)*A-NA* É.NA$_4$ *pí-ia-an-te-eš na-at-kán ša-aḫ-ḫa-na-za lu-zi-ia-za a-ra-u-e-eš a-ša-an-du*

(A obv. 7–8) (7)UR.GI$_7$-*aš wa-ap-pí-ia-zi a-pí-ia-ma-aš a-ri na-aš ka-ru-uš-ši-ia-zi* (8)ì-*an-ma-kán la-ḫu-*ut*-ta-ri*[283] *a-pu-uš-ma-kán pa-ra-a le-e ú-wa-an-zi*

its stipulations it echoes Ḫattusili III's Decree Regarding the Exemptions of the *ḫekur* of Pirwa (*CTH* 88), whereby the *ḫekur* is also some type of funerary monument (van den Hout 2002: 74–80, 86).

The "royal funerary structure" (see n. 284), often dubbed a "mausoleum," literally "stone building" (É.NA$_4$; van den Hout 2002: 80–89), along with other more or less closely related royal funerary structures and institutions, have been the subject of much discussion in recent years. The reader interested in further literature may consult, in addition to the new edition of the Royal Funerary Ritual (Kassian, Korolëv, and Sidel'tsev 2002), van den Hout 1994, 2002; Groddek 2001; Loretz 2001; Dietrich and Loretz 2004; Archi 2007; Kapełuś 2007; Torri 2008; Singer 2009b; Taracha 2009: 158–67; Mora and Balza 2010; and Balza and Mora 2012. The primary import of the present text clearly lies in its provision of exemptions from *saḫḫan*- and *luzzi*-levies for the royal funerary structure (l. 6). After two mysterious lines (8–9), the composition goes on to further define the exemptions: cattle and sheep may not be confiscated from it, and the property of those belonging to it reverts to the institution if they are convicted of a capital crime (9–12). Young women are allowed to be married into the sequestered institution, but no one belonging to it is to be married to a person from the outside (13–15), and no one can purchase property from them. A man of the royal funerary structure can apparently purchase such property, though it seems to have been subject to some further restrictions, now lost with the end of ms. A. What little can be gleaned from the remainder of ms. B seems to touch on farming (l. 10), labor (ll. 10–12), and again the *saḫḫan*- and *luzzi*-levies (15–17). The final lines mention potential lawsuits involving some lord (11′–17′) and seemingly a curse (18′).

TRANSLATION

(1)Thus (speaks) Ašmunikkal, Great Queen: The royal funerary structure[284] that we created, (2)the towns that have been given to the royal funerary structure, the craftsmen that have been given, (3)the ploughmen, cowherds and shepherds that have been given, (4)those who were taken from the *sari(ku)wa*-troops and along with their homes and their towns (5)given to the royal funerary structure, and the *ḫilammi*-cult personnel that had already (6)been given to the royal funerary structure, they shall be exempt from the *saḫḫan* and *luzzi*-levies.[285]

(7)A dog barks; he goes there/then, though, and he is quiet.[286] (8)Oil is poured out, but those shall not come forth.[287]

(A obv. 9–12; B obv. 1–3) (9)nu-uš-ma-aš-kán pé.-an GIŠe-ia-an ar-ta-*ru* pa-ra-a-ma-aš-kán le-e ku-iš-ki tar-na-i (10)GU$_4$ḪI.A-ia-aš-ma-aš UDUḪI.A *le-e* ku-iš-ki ap-pát-ri-ia-zi (11)na-at-kán ḫu-u-ma-an-ta-za a-ra-u-e-eš a-ša-an-du ma-a-an ŠA É.NA$_4$-ma (12)ḫi-in-ka$_4$-na-aš wa-aš-túl ku-iš-ki wa-aš-ta-i na-aš a-ki É-ZU-ma-aš-ši ŠA É.˻NA$_4$˼-pát

(A obv. 13–18; B obv. 3–9) (13)A-NA LÚMEŠ É.NA$_4$-ia-kán AŠ-ŠUM É.GI$_4$.A-TÌ an-da-an pé-eš-kán-du (14)pa-ra-a-ma-kán DUMU.NITA DUMU.MUNUS AŠ-ŠUM É.GI$_4$.A-TÌ LÚan-da-i-ia-an-da-an-ni-ia le-e (15)ku-iš-ki pa-a-i ŠA É.NA$_4$-ia-za[288] A.ŠÀ GIŠTIR GIŠMÚ.SAR GIŠKIRI$_6$.GEŠTIN (16)NA-AP-ŠA-TÙ-ia le-e ku-iš-ki wa-a-ši ma-a-an-za LÚ É.NA$_4$-ma ku-iš-ki (17)˻na˼-[(aš)]-˻šu A.ŠÀ˼ na-aš-šu GIŠTIR na-aš-šu GIŠMÚ.SAR na-aš-šu GIŠKIRI$_6$.GEŠTIN NA-AP-<ŠA>-TÙ-ia wa-a-ši (18)[…]x x x x x x x-˻ia an-da˼ a-ni-ia-az ku-iš-ki

(B obv. 9–17; A obv. 19–20) (9)[…]x x ⸢KIN?/ra? e?-eš?⸣-tu ma-a-an-ma-kán x x-˻ia?˼ an-da a-ni-ia-[az] (10)[… (ku-it KIN-an) …]x x x-iš?-š/ta?-ri? *x* na-aš-ma x x x ˻APIN?.LÀ?˼ ku-it-ki (11)[…]x x ku-⸢iš⸣ a-ni-ia-˻az˼ [n]a?-aš?-˻za?˼ x? x? (12)[…]x~ḫa?-a?-ni?-an? KIN?-an ˻le-e ku-e-da-ni˼-ik-ki (13)[…]x x x ⸢-a?-i ma⸣-a-an IŠ-⸢TU É?⸣.GAL-LÌ-ia (14)[…]˻na?-aš?-ma?˼ x-iš? im?-x~x-iš an-tu-uḫ-ḫa-x[…] (15)[…]x x ˻ŠA É.NA$_4$-ni?˼ [ša]-˻aḫ-ḫa˼-ni lu-uz-zi-[ia] (16)[…]x x ˻ḫu-it-ti-ia-az?-zi?˼ (17)[…]x x x x x ša-˻aḫ-ḫa?˼-[ni? l]u?-uz-zi?-ia (traces in 3–4 further lines)

(gap of ca. one-third of the tablet)

(B rev. 1′–20′) (traces in ca. 10 lines) (11′)[…]x x ˻ku?-e?-da?˼-ni A-NA ˻BE-LÍ?˼ x x[…] (12′)[…]x x x-⸢zi? nu-uš-ši?⸣ a-pa-a-aš BE-˻LÍ?/LU?˼ x x x[…] (13′)[…]x x x x ⸢e?-ep?⸣-du (14′)[…]x x-ru? ˻na?˼-an-kán IŠ-TU ˻DI˼-NI$_7$ aš-nu-⸢ud?-du??⸣[…] (15′)[…]x x ˻še˼-er ar-ḫa le-e wa-aḫ-nu-⸢zi⸣ (16′)[…]x x x x ˻le˼-e ša-me-nu-uz-zi (17′)[…]x x x ˻A??-NA? LÚ?˼MEŠ ˻É?.NA$_4$?-aš?-ma˼ ša?-a-ku-˻wa Ú-UL? ku?˼-x[…] (18′)[… ME]Š? ˻DUMU?MEŠ? ḫar?-ni˼-in-˻kán?˼-[d]u? (19′)[…]x x x-˻wa?-az?˼ ku-i-e-eš LÚ⸢MEŠ⸣ x x[…] (20′)[… k]u??-˻i??-e?-eš? ŠÀ??.BA?? É?.NA$_4$-ni?˼ pí-˻ia˼-an-te-eš (traces)

(9)An *eya*-tree shall be planted before them;[289] no one shall let them out. (10)And no one shall confiscate cattle and sheep from them. (11–12)They shall be free from it all. If, however, anyone from the royal funerary structure commits a capital crime, he will die. His estate, though, is still part of the royal funerary structure.

(13)They shall send (young women) in to the men of the royal funerary structure as brides,[290] (14–16)but no one shall send out (from there) a young man or a girl as a bride or a son-in-law. No one shall purchase a field, a woodland, a garden, an orchard, a vineyard or personnel from (those) of the royal funerary structure. If, however, some man of the royal funerary structure (17)purchases a field or a woodland or a garden or a vineyard and pers<on>nel, (18)whatever task in […][291]

(9)[…] *let it be* […]. But if in […] a task (10)[… (which task) …] or […] whatever *plough* […] (11)[…] which work/task, *and he/it* (12)[…] *task* shall to none whatsoever (13)[…]. If […] from the *palace* (14)[…] *or* […] man (15)[…] of the royal funerary structure for the [*s*]*aḫḫan* [and] *luzzi*-levies (16)[…] he shall extract/draw (17)[…] *saḫḫan* and *luzzi*-levies

(gap of ca. one-third of the tablet)

(traces in ca. 10 lines) (11′)[…] *to which* lord (12′)he […]-s, and that lord […] to him (13′)[…] *let him seize* (14′)[…], and *he shall* settle it/him by means of a law case (15′)[…] he shall not wave/turn it out over (16′)[…] he shall not *neglect* (17′)[…] *to the men of the royal funerary structure*, though, […] not the eye (18′)[…] may they destroy [… and] (his?) *sons*! (19′)[…] Whatever men (20′) […] *who/whatever* are given *within the royal funerary structure* […]

No. 17
Instructions of Arnuwanda I for the Frontier Post Governors
(*CTH* 261.I)

It is, on the one hand, very fortuitous that the several rather fragmentary mss. allow the reconstruction of a large portion of the original text, and on the other, a great pity that one is forced to reconstruct a composite text from mss. of widely varying dates and thus largely prevented from comparing mss., which surely would have revealed a highly interesting redactional evolution. Some preliminary considerations in this direction can be found in Miller 2011b.

The composition is preserved by four substantial fragment blocks (A–D) and two mid-sized groups of fragments (E–F) as well as a handful of smaller pieces (G_{1-3}, H–M). Ms. A was written in the MH period, all others are NH derivations.[292] All tablets whose findspots are known (A, C_{1-2}, D, F, G_1, G_2, H, J) originate in the Temple I complex. If one were to assume that the composition originally spanned two tablets (see n. 475), then the preserved text would represent nearly half of the original composition.

This text shows numerous similarities to Arnuwanda I's treaties with the Kaska (*CTH* 138 and 140), which is hardly surprising, as both these instructions and the treaties were probably written in the face of the same situation, that is, the Kaska's hostile reaction to the incessant pressure placed on them by a neighboring expansionist empire. Many passages of these instructions also find clear reflections in the letters from Tapikka/Maşat Höyük (Alp 1991; Hoffner 2009: 91–252; Marizza 2009: 37–129), which deal above all with the security of this northern border town at about the same time as the instructions must have been composed.

The text also deals with mundane daily tasks that have left their mark in other genres in the archives from Ḫattusa, such as the so-called Cult Inventories (*CTH* 500–530; Hazenbos 2003). It was presumably precisely obligations such as that expressed in §34′ that resulted in the accumulation of cult inventories from the time of Tudḫaliya IV. The passage here would perhaps suggest that the administrative processes evidenced in the texts preserved from Tudḫaliya's reign may well have been in place already long before his era, and thus that the recovery of those known to us would be as much the result of processes of preservation and destruction, as well as archaeological accident, than of any raised concern about the state of the cult on the part of Tudḫaliya.

As Beal (1992: 426) has pointed out, the duties of the "governor of the post," literally "lord of the watchtower" (Hitt. *auwariyas isḫas*; Akk. *BĒL MADGALTI*), certainly extended beyond the confines of the border bastion itself to its associated town and the entire province that it was to protect, and the term is therefore often translated "provincial governor."[293] Nevertheless, I have retained the more restricted translation for several reasons. First, Hittite has a further term, *utneyasḫas*, that more nearly fits a translation "provincial governor," literally "lord of the land," a term that occurs in the present text as well (§§55b′, 58′), and is thus to be distinguished from the "governor of the frontier post." As Beal notes, this official's duties would have overlapped to a significant degree with those of the *auwariyas isḫas*, "(frontier) post governor." Second, I have opted for "governor of the post" as opposed to, for example, "border town commander," as the "post" and the "town" are in fact differentiated in this text as well (e.g., §§9–10, 15, 18, 27′), as are the "governor of the post" and the "town magistrate" (LÚMAŠKIM.URUKI; §§33′, 37′). There are also passages that seek to regulate potential conflicts between these various authorities (e.g., §§37′, 55′b). It would seem perhaps that the *auwariyas isḫas* was the king's governing representative in the province (see, e.g., §27′), while the magistrate may well have been the local mayor. It is certain, however, that the *auwariyas isḫas* was the highest authority in the province. Finally, when "governor of the post" is explicitly modified with *ḫantezzi*-, "forward; frontier," I have translated "frontier post governor," though presumably *auwariyas ḫantezziyas isḫas* and *auwariyas isḫas* would both have referred to the "(frontier) post governor."

The first eighteen paragraphs deal primarily with the regular watch and with guarding the roads, getting the townsfolk and livestock into and out of the town mornings and evenings, and keeping track of the enemy. The following §§19–26′ consist of somewhat detailed instructions concerning the construction and maintenance of various defensive structures. Paragraphs 27′–30′ deal with supply and maintenance of the town's various secular structures and installations, while §§31′–36′ concern the upkeep and administration of the temples and cultic sites and their personnel. Paragraphs 37′–40′ move on to the matter of legal cases, whereby the first few sentences of §38′ revert to proper religious behavior and may thus represent a redactional slip. Paragraphs 40′–41′ touch on the provisioning of troops and deportees, while the fragmentary §§42′–45′ deal with agricultural matters. Paragraph 46′ returns to the provisioning and oversight of deportees, whereas §47′ deals with abandoned land lots. Paragraphs 48′–49′, again fragmentary, are concerned with horticulture and armaments, respectively. Paragraphs 50′–51′, only slightly less fragmentary, touch on troops, armaments, and military supplies, while §52′ switches to the management of labor contingents. Paragraphs 53′–55′ deal with the upkeep, maintenance, and security of the royal palaces and noble estates in the region, before §§56′–58′ return to agricultural issues. The final partially preserved paragraph, §61″, relates to fugitives.

A number of passages would seem to be of relevance for the question of the *Sitz im Leben* of the text and of its evolution (see Miller 2011b). First, some paragraphs seem to indicate that at least some portions of the text were envisioned as spoken to the governors gathered or summoned to Ḫattusa (e.g., §§31′ and 40′; see Introduction sub Envisioning the Setting). Second, while switching between the 1st and 3rd or between 2nd and 3rd person is well known in various genres of Hittite texts, the distribution of the switching in these mss. seems to be significant, and may suggest something about its original composition and its further compilation (cf. also n. 474). All of §§1–21 refer to the (frontier) post governor in the 3rd person, the only exception being C_1 i 5[!] (see n. 309). Thereafter one finds somewhat sporadic "slips" into the 2nd person from §22 to the first portion of §38′ (once each in §§22, 25′, 30′ and 35′ [in a duplicate]). The end of §39′ until nearly the end of §41′ is then entirely in the 2nd person, while the end of §41′ through §43′ (as far as preservation allows determination) are again in the 3rd person. Paragraph 44′ is entirely in the 2nd, §§45′–46′ in the 3rd. Paragraphs 47′–48′ are again mostly 2nd, §§49′–52′ exclusively 3rd, and §§53′–61″ are rather mixed. One suspects, therefore, that even the earliest ms. (A) represents a compilation of instructions gathered from varying oral and written sources, some perhaps spoken by the king to his governors and recorded at the time by scribes, some probably formulated by the scribes after consultation with the king and his courtiers, others perhaps lifted from existing textual sources. A thorough study of the *Sitz im Leben* of this and the other instructions—a task that has seen renewed efforts in recent years with regard to other genres—would surely yield interesting results.

The paragraph divisions among the various mss. differ markedly, sometimes seemingly almost randomly. In §§38′ and 40′, for example, can be seen passages where the paragraph division would not seem to correspond to the content. For the present treatment, the paragraph division of the best preserved fragment at any given point is adopted,[294] and this is indicated by the placement of its signature first in the list of preserved mss. Comments in the footnotes refer to the main (i.e., best preserved) ms. of the paragraph in question unless otherwise noted.

The various mss. also fluctuate seemingly almost haphazardly with regard to the use of 3rd sg. vs. pl. verb forms, not only in regard to the pl. neut., as expected, but also with regard to pl. comm., that is, groups of persons, which are often treated as pl. tant. or collectives. A thorough study of when persons or groups of persons are treated as plurals and when as a collective might also be a fruitful area of study. Variation of this sort among the mss. is generally not indicated in the present treatment.

The composition shows a comprehensible overall structure, though from one paragraph to the next or from one phrase to the next one sees almost a stream of consciousness style in its handling of a range of subjects. The most obvious case of this would be the afterthought concerning behavior in the temples inserted at the beginning of §38′ after the section regarding the administration of justice has already begun in §37′, or the admonition to heed the word of the scout at the end of §45′.

1. Incipit (§1)
2. Disposition and organization of the town watch (§2–§17)
   a. Early morning inspection of surrounding area (§3–§6)
   b. Opening up the town for the day (§7)
   c. Closing up the town for the night (§8–§9)
      i. Getting the populace into the town (§8–§9, 23)
      ii. Barring the gates, setting the watch for the night (§9, 23–28)
   d. Early inspection of surrounding area for the following day (§10–§11)
   e. Additional regulations and duties (§12–§17)
      i. Patrolling roads and watching for the enemy (§12)
      ii. Maximum extent of leave for the governor (§13)
      iii. Duty of reporting sign of the enemy (§14)
      iv. Closing and guarding town in face of enemy (§15, 7′–10′)
      v. Keeping track of the enemy; disposition of scouts and commanders (§15, 11′–12′)
      vi. Recording of commanders; tracking the enemy; arrest and extradition of slackers to the king (§16–§17)
3. Specifications regarding building fortification (§18–§26′)
   a. Re. the *ḫu*[*ri*]*ppata*-[(?)] and *ḫunipis*[*a* (§19)
   b. Re. the towers (§20)
   c. Re. the *mariyawanna*-structure (§21)
   d. Re. the *ḫūtanu*- and *ḫerītu*-trenches (§22)
   e. Plastering (§23)
   f. Re. postern gates and plastering (§24′)
   g. Re. *ḫakkunnai*-installation and the gate of the wall (§25′, 28′–30′)
   h. Injunctions against actions that could damage fortifications (§25′, 31′–§26′)
4. Provisioning the town, maintenance, internal infrastructure (§27′–§30′)
   a. Firewood provisions and furnishings (§27′)
   b. Sealing and inventory procedures (§28′, 11′–12′)
   c. Scrubbing out and replastering buildings (§28′, 13′–§29′, 18′)
   d. Proper construction of various internal elements (§29′, 18′–20′)
   e. Proper maintenance and inspection of waterworks (§30′)

5. Administration of religious institutions (§31′–§37′, §38′, 17–21)
   a. Responsibility for maintenance of temples with temple personnel (§31′–§32′)
   b. Responsibility of state officials for repairs (§33′, 36′–39′)
   c. Responsibility of local personnel for utensils of deities (§33′, 39′–41′)
   d. Recording of utensils of deities for state records (§34′, 42′–43′)
   e. Proper scheduling and staffing of festivals (§34′, ii 43′–iii 8)
   f. Proper veneration of cult stelae, springs, mountains, rivers (§35′–§36′)
   g. Proper behavior in temples (§38′, 17–21)
6. Administration of justice (§37′, §38′, 21–§40′, 32)
   a. Confirmation of local traditions concerning sexual offenses (§37′)
   b. Division of jurisdiction between province and capital (§38′, 21–24)
   c. Warning against corruption (§39′)
   d. Admonition to judge cases of common people as well (§40′, 29–32)

TRANSLITERATION

§1 (B_1 i 1–4; A i 1–3; C_1 i 1!–3!; E i 1′)[295] (1)[(*UM-MA* ^{d}U)TU-*ŠI* ^{m}*AR.NU.WA*]. *AN.DA* LUGAL.⸢GAL⸣[296] (2)[*ma-a-an*(?) *a-ú-ri-ia-aš*[297] EN^{M}]^{EŠ} [298] *ḫa-an-te-ez-zi-uš a-ú-ri-⸤uš⸥*[299] (3)[… (x-*aš-kán-z*)*i*[300] *nu-*(*uš-ma-a*)]*š iš-ḫi-ú-ul* (4)[(*ki-iš-ša-an*) …] *e-eš-tu*

§2 (A i 4–5; B_1 i 5–6; C_1 i 4!–5!) (4)*ḫa-an-te-ez-zi-*⸢*e*⸣-[*eš* (BÀ)D^{ḪI}]⸤.A⸥*-aš*[301] URU$^{DIDLI.ḪI.A}$*-aš* [*ḫa-*(*li-ia-az*) …][302] (5)*a-ša-an-du nu* ⸢*ḫa*⸣-[(*a-li* SIG$_5$)]*-in pa-aḫ-ḫa-aš-nu-wa-an*[303] [*e-eš-tu*][304]

§3 (A i 6–8; C_1 i 6!–7!) (6)*na-aš-ta ku-it-ma-an ḫ*[*a-li-i*]*a-az* $^{LÚ.MEŠ}$*ḫa-a-li-i*[*a-tal-le-e-eš*] (7)*kat-ta na-a-ú-i ú-wa-an-*[*zi n*]*a-aš-ta* URU*-az kat-ta* ^{L}[($^{Ú.MEŠ}$NÍ.ZU)] (8)*ku-it-ma-an* [*ú-wa-a*]*n-du* […]

§4 (A i 9–11; C_1 i 8!–10!) (9)*na-aš-ta ku-ra-an-na* SIG$_5$*-i*[(*n š*)]*a-an-ḫa-an-du nu me-mi-an* [ ] (10)EGIR*-pa ú-*⸢*da-ú*⸣ *na-aš-ta* ^{L}[(^{Ú}EN.NU)].UN[305] *kat-ta* {*ḪA*}*ḫa-li-ia-a*[*z*] (11)*QA-TAM-MA ú-ed-du* […]

§5 (A i 12–14; C_1 i 11!–13!) (12)*nu* $^{LÚ.MEŠ}$NÍ.ZU *ŠA* KASKAL GÍD.DA *a-⸤ú⸥-*[(*ri-i-e-e*)]*š e-ep-du na-aš-ta* $^{LÚ.MEŠ}$[…] (13)URU*-az kat-ta ku-ra-an-na ša-a*[*n-ḫu-wa-an-z*]*i* [(*u-u*)]*n-ni-⸤ia-an-du⸥* [ ] (14)*na-aš-ta ku-ra-an-na-an š*[*a-a*(*n-ḫa-an-du*)]

§6 (A i 15–16; C_1 i 14!–15!) (15)*nu* $^{LÚ.MEŠ}$NÍ.ZU *ku-iš ŠA* KASKAL GÍD.DA *a-*⸢*ú*⸣*-*[*r*(*i-ia-an ḫar-zi*(?) *na-at*(??))][306] (16)*pa-ra-a ú-e-mi-ia-az-zi nu ma-a-an* [… *ú-e-*(*mi-ia-an-du*)][307]

7. Administration of troops, deportees and *land tenants* (§40′, 33–§48′)
   a. Oversight of troops stationed in town (§40′, 33–35)
   b. Oversight of and provisions for settled deportees (§41′)
   c. Care of horticultural, agricultural resources (§42′–§45′)
   d. Seed and land allotment (§46′–§47′)
   e. Administration of "the works" (§48′)
8. Administration of military equipment and personnel (§49′–§51′)
   a. Maintenance and inspection of equipment (§49′–§50′)
   b. Provisioning of military personnel (§51′)
9. Administration of labor contingents (§52′)
10. Administration of royal and noble residences (§53′–§58′)
11. Re. fugitives (§61″)
12. Colophon

TRANSLATION

§1 (1)[(Thus) says His (Maj)esty, Arnuw]anda, Great King: (2–3)[When(?) (fron)tier post (governor)]s [(continually) …] the frontier posts, [(thei)]r duty shall be [(as follows)]:

§2 (4–5)The [(forti)fi]ed frontier towns shall be […[308] (with a) wa(tch)], and the w[(atch) shall be (wel)]l kept.[309]

§3 (6–8)As long as the wa[tchm]en have not yet come down from the w[at]ch,[310] let the [(scouts) come] down from the town in the meantime.

§4 (9–11)They shall inspect the *sectors*[311] well, he shall bring back word, and the w[(atchma)]n[312] shall likewise come down from the watch.

§5 (12)The scouts shall occupy the p[(ost)]s of the main road, and the […]-men (13)shall [(dr)]ive down from the town t[o inspe]ct the *sectors*, (14)and [(they shall)] i[n(spect)] the *sectors*.

§6 (15–16)The scouts who [(hold(?))] the p[(ost)] of the main road will "find out/forth,"[313] and if […, then th(ey shall fi)nd …].[314]

§7 (A i 17; C$_{1/2}$ i 16′) (17)*na-aš-ta* GU$_4$ UDU LÚ^{MEŠ} KIN URU-*az kat-ta* [*tar-na-an-du*][315]

§8 (A i 18–22; C$_2$ i 17′–21′) (18)*ma-a-aḫ-ḫa-an-ma ne-ku-uz-zi nu* $^{LÚ.MEŠ}$NÍ.Z[U …] (19)*i-ia-an-du nu a-ú-wa-ri-e-eš ap-pa-an-d*[*u* (IGI-*zi pal-ši-ma*)] (20) *ku-i-e-eš* $^{LÚ.MEŠ}$NÍ.ZU-*TÌ* UD-*az a-ú-i-*[*e-er* (*nu-za* LÚ^{MEŠ} KIN GU$_4$ U)DU] (21) ANŠE.KUR.RA$^{ḪI.A}$ ANŠE$^{ḪI.A}$ *pé-ra-an ḫu-u-i-*[(*nu-wa-an-du na-a*)*t-kán* URU-*ri*] (22)*ša-ra-a ni-ni-in-kán-*[*du*]

§9 (A i 23–28; C$_2$ i 22′–29′; D i 1′–5′; G$_1$ i 1′–3′) (C$_2$ i 22′)⸢*na*⸣*-aš-ta* GIM-*an* LÚ^{MEŠ} ⸢KIN GU$_4$⸣ UDU [ANŠE.KUR.RA$^{ḪI.A}$ ANŠE$^{ḪI.A}$] (23′)[UR]U-*ri ša-ra-a ta-ru-up-ta nu* […][316] (A i 23)*nam-ma* $^{LÚ.MEŠ}$NÍ.ZU-*TÌ ku-i-e-eš a-ú-w*[*a-ri-e-eš e-ep-per* (*na-at-kán* URU-*ri*)] (24)*ša-ra-a pa-a-an-du nu* KÁ.GAL$^{ḪI.A}$-*TÌ l*[(*u-uš-ta-ni-i-e-e*)*š-ša*] (25)*ḫa-tal-wa-an-du nu za-ak-ki-e-eš pé-e-eš-š*[(*i-ia-an-du*) *nam-ma*(?)] (26)*lu-uš-ta-ni-ia-aš* ÉRIN^{MEŠ} EGIR-*an ḫa-an-da-a-a*[*n-d*(*u*) *na-at* (*A-NA* KÁ.GAL-*TÌ*)] (27)EGIR-*an še-eš-ke-e-ed-du nam-ma-aš-ša-an* [($^{LÚ.MEŠ}$EN.NU.UN.NA [317]*lu*)*-uš-ta-ni-ia-aš*] (28)*ša-ra-a tar-na-an-du nu ḫa-a-li* *PA* SIG$_5$-*in* [*p*(*a-aḫ-ḫa-aš-ša-an-du*)]

§10 (A i 29–32; C$_{2-3}$ i 30′–34″; D i 6′–9′; G$_1$ i 4′–7′; H, 1′–4′) (29)*ma-a-aḫ-ḫa-an-ma lu-uk-kat-ta na-aš-ta* URU-*az* $^{LÚ.}$[(^{MEŠ}NÍ.ZU *kat-ta*) *ú-wa-an-du*] (30)⸤*na-aš*⸥*-ta ku-ra-an-nu-uš* SIG$_5$-*in ša-an-ḫa-*<(*an*)>*-*⸢*du*⸣ […] (31) [*nu*[318] (*a-ú*)*-w*]*a-ri-e-eš*[319] *ap-pa-an-du na-aš-ta* URU-*az k*[(*at-ta*)][320] (32) [(*QA-TA*)*M-M*]*A tar-na-an-du* […]

§11a (A i 33–34; D i 10′; G$_1$ i 8′–9′) (33) [(^{LÚ})$^{.MEŠ}$N]Í.ZU-*kán*[321] *ŠA* KASKAL GÍD.DA *a-ú-wa-ri-e-eš* EG[IR[322]*-pa a*(*p-pa-an-d*)*u*[323]] (34)[*nu* UR]U-*aš pa-aḫ-ḫa-aš-nu-wa-an-za e-eš-du*

§11b (C$_3$ i 34″–35″; D i 11′; H, 5′) (34″)⸢*nam-ma* ^{LÚ}⸣$^{.}$[^{MEŠ} …] (35″)*tu-u-wa ḫar-kán-du* x[… *p*(*a*[324]*-ra-a ar-*) …]

§12 (A i 35–36; B$_1$ i 1′–3′; C$_3$ i 36″–38″; D i 12′–14′; H, 6′–8′) (35)[(*a-ú-ri*)]-⸤*ia-aš-za*⸥[325] *ku-iš* ÉRIN^{MEŠ} *ḫar-zi na-aš pa-aḫ-ḫa-aš-nu-wa-*[*an-za e-eš-du* (*nam-ma-kán*)] (36)[(KASKAL$^{ḪI.A}$)]-*TI*[326] SIG$_5$-*in wa-ar-ši-ia-an-du nu* ^{LÚ}KÚR-*aš* [(*u-ur-k*)*i-i*(*n uš-kán-du*)]

§13 (A i 37–38; B$_1$ i 3′–4′; C$_3$ i 39″; D i 15′; H, 9′) (37)[(*nam-ma-aš*)]*-ša-an a-ú-wa-ri-ia-aš* EN-*aš* ÉRIN^{MEŠ} *a-ú-*⸢*ri*⸣*-*[*ia-aš* $^{LÚ.MEŠ}$NÍ].⸢ZU⸣*-ia*[ ][327] (38) [(*a*)*-ú-wa*]*-*⸤*ri-ia-aš*[328] *I-NA* UD.3[329]⸥.KAM *wa-ak-k*[*a-*(*re-eš*)*-ke-ed-d*]*u*?[330]

§14 (B$_1$ i 5′–6′; A i 39–40; C$_3$ i 40″–41″; D i 16′–17′; H, 10′–11′) (5′)⸢KASKAL⸣$^{ḪI.A}$*-ma-kán wa-ar-ša-an-te-eš ku-it nu ma-aḫ-ḫa-*⸢*an*⸣[331] $^{LÚ.MEŠ}$NÍ.⸢ZU⸣[332] (6′) *ŠA* ^{LÚ}KÚR *u-ur-ki-in ú-wa-an-zi nu me-mi-an ḫu-u-da-a-ak ú-da-an-zi*

§7 (17)And [they shall let] the cattle, the sheep (and) the workmen down from the town.

§8 (18–22)When night falls, though, the scouts shall make/do[333] [...], and they shall take (up) the posts. The scouts who observ[ed (the first stretch)] of the day, however, [(shall)] drive forth [(the workmen, the cattle, the sh)eep], the horses (and) the donkeys, [(and th)ey] shall move them up [into the town].

§9 (C_2 i 22′)And as soon as the workmen, the cattle, the sheep, [the horses and the donkeys] (23′)have gathered up in the [to]wn, then [...].[334] (A i 23–25) Further, the scouts who [took up] the pos[ts] shall go up [(into the town)], and they shall bar the gate [and] the p[(ostern)], and [(they shall)] throw the doorbolts. [Further], (26–28)behind the postern [they sh(all)] station troops,[335] [and they] shall sleep behind [(the gate)]. Further, they shall let the [(guards)] up [through the (po)stern]. And [(they shall keep)] the watch well.

§10 (29)But as soon as it dawns, the [(scouts) shall come (down)] from the town, (30)and they shall inspect the *sectors* well. [Then] (31–32)they shall take (up) the [(pos)]ts, and they sha<(ll)> [(like)wi]se release (them)[336] d[(own)] from the town.

§11a (33)The scouts [s(hall tak)e up] the posts on the main (lit. "long") road aga[in], (34)[and the tow]n shall be protected.[337]

§11b (34″–35″)Further, the [...]-men shall hold/take [...] from afar. [... f(orth)/o(ut)].

§12 (35–36)Whatever [(pos)]t has a garrison, it [shall thereby be] protect[ed].[338] [(Further)], they[339] must patrol the [(roads)] well, and [(they must watch for sign)] of the enemy.

§13 (37–38)[(Further)], the governor of the post [ma]y lea[(ve)] the troops [of] the post and the [sco]uts of the [(p)os]t alone for (up to) 3 days.

§14 (5′)But as far as the roads being covered is concerned, as soon as the scouts (6′)come upon sign of the enemy, they will bring word immediately.

§15 (B_1 i 7′–12′; A i 41–46; C_3 i 42″-48″; D i 18′–22′; K i 1′–4′) (7′)*nu* URU$^{\text{DIDLI.ḪI.A}}$ *an-da iš-tap-pa-an-du na-aš-ta* LÚ^{MEŠ} ŠE.KIN.KU_5 GU_4 UDU ANŠE.KUR.RA (8′)[AN]ŠE *kat-ta le-e tar-na-an-zi nu pa-aḫ-ḫa-<(aš)>-nu-an-du ḫa-an-te-⸤ez⸥-ze-e-eš-ma* (9′)*ku-<(i)>-e-eš MA-AD-GA-LA-TI nu ŠA* ^{LÚ}KÚR *ku-i-e-eš* KASKAL$^{\text{ḪI.A}}$ *na-aš-za* (10′)*BE-EL MA-AD-GAL₉-TI kap-pu-u-wa-an ḫar-du na-aš-za gul-aš-ša-an ḫar-du* (11′)*nam-ma* 1 KASKAL 3[340] $^{\text{LÚ.MEŠ}}$NÍ.ZU-*TÌ ḫar-kán-du še-er-ma-aš-ša-an* (12′)3 $^{\text{LÚ.MEŠ}}$⸤DUGUD⸥ *ú-e-ḫa-an-da-ru*

§16a (B_1 i 13′–19′; A i 47–51; C_3 i 49″–56″; K i 5′–11′) (13′)*a-ú-ri-ia-ša-aš-ši ku-iš* ÉRIN^{MEŠ} *na-an kap-pu-u-wa-id-du na-aš-za* (14′)*⸤gul⸥-aš-ša-an ḫar-du nu-za-kán* $^{\text{LÚ.MEŠ}}$DUGUD 2! *pé-e-da-an* 3 *pé-e-da-an* (15′)4 *pé-e-da-an pé-di ša-a-ak-ki ma-a-an* ^{LÚ}KÚR-*ma ku-wa-pí* (16′)*wa-al-aḫ-zi nu* ÉRIN^{MEŠ} ^{LÚ}KÚR *u-ur-ki-in* ⸤UD.3⸥.KAM *na-an-⸢na-ú⸣* (17′)KASKAL$^{\text{ḪI.A}}$-*TÌ* UD.2.KAM *ḫar-kán-du ku-i-ša-kán* ^{LÚ}KÚR-*ma Ú-UL ku-en-zi* (18′)*nu* ^{LÚ}*BE-EL MA-AD-GAL₉-TI* ^{LÚ}DUGUD 2 *pé-e-da-an* 3 *pé-⸢e-da⸣-an* (19′)⸤4⸥ *pé-e-da-an e-ep-du na-aš MA-ḪAR* ^{d}UTU-*ŠI ú-⸤up-pa-ú⸥*

§16b_1 (D i 23′–25′) (23′)*⸤a⸥-ú-ri-⸤e⸥-eš ku-⸤iš⸥* ÉR[IN^{MEŠ} …] (24′)*[n]a-an-za-an gul-ša-an ḫar-*[*du* …]x x[…] (25′)[*nu*]-*kán* $^{\text{LÚ.MEŠ}}$*wa-ak-ka₄-ru-na-⸢e⸣-*[*eš* …]x x x-*⸢te-eš a⸣-š*[*a-a*]*n-du*

§16b_2 (D i 26′–29′) (26′)[*nu*] URU-*an* ÉRIN^{MEŠ} *a-ú-ri-ia-aš-ša ⸢I⸣-*[*NA* UD].⸢2.KAM⸣ *wa-⸢ak⸣-ka₄-re-eš-ke-ed-du* (27′)[*m*]*a-a-an* ^{LÚ}KÚR-*ma ku-wa-pí* GUL-*aḫ-zi nu* ÉRIN^{MEŠ} *ŠA* ^{LÚ}KÚR *úr-ki-in I-NA* UD.3.KAM *na-an-na-ú* (28′)[KASKA]L^{MEŠ}-*ia I-NA* UD.3.KAM *⸤ḫar⸥-du ku-iš-ša-aš-kán* ^{LÚ}KÚR-*ma Ú-UL ku-en-zi* (29′)[*n*]*a-an* EN *MAD-<GAL₉>-TI ⸤e-ep⸥-du na-an MA-ḪAR* ⸤^{d}⸥UTU-*ŠI ú-up-pa-ú*

§17 (B_1 i 20′–21′; C_3 i 57″–58″) (20′)*ma-a-an* ^{d}UTU-*ŠI-ma ma-an-ni-in-ku-wa-an nu a-ú-⸤ri⸥-aš* ⸤EN⸥-*aš* (21′)*MA-ḪAR* ^{d}UTU-*ŠI u-un-na-ú wa-aš-túl-la-aš-ša* EN^{MEŠ}-*uš ⸢ú⸣-wa-te-⸢ed⸣-du*

§18 (B_1 i 22′–28′; A i 56′–63′) (22′)URU$^{\text{DIDLI.ḪI.A}}$ BÀD-*kán*[341] *ku-i-e-eš ma-ni-ia-aḫ-ḫi-ia an-da nu-za* (23′)*ḫu-ru-pa-an* EGIR-*an kap-pu-u-wa-an ḫar-kán-du ḫa-an-te-ez-zi-e-eš-ma* (24′)[*ku-i*]-*e-eš MA-AD-GA-LA-TI* URU$^{\text{DIDLI.ḪI.A}}$ ^{LÚ}KÚR-*ša-an ku-e-da-aš* (25′)[*ḫu-u-da*]-*⸤a-ak⸥ a-ar-ša-ke-ez-z*[*i n*(*u*)] *⸤ma⸥-aḫ-ḫa-an a-pé-e-da-aš* URU$^{\text{DIDLI.ḪI.A}}$-*aš* (26′)[*a-ú-wa*[342]*-r*]*i-ia-aš* EN-*aš ⸤ú⸥-*[*e-d*(*a*)]-*⸤i⸥ na-aš ku-it-ma-an* (27′)[*ḫu-u-d*(*a-a-ak*)-*pát*][343] *⸤ú-e-te⸥-*[(*ed-du*) *na-aš pa-a*]*ḫ-ḫa-aš-nu-ud-du na-aš an-da* (28′)[(*ḫi-i-la-aš i-wa-ar wa-aḫ-nu-ud-du*)]

§19 (A i 64′–69′; B_1 i 29′; D ii 1′–5′) (64′)[…]⸢4⸣ *gi-pé-eš-šar* 4 *še-e-kán-na* (65′)[… *e-e*(*š-du*) … *š*]*e-e-kán ḫu-u*[*r-i*]*p-⸤pa*?⸥*-ta-aš-m*[*a-pá*]*t*? x[…] (66′)[…]x $NA_4$$^{\text{ḪI.A}}$ GAL x[…*še-e-ká*(*n*? *e*?)-*eš-du*(?) …] (67′)[…] *ḫu-u-ni-pí-*

§15 (7′–8′)And they shall close up the towns. They shall not let the field workers, cattle, sheep, horses, (and) [don]keys down out (of the town). They shall pro<(te)>ct (them). The governor of the post, though, (9′–10′)shall keep track of and record the frontier posts and the enemy routes. (11′–12′) Further, three scouts shall hold each road, while three commanders shall supervise.

§16a (13′)He (i.e., the governor), however, shall keep track of the troops of the post (available) to him, and he (14′–16′)shall keep a record of them. He will know by rank the commanders of second rank, third rank, (and) fourth rank. But if the enemy attacks at some point, then the troops shall follow the track of the enemy for three days, (17′)(and) they shall hold the roads for two days. Whoever does not kill the enemy, though, (18′–19′) the governor of the post shall seize (them), (be he) a commander of second rank, third rank (or) fourth rank, and have them brought before His Majesty.

§16b$_1$ (23′)The posts [...] which tro[ops], (24′)he (i.e., the governor) [shall] keep a record of them [...]. (25′)[And] the *wakkaruna*-people shal[l b]e [...].

§16b$_2$ (26′)[And] the troops of the post as well shall leave the town f[or] (up to) two [days]. (27′)But if the enemy attacks at some point, then the troops shall follow the track of the enemy for three days, (28′)and they shall hold the [roa]ds for three days. But whoever does not kill the enemy, (29′)the governor of the p<os>t[344] shall seize him and have him brought before His Majesty.

§17 (20′)If His Majesty, however, is nearby, the governor of the post (21′)shall hasten to appear before His Majesty, and he shall bring the offenders.

§18 (22′)Concerning the fortified towns in the province, (23′–24′)they should keep track of the *ḫurupa*-.[345] But the towns of the frontier post [wh]ich the enemy (25′–26′)can reach [quic]kly, when the governor of the [post buil(d)]s in those towns, he shall during that time bu[(ild) very quic(kly), and] he shall [de]fend [them]. And [(he shall enclose)] them [(like a courtyard)] (is enclosed).[346]

§19 (64′)[... shal(l be)] 4 ell and 4 hands.[347] (65′)[... x h]ands, b[ut especia]lly(?) the *ḫu*[*ri*]*ppata*-(?) (66′)[...] large stones [... sha(ll b)e(?) ... *hand*(*s*)(?) ...] (67′)[...] *ḫunipis*[*a*~ ... (they shall) ...] (68′)[...] he/they shall, and [(they

š[a~ … (x-an-du)] (68′)[… -i]d-du nu-uš-š[a-an … (a-ša-an-du)] (69′)[… -w]a?-a[(n-zi)]

§20[348] (A i 70′–75′; C$_1$ ii 1–4; D ii 6′–9′) (70′)[…]-⸢i⸣ nu NA$_4$-an 2 še-e-k[án…] (71′)[… S]A$_x$?-A!?-TÙ nu ⸢nam⸣-ma NA$_4$-a[n … (gi-p)é-eš-šar … AN.Z(A.GÀR$^{\text{ḪI.A}}$ pár-ga-aš-ti)] (72′)[…^{GIŠ}i]š-pár-ru-uz-zi 4 še-e-k[án … (1-EN AN.ZA).GÀR ú-e-(da-i-ma 3 gi-pé-eš-šar)] (73′)[…] e-eš-du ku-*ú*-uz-za-ma k[at?-ta?… ar-(ḫa 4?/5? gi-pé-eš-šar e-eš-d)u …(Ú-UL an-da)] (74′)[na]m?-ma-aš-ša-an iš-tar-na […-i(a-aš AN.ZA.GÀR)] (75′)[pé-ra-a]n?[349] ⸤ar-ḫa 4 gi⸥-p[(é-eš-šar e-eš-d)u]

§21 (B$_1$ ii 1–4; C$_1$ ii 5–10; D ii 10′–14′; J ii? 1′–4″) (1)⸢ar!⸣[350]-ḫa-ma-aš ⸢4?/7?[351] gi⸣-pé-⸢eš⸣-š[(ar)] ⸢e-eš-tu⸣ nam-ma-aš (2)⸤^{URUDU}⸥ḫe-ia-wa-al-li-it ma-ri-ia-wa-an-ni-it an-da wa-aḫ-nu-wa-an-za (3)e-eš-tu ma-ri-ia-wa-an-na-ma-kán[352] pé-ra-an ar-ḫa (4)6 gi-pé-eš-šar e-eš-tu pa-ra-a-ma-at-kán 6[353] še-kán ú-wa-an e-eš-tu

§22[354] (D ii 15′–21′; B$_1$ ii 5–11; C$_1$ ii 11–17) (15′) [(nam-m)a URU-an ku-in][355] ú-e-te-eš$_{15}$-ke-*ši* nu-kán ḫu-u-ta-nu-e-uš[356] (16′)GAM-an-da ⸢2?⸣[357] gi-p[(é-šar)][358] da-an-te-eš a-ša-an-du še-er ar-ḫa-ia-⸢at⸣-k[án][359] (17′)2 gi-pé-šar a-ša-⸢an⸣-du ku-it-ma-an URU-an ú-i-du-⸢ma-an-zi⸣ (18′)ze-en-na-i nu-kán ḪÉ-RI-TU$_4$ GAM-an-*da* 6 gi-pé-eš-šar e-eš-⸢du⸣ (19′)še-er ar-ḫa-ia-at-kán 4 gi-pé-eš-šar e-eš-du (20′)ma-a-a[n] ⸤ú⸥-e-ti-na-an-za-ma[360] ša-ra-a Ú-UL ar-nu-zi (21′)⸤nu-u⸥-w[a?][361] ša-ra-a IŠ-TU *NA$_4$ {x x} [362]tal*-ḫa-a-an-du

§23[363] (B$_1$ ii 12–13; B$_2$ ii 15′–20′; C$_1$ ii 18–23; E ii 1′–2′) (B$_1$ ii 12)[(GIM-a)n-ma …] ⸤a-ú-ri⸥-uš ú-e-tum-ma-an-z[i] (13)[(ze-e)n-na-i … a-ú-r]i-ia-aš-kán [… (an-d)a? …] (B$_2$ ii 15′)[(na-) …] (16′)[(a?-š)]a?-an-du[…] (17′)[i]š-⸤ki⸥-ia-an-t[e?-eš? …] (18′)[x] gi-pé-eš-šar […] (E ii 1′)[(ku-uz-za-ma)] ⸢4 še-e-kán e-eš-du⸣ pár-ga-⸢aš-ti⸣ x x x[…] (2′)iš-ki-ia-an-ma 1-an-ki e-eš-du

§24′ (D ii 22′–27′; B$_2$ ii 19′–26′; E ii 3′–7′) (22′)nam-m[(a) Š]A ⸤KÁ⸥.GAL$^{\text{ḪI.A}}$-TÌ lu-uš-ta-ni-ia-aš i-la-na-aš SAG.DU^{MEŠ}-uš (23′)ŠA B[(À)]D.URU$^{\text{DIDLI.ḪI.A}}$ [364] ^{GIŠ}IG-an-te-eš ^{GIŠ}ḫa-at-tal-wa-an-te-eš (24′)a-ša-[a]n-du na-aš-ta ar-ḫa le-e ku-it-ki ḫar-ak-[(zi)] (25′)BÀD-ma pu-ru-ut ti-ia-u-wa-an-zi ⸤2?-an?⸥ al-la-⸤a⸥-a[(n[365] e-eš-du)] (26′)nam-ma-⸤at⸥ iš-tal-ga-an e-eš-du na-aš-ta ⸤šu⸥-u[(ḫ-ḫa le-e)] (27′)⸤wa-ar⸥-[(ḫ)]u-i[366] za-ap-pí-ia-at-ta-ri le-⸢e⸣[…]

§25′ (D ii 28′–34′; B$_2$ ii 27′–32′; E ii 8′–13′; G$_3$ ii 1′–6′) (28′)[(URU-an-m)]a[367] ku-in ú-e-te-eš-ke-ši nu ^{LÚ}TIBIRA [pé-r(a-an)] (29′)[(NA$_4$-a)]n?[368] ḫa-ak-ku-un-na-i[369] ú-e-te-ed-du nu B[(ÀD-eš)-na-aš] (30′) ^{GIŠ}KÁ.GAL-TÌ an-dur-za a-ra-aḫ-za NA$_4$-it QA-[(TAM-MA)] (31′)nam-ma-aš-ša-an BÀD^{MEŠ}-ni an-da

shall be) …] (69′)[… (they will) …].

§20 (70′)He will […], and a/the stone(acc.) 2 han[ds] (71′)[… *s*]*âtu*(?)-measure(s), and further, […] the ston[e(acc.) … (e)ll … to(wers … high)] (72′–73′)[… *i*]*sparuzzi*-beam 4 han[ds … (he) buil(ds a single to)wer, (though, 3 ell) …] it shall be. The wall, though, d[own? … (it shall be 4?/5? ell fo)rth … (not in) …]. (74′–75′)[Fu]rther?, inside [… (the tower of) … (it shall be)] 4 e[(ll)] out [fron]t?.

§21 (1)It shall, however, extend (lit. “be”) forth 3! el[(l)]. (2–4)Further, it shall be encircled by a gutter and a *mariyawanna*-structure. The *mariyawanna*-structure, though, shall extend (lit. “be”) 6 ell out in front, but it shall come out 6 hands.

§22 (15′–16′)[(Furth)er, as concerns the town that] you[370] build, the *ḫūtanu*-trenches shall be taken 2? e[(ll)] deep, and out above (17′–18′)they shall be 2 ell. By the time he finishes building the town, the *ḫerītu*-trench[371] shall be 6 ell deep, (19′)and out above it shall be 4 ell. (20′)But if/when *the water raises (it) up/over*,[372] (21′)they shall *sti*[*ll*][373] pave (it) over with stone.[374]

§23 (12–13)[But (as soon a)s he (fin)ishes] building […] the posts, […] of [the pos]ts [(in) …] (B2 ii 15′)[(and) …] (16′)they shall [(be) …] (17′)[p]laster[ed(pl.) …] (18′)[x] ell […] (E ii 1′)[(but the wall)] shall be 4 hands. The height […] (2′)but it shall be plastered once.

§24′ (22′–24′)Furth[(er)], *for* the heads of the stairways of postern gates of fo[(rtifi)]ed towns there shall be doors (and) bolts.[375] Nothing shall be missing. (25′)To apply plaster (to) the wall, though, [(it shall be)] 2? *alla*-? (*thick*?/*high*?). (26′)Further, let it be smoothed, and the ro[(of)] must [(not)] (be) (27′)*rough*. It must not leak![376]

§25′ (28′)Concerning the [(town)] that you build, [(tho)]ugh, the coppersmith (29′–30′)shall [*p*(*re*)]*fabricate* a [(*st*)*on*]*e* *ḫakkunnai*-installation,[377] also *for* the gate [of (the wal)]l inside and outside, lik[(ewis)e] with stone. (31′)Further, no one shall d[(i)g] at the wall, (32′)and no one shall burn

le-e ku-iš-ki ⸢pád⸣-[(d)a-i] (32′)an-da-ia-kán le-e ku-iš-ki wa-ar-nu-zi (33′) pu-ru-ut-ti-ia-aš-ša-an[378] GU$_4$ UDU ANŠE.KUR.RA *x* ANŠE.GÌR.NUN.NA (34′)an-da le-e tar-ni-iš-kán-zi[379]

§26′ (D ii 35′–41′; A ii 1′–4′; B$_1$ ii 1′–4′; E ii 14′–20′; G$_3$ ii 7′–9′; K ii 1′–4′) (35′) a-ra-aḫ-zé-na-aš-ša-kán an-tu-ri-ia-⸤aš-ša⸥ A-NA AN.*ZA*.GÀR (36′)GIŠ-ṢU GIŠzu-up-pa-ru an-da le-e ku-⸢iš⸣-ki da-a-i BÀDMEŠ-eš-ša[(r-r)a] (37′)ar-za-na-an-ni le-e ku-iš-ki e-ep-zi BÀD-eš-ni-ia-kán (38′)⸤an⸥-da le-e ku-iš-ki wa-ar-nu-uz-zi ANŠE.KUR.*RA* ⸤ANŠE.GÌR⸥.N[UN.NA-ia] (39′)[a]n-da le-e ku-iš-ki ti-it-ta-nu-zi nam-ma-kán U[(RU-ri ar-ta-aḫ-ḫi-uš)] (40′)[(le)]-⸤e⸥ ša-a-ḫi-iš-ket$_9$-ta-ri na-aš-kán MU.KAM-ti MU.KA[(M-ti)] (41′)[UGU[380] (š)]a-an-ḫi-iš-kán-du

§27a′ (B$_1$ ii 5′)a-⸤ú-wa⸥-ri-ia-aš-⸤ša⸥-kán EN-aš A-NA URUDIDLI.ḪI.A BÀD an-da wa-ar-nu-ma-aš (6′)GIŠ-ruḪI.A ki!(DI)-⸢iš⸣-ša-an ḫa-an-ta-id-du ḫa-an-ta-az-at-kán 12 ga-lu-lu-pa-aš (7′)⸤e⸥-[(eš)-t]u ⸤GÍD⸥.DA-aš-ti-ma-at 1 gi-pé-eš-šar 4 še-kán-na e-eš-tu (8′)[(GIŠm)a-…] x ḫa-an-da-az 3 ga-lu-lu-pa-aš e-eš-tu GÍD.DA-aš-ti-ma-at (9′)[(1 gi-pé-eš-ša)]r e-eš-tu an!(GIŠ)-dur-za[381] ŠA GIŠḪI.A me-ek-ki e-eš-tu (10′)[…]x[382] GIŠḫar-du-up-pí-iš nu ḫu-u-ma-an me-ek-ki e-eš-tu

§27b′ (A ii 5′; K ii 5′–7′) a-ú-⸢ri⸣-ia-š[a-ká]n EN-⸢aš A⸣-[NA …] (6′) wa-ar-nu-ma-aš GIŠḪI.A ḫa-an-d[(a-id-du) …] (7′)5 ⸢ŠU⸣.SIḪI.A e-eš-du GÍD.DA-aš-t[i-ma-at …] (8′)4 še-e-kán-na e-eš-du GIŠm[a-…] (9′)GÍD.DA-aš-ti-ma-at 1 gi-pé-eš-ša[(r e-eš-du) …] (10′) GIŠ⸤GUL⸥ḪI.A GIŠKA.BALḪI.A EŠ/30[…] (11′) IN.NUḪI.A GI.DUR$_5$!(KUN) nu ḫu-u-ma-an […]

§27c$_1$′ (D ii 42′)A-NA UR[U-L]Ì-kán še-er GIŠ-ṢU ⸢ŠA⸣ LUGAL ⸢ḫa⸣-an-da-an e-eš-[du] (43′)GIŠ-ṢU-[i]a-⸤kán⸥ nam-ma ar-ḫa-ia-⸢an⸣ A-NA URU-LÌ š[e-er] (44′) me-ek-k[i-pát[383] ḫ]a-an-da-an e-eš-du ma-a-an LÚKÚR k[u-it] (45′) URU-an ḫ[a-a]t-kiš-nu-zi [k]e-e-ez-za-an-kán U[R]U t[i-…][384]

§27c$_2$′ (D ii 46′)ŠA LUGAL-ia-kán ⸤na⸥-ak-ki-iš GIŠḫar-du-up-pí-iš […] (47′)la-aḫ-⸢ḫu-ra⸣-aš ⸢GIŠḫa-pu⸣-ti-ia URU-ri še-er ḫa-a[n-da-an e-eš-du]

§28′ (B$_1$ ii 11′–15′; A ii 12′–17′; C$_4$ ii 1′–6′; D ii 48′–52′) (11′)[(nu an-da ši-ia-an)] ⸤e⸥-eš-tu na-at-za EGIR-an MU.KAM-ti MU-ti (12′)k[(ap-pu-u-uš-ke-ed-du n)]u ša-ra-am-ni-it kat-ta zi-ik-ke-ed-du[385] (13′)É⸢MEŠ⸣ L[(UGAL É)]⸢MEŠ GU$_4$⸣ É NA4KIŠIBḪI.A Étar-nu-u-e-eš ku-e ka-ru-⸤ú⸥-[(i-l)]i (14′)na-at ⸢ar-ḫa⸣ ar-ri-ir-ra-an-du na-at da-a-an EGIR-pa ne-e-u-i[(t)] (15′)ú-i-la-ni-it ḫa-ni-iš-ša-an-du na-at ta-a-an EGIR-pa ne-wa-aḫ-ḫa-an-du

(anything) at (it). (33′–34′)And they shall not let cattle, sheep, horses, (or) mules near the *adobe*.[386]

§26′ (35′–39′)And no one shall place a torch on a wooden tower, outside or inside.[387] No one is to occupy the walls as a dwelling. And no one shall burn (anything) at the wall. No one shall quarter horse [and mu]le (there). Further, the [(drains in the tow)]n (40′–41′)must not become clogged. They must be cleaned [(up)] year for year.

§27a' (5′–7′)And the governor of the post shall organize the firewood in the fortified towns as follows: It s[(hall b)]e 12 fingers *in diameter*,[388] while it shall be 1 ell and 4 hands in length. (8′)The [*m*(*a-*…-wood)] shall be 3 fingers *in diameter*, while it (9′)shall be [(1 el)]l in length. There shall be lots of wood inside(?). (10′)[…] furniture; there shall be much of everything.

§27b' (5′–6′)A[nd] the governor of the post [(shall)] organize the firewood f[or …]. (7′–8′) It shall be 5 fingers […, while it] shall be […] and 4 hands in length. The *m*[*a-*…]-wood […], (9′) while it [(shall be)] 1 ell in length. […] (10′)*striking-tools* (and) *air-holes* […] (11′)straw (and) GI.DUR$_5^!$-*reed*, and […] everything.

§27c_1′ (42′)The king's wood [shall] be arranged up in the tow[n], (43′–44′)and further, [very] much wood *apart from* u[p] in the town shall be arranged. If s[ome] enemy (45′)b[es]ieges the town, [they shall …] the t[ow]n with this (wood).[389]

§27c_2′ (46′–47′)The heavy furniture […], the altar and the bed of the king [shall be] arr[anged] up in the town.

§28′ (11′–12′)[(And)] it shall remain [(under seal. He shall take)] s[(tock)] of it year for year, and he shall regularly store it with the bread provisions. (13′–15′)They shall scrub out those r[(oyal)] buildings, cattle [(barn)]s, storehouses, and baths that are ol[(de)]r, and they shall replaster them a second time with new plaster and renovate them a second time.

§29′ (B$_1$ ii 16′–20′; A ii 18′–23′; C$_4$ ii 7′–12′; D iii 1–3) (16′)*ḫa-ni-iš-šu-wa-ar-ma-kán ku-it a-wa-an kat-ta mu-um-mi-i-e-et-ta*[390] (17′)*na-at ku-ut-ta-aš a-wa-an ar-ḫa da-aš-kán-du na-aš-ta ša-ma-nu-uš* (18′)*te-ek-ku-uš-nu-uš-kán-du*[391] *nam-ma* KISLAḪ ^{É}IN.NU.DA ^{É}*ka-ri-im-mi* (19′) ^{É}*tar-nu-ú-e-eš ŠA* ^{GIŠ}TIR$^{\text{ḪI.A}}$ ^{GIŠ}MÚ^{SAR} ^{GIŠ}KIRI$_6$.GEŠTIN (20′)SIG$_5$-*in ú-e-da-an-te-eš a-ša-an-du*

§30′ (B$_1$ ii 21′–25′; A ii 24′–27′; C$_4$ ii 13′–18′) (21′)*ŠA* É.DU$_{10}$[392].ÚS.SA-*ia ŠA* É ^{LÚ}SAGI ^{É}*ḫi-lam-na-aš-ša* (22′)*a-ar-ta-ḫi-uš ú-e-ḫa-an-da-ru na-aš* ˻*uš*˼-*kán-du ku-i-ša-kán* (23′)*ú-e-te-na-za ša-ḫa-a-ri na-an-kán ša-ra-a ša-an-ḫa-an-du* (24′)*ma-ni-ia-ḫi-ia-ia-ták-kán*[393] *ku-i-e-eš* MUŠEN$^{\text{ḪI.A}}$-*aš lu-ú-li-ia-aš an-da* (25′)*na-at* SIG$_5$-*an-te-eš a-ša-an-du*

§31′ (B$_1$ ii 26′–31′; C$_4$ ii 19′–24′; L ii 1′–3′) (26′)*ku-e-da-*⸢*ni*⸣-*ma-aš-ša-an* URU-*ri a-ú-ri-ia-aš* EN-*aš* EGIR-*pa pé-en-na-i* (27′)*nu-za* $^{\text{LÚ.MEŠ}}$ŠU.GI $^{\text{LÚ.MEŠ}}$SANGA $^{\text{LÚ.MEŠ}}$GUDU$_{12}$ $^{\text{MUNUS.MEŠ}}$AMA.DINGIR *kap-pu-u-id-du* (28′)*nu-uš-ma-aš ki-iš-ša-an me-ma-ú ke-e-da-ni-wa-aš-ša-an* URU-*ri* (29′)*na-aš-šu ŠA* ^{d}10 *ku-it-*<(*ki*)> ^{É}*ka-ri-im-mi na-aš-ma ta-me-e-da-aš* DINGIR-˻*LÌ*˼-*aš* (30′)*ku-it-ki* ^{É}*ka-ri-im-mi ki-nu-na-at kat-ta mu-ta*[394]*-a-an* (31′)*na-at ar-ḫa ḫar-kán*

§32′ (B$_1$ ii 32′–35′; C$_4$ iii 1–4; L ii 3′–5′) (32′) $^{\text{LÚ.MEŠ}}$SANGA-*at-za* $^{\text{MUNUS.MEŠ}}$*ši-wa-an-za-an-ni-iš* $^{\text{LÚ.MEŠ}}$GUDU$_{12}$ EGIR-*an Ú-UL kap-pu-u-an-za*[395] (33′)*ki-nu-na-at* EGIR-*an kap-pu-wa-at-te-en na-at* EGIR-*pa i-ia-an-du* (34′)*na-at ma-aḫ-ḫa-an ka-ru-ú ú-e-da-an e-eš-ta* (35′)*na-at* EGIR-*pa QA-TAM-MA ú-e-da-an-du*

§33′ (B$_1$ ii 36′–41′; A iii 1′; C$_4$ iii 5–12; F$_1$ iii 1′–2′; L ii 6′–11′) (36′)*nam-ma-aš-ša-an* DINGIR^{MEŠ}-*aš na-aḫ-šar-az ti-ia-an e-eš-du A-NA* ^{d}10-*ma-aš-ša-an* (37′)*na-aḫ-šar-az me-ek-ki ki*$^{!}$(DI)-*it-ta-ru ma-a-an* É DINGIR-*LÌ-ia ku-it-*⸢*ki*⸣ (38′)*za-ap-pí-ia-at-ta na-at a-ú-ri-ia-aš* EN-*aš* ^{LÚ}MAŠKIM.URU^{KI}-*ia* (39′) EGIR-*pa* SIG$_5$-*aḫ-ḫa-an-du na-aš-ma-kán A-NA* ^{d}10 *ku-iš-ki BI-IB-RU* (40′)*na-aš-ma-kán ta-me-e-da-ni*[396] DINGIR-*LÌ ku-e-da-ni Ú-NU-TU*$_4$ *ḫar-kán* (41′) *na-at* $^{\text{LÚ.MEŠ}}$SANGA $^{\text{LÚ.MEŠ}}$GUDU$_{12}$ $^{\text{MUNUS.MEŠ}}$AMA.[397]-*ia* EGIR-*pa i-ia-an-du*

§34′ (B$_1$ ii 42′–46′; A iii 2′–8′; C$_4$ iii 13–16; F$_1$ iii 3′–8′) (B$_1$ ii 42′)*nam-ma ŠA* DINGIR-*LÌ Ú-NU-TU*$_4$ *a-ú-wa-ri-ia-aš* EN-*aš gul-aš-du* (43′)*na-at MA-ḪAR* ^{d}UTU-<*ŠI*> *up-pa-ú nam-ma* DINGIR^{MEŠ} *me-ḫu-na-aš iš-ša-an-du* (44′)*ku-e-da-ni-ia* DINGIR-*LÌ-ni ku-it me-ḫur na-an a-pé-e-da-ni me-ḫu-ni e-eš-*˻*ša*˼*-an-*˻*du*˼ (45′)*ku-e-da-ni-ma A-NA* DINGIR-*LÌ* ^{LÚ}SANGA *MUNUS*AMA. ^{LÚ}GUDU$_{12}$ NU.GÁL (46′)*na-an* EGIR-*pa ḫu-u-da-a-ak i-ia-an-du* (A iii 7′)*A-N*[(*A* ^{GIŠ}TIR$^{\text{ḪI.A}}$-*i*)*a*] (8′)[*šu*]-*up-pé-eš-na-aš na-aḫ-*šar*-*[*r*]*a-*˻*az*˼ *ki-it-ta-r*[*u*][398]

§29′ (16′)The plaster that crumbles down, though, (17′–18′)they shall regularly[399] remove from the walls, and they shall expose the foundation stones.[400] Further, the threshing floor, the straw barn, the shrine, (and) (19′)the *water installations*[401] for the orchards, gardens, (and) vineyards (20′)must be properly constructed.

§30′ (21′–22′)The (water of the) drains of the ritual purification building, of the house of the cupbearer, and the gate-house must *circulate* (freely),[402] and they shall inspect them regularly. That which (23′)is clogged due to the (sewer-)water, though, they shall clean up. (24′)Also the birds in the ponds[403] in your district (25′)shall be well.

§31′ (26′)But in whatever town the governor of the post drives back to, (27′)he shall count the *ritualists*,[404] the priests, the anointed ones and the mother-deity priestesses, (28′)and he shall speak to them thus: "In this town (29′–30′) either the temple of som<(e)> Storm God or the temple of some other deity is now neglected,[405] (31′)and it is dilapidated.[406]

§32′ (32′) "You priests, mother-deity priestesses (and) anointed ones, it (i.e., the temple) is not attended to![407] (33′)You(pl.) shall attend to it now!" And they shall restore it. (34′)As it was built before, (35′)so they shall rebuild it.

§33′ (36′)Further, reverence for the deities shall be maintained; for the Storm God, though, (37′)reverence shall be *firmly*[408] established. And if some temple (38′)leaks, the governor of the post and the magistrate (39′)must repair it; or if some rhyton of the Storm God (40′)or the paraphernalia of some other deity are missing, (41′)then the priests, the anointed ones and the mother-deity priestesses shall restore them.

§34′ (42′)Further, the governor of the post shall make a record of the paraphernalia of the deity, (43′)and he shall have it brought before <His> Majesty. Further, they shall venerate the deities in a timely (fashion): (44′)For whatever deity there is a (set) time, they shall venerate him/her at that time. (45′) For whatever deity there is no priest, mother-deity priestess (or) anointed one, (46′)they must immediately appoint one. (A iii 7′–8′)And reve[r]-ence must be established [fo(r)] the [sa]nctity of [(the forests)].

§35′ (A iii 9′–17′; B$_1$ iii 1–7; F$_1$ iii 9′–15′) (9′)[(URU-*L*)]*ì-ma-kán ka-ru-ú-i-l*[*i*] NA$_4$*ḫu-wa-š*[*i k*]*u-i*[*t*] (10′)[(EGI)]R-*an-ma-at*[409] *Ú-UL kap-*[(*p*)]*u-u-wa-an ki-nu-na-at-*⸢*za*⸣[ ] (11′)[(EGI)]R-*an kap-pu-u-wa-an-du* [(*n*)]*a-at ša-ra-a ti-it-*⸢*ta*⸣*-nu-an-du* (12′)[(*nu-u*)]*š-ši ka-ru-ú-i-li-ia-az ku-it* SÍSKUR *na-at-ši* (13′)[*e-eš*]*-ša-an-du*[410] *A-NA* URU-*LÌ-ia-aš-ša-an ku-e* PÚ.ḪI.A EGIR-*an* (14′)[*nu*[411] *k*]*u-e-da-ni A-NA* PÚ SÍSKUR *e-eš-zi na-at ši-pa-an-za-kán-du* (15′)[*ša-r*]*a-a-ia-at-kán a-ar-*aš*-kán-du ku-e-da-ni-ma* (16′)[(*A-N*)]*A* PÚ SÍSKUR NU.GÁL *na-at-kán ša-ra-a im-ma a-ar-aš-kán-du* (17′)[*na*]*-at-kán an-da le-e* IGI-*wa-an-da-ri-iš-ke-ez-zi*

§36′ (A iii 18′–19′; B$_1$ iii 8; F$_1$ iii 16′) (18′)[(*A-N*)]*A* ḪUR.SAG DIDLI!(AŠ).ḪI.A I$_7$ DIDLI!(AŠ).ḪI.A *ku-e-da-ni*[412] SÍSKUR *e-eš-zi* (19′)[(*n*)]*a-aš ši-pa-an-za-kán-du*

§37′ (B$_1$ iii 9–16; A iii 20′–30′; F$_1$ iii 17′–18′) (9)*nam-ma a-ú-ri-ia-aš* EN-*aš* LÚMAŠKIM.URUKI!(DI) LÚ.MEŠŠU.GI *DI-NA-*⸢*TÌ*⸣ (10)SIG$_5$-*in ḫa-aš-ši-kán-du nu-*⸤*uš-ša*⸥*-an kat-ta ar-nu-uš-kán-du* (11)*ka-ru-ú-li-ia-az-*⸤*ia ma*⸥*-aḫ-ḫa-an* KUR.KUR-*kán an-da ḫu-ur-ki-la-aš* (12)*iš-ḫi-ú-ul i-ia-an ku-e-*da-ni*-aš-kán* URU-*ri* ⸤*ku*⸥*-aš-ke-er na-aš-kán* (13)*ku-wa-aš-kán-du ku-e-da-ni-ma-aš-kán* URU-*ri ar-ḫa pár-ḫi-iš-ke-er* (14)*na-aš-kán ar-ḫa pár-ḫi-iš-kán-du nam-ma-za* URU-*aš* EGIR-*an-da wa-ar-*⸤*ap-du*⸥ (15)*nam-ma* ⸤*wa-tar-na*⸥*-aḫ-ḫa-an e-eš-du na-aš-ša-an* EGIR-*pa le-e* (16)*ku-iš-ki* ⸢*tar*⸣*-na-i ku-i-ša-an-ša-an* EGIR-*pa tar-na-i na-an ša-ku-wa-an-za*[413]

§38′ (B$_1$ iii 17–24; A iii 31′–33′; D iv 1–10; I, 1′–6′) (17)DINGIRMEŠ-⸤*ia ku-wa-pí e*⸥*-eš-ša-an-zi nu PA-NI* DINGIRMEŠ *le-e ku-iš-*⸤*ki*⸥ (18)*ni-ni-*⸢*ik-zi*⸣ *I-NA* É EZEN$_4$-*ia le-e ku-iš-ki ni-ni-ik-zi* (19)*nam-ma-aš-ša-an A-NA* LÚ.MEŠSANGA LÚ.MEŠ*UM-MI-IA-NU-TÌ* LÚ.MEŠGUDU$_{12}$ (20) MUNUS.MEŠAMA.DINGIR-*LÌ na-aḫ-šar-ra-az ki-it-ta-ru* LÚ.MEŠSANGA LÚ.MEŠGUDU$_{12}$ (21) MUNUS.MEŠAMA.-*ia A-*NA** DINGIRMEŠ *na-aḫ-ḫa-an-te-eš a-ša-an-du ma-a-an DI-NU-ma ku-iš* (22) GIŠ[414].ḪUR ⸤*tup*⸥*-pí-az ši-ia-an ú-da-i nu a-ú-ri-ia-aš* EN-*aš DI-NA$_7$* (23) SIG$_5$-*in ḫa-an-na-ú na-at-kán aš-ša-nu-ud-du ma-a-an-kán DI-NU-ma* (24) *šu-wa-*⸤*at-ta-ri na*⸥*-at MA-ḪAR* dUTU-*ŠI up-pa-ú*

§39′ (B$_1$ iii 25–28; D iv 11–16′) (25)*A-NA BE-LÍ-ma-at-ša-an le-e i-e-ez-zi A-NA* ŠEŠ-*ia-at-za-an*[415] (26)⸤NIN-*ŠU* LÚ*a*⸥*-ri-ši-ia le-e*[416] *i-ia-zi ma-aš-ga-an-na-za le-e ku-iš-ki* (27)*da-a-i* ⸢*DI-NA$_7$*⸣ *ša-ra-az-zi kat-te-ra-aḫ-ḫi le-e kat-te-er-ra*[417] (28)*ša-ra-az-ia-*⸤*ḫi*⸥ *le-e ku-it ḫa-an-da-an a-pa-a-at i-iš-ša*[418]

§40′ (B$_1$ iii 29–35; D iv 17′–24′) (29)*ku-e-da-ni-ma-aš-ša-an* URU-*ri* EGIR-*pa a-ar-ti nu* LÚMEŠ URU-*LÌ* (30)*ḫu-u-ma-an-du-uš pa-ra-a ḫal-za-a-i nu ku-e-da-ni DI-NA$_7$ e-eš-zi* (31)*na-at-ši ḫa-an-ni na-an-kán aš-nu-ut* ÌR.LÚ GÉME.

§35′ (9′)But [wha]te[ver] ancient[419] cult stele in a [(tow)]n that (10′–11′)has not been [(at)]tended to, they[420] shall now [(at)]tend to. They shall set it up, (12′–13′)[(and)] they shall [per]form for it whatever rite that (was performed) for it from ancient (days). And for whatever springs are behind the town, (14′)for [wh]atever spring there is an offering regimen, they must perform it regularly, (15′–16′)and they must come [u]p to visit it regularly. And they must even[421] come up to visit regularly any spring for which there is no offering regimen. (17′)They must never neglect it.

§36′ (18′)For whatever mountains (and) rivers there are offerings, (19′)they must regularly offer them.

§37′ (9–10)Further, the governor of the post, the magistrate, (and) the elders shall judge law cases properly, and they shall resolve (them). (11–12)And as the law regarding a sexual offense has been handled traditionally in the provinces, in a town in which they have executed, (13)let them execute, while in a town in which they have banished, (14)let them banish. Further, the town must bathe afterwards, (15–16)and moreover, let it be decreed: No one shall allow him/her[422] back. They will *sakuwai-*[423] whomever allows him/her back.

§38′ (17–18)And when they venerate the gods, no one shall misbehave before the gods, and no one shall misbehave in the festival building. (19–23)Further, reverence will be established for the priests, the (temple) personnel,[424] the anointed ones, (and) the mother-deity priestesses. (And) the priests, anointed ones, and mother-deity priestesses shall be reverent toward the gods. If, however, someone brings a law case, with a sealed writing board from a clay tablet,[425] then the governor of the post shall decide the law case properly, and he shall settle it. If, however, the law case (24)becomes (too) onerous, he shall have it brought before His Majesty.[426]

§39′ (25–28)He shall not, however, do it for a lord, nor shall he do it for a brother, his sister or his friend. And let no one accept a bribe.[427] He shall not make a superior case inferior; he shall not make the inferior superior. You shall do what is just!

§40′ (29–30)In whatever town to which you return,[428] though, call out all the people of the town, and for whomever a law case is (pending), (31–32) judge it for him/her and resolve (it for) him/her. If there is a law case

LÚ *wa-an-nu-mi-ia-aš* (32)MUNUS-*ni ma-a-an* DI-*ŠU-NU e-eš-zi nu-uš-ma-ša-at ḫa-an-ni na-aš-kán aš-nu-ut* (33)ÉRIN^MEŠ ^URU*KA.ŠI.IA-ia* ÉRIN^MEŠ ^URU*ḪI.IM.MU.WA* ÉRIN^MEŠ ^URU*TA.GA.RA.M*[*A*] (34)*Ù* ÉRIN^MEŠ ^URU*I.ŠU.WA-ia a-pí-ia nu-uš-ma-aš-ša-an* *x* (35)*ḫu-u-ma-*<*an*>*-da-az*[429] IGI^ḪI.A*-wa ḫar-ak*

§41′ (B₁ iii 36–41; J iii? 1′–5″) (36)*ar-nu-wa-*˻*la*˼*-ša-kán ku-iš* KUR*-ia an-da ar-za-na-an-za nu-uš-ši-ša-an* (37)*iš-ḫu-e-eš-ni-it* NUMUN^ḪI.A*-it* GU₄ UDU IGI^ḪI.A*-wa ḫar-ak nam-ma-an-kán* (38)*IŠ-TU* GA.KIN.AG *EM-ṢI* SÍG^ḪI.A *aš-nu-ut ar-nu-wa-la-ša-ták-kán* (39)*ku-iš* KUR*-az ar-ḫa ú-ez-zi pé-di-ma-aš-ši-ša-an ku-iš a-aš-zi* (40)*nu-uš-ši* ˻NUMUN˼^ḪI.A *a-ni-ia-pát nam-ma-aš-kán* A.ŠÀ^ḪI.A*-it šu-u-wa-an-za e-eš-*˻*tu*˼ (41)*n*[*u-u*]*š-ši pí-it-ta ḫu-u-da-a-ak ḫi-in-kán-du*

§42′ (B₁ iii 42–46′; J iii? 6″–9″) (42)[…]x x x-˻*ia*?*-ni*?˼*-kán BE-EL* LÚ ^GIŠTUKUL A.ŠÀ^ḪI.A*-an* ^GIŠTIR ^GIŠKIRI₆[…] (43)[…]x x x x-*ši* *x* *BE-*˻*EL*˼ É.GAL-*LÌ-ia-aš-ša-an* GU₄ UDU[…] (44)[…]x x x[…]x ˻*ŠA*˼ É.GAL-*LÌ-ia*[…] (45)[…]x-*ia*[…] (46′)[… (x-*ta-an*) …]x *a*-x[…][430]

§43′ (B₁ iii 47′–51′) (47′)[… U]DU ANŠE.KU[R.RA …] (48′)[… *ḫ*]*ar-du na-*[…] (49′)[… *Š*]*A* É.GAL-*LÌ*[…] (50′)[…]x-*wa-an ḫar-zi* x[…] (51′)[…]*-ia-an-za-an le-e k*[*u*?-…]

§44′ (B₁ iii 52′–56′; C₁ iii 1′–5′) (52′)[…]x-*it an-da ku-un-***ku**[431]*-uš-k*[*án*?*-du*(?)] (53′)[… (*ŠA*) … ^GIŠ]⸢TIR⸣^ḪI.A [432] *ku-ut-te-eš* SIG₅*-in ú-*⸢*e*⸣*-*[*da-an-te-eš*] (54′)[*a-ša-an-du* (*nam-ma-a*)]*t*? *ú-e-te-na-za ši-iš-ši-***u***-ri-iš-k*[*e*] (55′)[(*Ú-SAL-LU-i*)*a ú-e-te*]*-na-az ši-iš-ši-u-ri-iš-ke* [ ] (56′)[(*na-aš-ta* x)…]*-da*[433] *le-e ú-e-ši-ia-at-ta* [ ]

§45′ (B₁ iii 57′–59′; C₁ iii 6′–9′) (57′)[(*nam-ma* ^GIŠ)MÚ^SA]R[434] ⸢^GIŠKIRI₆⸣.GEŠTIN^ḪI.A SIG₅*-in a-ni-ia-an-te-eš* ⸢*ú-e*⸣*-d*[*a-an-te-eš*] (58′)⸢*a*⸣*-š*[(*a-an-d*)*u*] *nam-ma-kán ḫu-up-pí-da-nu-e-eš* PA₅^ḪI.A*-ša ša-ra-a* (59′)*ša-an-ḫ*[*a-an-t*]*e-eš a-ša-an-du* ⸢*nam-ma* ^LÚNÍ.ZU⸣*-aš ut-tar na-ak-ki-aḫ-ḫa-an* ⸢*e*⸣*-*[(*e*)*š-du*]

§46′ (B₁ iii 60′–65′; C₁ iii 10′–16′; G₂ iv 1′)[435] (60′)*A-NA* NA[(M.R)]A^ḪI.A*-ma ku-wa-pí* NUMUN^ḪI.A *an-ni-iš-kán-zi nu a-ú-wa-ri-aš* EN*-aš* (61′)*ḫu-u-ma-an-da-aš-ša* IGI^ḪI.A*-ŠU še-er ḫu-ia-an-za e-eš-tu ma-a-an ki-iš-ša-an-ma* (62′)*ku-*⸢*iš*⸣*-ki me-ma-i* NUMUN*-wa-mu pa-i nu-wa-ra-at-za-kán am-me-el* A.ŠÀ*-ni*[436]*-mi* (63′)*an-da a-ni-ia-mi*[437] *nam-ma-wa iš-*˻*ḫu-e*˼*-eš-šar iš-ḫu-eḫ-ḫi nu še-er* (64′)⸢*a*⸣*-ú-wa-*˻*ri-ia*˼*-aš-pát* EN*-aš* IGI^ḪI.A-[(*iš*)] *ḫu-ia-an-za e-eš-tu* (65′)*ma-aḫ-ḫa-an-*⸢*kán*⸣ BURU₁₄*-an-za ki-ša-ri na-aš-ta a-pu-u-un* A.ŠÀ*-LA*₁₂ *ar-ḫa wa-a*[*r-aš-du*]

§47′ (B₁ iii 66′–71′; C₁ iii 17′–18′; G₂ iv 2′–5′) (66′)˻*ḫar-kán*˼*-ta-aš-ša*[438] LÚ ^GIŠTUKUL *ku-iš* ⸢A⸣.ŠÀ^ḪI.A *ta*[439]*-an-na-a-at-ta-ia* (67′)˻*ku*˼*-e pí-e-*˻*et-ta*˼

(pending) for a male or a female servant or a woman without kin,[440] then decide it for them and resolve (it for) them. (33)Also the troops of Kasiya, the troops of Ḫimmuwa, the troops of Tagaram[a] (34–35)and the troops of Isuwa (which are) there, you[441] shall by all (means) keep an eye on them.

§41′ (36–39)You must keep an eye on a deportee who has been settled in the province with regard to *provisions*,[442] seed, cattle (and) sheep; further, you must provide him with cheese, sourdough, (and) wool. Whoever remains in place of a deportee who leaves your province, though, (40)you yourself must sow seed for him. Furthermore, he must be satisfied with regard to fields, (41)s[o] they shall promptly assign him a plot.

§42′ (42)[…] the supervisor of the *land tenants*,[443] fields, forest, orchard (43) […] and the palace supervisor […] cattle, sheep (44–46′)[…] of the palace […]

§43′ (47′)[… sh]eep, hors[es …] (48′)[…] he shall keep/hold, and (49′)[… o]f the palace […] (50′)[…] he keeps/will keep […]-ed (51′)[…] shall not […] it/him.

§44′ (52′)[…] t[hey?] shall continually *prepare* […] with (53′–54′)[… (*of*) …] the forests? (and) walls [shall be] well bu[ilt …]. [(Further)], you shall irrigate [(th)]em with water. (55′)[(Al)so (the pasture)] you shall irrigate with [wat]er. (56′)[(And)] you shall not let […] graze [(on it)].

§45′ (57′–59′)[(Further, the) garde]ns? (and) vineyards [(mus)]t be well made (and) bu[ilt]. Further, the *ḫuppidanu*-installations and the canals shall be cle[an]ed up. Further, the word/matter of the scout [must (b)]e taken seriously.

§46′ (60′)When, however, they sow seed for depo[(rte)]es, the governor of the post (61′–64′)must keep his eyes on all of them as well.[444] But if someone speaks thus: "Give me seed, and I will sow it in my field, then I will heap up stores (of grain)," then the governor of that very post must keep (his) eyes on (him). (65′)When the harvest arrives, then [he shall ha]rvest that field.

§47′ (66′–67′)Also the fields of a run-away *land tenant* and land allotments that are empty shall all be recorded for you. (68′–70′)But [w]hen they allocate

ne-et-ta ⸤*ḫu-u-ma*⸥*-an gul-aš-ša-an e-eš-tu* (68')[*m*]*a-aḫ-ḫa-an-ma* NAM.RAḪI.A *pí-an-*˹*zi nu*˺*-uš-ši* ˹*AŠ-RA*˺[445] *ḫu-u-da-ak* (69')⸤*ḫi*⸥*-in-kán-du gi-im-ra-aš-ša ku-i-e-*⸤*eš wa*⸥*-al-ḫu-u-wa-an-te-eš* (70')*nu-uš-ma-aš-ša-an ú-e-*⸤*tum*⸥*-ma-aš* ˹*ud-da-ni-i* IGIḪI.A˺*-wa ḫar-ak* (71')*na-aš* ⸤SIG₅⸥*-in ú-e-*⸤*da*⸥*-an-za* ⸤*e*⸥*-eš-*⸤*tu*⸥

§48′ (B₁ iii 72′–76′; G₂ iv 6′) (72')*nu* KIN˹ḪI˺.A*-aš ud-da-ni-i* ˹EGIR*-an ar-ḫu-ut na-aš-ta*˺ (73')˹*pí-iš-ta-li*˺*-ia* ˹*ka-pa*?*-a*?*-nu*?˺ x x x x-˹*ḫa*?˺*-a-an e-eš-tu* (74')*ú-li-*˹*li-ia-kán* KINḪI.A˺ x x x x x (75')[…]x ḪA x x x x x ˹*e-eš-tu*˺ *ma-a-an* É DINGIR*-LÌ-ma* (76')[…]x MA NI x[…]-˹*ia* 4 *gi*˺*-pé-eš-šar e-eš-tu*

§49′[446] (A iv 1′–5′) (1')[… ANŠE.KU]R.˹RAḪI.A˺[…] (2')[… TÚGGÚ].⸤È⸥.A ZABAR (3')[… ZAB]AR GIŠBANḪI.A (4')[…]˹GI˺[GAG.Ú.T]AG.˹GA˺Ḫ[I.A K]UŠ*ki-li-it*ḪI.A (5')[…] *e-*˹*eš*˺*-du*

§50′ (A iv 6′–9′; B₁ iv 1′–2′; E iv 1′) (6')[… *ku-i*]*š*? ÉRINMEŠ*-az na-aš IŠ-TU* KUŠÉ.MÁ.URU₅ḪI.A (7')[… K]UŠ*A-RI-I-TI* SAG.DULḪI.A *ar-ma-an-na-an-ti-it* (8')[… S]IG₅*-ia-aḫ-ḫa-an e-eš-du na-an-kán* (9')[(*a-ú-ri-ia-aš* EN*-aš*) …]x[447] **me-na-aḫ-ḫa***-an-da* **uš***-ke-du*

§51′ (A iv 10′–13′; B₁ iv 3′–6′; E iv 2′–4′) (10')[… (~*ti-ia-za* Š)A … LÚK]UŠ₇ KÙ.SIG₁₇!(ŠU.GI)[448] *ŠA* LÚKUŠ₇ ANŠE.KUR.RAḪI.A (11')[… -*š*]*a-an* NINDA KAŠ *le-e ti-an-zi* (12')[…]*-zi ma-a-an Ú-UL-ma* (13')[… *a-ú-*(*ri-ia-aš* EN*-an wa*)-…]x *ap-pa-an-zi*

§52′ (B₁ iv 6′–8′; A iv 14′; E iv 5′) (6')… ÉRINMEŠ KIN*-ia ku-iš* (7')[… *a*(*n-ni-i*)]*š-ke-ed-du a-ú-ri-ia-ša* (8')[(EN*-aš*) …]*a-ni-ia-zi*

§53′ (B₁ iv 9′–12′; A iv 15′–18′) (9')[…][449] ˹É.GAL*-LÌ*˺ḪI.A *ku-e ma-ni-ia-aḫ-ḫi-ia* (10')[(*an*)*-da nu-uš-ma-aš-ša-a*(*n*)[450] *ḫu*]*-*˹*u-ma*˺*-an-te-ia* IGIḪI.A*-wa ḫar-ak* (11')[(A.ŠÀ *te-ri-ip-pí-ia*)]*-*˹*ša*˺*-aš-ša-an* NUMUNḪI.A*-aš-ša* É.GAL*-LÌ*ḪI.A (12')[*ŠA*][451] ˹SAG˺.GÉME.˹ÌR˺MEŠ *ḫal-ku-iš-ša-na-ša* IGIḪI.A*-wa ḫar-ak*

§54′a (B₁ iv 13′–20′; E iv 6′–10′; F₁ iv 1′–9′) (13')[*m*]*a-ni-ia-aḫ-ḫi-ia-ták-kán*[452] *ku-e* É.GAL*-LÌ*ḪI.A*-TÌ*[453] ÉḪI.A *BE-LU-TI-ia* (14')[(*an-d*)]*a na-aš-ta* EGIR*-an ar-ḫa pu-nu-uš-ke na-aš-šu da₄-mi-iš-ḫa-a-an* (15')*ku-iš-ki ku-it-ki ḫar-zi* [454]*na-aš-ma-za da-a-an ku-iš-ki ku-it-ki ḫar-zi* (16')*na-aš-ma-za ḫa-ap-pí-ra-an*[455] *ku-iš-ki ku-it-ki*

§54′b (A iv 19')ÉḪI.A *BE-LU-TÌ* É.GAL*-LÌ-*⸤*ia an-da*⸥[…] (20')*na-aš-šu da₄-mi-iš-ḫa-a-an ku-iš-ki ku-it-ki* [*ḫar-zi* …] (21')*ku-it-ki ḫar-zi na-aš-ma-za ḫa-ap-pí-ra-*[*an* …] (22')ÉSAG *ku-iš-ki* ZI*-it ki-i-nu-an ḫar-z*[*i* …] (23')*ku-na-an ḫar-zi na-aš-ma* ŠEḪI.A*-in ku-i*[*š-ki* …] (24')*pé-ra-an ša-ra-a e-ep-du na-a*[*t* …]

deportees, they shall promptly assign them a place. And you shall keep an eye on the *walḫuwant*-[456] for the fields with regard to their construction, (71′)and they shall be well built.

§48′ (72′)And you shall take care of the matter of the works. And (73′)the *pistali*-(and?) the *kapanu*(?)-bulbs shall be […]-ed. (74′)And the foliage, the works […] (75′)[…] shall be […]. But if/when a/the temple […] (76′)[…] it shall be 4 ell.

§49′ (1′)[… hor]ses (2′)[… c]oat of bronze (3′)[… bron]ze, bows (4′)[… arr]ows, *kili*-leathers (5′)[…] it/they shall be.

§50′ (6′)[… as regar]ds(?) the troops, it […] with quivers (7′)[… l]eather shields, SAG.DUL-headwear, with *armannant* (8′–9′)[…] it/they shall be refurbished. And [(the governor of the post) …] shall inspect it regularly.[457]

§51′ (10′)[…] the gold (level) chariot fighter (and) the horses of the chariot fighter (11′)[…] they shall not give bread (and) beer. (12′)[He/They wi]ll […]. But if not, (13′)they will hold/grasp/take the [gove(rnor of the po)st …].[458]

§52′ (6′)And the labor contingents that are […] (7′–8′)[…] they shall regularly [w(or)]k/[m(ak)]e […]. But the [(governor)] of the post […] works/makes/will work/will make.

§53′ (9′–10′)You must [(also)] keep an eye on al[l the …] (and) the palaces [(i)n your] province. (11′–12′)You[459] must also keep an eye on the seed for the [(ploughed fields)] and the land allotments of the palace servants.

§54′a (13′–15′)And you shall inquire regularly into the palaces and noble estates that are in your [p]rovince, whether someone has damaged anything, or whether someone has taken anything, (16′–17′)or whether someone has sold anything, or whether someone has broken into a granary, or whether someone has killed royal

§54′b (19′–23′)[…] into the noble estates and the palaces […], whether someone [has] damaged anything, […] has […] anything, or […] sold […], […], someone has deliberately broken into a granary, […] has killed […], or whether some[one …] the grain stores […] (24′)he shall take […] up before […], and i[t …].

ḫar-zi na-aš-ma ÉSAG (17′)*ku-iš-ki ki-nu-wa-an ḫar-zi na-aš-ma-za-kán* GU$_4$ LUGAL *ku-iš-ki* (18′)*ku-na-an ḫar-zi na-aš-ma-kán* ÉSAG^ḪI.A^ *ku-iš-ki ša-ra-a* (19′)*a-da-a-an ḫar-zi nu-za* GIŠ.ḪUR^ḪI.A^ GÙB-*la-aš-ma ḫar-ni-in-kán ḫar-zi* (20′)*na-at-za* EGIR-*an kap-pu-u-i*

§55′a (B$_1$ iv 21′–26′; E iv 11′–15′) (21′)*na-aš-ma-⌞kán⌟ A-NA* SAG.GÉME.ÌR^MEŠ^ *ku-iš-ki ku-it-ki ar-ḫa* (22′)*da-a-an ḫar-zi na-an a-ú-wa-ri-ia-aš* EN-*aš e-ep-⌞du⌟* (23′)*na-an MA-ḪAR* ^d^UTU-*ŠI up-pa-ú gi-im-mi-ia-aš-ša-[a]n A-NA* GU$_4$^MEŠ^ LUGAL (24′)IGI^ḪI.A^-*wa ḫar-du nu gi-im-ma-an-da-aš* BURU$_{14}$-*aš* KIN-*ši*[460] ⌜EGIR⌝-*an ar-ḫu-ut* (25′)*ŠA* TU$_7$^ḪI.A^ *AŠ-RI*^ḪI.A^ SIG$_5$-*ia-aḫ-ḫa-an e-eš-tu e-kán ⌞da⌟-a-⌞an⌟* (26′)*e-eš-tu* É *ŠU-RI-PÍ ú-⌞e-da⌟-an e-eš-tu*

§55′b (A iv 25′–29′) (25′)*ma-a-an-kán* ^LÚ^KUR-*ia-aš-ḫa-aš A-NA* SAG.GÉM[E.ÌR^MEŠ^ …] (26′)**ḫar-zi na-an* EGIR-*pa ti-i-ia** *na-a[t…]* (27′)*ge-e-mi-ia-aš-ša-an a-ni-ia-at-ta-[aš …]* (28′)EGIR-*an ar-ḫu-ut na-at* SIG$_5$-[…] (29′)*A-NA* É.GAL-*LÌ*^ḪI.A^ *ḫu-u-ma-an-te-i[a …]*

§56′ (A iv 29′–36′; B$_1$ iv 27′–32′; E iv 15′–19′; M iv 1′–3′) (29′)[… (*nam-ma-za*)] (30′)*ŠA* ^GIŠ^KIRI$_6$^ḪI.A^-*az*[461] SAR^ḪI.A^ EGIR-*an ka*[(*p-pu-wa-an*) *ḫar-*(*ak na-at wa-ar-pí ti-ia-an e-eš-tu*)] (31′)*A-NA* GU$_4$^ḪI.A^ *pár-za-ḫa-an-na-aš* ḪA.LA 3-*i*[*š*? [462](*nu a-pu-u-un* ḪA.LA *az-zi-zi-kán-du*)] (32′)**kal-la-ra-an-ni-ia-aš-ma-aš* x x x* *le-e k*[*u-*(*iš-ki*)[463] *pa-a-i ku-*(*iš-ša-ma-aš*)] (33′)**kal-la-ra-an-ni-ma** (erasure) *pa-a-i n*[*a-* …] (34′)A.ŠÀ *te-ri-ip-pí-ia-aš-ša ku-wa-pí* x[… (*-zi-ma ku-wa-pí*) …] (35′)*ku-it-ma-an nu* A.ŠÀ^ḪI.A^-*an ar-ḫa* [… -(*ru*)] (36′)*nu du-wa-an* 1 *gi-pé-eš-šar* 5 *še-e-kán-n*[*a* …]

§57′ (A iv 37′–42′; F$_2$ iv 1′–6′; M iv 4′–10′) (37′)*ma-a-aḫ-ḫa-an-na* GU$_4$^ḪI.A^ *za-al-ka$_4$-nu-an-*ta-r**[*i n*(*am-ma ar-ḫa ša-ar-ru-*)[464] …] (38′)*nu du-wa-a-an* 1 IKU 5 *gi-pé-eš-šar-ra* [*du-wa-a-*(*an-na* 1 IKU A.ŠÀ 5[465] *gi-pé-eš-ša*)*r-ra*] (39′)*te-ri-ip-pí-iš-*kán-du* nam-ma ḫa-me-eš-ḫ*[*a*[466]*-an-za ki-ša-r*(*i* NUMUN^ḪI.A^ É.GAL-*LÌ*)] (40′)SAG.GÉME.ÌR^MEŠ^ *BE-EL* ^GIŠ^TUKUL EGIR-*an* [(*ar-ḫu-ut nu-kán* IGI^ḪI.A^-*wa ḫar-ak*)] (41′)*nam-ma ku-it-ma-an ḫa-me-eš-ḫa-an-*[*za ki-š*(*a-ri nu* ^GIŠ^*ti-i-e-eš-ni*)] (42′)*kat-ta-an ḫa-an-te-eš-⌞kán-du⌟*[…]

§58′ (A iv 43′–49′; F$_2$ iv 7′–9′; M iv 11′–14′) (43′)*ma-a-aḫ-ḫa-an-na ḫa-me-eš-ḫa-an-z*[*a ki-ša-ri* …(x-*kán*)] (44′)*ku-it a-aš-zi na-at* x[…]⌜*ma-a-aḫ-ḫa-an-na*⌝(?)[…][467] (45′)*ta-me-e-da-ni* URU-*ri*[…]^LÚ^APIN.LÁ-*ma-aš-⌞ša⌟-*[(*an*

cattle, (18′–19′)or whether someone has consumed the grain stores then illicitly destroyed the wooden writing boards. (20′)You shall keep track of it.

§55′a (21′–22′)Or if someone has taken something away from the servants, the governor of the post shall apprehend him, (23′–24′)and he shall have him brought before His Majesty. And in winter he must keep an eye on the royal cattle, and you shall tend to the winter (and) harvest labor. (25′)The kitchens shall be in order. Ice shall be collected, (and) an ice-house shall be built.

§55′b (25′–26′)If a *provincial governor* has […] to/from the serv[ants], you shall “step/stand back/again” him(acc.),[468] and […] it. (27′)And the *work* of winter […] (28′)you shall take care of, and it […] well. (29′)To/For all the palaces al[so …].[469]

§56′ (29′)[… (Further)], (30′)[(you shall) keep (track of)] the plants of the gardens,[470] [(and they shall be placed within a fence)].[471] (31′)A *threef[old?]*[472] portion is for the *parzaḫanna*-cattle, [(and they shall regularly eat that portion)]. (32′)And no o[(ne)] shall [give] them in excess (of that). [Who(ever)] (33′)gives [(them)] in excess (of that), though, […]. (34′) And where/when the/a cultivated field […, (but where/when) …] (35′)in the meantime, and the fields […] forth. […] (36′)And in one direction 1 ell and 5 hands […].

§57′ (37′)And when the cattle are late, (and) [f(urther) … (forth)], (38′–40′)they shall plough 10 m. and 5 ell in one way [(and 10 m.) and (5 ell land) the other w(ay)]. Further, (when) spr[ing arrive(s, you shall take care of the seed of the palace)], the servants (and) the chief *land tenant*, [(and you must keep an eye on)] (them). (41′–42′)Further, until sprin[g arri(ves)], they shall prepare down [(in the *tiyessar*-orchard)]. […].

§58′ (43′)And as soon as spring [arrives, …] (44′)that remains, it […]. And as soon as(?) […] (45′)in/to another town […]. The ploughman, though, [… (the work)]. (46′)And as soon as the provinci[al (governor)] comes b[ac]k,

KIN) ...] (46′)*ma-a-aḫ-ḫa-an-na* LÚKU[R-(*ni-ia-aš-ḫa-aš* E)GIR-*p*]*a*(?) *ú-ez-z*[*i* ...] (47′)⌞*a*⌟*-uš-zi nu-uš-š*[*i* … (*kap-p*)*u*-…]x x[...] (48′) [G]U₄ḪI.A*-ia-aš-ši*[...] (49′) [*ma*]*-a-an-za* KIN-*ma*[…][473]

§59″ (C_2 iv 3′) (traces)

§60″ (C_2 iv 4′–5′) (4′)⌜*zi*?*-ik*?⌝ m*Ú*-⌜*ra*⌝-x[…][474] (5′)⌜*pé-ra*⌝*-an* ⌜*ŠA*? AN?⌝ x ⌜IŠ?⌝ x[…]

§61″ (C_2 iv 6′–9′) (6′)[LÚ*p*]*ít-ti-ia-an-da-an-na-za* EN *MAD-GAL₉-TI* […] (7′)[…]x KUR LÚ *le-e ku-iš-*⌞*ki*⌟ *da-a-i ku-*x[…] (8′)[…-*m*]*a-aš-*⌞*ši ú-e*⌟*-mi-ia-an-zi na-an u*?*-t*[*a*/*g*[*a-* …] (9′)[…]⌞*A*?*-NA*?⌟ x x x ⌞DU⌟ x *ap-pa-an-zi* […]

Colophon

(C_2 iv 10′) DUB.1.KAM *iš-ḫi-ú-la-aš* [… *Ú-UL QA-TI*]

[…] (47′)he will see […], and [*he will* (*count/keep track of*) …] for hi[m]. (48′)And the cattle […] to him. (49′)But if/when the work […].

§59″ (3′) (traces)

§60″ (4′)*You, Ura*-[…] (5′)before […]

§61″ (6′)And the governor of the post [… a f]ugitive(acc.) […] (7′)[…] land, no one shall take the man […] (8′)but they find […] for him, and […] him, […] (9′)[…] they hold/seize […].

COLOPHON

(10′)Tablet One of the Obligations [… . Not finished.][475]

No. 18
Instructions and Oath Imposition for Military Commanders (*CTH* 268)

This composition is represented by two blocks of fragments that would seem to belong to a single tablet. If one were to assume that the text were finished with this tablet alone, the preserved text would represent less than a quarter of the original composition. The tablet is clearly a MH source, perhaps rather late than early MH, judging from both its paleography and language. A more concrete dating is not possible at present. As with so many of the instructions, the tablet fragments were found in the Temple I complex.

The first partially comprehensible paragraph (§2′) deals with personal loyalty to the king. The following two paragraphs continue in the same vein (§§3′–4′), whereby the military context of the prescribed duties becomes clear. In §5′ the speaker warns against failing to come to him when written to in time

---

Transliteration

(ca. first quarter of obv. missing)

§1′ (obv. 1′)[…]x x

§2′ (2′)[…]x-⸢*ia*⸣-*aš* ÉRIN^MEŠ.ḪI.A (3′)[…]x-*un nu-za a-ra-u*-x[ ] (4′)[… *š*]*a-aḫ-ḫa-an lu-uz*-[*zi-ia*] (5′)[…]x *pa-aḫ-ḫa-aš-tén* (6′)x[… -(*i*)]*a na-ak-ki*-x[ ] (7′)*am-me*-⸢*el*⸣[… *na-a*]*k*^?-*ki-iš e-eš-d*[*u*] (8′)*pé-ra-an* x[…]x *A-NA* SAG.DU^M[^EŠ-*KU-NU*] (9′)ZI^ḪI.A-*KU-NU* ⸢*A*^!-*RA*⸣-*M*[*A-NI-KU-NU* … *A-NA* S]AG.DU-*IA* (10′)ZI-*IA A-RA-MA-NI-IA* [… *pé-ra-a*]*n wa-aḫ-nu-an ḫar-d*[*u*]

§3′ (11′)*nu-mu-za* UD-*ti* GE$_6$-*an-ti ḫa*-[[476]… ^LÚ]*uš-ki-iš-ga-tal-li-iš-ša* (12′)*e-eš-tén nu-mu-za ma-a-an* URU~x[…] *a-pí-ia pa-aḫ-ḫa-aš-tén* (13′)*ma-a-an-mu-za la-aḫ-ḫi-ma ku-w*[*a-pí* …]x EGIR-*pa* ^UZUGABA-*aš* (14′)*wa-ar-ši-ia-an-za e-eš-du ma*-⸢*a-an*⸣-*m*[*u* … *i*]*š-ki-ša* (15′)*wa-ar-ši-ia-an-da e-e*[*š-du* …]

§4′ (16′)*ma-a-an-mu* ZAG-*az-ma* GÙB-*za ḫu-i-ia*-⸢*an-te*⸣-*eš nu-za* ⸢*ḫu*⸣[477]-[*u-m*]*a-an*-⸢*da-az*⸣ *wa-ar-ši*-⸢*ia*⸣-*an-za e-eš-li-it* (17′)*nu-mu I-NA* KUR ^LÚKÚR **a-wa-an ar-ḫa le-e ku-iš-ki* píd-da-a-i n*[*u*]-*mu-kán an-da le-e ku-iš-ki*[ ] (18′)*da-la-i nu ḫu-u-ma-an-za ḫu-u-da ḫar-du nu-kán* ^LÚKÚR *ku-w*[*a*]-*ni ku-iš-ma-mu a-wa-an ar-ḫa*~x[…] (19′)*píd-da-a-i šu-me-ša-an e-ep-tén nu ku-iš am-mu-uk* ^LÚKÚR *šu*-⸢*ma*⸣-*a-aš-ša-aš* ^LÚKÚR ⸤*e*⸥-*eš-du na-an la-aḫ-ḫi*-⸢*ia*⸣-*a*[*t-tén*] (20′)*ma-a-na-aš* 1 LÚ-*LU*$_4$ *ma-a-na-aš me-ek-ki-iš ma-a-na-aš* ÉRIN^MEŠ *ku*-⸤*iš-ki*⸥ *ma-a-na-at* KUR-*e ku-it-ki* (21′)*ma-a-na-at te-li-pu-ri-i ku-it-ki ma-a-na-aš* URU-*aš* ⸤*ku*⸥-*i-ša-aš im-ma ku-iš an-tu-u-*

of need, suggesting that the subordinates in question might be rather border commanders or military officers stationed outside the capital rather than personal bodyguards or the central military command. In the first two paragraphs of the rev. (§§8″–9″) the exact setting is no longer clear. It may continue with the theme of loyalty in a military situation. The final paragraph (§10″) invokes the thousand gods (of Ḫatti) to witness the oath that would have been taken before the king.

This MH text shows that personal loyalty to the king was very much a focus of the documentation during this period as well, and that it was not only in the insecure era toward the end of the empire that such texts were extant (e.g., Giorgieri 2005: 329–30). Though the unique features of the later texts must not be denied, the present text (cf. also No. 22) can serve as a caution against overinterpreting them when searching for clues concerning the reasons for the collapse of the Hittite Empire (cf. e.g., Giorgieri and Mora 2010: 139). For arguments against seeing this text as a continuation of No. 4, see discussion there.

TRANSLATION

(ca. first quarter of obv. missing)

§1′ (traces)

§2′ (2′)[…] the troops of (3′)[…] I did […], and *fre*[*e* …] (4′)[… *s*]*aḫḫan*- [and] *luz*[*zi*]-levies (5′)[…] you[478] must protect. (6′)[…] important, (7′)my […] shall be [impo]rtant. (8′)Before […] to [your] persons, (9′)to your souls, to [your] bod[ies, … to] my person, (10′)my soul, to my body […] shall be the [pri]ority.

§3′ (11′–12′)And you shall be […] and lookouts for me day and night. And when the/a city […] me, you must protect […] then/there. (13′)When at some poi[nt …] me on campaign, though, […] back/again/after the front (14′)shall be *cleared*; when […] m[e …] to the back (15′)[shall] be *cleared*.

§4′ (16′)If, however, there are *deserters* to my right (or) to my left, then I must be *kept free* from them a[l]l.[479] (17′–19′)And let no one flee from me in the land of an enemy, and let no one leave me in (that land). And everyone shall maintain preparedness, so that we kill the enemy. He who flees from me, though, you must seize him. And he who is an enemy to me must be an enemy to you. [You must] fight against him! (20′)Whether it is (only) one man, whether it be many, whether it is some army, whether it is some land, (21′)whether it is some province, whether it is some city, whoever the man is, (22′)all of you together must fight him unreservedly, and you must not relent!

wa-aḫ-ḫa-aš (22′)*na-an ḫu-u-ma-an-te-eš ták-ša-an kar-ši za-aḫ-ḫi-ia-ad-*[*du*]*-ma-at na-an le-e da-le-eš-te-ni*

§5′ (23′)*ma-a-an-mu i-da-la-u-wa-an-ni-ia ku-iš wa-ag-ga-ri-i*[*a-wa-a*]*n-zi ša-an-ḫa-zi šu-ma-a-ša* (24′)*ḫa-at-ra-a-mi nu-mu-uš-ša-an ma-a-an wa-ar-ri lam-n*[*i-i*] *Ú-UL e-er-te-ni na-aš-ma-at šu-me-eš-ma*[ ] (25′)[*i*]*š-ta-ma-aš-ta-ni na-at ma-a-an A-NA* dUTU-*ŠI ḫu-*[*u-da*]*-a-ak Ú-*UL me*-ma-at-te-ni* (26′)*a-pa-a-*aš-ša-aš-ma-aš* ma-a-an Ú-UL* LÚKÚR *x* *na-an la-aḫ-*[*ḫi-i*]*a-at-te-ni Ú-UL* *x* (27′)[*n*]*u-uš-ma-ša-at* ˻*ŠA-PAL NI-IŠ*˼ DINGIR-*LÌ ki-it-t*[*a-ru* x x x]~˻*ma*˼*-a-an* LUGAL-*uš*

§6′ (28′)[*na*]-˻*aš*˼*-ma-mu ku-i*[*š~… an-tu-w*]*a-*˻*aḫ*˼*-ḫa-aš i-d*[*a-la/u-* …] x-˻*an-ni*? *tu*˼-x x x[ ] (29′)[…]x x[…]x x[ ]

(remaining ca. quarter of obv. and first ca. quarter of rev. missing)

§7″ (rev. 1′)[…]x[…]

§8″ (2′)[*šu-ma*][480]*-aš-ma-aš-kán ma-a-an ki-iš-šu-wa-an*~x x[… *pé-ra-an*] (3′)[*pé-e*]*-ḫu-te-ez-zi na-aš-ma ma-a-an šu-m*[*e-* …] (4′)[*i-i*]*a-zi na-aš-šu tar-pa-ni-ia-aš ut-tar* x[…] (5′)[*iš-t*]*a-ma-aš-ta-ni nu ma-a-an* ˻*a*˼*-pé-ni-i*[*š-šu-wa-an~* … *Ú-UL*] (6′)[*te-e*]*k-ku-*˹*uš*˺*-ša-nu-*˹*ut*˺*-ta-ni* ˻*nu-uš*˼*-ma-ša-aš* x[…] (7′)[*šu-me-š*]*a-an*[481] *ma-a-an ḫu-u-da-a-ak Ú-UL e-ep-t*[*e-ni* …] (8′)[*an-t*]*u-uḫ-ši* EGIR-*an ti-ia-at-te-ni nu-uš-ma-aš-kán NI-I*[*Š* DINGIRMEŠ …] (9′)[*QA-D*]*U* DAMMEŠ-*KU-NU* DUMUMEŠ-*KU-NU ar-ḫa ḫar-ni-in-kán-du* [*nu-kán da-an-ku-wa-az*] (10′)[*ta-g*]*a-an-zi-pa-az* ŠUMMEŠ-˹*KU*˺*-NU* NUMUN-˻*KU-NU*˼*-ia ar-ḫa ḫar-*[*ni-in-kán-du*]

§9″ (11′)[*šu-me-e*]*n-za-an-na ku-iš ḫa-an-te-ez-zi-iš nu-uš-*˻*ma*˼*-aš ma-a-a*[*n* …] (12′)[*nu-u*]*š-ma-aš* dUTU-*ŠI-in pé-ra-an* SIG5-*in me-mi-iš-ke-ez-zi*[…] (13′)[*na-a*]*n iš-ta-ma-aš-ket9-tén* ˻*ma*˼*-a-an-ša-ma-aš-kán ki-iš-šu-wa-an-m*[*a* …] (14′)[*wa-a*]*g-ga-a-ri-ia-aš-ša-aš ut-tar pé-ra-an pé-e-ḫu-te-ez-zi* x[…] (15′)[*nu*] ˹*a*˺*-pé-ni-iš-*˹*šu*˺*-wa-an-ti an-tu-uḫ-ši* EGIR-˻*an ti-ia-at*˼*-te-ni n*[*u-uš-ma-aš NI-IŠ* DINGIRMEŠ] (16′)[EGI]R-*an le-e tar-na-an-zi* […]

§10″ (17′)[*nu k*]*a-a-ša ke-e-da-ni li-in-ki-ia-*{*aš*} *LI-IM* DINGIRMEŠ *tu-l*[*i-ia ḫal-zi-u-en* …] (18′)[dUT]U *ŠA-ME-E* dUTU URU*A.RI.IN.NA* d10 URU*ḪA.AT.TI* dIŠKUR URU*ZI.I*[*P.PA.LA.AN.DA* dIŠKUR UR]U*PÍT.TE.IA.RI.GA*[ ] (19′)[dIŠKU]R URU*NE.RI.IK* dIŠKUR URU*ḪA.LA.AB* dIŠKUR ˻URU*LI.IḪ.ZI*˼*.N*[*A* … dIŠKU]R URU*ŠA.RI.IŠ.ŠA* (20′)[dIŠKUR K]I.LAM d*ŠE.RI* ˻d˼[*ḪU.UR.RI*] x x x x[…]x[… dIŠKUR KAR]AŠ (21′)[dLAMMA KU]Š*kur-ša-aš* d[…] (22′)[…]x N[A? …]x (23′)[…]x x x d*ZA-BA4-BA4*

(ca. remaining quarter of rev. missing)

§5′ (23′–24′)If someone seeks [to] forsake me also with evil intent, but I write to you, and if you do not come to my aid in an instant, or you yourselves (25′)hear of it, and if you do not report it to My Majesty im[me]diately, (26′) and if that (enemy) is no enemy to you, so that you do not fi[gh]t against him,[482] (27′)[th]en [let it] be placed under oath for you. […] is the king.

§6′ (28′–29′)[O]r he who […] me [… ma]n ev[il …]

(remaining ca. quarter of obv. and first ca. quarter of rev. missing)

§7″ (traces)

§8″ (2′–3′)If he [pres]ents to [yo]u this kind of […], though, or if yo[u …] (4′) he [do]es […], or […] a matter of *revolt*, […] (5′–6′)you [he]ar (of it), and if in that w[ay …] you [do not de]nounce [him], and he […] (to) you, (7′) (and) if y[ou] do not seize him immediately, (8′)and you (even) support the [ma]n, then may (these) oat[h deities …] (9′–10′)utterly destroy you [alon]g with your wives (and) your sons, [and let them] eradi[cate] your names and your seed from the [dark ea]rth.

§9″ (11′)And he who is foremost amo[ng you], if […] (to) you, (12′)[and] he speaks positively about My Majesty to you, (13′)[then] you must listen to [h]im. If […] (to) you in this way […], though, (14′)and he presents the matter of his [reb]ellion, (15′–16′)[and] in that way you support the man, th[en] may [the oath deities] not [re]lease [you]!

§10″ (17′)[And he]reby [have we called] the asse[mbly] of the thousand gods for this oath […]: (18′)the [Sun G]od of heaven, the Sun Goddess of Arinna, the Storm God of Ḫattusa, the Storm God of Zip[palanda, the Storm God of] Pitteyariga, (19′)the [Storm G]od of Nerik, the Storm God of Ḫalab, the Storm God of Liḫzin[a … the Storm G]od of Sarissa, (20′)the [Storm God of the Gat]ehouse, Šeri, [Ḫurri …, the Storm God of the army c]amp, (21′–22′)[the protective deity] of the hunting bag, the deity […] (23′)[…] Zababa […]

(ca. remaining quarter of rev. missing)

No. 19
Āsḫapāla's Oath regarding an Obligation to Supply Troops
(*CTH* 270)

This text is preserved on a tablet in letter-like format, and indeed one should not exclude the possibility that it might have been sent to the administration in Ḫattusa as a missive of some sort from the northern frontier. Giorgieri (2005: 327, n. 31) has similarly suggested that its omission of any deities who would have witnessed the oath might be a function of its not being "ein Dokument offizieller, feierlicher Natur ..., sondern ... eine Art Nachtrag oder Fortsetzung zu einer größeren Vereidigung." It is a MH tablet, and might perhaps be linked with the well-known struggles of, for example, Arnuwanda I against the Kaska tribes. The nearly fully preserved tablet was found in Building A of the royal palace.

This composition represents one of three actual oaths in the volume, the others being Nos. 14 and 23. It is spoken in the 1st person by a certain Āsḫapāla

---

Transliteration

§1 (obv. 1)[*U*]*M-MA* ^{m}*A.AŠ.ḪA.PA.A.LA na*[*m-ma-ia* ÉRIN^{MEŠ}] (2)[*ku-i*]*-e-eš kat-ti-iš-ši l*[*i-in-ki-ia-aš-ma-ša-at*] (3)[*kat-t*]*a-an ki-iš-ša-an k*[*i-it-ta-ru*]

§2 (4)[^{URU}*Ḫa-a*]*t-tu-ši me-na-aḫ-*⸢*ḫa-an*⸣*-d*[*a*] (5)[^{LÚ}KÚR?] ⸤*Ú*⸥*-UL an-da ḫar-wa-ni* ⸢*Ù*⸣ [*ke-e* ÉRIN^{MEŠ}] (6)[*A-NA*] ^{d}UTU*-ŠI pé-ú-e-ni* 10 ÉRIN^{MEŠ} ⸢^{URU}*Ta*⸣*-pa-p*[*a-nu-wa-az*] (7)⸢10 ÉRIN⸣^{MEŠ} ^{URU}*Ta-pa-pa-aḫ-šu-wa-az* 10 ÉRIN$^{\text{⸢MEŠ⸣}}$ ^{URU}⸤*Ti-ia*⸥*-*[*aš-ši-il-ta-az*] (8)⸢ŠU.NIGIN⸣ 30 ÉRIN^{MEŠ} *I-NA* ⸤^{URU}*ḪA*⸥*.AT.TI ku-*⸤*iš*⸥ *ú-ez-*[*zi*]

§3 (9)*an-da-ma-az-kán ma-a-*⸤*an*⸥ ^{LÚ}KÚR*-aš* (10)*ku-wa-a-pí u-*⸢*wa*⸣*-al-ḫu-u-w*[*a-a*]*n-zi da-a-*⸢*i*⸣ (11)*ú-e-ša iš-ta-ma-aš-šu-*⸢*wa*⸣*-ni* (12)*nu A-NA* ^{LÚ}*BE-EL* <*MAD*>*-GAL*$_{9}$*-LA-TI me-mi-ia-an* (13)*ḫu-u-da-a-ak ú-du-um-me-ni*

§4 (14)*a-ap-pa-la-a-u-e-ni-ma-an Ú-UL nu-za-kán* (15) ^{LÚ}KÚR*-aš u-wa-al-ḫu-wa-an-zi da-me-e-te* (16)*pé-e-ti da-a-i ú-e-eš-ša-aš-ši* (17)*da-ma-i pé-e-da-an lam-ma-ni-i-e-u-e-ni* (18)*nu* ⸢*da*⸣*-ma-i pé-e-da-an pa-aḫ-*⸢*ḫa*⸣*-ša-nu-an-zi* (19) ^{LÚ}KÚR*-aš-ša da-ma-i pé-e-da-an* (20)*u-wa-al-aḫ-zi li-in-ki-ia-an-na-ša-at* (21)⸤*kat-ta*⸥*-an ki-it-ta-ru*

and his troops (§1), though introduced by an anonymous third person. It may be the case that Āsḫapāla here is to be identified with his namesake in No. 14.1 §10, where he is listed among many others as the commander (DUGUD) of the town S[ās]ana; and if so, the present document might constitute either an additional oath sworn by Āsḫapāla and his men or, perhaps more likely, a witness of the oath taken by them, which was then summarized and standardized for all the individuals named in No. 14, implying that any number of such individual oath documents could have been created at the time. Āsḫapāla and his men declare in this text that they will remain loyal to Ḫattusa and provide troops, ten each from three named towns (§2). They further assent to inform the provincial governor of any enemy mischief (§3), and moreover, they declare that their declaration will not be laced with disinformation (§4). All this is then to be placed under oath.

Oaths evincing similar features include the Loyalty Oath of a Scribe (*CTH* 124; Giorgieri 1995: 278–80; Glocker 2009) and the Oath of the SA.GAZ-troops or *ḫabiru* (*CTH* 27; Giorgieri 1995: 69–89).

TRANSLATION

§1 (1–3)[T]hus (speak) Āsḫapāla, [and] fu[rther, th]ose [troops] that are with him; thus [shall it be] pl[aced] for them [und]er o[ath]:[483]

§2 (4–6) "We will not hold to [*the enemy*] as opposed to [Ḫa]ttusa, and we will provide [these troops for] His Majesty: 10 troops [from] the town of Tapap[anuwa], (7)10 troops from the town of Tapapaḫsu, 10 troops [from] the town of Tiya[ssilta]; (8)altogether 30 troops, which [will] come to Ḫattusa.

§3 (9)Moreover, if an enemy (10)sets about to attack somewhere, (11)and we hear (of it), (12–13)then we will bring a message to the <pro>vincial governor immediately.

§4 (14–17)We will not trick him, though. Should the enemy set about to attack at another place, we will name for him that other place as well, (18)so that they can defend the other place. (19–21)Should the enemy attack at (yet) another place,[484] then that shall be placed under oath for us."

No. 20
Instructions for Priests and Temple Personnel (*CTH* 264)

The Instructions for Priests and Temple Personnel, being among the best preserved of the instruction texts as well as the first to enjoy a full edition (Sturtevant 1934), has long been regarded as one of the centrally important Hittite documents and has yielded a wealth of linguistic and cultural information.

The composition is preserved by one nearly complete tablet (A), two significant fragment blocks (B–C) and more than a dozen small to mid-sized fragments (cf. Sources, n. 20). All tablets and fragments for which a findspot is known were found in the Temple I complex (B_2, B_3, C_2 [KBo 50.283], E_2, I, J, K, L, N). Ms. A serves as the primary text except in the latter portion of §6′ and the beginning of §7′, where one must resort to C_1. As the text is complete with a single tablet, quite nearly the entire composition is extant, failing only its opening lines.

Though all extant manuscripts show a NH ductus, numerous graphic and morphological features suggest that they are based on an older text or texts, which likely would have been composed, like most of the other instructions, during the later Middle Hittite period (see, e.g., Starke 1995b: 81, n. 36; Pecchioli Daddi 2005b: 602).

Above all the composition bears witness, as attested in numerous other texts as well, to the Hittites' pronounced focus on fulfilling the every need and desire of their numerous deities and their ever-present fear that failing to do so would result in incurring their wrath.[485] It thus constitutes a rich source of information and a unique perspective on religious thought and practice, as well as the psychology of potentially irreligious mischief, among the Hittites. A major facet of fulfilling the desires of the deities was to approach them only in a pure state, which included what the modern observer would refer to as hygiene, as well as sexual purity and the avoidance of taboos.[486]

At the same time these instructions to the temple personnel hint at a rich repertoire of inventive tricks that presumably must have been attempted from time to time, as it was certainly suspected that they might be. The composition does not stop at forbidding such practices, however, but also makes some attempts at anticipating the psychological justification for such misdeeds and at providing arguments against any such devious thoughts. How successful the text would have been will of course remain a mystery, but what the modern observer would perceive as corruption and vice likely would have played a significant role in Hittite society, as it has in all societies to greater or lesser degrees throughout the ages.

Also implicitly and explicitly expressed in the composition is the Hittite conception of the divine world as comparable to Hittite society, while the relationship of the gods to man was envisioned as parallel to that of a master to his slave. Similarly, the dualistic natures of both god and man are explicitely compared, both being assumed to consist of a corporeal and an immaterial component.

The first three paragraphs of the composition concern the purity of those responsible for providing sustenance for the deities, whereby the latter two-thirds of §2′ and the whole of §3′ consist of fascinating attempts at providing a rationale for the required purity. In §4′ enters one of the central themes of the composition, corruption, and more specifically, the siphoning off of goods intended for the offerings to the gods for one's personal benefit. The text continues in this vein through §7′, whereby the most ingenious and creative methods of bilking the temple institution are anticipated and, on pain of death, warned against. Paragraph 8′ treats the precious metals and cult paraphernalia of the temples, prescribing rather elaborate measures to keep its riches under control. Paragraph 9′ emphasizes the importance of celebrating the cyclical festivals punctually, while §§10′–11′ stress the importance of keeping the watch during the night. Paragraph 12′ deals with avoiding fights and drunken brawls in the temple, §13′ with fire prevention. Paragraph 14′ returns to the issue of purity with regard to the preparation of the gods' food as well as bathing following sexual activity and before returning to service in the temple. Paragraph 15′ stresses bringing the deities their rations in a timely fashion, while §§16′–17′ return to the issue of corruption, the former in connection with honestly allotting personal and temple land yields, the latter regarding the use and misuse of the temple's plough oxen. Paragraph 18′ emphasizes bringing punctually the offerings of a given festival, and finally, §19′ forbids various ways of diverting livestock from the temple holdings for personal benefit. Paragraphs 5′–9′, 15′–19′ are echoed in the Prayer of Kantuzzili (Singer 2002: 32): "What is holy to my god and is not right for me to eat, I have never eaten and I did not thereby defile my body. § Never did I separate an ox from the pen, and never did I separate (lit. ditto) a sheep from the fold."

Also of interest is the lack of any hint that the priests and personnel were to take an oath to any secular power. Rather, at three points (§§6′, 18′, 19′) they are required to pronounce a self-deprecating oath and/or undergo a drinking ordeal directly to or in the presence of the deities,[487] which makes perfect sense in light of the fact that these persons were, in the Hittite perspective, employees or servants of the gods, not the king. Moreover, while secular punishment is stipulated for some misdemeanors as well as for some more serious capital crimes (e.g., §§11′, 15′), the personnel is repeatedly warned not to assume that punishment for crimes against the gods will not be punished just because retribution does not come immediately or because it may seem that one might not be found out (§§2′–3′, 7′, 9′, 16′). Death is the punishment for many a trespass against the gods, though it is not always entirely clear whether an actual terrestrial execution or the certainty that the gods will catch up to the person is envisioned.

Following is an outline of the content of the composition:

1. Fragmentary instructions pertaining to offerings for the deities (§1′, i 1′–13′)
2. Instructions for those who prepare the daily bread for the deities (§2′, 14′–§3′, 38′)
    a. Re. purity of those who prepare the daily bread (§2′, 14′–18′)
    b. Re. purity of the bakeries (§2′, 18′–20′)
    c. Rationale behind the need for purity (§2′, 21′–§3′, 38′)
        i. Identification of mind of man and mind of gods (§2′, 21′–22′)
        ii. Illustration of principle through master–servant metaphor (§2′, 22′–33′)
        iii. Application of metaphor to human–deity relationship (§3′, 34′–38′)
3. Instructions for the temple personnel on properly supplying the festivals (§4′, 39′–§7′)
    a. Enumeration of festivals of Ḫattusa (§4′, 39′–45′)
    b. Failure to properly supply them keeps the deities wanting (§4′, 46′–49′)
    c. Potential ways to cause the supplies to fall short (§5′, 50′–57′)
    d. Such behavior defined as capital offence (§5′, 58′–59′)
    e. Injunction against failing to supply bread, beer, wine (§6′, 60′–ii 16)
        i. Command and injunction (§6′, 60′–63′)
        ii. Oath to be spoken regarding the commodities (§6′, 64′–ii 5)
        iii. Regulations on when bread, beer, wine can be consumed by whom (§6′, 6–16)
    f. Injunction against failing to provide meat (§7′, 17–24″)
        i. Potential fraudulent actions enumerated (§7′, 17–17″)
        ii. Example of potential reasoning behind such fraud (§7′, 18″–19″)

        iii. Dissuasion and warning against such reasoning (§7′, 20″–24″)
4. Instructions to the custodians of the temple treasure (§8′)
    a. Exclusivity of the temple treasures (§8′, 25″–29″)
    b. Injunction against temple personnel owning valuables (§8′, 29″–32″)
    c. Procedure when temple employee receives valuable royal gift (§8′, 32″–50″)
        i. Proper labeling of gift (§8′, 32″–38″)
        ii. Proper procedure for public sale of the gift (§8′, 38″–44″)
        iii. Punishment for those involved in selling privately (§8′, 45″–50″)
    d. Restatement of exclusivity of the temple treasures (§8′, 50″–51″)
5. Further instructions for the temple personnel (§9′–§11′)
    a. Timely celebration of festivals (§9′)
    b. The temple watch (§§10′–11′)
6. Instructions for priests, anointed ones, mother-goddess priestesses and temple personnel (§12′–§13′)
    a. Regarding disorderly conduct in the temple (§12′)
    b. Regarding fire prevention (§13′)
7. Instructions for the kitchen personnel on purity (§14′)
    a. Keeping food, utensils, and kitchen pure (§14′, 55–68)
    b. Bathing after sex (§14′, 68–83)
8. Instructions to the temple ploughmen (§15′–§16′)
    a. Regarding bringing offerings punctually (§15′)
    b. Regarding temple lands and granaries (§16′)
9. Instructions to the keepers of the plough oxen (§17′)
10. Instructions to cowherds and shepherds on bringing livestock punctually and in full (§§18′–19′)

TRANSLITERATION

§1′ (A i 1′–13′; B1 i 1′–11″) (1′–2′)(traces) (3′)[…]-*an-te-eš* [… (DINGIR-*LÌ*) …] (4′)[…-*i*]*š-ke-ed-du-ma-at nu ma-a-*[*an* … N(INDA.GUR4.RA UD-*MI*) …] (5′) […] *ma-a-an ŠA* 1 *ŠA-A-TI ma-a-n*[*a* …] (6′)[*Š*]*A*? 2 *UP-NI* 1 *UP-NI* ½ *UP-NI* x[…] (7′)⌜*šu*?⌝-*un-nu-um-me-eš-šar ti-i*[(*a-an*) …] (8′)*pé-eš-kán-zi na-aš-ma-at*[…] (9′)*na-at ša-ra-a ti-ia-*[*an-ta-an* … -*n*(*i*?)] (10′)EGIR-*pa-ia-kán* ⌜*le-e*⌝ x[…] (11′)*A-NA* É.GAL *na-aš-ma a-p*[*é*]-*da-*[*ni* … -*n*]*a-an-zi* (12′)*le-e pa-it-*[*t*]*e-ni na-aš-ta* É.G[AL? …]x ⌜*ŠA*⌝[…]-*aš* (13′)*da-me-e-da-ni šar-ḫu-u-wa-an-da-az le-e ḫar-ni-*[*ik-t*]*e-ni*

§2′ (A i 14′–33′; B1 i 15″–30″; C2 i 1′–3′; L i 1′; O i 1′–3′) (14′)*nam-ma* NINDA.[GU]R4.RAḪI.A UD-*MI ku-i-e-eš e-eš-ša-an-zi na-at pár-*[*k*]*u-wa-iš a-ša-an-du* (15′)*wa-ar-*[*pa*]-*an-ti-ša-at kar-ta-an-te-eš a-ša-an-du iš-ḫi-*˻*i*˼-*ni-uš-ma-aš-kán*[488] (16′)UM[BIN-*i*]*a da-a-an e-eš-du pár-ku-wa-ia* TÚGḪI.A *wa-*˻*aš*˼-*ša-*˻*an*˼ *ḫar-kán-du* (17′)x[ ]x-*aš*? [489] *le-e e-eš-ša-an-zi ku-i-e-eš-za* DINGIRMEŠ-*aš* ZI-*an* NÍ.TE-*an-na* (18′)[…]-*kán-zi*[490] *na-aš a-pu-u-uš e-eš-ša-an-du I-NA* É ⌜LÚ⌝NINDA.DÙ.DÙ-*ma-aš-*˻*kán*˼ (19′)*ku-e-*⌜*da*⌝-*aš an-da-an e-eš-ša-an-zi na-at-kán* ˻*ša*˼-[*a*]*n-ḫa-an ḫar-nu-wa-an* (20′)*e-eš-du nam-ma-kán pár-šu-u-ra-aš pé-di* ŠAḪ-*aš* UR.GI7-*a*[*š*] KÁ-*aš le-e ti-ia-zi* (21′) UN-*aš* DINGIRMEŠ-*aš-ša* ZI-*an-za ta-ma-a-iš ku-iš-ki UL* ⌜*ki*⌝-*i-pát ku-it UL* (22′)ZI-*an-za-ma* 1-*aš-pát* ÌR-*ŠU* ˻*ku*˼-*wa-pí A-NA* EN-*ŠU pé-ra-*˻*an*˼ *ša-ra-a ar-ta-ri* (23′)*na-aš wa-ar-pa-an-za nu pár-ku-wa-ia wa-aš-ša-an ḫar-*⌜*zi*⌝ (24′)⌜*nu*⌝-*uš-ši na-aš-šu a-da-an-na pé-eš-ke-ez-zi na-aš-ma-aš-ši a-ku-wa-an-na* ˻*pé-eš*˼-*ke-ez-zi* (25′)*nu-za a-pa-a-aš* EN-*ŠU az-zi-ik-ke-ez-zi ak-ku-uš-*˻*ke*˼-*ez-zi ku-*˻*it*˼ (26′)*na-aš* ZI-*an*[491] *ar-ḫa la-a-an-za na-at*[492]-*ši-kán an-da* ˻*da*˼-*me-en-kiš-*˻*ke-et-ta*˼ (27′)*ma-a-na-aš an-da-ma ku-wa-pí* IGI-*wa-an-na-an-za*[493] *na-aš-*˻*kán*˼ *UL*˼ ≮*ḫa-an-ḫa-*⌜*ni-ia-i*⌝[494] (28′)ZI DINGIR-*LÌ-ma ta-ma-a-iš ku-iš-ki nu-kán ma-a-an* ⌜ÌR-*ŠU*?⌝ *ku-wa-pí* EN-⌜*ŠU*⌝ (29′)TUKU.TUKU-*nu-zi na-an-kán na-aš-šu ku-na-an-zi na-aš-ma-*⌜*kán*⌝ KIR14-*ŠÚ* IGIḪI.A-⌜*ŠU*⌝ (30′)GEŠTUḪI.A-*ŠU i-da-a-la-u-aḫ-ḫa-an-zi na-aš-ma-an-za-an-*⌜*kán*⌝ DAM-*ŠU* DUMUMEŠ-*Š*[*U*] (31′)ŠEŠ-*ŠU* NIN-*ŠU* LÚ*ka-i-na-aš*[495] MÁŠ-*ŠU na-aš-šu* ÌR-*Š*[*U*] ⌜*na*⌝-*aš-ma* GÉME-*ŠU* x x x[496] (32′)*na-aš-ta pár-ra-an-da ḫal-zi-an-zi-pát na-an UL* [*k*]*u-it-ki* DÙ-*an-zi* (33′)*ma-a-na-aš a-ki-ia ku-wa-pí na-aš UL* 1-*aš a-ki* MÁŠ-*ŠU-ma-aš-ši te-et-ti-*⌜*an-pát*⌝

§3′ (A i 34′–38′; B1/2 i 31″–34″; C2 i 4′–7′; L i 2′–7′) (34′)⌜*ma*⌝-*a-an-ma-aš-ta* ZI-*TU*4 DINGIR-*L*[(*ì-ma ku*)-*i*]*š* ⌜TUKU⌝.TUKU-⌜*ia-nu*⌝-*zi* (35′)*na-at-kán* DINGIR-*LÌ a-pé-e-da-ni-p*[(*át*)[497] 1]-˻*e*˼-*da-ni an-da š*[(*a-an-aḫ-z*)]*i* (36′) *UL-at-kán A-NA* DAM-*ŠÚ* D[UMUMEŠ-*ŠU* N]UMUN-*ŠU* MÁŠ-*ŠU* ⌜ÌR⌝MEŠ-*Š*[(*U*

TRANSLATION

§1′[498] (1′–2′)(traces) (3′)[…]s [… (to/for the deity) …] (4′)[…] you[499] should always […], and if [… d(aily bread loaf) …] (5′)[…] either of one *šâtu*-measure o[r …] (6′)[o]f two *upnu*-measures, one *upnu*-measure, half an *upnu*-measure […] (7′)the *filling* is se[(t) …] (8′)they deliver, or […] it/them, (9′)and […] the provis[ions …] it/them; (10′)and afterwards […] shall not […] (11′)they […] to/for the palace or to/for tha[t …], (12′)do not go! And […] the *pala*[*ce* …], (13′)do not des[tr]oy from/with a *sarḫuwant*- for another!

§2′ (14′)Further, those who prepare the daily bread [lo]aves should be pu[r]e. (15′)They should be wa[s]hed and *groomed*.[500] Their *hair* (16′)and na[ils] should be trimmed. They should wear pure clothes. (17′–18′)[…] should not prepare (it). Those who […] the spirit and the body of the deities should prepare them (i.e., the bread loaves). The bakeries (19′–20′)in which they prepare them, though, must be swept and sprayed. Further, no pig (or) dog should be allowed to set foot at the kitchen door. (21′)Is the mind of man and (that) of the gods somehow different? No! (And) in regard to this very (matter)? No! (22′)The mind is indeed one and the same. When a servant stands up [501] before his master, (23′)he is washed and he wears pure (clothes), (24′)and he gives him (something) to eat or he gives him (something) to drink. (25′)And since he, his master, eats (and) drinks, (26′)he is of a tranquil mind, and he is therefore attached to him. (27′)If, however, he is ever *neglected*, is he not *perturbed*? [502] (28′–31′)And is the spirit of a deity somehow different? [503] And if a servant ever angers his master, either they kill him or they mutilate his nose, his eyes (or) his ears, or [they …] him, his wife, h[is] sons, his brother, his sister, (or) the family *of his in-laws*, whether it's a male servant or a maidservant. [504] (32′)Do they merely "call him over," [505] or do they do nothing [a]t all to him? (33′)When he dies, he does not die alone; no, his family indeed accompanies him.

§3′ (34′)When, however, [(som)eo]ne angers the spirit of a deity, (35′)does the deity a[(venge)] it on j[(ust)] that person [al]one? (36′–38′)Does he not [av]enge it on his wife, [his] s[ons], his descendents, his family, h[(is)] male servants, his [(female serv)]ants, his cattle, his sheep, and (his) grain?

GÉM)]E^{MEŠ}-*ŠU* ⌜GU$_4$^{ḪI}⌝$^{\text{.A}}$-*ŠÚ* (37′)UDU^{MEŠ}-*ŠU ḫal-ki-it-ta* ⌜*an*⌝-[*da*[506] *š*]*a*-⸤*an*⸥-*aḫ-zi na-an-kán ḫ*[(*u-u-m*)]*a-an-da-az* (38′)⸤*ḫar-ni-ik-zi*⸥ *nu-za* *A*-⸤*NA*⸥ INIM ⌜DINGIR⌝-*L*[*Ì me-e*]*k-ki mar-ri na-aḫ-ḫ*[*a-a*(*n-t*)]*e-eš e-eš-tén*

§4′ (A i 39′–49′; B$_{1/2}$ i 35″–44″; C$_2$ i 8′–15′; L i 7′; N, 1′–6′) (39′)[(*an*)-*da-m*]*a* EZEN$_4$ ITU.KAM EZEN$_4$ MU-*ti* EZEN$_4$ *A-IA-LI* EZEN$_4$ *zé-n*[*a-an-d*]*a-aš* (40′) EZEN$_4$ *ḫa-me-eš-ḫa-an-da-aš* EZEN$_4$ *te-et-ḫe-eš-na-aš* ⸤EZEN$_4$⸥ *ḫi-ia-r*[(*a*)]-*aš* (41′)EZEN$_4$ *pu-u-da-ḫa-aš* EZEN$_4$ *i-šu-wa-aš* EZEN$_4$ [*š*(*a*)]-⸤*at*⸥-*la-aš-ša-aš* (42′)EZEN$_4$ *BI-IB-RI* EZEN$_4$^{MEŠ} *šu-up-pa-ia-aš* ^{L}[$^{\text{Ú.MEŠ?}}$]SANGA-*aš* (43′)EZEN$_4$^{MEŠ} $^{\text{LÚ.MEŠ}}$ŠU.GI EZEN$_4$^{MEŠ} $^{\text{MUNUS.MEŠ}}$AMA.DINGIR-*L*[(*Ì*)] EZEN$_4$ *da-ḫi-ia-aš* (44′) EZEN$_4$^{MEŠ} $^{\text{LÚ.MEŠ}}$*ú-pa-ti-ia-aš* EZEN$_4$^{MEŠ} *pu-u-*⌜*la*⌝-*aš* EZEN$_4$^{MEŠ} *ḫa-aḫ-ra-an-na-aš* (45′)*na-aš-ma-aš ku-iš im-ma ku-iš* EZEN$_4$-*aš* ^{URU}*Ḫa*-[(*a*)]*t-tu-ši-kán še-er* (46′)*na-aš ma-a-an IŠ-TU* GU$_4$$^{\text{ḪI.A}}$ UDU$^{\text{ḪI.A}}$ NINDA KAŠ *Ù IŠ-TU* GEŠTIN (47′)*ḫu-u-ma-an-da-az ša-ra-a ti-ia-an-ta UL e-eš-ša-at-te-ni* (48′)*na-*⌜*at*⌝ *pé-eš-kán-zi ku-i-e-eš nu-uš-ma-aš šu-me-eš* LÚ^{MEŠ} É DINGIR-*LÌ* (49′)*ḫa-ap-pár da-aš-ket$_9$-te-ni* DINGIR^{MEŠ}-**aš**-*ma-at-kán* ZI-*ni wa-ak-ši-ia-nu-ut-te-ni*

§5′ (A i 50′–59′; B$_{2/3}$ i 45″–53″; C$_2$ i 5″–13″; H i 1′–7′; J, 1′–6′) (50′)*na-aš-ma-at-kán ma-a-an ša-ra-a ti-ia-an-da ku-wa-pí da-at-te-ni* (51′)*na-at* DINGIR^{MEŠ}-*aš* ZI-*ni pa-ra-a UL ar-nu-ut-te-ni nu-uš-ma-ša-at ar-ḫa* (52′) *I-NA* É^{MEŠ}-*KU-NU pé-e ḫar-te-ni na-at šu-me-el* DAM^{MEŠ}-*KU-NU* DUMU^{MEŠ}-*KU-NU* (53′)SAG.GÉME.ÌR^{MEŠ}-*KU-NU ar-ḫa e-ez-za-a-i na-aš-šu-ma-aš-ma-aš* ^{LÚ}*ka-e-na-aš* (54′)*na-aš-ma a-aš-šu-wa-an-za ku-iš-ki* ^{LÚ}*Ú-BA*-⸤*RÙ*⸥ *ú-ez-zi na-at a-pé-e-*<*da*>*-ni* (55′)*pé-eš-te-ni A-NA* ZI-*TU$_4$* DINGIR-*LÌ-ma-at-kán da-at-te-ni* (56′)*na-at-ši pa-ra-a-pát UL ar-nu-ut-te-ni na-at ták-ša-an šar-ra-aš* (57′)*ták-ša-an šar-ra-an pé-eš-te-ni nu-uš-ma-aš ki-i šar-ru-ma-aš ut-tar* (58′)SAG.DU-*az* GAM-*an ki-it-ta-ru na-at-kán le-e šar-ra-at-te-ni* (59′) *ku-i-ša-at-kán šar-ra-a*-⸤*i-ma*⸥ *na-aš a-ku* EGIR-*pa wa-aḫ-nu-mar-ši le-e e-eš-zi*

§6′ (A i 60′–66′, ii 2′–3′; C$_1$ ii 1–16; H i 8′–19′) (60′)*IŠ-TU* NINDA KAŠ GEŠTIN *I-NA* É DINGIR-*LÌ ḫu-u-ma-an ša-ra-a pé-e ḫar-tén* (61′)NINDA.GUR$_4$.RA DINGIR-*LÌ-za-kán* NINDA.SIG *le-e ku-iš-ki da-a-li-ia-zi* (62′)KAŠ-*ma-kán* GEŠTIN *IŠ-TU* GAL-*ia še-er ar-ḫa le-e ku-iš-ki la-a-ḫu-u-i* (63′)*ḫu-u-ma-an-pát* DINGIR-*LÌ-ni* {EGIR-*pa*} *ma-ni-ia-aḫ-tén nam-ma-aš-ma-aš PA-NI* DINGIR-*LÌ me-mi-an* (64′)⸤*me*⸥*-mi-iš-tén ku-i-iš-wa-*⌜*kán tu*⌝*-e-el* DINGIR-*LÌ-az* NINDA *ḫar-ši-ia-az* (65′)[^{DUG}]⸤*iš*⸥-[(*pa*)]-⸤*an*⸥-*du-uz-zi*-⸤*az*⸥ *da-a-aš* ⸤*nu*⸥*-wa-ra-an-*^{kán} DINGIR-*LÌ* EN-*IA* EGIR-*an* (66′)[*ki-ia-*(*aḫ-ḫu-ut*)][507] *nu-wa-za-kán a-pé-e-el* ⌜É⌝-*er* GAM-*an ša-ra-a e-ep-du* (C$_1$ ii 6)[NINDA KAŠ GEŠTIN-*ia-m*]*a*[508] *ma-a-an a-pé-e-da-ni* UD-*ti a-da-an-na a-ku-wa-*[(*an-na*)] (7)[*tar-aḫ-te-ni*

He destroys them a[(l)]l along with him.[509] So be [ext]remely rev[er(e)]nt with regard to matter(s) of the deity!

§4′ (39′)[(Fur)therm]ore, the monthly festival, the yearly festival, the festival of the stag, the au[tum]n festival, (40′)the spring festival, the festival of thunder, the *ḫiyara*-festival, (41′)the *pūdaḫa*-festival, the *isuwa*-festival, the [*s*]*atlassa*-festival, (42′)the rhyton festival, the festivals of the holy priests, (43′)the festivals of the old men, the festivals of the mother-deity priestesses, the *daḫiya*-festival, (44′)the festivals of the *upati*-men, the *pūla*-festival, the *ḫaḫratar*-festivals, (45′)or whatever festival (is celebrated) up in Ḫattusa: (46′–47′)when you do not perform them with all the cattle, sheep, bread, beer, and wine, (i.e.,) the provisions, (48′)and those who deliver them, you temple personnel, (49′)take payment for yourselves (instead),[510] then you cause them to be insufficient for the desire of the deities.

§5′ (50′)Or if you at some point take them, the provisions,[511] (51′–52′)and do not deliver them to the deities themselves, and you keep them apart in your own houses, and your wives, your sons, (53′)(and) your servants consume them, or rather a relative (54′–55′)or some favorite foreign guest comes to you, and you give them to hi<m>, so that you take them from the deity himself, (56′–58′)and you do not deliver them to him at all, and you give (only) the half part of them,[512] then this matter of your dividing (them) up shall be considered as a capital (offense). So do not divide them up! (59′) Whoever does divide them up shall die! There will be no turning back for him.

§6′ (60′)Deliver all of the bread, beer, (and) wine up into the temple. (61′)No one shall *allow himself* a bread loaf (or) a flatbread of the deity. (62′)And no one shall pour beer (or) wine off the top of the pitcher. (63′–66′)Present absolutely everything {again}[513] to the deity! Further, you shall utter (these) word(s) regarding yourselves before the deity: "Whoever has taken from your divine bread loaf (and) from your wine pitcher, you, my god, my lord, shall [*tor*(*ment*)] him! May he seize his household below (and) above!" (C_1 ii 6–7)If, [howe]ver, [you are able (to)] eat and drink [*the bread, the beer, and the wine*] on that day, [then] eat (and) drink [i]t. But if y[(ou)] are not able, (8)[then] eat (and) drink [it …] the third day. (9–11)

na-a]t e-ez-za-tén e-ku-ut-tén ma-a-na-at Ú-UL-ma tar-aḫ-t[(e-ni)] (8)[na-at ...][514] UD.3.KAM az-zi-ik-ke-et-tén ak-ku-uš-ke-et-tén [ ] (9) [(NINDApí-ia-an-ta-al-la-an-ma) A-NA DAM]MEŠ-KU!(ŠU)-NU[515] DUMUMEŠ-KU!(ŠU)-NU SAG.GÉME.ÌRMEŠ-KU!(ŠU)-[NU le-e] (10)[pé-eš-te-n(i[516] KAŠ GEŠTIN[517]-ma-ká)]n DINGIRMEŠ-a[(š GI)]Škat-ta-lu-uz-zi le-e-pát [ ] (11)[pé-e-da-at-te-ni][518] ma-a-an LÚÚ-BA-RÙ-ma ku-e-da-ni ú-ez-zi [ ] (12)[(na-aš ma-a-an) I-NA] É DINGIR-LÌ ša-ra-a pa-a-u-wa-aš ˻DINGIRMEŠ-na˼-aš-kán LUGAL-aš-ša[519] [ ] (13)[GIŠ(kat-ta-lu-u)z-zi š]ar-ra-aš-ke-et-ta na-an [a-da-an-n]a[520] ša-ra-a (14)[pé-e-ḫu-te-(ed-du)][521] nu GU$_7$-ke-ed-du ak-ku-uš-[ke-ed-d]u ma-a-an-ma-aš [ ] (15)[UN-aš[522] a-ra-aḫ-zé]-na-aš Ú-UL-aš URUḪa-at-tu-ša-aš DUMU.˹LÚ.U$_{19}$˺.L[U DING]IRMEŠ-aš ti-[ia-(zi)] (16)[na-aš a-ku ku-i-ša-a]n[523] pé-e-ḫu-te-ez-zi-ma na-at-ši SAG.DU-aš ag-ga-t[ar]

§7′ (C$_1$ ii 17–33; A ii 6″–24″; B$_1$ ii 1′–16′; G, 1′–2′; M, 1′–10′) (C$_1$ ii 17) [ma-a-an GU$_4$ na-aš-ma] UDU ku-iš DINGIR-LÌ-ni a-da-an-na u-un-na-an-za (18) [(šu-ma-aš-ma-z)a?-kán n]a-aš-šu GUD.NIGA na-aš-ma UDU.NIGA ar-ḫa e-ep-te-ni (19)[(šu-ma-aš-ma-az ku-i)n] ma-ak-la-an-da-an mar-kán ḫar-te-ni na-an-kán an-d[(a)] (20)[(tar-na-a)t-te-ni nu a-p]u-u-un GU$_4$ na-aš-šu ar-ḫa e-ez-za-at-te-ni (21)[(na-aš-ma-an-za-an-kán ḫ)]a-a-li an-da tar-na-at-te-ni na-aš-ma-an-za-an-kán i-ú-˻ki?˼ (22)[kat-ta-(an[524] da-a-it-t)]e-ni na-aš-ma-za-kán UDU a-ša-u-ni an-da tar-na-at-te-ni (23)[(na-aš-ma-an-za-an-kán ku)]-en-na-at-te-ni nu-za ZIḪI.A-KU-NU SIG$_5$-in (24) [i-ia-a(t-te-ni na-aš)]-ma-an-kán ta-me-e-da-ni UN-ši wa-aḫ-nu-ma-an-zi (25)[(pé-eš-t)e-ni (nu-za-kán)] ŠÁM še-er da-at-te-ni na-aš-ta DINGIR-LÌ-ni (26)[(a-pé)-e-(el[525] ZI-aš) Ḫ]A.˻LA˼[526] KA×U-it pa-ra-a ḫu-u-it-ti-at-te-ni (A ii 17″)na-an-za [...[527] (n)]a-aš-ma-an ta-me-e-da-ni pé-eš-te-ni (18″)nu ki-iš-[(ša-an) an-da pé-e-(da-at-te-ni)][528] DINGIR-LÌ-wa-ra-aš ku-it nu-wa UL (19″)ku-it-ki [(me-ma-i nu-wa-an-n)a-a(š)] UL ku-it-ki ˻i-ia˼-zi (20″)nu-za UN-an-[(na a-ú ZI-aš-ták-ká)]n ku-iš ⸗zu-u-[(wa-an I)]GIḪI.A-wa-az (21″) pa-ra-a pít-t[(i-nu-zi) EG(IR-a)]n-da[529] ma-aḫ-ḫa-an ˻e˼-[(eš-š)]a-a-i (22″) DINGIRMEŠ-aš-ma Z[(I-an-za da-aš-šu)]-uš nu e-ep-pu-u-wa-˻an˼-zi UL nu-un-tar-nu-˻zi˼ (23″)e-ep-zi-[(ma ku-e-d)]a-ni me-e-ḫu-ni nu nam-ma ar-ḫa (24″)UL tar-na-a-˻i˼ [(nu-za)] DINGIRMEŠ-aš ZI-ni me-ek-ki na-aḫ-ḫa-an-te-eš e-eš-tén

§8′ (A ii 25″–51″; B$_1$ ii 17′–42′; C$_1$ ii 34–45; G, 3′–9′; E$_{1/2}$ ii 1′–9′; O i 1′–5′) (25″)an-da-ma DINGIRMEŠ-a[(š ku)]-it KÙ.BABBAR KÙ.SIG$_{17}$ TÚG-TU$_4$ Ú-NU-UT ZABAR (26″)šu-ma-aš ḫar-te-˹ni˺ nu-za LÚ.MEŠÙMMEDA-KU-NU[530] nu-za DINGIRMEŠ-aš KÙ.BABBAR-i KÙ.SIG$_{17}$-i (27″)TÚG-i Ú-NU-UT ZABAR e-eš-zi NU.GÁL ku-it-kán DINGIRMEŠ-aš pár-ni (28″)an-da NU.GÁL ku-it ku-it DINGIR-LÌ-ni-ma-at e-eš-zi-pát (29″)nu-za me-ek-ki na-aḫ-ḫa-an-te-eš e-eš-tén

[Yo(u) shall not, (however), give (the *piyantalla*-bread) to] your! [wive]s, your! sons, (or) yo[ur!] servants. And in no case are you to [carry (the beer and wine)] across the threshold of the deity. If, however, a foreign guest comes to someone, (12–14)[(and if)] he (the guest) normally crosses the [(thresho)ld] of the deities and of the king in order to go up [into] the temple, then [(he)] (the host) [(shall) lead] him (the guest) up [*to ea*]*t*, and he shall eat and drink.[531] But if (15)a [strang]er, a person not of Ḫattusa, ap[proach(es)] the [dei]ties, (16)[he shall die], and for [whomever] brought [hi]m (there) it is a capit[al] (offense).

§7′ (17)[When] some [cow or] sheep is driven (to the temple) for the deity to eat, (18)[(and)] you pick out either a fattened cow or a fattened sheep for [yours(elves)], (19–20)and [(you tu)rn] over (to the temple) a haggard one [(tha)t] you had slaughtered for yourselves, [and] you either consume [th]at cow (21–22)[(or)] you let [(it)] into a [(co)]rral [(for yourselves)], or you [(pla)]ce it [und(er)] the yoke for yourselves, or you let the sheep into a pen for yourselves, (23–26)[(or)] you [(ki)]ll [(it for yourselves)], and [(you) ser(ve)] your own interests, [(o)]r [you (give)] it to another man in a trade, [(and)] you take payment (for it), and you (thereby) snatch the deity's desired [sh]are out of (his) mouth, (A ii 17″)and you […] it yourselves, or you give it to someone else, (18″–19″)and [(you) arg(ue) th[(us)]: "Because he is a deity, he will not [(say)] anything [(and)] he will not do anything [(to us)];" (20″–21″)[(consider, too,)] that man who lets your desired sh[(are)] disap[(pear before your e)]yes! [Aft(erwa)]rds, as soon as it oc[(cu)]rs, (22″)the w[(ill)] of a deity is indeed [(fi)]rm. He does not hasten to seize (the offender), (23″–24″)[(but w)]hen he does seize (him), he does not let go again. [(So)] be extremely reverent with regard to the will of a deity!

§8′ (25″–28″)Moreover: You are the custodians of the silver, gold, clothing, (and) bronze utensils of the deities [(th)]at you keep. It belongs to the silver, gold, clothing, (and) bronze utensils of the deity. (*As far as you are concerned*) it does not (*even*) exist![532] What is in the temple (simply) does not exist! Whatever (is there) belongs exclusively to the deity, (29″–33″)so be extremely reverent! No silver (or) gold whatsoever shall belong to a

nu A-NA ⌞LÚ⌟ É DINGIR-LÌ KÙ.BABBAR KÙ.SIG$_{17}$ (30″)*le-e-pát e-eš-zi* A-NA NÍ.TE-ŠU-*za-at-kán an-da le-e-pát* (31″)*pé-e-da-a-i* A-NA DAM-ŠU-*ia-an-za-an* DUMU-ŠU ⌞*ú*⌟-*nu-wa-aš-ḫa-an* (32″)*le-e i-ia-zi ma-a-an-ma-aš-ši* IŠ-TU É.GAL-LÌ AŠ-ŠUM NÍG.BA-ŠU (33″)KÙ.BABBAR KÙ.SIG$_{17}$ TÚG-TU$_{4}$ Ú-NU-UT ZA-BAR *pí-an-zi na-at lam-ni-ia-an e-eš-du* (34″)*ka-a-aš-wa-ra-at-ši* LUGAL-*uš pa-iš* KI.LÁ.BI-ŠU-*ia*-⌞*at*⌟ *ma-ši-wa-an* (35″)*na-at i-ia-an-pát e-eš-du nam-ma ki-iš-ša-an-na i-ia-an e-eš-du* (36″)*ke-e-da-ni-wa-ra-at-ši* A-NA EZEN$_{4}$ SUM-*er ku-ut-ru-u-uš-ša* EGIR-*an* (37″)*i-ia-an-te-eš a-ša-an-du* SUM-*er-wa-at-ši*[533] *ku-wa-pí nu-wa ka-a-aš* (38″)*ka-a-aš-ša a-ra-an-ta-at nam-ma-at-za-kán* ŠÀ É-TI *le-e-pát* (39″)*da-a-li-ia-zi pa-ra-a-pát-za uš-ša-ni-ia-ad-du* (40″)*uš-ša-ni-ia-zi-ma-at-za ku-wa-pí na-at ḫar-wa-ši*[534] *le-e uš-ni-ia-zi* (41″)EN^{MEŠ} ^{URU}ḪA.AT.TI *a-ra-an-ta-ru nu uš-kán-du nu-za ku-it* (42″)*wa-ši-ia-zi na-at* GIŠ.ḪUR *i-ia-an-du na-at-kán pé-ra-an ši-ia-an-du* (43″)*ma-aḫ-ḫa-an-ma-kán* LUGAL-*uš* ^{URU}*Ḫa-at-tu-ši ša-ra-a ú-ez-zi* (44″) *na-at* I-NA É.GAL-LÌ *pa-ra-a e-ep-du na-at-ši ši-ia-an-du* (45″)*ma-a-na-at-za* ZI-*az-za-ma ḫa-ap-pí-ra-iz-zi na-at-ši* SAG.DU-*aš* ÚŠ-*tar* (46″)*ku-iš-ma-za* NÍG.BA LUGAL UL[535] *ḫa-ap-pí-ra-a-iz-zi* ŠUM LUGAL-*kán ku-e-da-ni* (47″)*gul-ša-an nu-za* QA-TAM-MA-*pát* KÙ.BABBAR KÙ.SIG$_{17}$ TÚG-TU$_{4}$ Ú-NU-UT ZABAR (48″)*ḫa-ap-pí-ra-a-iz-zi ku-iš-ma-an e-ep-zi na-an mu-un-na-a-iz-zi* (49″)*na-an* LUGAL-*an a-aš-ka* UL *ú-wa-te-ez-zi nu-uš-*<(*ma*)>-*ša-at* 2-*aš-pát* (50″)SAG.DU-*aš* ÚŠ-*tar* 2-*uš-pát-at ak-kán-du* DINGIR-LÌ-*na-ša-at* NU.*GÁL* [*l*]*e*?-⌞*e*?⌟[536] (51″)*nu-uš-ma-aš* EGIR-*pa wa-aḫ-nu-mar le-e-pát e-eš-zi*

§9′ (A ii 52″–72″; B$_{1}$ ii 43′; E$_{1/2}$ ii 10′–13′; F$_{1}$, 1′–2′; F$_{2}$, 1′–7′) (52″)*an-da-ma-za šu-ma-aš ku-i-e-eš* LÚ^{MEŠ} É DINGIR-LÌ *nu ma-a-an* EZEN$_{4}$M[EŠ] (53″) EZEN$_{4}$-*aš me-e-ḫu-u-ni* UL *e-eš-ša-at-te-ni nu* EZEN$_{4}$ *ḫa-me-eš-ḫ*[(*a*)-*an-da-aš*] (54″)[I]-NA *zé-e-ni i-ia-at-te-ni* EZEN$_{4}$ *zé-e-na-an-da-aš-m*[*a*] (55″) *ḫa-me-eš-ḫi e-eš-ša-at-te-ni nu ma-a-an* EZEN$_{4}$ *i-ia-u-an-zi me*-⌞*e*⌟-[(*ḫu-na*)-*aš*] (56″)*me-e-ḫu-u-ni a-ra-an-za na*-⌞*an*⌟ *i-ia-zi ku-iš na-aš šu-ma-aš* (57″)A-NA $^{\text{LÚ.MEŠ}}$SANGA $^{\text{LÚ.MEŠ}}$GUD[U$_{12}$ ^{M}]$^{\text{UNUS.MEŠ}}$AMA.DINGIR-LÌ Ù[537] A-NA LÚ^{MEŠ} É [DINGIR-LÌ] (58″)*ú-ez-zi nu-uš-ma-aš-za ge-e-nu-uš-šu-uš e-ep-zi* BURU$_{14}$^{MEŠ}-*wa*-⸢*mu*⸣-*kán* (59″)*pé-ra-an na-aš-šu ku-ša-a-ta na-aš-šu* KASKAL-*aš na-aš-ma ta-ma-i* (60″)*ku-it-ki ut-tar nu-wa-mu* EGIR-*pa ti-ia-at-tén nu-wa-mu-kán a-ši* (61″)*ku-it-ma-an me-mi-aš pé-ra-an ar-ḫa ti-ia-ad-du* (62″)*ma-aḫ-ḫa-an-ma-wa-mu-kán a-ši me-mi-aš pé-ra-an ar-ḫa ti-ia-zi* (63″)*nu-wa* EZEN$_{4}$ QA-TAM-MA *i-ia-mi na-aš-ta* UN-*aš* ZI-*ni le-e-pát* (64″) *i-ia-at-te-ni le-e-aš-ma-aš-kán u-wa-it-ta-ri* (65″)*nu-uš-ma-aš* DINGIR^{MEŠ}-*aš* ZI-*ni ḫa-ap-pár le-e da-at-te-ni* (66″)*nu-kán šu-ma-aš* UN-*aš u-wa-it-ta-ri ḫa-ap-pár-ra-aš-ma-aš da-at-te-ni* (67″)DINGIR^{MEŠ}-*ma-kán šu-ma-aš*

temple functionary. He is not even allowed to wear it on his person. He is not allowed to make it into jewelry for his wife (or) his son. If, however, they give him silver, gold, clothing, or bronze utensils from the palace as a gift, then let it be designated (as such): (34″)"This king gave it to him." How much it weighs (35″)must also be ascertained, and further, it shall be recorded like this, too: (36″–39″)"They gave it to him for this festival." The (names of) the witnesses shall also be appended (thus): "This and that person were present when they gave it to him." Further, in no case shall he leave it inside his own house. He must sell (it) off. (40″)When he sells it, though, he shall not sell it in secret. (41″–42″)The lords of Ḫattusa shall be present, and they shall watch. They shall record what he sells on a wooden writing board, and they shall pre-seal it.[538] (43″)As soon as the king comes up to Ḫattusa, though, (44″)he (the seller) shall present it in the palace, and they shall seal it for him. (45″)If he sells it on his own volition, however, it is a capital offense for him. (46″)Whoever does not sell a royal gift on which the name of the king (47″–48″)is inscribed, however, and as mentioned, he sells silver, gold, clothing, (or) bronze utensils (privately), then whoever catches him, but conceals him, (49″–50″)and does not bring him to the king's gate, it is a capital offense for both of t<(he)>m. Both of them shall die. That (property) of the deities does not exist (for you), [*no*]*t at all*! (51″)There will be absolutely no turning back for them!

§9′ (52″–61″)Moreover, you who are the temple personnel: if you do not celebrate the festivals at festival time, (e.g.,) you perform the spring festival [i]n autu[mn], bu[t] then you celebrate the autumn festival i[n] the spring;[539] or when the p[(ro)]per time to celebrate a festival has arrived, and the one who is to perform it either comes to you priests, anoint[ed] ones, mother-deity priestesses and te[mple] personnel, and he grabs your knees (crying): "The harvest is before me;" or a dowry or a journey or some other matter, (or he says): "Stand behind me! Let me take care of this matter in the meantime, (62″)and as soon as I have taken care of this matter, (63″–64″) I will perform the festival as such." In no case shall you act according to the man's wishes! He shall not make you feel sorry for him.[540] (65″)And do not accept payment (in a matter concerning) the will of the deities! (66″) The man will make you feel sorry for him, so that you accept payment; (67″)but the deities will avenge (it) upon you some day. (68″–70″)They will most malevolently confront you yourselves, your wives, your sons (and) your servants. You should act exclusively for the will of the deities. Eat

I-NA EGIR UD-MI an-da ša-an-ḫi-iš-kán-zi (68″)nu-uš-ma-ša-at A-NA ZI$^{\text{ḪI.A}}$-KU-NU DAM^{MEŠ}-KU-NU DUMU^{MEŠ}-KU-NU SAG.GÉME.ÌR^{MEŠ}-KU-NU (69″)i-da-a-la-u-an-ni-pát a-ra-an-ta-ri na-aš-ta DINGIR^{MEŠ}-aš-pát ZI-ni (70″)i-ia-at-tén nu NINDA-an e-ez-za-at-te-ni wa-a-tar-ma e-ku-ut-te-ni (71″)É-er-ra-za i-ia-at-te-ni UN-aš-ma-at-kán ZI-ni le-˻e˼-[pát i-i]a-at-te-ni (72″)nu-za ÚŠ-tar le-e uš-ni-ia-at-te-ni ÚŠ-tar-ma-za wa-a-ši-i[a-te]-ni le-e

§10′ (A ii 73″–iii 20; D_1 iv 1′–17′; D_2 iv 1″–2″; F_1, 3′–7′; K, 1′) (73″)an-da-ma-za šu-me-eš ku-i-e-eš LÚ^{MEŠ} É DINGIR-LÌ nu-za ḫa-li-i[a-aš] (74″)ud-da-ni-i me-ek-ki pa-aḫ-ḫa-aš-ša-nu-wa-an-te-eš e-eš-tén (75″)nu ne-ku-uz me-e-ḫu-u-ni ḫu-u-da-a-ak GAM pa-it-tén (76″)nu e-ez-za-tén e-ku-ut-tén ma-a-an-na MUNUS-aš ut-tar ku-e-da-ni-i[k-ki] (77″)[…]x-˻zi˼ na-aš-za MUNUS-ni-i GAM-an še-eš-du (iii 1)[na]m-ma-aš-ta ku-it-ma-an x[… wa-ar-ap]-⸢du⸣[541] (2)[n]a-aš I-NA É DINGIR-LÌ še-e-šu-u-an-zi ⸢ḫu-u⸣-[da-a-ak š]a-ra-a ú-ed-du (3)ku-i-ša-aš ku-iš LÚ É DINGIR-LÌ $^{\text{LÚ.MEŠ}}$SANGA ⸢GAL.GAL ^{LÚ}⸣$^{\text{.MEŠ}}$SANGA TUR.TUR (4) $^{\text{LÚ.MEŠ}}$GUDU$_{12}$ ḫu-u-ma-an-te-eš ˻ku˼-iš-pát-kán ⸢im-ma ku⸣-iš DINGIR^{MEŠ}-aš (5) ^{GIŠ}kat-ta-lu-uz-zi šar-re-eš-ke-ez-zi nu 1-aš 1-aš I-NA É DINGIR-LÌ (6)ša-ra-a še-e-šu-u-wa-an-zi le-e-pát kar-aš-ta-ri (7)nam-ma-kán GE$_6$-az $^{\text{LÚ.MEŠ}}$ú-e-<ḫi>-ìš-ket$_9$-tal-li-iš da-an-te-eš[542] a-ša-an-du (8)nu GE$_6$-an ḫu-u-ma-an-da-an ú-e-ḫi-ìš-kán-du (9)nu a-ra-aḫ-za ḫa-a-li $^{\text{LÚ.MEŠ}}$ḫa-li-ia-at-tal-liš uš-kán-du (10)an-˻dur˼-za-ma É^{MEŠ} DINGIR^{MEŠ} LÚ^{MEŠ} É DINGIR-LÌ GE$_6$-an ḫu-u-ma-an-˻da˼-an (11)ú-e-ḫi-ìš-kán-du nu-uš-ma-aš Ù-aš le-e e-eš-zi (12)GE$_6$-ti GE$_6$-ti-ma 1 ^{LÚ}SANGA GAL $^{\text{LÚ.MEŠ}}$ú-e-ḫi-ìš-ga-at-tal-la-aš (13)pé-ra-an ḫu-u-˻ia˼-an-za e-eš-du nam-ma-ma ku-i-e-eš $^{\text{LÚ.MEŠ}}$SANGA (14)nu-za ku-iš ŠA KÁ É DINGIR-LÌ e-eš-du nu-za É DINGIR-LÌ pa-aḫ-ša-ru (15)ŠÀ É-ŠU-ma-za-˻*kán˼[543] IT-TI DAM-ŠU* le-e ku-iš-ki še-eš-zi (16)ku-in-ma I-NA É-ŠU GAM-an ú-e-mi-an-zi na-at-ši SAG.DU-aš wa-aš-túl (17)nu É^{MEŠ} DINGIR^{MEŠ} me-ek-ki mar-ri pa-aḫ-ḫa-aš-tén nu-uš-ma-aš te-eš-ḫa-aš (18)le-e e-eš-zi nam-ma-aš-ma-aš ḫa-a-li ar-ḫa šar-ra-an e-eš-du (19)na-aš-ta ku-e-da-ni ḫa-a-li wa-aš-túl an-da ki-i-ša (20)na-aš a-ku le-e-ia-aš-kán ú-e-eḫ-ta-ri

§11′ (A iii 21–34; C_1 iii 1′–5′; D_2 iv 3″–13″; E_1 iii 1′–6′; K, 2′–6′) (21) ^{URU}Ḫa-at-<tu>-ši-ma-kán ku-e-da-ni ku-iš ša-ak-la-a-iš še-er (22)ma-a-an ^{LÚ}SANGA ^{LÚ}GUDU$_{12}$ $^{\text{LÚ.MEŠ}}$ḫa-li-ia-at-tal-le-e-eš ku-i[š-ša-aš][544] (23)tar-ni-ìš-˻ke˼-ez-zi na-aš tar-ni-iš-ke-ed-du-pát ma-a-an ^{LÚ}ḫa-li-⸢ia-at⸣-tal-[…] (24) ku-e-da-ni-ik-ki e-eš-zi na-aš ḫa-a-li pa-id-du-pát (25)ki-iš-ša-an le-e-pát te-ez-zi am-mu-uk-wa-za É DINGIR-LÌ-IA (26)pa-aḫ-ḫa-aš-ḫi a-pí-ia-ma-wa UL pa-i-mi nu ma-a-an INIM ^{LÚ}KÚR ku-iš-ki (27) ^{URU}Ḫa-at-tu-ša-an-za-kán za-am-mu-ra-u-wa-an-zi ku-iš-ki ti-iš-ke-ez-zi (28)na-an a-ra-aḫ-zé-na-aš BÀD-aš UL ú-wa-an-zi nu a-pu-u-uš LÚ^{MEŠ} É DINGIR-LÌ (29)an-dur-za

bread and drink water, (71″)establish your household, too, but [in no case] shall you [d]o it according to a man's wishes! (72″)You shall not sell death, but [y]ou shall not bu[y] death either!

§10′ (73″–74″)Moreover, you who are the temple personnel, be very mindful in the matter [of] the watch. (75″)In the evening you shall go down punctually (76″–77″)and you shall eat and drink. And if anyo[ne …] the matter of a woman, then let him sleep with a woman. (iii 1)[Th]en, as long as […], [let him bat]he, (2)and let him come up pun[ctually] to sleep in the temple. (3–6)Whoever belongs to the temple personnel, all the major priests, minor priests (and) anointed ones, whoever normally crosses the threshold of the deities, neither the one nor the other shall neglect to sleep up in the temple. (7)Furthermore, p<at>rols shall be *posted* in the night, (8)and they shall patrol the whole night. (9)And the watchmen are to keep watch outside. (10–11)Inside the temple, though, the temple personnel shall patrol through the whole night. There will be no sleep for them. (12–14)And night for night a major priest shall be the leader of the patrols. Furthermore, one of the priests shall be assigned to the temple gate,[545] and he shall protect the temple. (15)No one, however, shall sleep in his own house with his wife. (16)Whomever they find down in his house commits a capital offense. (17–18)Above all you must protect the temple! There shall be no sleep for you! Furthermore, the watch shall be divided among you. (19)In whose[546] watch an offense occurs, (20)he shall die; he shall not *escape*.[547]

§11′ (21–24)He who is responsible for letting in someone who has some duty up in Ḫat<tu>sa, though – be he a priest, an anointed one, (or) the watchmen – he must let only them in.[548] If anyone *has guard duty*,[549] then by all means let him go on the watch.[550] (25–26)In no case shall he speak as follows: "The temple of my own god I will protect, but to (the temple) there I will not go." And if it is a matter of some enemy, (i.e.) (27)someone endeavors to harm Ḫattusa, (28–29)and (the guards) of the outer wall do not see him, but those temple personnel inside do see (him),[551] then the watchman must certainly go to him. (30)But the aforementioned must not

ú-wa-an-zi ^{LÚ}*ḫa-li-ia-at-tal-la-aš-ši pa-id-du-pát* (30)*a-pa-a-aš-ma A-NA* DINGIR-*LÌ-ŠU ša-ra-a še-e-šu-u-an-zi le-e kar-aš-ta-ri* (31)*ták-ku-wa-aš kar-aš-ta-ri-ma na-an-kán ma-a-an* UL *ku-na-an-zi* (32)*lu-ri-ia-aḫ-ḫa-an-du-ma-an nu ne-ku-ma-an-za* TÚG-*aš-ši-kán* NÍ.TE-*ši* (33)*an-⸤da⸥ le-⸢e⸣-pát e-eš-zi nu wa-a-tar* 3-*ŠU la-ba-ar-na-aš lu-li-ia-za* (34)**I-NA** É DINGIR-*LÌ-ŠU pé-e-da-a-ú nu-uš-ši a-pa-a-aš lu-ú-re-eš e-eš-du*

§12′ (A iii 35–43; C_1 iii 6′–14′; E_1 iii 7′–15′) (35)*an-⸤da⸥-ma-za n[am-m]a*[552] *šu-me-eš* $^{LÚ.MEŠ}$SANGA $^{LÚ.MEŠ}$GUDU$_{12}$ $^{MUNUS.MEŠ}$AMA.DINGIR-*LÌ* (36)LÚ^{MEŠ} ⸤É⸥ DINGIR-*LÌ* x x x~*túḫ*?-*me*?-*ia-an-za*[553] ŠÀ É DINGIR-*LÌ na-aš-*ma* ta-me-e-da-ni* (37) ^{É}⸤*ka-ri-im-me ku-iš-ki*⸥ *ni-ik-zi*[554] *na-aš-kán ma-a-an* ŠÀ É DINGIR-*LÌ* (38)⸤*ni-ni-ik-ta-ri nu ḫal-lu-u*⸥*-wa-a-in i-ia-zi na-aš-ta* EZEN$_4$ *za-aḫ-zi* (39)⸤*na-an za-ḫa-an-du*⸥ [EGI]R-[*a*]*n*[555] *a-pu-u-un* EZEN$_4$ *QA-DU* GU$_4$ UDU NINDA KAŠ *ša-ra-a* (40)⸤*ti-ia-an-da-an*⸥ [(*i*)]-⸤*ia-ad*⸥*-du* NINDA.SIG-*ia-kán le-e wa-ak-ši-ia-nu-zi* (41)⸤*ku-iš*⸥-[(*ša-a*)]*n*-⸤*za-an-kán mu-ta*⸥*-a-iz-zi nu* EZEN$_4$ *ša-ra-a ti-ia-an-ta-an* (42)⸤UL⸥ *i*-⸤*ia-zi na-at a-pé*⸥*-e-da-ni me*!(PI)-*ek-ki wa-aš-túl e-eš-du* (43)⸤*na-aš-ta* EZEN$_4$-*an*?⸥ *ḫa-pu-uš-du nu-za ḫal-lu-wa-ia-za me-ek-ki na-aḫ-ḫa-an-te-eš e-eš-tén*

§13′ (A iii 44-54; B_1 iii 1′–6′; C_1 iii 15′–25′) (44)⸤*an-da-ma-za pa*⸥*-aḫ-*⸤*ḫu*⸥*-u-e-na-aš-ša ud-da-ni-i me-ek-ki na-aḫ-ḫa-an-te-eš e-eš-tén* (45)*na-aš-ta* ⸢*ma-a*⸣*-an* Š[À?] DINGIR-*LÌ* EZEN$_4$ *nu* IZI *me-ek-ki pa-aḫ-ḫa-aš-tén* (46)*ma-aḫ-ḫa-*⸤*an-ma*⸥ GE$_6$-⸤*an*⸥*-za ki-i-ša na-aš-ta pa-aḫ-ḫur ku-it A-NA* GUNNI (47)*a-aš-zi na-at-kán ú-e-da-an-da* SIG$_5$-*in ke-eš-ta-nu-ut-tén* (48)*ma-a-an* INIM IZI-⸤*ma*⸥ *ša-an-na-pí ša-an-na-pí*[556] *ku-it-ki* ⸤*ḫa*⸥*-da*!(MA)-*an-ma* GIŠ-*ru* (49)*na-at ku-*⸤*iš kiš-ta*⸥*-nu-zi na-aš-ta ku-e-*⸢*da*⸣*-ni* ŠÀ É DINGIR-*LÌ-ŠU* (50)*wa-aš-túl ki-ša-ri nu* É DINGIR-*LÌ-*⸤*ŠU*?⸥[557] *im-ma* 1-*an ḫar-ak-zi* ^{URU}*Ḫa-at-tu-ša-aš-ma* (51)LUGAL-*aš a-aš-*⸢*šu*⸣ UL ⸢*ḫar*⸣*-ak-zi nu wa-aš-túl ku-iš i-ia-zi na-aš QA-DU* NUMUN-*ŠU* (52)*ḫar-ak-zi-pát ku-e-*⸤*ša*⸥*-at-kán ku-i-e-eš im-ma* ŠÀ É DINGIR-*LÌ nu* 1-*aš-ša* (53)TI-*nu-ma-aš* UL *e-*[*eš*]*-zi QA-DU* NUMUN-*ŠU-at ḫar-kán-zi-pát* (54)*nu-za pa-aḫ-ḫu-u-e-na-*⸤*aš*⸥ *ud-da-ni-i me-ek-ki-pát mar-ri pa-aḫ-ḫa-aš-ša-nu-an-*⸤*te*⸥-[(*eš*)] *e-eš-tén*

§14′ (A iii 55–83; B_1 iii 7′–32′; C_1 iii 26′–51′; I, 1′–7′) (55)*an-da-ma-za šu-ma-aš k*[*u-i*]*-e-eš* EN^{MEŠ} TU$_7$ DINGIR^{MEŠ}-*aš ḫu-u-ma-an-da-aš* (56) ^{LÚ}SAGI.A LÚ ^{GIŠ}BANŠUR ^{LÚ}MUḪALDIM ^{LÚ}NINDA.DÙ.DÙ ^{LÚ}KÚRUN.NA *nu-uš-ma-aš* DINGIR^{MEŠ}-*aš* (57)ZI-*ni me-na-aḫ-ḫa-an-da me-ek-ki na-aḫ-ḫa-an-te-eš e-eš-tén* (58)*na-aš-ta* DINGIR$^{⸢MEŠ⸣}$-*aš* ^{NINDA}*ḫar-*⸢*ši*⸣ ^{DUG}*iš-pa-an-tu-uz-zi na-aḫ-ša-ra-at-ta-an* (59)*me-ek-ki ti-ia-an ḫ*[(*ar-tén*)] *nu-uš-ma-aš-kán pár-šu-u-ra-aš pé-e-da-an* (60)*ša-an-ḫa-an* ⸤*ḫar-nu*⸥*-wa-an* ⸤*e-eš-du*⸥ *na-aš-ta* ŠAḪ-*aš* UR.GI$_7$-*aš* ^{GIŠ}*kat-ta-lu-uz-zi* (61)*le-e šar-ri-ìš-ket$_9$-ta*

neglect to sleep up by his deity. (31)If he neglects it, though, and if they do not kill him, (32–34)then they shall humiliate him. Naked – there will be no clothing at all on his body[558]—he shall carry water from the Labarna spring into the temple of his deity three times. That shall be his humiliation.

§12′ (35)Moreover: *F*[*urth*]*er*, you priests, anointed ones, mother-goddess priestesses (and) (36–38)temple personnel: someone [...] gets drunk in the temple or in another shrine, and if he arises in the temple and starts a brawl, and he ruins the festival, (39–40)then they shall ruin him. [Afterw]ards, he shall [(pe)]rform that festival with all the cattle, sheep, bread, beer, (and) provisions. And he shall not skimp on the flatbread. (41–42)Whoever neglects it, and does not provide the festival provisions, is guilty of a serious offense. (43)He must make amends for the festival. So be very careful regarding a brawl.

§13′ (44)Furthermore: You must also be very careful in the matter of the fire. (45)When a festival (takes place) *in*[*side*] the temple, take great care with the fire. (46–47)As soon as night falls, you must douse well with water the fire that is left in the hearth, (48)be it some *scattered* burning *pieces* or dry wood; (49–52)he who douses it, and for whom a disaster occurs in his temple, and only *his* one temple is destroyed, while the goods of the king of Ḫattusa are not destroyed, whoever caused the disaster will be completely destroyed along with his descendants. Whoever else (was) in the temple, not one of them (53)will re[ma]in alive. Along with his descendants they will be completely destroyed. (54)So you must be extremely careful in the matter of fire.

§14′ (55)Furthermore: all you w[h]o are kitchen personnel of the deities: (56–57)cupbearer, waiter, cook, baker, beer brewer: you must be extremely reverent with regard to the will of the deities. (58–59)And main[(tain)] great respect for the bread loaf (and) wine pitcher of the deities. The kitchen (60–61)shall be swept and sprayed for you. A pig (or) a dog shall not cross the threshold. And [(yo)]u yourselves must be washed, (62)and you must [(we)]ar clean clothes. Further, your *hair* and nails (63)must be trimmed. The soul of the deities shall not *ḫanḫaniya-* y[(ou)].[559] (64–65)If a pig (or)

[(šu-m)]a-ša$^{!}$(TA)-za wa-ar-pa-an-te-eš e-eš-tén (62)nu TÚG$^{\text{ḪI.A}}$ pár-ku-wa-ia [(ú-e-eš)]-tén nam-ma-aš-ma-aš-kán iš-ḫi-e-ni-uš UMBIN^{MEŠ}-ia (63)da-a-an e-eš-du[560] nu-uš-m[(a-aš)]-kán DINGIR^{MEŠ}-aš ZI-an-za le-e ≮ḫa-an-ḫa-ni-ia-i (64)ma-a-an Ú-NU[(TE)]^{MEŠ} GIŠ-ṢI ⸤Ú⸥-NU-TE^{MEŠ} GIR$_4$ ku-e ḫar-te-ni (65)na-aš-ta ma-a-an ŠAḪ-aš ⸤UR.GI$_7$⸥-aš ku-wa-pí-ik-ki an-da ša-a-li-ka$_4$ (66)EN TU$_7$-ma-at ar-ḫa UL pé-eš-še-ia-zi nu a-pa-a-aš DINGIR^{MEŠ}-aš pa-ap-ra-an-da-za (67)a-da-an-na ⸤pa⸥-[(a)]-i a-pé-e-da-ni-ma DINGIR^{MEŠ}-eš za-ak-kar ≮du-ú-úr (68)a-da-an-na ⸤a-ku-wa⸥-an-na pí-an-zi ma-a-an-na-za MUNUS-i ku-iš GAM-an še-eš-zi (69)nu-kán ma-aḫ-ḫa-an DINGIR^{MEŠ}-aš ⸤ša-ak⸥-la-in aš-ša-nu-zi DINGIR-LÌ-ni a-da-an-na (70)a-ku-wa-an-na pa-a-i na-aš⸤ IT⸥-TI MUNUS-TI QA-TAM-MA pa-id-du (71)⸤nam-ma⸥ x x x x x x-⸤pát⸥[561] na-aš-ta ku-it-ma-<(an)> ^{d}UTU-uš ša-ra-a (72)nu-za ⸤ḫu-u-da⸥-a-⸤ak wa-ar⸥-[ap]-⸤du⸥ na-aš-kán lu-uk-kat-ti DINGIR^{MEŠ}-aš (73)[(a-da-an-n)]a-aš me-e-ḫu-u-ni ḫu-u-da-a-ak a-ru[562] ma-a-an-ma-aš kar-aš-ta-ri-ma (74)[(na-at-š)]i wa-aš-túl ma-a-an-ma-za IT-TI MUNUS-TI ku-iš še-eš-zi (75)[na-a]n-kán[563] ⸢MAḪ⸣-RI-ŠU ^{LÚ}GAL-ŠU EGIR-an ta-ma-aš-zi[564] nu me-ma-ú-pát (76)[m(a-a)-a]n a-pa-a-aš-ma me-mi-ia-u-an-zi UL ma-az-za-az-zi (77)⸢nu⸣ ^{LÚ}a-ri-iš-ši me-ma-a-ú nu-za wa-ar-ap-tu$_4$-pát {*ma-a-an*} (78)ma-a-an še-ek-kán-ti-it-ma ZI-it pa-ra-a da-a-i (79)wa-ar-ap-zi-ma-za na-a-ú-i na-aš DINGIR^{MEŠ}-aš ^{NINDA}ḫar-ši (80)⸤^{DUG}iš⸥-pa-an-tu-uz-zi ma-ni-in-ku-wa-an ša-ak-nu-$^{\text{an-za}}$ ša-a-li-ka$_4$ (81)[(na)]-aš-ma-an ^{LÚ}a-ra-aš-ši-iš ša-ak-ki na-aš-ták-kán u-wa-it-ta (82)[(na-an[565] š)]a-an-na-a-i EGIR-zi-an-ma-at iš-du-wa-a-ri (83)[(nu-uš-ma-ša-a)]t SAG.DU-aš ÚŠ-tar 2-uš-ša-at ak-kán-d[u]

§15′ (A iv 1–11; B$_1$ iii 33′–39′; H iv 1–5) (1) [(an-da-ma-za šu-ma-aš) …] x x[…] (2)[(n)]u ma-a-[(an DINGIR-LÌ-ni) …]x ⸢ku⸣-it-ki e-eš-⸢zi na-aš-šu⸣ NINDA.G[UR$_4$].RA […]x[566] (3)[(n)]a-aš-m[(a ku-it) im-ma] ku-it ḫu-u-el-pí šu-ma-a-aš $^{\text{LÚ.MEŠ}}$APIN.LÁ ⸤DINGIR^{MEŠ}-aš⸥ [ ][567] (4)pé-e ⸢ḫar-te⸣-[(n)i na-a]t ḫu-u-da-a-ak me-e-ḫu-u-na-aš me-e-ḫu-ni ⸢pé-e ḫar-tén⸣ (5)ku-it-ma-na-at [UN-a]š[568] na-a-ú-i e-ez-za-a-i na-at-kán DINGIR^{MEŠ}-⸢aš ZI-ni⸣ (6)ḫu-u-da-a-ak ar-[(nu-u)]š-ke-et-tén na-at DINGIR^{MEŠ} me-na-aḫ-ḫa-an-da ⸢le⸣-[e] (7)uš-kán-zi ma-a-an-[(na-a)]t iš-ta-an-ta-nu-uš-ket$_9$-te-ni (8)nu-uš-ma-ša-at wa-aš-⸢túl⸣ nu-uš-ma-aš a-ri-an-zi nu-uš-ma-aš DINGIR^{MEŠ} EN^{MEŠ}-K[(U-NU)] (9)ma-aḫ-ḫa-an ta-pa-ri-ia-an-zi nu-uš-ma-aš QA-TAM-MA i-en-z[(i)] (10)IŠ-TU GU$_4$-ia-aš-ma-aš 10 UDU-ia za-an-ki-la-an-zi (11)nu DINGIR^{MEŠ} ZI-an wa-ar-ša-nu-an-zi

§16′ (A iv 12–24; H iv 6–14) (12)an-da-ma ma-a-an ḫal-ki-in a-ni-ia-at-te-ni nu-uš-ma-aš ma-a-an ^{LÚ}SANGA (13)A-NA NUMUN a-ni-ia-u-an-zi UN-an EGIR-an UL u-i-ia-zi šu-ma-a-ša-at (14)a-ni-ia-u-wa-an-zi ma-ni-ia-a dog ever does touch the wooden uten[(sil)]s (or) the ceramic wares that you have, (66–68)but the kitchen foreman does not throw them out, and he gives the deities to eat from unclean (utensils/wares), then the deities will give him feces (and) urine to eat (and) drink. Also, when someone goes to sleep with a woman, (69–70)as soon as he performs the rite(s) for the deities, gives the deity to eat (and) to drink, then let him thus go with the woman. (71)Further, [...] and by the ti<(me)> the sun (comes) up, (72–73) let him bat[he] punctually, and in the morning, by [(feedi)]ng time for the deities, let him appear punctually. If he neglects to do so, however, (74)[(then)] he commits an offense. If, however, someone sleeps with a woman, (75)[bu]t his *foreman*, his boss *presses* [hi]m (about it), he must certainly tell. (76)But [i]f he does not dare to tell, (77)then let him tell his colleague. And he shall bathe in any case. (78)But if he knowingly *postpones* (it),[569] (79–80)he has not yet bathed, and he approaches the bread loaf (and) the wine pitcher of the deities unclean, (81)or his colleague notices him, and you[570] feel sorry for him, (82)[(and)] he conceals [(him)], but it later becomes known, (83)[(then they)] commit a capital (offense). Both shall die.

§15′ (iv 1)[(Furthermore, you) ...]: (2)[(an)]d if there is any [... (to/for the deity)], or a bread lo[a]f [...] (3–4)o[(r a)n]y young animal [that] you ploughmen of the deities bring, [then] bring [i]t punctually at the proper time. (5–7)Before a [perso]n eats it, br[(i)]ng it punctually in accordance with the will of the deities. The deities will not be kept waiting. If you delay [(i)]t, (8–9)you commit an offense. They will consult an oracle concerning you, and as the deities, y[(our)] lords, command regarding you, thus they will do to you, (10)and they will impose a fine of one cow and ten sheep on you, (11)and (thereby) they will appease the ire of the deities.

§16′ (12–14)Furthermore: When you plant grain, and the priest does not send a man after you to plant the seed, (and) he distributes it to you to plant, and you plant much, (15)but you tell the priest it was little; or the field of the

aḫ-ḫi[571] *nu me-ek-ki a-ni-ia-at-te-ni* (15)*A-NA* ^{LÚ}SANGA-*ma-at pé-ra-an te-pu me-ma-at-te-ni na-aš-ma* A.ŠÀ DINGIR-*LÌ* (16)*mi-ia-an-za* A.ŠÀ ^{LÚ}APIN.LÁ-*ma-kán an-da ḫar-kán-za nu-za* A.ŠÀ DINGIR-*LÌ šu-me-e-el* (17)*ḫal-zi-ia-at-te-ni šu-me-el-ma-za* A.ŠÀ DINGIR-*LÌ ḫal-zi-ia-at-te-ni* (18)*na-aš-ma ḫal-ki-uš ku-wa-pí šu-un-na-at-te-ni nu ták-ša-an šar-ra-an* (19)*me-ma-at-te-ni ták-ša-an šar-ra-an-ma-za-kán an-da ša-an-na-at-te-ni* (20)*nu-uš-ma-ša-an ú-wa-at-te-ni* EGIR-*zi-an ar-ḫa šar-ra-at-te-ni* (21)*ap-<pé>-zi-an-ma-aš iš-du-wa-a-ri na-an-kán* UN-*ši im-ma ta-a-it-te-ni UL-an-kán* (22)*DINGIR$^{?}$-*LÌ*$^{?}$-*ni*$^{?}$ x* *ta-ia-at-te-ni nu-uš-ma-ša-at wa-aš-túl šu-me-el-ma-aš-kán* (23)*ḫal-ki-uš ḫu-u-ma-an-du-uš ar-ḫa da-an-*˻*zi*˼ *na-aš-kán* DINGIR^{MEŠ}-*aš* (24)˻É.SAG˼^{MEŠ}-*aš*[572] *an-da iš-ḫu-u-wa-an-zi*

§17′ (A iv 25–33) (25)*an-da-ma ŠA* KI[SLAḪ] GUD.APIN.LÁ$^{\text{ḪI.A}}$ *ku-i-e-eš* [*ḫar-t*]*e-ni nu ma-a-an* GUD.A[PIN.L]Á (26)*uš-ni-ia-at-te-ni na-aš-ma-an-za-an-kán k*[*u-e*]*n-na-at-te-n*[*i*] (27)*na-an ar-ḫa e-ez-za-at-te-ni šu-ma-aš-ma-an-kán* DINGIR^{MEŠ}-*aš ta-a-iš-te-ni* (28)*ma-ak-la-an-*˻*na-az*˼*-wa-ra-aš* BA.ÚŠ *na-aš-šu-wa-za du-wa-ar-ni-ìš-ke-et* (29)*na-aš-šu-wa-ra-aš* ˻*pár*˼*-aš-ta na-aš-ma-wa-ra-an* GUD.NÍTA GUL-*aḫ-ta* (30)*šu-ma-aš-ma-an ar-ḫa e-ez-za-at-te-ni* EGIR-*zi-an-ma-aš iš-du-wa-*˻*a*˼*-ri* (31)*nu a-pu-u-un* GU$_4$ ˻*šar*˼*-ni-ik-te-ni-pát ma-*[*a-an-m*]*a-aš UL-ma iš-du-wa-a-ri* (32)˻*nu* DINGIR-*LÌ-ni pa-it*˼*-te-ni ták-ku pár-ku-e*[*š-t*]*e-ni šu-me-el* ^{d}LAMMA-*KU-NU* (33)*ták-ku pa-ap-re-*[*eš-te-ni*]*-ma nu-uš-ma-ša-at* SAG.DU-*aš wa-aš-túl*

§18′ (A iv 34–55; B$_1$ iv 1′–16′) (34)*an-da-ma-z*[*a š*]*u-ma-aš ku-i-e-eš* $^{\text{LÚ.MEŠ}}$SIPA GU$_4$ DINGIR-*LÌ* $^{\text{LÚ.MEŠ}}$SIPAD.UDU DINGIR-*LÌ* (35)*nu *ma-a-an* ḫa-aš-ša-an-na-aš m*[*e-e*]*-ḫu-u-ni* DINGIR-*LÌ-ni ku-e-da-ni-ik-ki* (36)*ša-ak-*˻*la*˼*-a-iš nu-uš-ši na-aš-šu* AMAR SILA$_4$ MÁŠ.TUR *na-aš-ma* ^{UZU}*ŠA-LI-T*[*E*^{M}]^{EŠ} (37)*ḪA-A*[*K-KÚ*]*R-RA-TE*^{MEŠ} *pé-e ḫar-te-ni na-at le-e iš-ta-an-ta-nu-uš-ket*$_9$*-te-ni* (38)*me-e-*[*ḫu*]*-u-na-ša-at me-e-ḫu-u-ni pé-e ḫar-tén na-at-kán* DINGIR^{MEŠ} (39)*me-na-aḫ-ḫa-an-da le-e uš*[573]*-kán-zi ku-it-ma-an* UN-*aš ḫu-u-el-p*[(*í*)] (40)*na-a-ú-i e-ez-za-az-zi na-at* DINGIR^{MEŠ}-*aš ḫu-u-da-a-ak ú-da-at-tén* (41)*na-aš-ma ma-a-an* DINGIR-*LÌ-ni ku-e-da-ni* EZEN$_4$ GA *e-eš-zi* (42)GA *ku-wa-pí šap-pé-eš-kán-zi na-an-kán le-e ša-ku-wa-an-ta-ri-ia-nu-ut-te-ni* (43)*na-an-ši i-ia-at-tén ma-a-an ḫu-u-*˻*el-pí*˼ DINGIR^{MEŠ}-*aš ḫu-u-da-a-ak UL* (44)*ú-da-at-te-ni na-at* ˻*šu-ma*˼*-*[(*aš*)] *ḫu-u-da-ak ez-za-at-te-ni* (45)*na-aš-ma-at A-NA MAḪ-RI-*˻*KU*˼*-NU* ˻*up-pa-at-te*˼*-ni* EGIR-˻*ez-zi-an-ma-at*˼ (46)˻*iš*˼*-du-wa-a-ri nu-uš-ma-ša-*˻*at* SAG˼.DU-*aš wa-aš-túl ma-a-an-ma-at UL-m*[(*a*)] (47)*iš-du-wa-a-ri na-at ú-da-at-te-ni ku-e-da-ni me-e-ḫu-ni* (48)*nu-uš-ma-aš-kán*[574] *PA-NI* DINGIR-*LÌ ki-iš-ša-an an-da* ˻*pé-e-da-at*˼*-te-ni* (49)*ma-a-an-wa-za ki-i ḫu-u-el-pí an-ze-el* ZI-*ni*

deity (16–17)is prosperous, while the field of the ploughman fails, and you designate the field of the deity yours and yours you designate the field of the deity; (18–19)or you store the grain at some point, and you report half of it, but you conceal the (other) half, (20)and thereafter you divide it among yourselves, (21–24)but aft<er>wards it becomes known: are you stealing it from just a man? Are you not stealing it from the deity? You commit (thereby) an offense. So they will take it, (i.e.) all of your grain,[575] away and pour it into the storage pits of the deities.

§17′ (25–26)Furthermore: Those of you who [kee]p the plough oxen for the thre[shing floor]: if you sell a p[loug]h ox, or you k[il]l it (27)and you consume it, but then you *place*[576] it before the deities (and you say), (28)"it died of emaciation," or[577] "it *suffered a serious injury*," (29)or "it fled," or "a bull gored it," (30)but you yourselves consume it, and afterwards it becomes known, (31)then you will certainly replace the ox. I[f] it does not become known (*who has done it*),[578] though, (32)then you will go before the deity. If you are innocent, (then it is due to) your patron deity. (33)But if [you are] guilty, it is a capital offense for you.

§18′ (34)Furthermore: You who are the cowherds of the deity (and) shepherds of the deity: (35–37)If there is a rite for some deity during the birthing season, and you bring him a calf, a lamb, a kid or the afterbirth (and) *ḫa*[*kku*]*rrāte*,[579] then you will not delay it. (38–40)Bring it at the proper time. The deities should not be kept waiting for it. Before a person consumes the young animals, bring them punctually to the deities. (41)Or if there is a milk[580] festival for some deity, (42)do not neglect it (the festival) while they churn the milk. (43–44)Carry it out for him. If you do not bring the young animals to the deities immediately, but rather you hastily consume them yourselves, (45)or you bring them to your foreman, and afterwards it (46)becomes known, you commit a capital offense. But if it does not (47)become known (*who has done it*), then at the season in which you (are to) bring them, (48)you shall proclaim before the deity as follows: (49–51)"If we hastily claimed these young animals for ourselves, or we have given them to our foreman, or to our wives, sons, or another person, (52–53)so that we have wronged the deities themselves, …."[581] Then you will drink empty the rhyton of the deity himself.[582] If you are innocent,

ḫu-u-da-a-ak (50)*pí-ia-u-e-en na-aš-ma-wa-ra-aš A-NA MAḪ-RI-NI na-aš-ma A-NA* DAM^{MEŠ}-*NI* (51)DUMU^{MEŠ}-*NI na-aš-ma ta-me-e-da-ni* UN-*ši pí-ia-u-e-en* (52)DINGIR^{MEŠ}-*aš-ma-wa-kán* ZI-*an za-am-mu-ra-a-u-e-en na-aš-ta BI-IB-RU* DINGIR-*LÌ* (53)ZI-*aš ar-ḫa e-ku-ut-te-ni nu-za ma-a-an pár-ku-wa-e-eš* (54)*šu-me-el* ^{d}LAMMA-*KU-NU ták-ku-za *pa*-ap-ra-an-te-eš-ma na-aš-ta QA-DU* (55)DAM^{MEŠ}-*KU-NU* DUMU^{MEŠ}-*KU-NU ḫar-ak-te-ni*

§19′ (A iv 56–77; B_1 iv 17′–34′) (56)*an-da-ma-aš-ta ma-a-an kar-ša-at-tar ku-wa-pí kar-aš-te-ni* (57)*na-at* DINGIR^{MEŠ}-*aš A-NA* EN^{MEŠ}-*KU-NU u-un-na-an-zi nu kar-ša-ad-da-⸤ni⸥* (58)GAM-*an* ^{LÚ}SIPAD.GU_4 ^{LÚ}SIPAD.UDU-*ia i-ia-an-ta-ru* (59)*na-at-ša-an ḫa-li-ia-az a-ša-u-na-az ma-aḫ-ḫa-an kar-ša-an* (60)*na-at-kán* DINGIR^{MEŠ}-*aš QA-TAM-MA an-da ar-nu-wa-an-du* (61)EGIR KASKAL-*NI-ma-at-kán le-e wa-aḫ-nu-uš-kán-zi ma-a-an-ma-kán* ŠÀ KASKAL-*NI* (62) ^{LÚ}SIPAD.GU_4 *na-aš-ma* ^{LÚ}SIPAD.UDU *mar-ša-tar ku-iš-ki i-ia-zi* (63)*na-aš-ta na-aš-šu* ⸤GUD⸥.NIGA *na-aš-ma* UDU.NIGA *wa-aḫ-nu-zi nu-za-kán ḫa-ap-pár* (64)*ša-ra-a da-a-i na-aš-ma-an-za-an-kán ku-en-zi na-an ar-ḫa* (65)**a**-*da-an-zi pé-di-iš-ši-ma ma-ak-la-an-ta-an tar-na-an-zi* (66)*na-at iš-du-wa-a-ri nu-uš-ma-ša-at* SAG.DU-*aš wa-aš-túl* (67)DINGIR^{MEŠ}-*aš-kán* ZI-*aš-ša-aš ša-ne-ez-zi-in* ⊀ *zu-u-wa-an da-a-er* (68)*ma-a-an-ma-at UL-ma iš-du-wa-a-ri na-at ku-e-da-ni me-e-ḫu-u-ni* (69)*a-ra-an-zi na-aš-ta BI-IB-RU* DINGIR-*LÌ* ZI-⸤*TI*⸥ ^{GIŠ}*iš-ta-na-*<(*na*)>*-az* GAM (70)*da-an-du nu-za-kán an-da ki-iš-ša-an pé-e-da-an-du* (71)*ma-a-an-wa-kán* DINGIR^{MEŠ}-*aš ša-ne-ez-zi-in* ⊀ *zu-u-wa-an* KA×U-*az* (72)*pa-ra-a an-za-a-aš ḫu-u-it-ti-ia-u-en nu-wa-ra-an-na-ša-an*[583] *an-ze-el* (73)ZI-*ni pí-ia-u-e-en na-aš-ma-wa-an-na-ša-an uš-ša-ni-ia-u-e-en* (74)*na-aš-ma-wa-ra-an-kán wa-aḫ-nu-um-me-en nu-wa-an-na-⸢aš⸣ ḫa-ap-pár da-a-u-e-en* (75)*pé-di-iš-ši-ma-wa ma-ak-la-an-da-an tar-nu-⸤um-me-en⸥* (76)*nu-wa-an-na-aš zi-ik* DINGIR-LU_4 *tu-el* ZI-*aš* ⊀ *zu-u-wa*[584] *še-er* (77)*QA-DU* DAM^{MEŠ}-*NI* DUMU^{MEŠ}-*NI pár-ḫi-iš-ke*

COLOPHON

(A iv 78–81) (78)DUB.1.KAM *ŠA* LÚ^{MEŠ} É DINGIR-*LÌ ḫu-u-ma-an-da-aš* (79)*ŠA* EN^{MEŠ} TU_7 DINGIR^{MEŠ} LÚ^{MEŠ} APIN.LÁ DINGIR^{MEŠ} (80)*Ù ŠA* $^{\text{LÚ.MEŠ}}$SIPAD.GU_4 DINGIR-*LÌ* $^{\text{LÚ.MEŠ}}$SIPAD.UDU DINGIR-*LÌ* (81)*iš-ḫi-ú-la-aš QA-TI*

(54–55)(then it is due to) your patron deity. But if you are guilty, then you will be destroyed along with your wives and your sons.

§19′ (56)Furthermore: If you select at some point a selection (of the animals), (57–58)and they drive them to the deities, your lords, then the cowherds and the shepherds shall go along with the selection. (59)And just as they were selected from the corral (and) from the pen, (60)so they shall bring them in to the deities. (61)Following (the selection) they shall not exchange them along the way. But if along the way (62)some cowherd or shepherd commits fraud, (63–65)and he exchanges a fattened cow or a fattened sheep, and he accepts payment (for it), or he kills it and they consume it, and they replace it with an emaciated animal, (66)and it becomes known, then it is a capital offense for you. (67)They have taken the savory share of the deities themselves. (68)But if it does not become known (*who has done it*), then whenever (69–70)they arrive, they shall take the rhyton of the deity itself down from the alt<(ar)>, and they shall proclaim as follows: (71–73)"If we have snatched for ourselves the savory share from the (very) mouth of the deities, and claimed it for ourselves, or we have sold it for ourselves, (74)or we have exchanged it and taken payment for ourselves, (75)and replaced it with an emaciated one, (76–77)then may you, o deity, continually haunt us, along with our wives and our sons on account of your own share!"

COLOPHON

(78–81)Tablet One of the Obligations for All the Temple Personnel, the Kitchen Personnel of the Deities, the Ploughmen of the Deities and for the Cowherds of the Deity (and) the Shepherds of the Deity. Finished.

Chapter 3
Empire Period Sources

No. 21
Instructions for Supervisors (*CTH* 266)

The only extant fragment preserving this composition shows a NH script and is one of the rather few instructions found in the palace, in Building A. The phonetic writing of *parn-* in 7′ and 10′ might perhaps be an indication that it was copied from an older ms., but much more than this would be necessary to confirm such a suspicion. The use of the potentialis particle *man-* in §2′, 11′ and 16′– if not simply a rare non-plene writing of the conj. *mān* – is rather unexpected, while the writing of *-asta* with *-aš-da* (11′), if indeed to be interpreted as the local particle, is unique, and perhaps to be seen as a scribal mistake rather than a variant.

Of note is the royal interest in having the town commanders or mayors, to whom the composition seems to be addressed (§3′, 16′), attempt to uncover corruption, a theme most common in the oldest texts of the corpus (cf., e.g., No. 1).

TRANSLITERATION

§1′ (iii? 1′)[…]x x[…] (2′)[… -*n*]*a-az-ma ku-iš e-ku-*[*zi* …] (3′)[*pát-te-e*]*š*$_{15}$*-ni pu-ru-ut pád-da-an* x[…] (4′)[*ka*]*r*?*-pa-an-ti-ma* MA-ḪAR GUNNI x[…]

§2′ (iii? 5′)*na-aš-ta ma-a-an* É*-ri* 4 LÚ^{MEŠ} [*an-da-an*] (6′)*nu* 2 LÚ^{MEŠ} ŠA É.GAL-LÌ KIN*-an a-*[*ni-ia-an-du*] (7′)⌜2⌝ LÚ^{MEŠ}*-ma-aš*[1] *pár-na-aš* KIN*-an a-n*[*i-ia-an-du*] (8′)[*ma*]-⸤*a*⸥*-an-kán* É*-ri-ma* 2 LÚ^{MEŠ} *an-d*[*a-an*] (9′)[*nu*][2] 1 LÚ ⸤ŠA⸥ [É].⸤GAL⸥-LÌ KIN*-an a-n*[*i-ia-ad-du*] (10′)[1 LÚ*-a*]*š-ma pár-na-*⌜*aš-ma*⌝*-aš* KIN*-an* *an-ni*-[*ia-ad-du*] (11′)[*ma-n*]*a*[3]*-aš-da* É*-ri-ma* 1 LÚ *an-da-an* [ ] (12′)*nu* I-NA UD.4.KAM ŠA É.GAL-LÌ KIN*-an*[ ] (13′)*a-ni-ia-ad-du* I-NA UD.4.KAM*-ma* *x*[ ] (14′)KIN ŠA É-TI-ŠU *a-ni-ia-ad-du* [ ] (15′) MUNUS.MEŠ*wa-an-nu-um-*mi*-uš* KIN*-an iš-ḫa-a-*⸤*i*⸥[ ]

§3′ (iii? 16′)*ma-na-ša-an ku-wa-pí* URU*-ri-ia* EGIR*-pa* [*a-ar-ti*] (17′)*nu* LÚ^{MEŠ} ^{GIŠ}TUKUL $^{\text{LÚ.MEŠ}}$ŠU.GI *an-da ḫal-za-a-*⌜*i*⌝[ ] (18′)[*nu*]*-uš-ma-aš ki-iš-ša-an me-mi* (19′)[^{LÚ}]*ḫa-at-tal-wa-al-li-iš*[4] *mar-ša-an-te-eš* (20′)[LÚ^{M}]^{EŠ} ŠA É-IA[5] *mar-ša-an-te-eš* (21′)[*nu-uš-m*]*a-aš* GEŠTIN*-an da-aš-kán-zi* (22′)[*šu-me-eš*(?)] *me*-*na-aḫ-ḫa-an-da wa-a-tar* (23′)[*la-a-ḫ*]*u-u-wa-an-zi* $^{\text{LÚ.MEŠ}}$NU.GIŠ.KIRI$_6$ (24′)[x x x x] ⸤Ù⸥ ^{GIŠ}KA×GIŠ *da-aš-kán-zi* (25′)[*na-at* A-NA L]Ú^{MEŠ} ^{GIŠ}TUKUL *pé-eš-kán-zi* (26′)[x x x x ^{LÚ}NU].GIŠ.KIRI$_6$ A-NA LÚ ^{GIŠ}TUKUL (27′)[x x x *ku-e-da-ni-i*]*k-ki ku-it-ki pa-a-*⸤*i*⸥[ ] (28′)[… A-NA L]Ú ⸤^{GIŠ}⸥TUKUL *pa-a-i*[ ] (29′)[…]x x x x[…]

TRANSLATION

§1′ (2′)[...] but he who eat[s ...] (3′)[...] mud excavated in a [pi]t, (4′)but in front of the [ra]ised hearth [...]

§2′ (5′)And if there are four men [in] a household, (6′)then two men [shall] pe[rform] work for the palace, (7′)while two men [shall] per[form] work for (their) household. (8′)[I]f, however, there are (only) two men i[n] a household, (9′)[then] one man [shall] per[form] work for the [pa]lace, (10′) while [one] man [shall] perfo[rm] work for their households. (11′)[Should] there be (only) one man in the house, though, (12′–13′)then he shall perform work for the palace for four days, while for four days (14′)he shall perform work for his house. (15′)You[6] shall impose work upon women with no family, (too).

§3′ (16′–17′)Should [you] at some point re[turn] to the city, then you shall call out the *land tenants* (and) the elders, (18′)[and] you(sg.) shall speak to them as follows: (19′)“Are the guards of the gates corrupt? (20′)Are the [me]n of my household corrupt? (21′)Do they take wine for [thems]elves? (22′–24′)Do they [pou]r water [*for you*]? Do the gardeners take the [... a]nd the container (25′)[and] give [them to] the *land tenants*? (26′–27′)[... a ga]rdener give something to [som]e *land tenant* (28′–29′)[...] give [to] a *land tena*[*nt*? ...]”

No. 22
Instructions of Suppiluliuma I for the Military and a Corresponding Oath (*CTH* 253)

These instructions and oath fragments are very incompletely preserved on (1) a late MH tablet fragment and (2) a NH copy of a (presumably late) MH text; they might, but do not necessarily, belong to the same composition. No archaeological findspot for either of the fragments is known. Since the first tablet seems to contain instructions and perhaps an oath imposition, while the second appears to consist of an oath expressed in the 1st pl. (No. 22.2 §2′, 8′), this might conceivably be a unique case of the obligations/instructions being recorded on one tablet and its corresponding oath on another, but far too little is preserved of both for any more than speculation in this direction.

TRANSLITERATION (22.1)

§1′ (1 iv? 1′) ⸢*ku-i*⸣*-ša-aš* ⸢*im-ma*⸣ *ku*-x[7][…]

§2′ (1 iv? 2′–9′) (2′)*an-da-ma A-NA* LUGAL MUNUS.LUGAL[…] (3′)⸤*me*⸥*-eg-ga-e-eš nu-za ma-a-an A*-[*NA* …] (4′)*i-da-a-lu-un me-mi-an ku-iš-ki*[…] (5′)⸤*za*⸥*-am-mu-ra-iz-zi šu-me-ša* x[…] (6′)[É]RIN^{MEŠ} *ša-ri-ku-wa-aš* ÉRIN^{MEŠ} ANŠE.KUR.RA[…] (7′) ^{m}*ŠU.UP.PÍ.LU.LI.U.MA* LUGAL.GAL […] (8′)*nu AŠ-ŠUM BE-LÍ-KU*!(MA)*-NU I-NA* EGI[R.UD-*MI*(?) …] (9′) ^{d}UTU-*ŠI-in-pát* […][8]

§3′ (1 iv? 10′–22′) (10′)⸤*ku*⸥*-i-ša-kán A-NA ŠA* LUGAL x[…] (11′)⸤*ḫa*⸥*-aš-ša-an-na-aš-ši i-da-*⸤*a*⸥*-*[*lu* …] (12′)⸤*na*⸥*-an mu-un-na-a-***iz-zi**[…] (13′)*te-ek-ku-uš-*{*ku-uš*}*-š*[*a-nu-* …] (14′)EGIR-*an da-a-i* […] (15′)EGIR *ša-ra-*⸤*a*⸥[…] (16′) *am-mu-uk-wa*[…] (17′)⸤*ut*⸥*-tar am-mu-u*[*k* …] (18′)*zi-ik* x[…] (19′)*na-aš-m*[*a* …] (20′)*ti-i*[(*a*)- …] (21′)*ma-*⸤*a*⸥*-*[…] (22′)DUM[U …]

If indeed No. 22.1, §2′, 2′ is to be understood as referring to the many royal relatives, as would seem likely, it would provide a close parallel to those later texts that so urgently demand personal loyalty in the face of the many potential royal contenders (e.g., No. 26, *passim*; No. 27, §§2, 3, 25″), and would thus constitute a further caution (cf. No. 18) about seeing the late loyalty oaths as witnessing a unique scenario at the end of the Empire (cf., e.g., Giorgieri and Mora 2010: 139). No. 22.2 has received attention in the scholarly literature primarily due to the fact that it is addressed to Suppiluliuma I and Tadu-Ḫepa, who as the widow of the preceding king, Tudḫaliya III, played the role of queen mother and *tawannanna* during the first part of the reign of Suppiluliuma I.

TRANSLATION (22.1)

§1′ (1′)Whoever […] them […]

§2′ (2′)Furthermore, the […] of the king (and) queen (3′–4′)are many, and if anyone […] an evil matter t[o …] (5′)s/he insults, but you(pl.) […] (6′)*sarikuwa*-[tr]oops, soldiers, chariotry […] (7′)Suppiluliuma, Great King, […] (8′)and for the sake of your(pl.) lord in *fut*[*ure*…] (9′)only My Majesty […]

§3′ (10′–11′)But whoever […] ev[il] to the king's […] and of his descendents […], (12′)and he hides him, […] (13′)reve[al …] (14′)he takes/places back […] (15′)back up […][9] (16′) "I […] (17′)word/matter I […] (18′)you(sg.) […] (19′–20′)or […] (21′)i[f …] (22′)so[n…]

TRANSLITERATION (22.2)

§1′ (2 i 1′–7′) (1′–2′)(traces) (3′)[... M]EŠ ÉRINMEŠ *ša-ri-⸢ku-wa-aš⸣* (4′)[...]-*zi-iš*[10] *ḫu-u-ma-an-za* (5′)[... -(I)]A LÚ*ar-nu-wa-la-aš-ša-k*[*án*?][11] (6′)[...]KUR.KURMEŠ-*aš ḫu-u-ma-an-da-aš* (7′)[...]⸢KUR URU*ḪA*⸣.*AT.TI an-da e-eš-zi*

§2′ (2 i 8′–13′) (8′)[*nu ka*]-⸤*a*⸥-*ša* ITU-*mi* ITU-*mi A-NA* SAG.DU mŠ*U.UP.PÍ.LU.LI.U.MA* (9′)[LUGAL.GAL *Ù A-NA*] ⸤f⸥*TÁ.DU.ḪÉ.PA* MUNUS.LUGAL.GAL *Ù A-NA* DUMU!MEŠ! LUGAL (10′)[DUMU.DUMUMEŠ LUGAL(?) *k*]*at-ta ḫa-aš-ša ḫa-an-za-*aš*-ša* (11′)[*še-er li-in-k*]*i-iš-ke-u-wa-ni nu ka-a-ša* (12′)[*ke-e-da-ni li-in-k*]*i-ia LI-IM* DINGIRMEŠ (13′)[*ku-ut-ru-u-uš*(?)][12] *ḫal-z*]*i-*⸤*ú*⸥*-en*[13]

§3′ (2 i 14′–16′) (14′)[... dUTU URU*A.RI.I*]*N.NA*[14] (15′)[... GUD/d*Š*]*E.*⸤*E*⸥*.RI* (16′)[GUD/d*ḪUR.RI* ...]x x[...]

TRANSLATION (22.2)

§1′ (3′)[...]s, the *sarikuwa*-troops, (4′)[...] the whole (5′)[...] and a civilian captive (6′)[...] all the lands (7′)[...] is in the land of Ḫattusa.

§2′ (8′–13′)[And] month for month we will hereby [swe]ar this oath to the person of Suppiluliuma, [Great King, and to] Tadu-Ḫepa, Great Queen, and to the sons of the king, [the grandsons of the king],[15] (and) thereafter also to (his) descendents. And hereby have we [call]ed the thousand gods [as witnesses] to [this oat]h.

§3′ (14′)[... the Sun Goddess of Ari]nna, (15′)[... the divine bull Š]ēri, (16′)[the divine bull Ḫurri, ...]

No. 23
Oath of the Men of Ḫattusa to Ḫattusili III and Pudu-Ḫepa
(*CTH* 254)

Though only the ends of the lines of the first two paragraphs are preserved on a single fragment, this oath to the royal couple, Ḫattusili III and Pudu-Ḫepa, shows such similarities in formulation to some of its forerunners (see nn. 17 and 18) that one suspects that already by this time at the latest the oath ceremony, or at least its prescription, had evolved into very much a standard procedure, and that the scribes to a significant degree were copying their texts from earlier compositions, changing them only where needed or desired. No findspot is known for the fragment.

Curiously, this is the only instruction or oath fragment known from the age of Ḫattusili III, a king otherwise so well attested in his desperate desire for legitimacy.

Transliteration

§1 $^{(\text{i }1)}$[... ^{m}*ḪA.AT.TU.ŠI.L*]*I* LUGAL.GAL LUGAL KUR *ḪA.AT.TI* $^{(2)}$[...]x DUMU^{MEŠ}.LUGAL $^{(3)}$[...]x ÉRIN^{MEŠ} ANŠE.KUR.RA^{MEŠ} $^{(4)}$[...]*UN$^{?}$*^{MEŠ}-*uš* $^{\text{LÚ.MEŠ}}$MAŠDA $^{(5)}$[... *ḫu-u-ma-a*]*n-za ku-iš-kán INA* KUR ^{URU}*ḪAT.TI an-da* ⸢*e-eš-zi*$^{?}$⸣

§2 $^{(\text{i }6)}$[*nu ka-a-ša* ITU-*mi* ITU-*mi*] *A-NA* SAG.DU ^{m}*ḪA.AT.TU.ŠI.LI*$^{!}$ $^{(7)}$[LUGAL.GAL *Ù A-NA* SAG.DU ^{f}*PU.DU.ḪE*].*PA* MUNUS.LUGAL.GAL (erasure) $^{(8)}$[*Ù A-NA* DUMU^{MEŠ}-*ŠU-NU* DUMU.DUMU^{MEŠ}-*ŠU-NU kat*]-⸢*ta*⸣ *ḫa-aš-ša ḫa-an-za-aš-ša še-er* $^{(9)}$[*li-in-ku-u-e-ni nu ka-a-ša ke-e-da-ni*] ⸢*li-in*^{16}*-ga-i*⸣ $^{(10)}$[*LI-IM* DINGIR^{MEŠ} *tu-li-ia ḫal-zi-ia-an-te-eš nu uš-kán-d*]*u iš-ta-ma-*[*aš-kán-du*] $^{(11)}$(traces)

TRANSLATION

§1 (1)[... Ḫattusil]i, Great King, King of the Land of Ḫattusa, (2)[...] sons of the king, (3)[...] troops, chariotry, (4)[...] *men* (and) peasants (5)[enti]re [...], he who is in the land of Ḫattusa.[17]

§2 (6–11)[Hereby do we swear, month for month], to the person of Ḫattusili, [Great King, and to the person of Pudu-Ḫe]pa, Great Queen, [and to their sons and grandsons, (and) there]after to further generations, [and hereby are the thousand gods called to assembly for this] oath, [so that they m]ay [see, that they may] hear.[18]

No. 24
Instructions for Priests and Diviners (*CTH* 275)

This composition is represented by one mid-sized fragment and a small duplicate. It is not entirely certain that this fragmentary text represents an instruction composition, as there are also ritual and festival texts that occasionally switch between a prescriptive third sg. or pl. to the second person (for the rituals, see Miller 2004: 488–92), and this could conceivably be such a case. Some features, however, might support the interpretation as an instruction, such as the first line, in which it seems that a rare occurrence of the verb *isḫiyaḫḫ-*, "to impose obligations; to issue instructions," from *isḫiul-*, "obligation; instruction," can be recognized. (Another festival text that shows elements of an instruction is KUB 57.29 // KUB 55.21; see Popko 1994: 280–84; Taggar-Cohen 2006: 180–81.) Further, while the rituals occasionally slip into the second person, they do not as a rule employ the imperative (Torri 2007), and as far as I know

---

Transliteration

§1′ (A 1′–7′) (1′)[*me*?]-*ek-ki* ⸢*iš*⸣-*ḫi*-⸢*ú-la-aḫ*?-*ḫa*?⸣-*a*[*n*?-*zi*[19] …] (2′)*ú-e-da-ar ku-e A-NA* *URU-*LÌ** *a*-⸢*ra-aḫ-za*⸣[…] (3′)*ša-ra-a-*kán* x x* *ku-it wa-a-tar na-at* *x*[…] (4′)*na-at ŠA* DINGIR-*LÌ* *ša-ak-la-a-i le-e da-aš-ga-at-*[*tén*] (5′) [*w*]*a-a-tar ŠA* DINGIR-*LÌ* NINDA.GUR$_4$.RA UD-*MI* ^{GIŠ}TIR *ga*-*ú-ri-*[*ia-za*] (6′) [^{GI}]^{Š}⸤TIR⸥ *du-un-na-ri-ia-za píd-da-iš-ke-et-tén* [ ] (7′)*nu* *ŠA* DINGIR-*LÌ** *ša-ak-la-a-i a-pa-a-at* *da-aš-ket$_9$-té*[*n*]

§2′ (A 8′–17′; B obv.? 1′–4′) (8′) ^{d}UTU-*ŠI-ia-kán ku-in* *NINDA.GUR$_4$*.RA UD-*MI A-NA* DINGIR-*LÌ pí*[*d-da-iš-ke-mi*] (9′)*nu šu-um-ma-aš* $^{\text{LÚ.MEŠ}}$SANGA *ki-iš-ša-an e-eš-še-eš-tén*[ ] (10′)GIM-*an* $^{\text{LÚ.MEŠ}}$SANGA ^{LÚ}ḪAL-*ia ka-ri-wa-ri-wa-a*[*r*] (11′)*PA-NI* É DINGIR-*LÌ pa-a-an-zi nu A-NA* DINGIR-*LÌ* NINDA.GUR$_4$.RA [UD-*MI*] (12′)*pé-ra-an ar-ḫa da-an-zi nu-kán* É DINGIR-*LÌ p*[*a-ra-a*] (13′)*ša-an-ḫa-an-zi pa-ap-pár-ša-an-zi nu-kán* NINDA.GUR$_4$.[(RA UD-*M*)*I*] (14′)*ti-ia-an-zi* GIM-*an ne-ku-uz-za me-ḫur ki-ša-r*[*i*] (15′)*nu-kán ša-ša-an-na-aš da-a-i nu-kán* É DINGIR-*LÌ* [ ] (16′)[(*p*)]*a-ra-a* SUD-*an-zi* ^{LÚ}⸤SANGA⸥-*ma-kán* ^{LÚ}ḪAL-*ia* [ ] (17′)[(*P*)]*A-NI* KÁ-*aš še-ša-an-zi* [ ]

§3′ (A 18′–21′; B obv.? 5′–9′) (18′)[*n*]*am-ma-ia ku-e* É^{MEŠ} DINGIR^{MEŠ} *nu* ⸤GIM⸥-*an ka-*[*ri-wa-ri-wa-ar*] (19′)[^{LÚ}SA]NGA ^{LÚ}ḪAL-*ia pa-an-zi nu-kán* ⸢É⸣^{MEŠ} DING[IR^{MEŠ} *a-r*(*a-aḫ-za-an-da*)] (20′)[(*ú*)]-⸤*e*⸥-*ḫa-an-du nam-ma-at-kán pa-ra-a š*[(*a-an-ḫa-an-du*)] (21′)[(*pa*)-*ap-pár*]-*aš-ša-an-du na-at-kán pa-ra-a* S[UD-*an-zi*]

this applies to the festivals as well, though no systematic or exhaustive study on this question is available. Further, one would expect the king to be referred to with LUGAL in the festivals rather than with ^{d}UTU-*ŠI*, as in l. 8′ here. Finally, there is of course the general similarity to the Instructions for Priests and Temple Personnel (No. 20).

In any case, the instructions in this composition are issued partly in the 2nd pl., partly impersonally in the 3rd sg. or pl. The king is also mentioned as an actor, but since the verb ending is lost, it is impossible to tell if he is speaking in the first person or whether he is referred to in the third (see n. 20). It is a NH tablet, of unknown provenience, and there seem to be no clear indications of original antiquity (cf. Taggar-Cohen 2011b: 15), so that one suspects it could represent another text from the time of Ḫattusili, in whose reign so much interest in the Storm God of Nerik (cf. §4′) is witnessed, a possibility which remains quite speculative.

TRANSLATION

§1′ (1′)[*the*]*y impose* [*m*]*any* obligations [...] (2′)the waters that [...] outside the city, (3′)the water that is up above, [...] it. (4′)For the rites of the deity yo[u(pl.) must] not take it. (5′–6′)The [w]ater of the deity (and) the daily bread you(pl.) must carry from the *gauri*[*ya*]- (and) *dunnariya*-forests. (7′) You(pl.) must always take those for the rites of the deity.

§2′ (8′)And the daily bread which *I*, My Majesty, *b*[*ring*][20] for the deity, (9′) you(pl.) priests must prepare as follows: (10′14′)As soon as the priests and the diviner go to the temple early in the morning, they take the (old) [daily] bread away from in front of the deity, and they sweep o[ut] (and) sprinkle the temple, then they place the [(dail)y] bre[(ad)] there. As soon as evening arrives, (15′–16′)he places the lamps and they pull the temple (gate) shut. A priest and a diviner, though, (17′)sleep in [(fr)]ont of the gate.

§3′ (18′–20′)And [fu]rther, whatever temples there are, as soon as the [pri]est and the diviner go (there) ear[ly in the morning], they must take a [(l)]ook around [ou(tside)] the tem[ple]s. Further, they must s[(weep)] them out (and) (21′)[(sp)rink]le them, then they p[ull] them shut.

§4′ (A 22′–26′) (22′)[…] GIM-*an* *A-NA* d10 URU*NE.RI.I*[*K* …] (23′)[… NINDA.GU]R$_4$.RA-*ia* *kat-ta* *ḫa-ma-an-ku*-x[…] (24′)[…]-*iš* IGI-*zi-iš* UD-*az* LÚSANGA […] (25′)[…]*ḫu-u-ma-an-ti-iš* *wa-ar-p*[*a-an-zi* …] (26′)[…]x 1 GA SISKUR *pé-e*[*š-kán-zi* …]

(gap of indeterminate length)

§5″ (B rev.? 1′–3′) (1′)[…]⸢*Ú-UL*⸣ *ḫal-zi*-x[…] (2′)[…]x LÚDUB.SAR.GIŠ-*ia*[…] (3′)[…]x-*an-zi* *šu-u*[*m*?- …]

§4′ (22′)[…] as soon as […] to the Storm God of Neri[k …] (23′)[…] and the [thick b]read […] *tying down* […] (24′)[…] the first day, the priest […] (25′)[…] everyone wash[es …] (26′)[… they] give one milk offering. […]

(gap of indeterminate length)

§5″ (1′)[…] not cry out […] (2′)[…] and a scribe for wooden writing boards […] (3′)[…] they […]

No. 25
Instructions for the UKU.UŠ-Troops (*CTH* 267)

This NH fragment, which may perhaps be based on older texts,[21] preserves only a few lines of a king's instructions to military personnel, in the preserved passages the UKU.UŠ-troops.[22] The text shows some similarities to No. 17, the Instructions for the Frontier Post Governors,[23] but a more precise attribution remains difficult. The emphasis of the single preserved passage seems to be that the UKU.UŠ-troops, apparently a higher level military category (see Beal 1992: 43–44, n. 172), take part in labor duties alongside the regular soldiers. No findspot is known.

Transliteration

§1′ (entirely lost)

§2′ (1′)[...]x *ku-iš-ki* (2′)[...] É.GAL-*LÌ* (3′)[...] É.GAL-*LÌ-ia-aš-kán* (4′)[...]-*in le-e ku-iš-ki* (5′)[...]x x x x x [*ka-r*]*u-ú an-tu-u-ri-ia-aš* KIN (6′)[...] *ḫu-up-pí-da-nu-uš* PA$_5$$^{\text{ḪI.A}}$ [24] *da-aš-ket$_9$-tén* *x* ^{GIŠ}*ti-i-e-eš-šar-ra* (7′)[... *ku-it*] *im-ma ku-it* KIN[25] *ša-ra-a wa-at-ku-uš-ke-et-ta* (8′)[... -*a*]*t-tén-pát ki-nu-na tu-uk A-NA* ÉRIN^{MEŠ} UKU.<UŠ>[26] *ki-iš-ša-an* (9′)[... -*m*]*a*? *ma-a-an* ^{d}UTU-*ŠI ku-wa-pí ḫa-an-te-ez-zi a-ú-ri-ia* URU-*an* (10′)[... *šu-m*]*eš-ša*[27] ÉRIN^{MEŠ} UKU.UŠ ÉRIN^{MEŠ}-*ti an-da* KIN-*an ú-e-te-eš-ke-te-ni* (11′)[...]x *ku-wa-pí* URU-*an tu-zi-it ú-e-da-an-zi* (12′)[... *šu-meš-ša* ÉRIN^{MEŠ} UK]U.UŠ ÉRIN^{MEŠ}-*ti an-da* KIN-*an ú-e-te-eš-ke-ta-ni* (13′)[... *ku-w*]*a*?-*pí an-dur-za* *x* *I-NA* ŠÀ.BI KUR ^{URU}*ḪA.AT.TI* KIN-*ti* (14′)[... *t*]*i-ia-an-na na-aš-ma* *x* PA$_5$ (15′)[...]x KIN-*az nu-uš-ma-aš* ^{d}UTU-*ŠI* (16′)[...]x *a-ni-ia-at-te-e-ni*

TRANSLATION

§1′ (entirely lost)

§2′ (1′)[…] whoever (2′)[…] the palace (3′)[…] s/he/them […] the palace (4′)[…] no one shall (5′)[… ear]lier […] the interior work (6′)[…] you(pl.) shall "take" *ḫuppidanu-* (*and*) canals. The forest, too, (7′)[… wha]tever work "springs up." (8′)You(pl.) shall indeed […]![28] But now to you(sg.), to the UKU.UŠ-troops, thus (9′)[…]: If My Majesty ever/somewhere […] a town by/for a frontier post (10′)[…, yo]u UKU.<UŠ>-troops, too, will carry out the construction work for/with the soldiers (11′)[…] ever/somewhere they construct a town employing the army, (12′)[… you UK]U.UŠ-[troops, too], will carry out the construction work for/with the soldiers. (13′)[… *ev*]*er/some*]*where* […] to/for work within the Land of Ḫattusa (14′)[…] to place or […] a canal (15′)[…] is work, and for you/them My Majesty (16′)[…] you(pl.) will work […]

No. 26

Tudḫaliya IV's Instructions and Loyalty Oath Imposition for Lords, Princes, and Courtiers (*CTH* 255.1)

This composition is represented by one substantial block of fragments (A) and two smallish fragments (B–C). No findspot for any tablet or fragment of No. 26 is known, while two small fragments of the closely related No. 27 (F, G) were found in the Temple I complex. The format of ms. A of the present text is of special interest, as it would seem to be a *Sammeltafel* of sorts (Giorgieri 1995: 49, 274; Hawkins 2002: 221). The first twenty paragraphs (up to A iii 35), in which the courtiers do not appear at all, are addressed to the lords and princes, after which a double paragraph divider is found. The remainder of the composition is addressed to the courtiers, princes, and lords (for "courtiers" rather than "eunuchs," see the introduction to No. 27). Unfortunately, since the text breaks off almost immediately following the double paragraph divider before resuming again in col. iv, the transition between the two is not entirely clear. That said, the fact that the upper portion of C i duplicates the upper portion of A iv (§§23″–24″) suggests that there was likely at least one tablet preceding C, so that the composition would have been at least two tablets long. If so, then the preserved text would constitute about one third of the original composition(s) at most.

In any case, as with No. 27, the prevailing theme of this composition is undivided loyalty toward Tudḫaliya as opposed to any pretender to the throne, whereby the "many brothers" and descendents of Tudḫaliya's royal predecessors are mentioned specifically (§§3′–5′, 9″, 24″). The rest of the document, for the most part in the 2nd pl., consists in further defining exactly how the subjects' loyalty is to be expressed in a series of conceivable situations, whereby the stipulations can be said to be the most demanding of the corpus vis-à-vis its subordinates. Again, like No. 27, it occasionally attempts to anticipate treasonous thinking and/or utterances and to argue against and forbid them (§§3′,

---

Transliteration

(first ca. one-third of col. i missing entirely)

§1′ (A i 1′–3′; B i 1′–3′) (1′)[…]x x x x-*kán* x x x x[…] (2′)[(*A-NA MA-ME-TU*$_4$ x) …]x *me-ma-ú* (3′)[(*ku-iš-ma-at Ú-U*)*L* *me-ma*]-*i* GAM-*an* *NI-ÌŠ* DINGIR-*LÌ* GAR-*ru*

4′, 9″, 12″, 15″, 16″, 20″?, 27″, 28″?). Several of these attempts seem to demonstrate that Tudḫaliya must have been haunted by the suspicion that many within his innermost circle would have realized what he clearly knew himself, i.e., that one could easily argue that the "rightful" king, Kuruntiya, resided in Tarḫuntassa, not in Ḫattusa. He seems, moreover, to have been wary of his own brothers, too, or at least of the potential for his courtiers to prefer one of them for the throne, since the "progeny of Ḫattusili as well as the brothers of My Majesty born of the queen" (§§3′, 5′, 9″, 24″) are noted among his latent rivals. Brothers of other wives are mentioned as well (§§4′, 5′, 9″, 24″).

It has often been noted (e.g., Liverani 2001: 130–31) that Tudḫaliya IV was with documents such as this demanding of his subordinates precisely the kind of loyalty that would have precluded his reign as king (e.g., No. 26, §3′). That is to say, if the courtiers and other grandees of Mursili III / Urḫi-Teššub had behaved as Tudḫaliya demands with this composition, they never would have permitted Tudḫaliya's father, Ḫattusili III, to dethrone their lord. At the same time, Tudḫaliya demands explicitly that his subordinates discard any oath they are obliged to swear to anyone else, remaining loyal only to him (§24″), a remarkably explicit endorsement of duplicity.

In fact, in his vassal treaty for Šaušgamuwa of Amurru, Tudḫaliya IV condemns a certain Masturi for siding with his own father, Ḫattusili III, following his coup d'état against his nephew, Mursili III/Urḫi-Teššub, the "rightful" king and son of Muwattalli II (KUB 23.1++ ii 15–30):

> You shall not behave like Masturi: Muwattalli took Masturi, who was king of the land of the Seḫa River, and made him his brother-in-law, giving him his sister Massanuzzi in marriage. And he made him king in the land of the Seḫa River. But when Muwattalli died, then Urḫi-Teššub, son of Muwattalli, became King. [My father] wrested the kingship away from Urḫi-Teššub. Masturi committed treachery. Although it was Muwattalli who had taken him up and had made him his brother-in-law, afterwards Masturi did not protect his son Urḫi-Teššub, but went over to my father.... Will you perhaps behave like Masturi? (trans. Beckman 1999: 105)

TRANSLATION

(first ca. one-third of col. i missing entirely)

§1′ (2′)[(to/for the oath) ...] he shall tell/say. (3′)[(Whoever does no)t te]ll/[s]ay [(it, though)], (it) shall be placed under oath.

§2′ (A i 4′–10′; B i 4′–11′) (4′)[(nam-ma-aš-ma-aš šu-um-m)e-eš k]u-i-e-eš BE-LUḪI.A KARAŠḪI.A (5′)[(Ú-UL-ia ku-i-e-eš B)E-LUḪI.A K]ARAŠḪI.A ku-[i]š-⸤ša⸥ GAL-iš (6′)[(ku-iš-ma Ú-UL nu A-NA) dU]TU-ŠI ku-it-ki ˹na-ak-ke-eš˺-zi (7′)[(šu-um-me-eš-ma Ú-UL wa-a)]r-re-eš-ša-at-te-ni (8′)˹na-aš-ma˺-a[(š-ši šu-um-me-eš) k]u-i-e-eš MÁŠ LUGAL nu-uš-ši-ká[(n ḫ)]u-u-da-ak (9′)Ú-UL e-er-te-n[i (nu-uš-ši-k)]án pa-ra-a a-ut-te-ni (10′)nu-uš-ma-aš a-pa-a-aš me-m[(i)]-aš GAM NI-IŠ DINGIR-LÌ GAR-ru

§3′ (A i 11′–21′; B i 12′–20′) (11′)[(na)]m-ma-ia ku-i-e-eš NUMUN LUG[(AL-UT-T)I NUM]UN mMUR.ŠI-DINGIR-LÌ NUMUN mNIR.GÁL (12′)NUMUN mḪA.AT.⸤TU⸥.ŠI-DINGIR-LÌ ŠEŠMEŠ dUTU-ŠI-ia ku-i-e-eš (13′)[(I)]Š-TU MUNUS.LUGAL ḫa-aš-ša-an-te-eš nu šu-um-ma-aš BE-LUḪI.A a-p[a]-⸤a-at⸥ (14′)[k]u-wa-at-ka$_4$ ku-iš-ki me-ma-i DUMUMEŠ ENMEŠ-ia-wa-an-n[a-aš] (15′)[a]n-⸤da⸥ Ú-UL im-ma NUMUN EN-IA nu-wa-an-na-aš ke-e-da-n[i] (16′)[(GIM)]-an še-er li-in-ga-nu-uš-ke-er ke-e-da-ni-ia-w[(a-an-na)-aš] (17′)[QA-T]AM-MA še-er li-in-⸤ga⸥-nu-uš-kán-zi nu-wa-an-na-aš ka-⸤a⸥-[(aš)] (18′)[(E)N]-aš-pát na-at-ši GAM ˹NI-IŠ˺ DINGIR-LÌ GAR-ru dUTU-ŠI PAB-aš-tén (19′)[kat-t]a-ma NUM[UN] dUTU-ŠI pa-aḫ-˹ḫa˺-aš-tén ta-˹me-e-da˺-ma (20′)[le]-⸤e ku⸥-iš-[k]i a-uš-zi ku-iš-⸤ma-za ta-ma⸥-i (21′)[EN-U]T-⸤TA i⸥-la-li-ia-zi na-at GAM NI-IŠ DINGIR-LÌ GAR-ru

§4′ (A i 22′–26′) (22′)˹na-aš-ma-aš-ma˺-aš ŠEŠ dUTU-ŠI ḫa-aš-ša-an-za (23′)˹na-aš-ma DUMU˺ *MUNUS*NAP-ṬÍR-TI ku-iš-ki a-pa-a-at me-ma-i (24′)am-mu-uk-⸤ka$_4$⸥[29]-wa-za Ú-UL DUMU *x* EN-KA nu-wa am-mu-uk (25′)PAB-aš-tén na-˹at ku˺-iš iš-ta-ma-aš-zi na-at mu-un-na-iz-zi (26′)[na-a]t I-NA É.GAL-LÌ UL me-ma-i na-at-ši-at!(AB) NI-IŠ DINGIR-LÌ GAM GAR-r[u]

§5′ (A i 27′–32′; C iv 1′–2′) (27′)[na-aš]-˹ma˺-kán ŠA dUTU-ŠI ḪUL-lu ŠEŠ dUTU-ŠI ku-iš-ki (28′)[MUNUS.LUGA]L[30] ḫa-aš-ša-an-za na-aš-ma ŠEŠ DUMUMEŠ MUNUSNAP-ṬÍR-TI (29′)[k]u-˹iš˺-ki na-aš-ma BE-LU ku-iš-ki ku-e-da-ni-ik-ki (30′)GAM-an ḫar-zi na-at ša-ak-ki!(DI)[31] ke-e-da-ni-ma-za-kán (31′)⸤A-NA⸥ NI-IŠ DINGIR-LÌ pa-ri-ia-an Ú-UL me-ma-i (32′)[na-at-š]i a-pád-da-ia GAM NI-IŠ DINGIR-LÌ GAR-ru

§6′ (A i 33′–35′) (33′)[na-a]š-ma-aš-ma-aš EGIR-zi-az iš-ta-ma-aš-zi ku-iš-ki (34′)[k]u-it-ki I-NA É.GAL-LÌ-ma-at Ú-UL me-ma-i (35′)nu-uš-ši a-pád-da-ia NI-IŠ DINGIR-LÌ GAM-an GAR-ru

§7′ (A i 36′–40′) (36′)AŠ-ŠUM EN-UT-TI dUTU-ŠI pa-aḫ-ḫa-aš-tén kat-ta-ma NUMUN dUTU-ŠI (37′)pa-aḫ-ḫa-aš-tén da$_4$-me-e-da-ma le-e a-ut-*te*-ni (38′)ta-ma-a-i-<ša>-ma-aš[32] EN-UT-TA le-e i-la-li-ia-at-te-ni (39′)[k]u-⸤iš⸥-ma-⸤za⸥ i-la-li-ia-zi na-aš-ši kat-ta-an (40′)NI-IŠ DINGIR-LÌ ki-it-ta-ru

§2′ (4′)[(Further, yo)u[33] w]ho are field commanders (5′)[(as well as those who)] are [(not) f]ield [(co)mmanders], and he who is a grandee, (6′)[(but also he who is not)]; (if)[34] something becomes too difficult [(for) My Maj]esty, (7′)[(but you do not ru)]sh to (my) aid; (8′–9′)or [(you) w]ho are royal family [(to him)], you do not come to him [(im)]mediately, [(and)] you ignore [(him)], (10′)then that matter shall be placed under oath for you.

§3′ (11′)[(Fur)]ther, (concerning) whatever progeny of the kin[(gshi)p] there is, (i.e.,) [prog]eny of Mursili, progeny of Muwattalli (and) (12′)progeny of Ḫattusili, as well as the brothers of My Majesty (13′–14′)born [(o)]f the queen; (if) [p]erhaps someone tells you lords this: "Are the sons of the lords among u[s] (15′–17′)not progeny of my lord as well?[35] So [(just li)]ke they swore each of [(u)s] to this (man), they will [lik]ewise swear each of us to that (man), too (in this way): 'Th[(is)] is our (18′)only [(lo)rd].'" Then that shall be placed under oath for him. You must protect My Majesty, (19′–20′)and [aft]er (me) you must protect the prog[eny] of My Majesty. [N]o one shall seek someone else. He who does wish for another (21′)[lords]hip, it shall be placed under oath (for him).

§4′ (22′–23′)Or (if) a brother of My Majesty, born (of the queen) or some son of a secondary wife says this to you: (24′–25′)"Am I not also a son of your(sg.) lord? Then support me!" He who hears this, and conceals it, (26′)[and] does not report it in the palace, it shall be placed under oath for him.

§5′ (27′–30′)[O]r (if) some brother of My Majesty, born of the [quee]n, or [s]ome brother, (i.e.,) sons of a secondary wife, or some lord proposes[36] the ruin of My Majesty to someone, and *he* knows of it, (31′)but he does not divulge (it) over this oath,[37] (32′)[then] also for this reason[38] shall [it] be placed under oath for [hi]m.

§6′ (33′–34′)[O]r if any one of you hears [an]ything afterwards, but he does not report it in the palace, (35′)then also for this reason shall (it) be placed under oath for him.

§7′ (36′–37′)For the lordship you shall support My Majesty, and after (me) you shall support the progeny of My Majesty. You shall not seek someone else, (38′)you shall not wish another lordship for <you>rselves. (39′–40′)He who wishes for (it), it shall be placed under oath for him.

(gap of ca. one-third of a col.)

§8″ (traces)

§9″ (A ii 2′–11′) (2′)*na-aš-ma-kán* x[…] (3′)*na-aš-ma* ŠEŠ ^{d}[UTU-*ŠI* MUNUS.LUGA]L *ḫ*[*a-aš-ša-an-za na-aš-ma*] (4′)ŠEŠ^{MEŠ} DUMU^{MEŠ} ^{MUNUS}*NA*[P-*TÍ*]*R*-⸢*TI an*⸣*-da i*[*š-ta-ma-aš-* …][39] (5′)*nu ki-i me-ma-i* EGIR-*an-wa-mu ti-*[*ia~* …] (6′)*a-pa-a-aš-ma a-pa-a-at me-ma-i* EGIR-*a*[*n-wa-*…] (7′)*Ú-UL ti-ia-mi ḫa-an-ti-ia-wa-aš-ši-*[*kán*][40] (8′)*Ú-UL ti-ia-mi* ⸗ *ḫu-uḫ-ḫu-pa-aš-ša-*[*wa-aš-ši Ú-U*]*L* (9′)*kiš-ḫa-ḫa-ri nu ku-iš I-NA* É.G[AL-*LÌ Ú-UL me-m*]*a-i* (10′)*ku-iš a-pa-a-at i-ia-zi* {**na-an**} […]x (11′)*n*[*a*]*-an-kán ku-u-uš* DINGIR^{MEŠ} *ḫar-ga-nu-a*[*n-du*]

§10″ (A ii 12′–22′) (12′)[*n*]*am-ma-aš-ma-aš šu-me-e-eš ku-i-e-eš BE-LU*$^{HI.A}$ (13′) [*ḫ*]*a-an-te-zi-*<*uš*> *a-ú-ri-uš ma-ni-ia-aḫ-ḫi-iš-ket*$_9$*-te-ni* (14′)*IŠ-TU* KUR ^{URU}*AZ.ZI* KUR ^{URU}*GA.AŠ.GA* (15′)*IŠ-TU* KUR ^{URU}*LU.UK.KA*$_4$*.A nu* ZAG *še-ek-kán-te-et* (16′)ZI-*it an-da le-e ku-iš-ki za-a-ḫi ar-ru-*⸢*ša*⸣ (17′)*pa-a-u-wa-*⸢*ar*⸣ *ša-an-aḫ-zi le-e ku-iš-ki* (18′)*na-aš-ma-kán wa-aš-du-la-aš* UN-*aš* EGIR-*pa an-da* (19′)*ú-ez-zi na-an-za-an-kán an-da tar-na-ti* (20′)*na-aš-ma-za-an-kán a-wa-an ar-ḫa tar-na-at-ti* (21′)*na-aš da-me-e-da-ni* KUR-*e ŠA* ^{LÚ}KÚR *pa-iz-zi* (22′)*na-an-kán ku-u-uš* DINGIR^{MEŠ} *ar-ḫa ḫar-ni-in-kán-du*

§11″ (A ii 23′–28′) (23′)*na-aš-ma-kán A-NA* ^{d}UTU-*ŠI ku-iš-ki wa-at-ku-wa-an-za* (24′)[*n*]*a-aš-kán A-NA* ZAG *ku-e-da-ni-ik-ki an-da* (25′)[*š*]*u-me-e-eš-ša-aš a-aš-šu-*⸢*uš*⸣ *ku-e-da-ni-ik-ki* (26′)*nu-*⸢*uš-ši-kán me-mi-an*⸣ GAM-*an ar-ḫa wa-*⸢*tar-na*⸣*-aḫ-zi* (27′)*nu* ⸢*a*⸣*-pa-a-an* ZAG-*na da-a-i* ^{d}UTU-*ŠI-ma* GÙB-⸢*la da-a-i*⸣ (28′)*na-an-kán ku-u-uš* DINGIR^{MEŠ} *ḫar-ni-in-kán-du*!(GÁN)

§12″ (A ii 29′–36′) (29′)*nam-*⸢*ma*⸣ *a-pa-a-at ku-it e-eš-ša-at-te-*⸢*en*$_6$⸣[41] *nu* KUR.KUR$^{HI.A}$ (30′)BA[L *d*]*a-pí-an-da* 1-*e-et*!(DA)*-ta na-iš-ke-et-tén* (31′)*nu* K[UR.KUR]$^{HI.A}$ ^{LÚ}KÚR *da-aš-ša-nu-uš-ke-et-tén* (32′)KUR.KUR ⸢^{URU}⸣*ḪA.AT.TI-ma ma-li-iš-ku-nu-ut-tén* (33′)*nu a-pa-a-at me-mi-iš-ket*$_9$*-te-ni ma-a-an-wa-an-na-aš* (34′)*na-ak-ke-eš-zi nu-wa-kán a-pé-e-da-ni* EGIR-⸢*an-da*⸣ (35′) *ti-ia-u-e-ni na-at ku-iš i-ia-zi* (36′)*na-a*[*t-š*]*i-ia-at* GAM-*an NI-ÌŠ* DINGIR-*LÌ* GAR-*ru*

§13″ (A ii 37′–iii 2) (37′)*na*[*m*?*-ma-i*]*a-za* UN-*an ŠA MA-ME-TI le-e* x[ ]-⸢*tu*?⸣-[ ] (38′)A[N? … *n*]*am-ma PA-NI A-BI* ^{d}UTU-*ŠI ku-it* x[ ] (39′)T[I? … -*a*]*t*?*-tén nu-za* EN LUGAL 1-*aš* 1-*e-da-*[*ni*] (40′)x[…]-*ke-et ki-nu-un-*⸢*ma*⸣-x[ ][42] (iii 1)*le-*⸢*e*⸣[… *k*]*u*?-⸢*iš*?⸣*-k*[*i*? …] (2)*ku-i*[*š-m*]*a-at* DÙ-*zi na-at* GAM-*an N*[*I-ÌŠ* DINGIR-*LÌ* GAR-*ru*]

(gap of ca. one-third of a col.)

§8″ (traces)

§9″ (2′–4′)Or (if) […] or […] l[isten(s)] to a brother of M[y Majesty], b[orn of the quee]n, [or] brothers, (i.e.,) sons of seconda[ry w]ives, (5′)and he say this: “St[and] behind me!” (6′–9′)But that man says this: “I will not stand behind […], but neither will I stand against him, [no]r will I be(come) *ḫuḫḫupa* [to him].” He who does [not[43] rep]ort (it) in the pal[ace], (10′)he who does that, (11′)m[ay] these gods destroy him.

§10″ (12′–13′)[F]urther, whoever of you lords who command the fronti<er> posts[44] (14′)opposite the land of Azzi, opposite the land of Gasga (or) (15′–17′)opposite the land of Lukka, no one shall knowingly violate the border; no one shall attempt going *arrusa*.[45] (18′–19′)Or (if) a malefactor (seeks to) reenter, and you(sg.) let him in, (20′)or you(sg.) even let him go on his way, (21′)and he goes into another enemy land, (22′)then may these gods completely destroy him.[46]

§11″ (23′)Or (if) someone has escaped from My Majesty, (24′)[an]d he is in some border region, (25′)and he is on good terms with any one of [y]ou, (26′)and he divulges the matter to him, (27′)and he acclaims that (man), though he denigrates My Majesty,[47] (28′)then may these gods destroy him.

§12″ (29′–30′)Further, what (will) you have done (thereby)?[48] You (will) have united all the reb[el] lands into one, (31′)and you (will) have made the enemy l[and]s strong, (32′)while you (will) have made the lands of Ḫattusa weak; (33′–35′)and (if) you say this: “If it gets difficult for us, we will stand behind that (man).” Whoever does this, (36′)it shall be placed under oath for him.

§13″ (37′–40′)An[d furth]er, […] shall not […] a man of the oath. [Mo]reover, because you(pl.) […]-ed before the father of My Majesty, and he […]-ed […] as one lord of the king to the oth[er]; but now (iii 1)[n]o on[e] shall […]. (2)Whoe[ver] does that, it [shall be placed] under o[ath].

§14″ (A iii 3–6) (3)*na-aš-ma-za ku-i-e-eš* EN^{MEŠ} DUMU^{MEŠ} LUGAL-*ia nu-za* (4)*ŠA MA-ME-TI le-e ku-iš-ki ku-e-da-ni-ik-k*[*i*] (5)*ki-ša-ri* [*k*]*u-iš-ma-za ŠA MA-ME-TI ku-e-*˻*da-ni-ik*?˼*-*[*ki*?][49] (6)*ki-ša-ri na-at* GAM-*an NI-ÌŠ* DINGIR-*LÌ* GAR-*ru*

§15″ (A iii 7–12) (7)*na-aš-ma ki-i ku-iš-ki* DÙ-*zi na-aš-šu BE-LU* (8)*na-aš-ma* DUMU LUGAL *na-aš-ma* ŠÀ.MÁŠ *na-aš-ma* ŠÀ x[ ]x$^{\text{HI?.A?}}$[50] (9)*ku-iš-ki*[51] EME-*an* BAL-*nu-zi* ḪUL-*u-e-eš-ta-*˹*wa*?˺*-ra-*˹*aš*?˺[52] (10)*nu-wa-*˹*kán*˺ *e-ḫu ta-me-e-da-ni an-da ti-ia-u-*˻*e*˼*-ni* (11)*me-ma-i-ma-at* [*k*]*u-*˻*e-da*˼*-ni na-an-kán ḫa-an-ti-i* (12)*Ú-UL ti-ia-*˹*zi*˺ [GAM *NI-Ì*]*Š* [DI]NGIR-*LÌ* GAR-*ru*

§16″ (A iii 13–20) (13)*na-aš-ma šu-me-e-eš ku-i-*˹*e*˺*-*[*e*]*š BE-LU*$^{\text{ḪI.A}}$ DUMU^{MEŠ} LUGAL (14)*ma-ni-ia-aḫ-ḫi-ìš-ket₉-te-ni* [*n*]*u* ˻*A-NA*˼ $^{\text{LÚ.MEŠ}}$*MU-IR-TU₄* (15)*ku-e-el-ka₄ ša-aḫ-ḫa-na-za* ḪUL-˹*lu*˺*-u-e-*˻*eš-zi*˼ (16)*a-pa-a-aš-ma a-pa-a-*˻*at*˼ *me-ma-i A-NA* ^{d}UTU-*ŠI-wa* (17)*me-mi-iš-ke-mi nu-wa-mu Ú-*˻*UL*˼ *iš-da₄-ma-aš-zi* (18)*nu-wa-za zi-ik a-aš-šu-uš ḫal-zi-ia-at-ta-ri* (19)˻^{d}˼UTU-*ŠI-ma-wa-kán* ˻ḪUL˼*-u-an-ni* *GAM* *ma-ni-ia-aḫ-zi*[53] (20)˻*na-at*˼ GAM-*an NI-ÌŠ* DINGIR-*LÌ* GAR-*ru*

§17″ (A iii 21–23) (21)*n*[*a-aš-m*]*a* ^{d}UTU-*ŠI ku-in-ki* [S]IG₅*-aḫ-mi* (22)*z*[*i-i*]*k-ka₄-an-za-an tu-e-el aš-šu-la-an* (23)[*ḫal*]*-*˹*zi-ia*˺*-ši na-at* GAM-*an NI-ÌŠ* DINGIR-*LÌ* GAR-*ru*

§18″ (A iii 24–28) (24)[*na-aš*]*-*˻*ma*˼ *šu-me-e-eš ku-i-e-eš BE-LU*$^{\text{ḪI.A}}$ DUMU^{MEŠ} LUGAL (25)[*nu A-N*]*A* ^{d}UTU-*ŠI ku-iš-ki a-aš-šu-uš na-aš A-NA* ˹LUGAL?*-i*?˺[54] (26)[*ša-ku-w*]*a-aš-šar-it* ZI-*it ar-ta-ri* (27)[*ku-iš-ma-a*]*n*[55] *A-NA* LUGAL *pu-uk-ka₄-nu-zi* (28)*n*[*a-at* GAM-*a*]*n NI-ÌŠ* DINGIR-*LÌ* GAR-*ru*

§19″ (A iii 29–31) (29) ^{d}[UTU-*ŠI ku-wa-p*]*í A-NA PU-UḪ-RI ḫal-zi-aḫ-ḫi* (30)GI[M-*an* ...]x-*li ku-iš-ki ti-ia-zi* (31)*na-*[*at-ši* GAM-*an NI*]*-ÌŠ* DINGIR-*LÌ* GAR-*ru*

§20″ (A iii 32–35) (32)*na-*[*aš-ma ki-i ku-i*]*š-ki me-ma-i* **ki-i-wa-za-*˻*kán*˼ *ku-wa-pí** (33)*na-*[…]x*-uš ku-iš-ki ku-e-da-*˹*ni-ik*˺*-k*[*i*] (34)[…]x *na-aš-ma-za-***at** *ar-ḫa* (35)[… *na-a*]*t* GAM *NI-ÌŠ* DINGIR-*LÌ* GAR-*ru*

§21″ (A iii 36–39) (36)[…]˻LÚ˼^{MEŠ} SAG^{MEŠ} *nu-uš-ma-aš-z*[*a*?] (37)[… N]Í?.˻TE?˼^{MEŠ} *šu-me-e-e*[*š*~…] (38)[…]x-*tén* GAM-*an* x[…] (39)[…]x[…]

(gap of ca. one-third of a column)

§22″ (A iv 1–2) (iv 1)[…*-a*]*n-na iš-ta-ma-aš-zi* (2)[*A-NA* LUGAL-*ma Ú-UL me-ma-i* G]AM-*an NI-ÌŠ* DINGIR-*LÌ* GAR-*ru*

§23″ (A iv 3–15; C i 1–4) (3)*n*[*a-aš-m*]*a-kán*[56] ŠÀ É.ŠÀ *ŠA* LUGAL GÙB-*an ut-tar ku-it-ki* (4)˹*a-ut-te*˺*-ni šu-me-eš-ša pa-ra-a ku-e-da-ni-ik-ki me-ma-te-ni*

§14″ (3–6)Or you who are lords and princes; no one shall pledge allegiance to anyo[ne] (else). He who does pledge allegiance to whomev[er] (else), that shall be placed under oath.

§15″ (7)Or (if) someone does this, be it a lord (8)or a prince or a family member or [...]members, (9)whoever twists words[57] (thus): "*He* has become evil. (10)So come and let us *collaborate* with someone else!" (11–12)Whoever does not denounce a person who has told him such a thing,[58] (it) shall be placed [under oa]th.

§16″ (13)Or you lords (and) princes who (14–15)carry out the administration: (if) it becomes dire for the *administrators*[59] due to someone's *saḫḫan*-levy, (16–17)but that (man)[60] says this: "I keep reporting it to His Majesty, but he does not listen to me. (18)You *can call yourself good*, (19)but His Majesty *is administering poorly*!"[61] (20)Then that shall be placed under oath.

§17″ (21)O[r] (if) I, My Majesty, [pr]omote someone, (22–23)and y[o]u(sg.) [ca]ll it!(text: him)[62] your(sg.) own benevolence, then that shall be placed under oath.

§18″ (24)[O]r you who are lords (and) princes: (25–26)(If) someone is dear [t]o My Majesty, and he stands *by the king* [whol]eheartedly, (27)[then whoever] makes [hi]m despised by the king, (28)[that] shall be placed [unde]r oath.

§19″ (29)[Whe]n I, [My Majesty], call together the assembly, (30)as s[oon as] someone steps [...], (31)then [that] shall be placed [under oa]th [for him].

§20″ (32)O[r] (if) [some]one says [this]: "When/Where this [...] (33)[...] someone to someone [...]," (34)[...] or it away, (35)[then i]t shall be placed under oath.

§21″ (36)[...] courtiers, and (to) them/you (37)[... *bo*]*dies* you (38)you shall [...] under/with [...].

(gap of ca. one-third of a col.)

§22″ (1)[...] and [...] he hears [...],(2)[but he does not report it to the king], (it) shall be placed [un]der oath.

§23″ (3–4)O[r] (if) you observe some inopportune matter in the king's inner chamber, and you divulge (it) to someone; (5–6)or a colleague hears an

(5)[n]a-aš-ma-kán LÚa-ra-aš a-ri ŠA LUGAL GÙB-an ut-tar (6)⌜x⌝ ku-gur-ni-ia-ma-an an-da iš-ta-ma-aš-zi (7)A-NA LUGAL-ma-at Ú-UL me-ma-i na-aš-ma!(DAG)-kán[63] LUGAL pa-ra-a (8)ku-e-da-ni-ik-ki wa-tar-na-aḫ-zi ŠA LUGAL ut-tar (9)wa-*aḫ-nu*-zi ta-ma-a-i-in me-mi-an me-ma-i (10)na-aš-ma-za LUGAL-uš ŠA ZI-*TI* me-mi-an ku-e-da-ni-ik-ki (11)a-wa-an GAM me-ma-i ma-a-an-na LUGAL LÚ SAG ku-in-ki (12)A-NA ZAG KUR a-ra-aḫ-zé-na-<aš> LUGAL-i u-i-ia-zi (13)a-pa-a-aš-ma-kán INIMMEŠ LUGAL wa-aḫ-nu-zi na-<aš-ma>-*at!* ta-me-*da* <(me-ma-i)>[64] (14)na-aš-ma-za ŠA LUGAL NÍ.TE pa-ra-a me-mi-ia-u-an-zi (15)*me-ma-i x*[65] ŠA-PAL ME-ME-⌜TU_4⌝[66]

§24″ (A iv 16–32; C i 5–10) (16)ŠEŠMEŠ dUTU-ŠI-ia ku-i-e-eš ša-ku-wa-aš-ša-ra[67] ŠA MUNUS.LUGAL (17)a-wa-an GAM ḫa-aš-ša-an-te-eš ŠA A-BI dUTU-ŠI-ia ku-i-e-eš (18)DUMU*MEŠ MUNUS*NAP-ṬÍR-TI nu-uš-ma-ša-aš le-e še-ek-te-ni {*UTU-ŠI x*} (19) dUTU-ŠI-pát AŠ-ŠUM EN-UT-TI GAM-ma-aš-ši DUMUMEŠ-ŠÚ DUMU.*DUMU*MEŠ-ŠÚ PAB-aš-tén (20)A-NA ŠEŠMEŠ dUTU-ŠI-ia-aš-ma-aš ku-e-el še-er ˻li˼-in-˻ga˼-nu-zi (21)nu a-pu-u-un MA-ME-TU_4 ar-ḫa pé-eš-ši-ia-at-tén ⌜nu dUTU-ŠI-pát⌝ (22)DUMUMEŠ dUTU-ŠI-ia AŠ-ŠUM EN-UT-TI PAB-aš-tén na-aš-ma ˻ke-e-el˼ (23)ŠA ŠEŠMEŠ dUTU-ŠI ḫa-aš-ša-an-te-eš na-aš-ma DUMU MUNUS⌜NAP-ṬÍR-TI⌝ (24)m[e]-mi-an GÙB-an!(TAR) ku-in!(IŠ)-ki DÙ-an <ḫar-zi> MUD na-aš-ma BAL (25)[na]-aš-ma ku-in-<ki> me-mi-an GÙB-an a-wa-an GAM I!-DE (26)[na-a]š-ma-za DUMU LUGAL ku-iš-ki GÙB-an ut-tar A-NA LÚ SAG (27)[a-w]a-an GAM me-ma-i na-aš-ma-at-ta ka-ru-ú-ia (28) [me-m]a-an[68] ḫar-zi A-NA LUGAL-ma-at Ú-UL me-ma-at-te-ni (29)[na-aš]-ma LÚ SAG ku-in-ki DUMU LUGAL ŠEŠ LUGAL ku-˻iš˼-ki (30)[LÚa-r]a-an DÙ-zi! nu-uš-ši ŠA LUGAL ku-it-ki ḪUL-lu (31)[ut-tar[69] GÙ]B-tar pa-ra-a me-ma-i A-NA LUGAL-ma-˻at˼ Ú-UL (32)[me-ma]-˻i˼ ŠA-PAL MA-MI-TU_4

§25″ (A iv 33–37; B iv 1′–5′) (33)[na-aš-m]a-aš-ma-aš šu-me-eš ku-i-e-eš ⌜LÚ⌝MEŠ SAG A-NA LUGAL-kán (34)[NÍ.TE-Š]U?-i[70] šu-up-pa-i ša-˻li-kiš˼-ket_9-te-ni nu-uš-ma-aš šu-up-pé-eš-ni (35)[x x x]-da[71] ti-iš-ḫa~⌜an-te⌝-eš e-eš-tén ma-a-an-na-kán A-NA LÚ SAG (36)[ku-e]-da-ni-ik-ki ḪUL-lu-uš mar-ša-aš-tar-ri-iš (37)[a-p]a-a-aš-ša[72] A-NA LUGAL NÍ.TEMEŠ-ŠÚ ša-li-ga-i GAM MA-MI-TI

§26″ (A iv 38–42; B iv 6′–11′) (38) dUTU-ŠI-ia ku-i-e-eš EGIR-pa SUM-an ḫar-zi nu-za ma-a-an EGIR-pa (39)SUM-an-tan_x(DIN) ku-iš-ki TI-tar i-la-li-ia-zi [(n)]a-aš-ma-an-za-an (40)ar-ḫa wa-at-ku-wa-ar i-la-li-ia-zi [(na-a)š-ma-(aš)]-ši ˻LÚṬE-MU˼ (41)ku-iš-ki u-i-ia-zi a-pa-a-aš-ma-a[n (an-da) m(u-un-na-iz-zi)] (42)A-NA LUGAL-ma-an Ú-UL me-ma-i GAM-a[(n NI-ÌŠ DINGIR-LÌ GAR-ru)]

evil thing, (i.e.,) *calumny*, concerning the king from a(nother) colleague, (7)but he does not report it to the king; or the king (8–9)gives someone an order, (but) he twists the king's word (and) he tells another tale; (10–12)or the king entrusts a personal matter to someone, and if the king sends some courtier to the king <of> a neighboring land, (13)but he twists the words of the king, o<r> he <(tells)> them to someone else, (14–15)or he begins to inform (him) about the king's person: under the oath.

§24″ (16–18)And you shall not recognize My Majesty's full brothers,[73] born of the queen subsequently, nor those who are sons of a secondary wife of the father of My Majesty. (19)For the lordship you shall support only My Majesty and after (him) his sons (and) grandsons. (20–23)You shall discard the oath of the person who makes you swear[74] to the brothers of My Majesty, and you shall support only My Majesty and the sons of My Majesty for the lordship;[75] or (if) the full brothers of My Majesty or a son of a secondary wife (24)<has> done some wi[ck]ed thing,[76] (e.g.,) blood(shed) or rebellion, (25)[o]r he *has foreknowledge*[77] of some wicked matter; (26–28)[o]r some prince divulges a wicked matter to a courtier, or he has also already [to]ld you, but you do not report it to the king; (29–32)[o]r some prince (or)[78] brother of the king makes some courtier (his) [ass]ociate, and he divulges to him some evil, [inopp]ortune [matter] regarding the king, but he does not [repo]rt it to the king: under the oath.

§25″ (33–36)[O]r you who are courtiers; (when) you approach the undefiled [perso]n of the king, be *mindful*[79] [...] of (your) purity. And if evil contamination (afflicts) [so]me courtier, (37)and [h]e approaches the person of the king; under oath.[80]

§26″ (38–41)And if someone hopes that some extradited person among those who My Majesty has extradited should survive, or he wishes him an escape, [(o)r] someone sends him a messenger, but that person [c(onceals) hi]m, (42)but he does not report him to the king, (it) [(shall be placed)] unde[(r oath)].

§27″ (A iv 43–50; B iv 12′–19′) (43)*ma-a-an-na* ŠEŠ LUGAL *ku-i-e-eš* EN DUMU L[(UGAL LÚ SAG) ...] (44)⌞*ŠA*⌟ LUGAL ḪUL-*lu ut-tar an-da iš-t*[*a-*(*ma-aš-zi a-pa-a-a*)*š-ma-at*] (45)[*A-N*]*A* LUGAL *UL me-ma-i nu ki-i te-e*[(*z-zi*) ... *-wa-kán* ...] (46)[(*a-aš*)]*-šu-wa-an-ni UL ḫar-pí-ia-nu-un*[81] ⌞*nu*⌟*-w*[*a-* ...] (47) [(*U*)]*L ḫar-pí-ia-mi ma-a-an-ma-wa-ra-a*[*t* ... (*ku-wa-pí*)] (48)[(*Š*)*A*?][82] *ut-tar ú-e-mi-ia-an-du-wa-ra-*[*at* (*ma-a-an-ma-wa*)-...] (49)[x x *-i*]*a*?-*zi am-mu-*⌞*uk*⌟*-ma-wa-aš-š*[*i* (≮ *ḫu-ḫu-pa*)*-aš Ú-UL*] (50)[*kiš-ḫa-ḫa-r*]*i*[83] GAM-*an NI-ÌŠ* DINGIR-*LÌ* [GAR-*ru*]

§28″ (B iv 20′–22′; A iv 51–52) (20′)*na-aš-ma ki-*[*i* ...] (21′)*li-in-ku-w*[*a-an-ni* ...] (22′)*ar-ḫa a-*[...]

§29″ (B iv 23′–25′) (23′)*na-aš-ma*[...] (24′)*BI-I*[*B-*...] (25′)⌞*na*⌟-[...]

§30″ (A left edge i 1)*šu-***me***-e-eš ku-i-e-eš* LÚ.MEŠ ⸢SAG⸣[ ][84] (2)LUGAL-*ma-aš A-NA* INIM MUNUS-*TI pa-ra-a u-i-iš-k*[*e-et*] (3)*nu ma-a-an* LÚ*a-ra-aš* LÚ*a-ra-an A-NA* INIM MUNUS-*T*[*I*] (4)≮*ma-za-al-la a-uš-zi A-NA* LUGAL-*ma UL me-ma-*[*i*] (5)*na-an an-da mu-un-na-iz-zi* GAM *NI-ÌŠ* DINGIR-*LÌ* G[AR-*ru*]

§31″ (A left edge ii 1)[*m*]*a-*⌞*a*⌟*-an-na-za* d[UTU-*ŠI* ...] (2)[...]x x x[...]

§27″ (43)And if (one of) those who are a brother of the king, a lord, a prin[(ce, a courtier) …], (44–45)he[(ars)] of an evil matter regarding the king, [but (h)e] does not report [it t]o the king, and he sa[(ys)] this: (46)"Out of [(*int*)]*egrity* I did not support […], and (47)I will [(no)]t support […]. If, however, i[t … (somewhere/sometime)] (48)[(*o*)*f*] the matter, let them find [it. (But if)] he (49–50)[…]-s, then I, in contrast, wi[ll not be/beco]me [*ḫuḫupa-*] to him." (It) [shall be placed] under oath.

§28″ (20′)Or […] thi[s …] (21′)w[e] swear […] (22′)away […]

§29″ (23′)Or […] (24′)rhy[ton? …] (25′)and […]

§30″ (1)You who are courtiers, […]: (2)(If), however,[85] the king has sen[t] them out in the matter of a woman, (3–4)and if one colleague sees another colleague *mazalla* in the matter of the woman, but [he] does not tell the king, (5)and he conceals him, (it) [shall be] pl[aced] under oath.

§31″ (1–2)And if My [Majesty …]

No. 27
Tudḫaliya IV's Instructions and Oath Imposition for Courtiers (*CTH* 255.2)

This composition is preserved by one very substantial block of fragments (A), a second rather less substantial block (B) and five small fragments (C–G). Assuming that the composition covers only a single tablet, then slightly more than half of the original composition would be preserved. Findspots for only two small fragments (F and G) are known, and these come from the Temple I complex.

The text is the only one of the corpus that preserves an explicit reference to the swearing of the oath occurring at the coronation of the king (§1), though it is quite possible that this would have been the case with at least some of the others as well. This reference is then followed by a citation of the oath to be taken, in the 1st person pl., or perhaps a short summary thereof (§1, 3–4), styled as if dictated by the king himself. The remainder of the document, for the most part likewise addressing its audience in the 2nd pl., consists in further defining exactly how the subjects' loyalty is to be expressed in a series of situations, descriptions that can be understood as the instructions, directives, or obligations to which they are to swear their oath. It occasionally attempts to anticipate treasonous thinking and/or utterances and to argue against and forbid them (§§3, 5′?, 10″, 19″, 20″, 29″?, 35″).

The directives are addressed to the "courtiers" (LÚ^MEŠ^ SAG, lit. "men (of) the head"; Akk. *ša rēši*, lit. "(man) of the head"), that is, the innermost circle of state administrators (see introduction to No. 26), a term that requires some comment. Though LÚ SAG is often translated as "eunuch," it is here rendered as "courtier," since (a) it continues to be debated if the translation "eunuch" is appropriate in general, and if so, if it can therefore be translated as such wherever it is attested throughout the cuneiform world (Peled, in press), and since, (b) even if it can be legitimately translated as such, the passages in the present text relate to these officials not with regard to the status of their genitals but with regard to their function as close and personal servants of the king, as Starke (1996: 144, n. 21) has argued; in other words, the translation "courtier" is correct whether each and every one of the addressed subordinates is also a eunuch or not, while "eunuch" would be correct only if they were, for the most part at least, eunuchs (cf. also Pecchioli Daddi 2006: 121–25; Miller 2004: 318–19; Giorgieri 2008: 355–56; Mora 2010a). Largely on the basis of this text, No. 27, Hawkins (2002: 221–24) has recently argued for the interpretation as "eunuch," whereby his assumption (p. 223) that those who are forbidden to maintain a relationship with the king's women are not those LÚ^MEŠ^ SAG being addressed (No. 27, §§31″–33″), but other, not castrated, men, plays a central role in his analysis. The paragraphs in question, however (No. 27, §§31″–33″), do indeed relate to the LÚ^MEŠ SAG being addressed, that is, they are forbidden from having relationships with the women of the palace.[86] Hawkins apparently assumes that some other individuals are being referred to because of the change from the 2nd to the 3rd person in mid-paragraph, but in fact it is common in this text and many others of this genre that those being addressed are referred to sometimes in the 3rd person, sometimes in the 2nd; §§9″–10″, 16″–17″, 19″, 25″ are just a few examples. Also a paragraph such as §30″ can hardly be understood any other way. The first half of the paragraph is phrased in the 2nd sg., clearly directed toward the, or a, LÚ SAG. The second half of the same paragraph is phrased in an impersonal 3rd person, but it must still refer to the LÚ SAG or LÚ^MEŠ SAG to which the composition as a whole is addressed. Why would the king otherwise place the passage in the directives for the LÚ^MEŠ SAG? And why would someone else's refusal to agree to the stated restriction be put under an oath for the LÚ^MEŠ SAG? Moreover, Hawkins (p. 223, commentary to l. 29) freely admits the import of the even more conclusive statement from the beginning of §31″, which reads, "[No]w, since woman are to be let [(into yo)] ur [(houses)]," but he does not comment further on the point. Here it is in fact clearly stated that the LÚ^MEŠ SAG are allowed to have women, and one can safely assume that it is not a scrabble partner that is at issue.[87] It is women employed in the royal palace that the LÚ^MEŠ SAG are not to have relations with, as made clear in the ensuing clauses: "[(but, becau)se (this)] is the palace, then whatever [pa]lace [(woman)] is (concerned), be she a chambermaid (or) be she a [(free person)…." The LÚ^MEŠ SAG are thus prohibited from having a palace employee as a lover, presumably in order to prevent them from having access to an insider who could serve them as a mole. The relevant passages of these instructions texts thus lend no support to, inceed clearly militate against, the suggestion that the LÚ^MEŠ SAG at the Hittite court are to be regarded as eunuchs.

The overriding theme of the composition is loyalty toward Tudḫaliya as opposed to supporting some other pretender to the throne, whereby the "many brothers" and descendents of Tudḫaliya's predecessors are clearly viewed as a real and present threat (§§2, 25″). The king's paranoia, as well as that of his predecessors and parents, Ḫattusili III and Pudu-Ḫepa, is otherwise well documented, and complements nicely the present composition. Ever since Ḫattusili had driven his nephew Mursili III / Urḫi-Teššub, the son of Ḫattusili's older brother Muwattalli II, from the throne and usurped it himself, he and his wife Pudu-Ḫepa had been intensely preoccupied with legitimizing their rule and the succession of their son as well as sidelining all alternatives (van den Hout 1997; 1998; Bryce 2005: 268–73; Singer 2006; Bányai 2010). This paranoia has often been linked with a certain instability within the Hittite state structure, which in turn has been seen as a factor in the final collapse of the Empire in the generation following Tudḫaliya IV.

Of further interest is the distinction (§§23″–24″) between those courtiers "who were here promptly" and had already sworn the oath and those "who were not here," both of which groups were apparently required to jointly swear

---

TRANSCRIPTION

§1 (A i 1–5) (i 1)[*U*]*M-MA* ^{m}*TU.UD.ḪA.*⸢*LI*⸣*.IA* ⸢LUGAL⸣.GAL LUGAL-*ez-zi-aḫ-ḫa-at-wa* (2)[*nu*]-*wa šu-um-me-eš*$_{15}$ LÚ^{MEŠ} SAG *A-NA* SAG.DU ^{d}UTU-*ŠI* (3)[*še*]-*er kiš-an li-in-ik-<tén>* ^{d}UTU-*ŠI*-˻*wa AŠ-ŠUM*˼ EN-*UT-TI* (4)[*p*]*a-aḫ-šu-u-e-ni kat-ta-ma-wa* DUMU^{MEŠ} ^{d}UTU-*ŠI* (5)*ḫa-aš-ša ḫa-an-za-aš-ša AŠ-ŠUM* EN-*UT-TI pa-aḫ-šu-u-e-ni*

§2 (A i 6–16; B i 1′–6′) (6)*šu-um-me-eš-ma-aš ku-i-e-eš* LÚ^{MEŠ} SAG *nu-uš-ma-*⸢*aš* AN? DI/KI? LU? x[ ][88] (7)UN^{MEŠ}-*uš* ^{d}UTU-*ŠI-kán šu-um-ma-aš* ŠU-*aš* (8)˻*nu*˼ ^{d}UTU-*ŠI pa-aḫ-ḫa-aš-tén kat-ta-ma* NUMUN ^{d}UTU-*ŠI pa-aḫ-ḫa-aš-tén* (9)*A-NA* ^{d}UTU-*ŠI* ŠEŠ^{MEŠ} ˻*me-ek-ka*$_{4}$*-uš*?˼[89] ˻*A*˼-*BI*^{MEŠ}-*ŠU-ia-aš-ši* (10)*me-ek-ka*$_{4}$*-e-eš* KUR ^{URU}*ḪA.A*[*T.TI-kán IŠ-T*]*U* NUMUN LUGAL-*UT-TI* (11)*šu-wa-an* ŠÀ ⸢^{URU}*ḪA*⸣.[*AT.TI-kán* NUMUN ^{m}*Š*]*U.UP.PÍ.LU.LI.U.MA* (12)NUMUN ^{m}˻*MUR.ŠI*˼.*LI* NUMUN ^{m}⸢NIR.GÁL NUMUN ^{m}⸣[(*ḪA.A*)]*T.TU.ŠI.LI* (13)*me-ek-ki nu-uš-ma-aš AŠ-ŠUM* E[N-*U*]*T-TI ta-ma-a-*˻*in*˼ (14)⸢UN⸣-*an le-e ku-in-ki še-ek-*[(*t*)]*e-ni* (15)[*A*]*Š-ŠUM* EN-*UT-TI kat-ta ḫa-aš-š*[(*a ḫ*)]*a-*˻*an-za-aš*˼-*š*[(*a*)] (16)NUMUN ^{m}*TU.UD.ḪA.LI.IA-pát pa-aḫ-aš-t*[(*én*)]

§3 (A i 17–29; B i 7′–20′) (17)˻*ma*˼*-a-an-na-za ŠA* ^{d}UTU-*ŠI* ḪUL-*lu k*[*u-wa-*(*pí ki-ša-r*)*i*] (18)˻*A*˼-*NA* ^{d}UTU-*ŠI-*ma* ŠEŠ*^{MEŠ} *me-ek-ka*$_{4}$*-e-e*[(*š*)] (19)[*n*]*u a-pa-a-at ku-wa-at-ka*$_{4}$ *i-ia-at-te-*[(*ni*) *nu-ká*(*n*? *ta-me-e-da-ni*)] (20)[*k*]*u-e-da-ni-ik-ki an-da-an pa-it-t*[(*e-ni*)] (21)[(*n*)]*u kiš-an me-ma-at-te-ni ku-in-w*[(*a-an-na-aš im-ma*)] (22)*ša-ra-a du-um-me-e-ni nu-wa-an-na-*[(*aš a-pa-a-aš*)] (23)*Ú-UL im-ma* DUMU EN-*E-NI nu a-p*[(*a-a-aš me-mi-aš*)] (24)*le-e e-eš-zi AŠ-ŠUM* EN-*UT-TI* [(*kat-ta* NUMUN ^{d}UT)U-*Š*(*I-pát*)] (25)[(*pa-a*)]*ḫ-ḫa-aš-tén an-da-kán ta-me-e-d*[(*a-ni le-e ku-e-da-ni-ik-ki*)] (26)[*pa-*(*i*)]*t-te-ni AŠ-ŠUM* EN-*UT-TI* ^{d}U[TU-*ŠI* NU(MUN ^{d}UTU-*ŠI-ia*)] (27)[PAB-*aš-té*]*n ḫu-u-ma-an-da-*az-zi*-ia* […] (28)[*ta-me-e-d*]*a-ni-kán* UN-*ŠI an-d*[*a-an le-e*] (29)[*ku-e-da-ni-i*]*k-ki pa-*˻*it-te-ni*˼[ ]

§4 (A i 30) (30)[…]x x[…]

(gap of perhaps only some 2–3 lines)

the oath when this tablet was written up. Moreover, the colophon reveals where "here" was, that is, in Ūssa, a city of Tarḫuntassa, the secondogeniture in which Tudḫaliya's cousin, Kuruntiya, ruled as king. This situation prompts an entire series of questions, such as why Tudḫaliya should have sworn in the courtiers of Ḫattusa in a city of Tarḫuntassa, and why they were apparently summoned so hurriedly that some had taken the oath even before the rest arrived.

TRANSLATION

§1 (1)[T]hus (speaks) Tudḫaliya, Great King: I have become king, (2–5)[so] you courtiers <must> swear an oath [up]on the person of My Majesty as follows: "We will [p]rotect His Majesty with regard to the lordship, while thereafter we will protect the sons of His Majesty (and his) sons and grandsons with regard to the lordship."

§2 (6–7)You who are courtiers and you are […]-men: My Majesty is accessible to you,[90] (8)so you[91] must protect My Majesty, while after (me) you must protect the progeny of My Majesty! (9–11)My Majesty has many brothers, and *they*[92] have man[y] fathers. The land of Ḫa[ttusa] is full [o]f royal progeny. In Ḫa[ttusa] the [progeny of S]uppiluliuma, (12)the progeny of Mursili, the progeny of Muwattalli (and) the progeny of [(Ḫa)]ttusili (13–14)are numerous, and (yet) you shall recognize no other man for the lo[rds]hip, (15–16)and after (me) yo[(u must)] protect the sons and grandsons, the seed of Tudḫaliya alone, for the lordship!

§3 (17)And if evil e[ve(r befall)s] My Majesty—(18)My Majesty (has), after all, many brothers—(19–20)[a]nd perhaps you even do this: [(you)] support someone [(else)],[93] (21–23)[(an)]d you speak thus: "Whom[(ever)] shall we raise up (as king) [(for ourselves)]? Is [(that other man)] not in fact a son of our lord?"[94] Such an utterance (24–27)shall not be made! For the lordship [(pro)]tect [(hereafter only the progeny of M)y Ma(jesty)]! You shall [(not) su(ppo)]rt an[(yone else)]! [Protec]t My Maj[esty (and the) pro(geny of My Majesty)] for the lordship! But by no means […]! (28–29) You [shall not] support any [oth]er man!

§4 (traces)

(gap of perhaps only some 2–3 lines)

§4′ (B i 23′–32′; E i 1′–4′) (23′)⸢*ta-me-e-da*⸣-[*ni*[95] …] (24′)INIM^MEŠ GAM x[96][…] (25′)*e-*⸢*eš-zi*⸣ *ag-g*[*a*?- …] (26′)*IŠ-*⸢*TU*⸣ ZI LUGAL x[…] (27′)*le-e ku-iš-ki a-uš-z*[*i* …] (28′)*ku-e-da-ni-ik-ki* x[… (*a*)*r*-? …] (29′)*nu-za A-NA* dUTU-*ŠI* x[… (*ar*)-…] (30′)*ḫa-at-te₉-eš-šar*~x[… (*i-i*)*a*-…] (31′)*na-aš-kán ta-me-*⸤*e*⸥-[…] (32′)*le-e ku-e-da-*[…]

§5′ (B i 33′–37′; E i 5′–8′) (33′)⸢*na-aš-ma*⸣ LÚ*a*?-x[97…] (34′)*a-aš-šu-uš* AN[… (*me-m*)*a-i*] (35′)[(E)]GIR GAM-⸢*wa*⸣-*ra-a*[*n* … (*BE*?-)*L*(*I*?*-an-kán*)] (36′)[E]GIR ⸤GAM⸥ *Ú-UL*[…] (37′)⸢*na*⸣*-at* GAM *NI-ÌŠ* D[INGIR-*LÌ* GAR-*ru*]

§6′ (E i 9′–14′; B i 38′–42′) (4′)INIM dUTU-*ŠI-ia-aš-ma-aš me-*x[…] (5′)*e-eš-tén* ∠ *ku-ku-pa-la-tar l*[*e*?*-e* …] (6′)*IŠ-TU* É.LUGAL-*kán me-mi-*x[… (*pé-e*)- …] (7′)*A-NA BE-LI* DUMU LUGAL-*kán* A[N …] (8′)*A-NA* ZI LUGAL-*ma-aš* IGI-*an-da* x[98…] (9′)⸤*pa*⸥-*a*[*ḫ*]-*ḫa-aš-tén ta-me-e-da-ma le-e*[…]

§7′ (E i 15′–20′) (15′)[…]x[99]*-an-ti-ia-an-te₉-eš-ma-aš ku-e*~[…] (16′)[… LU]GAL LÚ.MEŠ*ḪA-TÁ-AN* LUGAL […] (17′)[…]x-*ša-aš QA-TAM-MA* LÚ*Ḫ*[*A*-…] (18′)[… -*i*]*k-tén ma-a-an-ma* x x[…] (19′)[…]x *me-mi-an*[…] (20′)[…] x[…]

(gap of some few lines)

§8″ (A i 54′–55′) (54′)[…]-⸢*iz-zi*⸣ (55′)[…]-*ú*

§9″ (A i 56′–62′) (56′)[*na-aš-ma-za* dUTU-*ŠI k*]*u-e-da-ni-ik-ki ku-*⸢*in*⸣*-ki* (57′) [*me-mi-an a-wa-an kat-t*]*a me-ma-aḫ-ḫi na-an-za-an-kán pé-ra-an* (58′) [*ku-ut-ru-w*]*a-aḫ-mi le-e-wa-ra-an-za-an*[100] *ku-e-da-ni-ik-ki* (59′)[*pa-ra-a*] *me-ma-at-ti na-an-za-an ku-it-ma-an a-pé-e-el* (60′)[UD.KAM-*za*][101] *ar-ḫa pé-e-da-i a-pa-a-aš-ma-an-za-an* (61′)[*pa-r*]*a-a me-ma-a-i na-at-ši-ia-at* (62′)[GAM *N*]*I-ÌŠ* DINGIR-*LÌ ki-it-ta-ru*

§10″ (A ii 1–9; B ii 1′–2′; C i 1′–6′) (A ii 1)[…]⸤d⸥UTU-⸤*ŠI*⸥ *ku-wa-a*[*t*?*-ka₄*?] (2) […]x-⸤*kán*⸥ *me-ma-*⸢*i*⸣ *a-pí-i*[*a*] (3)[… (*nu a-pa-a*)*-aš* ...] *pa-it* (4)[(*nu-wa-r*)*a*- …]x-*ia-*⸢*u*⸣*-wa-an-zi* (5)[… (*ki-ša-at*) … *-wa-r*]*a-*[*a*]*n-za-an* (6)[… *a-pa-a-*(*aš m*)]*e-mi-aš le-e* ⸢*e-eš*⸣*-z*[*i*] (B ii 1′)[…-(*ma-za m*)]*e-mi-an pa-*⸢*ra-a*⸣ [(*l*)*e-e*] (2′)[*ku-e-da-ni-ik-*(*k*)]*i me-ma-i* GAM *NI-ÌŠ* DINGIR-*LÌ* GAR-*ru*

§11″ (B ii 3′–8′; A ii 10-15; C i 7′–8′) (3′)[… N]Í.TE-*ŠU ḫu-u-ma-an* GIM-*an* (4′)[… *š*]*u-um-ma-aš A-NA* LÚMEŠ SAG ŠU-*i* (5′)[…]x-⸢*ma*⸣ *ku-it* GIM-*an *uš*-ket₉-te-ni* (6′)[*nu-za m*]*e-mi-an pa-ra-a* ⸤*le*⸥*-e ku-e-da-ni-ik-*⸤*ki*⸥ (7′)[*me-ma*]*-at-te-ni zi-la-du-wa ku-it-ma-an* (8′)[*šu-m*]*e-el* UD-*za* GAM *NI-ÌŠ* DINGIR-*LÌ-at* ⸤GAR-*ru*⸥

§12″ (A ii 16–20′; B ii 9′–12′) (16)[… (x-*aš-kán e-ni ku-it*) … *-z*]*i*? (17)[…

§4′ (23′)[… to] another […] (24′)words/affairs beneath/with […] (25′)he/it is […] (26′)by the *will* of the king […] (27′)no one shall seek! […] (28′)to/for whomever […] (29′)and to/for My Majesty […] (30′)a ditch/pit […] (31′)and he/them anoth[er …] (32′)shall not […] some[one …]!

§5′ (33′)Or (if) a *co[lleague* …] (34′)good [… (say)s]: (35′)"[… (b)]ack/[(ag)]ain with/below." [*To/For a lo(rd)* …] (36′)not […] [(him) b]ack/[ag]ain with/below, (37′)then that [shall be placed] under oa[th].

§6′ (4′)And the word/matter of My Majesty […] (5′)you must be. […] *n[o] kukupalatar*![103] (6′)[…] from the palace (7′)[…] for a lord (or) a prince […] (8′)against the *will* of the king […] (9′)you must pr[ot]ect! To another […] shall not […]!

§7′ (15′)[…] which you (16′)[… the k]ing, sons-in-law of the king (17′)[…] likewise […]-man, (18′)you shall […]. But if (19′–20′)[…] word/affair […]

(gap of some few lines)

§8″ (54′)[…] he/it […]s (55′)[…] he shall […].

§9″ (56′–57′)[Or] (if) I, [My Majesty], reveal some [matter in confidence] to someone, and I (58′–59′)[swe]ar him to secrecy[104] (saying): "Do not [dis]close this to anyone!" (60′–62′)And before his (final) [day] carries him away he nonetheless [di]scloses it, then it shall be placed [under o]ath for him.

§10″ (1)[…] My Majesty *perha[ps* …] (2–3)he says, "The[re … (and he) …] went, (4–5)[(and) …] to do [… (it happened) …] him." (6)[… tha(t ut)]terance shall not be made! (1′–2′)[(But)] he must [(n)ot] tell the matter to [anyo(n)]e! (It) shall be placed under oath.

§11″ (3′)[…] like his entire [p]erson (4′)[…] to/for you courtiers in the hand[105] (5′)[…], but when you observe something, (6′–7′)[then] you must not [divul]ge the [m]atter to anyone, forever, until (8′)[yo]ur (final) day (arrives). It shall be placed under oath.

§12″ (16)[… (with regard to that)[106] …] (17)[… (disapprov)al …] from the (x *mar-ki-ia-u-*˹*wa*˺*-a)r* ...]x KA×U!*-za* (18)[... -(*ni ú-ez-zi* GI)M?*-an* ... *i*]*š-da*$_4$*-ma-aš-zi*[102] (19′)[...] (20′)[... GAM *NI-ÌŠ* DINGIR-*LÌ*]*-at* GAR-*ru*

§13″ (A ii 21′–42′) (21′)[...] ḪUL-*lu* (22′)[...] (23′)[...] (24′)[...]*-uš* (25′)[...] (26′)[...]*-te-ni* (27′)[...]*-aš* (28′)[...] *e-eš-zi* (29′)[...] (30′)[... *ku-e-da-n*]*i-ik-ki* (31′)[...] (32′)[...] (33′)[... *-a*]*t-tar* (34′)[...] (35′)[...] (36′)[... *k*]*i-ša-ri* (37′)[...] (38′)[...] (39′)[...]x*-ket*$_9$*-te-ni* (40′)[... *le*]*-e ḫar-ak* (41′)[... *A*]*-NA* ^{d}UTU-*ŠI* (42′)[... GAM *NI-ÌŠ* DINGIR-*LÌ-at* GAR]*-ru*

§14″ (A ii 43′–47′) (43′)[...]x *ku-it-ki* (44′)[...]x*-zi* (45′)[... *-wa*]*-*˹*ra*˺*-aš-mu* (46′)[...]˹*ḫa-an*˺*-ti-i ti-ia-mi* (47′)[... *a-pa-a-aš m*]*e-mi-aš* GAM *NI-ÌŠ* DINGIR-*LÌ* GAR-*ru*

§15″ (A ii 48′–53′) (48′)[*nu šu-um-ma-aš*][107] LÚ^{MEŠ} SAG *ku-it nu-kán* ^{d}UTU-*ŠI* (49′)[*ku-in-ki ku*]*-e-da-ni-ik-ki A-NA* INIM^{MEŠ} (50′)[*u-i-iš-ke-m*]*i*[108] *nu-kán* INIM^{MEŠ} ^{d}UTU-*ŠI wa*!*-aḫ-nu-ši* (51′)[*na-aš-ma-ká*]*n*[109] *a-pé-e-el* INIM^{MEŠ} *wa-aḫ-nu-ši* (52′)[*na-at ta*]*-me-um-ma-an i-ia-ši* (53′)[*nu-uš-ši*[110] *a-pa*]*-*˻*a*˼*-aš me-mi-aš* GAM *NI-ÌŠ* DINGIR-*LÌ* [GAR-*r*]*u*

§16″ (A ii 54′–58′) (54′)*na-aš-m*[*a k*]*i-i ku-it* INIM MUD [*ki-ša-ri*(?)] (55′)ÌR^{MEŠ}*-mu-*˹*kán*˺ *ku-i-e-eš* GAM*-an ne-*[*ia-an-ta-at*] (56′)*na-at ma-a-an ka-ru-ú ku-i*[*š-ki iš-da*$_4$*-ma-aš-ta*][111] (57′)*A-NA* ^{d}UTU-*ŠI-ma-at Ú-UL m*[*e-ma-i*] (58′) GAM *NI-ÌŠ* DINGIR-*LÌ-at ki-i*[*t-ta-ru*]

§17″ (A ii 59′–64′) (59′)*e-ni-ia ku-it ut-tar ma*[*r*?-[112] ...] (60′)*ku-it lu-ut-ti-ia-za an-da*[...] (61′)*na-an ku-iš ša-ak-ta n*[*a-*...] (62′)*ki-nu-un ku-iš-ki* EGIR*-an-da*[...] (63′)*me-ma-i-ma-an Ú-UL na-*[*at* GAM *NI-ÌŠ* DINGIR-*LÌ*] (64′)*ki-it-ta-r*[*u*]

§18″ (A iii 1–10) (1)*ku-u-uš-ša ku-i-e-eš* UN x[[113]...] (2)*na-aš* ^{d}UTU-*ŠI* EGIR*-pa pí-*x[...] (3)*a-aš-šu-u-wa-an-za* *x* *ku-e-da-ni~*[...] (4) LÚ*a-ra-aš e-eš-ta na-*[...] (5)EGIR *GAM *kar*!?**-aš-du*[114] *nu-za-kán*[...] (6)GIM*-an* GÍR ZABAR *a*[*r-*...] (7)*a-pa-a-aš-ma-za-kán* ˻A˼[...] (8)*ar-ḫa* ˹*uš-ke*˺*-e*[*t*?[115] ...] (9) *a-ša-an-du n*[*u~*[116] ...] (10)*le-e ku-iš-*[*ki* ...]

§19″ (A iii 11–25) (11)*šu-me-eš-ma ku-i-e-*[*eš* ... *k*]*u*??*-*˹*i*??*-e*??*-eš*??˺ x[...] (12)*nu-uš-ma-aš ḫu-u-ma-a*[*n~* ...]*-*˹*e-eš*˺ (13)*nu A-NA* ^{d}UTU-*ŠI ḫ*[*u*]*-*˹*u-ma-an-te*˺*-eš-pát pé-ra-an* (14)*ḫu-u-i-*˹*ia-an*˺*-te-eš e-eš-tén ma-a-an* UD.KAM (15) *A-BI-ŠU* AMA-˹*ŠU*˺ *ku-e-da-ni-ik-ki* GÍD.DA*-aš* (16)*nu-za ku-it* GIM*-an ki-ša-ri nu a-pa-a-at* (17)*ku-iš-ki me-ma-i le-en-ga-nu-ut-wa-mu ku-iš* (18)*nu-wa ka-ru-ú* ⸗*ḫal-li-ia ú-e-eḫ-ta-at* (19)*nu-wa-ra-at Ú-UL nam-ma ku-it-ki* (20) *nu-wa-za ke-e* INIM^{MEŠ} *ke-e-da-ni me-e-ḫu-ni* (21)*pa-ra-a nam-ma me-ma-aḫ-ḫi nu ku-it-ma-an* (22)*a-pé-e-el* UD.KAM*-za ku-it-ma-na-aš a-ki* (23)*ŠA*

mouth (18)[… (comes to, wh)en …] he hears (19′)[…]. (20′)It shall be placed [under oath].

§13″ (21′–25′)[…] evil […] (26′–27′)[…] you do […] (28′–29′)[…] he/it is […] (30′–35′)[…] to [whom]ever […] (36′–38′)[…] he/it [be]comes […] (39′)[…] you continually (40′)[…] *you*(sg.) *must* [*no*]*t* hold/keep (41′)[… t]o My Majesty. (42′)[It] shall be [placed under oath].

§14″ (43′–45′)[…] whatever […] "He […] me, (46′)[…] I will denounce." (47′)[… that m]atter shall be placed under oath.

§15″ (48′)[And you], since you are courtiers: (If) I, My Majesty, (49′–50′)[dispatch someone] in connection with [s]ome matter, and you(sg.) twist the words of My Majesty, (51′)[or] you(sg.) twist his[117] words, (52′)[and] you(sg.) [di]stort [them], (53′)[then th]at affair [sha]ll be [placed] under oath [for him].

§16″ (54′)Or in [th]is regard, (if) a matter of blood(shed) [*occurs*], (55′–56′)and if some[one] has already [heard about] some servants who have tu[rned] against me, (57′)but he does not r[eport] them to My Majesty, (58′)then it [shall be] placed under oath.

§17″ (59′)And with regard to that […] matter, (60′)which […] in through the window, (61′)he who knew/recognized him/her, an[d …] (62′)now someone afterwards […], (63′–64′)should he not report (it), then [it] shall be placed [under oath].

§18″ (1)And those *m*[*e*]*n* who […] these […], (2)and them […] behind/back My Majesty […] (3)a favored person […] to someone/something (4)was a colleague, and […] (5)he shall *stay clear of*, and […] (6)like a bronze knife […], (7)but that (person) […] (8)looke[d] the other way […] (9)they shall be, an[d …] (10)no on[e] shall […].

§19″ (11)You wh[o] are […], though, […] *who* […], (12)and to you […] all […] (13–15)and you must every one of you be loyal supporters[118] of My Majesty. If someone should live to a great age,[119] (16–17)and should something happen, so that someone says this: "He who swore me in (18)has already passed away,[120] (19)and it does not matter any longer, (20–21)so I will speak out about these affairs again at this time." Until (22)his (final) day, until he dies, (23)as far as My Majesty and the person (and) life of My Majesty are concerned, (24–25)no one shall divulge them to anyone.

^{d}UTU-_ŠI-ma ku-it_ NÍ.TE-_ŠU_ ZI ^{d}UTU-_ŠI-ia_ (24)_na-at-za pa-ra-a le-e ku-iš-ki_ (25)_ku-e-da-ni-ik-ki me-ma-i_

§20″ (A iii 26–31) (26)_na-aš-ma-at ku-it im-_⸢_ma_⸣ _ku-i_[_t_] ḪUL-_lu_ (27)_ŠA_ ZI ^{d}UTU-_ŠI zi-ik-ma-at ša-ak-ti_ (28)_na-at pa-ra-a ar-mi-iz-zi-ia-ši nu kiš-an me-ma-at-ti_ (29)_ke-e-da-ni-wa_ UD.KAM _ú-uk ku-e-da-ni ša-ak-la-a-i_ (30)_Ú-UL_! _ar-ḫa-ḫa-at nu-wa-ra-at-mu Ú-UL_ (31)_wa-aš-túl na-at_ GAM _NI-ÌŠ_ DINGIR-_LÌ_ GAR-_ru_

§21″ (A iii 32–36) (32)_na-aš-ma šu-um-ma-aš ku-it_ LÚ^{MEŠ} SAG x[ ][121] (33)_IT-TI_ DUMU^{MEŠ} LUGAL _BE-LU_$^{ḪI.A}$ _A-NA_ INIM _a-ra-aḫ-zé-na-aš_ (34)⸤_ta_⸥_-pár-ri-ia_ GAM-_an u-i-iš-ke-mi_ (35)_nu-kán_ INIM LUGAL _le-e wa-aḫ-nu-ut-te-ni_ (36) GAM _NI-ÌŠ_ DINGIR-_LÌ-at_ GAR-_ru_

§22″ (A iii 37–44; B iii 1′–6′) (37)_na-aš-ma-*kán A-NA*_ ^{d}UTU-_ŠI a-aš-šu-wa-an-ni ku-iš-ki_ (38)⸢_an-da_⸣-⸤_an_⸥ _ne-an-za tu-_⸤_uk_⸥_-ma-kán ŠA_ ^{d}UTU-_ŠI_ ^{LÚ}KÚR-_aš_ (39)EGIR-_pa_ ⸢UGU⸣ ⸤_da_⸥_-a-i a-ši-wa-kán PA-AN_ *^{d}UTU*-_ŠI_ (40)_la-ak-nu-ut zi-ik-_⸤_ma_⸥_-a_[_t_? _i_?_-i_]_a_?_-ši_ (41)_na-an-kán la-ak-nu-š_[_i_] _na-aš-m_[_a t_]_u-uk ku-iš-ki_ ḪUL-_lu-uš_ (42)_PA-NI_ ^{d}UTU-_ŠI-ma-aš_ SI×SÁ-[_a_]_n-za zi-_⸢_ik_⸣_-ma-an-_⸢_kán_⸣ (43)_in-na-ra-a *la*-ak-nu-ši nu-uš-ši-kán ḫu-wa-ap-ti ku-it-ki_ (44)_nu-ut-ták-kán ku-u-uš_ DINGIR^{MEŠ} _ḫar-ni-in-kán-du_

§23″ (A iii 45–52; B iii 7′–14′) (45)_šu-um-ma-aš-ma-aš ku-i-e-eš_ LÚ^{MEŠ} SAG _ḫu-u-da-ak_ (46)_ka-a e-eš-tén nu-uš-ma-aš_ ^{d}UTU-_ŠI ku-it_ (47)_le-en-ga-nu-nu-un ma-a-an-wa-kán ŠA_ ^{d}UTU-_ŠI_ (48)⸤ḪUL-_lu_⸥_-un me-mi-_⸤_an_⸥ _na-aš-ma_ GÙB-_tar ku-e-da-ni-ik-ki_ (49)[(_an-da_) _i_]_š-da_$_4$_-ma-aš-*te-ni* nu-wa-*ra*-an A-NA_ ^{d}UTU-_ŠI_ (50)_me-m_[_i-iš-t_(_én š_)]_u-um-ma-aš-ma ku-it_ GIM-_an_ (51)_iš-da_$_4$_-ma-aš-tén na-at A-NA_ ^{d}UTU-_ŠI Ú-UL_ (52)_me-ma-at-te-ni_ ⸤_na_⸥_-at_ GAM _NI-ÌŠ_ DINGIR-_LÌ_ GAR-_ru_

§24″ (A iii 53–57; B iii 15′–17′) (53)_ki-nu-na-aš-ma-aš Ú-UL ku-i-e-eš ka-a_ ⸤_e_⸥_-eš-tén_ (54)_nu-kán_ 1-_e-da le-*en*-_⸤_ik_⸥_-tén nu-kán ma-a-an_ (55)_ŠA_ ^{d}UTU-_ŠI ku-e-da-ni-ik-ki_ ḪUL-_lu an-da_ (56)_iš-da_$_4$_-ma-aš-te-ni na-at le-e mu-_⸤_un-na_⸥_-it-te-ni_ (57)GAM _NI-ÌŠ_ DINGIR-_LÌ-at_ GAR-_ru_

§25″ (A iii 58–66) (58)_A-NA_ ^{d}UTU-_ŠI-ia_ ŠEŠ^{MEŠ}-_ŠU me_!(KU)[122]_-ek-ka_$_4$_-uš_ (59) _pa-ra-a_ ŠEŠ^{MEŠ}-_uš-ša-mu_[123] _me-ek-ka_$_4$_-e-eš_ (60)LUGAL^{MEŠ} _a-ra-aḫ-zé-nu-uš-ša me-ek-ka_$_4$_-uš_ (61)_šu-_⸤_um-ma_⸥_-aš-ma ku-i-e-eš_ LÚ^{MEŠ} SAG (62)_nu-za pa-ra-a ku-in-ki ku-e-da-ni-ik-ki_ (63)_u-i-ia-mi a-pa-a-aš-ma-an_ SIG$_5$-_aḫ-ḫi_ *x x* (64)_a-pa-a-*aš*-ma_ {*AŠ*} KA×U-_iš du-wa-ar-na-a-i_ (65)_nu-uš-ši_ INIM^{MEŠ} *LUGAL _pa-ra-a_* _me-ma-_⸤_i_⸥ (66)_na-at_ GAM _NI-ÌŠ_ DINGIR-_LÌ_ [GAR-_ru_]

§20″ (26)Or whatever evil (27)(concerning) the life of My Majesty (there may be), (if) you(sg.) know about it, (28)and you(sg.) also facilitate it,[124] and you(sg.) say this: (29)"Whatever regulation (announced) on a day (30–31) (when) I myself was not present is no crime for me."[125] That shall be placed under oath.

§21″ (32–34)Or, since I send you courtiers [...] along with princes (and) lords in a matter of foreign affairs with authority, (35)you must not twist the word of the king. (36)It shall be placed under oath.

§22″ (37–40)Or (if) someone is favorably disposed to My Majesty, but an enemy of My Majesty takes you(sg.) aside (saying), "Undermine him before His Majesty," and you(sg.) [*do i*]*t*, (41)y[ou](sg.) undermine him; or in your(sg.) view someone is corrupt, (42–43)while in My Majesty's view he is trustworthy, and you(sg.) vigorously undermine him, so that you(sg.) harm him in some way, (44)then may these oath deities destroy you(sg.).

§23″ (45–46)You courtiers who were here promptly, though; since I, My Majesty, have made you (47–52)swear an oath (whereby I said), "If you hear of any evil matter regarding My Majesty or of malevolence in someone,[126] then you must re[po(rt)] it to My Majesty;" but when you have heard something, and you do not report it to My Majesty, then it shall be placed under oath.

§24″ (53)Now, however, those of you who were not here, (54)you shall swear the oath as one.[127] And if (55–56)you hear about evil in anyone concerning My Majesty, then you must not conceal it. (57)It shall be placed under oath.

§25″ (58)I, My Majesty, have many brothers,[128] (59)and also many *parā*-brothers,[129] (60)and there are many neighboring kings. (61)You who are courtiers, though, (62–63)(if) I send someone out to someone, but that man favors him, (64)so that that man flaps his mouth (65)and he divulges the affairs of the king to him, (66)then that [shall be placed] under oath.

§26″ (A iv 1–2) $^{(iv\ 1)}$[*n*]*a-aš-ma a-*⸢*pé*⸣*-el ku-*⸢*it*⸣*-ki* GÙB*-tar* ⸢*a-uš-zi*⸣ $^{(2)}$*na-at mu-un-na-a-zi* GAM *NI-ÌŠ* DINGIR*-LÌ-at* GAR*-ru*

§27″ (A iv 3–6) $^{(3)}$*na-aš-ma ki-i ku-it* LÚ^{MEŠ} ^{URU}*ḪA.AT.TI e-eš-ša-an-zi* $^{(4)}$[*nu*]*-za ŠA* ^{d}UTU*-ŠI* EN*-ma-an-ni* EGIR*-an ar-ḫa* $^{(5)}$[*t*]*a-me-el* UN*-aš* EN*-UT-TA i-la-li-ia-zi* $^{(6)}$*na-at* GAM *NI-ÌŠ* DINGIR*-LÌ ki-it-ta-ru*

§28″ (A iv 7–10; C iv 1′–4′) $^{(7)}$*na-aš-ma-kán* ^{LÚ}*a-ra-aš* ^{LÚ}*a-ri an-da Š*[*A*] ^{d}UTU*-ŠI* $^{(8)}$[*k*]*u-in-ki* ḪUL*-lu-un me-mi-an iš-da₄-ma-aš-zi* $^{(9)}$[*n*]*a-an-kán ḫa-an-ti-i Ú-UL ti-ia-zi* $^{(10)}$[(GAM)] *NI-ÌŠ* DINGIR*-LÌ* GAR*-ru*

§29″ (A iv 11–19; B iv 1′–7′; C iv 5′–14′; E iv 1′–8′) $^{(11)}$[(*n*)]*a-aš-ma ma-a-an me-mi-aš ku-iš-ki e-eš-zi* $^{(12)}$[(*n*)*a-a*]*š-ma-aš* ≮*ku-ni-iš-ta-ia-al-li-iš-pát ku-iš-ki* $^{(13)}$[(*na-a*)]*š-ma-aš ŠA* MUNUS*-TI* ^{d}UTU*-ŠI-ma-at-ta pu-nu-uš-mi* $^{(14)}$[(*na-a*)]*n* ⸤*le*⸥*-e ša-an-na-at-ti me-mi-an* $^{(15)}$[(*nu-za-kán*)] ^{d}UTU*-ŠI pe-ra-an ku-ut-ru-wa-aḫ* $^{(16)}$[(*me-mi-ia-n*)]*i-ia-mu ku-e-da-ni pu-nu-uš-šer* $^{(17)}$[(*nu-wa-ra-a*)]*š*[130] *me-mi-aš-pát* ≮*ku-ni-iš-ta-ia-al-li-iš* $^{(18)}$[(*am-mu-uk-m*)]*a-wa pu-nu-uš-šer ku-it nu-wa-ra-an* $^{(19)}$[(*me-ma-aḫ-ḫi* z)]I*-aš-ma ša-an-nu-um-mar le-e e-eš-zi*

§30″ (A iv 20–28; B iv 8′–15′; D, 1′–7′; E iv 9′–15′) $^{(20)}$[(*ma-a-an-na-a*)]*d-du-za* ^{d}UTU*-ŠI ku-e-da-ni-ik-*<*ki*> *me-mi-ia-ni* $^{(21)}$[(*pa-ra-a u-i*)]*-ia-mi na-aš-ma-at-ta tu-e-el* $^{(22)}$[(*ku-e-da-ni-i*)]*k-ki* **me-mi-ni** *pu-nu-uš-mi* $^{(23)}$[(*na-an le*)]*-*⸤*e*⸥ *ša-an-na-at-ti na-aš-ma-kán* **ut-tar** $^{(24)}$[(*ku-e-da-ni-i*)]*k-ki* **mar***-ki-ia-mi nu-uš-ši me-ma-aḫ-ḫi* $^{(25)}$[(*le-e-wa-r*)*a-a*]*t nam-ma ku-wa-pí-ik-ki i-ia-ši* $^{(26)}$[(*a-pa-a-aš P*)]*A-NI* ^{d}UTU*-ŠI me-ma-i Ú-UL-wa-ra-at* $^{(27)}$[(*i-ia-mi*) E]GIR*-az-ma-at i-ia-zi* $^{(28)}$[(GAM *NI-ÌŠ* DINGIR*-LÌ*)] GAR*-ru*

§31″ (A iv 29–37; B iv 16′–24′; E iv 16′–17′) $^{(29)}$[(*INA* É^{MEŠ}*-KU-N*)*U*?[131]*-m*]*a***-aš-ma-aš** *ku-it* MUNUS^{MEŠ} *tar-na-an e-eš-***du**[132] $^{(30)}$[(*ki-i-ma ku-i*)*t*][133] É.LUGAL *na-aš ma-a-an ku-iš im-ma ku-iš* $^{(31)}$[(MUNUS*-TU₄ ŠA*) É].LUGAL *ma-a-na-aš* ^{MUNUS}SUḪUR.LA₅ *ma-a-na-aš* $^{(32)}$[(*EL-LU nu-za*) *ma*?*-a*?*-a*]*n*[134] *ša-ak-ta ku-iš-ki ku-in-ki* $^{(33)}$[(*ki-nu-un-m*)*a-an-za-a*]*n-kán*[135] *Ú-UL* EGIR GAM *kar-aš-zi* $^{(34)}$[(*na-an-š*)*i*~[136] x x x]x **ar***-ḫa iš-da₄-ma-aš-ša-an-zi* $^{(35)}$[(*na-at*)~ x x x x]x[137] *ke-e-ez-za-kán* UD.KAM*-za ar-ḫa ta-me-e-*[*d*]*a-ni* $^{(36)}$[(*A-NA*) MUNUS?*-TI*? *ŠA*? É.L]UGAL[138] *ma-ni-in-ku-wa-an* *x x* $^{(37)}$[(*k*)*u-iš-ki* x x x *pa-iz-z*]*i* GAM *NI-ÌŠ* DINGIR*-LÌ* GAR*-ru*

§32″ (A iv 38–41; B iv 25′–28′) $^{(38)}$[*ma-a-an-na-kán*[139] L]Ú*a-ra-an-ma ku-iš Ú-UL ḫa-an-*⸢*ti-i*⸣ $^{(39)}$[*ti-ia-zi*][140] ^{d}UTU*-ŠI-ma-at iš-da₄-ma-aš-mi* $^{(40)}$[*na-an pu-nu-u*]*š-mi na-at-mu-kán le-e ša-an-na-a-i* $^{(41)}$[*ma-a-an-n*]*a-at ša-an-na-a-i-ma* GAM *NI-ÌŠ* DINGIR*-LÌ* GAR*-ru*

§26″ (1)Or if he sees some malevolence of his, (2)and he conceals it, it shall be placed under oath.

§27″ (3)Or as concerns what the men of Ḫattusa are prone to do, (4–5)(i.e.,) they *secretly* wishes for the lordship of [an]other man instead of the lordship of My Majesty,[141] (6)that shall be placed under oath.

§28″ (7–8)Or (if) a colleague hears from a(nother) colleague [s]ome evil matter conce[rning] My Majesty, (9)[a]nd he does not denounce him, (10)(then it) shall be placed [(under)] oath.

§29″ (11)Or if there is some matter, (12)[o]r even some *kunistayalli*-,[142] (13)[(o)]r it (regards) a woman, and I, My Majesty question you(sg.), (14)[(then)] you(sg.) shall not conceal [(i)]t, the matter. (15)Testify(sg.) before My Majesty (as such): (16)"[(The matter)] they are questioning me about (17)is indeed a *kunistayalli*-matter, (18–19)but since they are questioning [(me, I will divulge)] it." There shall be no [(will)]ful dissimulation.

§30″ (20–22)[(And if)] I, My Majesty, [(se)]nd you(sg.) [(out)] for som<e> matter, or I question you(sg.) about [(som)]e affair of yours(sg.), (23–24)[(then)] you(sg.) must [(no)]t conceal [(it)]. Or if I forbid some matter to [(someo)]ne, and I tell him, (25)"You(sg.) must [(not)] do [i]t for anyone any longer!" (26f.)[(He)] will say [(be)]fore My Majesty, "I [(will)] not [(do)] it." If thereafter he does it, though, (28)(it) shall be placed [(under oath)].

§31″ (29)[No]w, since women are to be let [(into yo)]ur [(houses)], (30–31)[(but, becau)se (this)] is the palace, then whatever [pa]lace [(woman)] is (concerned), be she a chambermaid (or) be she (32)a [(free person), *i*]*f* anyone (of you) has known any one (of them), (33)[(b)u]t he does not [(now)] break it off with [he]r, (34)[(and)] they hear [… (*about him*)] *from* [(*he*)*r*], (35–36)[(and it/they) …], then from this day on whoever [… goe]s near another [*woman of* the pa]lace, (it) shall be placed under oath.

§32″ (38–39)[*And if*] someone does not *de*[*nounce*] a colleague, on the other hand, and I, My Majesty, hear about it, (40)[and] I [quest]ion [him], he shall not conceal it from me. (41)A[nd if] he nonetheless conceals it, (it) shall be placed under oath.

§33″ (A iv 42–45; B iv 29′–32′) (42)[*ma-a-an-m*]*a*[143] *ma-ni-in-ku-wa-an-ma ku-iš-ki* (43)[*ku-e-da-n*]*i-ik-ki pa-iz-zi* LÚ*a-ra-aš-ma-an-kán* (44)[EGIR-*an*]-*da*[144] *a-uš-zi na-an-kán ḫa-an-ti-i* (45)[*Ú-UL*] *ti-ia-zi na-at* GAM *NI-ÌŠ* DINGIR-*LÌ* GAR-*ru*

§34″ (A iv 46–48; B iv 33′–35′) (46)[(*na-aš-ma-za*)] *ki-i MA-ME-TU*$_4$ *še-ek-nu-uš pí-ip-pu-wa-ar* (47)[(*ku-iš-ki i*)]-*ia-zi na-aš-ma-za-at ar-ḫa* (48)⌜*a-ni-ia-zi*⌝ GAM *NI-ÌŠ* DINGIR-*LÌ* GAR-*ru*

§35″ (A iv 49–53; B iv 36′–40′; F iv 2′–5′) (49)*na-aš-ma ki-i ku-iš-ki me-ma-i ke-e-da-ni-wa-kán TUP-PÍ* (50)*ke-e* INIM^{MEŠ} *Ú-UL* GAR-*ri nu-wa-ra-at-mu-kán* (51)*pa-ra-a tar-na-an e-eš-du nu a-pa-a-aš me-mi-aš* (52)*le-e e-eš-zi ku-it im-ma ku-it* ⅃ *ku-ku-pa-la-tar* (53)GAM *NI-ÌŠ* DINGIR-*LÌ* GAR-*ru*

Colophon

(A iv 54–56; B iv 41′–42′; F iv 6′) (54)DUB.1-*PU ŠA MA-ME-TI* (55)*I-NA* URU*U.UŠ.ŠA* (56)*ŠA* LÚ^{MEŠ} SAG

§33″ (42–45)[*B*]*ut* [*if*] someone is having an affair with [some]one, but a colleague sees him [*by chan*]*ce* and he does [not] denounce him, then it shall be placed under oath.

§34″ (46–48)[(Or) if (anyone)] spits upon[145] this oath or does away with it, (it) shall be placed under oath.

§35″ (49)Or (if) someone says this: "On this tablet (50–51)these words are not to be found, so it shall be permissible for me." That utterance (52)shall not be made! Any and every *kukupalatar* (53)shall be placed under oath!

COLOPHON

(54)Tablet One of the Oath; (55)in the city of Ūssa,[146] (56)for the Courtiers.

No. 28
Suppiluliu/ama II's Instructions and Oath Imposition for the Men of Ḫattusa (*CTH* 256)

This fragmentary text belongs to the very latest of the genre. No findspot for the lone extant tablet is known. Since the text was not complete with this single tablet, only some ten percent at most of the original composition is preserved.

Its structure is as intriguing as it is unique. The first paragraph introduces the composition as a plea or prayer of Suppiluliu/ama II[147]—whose pedigree back to Suppiluliuma I is provided—to the gods listed in its first four lines. At least the following two paragraphs, which seem to argue the matter of the ensuing oath before the gods, are then in fact formulated in the 1st sg. and addressed to the gods. Paragraph four, though still within the context of the prayer, would

---

Transliteration

§1 (i 1)[… d10 URU*Z*]*I.IP.*PA*.LA.A*[*N.DA*] (2)[… d10 URU*NE*].*RI.IK.KA*4 (3)[… d*T*]*A.RU.UP.PA.ŠA.NI* (4)[… ḪUR].SAGMEŠ I7MEŠ *ŠA* KUR URU[GN] (5)[… m*Šu-up-pí-lu-li-i*]*a-ma-aš* LUGAL.GAL LUGAL KUR URUKÙ.BABBAR (6)[UR.SAG DUMU m*TU.UD.ḪA.LI.IA* LUGAL.GAL LUG]AL KUR URUKÙ.BABBAR UR.SAG (7)[DUMU.DUMU-*ŠU ŠA* mGIŠGIDRU.DINGIR-*LÌ* LUGAL.GAL UR].SAG ŠA!.BAL.BAL m*ŠU.UP.PÍ.LU.*[*LI.U.MA*] (8)[LUGAL.GAL UR.SAG … *ar-k*]*u-wa-ar i-ia-at*

§2 (i 9)[…]x *šu-me-eš* DINGIRMEŠ *ti-ia-at-tén* (10)[…]x-*ta šu-um-me-eš* DINGIRMEŠ-*aš* (11)[… *k*]*a-ru-ú ar-ku-wa-ar i-ia-nu-un*

§3 (i 12)[…]x ˹*ta*˺-*pa-ra-ma-ḫi-ta-ti* (13)[…]x x ˹GIM˺-*a*[*n*] ˻*ar-ḫa*˼ x x (14)[…] x-*aš ka-a-aš-ša šu-u*[*m-* …] (15)[…]x-*in* KASKAL-*an ap-pa-an-zi* (16)[…]x[ ]x-*kán li-in-ki-ia* (17)[…]x-˹*wa*?/*ši*?-*du*?˺[ ]

§4 (i 18)[…]-*aš ki-i-i*[*a*?-*a*]*š*?[149] *ku-*˹*it* *MA-MIT*˺ (19)[…]x *ma-a-an k*[*iš-a*]*n ku-iš-ki me-ma-*˹*a-i*˺ (20)[… -(*i*)]*a-*aš** GEŠTU?-˹*an*?˺ *UL pa-ra-a e-ep-mi-p*[*át*?] (21)[…]*pé-e-da-aḫ-ḫi nu-wa-mu u-ni-iš* (22)[… -*i*]*š*?-*zi n*[*u-w*]*a*? *da-pí-an-za* (23)[… *ša-ku-wa-aš*]-*ša-ra-za* ˹ZI˺-*za* ˹GEŠTU?-*ŠU*?˺ *pa-ra-a e-ep-du* (24)[…]x-*da-ú ku-*˻*iš*˼-*ma ke-*˻*e-da*˼-*n*[*i*] (25)[… *ša-ku-wa-aš-ša-ri-i*]*t* ZI-*it* GEŠTU-*an* ˻*UL*˼ [*pa-ra-a*] (26)[*e-ep-zi* …]x *le-en-*˻*ki-ia*˼-*aš* ˻*le/iš*˼-x[…] (27)[… -*u*]*d*?-*du*

§5 (i 28)[…]-*ti* KUR.KURM[EŠ …] (29)[…]x x x[…]

(ca. latter half of col. i lost)

seem already to begin enumerating the potentially disloyal types of behavior to be placed under oath. Most of the four partially preserved paragraphs of col. ii contain the deities called to witness the imposition of the oath. Before the text of col. ii breaks off the prayer to the gods ends and the text continues by addressing the men of Ḫattusa (§10′). The remainder of the composition deals primarily with the status of the towns or communities dedicated to the presumably royal ancestors and with the addressees' obligations toward them.[148] Various duties and obligations incumbent upon the men of Ḫattusa are described, which are to fall under the divine oath if neglected.

Of interest are the references to "kingship of the Land of Ḫattusa" alongside the "kingship of the borders" and the "minor kingship," as well as the seemingly related phrase "made by men," all of which is unfortunately too fragmentary to allow reliable inferences.

TRANSLATION

§1 (1)[… Storm God of Z]ippala[nda], (2)[… Storm God of Ne]rikka, (3)[… T]aruppasani, (4)[… moun]tains, rivers of the Land of […] (5)[… Suppiluliy]ama, Great King, King of the Land of Ḫattusa, (6)[Hero, Son of Tudḫaliya, Great King, Ki]ng of the Land of Ḫattusa, Hero, (7)[Grandson of Ḫattusili, Great King, He]ro, Descendant of Suppilu[liuma], (8)[Great King, Hero …], made a [pl]ea.

§2 (9)[…] you gods placed/arrived[150] (10)[…] you gods (11)[… e]arlier I made a plea.

§3 (12)[…] with authority (13)[…] like/as soon as away/out (14)[…] this one, too, yo[u][151] (15)[…] they take the road […] (16f.)[…] to/for the oath […]

§4 (18)[… *a*]*nd since* [*h*]*e* […] *this* oath (19)[…] If anyone says the fol[low] ing: (20)"[…] I will not *listen a*[*t all*]! (21)I will carry/take […], and that (person) to/for me […], (22)a[nd] the entire […] (23)with an [upri]ght spirit make him *listen* […], (24)he shall […]!" But he who to this (person) (25–26)[…] with an [uprigh]t spirit does not *li*[*sten* …] of the oath […] (27)[…] let him […]!

§5 (28–29)[…] lands […]

(ca. latter half of col. i lost)

§6′ (ii 4′)[…]x x[…] (5′)[…]x-⌜*iš*⌝ d*NA.A*[*M.NI* d*ḪA.AZ.ZI* …] (6′)⌜d10 URU⌝*PÍT.TI.IA.RI.GA*[…] (7′)⌜d⌝10 URU*LI.IḪ.ŠI.NA* dx152[…] (8′)⌜d⌝10 URU*ŠA.RE.EŠ.ŠI.IA* d[…] (9′)⌜d⌝10 URU*ḪI.IŠ.ŠA.AŠ.PA* d10 UR[U …]

§7′ (ii 10′)[dLAMMA U]RU⌜KÙ.BABBAR⌝-*TI* d*ZI.IT.ḪA.RI.I*[*A* …] (11′)[dLAM]MA URU*GA.RA.AḪ.NA* *dLAMMA* U[RU…] (12′)⌜d⌝*É-a-aš* d*Le-el-wa-ni-iš*[…] (13′) URU**DA.WI*$_5$*.NI.IA* x* URU*DUR.MI.IT.T*[*A* …] (14′) d*Pí-ir-wa-aš* MUNUS.LUGAL-*aš* MUNUS.LUGAL[…] (15′) d30 *MA*!-*MIT* d*TA.RU.UP.PA.ŠA.NI*[…] (16′) d*Ma-am-mi-iš* d10 URU*TI.I.ŠA.M*[*A* …]

§8′ (ii 17′) d*ḪÉ.BAT* d*ḪÉ.BAT*-dLUGAL-*ma-aš* d*IŠTAR*[…] (18′) d*IŠTAR* URU*NE.NU.WA* d*IŠTAR* URUx[…] (19′) d*Ni-na-at-ta-aš* d*Ku-li-it-ta-*[*aš* …] (20′) d*ZA-BA*$_4$*-BA*$_4$ d*ZA-BA*$_4$*-BA*$_4$[…] (21′) d*ZA-BA*$_4$*-BA*$_4$ URU*A.AR.ZI.*[*IA* …]

§9′ (ii 22′)⌜*ŠA*⌝ URU*ḪUR.MA* d*ḪA.*<*AN*>*.TI.T*[*A.AŠ.ŠU* …] (23′) URU*An-ku-wa-aš* d*Ḫa-at-ta-k*[*a*~ …] (24′)*ŠA* URU*TU.UN.NA* d*Ḫal-la-a-*[*ra-aš* …] (25′)DINGIRMEŠ *Lu-la-ḫi-iš* DINGIRMEŠ *Ḫa-pí-*[*ri-iš* …] (26′)*ḫu-u-ma-an-te-eš ŠA* KUR URU*ḪA.*[*AT.TI* …] (27′) dEREŠ.KI.GAL *ka-ru-ú-i-*[*le-eš* DINGIRMEŠ …] (28′) d*Na-ra-aš* d*Na-ap-ša-ra-a*[*š* …] (29′) d*A-la-lu-uš* d**A-nu-uš** x[…] (30′)ḪUR.SAGMEŠ I$_7$MEŠ *šal-li-i*[*š a-ru-na-aš* …] (31′)*x x x *na-at* x x *ke**-*e-d*[*a-ni li-in-ki-ia* …] (32′)*nu uš-kán-du iš-da*$_4$[*-ma-aš-kán-du*]

§10′ (ii 33′)[*šu-u*]*m-me-eš-ma-aš* LÚMEŠ URU*ḪAT.T*[*I* …] (34′)[ ]**Ú**-*UL ar-ḫa tar-n*[*a*?- …] (35′)[ ]x-⌞*ni*?⌟*-e-eš* ≮*za-an-t*[*a-* …] (36′)[…]⌞*kap*⌟*-pu-u-wa-te-e*[*n* …]

(latter half of col. ii and first half of col. iii lost)

§11″ (iii 1′)(traces)

§12″ (iii 2′)⌜*ŠA*⌝ KUR.KUR URU*ḪAT.TI-ma* […] (3′)*nu-uš-ma-aš an-na-li-uš* x[…]

§13″ (iii 4′)ÉMEŠ *ŠA* GIDIMḪI.⌜A⌝[…] (5′)*lu-uz-zi-ia-za-at* x[…] (6′)*nu* GIDIM⌜ḪI⌝.[A*-a*]*š ku-*⌞*iš*⌟ *ku-it* […] (7′)*A-NA* ⌜É⌝MEŠ GIDIMḪI.A *ku-e*~[…] (8′)*ad-da-aš ḫu-uḫ-ḫa-aš ku-*⌜*e*⌝~[…] (9′)*ŠA* GIDIM⌜ḪI.A⌝ **iš*-*ḫi-ú-ul*[…] (10′)*lu-u-zi ḫar-zi nu-kán k*[*u*?- …] (11′)*pa-ra-a ú-da-an-zi nu* x[…] (12′)*a-pa-a-at lu-uz-zi e-e*[*š-* …] (13′) ≮*gal-la-ar-ma-aš-ma-aš-kán* x[…] (14′)*da*$_4$*-me-eš-ḫa-iz-zi-ia-aš le-*⌜*e*?⌝[…] (15′)*ka-a-aš-ma-aš* INIM-*aš* GAM *MA-MI*[*T* GAR-*ru*]

§14″ (iii 16′)*ŠA* GIDIMḪI.A *ku-iš* URU-*LU*$_4$ […] (17′)*pé-eš-du Ú-UL-ma-an ku-iš*[…]

§6′ (5′)[…] Na[mni, Ḫazzi, …] (6′)the Storm God of Pittiyariga, […], (7′)the Storm God of Liḫsina, the […]-Deity of […],(8′)the Storm God of Saressiya, the […]-Deity of […], (9′)the Storm God of Ḫissaspa, the Storm God of […]

§7′ (10′)[The protective deity of] Ḫattusa, Zitḫariy[a, …], (11′)[the prot]ective deity of Garaḫna, the protective deity of […], (12′)Ea, Lelwani, [… deity of] (13′)Dawiniya (and?) Durmitt[a …], (14′)Pirwa the queen, queen [of …], (15′)the Moon God of the oath, Taruppasani, […], (16′)Mammi, the Storm God of Tīsam[a …].

§8′ (17′)Ḫebat, Ḫebat-Šarruma, Ištar […] (18′)Ištar of Nineveh, Ištar of […], (19′)Ninatta, Kulitta […], (20′)the War God, the War God of […], (21′)the War God of Arzi[ya, …]

§9′ (22′)Ḫa<n>tit[assu] of Ḫurma, [… of] (23′)Ankuwa, Ḫattak[a~ of …] (24′)of Tunna, Ḫallā[ra …] (25′)the gods (of) the Lulaḫi-(people), the gods (of) the Ḫapi[ru]-(people) […] (26′)altogether, […] of the Land of Ḫa[ttusa, …] (27′)Ereškigal, the primev[al deities, …], (28′)Narā, Napsara, […], (29′)Alalu, Anu, […], (30′)the mountains, the rivers, the great [sea …]: (31′)They [… to] thi[s oath]. (32′)Let them observe! [Let them] lis[ten]!

§10′ (33′)[Yo]u men of Ḫattu[sa], though, […] to them […] (34′–35′)not *let loose* […] (36′)take account! […]

(latter half of col. ii and first half of col. iii lost)

§11″ (traces)

§12″ (2′)Of the Lands of Ḫattusa, though, […] (3′)to you/them the earlier/ancient […]

§13″ (4′)The houses of the ancestors […] (5′)and of the *luzzi*-levy they/it […]. (6′)And he who something of/to the ancestors […] (7′)to the houses of the ancestors which […] (8′)to the fathers (and) the grandfathers which […] (9′)levies concerning the ancestors […] (10′)has a *luzzi*-levy, and […] (11′)they bring out, and […] (12′)that *luzzi*-levy i[s …], (13′)but to you/them a misfortune […] (14′)he/it shall not oppress them, […] (15′)(then) this matter [shall be placed] under oath for you.

§14″ (16′)The town of the ancestors which […] (17′)he shall give! He who does

(18′)*nu a-pa-a-aš* URU-*aš ku-it A-NA*[…] (19′)*nu* ˻URU˼-*LU*$_4$ ˻GIDIM$^{\text{ḪI.A}}$ *ku-iš*˼ x[…] (20′)⌜*e*⌝-*eš*!?-⌜*du*?⌝ […]

§15″ (iii 21′)*nu šu-um-me-eš* LÚ^{MEŠ} ^{URU}KÙ.BABBAR[…] (22′)*A-NA* GIDIM$^{\text{ḪI.A}}$ *kiš-an še-er* x[[153] …]

§16″ (iii 23′)LÚ^{MEŠ} KUR.KUR ^{URU}*ḪAT.TI-ma-aš-ma-aš at*-[…] (24′)*iš-ḫi-ú-ul ku-wa-at-tan*$_{\text{x}}$?(DIN)[154] *ar-ḫa* […] (25′)LUGAL-*UT-TA ŠA* KUR ^{URU}*ḪAT.TI* DINGIR^{ME}[^{Š} …] (26′)LUGAL-*UT-TA ŠA* *x* ZAG$^{\text{ḪI.A}}$-*ma ku*-[*e* …] (27′)*na-at* UN^{MEŠ}-*za i-ia-an*~[…] (28′)LUGAL-*UT-TA te-e-pa-u-wa* A[…] (29′)*ku-i-e-eš* ^{GIŠ}*al-kiš-ta-nu-u*[*š* …] (30′)*iš-ḫi-ú-li a-pu-u-uš*[…] (31′)*ki-nu-na ŠA* KUR ^{URU}*ḪA*[*T.TI* …] (32′)*a-pu-u-uš ḫar-kán*-[*du* …]

(gap of ca. half a col.)

§17″ (iv 1′)[…]x x ⌜*ku-wa-ia-an-te*⌝-[*eš*] (2′)[… *m*]*a*?-*a-an* LUGAL-*i* (3′)[… *ki*]*š-an le-e* DÙ!(NI)-*zi* (4′)[…]x-*ti-ia-zi*[155] (5′)[… *k*]*iš-an le-e me-ma-i* (6′)[… *a*]*m-me-el* ⸔*wa-aš-ku-u-i*-⌜*ša*⌝ (7′)[… -*V*]*ḫ-ḫi ku-it-ma-an-wa-za* (8′)[…]x-*un nu-un-tar-aš* (9′)[… *a-pa-aš* I]NIM-*aš* GAM *MA-MIT* GA[R-*r*]*u*

§18″ (iv 10′)[… *i*]*š-ḫi-ú-ul-ma* x[ ]x *kap*-[*pu-wa-i*]*t-tén* (11′)[…]x *e-ep-tén nu* LUGA[L]x x x[…] (12′)[…]x ḪUL-*u-wa-aš* x[…] (13′)[… *ḫ*]*ar*?-*ku-e-ni* x x[…] (14′)[…]x *le-e*-x[…] (15′)[… *a-pa-aš* INI]M-*aš* GAM *M*[*A-MIT* GAR-*ru*]

Colophon

(iv 16′)[DUB.1.KAM] *UL* [*Q*]*A-TI* (17′)[*li-in*]-*ki-ia-aš* (18′)[*ŠA* ^{m}*Š*]*U.UP.PÍ.*[*LU.L*]*I.U.MA* (19′)[DUMU ^{m}*TU.U*]*D.ḪA.LI.IA*

not […] him/it, though, […] (18′)and *because* that town to […], (19′)and the town of the ancestors which […] (20′)let him/it *be* […]!

§15″ (21′)And you men of Ḫattusa, […] (22′)to the ancestors thus […]

§16″ (23′)You men of the lands of Ḫattusa, though, to them/yourselves […] (24′)*where* the obligation […] away […]. (25′)The kingship of the Land of Ḫattusa, the gods […] (26′)the kingship/kingdom of the borders whi[ch …], though, (27′)*are made by men.* […] (28′)the *minor* kingship/kingdom […] (29′)those who […] the branches […] (30′)those to the obligations […], (31′)but now […] of the Land of Ḫatt[usa …] (32′)[… may] they destroy those (persons)![156]

(gap of ca. half a col.)

§17″ (1′)[…] are afraid (2′)[… i]f to the king (3′–4′)[… t]hus he shall not do! (5′)[…] he shall not speak thus: (6′)"[… *m*]*y* misdeed, though, […] (7′)I will […], so long as (8′)[…] quickly […]." […] (9′)May [this] matter be placed under oath!

§18″ (10′)[…] the obligation, though, you shall […] tak[e acco]unt of (11′)[…] you shall seize/hold, and the kin[g …] (12′)[…] of evil […] (13′)[…] we will be [*ru*]*ined* […] (14′)[…] shall not […] (15′)[… this mat]ter [shall be placed] under o[ath].

COLOPHON

(16′) [Tablet One], not [fi]nished, (17′)of the [Oa]th (18′)[of S]uppiluliuma, (19′)[Son of Tu]dḫaliya.

Sources[1]

Old Kingdom Sources

1. A Royal Reprimand of the Dignitaries
   Text: *CTH* 272: KBo 22.1.
   Edition: Archi 1979: 43–48.
   Transliteration: Groddek 2008b: 1–4.
   Translations: Klinger 2001a: 71–72; Marazzi 1988: 127–28; Gilan 2009: 132–34.
   Selected Discussions: Hoffner 1976: 335; Neu 1984: 99; Marazzi 1988; Beal 1988: 280–81.

2. Instructions and Oath Imposition for Royal Servants concerning the Purity of the King
   Texts: *CTH* 265: A. KUB 13.3;[2] B. KBo 50.282+Bo 4410.[3]
   Editions: Pecchioli Daddi 2004; Marazzi 2013; cf. Friedrich 1928/9: 46–58.
   Partial Transliterations: Otten and Rüster 1977: 55–56; Groddek 2008a: 190–91.
   Translations: Goetze 1950: 207; von Schuler 1982: 124–25; Haase 1984: 63–64.
   Selected Discussions: Giorgieri 1995: 231–33.

3. Protocol for the Palace Gatekeeper
   Texts: *CTH* 263: A. KBo 5.11(+)KUB 26.23(+)KBo 50.275; B. KUB 26.28; C. KBo 50.270.
   Partial Editions: Hrozný 1920: 26–30; Bossert 1944: 16–17.
   Partial Transliterations: Otten 1953b: 12; Groddek 2008a: 177, 181.
   Selected Discussions: Otten 1953a: 21–22; Klinger 1996: 200–207, 249–52; Yakubovich 2009: 264–68.

4. Protocol for the Royal Body Guard
Text: *CTH* 262: IBoT 1.36.[4]
Editions: Jakob-Rost 1966; Güterbock and van den Hout 1991.
Translation: McMahon 1997: 225–30.
Selected Discussions: Singer 1975: 84–87; Alp 1983: 106–11; Beal 1992: 212–16, 528.

5. Royal Decree on Social and Economic Matters
Texts: *CTH* 269: A. KUB 29.39+KBo 50.284; B. IBoT 3.75.
Edition: Košak 1988a.
Discussion: Marazzi 1994.

6. An Akkadian Fragment Mentioning an Oath
Text: *CTH* 275: KUB 3.20.
Edition: Weidner 1923: 148–49.
Treatment: Giorgieri 1995: 324–26.
Discussion: Carruba 1988: 209.

Sources from the Reigns of Tudḫaliya I and Arnuwanda I

7. Instructions for Military Officers and Frontier Post Governors
Text: *CTH* 261.II: KUB 26.17.
Partial Edition: Alp 1947.
Transliteration, Commentary: Giorgieri 1995: 206–11.
Discussion: Del Monte 1975a: 137–39.

8. Tudḫaliya I's Decree on Penal and Administrative Reform
Texts: *CTH* 258.1: A. KUB 13.9+KUB 40.62; B_1. KBo 27.16; B_2. KBo 50.260; B_3. KBo 50.259.
Editions: von Schuler 1959: 445–72; Westbrook and Woodard 1990; Marazzi 2012.
Partial Transliterations / Editions: Otten 1952: 236; Otten 1979; Marazzi and Gzella 2003; Groddek 2008a: 165–66; Dardano 2009: 5.
Translation: Haase 1984: 56–57.
Selected Discussions: Riemschneider 1961: 28–29; Freydank 1970; Otten 1979; Güterbock 1983: 78–80; de Martino and Imparati 1998: 395–400.

9. Tudḫaliya I's Decree on Judicial Reform
Text: *CTH* 258.2: KUB 13.7.[5]

Editions: Giorgieri 1995: 122–36; Marazzi 2004.
Selected Discussions: Y. Cohen 2002: 136–40; Archi 2008: 291–92.

10. Tudḫaliya I?'s Instructions and Oath Imposition for All the Men
Texts: *CTH* 259: A. KUB 26.11; B. KUB 13.20; C. KUB 13.21+KBo 50.268; D_1. KUB 31.107+KBo 50.265; D_2. Bo 8570.
Editions: Giorgieri 1995: 137–205; cf. Alp 1947; von Schuler 1956: 213–14.
Partial Transliterations: Miller 2007b: 128–29; Groddek 2008a: 169–70, 173–76.
Selected Discussions: Del Monte 1975a; Gonzáles Salazar 1999; Giorgieri 2005: 327 and n. 22, 343–44.

11. Instructions and Oath Impositions for the Successions of Tudḫaliya I and Tudḫaliya III
Texts: *CTH* 271 (and 275): A_1. KUB 36.114; A_2. KUB 34.40+KUB 34.41[6]; A_3. KUB 36.113; A_4. KUB 36.112; A_5. KUB 36.116; A_6. KBo 50.285; A_7. KBo 38.91; B_1. KUB 36.109; B_2. KBo 40.16; C_1. KUB 36.118+KUB 36.119; C_2. KUB 34.58.[7]
Editions: A_1: Carruba 1971: 91–93; 1977: 188–91; Giorgieri 1995: 117–19; 2005: 332–33. A_2: Bin–Nun 1975: 266–68; Carruba 1977: 184–87. A_3: Carruba 1977: 188–89. A_4: Carruba 1977: 187–88. A_5: Carruba 1977: 188–89. B_1: Carruba 1977: 190–91. C: Carruba 1977: 192–93; Otten 1990: 224–26; Giorgieri 1995: 119–21.
Partial Transliterations: Groddek 2008a: 192–93.
Selected Treatments and Discussions: Carruba 1971, 1977; Gurney 1979; Otten 1987: 29–31; de Martino 1991; Giorgieri 1995: 117–21; Klinger 1988: 33; 1995: 95–97; Houwink ten Cate 1995–96: 58–69; Taracha 1997: 76 and n. 10; 2004: 635–36; Freu 2004; 2007a: 177–81; 2007b: 36–41, 60–68, 148–58; Giorgieri 2005: 332–35; Marizza 2007: 25–33; Carruba 2008: 107–15, 122–24; Hawkins 2011: 86–90.

12. Instructions and Oath Imposition for Princes, Lords, and Military Officers
Texts: *CTH* 251: A. KBo 16.24(+)KBo 16.25; B_1. KBo 16.102; B_2. KBo 50.256; B_3. KBo 50.257; B_4. Bo 6830.
Editions: Giorgieri 1995: 96–116; cf. Carruba 1977: 182–87; Rizzi Mellini 1979.
Partial Transliteration: Groddek 2008a: 163–64.
Selected Discussions: Kammenhuber 1970b: 550–51; Pecchioli Daddi

1979; Košak 1980; Giorgieri 2005: 326 and n. 20, 330–32; Y. Cohen 2002: 140–43; Freu 2007b: 34–36, 62–63; Christiansen 2008: 266–72.

13. Instructions of Arnuwanda I for the Mayor (of Ḫattusa)
Texts: *CTH* 257: 1.A. KBo 13.58; 1.B.[8] KUB 23.64; 1.C. KBo 50.262; 1.D.[9] KBo 10.5; 1.E.[10] KUB 26.9+KBo 50.264; 2. KBo 10.4; 3.A.[11] KUB 31.112+Bo 4007; 3.B. KBo 50.261+Bo 4468; 3.C. Bo 3977; 4.A. KUB 31.100; 4.B. Bo 3683.[12]
(Partial) Editions: 1–3: Pecchioli Daddi 1975; 1: Otten 1983a; 1983c: 48–52; 4: Košak 1993; Ünal 1993: 129–36.
Transliteration: Groddek 2008a: 166–69.
Translation: 1: Houwink ten Cate 1983: 163–64.[13]
Selected Treatments and Discussions: Otten 1964; Ünal 1992: 215–23; Singer 1998.

14. Loyalty Oath of Town Commanders to Arnuwanda I, Ašmunikkal, and Tudḫaliya
Texts: *CTH* 260: 1. KUB 31.44+KBo 50.273+KBo 51.4+Bo 4670; 2. KUB 31.42; 3.A. KUB 26.24+KUB 40.15+KBo 50.266b+Bo 7020(+)KUB 26.24+KBo 50.266a; 3.B_1. KBo 50.151+KBo 50.269; 3.B_2. KBo 50.62; 3.B_3. 2099/g.[14]
Editions: Giorgieri 1995: 212–30; cf. von Schuler 1956: 223–40.
Partial Transliterations: Otten and Rüster 1978: 270; Miller 2007b: 129–30; 2007c: 134–35; 2008: 126; Groddek 2008a: 53–55, 167–68, 170–72, 179–80; Lorenz 2010: 260–62.
Translation: Houwink ten Cate 1983: 168–71.
Selected Discussion: Giorgieri 2005: 336–38.

15. Instructions and Oath Imposition(s) of Arnuwanda I
Texts: *CTH* 275: 1. KUB 26.10; 2. KUB 26.42.
Edition: 1. Pecchioli Daddi 2002a.

16. Decree of Queen Ašmunikkal concerning the "Royal Funerary Structure"
Texts: *CTH* 252: A. KUB 13.8; B. KUB 57.46.
Edition: Otten 1958: 104–7.
Translations: del Monte 1975b: 324; Klinger 2001a: 72–73.
Selected Discussions: Otten 1974; del Monte 1975b.

17. Instructions of Arnuwanda I for the Frontier Post Governors
Texts: *CTH* 261.I: A. KUB 13.1+KBo 50.280a(+)KUB 31.87+KUB

40.56+KUB 31.88+Bo 7192(+)KUB 40.55+KBo 50.280b[15]; B_1. KUB 13.2+KUB 31.84+KUB 40.60+E 1489; B_2. Bo 6558; C_1. KUB 31.108(+) KBo 50.277; C_2. KUB 40.57; C_3. KUB 31.85(+)Bo 7770; C_4. KUB 31.90+KUB 31.91; D. KUB 31.86+KUB 40.58+KUB 48.104+KUB 40.78+KBo 50.272+KBo 57.10+Bo 5391+Bo 69/105(+)KUB 13.25[16]; E. KUB 31.89(+)KUB 13.24(+)E 1478; F_1. KBo 53.255; F_2. KBo 50.271[17]; G_1. KBo 22.44[18]; G_2. KBo 60.11; G_3. Bo 8182;[19] H. KBo 50.267; I. KBo 48.238; J. KBo 58.3; K. Bo 8326; L. Bo 8274; M. Bo 9110.

Editions: von Schuler 1957: 36–59; Pecchioli Daddi 2003a.

Partial Transliterations: del Monte 2003: 56–58; Groddek 2008a: 172–73, 177–79, 183–89; Miller 2008: 125.

(Partial) Translations: Goetze 1950: 210–11; Houwink ten Cate 1983: 166–68; McMahon 1997: 221–25; del Monte 2003: 56–58; Singer 2009a: 44–51.

Selected Discussions: Laroche 1957: 126–28; Goetze 1959: 69–70; 1960; Hoffner 1971; Kammenhuber 1970a: 63–65; 1972: 434–38; Kühne 1972: 255–56; Marazzi 1979; Beal 1992: 426–36 and *passim*; González Salazar 1999; Singer 2008: 251–57.

18. Instructions and Oath Imposition for Military Commanders

    Texts: *CTH* 268: KUB 21.47+KUB 23.82(+)KBo 19.58.

    Editions: Košak 1990; Giorgieri 1995: 237–53.

19. Āsḫapāla's Oath Regarding an Obligation to Supply Troops

    Text: *CTH* 270: KBo 16.50.

    Editions: Otten 1960; Giorgieri 1995: 234–36.

20. Instructions for Priests and Temple Personnel

    Texts:[20] *CTH* 264: A. KUB 13.4; B_1. KUB 13.6+KUB 13.17+KUB 13.19+FHL 100; B_2. KUB 31.120+KBo 50.276b; B_3. KBo 50.276a; C_1. KUB 13.5; C_2. KUB 31.92+KBo 50.283; C_3. KUB 31.95; D_1. AnSt 20; D_2. KUB 26.31; E_1. KUB 13.18; E_2. KBo 50.279; F_1. KUB 31.94; F_2. HT 28; G. KUB 31.93; H. KUB 40.63; I. KBo 57.232; J. KBo 50.274; K. KBo 57.11; L. KBo 50.278; M. Bo 8054; N. KBo 54.214; O. E 1401.

    Editions: Taggar-Cohen 2006: 37–139; cf. Sturtevant 1934; Sturtevant and Bechtel 1935: 127–74; Süel 1985.

    Partial Transliterations: Miller 2007b: 130–32; 2008: 125–26; Groddek 2008a: 180–89, 191–92.

    Translations: Goetze 1950: 207–10; Vieyra 1970: 511–12; Kühne 1975; Klinger 2001a: 73–81; McMahon 1997: 217–21.

Selected Discussions: Hulin 1970; Kammenhuber 1972: 434–41; Korošec 1974; Milgrom 1970; 1976: 242–47; Hoffner 1998: 35–36; Schwemer 2009; Taracha 2010; Taggar-Cohen 2011b.

Empire Period Sources

21. Instructions for Supervisors
Text: *CTH* 266: KBo 16.54+ABoT 1.53.
Edition: Riemschneider 1965: 336–40.

22. Instructions of Suppiluliuma I for the Military and a Corresponding Oath
Texts: *CTH* 253: 1. KUB 21.41; 2. KUB 26.57.
Editions: Giorgieri 1995: 254–60; cf. Laroche 1957: 125–26.
Translation: 2. Freu 2007b: 209–10.

23. Oath of the Men of Ḫattusa to Ḫattusili III and Pudu-Ḫepa
Text: *CTH* 254: KUB 21.46.
Edition: Giorgieri 1995: 261–67.

24. Instructions for Priests and Diviners
Texts: *CTH* 275: A. KUB 31.113; B. KUB 57.36.
Edition: Haas 1970: 130–33.
Discussion: Taggar-Cohen 2006: 178–82.

25. Instructions for the UKU.UŠ-troops
Text: *CTH* 267: KUB 13.28+KUB 40.61.
Treatments: Rosi 1984: 113–14; Beal 1992: 43–44, n. 172.

26. Tudḫaliya IV's Instructions and Loyalty Oath Imposition for Lords, Princes, and Courtiers
Texts: *CTH* 255.1: A. KUB 21.42+KUB 26.12; B. KUB 21.43+KUB 26.13; C. KUB 40.24.[21]
Edition: von Schuler 1957: 22–33.
Selected Discussions: Otten 1957/58: 389–90; Goetze 1959: 68–69; Giorgieri 1995: 274; Starke 1995b, 1996; Hawkins 2002: 221; Pecchioli Daddi 2006: 119–25.

27. Tudḫaliya IV's Instructions and Oath Imposition for Courtiers
Texts: *CTH* 255.2: A. KUB 26.1+KUB 23.112; B. KUB 26.8; C.[22] KUB

31.97; D. KUB 23.67; E. KUB 26.1a+Bo 4744(+)KBo 50.258; F. KBo 22.46; G. KBo 50.258.
Edition: von Schuler 1957: 8–21.
Partial Transliterations: del Monte 2003: 75–76; Groddek 2008a: 164–65.
Translation: del Monte 1988; 2003: 75–76.
Selected Discussions: Otten 1957/58: 388–89; Goetze 1959: 66–68; Giorgieri 1995: 275–76; Starke 1996; Hawkins 2002: 221–24; Pecchioli Daddi 2006: 119–25; Akdoğan 2013.[23]

28. Suppiluliu/ama II's Instructions and Oath Imposition for the Men of Ḫattusa
Text: *CTH* 256: ABoT 1.56.
Edition: Giorgieri 1995: 292–319.
Partial Treatments: Otten 1958: 102–5; 1963: 2–5; Meriggi 1962: 92–93.
Selected Discussions: Giorgieri and Mora 1996: 64–65; Singer 2009: 184–86.

Notes

Notes to the Introduction

1. Current English language overviews of Hittite history, culture, society, and religion include Bryce 2002, 2005; Collins 2007 and the various contributions in Genz and Mielke 2011.

2. My comment (Miller 2011a: 8) in this regard, "Naturally, the king took no oath of obligation toward his subordinates," should thus be stated more precisely as referring to the internal documentation of the state.

3. For relevant cautionary comments on the use of "contract" (and by implication "treaty") see Hoffner 2004b: 307.

4. In the Akkadian language treaties from Ḫattusa the terms *isḫiul-* and *lingai-* are replaced with *rikiltu/rikistu/riksu* and *māmītu*, respectively. These occur occasionally as Akkadograms in Hittite texts as well, though only the latter term is found in the instructions, and only in the compositions of the last Hittite kings, Tudḫaliya IV and Suppiluliu/ama II (Nos. 26, 27, and 28), or in late copies of earlier compositions (e.g., No. 9).

5. For a recent discussion of genre and category in the Hittite textual material in general, see Hutter 2011.

6. One does not, however, see purely prescriptive instruction texts labeled with *lingai-* (Christiansen 2008: 261; Giorgieri 1995: 27).

7. Similarly, e.g., Giorgieri 2005: 325, n. 17; d'Alfonso 2006b: 328; and Wilhelm 2011: 47. Tadmor (1982: 132) has pointed out that the situation is similar with the Neo-Assyrian treaties, where "*pars pro toto*, 'oath' or 'imprecation' would often stand for the whole phrase and imply 'treaty', 'covenant', 'allegiance'. Similarly, *ṭuppi niš ilī* ('tablet of the oath') and especially *ṭuppi mamīti* ('tablet of the imprecation') could stand for *ṭuppi riksi u mamīti* or *ṭuppu ša rikilti u ša mamīti*." Of interest in this context is Zaccagnini's (1990: 66–67) observation that the doublet *riksu-māmītu* occurs in the Akkadian language versions of Hittite treaties, but not in their Hittite language counterparts. Perhaps the scribes of the Hittite versions adopted the practice of using one of the terms *pars pro toto*, while the scribes of the Akkadian versions adhered to the convention of employing them in tandem.

8. As noted by Parpola (2011: 41), this was the case with the Neo-Assyrian treaty documents as well.

9. See also p. 33: "In den Vasallenverträgen ist jedoch die Aufstellung des Vertragsentwurfs (ak. *rikiltu*, h. *išḫiul*) Sache des Königs, seine Annahme durch Beeidigung (ak. *mamītu*, h. *lingaiš*) Sache des Vasallen" and p. 34; similarly Tadmor 1982: 139–40; Watanabe 1989: 269; Zaccagnini 1990: 64; Christiansen 2008: §5.3.1.

10. As noticed already by Taggar-Cohen (2006: 130). Wilhelm (2011: 48) likewise sees the obligation of loyalty as the most important among the various obligations incumbent upon the vassals of the state treaties.

11. For a differentiation between casuistic and legalistic regulations see, e.g., Riemschneider 1961: 28. Further discussion of the edicts and the question of the definition of the genre as well as ancient Near Eastern parallels can be found in Marazzi 2007 and d'Alfonso 2008: 331–42. It should perhaps be noted that Marazzi (2007) suggests a definition of the genre "edict" that leads to the exclusion of a number of texts often, and probably correctly, regarded as edicts, such as *CTH* 46, 47, and 65, composed by Suppiluliuma I and Mursili II for Niqmaddu and Niqmepa of Ugarit (cf. Devecchi 2012) and *CTH* 87, 88, and 89, from Ḫattusili III.

12. As noted, there is no reference to an oath imposition in the nearly completely preserved No. 20. It does, however, repeatedly refer to "the deities" destroying or otherwise punishing those temple personnel (and sometimes their decendents) who would fail in their duties (e.g. §9′, 67″; §13′, 53; §15′, 8–11; §18′, 55; §19′, 76–77), and one wonders if simply the deities for which the personnel happen to be working are intended or whether the text's composer assumed it would have been the "oath deities" that would have done so, implying that the personnel would indeed have been under oath regarding the instructions, even if not explicitely mentioned in the text. Some passages would seem to imply the former.

13. A further text, long thought to be a loyalty oath of a high official, has recently been shown to be a fragment of a treaty with Karkamiš (Singer 2001a; d'Alfonso 2007).

14. Von Schuler (1965b: 453–54) wrote that "gerade die Hapiru-Verträge und der Ashapala-Eid zeigen, wie fließend die Grenzen zwischen Diensteid und Vertrag mit auswärtigen Volksgruppen sind."

15. Zaccagnini (1990: 65) already queried whether such might be the case, but reasonably refrained from offering a firm answer, due to the lack of any substantiating documentation. Wilhelm (1978: 96), similarly, pointed out that the so-called *zweite militärischer Eid* could in fact have related to any group of officials, not just soldiers, since nowhere is any entirely unambiguous designation of its addressees preserved. For a thorough discussion of rites associated with oaths, see Giorgieri 2001; 2005: 338–42; and Christiansen 2008. Christiansen suggests that at least the so-called First Military Oath in fact "keine Elemente aufweist, die ihn als einheitliches Ritual erscheinen lassen" (p. 459); rather, it would seem to constitute "eine Sammlung von Eidesriten," and these "scheinen über einen längeren Zeitraum gesammelt worden zu sein und schließlich auf einer Tafel vereinigt worden zu sein."

16. In Cammarosano's (2006: 10) view, "il carattere estremamente dettagliato dei dettami contenuti nelle sezioni 'prescrittive' e la presenza di *tutti* gli elementi peculiari

dei testi *isḫiul* potrebbero autorizzare a parlare del documento come di un vero e proprio *testo d'istruzione*."

17. *CTH* 8–9; see Dardano 1997; Klinger 2001a: 61–64; Gilan 2007.

18. Gilan (2009: 134) categorizes the text as an instruction, and further, sees in §6, where the speaker refers to a tablet given to the addressees, i.e., the dignitaries, a reference to an instruction text. While this may perhaps be the case, the tablet in question is not designated as such, leaving open the possibility that it might, e.g., have been a letter of rebuke or similar.

19. *Pace* Starke (2002: 316–17), who has repeatedly and anachronistically insisted on unfittingly labeling it a *Verfassung*.

20. See the discussion on genre and *Sitz im Leben* by Gilan (2007).

21. A similar anecdote recalling a river ordeal, e.g., is found in KBo 3.28, §§2′–3′; see Dardano 2002: 365 and the online edition by Marazzi at hethiter.net/: *CTH* 9.6 (INTR 2011-09-18).

22. Whereby I revise my earlier acceptance (Miller 2011a: 8) of the common assumption that they are attested only beginning with Tudḫaliya I and his successor Arnuwanda I. See similarly Cammarosano 2006: 10–12.

23. In contrast, Pecchioli Daddi (2005a: 285) has suggested that "Während der Herrschaft von Arnuwanda hielt man den Eid allein, mit seinem kodifizierten Verfahren, für nicht mehr angemessen, um Verbindlichkeiten zu begründen, die nun von dauerhafter Geltung sein sollten."

24. KUB 40.31, which Giorgieri (2005: 324–25 and n. 13) speculated might also be an OH fragment containing an oath, has since been joined to KUB 26.20+KBo 22.132, a Treaty of Arnuwanda I with the Kaskaeans.

25. Nos. 21, 24, and 25, which do contain some rather detailed instructions, either show elements that might date their forerunners to the MH period (No. 21) or are too fragmentary to support robust conclusions (Nos. 24, 25).

26. Intriguingly, Schachner (2012a) has recently argued that the major changes in the state apparatus as far as can be identified in the artistic arena occurred in the later OH and early MH phase rather than in the later MH period.

27. It has been suggested that the land grants did not actually cease to be produced, but that the medium upon which they were inscribed changed from clay to wooden writing boards, which naturally have not been preserved (e.g., Bittel 1952; cf. Herbordt 2005: 25–39; van den Hout 2010: 257–58; Herbordt et al. 2011: 25; Mora 2010b).

28. "My/His Majesty" is in this volume used to translate ᵈUTU-*ŠI* (Akk. *šamšī*), lit. "My Sun" or "My Sun-God" (see, e.g., Beckman 2002; Sürenhagen 2001). Since, however, the title is employed not only by the king when he is speaking, i.e., when "My" is appropriate, but also by persons referring to the king, the epithet has been translated "His Majesty" when used to refer to the king in the third person and "Your Majesty" in the second.

29. One might object that the locution "whatever town" would militate against this

interpretation, as, e.g., opposed to "to his town," but this presumably refers in the context of a gathering of numerous governors to the various towns to which the several governors will return.

30. Giorgieri (1995: 276) refers to this fact as a possible explanation for the lack of divine witnesses and curses, suggesting these might have been found in the original document but not copied in the later tablets.

31. Oettinger (1976: 81) assumes that in No. 2 and in ii 19–20 in particular "nicht die Eidgötter, sondern Menschen die angedrohte Strafe vollziehen sollen." While it is indeed difficult in some cases to determine if the prescribed punishment is envisioned as being carried out by the gods or by men, in this text it seems in general to be the gods when "they" are the subject of such clauses. This is shown, *inter alia*, by §6″, where the gods are specifically mentioned; by the oath spoken directly to the sun-deity in §8″; by the validity of the curse not only for the perpetrator but also for his wife, sons, and even further generations (e.g., §9″); as well as by the distinction between these curses and the threat of presumably secular execution found in §§1′ and 4′. That said, whether these gods are limited to specifically the "king's gods" mentioned in ii 10′ or whether the term "king's gods" is employed here to refer to the "oath gods"—otherwise nowhere designated as such in the preserved text—who would presumably be invoked to assure adherence to the obligations, remains uncertain.

32. Monthly repetition of an oath also seems to be required in the fragments KUB 26.15, 5′–12′, twice yearly in KUB 26.3 iv 5. Such periodical reading is known also from other text genres, such as, e.g., the Political Testament of Ḫattusili (KUB 1.16 iii 57) and in the Treaty of Mursili II for Kupanta-Kurunta of Mira and Kuwaliya (KUB 19.52++ iv 1′).

33. On hiding and concealing, *munnai*- and *sanna*-, see recently Puhvel 2004.

34. (1) una formulazione di tipo apodittico, che salvo rare eccezioni ricorre all'uso dell'imperativo; (2) una formulazione con nesso relativo; (3) una formulazione introdotta da proposizione temporale o facente ricorso al periodo ipotetico; (4) (una) formulazione fa anch'essa ricorso ad una proposizione temporale o al periodo ipotetico, è però accostabile alla formulazione che ricorre nella raccolta di leggi: illecito (ovverossia norma negata) nella protasi e riferimento alla sanzione nell'apodosi; (5) formulazioni attraverso periodo ipotetico o nesso relativo, nelle quali l'apodosi definisce l'insieme a cui appartiene un determinato illecito; (6) formulazione fa ricorso a un *exemplum* tratto o dall'aneddotica o da un evento storico ben noto (d'Alfonso 2008: 348–50).

35. Several 2nd sg. forms are preserved in fragmentary §2′ as well, but these may well be in the context of quoted speech in an anecdote, as in §13″.

36. That the divine witnesses are placed toward the beginning of the text would appear to be the case with fragmentary Nos. 22.2 and 23, as well.

37. One wonders, of course, whether this distribution might suggest a certain redactional history, but this question could not be pursued for present purposes, and it is questionable whether the state of preservation of the two available manuscripts would allow significant results.

38. Texts beginning with *UMMA*: Nos. 8, 13, 14 [not king], 15, 16 [queen], 17, 19

[not king], 27. Texts with beginning preserved that do not begin with *UMMA*: No. 3. Texts without preserved beginning: Nos. 1–2, 4–7, 9–12, 18, 20–26, 28.

39. For similar usage of *UMMA* in the ritual corpora, see Miller 2004: 493–96.

40. Cf. No. 8, n. 15 there for the possibility that the tablet should be regarded as a *Sammeltafel*.

41. With "sovereign" I have translated the Hittite title *t/labarna*, concerning which there has been much discussion, most recently by Yakubovich (2009: 229–32; *EDHIL*, 830–32).

42. Singer (2011) has written and lectured (8th International Congress of Hittitology, Warsaw, Sept. 5–9) in a similar fashion on the Hittite predilection for justifying their actions on the international scene, a habit likely derived from a world view in which the Hittites were given by the gods a territory with concrete borders to govern, as opposed to, e.g., Assyrian and Egyptian conceptions, according to which their respective kings were commissioned with ruling the entire universe, regardless of how far their effective control actually reached at any given juncture. Overstepping these boundaries required justification in the Hittite view; naturally, the Hittites could be quite adept at finding just such justification if need be, while in other cases guilt for transgressions was simply accepted, as in the case of Mursili II's acceptance of the guilt of his father's attack on the Amqa.

43. The sources in the present volume seem to restrict such broad collective punishment to divine prerogative. Punishment meted out by the state seems to be directed solely at the guilty party. Collective punishment is, however, known from other Hittite sources to be called for by earthly powers in rare cases; see Haase 2003: 651. In some Hittite prayers the ethics of the concept of collective punishment is called into question (Singer 2004).

44. Why these two crimes are treated in such a lenient manner is not clear, as seemingly parallel crimes are treated with a summary death sentence, e.g., in No. 20, §§18′–19′.

45. It is indeed fascinating to contemplate how much of human history, from Alexander's conquests of the East to Cesar's crossing of the Rubicon, may have been conditioned by the common topics of historical inquiry, such as the brilliance and stupidity of great and foolish men, the nature of state and society, the impact of technology and trade, etc., and how much will have been influenced or determined, to at least some degree, by the occasional bump on a sheep's liver or a small wayward stone entering the earth's atmosphere at high speeds.

46. No. 18, §2 might at first glance seem to suggest a tripartite structure, but one should probably see this as a partitive apposition: "[…] to [your] persons, (9′)(i.e.,) to your souls, to [your] bod[ies, … to] my person, (10′)(i.e.,) my soul, to my body […]."

47. Goodnick Westenholz (2012) has recently provided a current account of the dualistic conception of the person in Mesopotamian thought.

48. Starke's (1996: 177–82; 1997: 480–81) insistence on translating the term as it relates to the king as the "will of the king" and understanding it, in Giorgieri's (2001: 429–30 and n. 18) words, "non da intendersi tuttavia come 'persönlicher Wille des Königs', bensì come un'entità di origine divina, rappresentativa della sovranità dello stato, un concetto

paragonabile dunque a quello di 'corona' sviluppatosi in epoca medievale," is surely to be rejected, as Giorgieri capably demonstrates (also in 2005: 339–40; 2006: 319, n. 54).

49. Akk. *tuppu(m)*, borrowed as Hitt. *tuppi-*, is as a rule to be understood as a clay (or, rarely, metal, e.g., No. 14.3.A, §2′) tablet bearing cuneiform writing. For Akk. *tuppu(m)* instead of *ṭuppu(m)*, see Streck 2009.

50. For the current debate within Hittitological circles concerning when the Hittites would have begun writing in the Hittite language, see above all van den Hout 2006, 2008, 2009a, 2009b, and cf., e.g., Archi 2010; Weeden 2011; and Waal 2011, 2012.

51. Among the voluminous literature on the convoluted history of the period, see recently Klinger 2007: 44–48; Marizza 2007; Giorgieri 2008; de Martino 2010; Hawkins 2011: 86–90.

52. Presumably those addressed with the phrase "your$^{(pl.)}$ mother" are not the "sons of Ḫimuili and Kantuzili" addressed in No. 11.A_1, §2′$^?$, §4′, unless one prefers to assume that both Ḫimuili and Kantuzili fathered sons with this queen. Rather, the speaker seems to turn to various individuals and groups of individuals one after the other as the text unfolds.

53. I.e., counting Nos. 1$^?$, 2, 3, 5, 8$^?$, 10, 12, 13, 14, 17, 18, 20, 26, and 27 for T. I; Nos. 8$^?$, 11, 12, 13 (x2), 19, and 21 for Büyükkale and the House on the Slope.

54. For a similar estimate based on the Mastigga ritual corpus, see Miller 2004: 36 and n. 60.

55. For a brief overview of Egyptian literature, see Redford 1995: 2226–29. For a summary of Egyptian didactic literature, see Lichtheim 1996.

56. English treatments of the Oath for Diviners can be found in Heimpel 2003: 174 and Lenzi 2008: 42–43.

57. The editors of these texts have referred to the oath takers in pl., e.g., "serment des intendants," which is surely correct in that the oath could be and presumably was pronounced by any and all individuals who were placed in the office in question, but since they are formulated in the 1st sg., the sg. is retained in the titles of the compositions here.

58. An essentially complete tablet of a loyalty oath to Aššur-aḫḫe-iddina (Esarhaddon) was found in 2010 at Tell Taʿyinat ca. 45 km east of Antakya in southeastern Turkey (Lauinger 2012). For recent discussions of the biblical covenant and its postulated connection with the Hittite *isḫiul-* genre, see Taggar-Cohen 2011a, 2011b; Christiansen and Devecchi 2013.

59. Typologically one can thus certainly agree with Giorgieri (2005: 325–26) when he writes, "Innerhalb der altorientalischen Überlieferung der Treueide stellen die hethitischen Bevölkerungs- und Beamteneide eine Zwischenstufe zwischen den sogenannten „protocoles jurés“ aus Mari der altbabylonischen Zeit und den neuassyrischen Treueiden aus der Zeit Sennacheribs und Asarhaddons dar," while there seems to be no compelling evidence that would lead one to suggest any genetic relationship.

60. See von Schuler 1976–80: 117; Tadmor 1982; Brinkman 1990; Zaccagnini 1990; Weeks 2004: 55–98; Beckman 2006; d'Alfonso 2006b; 2008; Balza 2008; Koch 2008: 19–105; Altman 2010; 2011: 153–86; Eidem 2011b; Wilhelm 2011; Christiansen and Devecchi 2013. None of these treatments were able to incorporate the evidence of the highly

important Old Babylonian treaties from Tell Leilan, recently published by Eidem (2011a: 310–438).

61. Christiansen (2008: 467), e.g., has recently concluded concerning the Hittite curse formulae that "Eine Durchsicht der Formeln beispielsweise des mesopotamischen Raumes anhand der hier vorgelegten Klassifikationskriterien zeigt jedoch deutlich, welche große Unterschiede die dort belegten Formeln zu dem Gros der hethitischen Formeln aufweisen. Diese Unterschiede betreffen nicht nur die Ebene des Inhalts, sondern auch Medien, Formen, Kontexte und Funktion."

62. Among the vast literature on the subject, see, e.g., Malul 1990; Tigay 1993; Miller 2004: 458–61; Weeks 2004: 93–97; Taggar-Cohen 2011a.

NOTES TO CHAPTER ONE

NO. 1. A ROYAL REPRIMAND OF THE DIGNITARIES (*CTH* 272)

1. Rose's (2006: 277, n. 214) attribution to Ḫattusili III's Accounts of Suppiluliuma I's Campaigns (*CTH* 83.01) is presumably an editing error. Also, the **me-ma-a-ḫi-ḫi-i* in Rose's (2006: 333) quote of Melchert (1994: 107) does not exist. This is an error-ridden representation of *me-ma-aḫ-ḫi-i*, which is wrongly attributed to KBo 22.1 by Melchert (1994: 107), presumably for KBo 18.22 obv. 6.

2. Klinger (2001a: 71), following previous treatments, translates "[sie] versammel[ten (sich)," but the traces following *-pé-* do not allow ⸢*er*⸣ or ⸢*e-er*⸣ (see already *HEG* T/D, 240), or -⸢*eš*⸣- or -⸢*šar*⸣ for that matter. They are, however, quite amenable to -*t*[*e*-, and since there are ten other *-teni* (and one other *-ten*) forms in this text, little speaks against *-teni*. According to *GrHL* §12.50 the chronology of the various stem forms of the verb (i.e., *tarrup-/taruppai-/taruppiya-*) is unclear, a problem to which the present attestation would thus be pertinent.

3. While one would generally want to transcribe -*ket*$_9$- in order to indicate the *e*-vocalism of the *-ske*-morpheme, *GrHL*, 205, n. 109, shows that at least in the older texts this may well have been an *a*-vowel, at least when the stress fell on the ensuing syllable.

4. Archi (1979: 45) opted for *a-pé-e-ma*, while Neu (1984: 99a) corrected the reading to *a-pé-e-ia*, and indeed both verticals of IA are clearly visible. An object would presumably have been written on the edge, as recognized, e.g., by Beal (1988: 280) and Marazzi (1988: 127), but ignored or glossed over, e.g., by Archi (1979: 46), Tjerkstra (1999: 146), and Goedegebuure (2003: 218). Cambi (2007: 201–2, 251) assumes an unexpressed 2nd pl. object, "hanno cominciato ad opprimer<vi>," which must be considered contextually unlikely. As *dames-* does not take *kattan* as a preverb in ll. 3′ or 19′, and, *pace* Goedegebuure (2003: 267) and García Ramón (2007: 286), *kattan* can hardly be understood as the object, i.e., "subordinates," it is presumably to be understood here as "later; accordingly."

5. On the syntax of this paragraph see Neu 1974: 53–54; similarly Beal 1992: 130, n. 479.

6. Likely so, with Beal (1988: 280), rather than LÚ-*iš* (e.g., Cambi 2007: 250; Groddek 2008b: 3).

7. Presumably abl., with Neu (1980a: 30), *pace* Starke (1977: 182).

8. While it is conceivable that one could see here a d.l. pl. and translate "to the assemblies," with *CHD* L–N, 149b, one otherwise finds, as far as I can ascertain, only calling the assembly with the sg. acc. *tuliyan* or calling to the assembly with the d.l. sg. *tuliya* (Beckman 1982; Imparati 1991; *HEG* T/D, 429–30, where the statement "In altheth. Originalen bisher nicht belegt" must be disregarded), so that Beckman (1982: 441 and n. 69), followed by Dardano (2002: 372), is probably correct to emend the passage.

9. All cases of "you" in this translation are pl. unless marked as sg. (in §§6′–7′).

10. For these "land tenants" (LÚ^{MEŠ} ^{GIŠ}TUKUL), literally "men of the weapon," see Beal (1988), who summarizes their status as "men who worked for the government or others and received their pay in the form of land whose produce supported them" (p. 304). Cf. Archi (1979: 45), "la population libre, indépendante de l'organisation du palais."

11. I.e., presumably one of the old men, with, e.g., Goedegebuure (2003: 218). See similarly *GrHL* 420, n. 18 and Hoffner 2007b: 394, where, however, ^{LÚ}ŠU.GI-*ešš=a* is translated as a sg.; cf. Otten 1973: 27 and Neu 1982b: 210–11, who assumed ^{LÚ}ŠU.GI-*ešša<r>*. The paragraph is misunderstood by Prins (1997: 36–37) and Zeilfelder (2001a: 255).

12. For "sourdough" see now Fritzsche 2011.

13. Tjerkstra's (1999: 37) interpretation, "fifty breads, ten from each house," is contextually attractive, and may perhaps be correct, but "from each house" would likely be expressed by *kuezziya parnaz*. As the distributive marker is attached to the numeral, "10 (to) each (person)" is probably intended.

14. The sense of §§3′–4′ and especially this last clause is difficult to grasp. A *kapunu* is a large area of several hundred hectares, at least 720 according to *HHw*, 79, which the subject "took out/forth," "selected" (*CHD* P, 115a), perhaps "appropriated." It seems that these two paragraphs are contrasting what a person is entitled to take, presumably from state funds or stores, vs. what Tās in fact took, providing such a poor example. The final sentence containing the huge "selection/appropriation" seems to be added possibly for literary, even satirical, effect. Perhaps Tās's story is related as an example of a trader who provisioned his employees with the poorest imaginable equipage, turning a large enough profit to allow him to buy a huge piece of land.

15. I am aware of no justification for Boley's (2005: 46) "correggervi"; for *gullakkuwan*, see *HED* K, 236–37.

16. Many treatments, not entirely without reason, have begun the quoted speech with the previous clause. As *natta* can be interpreted as being fronted and since *-kunu* is written plene, often interpreted as clause-final intonation, it has been understood as a rhetorical question, e.g., by Neu (1984: 99a) and Beal (1988: 280; see also Hoffner 1986: 90), who translates "When my father calls assemblies, he will seek wrong-doing … in you$^{(\text{pl.})}$: 'Is it not your provision carriers?'" On the other hand, the quoted speech particle occurs only with the following clause, forcing one to decide which hints should be given grea-

ter weight. The present solution agrees essentially with Archi (1979: 47), Goedegebuure (2003: 185–86), Cambi (2007: 250), and Boley (2004: 86; 2005: 46). Dardano (2002: 372), following Marazzi (1988: 127), translates the passage differently still, "Lorsque mon père convoqu(ait) le *tulii̯a-* et examinait votre comportement immoral, n'(était)-ce pas (à cause des vexations) à l'égard de vos contribuables?"

17. The translation of this sentence and that in l. 24′ with *kāsatta=wa* follows Rieken 2009.

18. *Pace*, e.g., Neu 1984: 99a and Zeilfelder 2001a: 29, the absence of the determinative LÚ in both cases of ^{GIŠ}TUKUL in this clause should not obscure the likelihood that the "land tenants" (cf. in l. 3′) are at issue here rather than "weapons"; see Beal 1988: 281–82, n. 61.

19. Or to be understood as rhetorical questions within the father's speech, i.e., "So are you (perhaps) a *land tenant*? And is he (perhaps) a *land tenant*?" The implication would probably thus be, "No, of course not, you are dignitaries!" (pers. comm. M. Giorgieri). This first sentence of the paragraph is in fact also marked as part of the quoted speech, which the present treatment assumes is an errant carryover from the previous paragraph, an interpretation perhaps supported by the use of *ta* in 20′ followed by the conjunction *-a* in 21′, which should indicate the end of a series of phrases (Rieken 1999b). Fortson (1998: 23, but cf. 32, n. 37) includes KBo 22.1 among those texts that show a "more sporadic usage [of *wa*(*r*)], amounting to virtual omission of the particle in some cases." As far as I can see, however, it does not seem necessary to assume any omissions (cf. n. 16). With the interpretation suggested here, the speaker would seem to be saying to his listeners that they, too, are land tenants just like those they are said to be oppressing in l. 3′. For this paragraph see also Neu 1974: 83–84; Starke 1977: 34, 38, 192; Beal 1992: 500, n. 1847.

20. To be translated thus (*CHD* L–N, 111b), not "e quando vi scrive separatamente" (Boley 2005: 46), regardless of whether *ma-a-an-ḫa-an-da* or *ma-a-an ḫa-an-da* is to be read, either of which is graphically possible.

21. Cf. Boley's (2005: 46; also 1984: 33) contextually unlikely "non vi ha inciso la tavoletta dei LÚ^{MEŠ} DUGUD?"

22. The syntax suggests that the quoted speech runs from 24′ at least through 27′, and that it might even continue through the first clause of 30′; see Rieken 1999b: 65–66; cf. Hoffner 1995: 561, who understands this sentence as a rhetorical question.

23. I.e., *piyannazzi=a=tta*, "and he rewards you," with, e.g., Beal (1988: 281, n. 59) and *HEG* P, 609–10; for discussion and a possible alternative, i.e., *piyannazziyatta* as a 2nd sg. med.-pass. form, "you are rewarded," from *piyanazziya-*, see *CHD* P, 251, following Neu (1984: 99b); see also *EDHIL*, 663.

24. The second verb is clearly the 2nd sg. pres. of *dai-*, "take," presumably with the meaning "take (for a ride); exploit." Goedegebuure (2006a: 181–82) interprets *siyet* as an instr. from *siya*, "one." Though her suggestion for *siya-* for most passages is quite convincing, it seems a bit of a stretch here, where she translates "take him to one (side)," i.e., "take/set him aside," "ignore him." Giorgieri (pers. comm.) wonders if one might read ḪUL$^{!}$-*it* and understand "You exploit the poor man evilly." Cf. Neu (1984: 99b; also 1983: 167 and n. 489; 1980a: 49–53), who opts for an endingless loc. of the dem. pron. *si-* or

siya-, "(jem.) dorthin (mit)nehmen"; Starke (1977: 176), similarly; Melchert (1977: 173–74), who suggests an instr. of *si/sa-*, hence "thereby"; Beal (1988: 281, n. 59), "fee(?)," "based solely on context"; D. Yoshida (1987: 35–36); Melchert (1994: 107) "his," i.e., an orthotonic version of enclitic *-set*. Melchert's interpretation as the 3rd sg. instr. of a pron. *siya-* requires a somewhat forced, as he admits, reading *da-a-la*$^{!}$*-ti*, "you abandon." Gilan (2009: 134 and n. 123) opts for ^{LÚ}*asiwandan=sset* (better ^{LÚ}*asiwandan=a=sset*), translating "den Armen das Seine nimmst du (weg)," which is perhaps not the worst solution, despite its ignoring the space as well as the vowel between the two morphemes.

25. On the difficulties with *ar-ḫa-a-an ḫar-te-ni-i*, see Neu 1984: 99b; Boley 1984: 32–33; Hoffner apud Beal 1988: 281, n. 59; *GrHL* §27.2.

No. 2. Instructions and Oath Imposition for Royal Servants concerning the Purity of the King (*CTH* 265)

26. In Miller 2009a, I followed the *communis opinio* in assuming that the text would be MH. Shifting it to the OH period removes the only text from the post-OH period in which Sanaḫuitta plays any significant role in the Hittite state, except perhaps KBo 50.51, 8' and 50.55, 4′, 7′, assumed to belong to Ḫattusili III's Accounts of Suppiluliuma I's Campaigns.

27. Depending on whether an earlier or a later OH date for this composition is assumed, it might form an interesting test case for the question of when the Hittites began to compose Hittite language texts. For recent remarks on the issue see Miller 2004: 463–64 n. 773; Popko 2005; van den Hout 2006, 2008, 2009a, 2009b; and Archi 2010. This question was also the topic of a lively and productive workshop, organized by A. Kloekhorst and W. Waal and held during the 58th Rencontre Assyriologique Internationale in Leiden, July 17, 2012.

28. E.g., *takku* in iii 18, 43; the nom. pl. c. pron. *-e* in B, 7′; the frequent plene writings of the 2nd pl. pres. *tēni* in i 1′, 14′, ii 8′, iii 4, 6, 11, 14, 18; the presence of the king in Sanaḫuitta. *CHD* (e.g., L–N, 14a; P, 372b; Š, 129b) refers to it as MH/NS, MH?/NS or pre-NH/NS, while *EDHIL* (e.g., pp. 245, 870) labels it as OH/NS. The nom. pl. c. pron. *-e* and *takku*, it must be granted, are found, e.g., in No. 8, dated to Tudḫaliya I (see introduction to No. 8 and n. 16), and No. 17 (§47′, 67′), dated to Arnuwanda I, so that a dating of the present text to a phase older than Tudḫaliya I depends essentially on the mention of the king in Sanaḫuitta and the use of what is often understood as a typical OH anecdote.

29. For further discussion on this typology, see Introduction, Defining the Genre(s), and The Origins and Development of the "Obligation and Oath" Texts.

30. This fact leads M. Giorgieri (pers. comm.) to wonder if the composition might be connected with No. 15.2, a fragmentary instruction (and oath imposition?) text of Arnuwanda I, in which the locutions "obligat[ion] of purity" (iii 3) and "[... obligation of] purity of this tablet" (iii 4) occur. He also points to the occurrence there of DUMU^{MEŠ}-*ŠU i-da-a-lu ḫi-in-kán* [*pí-ia-an-zi*], "(the gods) [will allot] his sons an evil death!" (iii 6), which parallels the locutions here in ii 19′ and iii 20 (cf. also iii 8 and iv 5′). If these two

compositions were in fact to be linked, it would of course render moot the considerations expressed here about the dating of No. 2 and the consequences thereof for the genre.

31. There would seem to be insufficient room for the *u-* of Pecchioli Daddi's (2004: 260) *u-ni-*, while the LUGAL read by others (e.g., Friedrich 1928/9: 46) fits quite well, even if one might like to see a bit of a leading horizontal.

32. So, not GI, "reed; arrow," as has been read in several treatments, e.g., Haas 1982: 110; Polvani 1988: 98–99; Boley 2000: 296.

33. So, thus lit. "lords of the soup," not *BE-LU*$^{\text{MEŠ.KAM}}$, as in Boley 2000: 327–28.

34. The sign here (and in iii 1, 22, 23, 37, 39) is wi_5 (GEŠTIN), not *wi* (PI), as in Pecchioli Daddi 2004: 460.

35. All second person verbs/pronouns in this text are plural unless marked otherwise.

36. A similar list of personnel is found in KBo 50.281 (558/u+1968/u), discussed by Pecchioli Daddi (2004: 452–53).

37. For DAM as da_4 in *damāi-* and *damāiss-*, see *EDHIL*, 832.

38. The passage quoted as KUB 13.3 iii 9–11 in Cotticelli-Kurras 1991: 76 is in fact KBo 4.14 iii 9–11.

39. So, not UZ_6, as in Pecchioli Daddi 2004: 461.

40. So, without ^{MEŠ}, as in Pecchioli Daddi 2004: 461.

41. Cf. Otten and Rüster 1977: 55–56; Pecchioli Daddi 2004: 464, 467–68; and Groddek 2008a: 190–91, where the size of the gap up to the column divider (or edge)—determined by the restoration of [*ti-i*]*t-ta-nu-er* in 10'—is not taken into account

42. One could, following A, restore *kartimmiyanu*]*n*=*wa* before the break. The trace following *ki-i*, however, is neither a *w*[*a* nor a *g*[*ul-*, suggesting caution. Neither does it seem to be a *k*[*u-*, the only other initial sign attested for *gullakuwan*. A *k*[*ul-* would fit the trace, but this is a rarely used value.

43. Or *-m*[*a*. In such cases it can be uncertain whether following *UMMA* an Akk. *-MA* or a Hitt. *-ma* is to be understood, since Hittite scribes often omit the Akk. element even when required.

44. Reichardt (1998: 49) inadvertently omits DINGIR^{MEŠ} from her transliteration, unnecessarily deducing that "the morphology of a curse in the Instructions for Palace Servants suggests that the agents are deities.... As the verb is a 2nd. pl. imp., the agents must be the gods, whether they are overtly stated or not." For the debate on whether this curse might be linked with Homeric passages, see Starke 1997: 483; Giorgieri 2001: 428–31; 2005: 339–40; Rollinger 2004; Haas 2007.

45. Beal (1992: 138 and n. 506, 187–88) and *HEG* T/D, 226, treat this syntactically cumbersome paragraph and discuss the occupational title *tarsip*(*iy*)*ala-*, here tentatively translated "coachman"; cf. Neu (1983: 192 and n. 561), who translates simply "Palastangestellter."

46. So, not "but (if) you had told the king about it," as in Pecchioli Daddi 2004: 466, as there is no irrealis particle (*man*).

47. Ünal (1993: 123, n. 12) points out a passage (KUB 35.2(+)35.4 iii 1′–4′; Starke 1985: 357) in a fragmentary festival ritual in which a hair in a rhyton is cause for alarm.

48. Earlier treatments translated "careless" or similar, e.g., Goetze 1950: 207; Laroche 1973: 186, but cf. n. 22; von Schuler 1982: 125; Haase 1984: 63; cf. now *CHD* P, 110–11, 142–43.

49. The river ordeal, common throughout much of the ancient Near East, was an oracular/juridical method by means of which the guilt/impurity or innocence/purity of a person was thought to be revealed, the gods rendering the verdict. The accused was thrown into a river, his/her escape supposedly demonstrating innocence rather than aquatic prowess, at least in most cases. The present situation seems perhaps to constitute an exception, as the accused, if found guilty, is thereupon to die; and indeed, once Zuliya (in A) and Zuliya and Arnili (in B) are found guilty, they are thereupon "dealt with," whereby the king does something to them, so that they die. This would seem to suggest that it was in fact those who had drowned who were to be considered innocent, which might in turn shed light on the puzzling phrase, according to which the innocent—and presumably deceased—should then "purify his soul" (*nu-za* ZI-*ŠU* *pár-ku-nu-ud-du*). Marazzi (2010: 209) understands this enigmatic phrase as meaning "then let his life be spared." Perhaps the deceased but innocent suspect was to attain a pure soul in the afterlife, quite like later European conceptions of the river ordeal? For a concise summary of the Mesopotamian evidence, see van Soldt 2003, as well as Paulus (in press)—whom I wish to thank for kindly giving me a preprint of her paper—for the revealing Middle Babylonian material, and for the Hittite, Marazzi 2010; van den Hout 2003b; and Kammenhuber 1964: 176.

50. Pecchioli Daddi (2004: 461, n. 66) suggests *n*[*atta ḫuesnut*, "and the king [did] n[ot let] him [live]," comparing KBo 3.28 ii 19' of the Palace Anecdotes (*CTH* 8–9).

51. In the copy seemingly AḪ, and even on the photos one can see what might be interpreted as a trace of a horizontal, but this is hardly certain, and *-tén* is presumably the correct reading.

52. Singer (1984: 107 and n. 58) makes the interesting and seemingly inexplicable observation that only here among all the instruction texts does this ^{LÚ}AGRIG, "administrator," appear. The question naturally arises whether these administrators enjoyed some special status so that they were not bound to such a set of obligations or whether, e.g., they were of too low a rank to have been sworn directly to the king.

53. Pecchioli Daddi (2004: 462 and n. 73) reads KAŠ-*iš-na-an-ni-eš-ši*, interpreting it as *šieššnanni=šši*, "to/in his beer." *CHD* L–N, 395b, P, 328a, opts for *pišnanni=šši*, "to/for his virility." Without context it is naturally impossible to decide if either might be correct; neither is entirely satisfying. With an exclamation mark *CHD* acknowledges that there is a clear space between the first two signs and the rest, and of course BI.IŠ yield ŠIM, "aroma, scent." What one would then do with *na-an-ni-eš-ši* would remain a mystery. A 2nd sg. pres. of *nanna-*, unexpectedly conjugated as a *mi*-stem? A d.l. of an otherwise unattested *natar*, from *ne-/nai-/neya-*, or from a likewise unattested verb *na-*? Certainly not solutions that one would be eager to defend.

54. Or a botched attempt at writing *iyann(iy)anzi* or *iyandari*, both "to go/walk"? The traces after the break do indeed make a good ^{UD}]^{U}.

55. So, not *uš*, as in Pecchioli Daddi 2004: 462.

56. Pecchioli Daddi's (2004: 463) G]IM-*an* can be all but excluded.

57. The traces would fit Pecchioli Daddi's (2004: 463) *p*]*u*- better than *CHD*'s, P, 373a, GE_6-*an l*]*u*-; moreover, causing someone to be despised is a common theme in the instructions, while passing the night is not.

58. The word used, *tittanu*-, means simply "to place, set; arrange," but in context presumably "to deal with; dispatch; kill." On the other hand, as M. Giorgieri (pers. comm.) has pointed out to me, one might expect the verb *essa*-, "to treat (badly)," for such a euphemism, as found, e.g., in KBo 3.34 ii 7 of the palace anecdotes. As an alternative, then, one could, with Pecchioli Daddi (2004: 467–68) or Marazzi (2010: 209), translate *tittanu*- in its more literal sense, assuming that the punishment followed in the break, i.e., "And they settled / placed him in Surest[a], and the king [killed] him / [did not let] him [live], and he died." One might, however, rather expect *ases*-, to "settle (people)," for Pecchioli Daddi's translation.

59. Divergence from ms. A in bold.

60. For this possibility, see Neu 1980b.

61. Where the quoted speech ends is impossible to determine.

No. 3. Protocol for the Palace Gatekeeper (*CTH* 263)

62. See join sketch on the *Konkordanz*, sub 1344/v. This format is perhaps conditioned by the bilingual nature of the paragraphs in question. Cf. e.g., the Hurrian-Hittite bilingual KBo 32.14, the obv. and first twenty-two lines of the rev. of which are divided into two columns, but whose remaining forty-nine lines stretch across the entire lower rev.

63. The scribe of this tablet, a certain Sakkapi, is also known to have penned KUB 50.72+KBo 53.107, which does not show any radical slanting. Sakkapi was active during the reign of Tudḫaliya IV (ca. 1240s–1210s); see Gordin 2008. Košak (*Konkordanz*, sub 32/a) notes four other tablets with similar formatting.

64. Yakubovich (2009: 265) is likely correct in assigning KBo 30.187 to this composition rather than to the Instructions for the Royal Body Guard (No. 4), but since it is such a tiny fragment, it is not treated here.

65. The Hittites called their own language Nasili or Ne/isili, that is, the language of the city of Nesa, a variant of the name of the city Kaneš (the ruins now known as Kültepe a few km northeast of Kayseri), the lower town of which formed the Old Assyrian trading colony that has yielded ca. twenty thousand cuneiform tablets, mostly business letters. The Hittites thus saw the roots of their language and much of their history in this city. For recent overviews and bibliography see Veenhof 1995; Michel 2003; Veenhof and Eidem 2008.

66. What is known today as Hattian was the language of an indigenous people of central Anatolia when the Indo-European groups arrived perhaps sometime in the middle or toward the end of the third millennium B.C.E.. It is known in the texts from Ḫattusa as

ḫattili, the language of the land of Ḫatti, i.e., central Anatolia. It has not been convincingly related to any other known language. For recent treatments see Klinger 2005b; Goedegebuure 2010. There is no current summary of the Hattians' part in Hittite history and culture, but one can consult the short section in Bryce's (2005: 12–15) general treatment of the Hittites or Taracha's (1995) overview of the state of the art of Hattian studies. For exhaustive treatments one can consult Klinger 1996; O. Soysal 2004; and Stivala 2003.

67. Luwian was an Indo-European language closely related to Hittite. For a current overview of all aspects of Luwian and the Luwians, see Melchert 2003 and Yakubovich 2009. That the passages in Nos. 3 and 4 referring to the speaking of Luwian should be interpreted as indicating that the "use of the Luvian language in official written discourse was systematically discouraged in the early fourteenth century Hattusa" (Yakubovich 2008; 15–16) seems quite doubtful.

68. At this point it seems no -*aš* is to be restored; after l. 12 it is uncertain whether -*aš* was placed at the end of the lines or not.

69. O. Soysal (2004: 405) reads ^{LÚ}x̣-x̣-x̣-el and writes, "Die in der Literatur bisher vorgeschlagenen Lesungen †^{LÚ}*duduel* bzw. †^{LÚ}*duwel* überzeugen nicht. Man würde hierfür eher ein *^{LÚ}*zilipurel* erwarten." It is of little consequence, however, that one might expect *zilipurel*, since this is clearly not what was written. The sign traces, while admittedly uncertain, are quite amenable to the reading here; cf. e.g., Klinger 1996: 202.

70. For recent studies on the *zilipuriyatalla-* and *akuttara-* see Arıkan 2003, 2004.

71. For *uwat*, see now *HEG* U, 161–62, 177.

72. Yakubovich (2009: 265) is surely correct in seeing a dittograph here. I suspect, further, since "be careful with the king" makes little sense in the context, and due to the odd syntax, that LUGAL-*it* might be a mistake for IZI-*it*, as LUGAL resembles IZI without its final vertical, and further, that the second *paḫsanuwan* is also a dittograph. These errors, in turn, may well be the reason why only *mar*-[*ri*] appears instead of the well-attested *mekki marri* in similar contexts; see *CHD* L–N, 185b. The original text would thus have read simply *paḫḫunit mekki marri paḫḫasnuwan esten*, "Be extremely careful with the fire!" There is therefore probably no need to restore unlikely *mar*[*set*?], "evil" (Bossert 1944: 16), or *mar*-[*ri-it*?] (*CHD* L–N, 185b; P, 9b). Neither would "[Let] it be protected by the king" (Melchert 1977: 417; *HEG* U, 161) be at all likely, even if one retains LUGAL-*it*, in which case an instr. of inclusivity, i.e., a comitative (*GrHL* §16.108), or Melchert's (1977: 417) instr. of respect would presumably be the correct interpretation.

73. Judging from the gradually decreasing thickness of the tablet fragment, it would seem that the first lines of KUB 26.23 obv. ii, if in fact the obv. has been correctly identified, should be placed not too very far from the original top edge. The surviving paragraph divisions on KBo 5.11 ii and KUB 26.23 ii suggest that the latter cannot be placed in a line with the former, so that KUB 26.23 must presumably be placed with only a very small (vertical) gap between them, indeed as seen in the join sketch in the *Konkordanz*. I am unaware of any means by which one could establish that KBo 5.11 iii 1 = KUB 26.23 iii 16, as M. Çiğ is supposed to have determined according to Otten (1953a: 21, n. 23).

74. Presumably more likely than interpreting as a form of *esseszi*, otherwise written *e-eš-še-eš-zi* (*EDHIL*, 388).

75. For discussions of *ub/pati*, see Beal 1992: 539–49; Singer 2005: 449; *HEG* U, 79–83.

76. For 10-*anza*, "a set of 10 …," see *GrHL* §9.35 and n. 31.

77. Perhaps an error for DINGIR^{MEŠ}.

78. What one might want to read *tar-n*[*a*- on the hand copy does not appear as such on the photo.

79. Cf. Boysan-Dietrich 1987: 134–35; Y. Soysal 2001: 665, with a Turkish translation.

80. It has been suggested (e.g., O. Soysal 2004: 559) that a *kazzue* might be a kind of cup; cf. the meaning "bed" assumed, e.g., by Alp (1983: 110–11 and n. 140) and Klinger (1996: 251–52).

81. The writing here, even if only partly preserved, seems likely to be corrupt. Both *na-aš-t*[*a* ^{L}]^{Ú}˻ŠU˼.I, provided by the duplicate, and *na-aš-t*[*a* $^{\text{LÚ.ME}}$]^{Š}˻ŠU˼.I, suggested by l. 21', where the duplicate again shows ^{LÚ}ŠU.I, are excluded by the head of a vertical before ŠU. The verb in any case is sg.

82. As suggested in *CHD* L–N, 296b.

83. The reading is assured by the duplicate, which has a clear ÌR LÚ-*ši*.

84. For this name and the two colophons in general see Gordin 2010: 164–65 and n. 36; Neu and Rüster 1975: 4, n. 9. It has been suggested that the tablet catalogue entry in KUB 30.51++ iv 23′ might refer to this composition, for which see Dardano 2006: 134–35, 148.

85. For this paragraph and a thorough treatment of the expression *miššā*, see Klinger 1993.

86. For a similar passage, cf. OH$^{?}$/early MH$^{?}$ No. 4, §12a, a parallel that adds credence to the assumption that the present composition is dependent on earlier forerunners. Cf. Klinger 1996: 249–50 and n. 460.

87. In consideration of the general context of the composition, and especially the mention of those sleeping in the palace (§2) and the collecting of the beds (§§33″, 35″), Neu's (1982a: 131) "erste Tafel vom Oben-Verweilen" is less apt.

No. 4. Protocol for the Royal Body Guard (*CTH* 262)

88. D'Alfonso (2005: 33–34) unfortunately follows long outdated literature in ascribing the tablet to the late thirteenth century. Cf. most recently Popko (2003b: 94), who suggests dating the text paleographically to Tudḫaliya I. This dating is supported generally by the *terminus post quem* of the mention of the Kaskaens (§37), who first appear in Hittite history during the reigns of Muwattalli I and Tudḫaliya I (Klinger 2002, 2005a).

89. The recent considerations expressed by Schachner (2012b: 92–94) concerning the layout of the palace on Büyükkale are based on an understanding of this Protocol for the Royal Body Guard that diverges significantly from that espoused here, primarily as

regards Schachner's assumption of two separate palace courtyards and concerning what sections of the text can be related to the Büyükkale.

90. The sign traces in the photographs would seem to suggest a TI rather than Güterbock and van den Hout's (1991: 4) *-TI[M*. As with all readings based on collations of photos noted here that vary from Güterbock and van den Hout's readings, this suggestion is to be understood as tentative pending further collation of the original, since Güterbock was able to collate both photos and the original.

91. Güterbock and van den Hout (1991: 4) restore *ḫuiyanzi* here and "they run" at the end of l. 7 based on *peran ḫuwai-* in ii 4, 8, 13, 18, 32, iv 2 (cf. iii 26, 29, 32, 52), but these occurences all relate to processions, whereas the context here seems to be one of entering, coming and/or going.

92. Traces and spacing favor *ne-i*[*a-an-t*]*e-eš*, which corresponds well with the attestations found in *CHD* L–N, 350b, over Güterbock and van den Hout's (1991: 4) *ne-e*[-*an*]-⌜*te*⌝-*eš*.

93. Significantly, the traces thus far read as *-z*[*i* here are located up above the line and clearly belong to the additions, raising a number of questions. One possibility would be to see in *sanḫan* a participle, yielding "and/so that it is watched/swept." Since the subject would presumably be *ḫila-*, however, one would naturally expect *sanḫants*. Alternatively, one could read *sanḫan*^{z}[^{i}, a 3rd pl. pres. indic., as in previous treatments. This assumes, though, that the scribe originally failed to complete the verb and that the *-zi* was added later as part of the corrections or additions, which is a possibility. If so, however, one wonders why the editor wrote the *-zi* up above the line when there was ample space behind the *-an* to write it normally. That there is clearly a fair bit of space between *-an* and the break may suggest that the original *zi* of *sanḫanzi* is actually completely lost in the break. As can be seen, e.g., in i 15, 47, 59, the scribe often pulled the last *-zi* of a paragraph to the right; and in fact, the tail of a wedge following the break and pointing up into the *-tu-* of the previous line would fit the end of a *-zi* perfectly. The rest of the signs added above the line would thus constitute the beginning of the adjunct paragraph. This latter possibility is preferred in the present treatment, though any solution must admittedly remain quite tentative.

94. Reading [*t*]*a* ⌞*lu-uk-kat*⌟*-ta* here must be considered extremely optimistic. Pecchioli Daddi's (1996: 141) suggestion to place this addition at the beginning of the text falters, *inter alia*, on the unlikelihood of the reading. Moreover, "in the morning" makes little sense in the context, as one hardly expects the passing of a night here. Further, any occurrence of *ta* should be considered highly unlikely, as it is found nowhere else in this text, including in ii 43, where *ŠA* should be read instead (see n. 137).

95. Both Jakob-Rost's (1966: 174) and Güterbock's readings (1991: 4), which diverge radically, seem highly optimistic, as are Alp's (1983: 106) as well. The sign traces are not only small and poorly preserved, they are written over other sign traces that all but prohibit any credible reading. For a further attempt at restoring and understanding these lines, see Pecchioli Daddi 1996: 141.

96. Jakob-Rost (1966: 174) implies with her reading *-m*[*a* that some traces of the sign are visible. Güterbock and van den Hout (1991: 4) are presumably correct, however,

when they interpolate it instead, as the spot is well preserved, and one would surely expect to see much more of it if it in fact had been there.

97. In contrast to previous treatments, the additional traces following *aranta* here have not been retained. Of the signs read *I-NA* É-*ma* by others, only -*ma* is relatively convincing on the photographs. In any case, the position and orientation of the signs of this addition seem clearly to indicate that it was intended to have supplemented the end of l. 16, with Jakob-Rost 1966: 174, rather than as an extension of the latter part of l. 19, as in Güterbock and van den Hout 1991: 6.

98. Güterbock and van den Hout (1991: 5) have "they sweep," but there does not appear to be a subject change here, so the meaning "search" seems to be more likely. On the other hand, all the examples in *CHD* sub *sanḫ-* 7 show an object, so that one must assume an implied object with this translation.

99. *Pace* Güterbock and van den Hout (1991: 6), I have accepted -*ma* here as an intentional addition, but rejected the reading 1-*za* and its interpretation as an abl. The -*ma* fits nicely syntactically and contextually, while 1-*za* would be a very rare writing for expected 1-*e-da-az/za* (or 1-*e-ez*, attested only once; see, e.g., *GrHL* §9.7; cf. also the single attestation of 1-*za-ma-kán* in *HT* 1 i 45, a ref. for which I would like to thank S. Košak) and would yield no immediately apparent sense. Further, the insertion seems clearly aimed at supplementing the end of l. 18, not as an extension of the latter part of l. 19.

100. The continuation of the paragraph is formed first by two lines (21a–b in IBoT 1.36) written through the column divider into the blank space at the end of the third paragraph in col. ii (between ll. 14 and 15). The text apparently continued from here onto the right edge of the tablet, which is no longer preserved at this point. How much text is lost here is difficult to estimate, but one suspects that several lines may have been written on the edge. In any case, once this space was filled as well, the scribe continued with one further line (21c here; B–C in IBoT) through col. iii (between ll. 75 and 76) and into the blank space at the bottom of col. iv beneath the colophon. Here the scribe added five further lines (21d–h here; D–E in IBoT), whereby these additional lines in rev. iii–iv are inverted vis-à-vis the normal text of the reverse. Compared with Güterbock and van den Hout's reconstruction (1991: 4–7), which jumps from the additions at the end of §1 to those at the end of §3—which bleed into col. ii—from where it jumps back to §§2–3 and then on to the additions on the rev. before finally returning to §4, the arrangement suggested here has several advantages: It provides a reasonable and continuous pathway for the writing on the tablet's surface; it assumes that each of the tablet's additions was inserted in immediate proximity to the text it is supposed to follow (cf. Güterbock and van den Hout 1991: 43), and in fact, nowhere else does it seem that the scribe inserts his additions at some random point on the tablet, but always leading off from the text they are supposed to supplement; and finally, it results in a satisfyingly coherent context, at least as far as the state of preservation of the tablet allows. For a more thorough explanation and graphic representations see Miller 2011a: 12–16, with figs. 1–4, unfortunately printed much smaller than intended.

101. The GAG portion of the sign is added above the line.

102. Cf. *nu* GAL *MEŠEDI* ^{GIŠ}ŠUKUR *ANA* ^{LÚ}*MEŠEDI para pai* in KBo 21.85 i 7 + KBo 8.109 left. col. 2 (in an OH/MS festival); see *CHD* P, 54a–54b.

103. Surely $^{\text{LÚ.MEŠ}}$ rather than Güterbock and van den Hout's ^{LÚ} (1991: 8), due to space considerations and since the abstractum in this text always occurs with the plural marker; cf. also i 34.

104. As it would yield an odd syntax and a very tight physical fit, Güterbock and van den Hout's restoration (1991: 8), ⸢*ḫu-u*⸣*-ma-an-te-eš k*[*u-i-e-eš ḫar-kán*]*-zi* [*n*]*a-at-kán*, seems unlikely. Moreover, the sign trace after *-eš* follows it immediately, suggesting an enclitic rather than a subsequent word, and the sign is placed in the middle of the line of text, so that a *ku-* would had to have been placed oddly halfway below the line. Jakob-Rost's (1966: 177) translation assumes that *ḫūmantes* would be an acc. pl., but this is hardly to be expected in a text of this date (but cf. Melchert 2008: 531), and indeed occurs nowhere else here. It must therefore be nom. and modify the pl. subj., as Güterbock and van den Hout assume (1991: 9, 46). Perhaps the least problematic solution would be to see the subj. as a status constructus, "the bodyguards of the staffs," thus modified by *ḫūmantes=pat*, followed in turn by the verb. For the verb one would perhaps like to see *sarā uwanzi*, but this would very likely be too long. A possibility that would fit the space nicely could be *-p*[*át* ^{GIŠ}GIDRU$^{\text{ḪI.A}}$ *pí-an*]*-zi*, resulting in "All the bod[ygu]ards of the staffs witho[ut exception], though, [relinqui]sh (their) [staffs]; (i.e.) when they come up, they give the staffs [… to] the gatekeeper."

105. Traces would seem to speak against Güterbock and van den Hout's (1991: 8) ^{L}]$^{\text{Ú.MEŠ}}$*M*[*E-ŠE-DI*, but would fit ^{GI}]^{Š}⸤GIDRU$^{\text{ḪI.A}}$⸥[perfectly. The rest of the space might then be filled with *ḫu-u-ma-an-du-uš*, which, however, would leave no space for *A-NA*.

106. The gap is far too long for Güterbock and van den Hout's (1991: 8) *UL-pat paizzi* alone. Cf. *HW*^{2} A, 419b.

107. Available space requires a further sign, *-kán* suggesting itself as a common companion of *arnu-*.

108. Güterbock and van den Hout (1991: 5) translate "key" according to their understanding of the context: "If on the inside (added: on one side in a building) some doorbolt has not been lifted, or (if) they open some storehouse and the key is lacking, (then) if a palace attendant of the lowest rank comes out, the gold-spear-man does not give it to him; (but) when a high palace attendant comes out—either (*col.* ii) a commander-of-ten or an army-bailiff (or) a [gu]ard comes—then they give the *key*(?) to that one." Similarly *CHD* L–N, 408b, suggesting the reading MUD rather than GI. If the key was missing, though, how could it be withheld from one person then given to another? Further, for "there is no key," one might expect NU.GÁL rather than *waksiya-*. Finally, GI is otherwise not attested as representing a key. Thus, whatever GI might be, it seems that the issue at hand is a shortage (*waksiya-*)—either due to some door not being unlocked or, if the door in question is unlocked, there is simply not enough GI—leading to the dilemma of who should be provided with GI when there is not enough to go around. What exactly is intended with GI, literally "reed," remains uncertain. One might consider various objects potentially made of reed, such as a stylus, or perhaps reed as firestarter. In light of the appearance of a bow, quiver, and arrows in ii 39–43, one might think of arrows as well. For GI as "arrow" elsewhere,

see Christiansen 2006: 92–95; Miller 2009b: 154. Still, there seems to be nothing directly linking the "reed" here with the archery equipment in ii 39–43. Perhaps reed as firestarter could be a solution, especially since the palace personnel seem to be coming out of the palace to fetch some of it rather than anything associated with the duties of the guards, and further, since in case supplies are short only high-ranking palace personnel are to receive it (presumably to heat the rooms of the royal family) as opposed to low-ranking personnel (perhaps to heat the servants' quarters). The suggestion also has the advantage of remaining with the basic meaning for GI, "reed." For the provisioning of the king's residence with firewood, cf. No. 17, §27'. Singer (pers. comm.), starting from the fact that the insertion likely relates to the topic of §§2–3, wonders if GI might refer back to the spears, which would of course make very good sense in the context. GI, however, does not seem to be associated with spears in particular, at least in HZL or MesZL; neither does there seem to be any immediately apparent reason why the scribe should suddenly begin using GI here rather than ŠUKUR.

109. Though there is a relatively clear GI at the end of the line, it is syntactically orphaned, rendering the suggested translation quite uncertain.

110. Meaning of verb (*dudduske-*) uncertain. Güterbock and van den Hout (1991: 7) suggest "to be in command of," which is a purely contextual reading. Pecchioli Daddi (1996: 142) suggests "comandare con clemenza." The basic meaning of the verb is generally taken to be "have/show mercy" (*HEG* T/D, 475–80), but since this would seem to make little sense in the admittedly fragmentary context, perhaps the semantically closely related concept of "excusing," i.e., "giving leave" to the bodyguards is at issue here.

111. For this deity, see Popko 2003b: 93–97.

112. *Pace* Güterbock and van den Hout (1991: 9), the sense of the latter part of the passage seems to be that not just anyone, but only the king is to designate and dispatch the official. See also *CHD* L–N, 39a.

113. Written over a KÁ.

114. Following this wedge—presumably a text divider, not the number 10, *pace*, e.g., Alp 1983: 106—are some one and two-thirds lines added after the fact. Their script is only minimally smaller than that of the main text. The following paragraph divider also seems to have been added, or perhaps redrawn after having been erased, and this is reflected in the paragraph designations 12a and 12b. The first one and one-third lines or so of the ensuing paragraph seem to be for the most part written over erased signs and are also slightly smaller than the original script.

115. Why the guard subsequently asks if he can go urinate even though the lexeme here indicates that he needs to defecate remains uncertain.

116. Cf. Ünal 1993: 127: "His Majesty needs to notice the watchman who goes to relieve himself, (therefore) the matter of relieving oneself must be reported to the (royal) palace." It seems unlikely, however, that it was to be reported to the king every time a guard had to urinate. Rather, they were to do so when and where allowed, so as not to disturb the king and raise his ire.

117. The translation is a paraphrase; cf. most recently Cambi 2007: 327; Melchert

1977: 289–90. For *naḫsaraz* as nom. sg., see Rieken 1999a: 115–16; *CHD* L–N, 343a, 344b.

118. For *sarkant*(*i*)- as "petitioners," see Melchert 1996: 135b.

119. For UGULA *LIM* as "clan chief" and *LĪM ṢĒRI* as "clan of the countryside" (e.g. in §15), see Beal 1992: 92–104; Beckman 1996: 62 and n. 73;

120. For a similar passage, cf. No. 3, §36″. For the meaning "cleaner" instead of "barber," see Klinger 1996: 251 and n. 461; cf. *HEG* T/D, 16–17.

121. The "carriage," Hitt. *ḫuluganni*-, is a two-wheeled vehicle, as is the "chariot," below; for royal wheeled transport, see Hagenbuchner-Dresel 2004: 364–69.

122. For "passageway," see Singer 1983: 106–11.

123. Seemingly written over *ma-a-aḫ-ḫa-an*.

124. ZAG-*az tiyenzi* here, which has been erased but not written over like the rest of the first ca. one and one-third lines of the paragraph, seems to represent the original active formulation, while the nominal sentence with the verbal substantive (*tiyawa*[*r* ZAG-*a*] *z=pat*) resulted from the rewriting process.

125. As the traces suggest ŠU]KUR or -*T*]*I*, either [^{GIŠ}ŠU]KUR or [SÍG-*T*]*I* has been restored in previous treatments, the latter in comparison with ii 49 and 53, which, however, are not directly comparable.

126. The traces could support either LÚ ŠUK[UR, which is how the copyist of IBoT 1.36 clearly understood them, or with Güterbock and van den Hout (1991: 14) ˹GÙB˺-. The phraseological construction (cf. ii 42–43, iii 10–11, 34, iv 11–12) would seem to speak for the latter, whereby the traces and the other attestations of GÙB (i 71, ii 43, 61, iii 23, iv 11) would suggest rather GÙB-*l*[*a-az*] than Güterbock and van den Hout's ˹GÙB-*za*˺.

127. The traces seem much more amenable to TI than to TE, which would also eliminate this lone attestation of -*te*- from the indicative paradigm; cf. *CHD* P, 352b–353a.

128. *Pace* Güterbock and van den Hout (1991: 16, n. 11), the traces would seem to match LÚ ŠUKUR neatly, with no trace of or room for GIŠ; cf. n. 136.

129. Literally "chair." For discussion of whether the object in the present context would be a chair or a step stool, see Hagenbuchner-Dresel (2004: 368–69), who argues against it being a step stool.

130. An IKU appears to have been somewhere between 10 and 15 m; cf. Melchert 1980; Starke 1995a: 21–22; van den Hout 1989/90: 520b–21a.

131. For "heavy-spearmen," see Beal 1992: 227 and n. 861.

132. Schuol (2004: 16–17, 120–21) suggests that the *mukar*-instrument may have been a rattle.

133. I can see no trace of the additional -*ri* assumed by Güterbock and van den Hout (1991: 16), though one would expect to see it, if it were there, judging from the appearance of the surface.

134. *Pace* Güterbock and van den Hout (1991: 18), *iya*- (and *iyanna*-) never take a local enclitic in this text (ii 19, 24, 27, 31, 32, 38, 45, 50, 54, 58, 62, iii 19, 22), so that one

thinks rather of a local adverb (which is always present), whereby *āppa* suggests itself in part due to its occurence three lines later in 38. The badly damaged signs do not seem to militate against the suggestion, but neither can they be said to demand it.

135. For the TIM, cf. iii 12. The break would seem to be a bit long to exclude the MEŠ, but quite a bit too short to include it; either way the traces before the break are a poor match for either MEŠ or É, and seem to be written over other traces.

136. The traces do not seem amenable to Güterbock and van den Hout's (1991: 18) *ŠA* LÚ GIŠŠUK[UR]; moreover, when referring to the person rather than the staff, only one other time (i 66) does it occur with GIŠ; otherwise it is attested only without (cf. n. 128); for a further attempt, see Hoffmann 1984: 138–39.

137. The sign is surely to be read *ŠA*, not *ta*. The ostensible first internal vertical is undoubtedly some damage or wayward trace, since the first five to six signs of the line seem to be written over previous traces. Note as well that this passage was a prime example used by van den Hout (2003a: 194, exx. 48 and 48b) to show that the difference between the phraseological or serial construction and phrases without a conjunction must have been slight. See also Rieken 1999b: 81 and n. 33.

138. As Güterbock and van den Hout (1991: 20, n. 20) astutely observed, the first signs are written over UGULA *LI-IM ṢE-RI*, whereby the *-RI* was not erased and not superimposed by any subsequent signs.

139. Melchert (1996: 135a), similarly, suggests "pass beside" for *awan arḫa pāi-*.

140. The traces seem perhaps to suggest *-na-* rather than *-an-*, so that one would have to parse *mān=as=(s)i*, "but if it, the road, is at some point ahead too narrow for him...."

141. Since there is still room for some 6+ signs after *widaizzi*, there may well have been some short sentence after the verb.

142. Giorgieri (1995: 126, n. 13) reads/restores LÚ*MEŠED*[*I parā*? *karapzi*?], *d*[*āi n=at kuit*?] and [LUGAL-*i memai*?] at the ends of ll. 3–5, respectively, translating "la guardi[a] lo [sceglie (lett. tira fuori)] e lo p[one] in mano al capo delle guardie; [di qualunque] caso (si tratti), lo dice al capo delle guardie e lo capo delle guardie [(lo) dice al re]."

143. Both Güterbock and van den Hout's (1991: 24) and my readings of the inserted text are somewhat suspect at certain points; the writing *ma-a-an-na-at* assumed by them would in any case be very odd. Contextually it makes little sense to say "two lords (whether they be lords or bodyguards)," i.e., the two possibilities should be subcategories of "lords." Hence, "two lords (whether they be spearmen or bodyguards)" is contextually more satisfying.

144. For discussion of the passage, see also Tjerkstra 1999: 76–77.

145. For *karp-* in legal contexts, see Beal 1993: 32–33; Marazzi 2004.

146. For the inversion of the enclitic pronouns, see *GrHL* §30.19.

147. For the law case being against the guard or the palace servant, see Melchert 1996: 135b.

148. In contrast to previous treatments, a change of subject is assumed here.

149. Literally "wrapping/surrounding." Cf., e.g., Klinger 1992: 195, "Bedeckung"

(where, incidentally, *halzāi* is translated "inspiziert"); Neu 1968: 59 and n. 3, "Begleitmannschaft, Gefolge," and below, n. 152.

150. Y. Cohen's (2002: 133) understanding of the passage is the most convincing, for which, however, one should restore *ḫa-an-da-˻a˼-*[*it*]-*t*[*a-r*]*i rather than ḫa-an-da-˻a˼-*[*an*]-*t*[*a-r*]*i.*

151. The traces beneath *na-* strongly suggest *te-*, so that one can assume that *te-ez-zi*, rewritten at the end of the addition, originally stood here.

152. Güterbock and van den Hout's (1991: 32) restoration [*ŠA* LÚ.MEŠ Š]UKUR.KÙ.SIG$_{17}$-*ia* is certainly too long.

153. Literally "it/he was surrounded/wrapped." Cf. Neu 1968: 59, "Eine Suite (Begleitmannschaft) hat man gebildet"; Melchert 1996: 135b; and above, n. 149.

154. Literally "it/he was united/collected." Cf. Neu 1968: 170, "man hat sich ge-/versammelt"; Melchert 1996: 135b.

155. Literally "the bodyguard who is (one) of cutting," so that one thinks either of a groom who is specifically responsible for cutting or trimming the horses hooves or one that grooms and cuts their hair and mane.

156. The translation treats ^{GIŠ}GIDRU-*z=an* as an abl. functioning as an instr. with acc. *-an* referring to the horse; cf. e.g., *HEG* T/D, 75.

157. I.e., assuming *parnass=a*, with *parnass* in the d.l. pl. Equally possible would be *parna=ssa*, in the allative, yielding, "As soon as the carriage *goes to* his (the king's) residence," as preferred by *CHD* P, 274b.

158. Cf. n. 170.

159. Lit. "The spears of the spear-men and the gold-spear[men] are fore-runners ..." The clause is certainly faulty, the translation an attempt to ascertain its intent. For the same error, cf. §26, 57.

160. The "accordingly" represents the KI.MIN written between ll. 1 and 2.

161. Space seems a bit tight for Güterbock and van den Hout's (1991: 32) *ŠA* along with some space between it and LÚ, though it cannot be ruled out categorically.

162. Güterbock and van den Hout's (1991: 32) *ša-a-r*[*i-ia-aš*]-*pát* is excluded by the traces. The suggested 3rd sg. pres. here is certainly incongruent with the pl. comm. subject, but any attempt to piece the paragraph together will deal with the same problem, as at least *paizzi* in the addition and either *tiyazi* or *paizzi* in 10 make clear. Probably the spearmen are simply treated as a collective. Pecchioli Daddi (1996: 144) suggests "Quando una parte della fila degli uomini della lancia passano il portico, il (loro) capo dove (va)? Entra proprio là, dove gli uomini della lancia — depositate le lance — vanno...."

163. The signs *-pí pa-* written over what seems to have been a *-zi*.

164. The signs *-an*$^{?}$*-zi*$^{?}$ likely written over *na-aš*.

165. (1) *a-pé*-t*[*a*$^{?}$*-a*]*z*$^{?}$*-*˹*pát*$^{?}$˺ is tentatively suggested, since in the traces immediately following *pé-* the heads of two inset verticals would seem to be visible, and since the next visible trace, the vertical, is too far to belong to the *e-* if one were to read *a-pé-e-da-ni*,

even accounting for the extra space in the split in the tablet, but not far enough for it to belong to the *-da-* in *a-pé-e-da-ni*. (2) From the position of the addition one would initially assume that it belongs to the first line of the paragraph, while not excluding that it could follow the second. As the first line ends with a verb, it seems one must opt for the latter.

166. Güterbock and van den Hout's (1991: 32) [*an-d*]*a-an* would seem a bit long for the space available, [*kat-t*]*a-an* only slightly better. In any case, I believe I am able to see traces of one or even two inset verticals before the wedge, which would assure the *-t*]*a-*.

167. The traces suggest (1) a *pa-* written over a *ti-* or vice versa, (2) an *-e-*, *-iz-* or an *-ia-* written over one of the others, and (3) a *-zi*, also over previous traces.

168. Though the syntax would seem to require it, there is not enough space for *-ma*.

169. Traces of what would seem to be two verticals are visible.

170. The only two obvious possibilities would be [*ap*]*-pa-an-zi* and [*kar*]*-pa-an-zi*. *CHD* P, 118b, and Güterbock and van den Hout (1991: 32) opt for the former but are thus forced to assume a meaning, "to reach," which, though suitable to the context, can neither be derived from the basic meaning of *parā ep-* nor is it attested elsewhere. If the verb is in fact *ep-*, one should presumably follow *HW*[2] E, 82, and assume that the mules are the object and translate "they take the mules out at the gate." Since *parā ep-* in iii 76–77, in a seemingly similar context, takes *-kan*, and since *parā karp-* here and in its other attestation does not (*CHD* P, 120a; see also *HED* K, 94, referring to plucking a stringed instrument), I have opted for *karp-*.

171. See n. 154.

172. This addition, which repeats verbatim the first clause of the ensuing paragraph, is difficult to explain. Why would the correcting scribe, if this interpretation of the additions is apt, add this clause at this point if it is already included? Did he hastily add it when he arrived at the end of the paragraph but before beginning the following section? And once he did continue to the ensuing paragraph, why did he then not erase his superfluous addition?

173. For this passage and the place of Luwian and Luwians in Hittite society, see most recently Yakubovich 2009: 264; Singer 2005: 448–49.

No. 5. Royal Decree on Social and Economic Matters (*CTH* 269)

174. The exploitation of the poor is addressed in later texts, too, e.g., in No. 9, §1.

175. All 2nd pers. verbs and pronouns in this text are pl.

176. For this interpretation, see Marazzi 1994; cf. *GrHL* §9.64, ns. 54 and 55; Floreano 2001: 211, n. 5.

No. 6. An Akkadian Fragment Mentioning an Oath (*CTH* 275)

177. A double paragraph line follows.

NOTES TO CHAPTER TWO

NO. 7. INSTRUCTIONS FOR MILITARY OFFICERS AND FRONTIER POST GOVERNORS (*CTH* 261.II)

1. Space is insufficient for Giorgieri's (1995: 206) [*ḫa-an-te-ez*]-⸢*zi-iš*⸣. Perhaps (*n=an*) *tu-uz-zi-iš ḫu-u-ma-an-za* (*istamaskeddu*) in No. 10, §9″, 15 and §10″, 18 points in the right direction, though the traces following *ḫu-u-ma-an-*[*za* do not seem to suggest *iš-ta-ma-*.

2. Based on l. 8′, below, and on No. 10, §9″, 11, Giorgieri (1995: 206) restores *arḫa tarnaḫḫi*, "I will release," but it is not entirely clear how this would fit the traces visible here.

3. On the necessity of emendation, see Rieken 1999a: 471, n. 2320.

4. Giorgieri's (1995: 207) [*e-eš-t*]*u* certainly to be favored over Alp's (1947: 391, n. 10a) [*iš-ša-an-d*]*u*, which would be far too long.

5. Also possible would be *iš-ta-ma-aš-ket*$_9$*-t*[*e-en* or perhaps *-ket*$_9$*-t*[*én*.

6. Alp's (1947: 394) **na-aš-ta-še-ia* is syntactically impossible. The damaged sign would seem to fit a ŠE better than a KUR, but neither is entirely satisfying. In context Giorgieri's (1995: 207) KUR-*ia* is surely preferable.

7. Though nothing appears in the drawing, I believe I am able to see rather clear traces on the photo that can be read as such. While Alp's (1947: 394) restoration is far too short, if one added *idalus* at this point, the signs along with Alp's suggestion would in fact fit perfectly, yielding [*nu* LÚ*ḫu-ia-an-za i-d*]*a-*⸤*a-lu*⸥*-*[*uš še-e*]*k-kán-za*, "[And a b]a[d fugitive, a kn]own man...."

8. Giorgieri (1995: 211) notes that KBo 22.235 rev. 3′–4′, which presumably have nothing to do with the present text, offers]KUR-*e iš-tar-na ar-ḫa i-ia-at-ta* / [... *me-na-a*]*ḫ-ḫa-an-da ú-e-mi-ia-an-zi na-aš-ta*; and curiously, restoring *iyatta menaḫḫanda* at the beginning of l. 9′ here would fit the space perfectly.

9. I believe I am able to see a trace of a wedge after the break, and without the extra sign the space between the *-zi* and the *nu* would have been inordinately long.

10. It seems that the head of a horizontal can be seen following *-šu*, so that Alp's (1947: 394) *punussuwar* can be eliminated, leaving only *punussueni*, *punussuen*, *punussun*, and *punussuanzi* as options.

11. Traces and space exclude the oft-restored *n*[*a-aš-m*]*a*. Alternatives include *a*[*n-d*]*a* and *k*[*u-i*]*t*. The former would seem to fit the traces better, the latter the context; *nu-uš* would seem a bit too short.

12. Alp's (1947: 396) *a*[*n-tu*]*-uḫ-ša-an* is too long and assumes an unlikely stem for this MH text, where *antuwaḫḫ-* is otherwise found (ii 8′, iv 5′). The only other stem ending with *-ḫsa-* to be found in Jin Jie 1994: 18 is *palaḫsa-*, which *CHD* P, 60a, defines as "a garment characteristic of d*IŠTAR*/dŠaušga and her two maidservants Ninatta and Kulitta." Sub usage a, *CHD* presents two passages in which Ištar is said to place her *palaḫsa*-garment

over a person in order to protect him, in the latter in the context of an escape across a river in a hail of arrows. As the *palaḫsa*-garment is thus associated with protection for the oppressed and/or fugitives, and since the signs would fit the space nicely, the restoration here seems apt. All other attestations, it must be noted, are from NH texts; the denominal verb *palaḫsiya-/palaḫsai-* occurs regularly in the MH horse training manuals (*CHD* P, 61). Against this interpretation might speak the following *dayan*, which must be the nom.-acc. sg. neut. participle, while one would expect *dayandan* for the acc. sg. comm. *palaḫsan*. There are, however, no n-stem neutra in Jin Jie's glossary that would fit the bill.

13. The writing is ambiguous, and could conceivably be read *BE-TU*$_4$, "lady," whereby one might expect ^{MUNUS}*BE-TU*$_4$ (cf. *HZL*, 97), or *BI*$_4$*-TU*$_4$, "house," among other possibilities. All, of course, would be errant for gen. *-TI*. One cannot simply translate "goods of the lord," as do Prins (1997: 44) and Watkins (1982: 251), without comment, for which one would expect *BE-LÌ*.

14. Perhaps ^{LÚ}*ḫu-ia-a*]*n-za*.

No. 8. Tudḫaliya I's Decree on Penal and Administrative Reform (*CTH* 258.1)

15. In view of the clear distribution of the prologue and impersonal lawgiving in cols. i–ii vis-à-vis the direct address in the 2nd pl. and the references to specific offices in cols. iii–iv, one might even suspect that this may be a *Sammeltafel*, i.e., a single tablet containing two entirely different compositions, the Decree of Tudḫaliya I on Penal and Administrative Reform (cols. i–ii) and something akin to Instructions for the Men of Ḫattusa (cols. iii–iv).

16. Hoffner (1992: 147) regards KUB 13.9+ as a "sloppy copy of a MH archetype." Perhaps supporting the suspicion that even the composition from the time of Tudḫaliya I might have incorporated earlier elements is the likelihood that the pl. (nom. comm. or nom.–acc. neut.) enclitic pronoun *-e* in 1.A iii 16′ is errantly employed, as no pl. substantive is apparent in the sentence, unless it refers obliquely to the court proceedings concerning the affair that do not reach their conclusion; see also ns. 37–38. Cf. now Marazzi 2012, n. 10: "Wörtlich fassen wir den Satz syntaktisch und semantisch folgendermaßen auf: „so dass es (*n=e=za=šan*) hinter der Sache (*uddanī appan*) angemessen/in angemessener Weise (*takšan*) nicht fertig wird (*natta appiyazi*)."

17. Presumably not [*ka*]-⌞*a*⌟-*aš-ša-wa-kán*, as usually restored (e.g., von Schuler 1959: 446; Marazzi 2012), since *kāsa* (for which see Rieken 2009) never shows gemination. A possible alternative would be [URU-*i*]*a-aš-ša-wa-kán*, i.e., [*ḫappiri*]*ass=a=wa=kan*, "... so you have not been able to render judgment concerning law cases, and evil persons of [the city] have utterly destroyed [...]." Similarly, KUR ([*utni*]*ass=a=wa=kan*), "of the land," would be a possibility.

18. Perhaps *ŠA BE-L*]*Í-NI*, "of our Lord."

19. As there is no space between *-e-eš-ta* and the preceding traces, a fientive in *-es*(*s*)- suggests itself, and in view of the "evil people" mentioned in l. 9 (*idalauies* UN^{MEŠ}-*sis*),

the suggested restoration seems not unlikely; cf., e.g., von Schuler 1959: 446 and Marazzi 2012.

20. *CHD* P, 125a, followed by Marazzi and Gzella (2003: 77) and Marazzi (2012), suggests ⌜*pi*⌝[*yan ḫarzi*], but this is entirely excluded by the traces visible on the photos.

21. Either [*na-an-ši-iš-ta pa-ra-a tar*]-*na-an-zi* (cf. e.g., ii 15), as preferred by Marazzi and Gzella (2003: 77) and Marazzi (2012), or [*na-aš-ta pa-ra-a* Ú-UL *tar*]-*na-an-zi* (cf. e.g., ii 10) would be expected; [*na-an-ši-iš-ta pa-ra-a* Ú-UL *tar*]-*na-an-zi* would be too long. De Martino and Imparati (1998: 400) argue for a negated clause.

22. For the translation of *-asta ... parā tarna-* in this text, see de Martino and Imparati 1998: 395–400, where the authors also argue for a distinction between handing the criminals in question over to the injured parties and handing them over to the state judicial system; cf. Haase 1965: 253–57; Freydank 1970; Marazzi and Gzella 2003: 77; and Marazzi 2012, who translates "überlassen (d.h. die als Buße gegebenen Güter zurückgeben)."

23. For this and the beginning of the following paragraph, see *CHD* Š, 280; Marazzi and Gzella 2003: 76–78.

24. (1) Westbrook and Woodard's (1990: 643) "from you," which goes back to von Schuler (1959: 449), is a misinterpretation of *nu=z=a(s)ta* as *nu=za=ta* (cf. already Otten and Souček 1965: 37, n. 5). Only in cols. iii and iv are persons addressed in the 2nd person in this text, in the pl. except for §11″, 14′, and §13″, 3′. (2) Melchert's interpretation of *wasta* as the 3rd sg. pret. of *was-*, "to buy, redeem" (quoted in Westbrook and Woodard 1990: 644–45 and n. 5; see now Marazzi and Gzella 2003) is followed here. Hoffner (in *GrHL* §28.22; cf. Hoffner 1997a: 170) seems now to have revised his earlier interpretation accordingly. Cf. Riemschneider 1961: 28; Catsanicos 1991: 13–18.

25. There should be no question regarding whether *-as-* in *mān=as=za* should be interpreted as a nom. sg. or an acc. pl. (cf., e.g., de Martino and Imparati 1998: 397), as a subject pronoun in this transitive sentence is excluded.

26. Melchert (cited in Westbrook and Woodard 1990: 645, n. 8; see also *GrHL* §4.65) suggests that *-an-* in *n=an=si=sta* refers to acc. comm. *sarnikzel*, i.e., the field and person paid as compensation. De Martino and Imparati (1998: 397; also Marazzi and Gzella 2003: 77) suggest that *-an-* might refer to the wives and children as a collective. Contextually, Melchert's solution would result in the injured party returning to the murderer the field and person, presumably a slave, but retaining the murderer's wives and sons, which strikes one as very odd. De Martino and Imparati's solution, which seems contextually most satisfying but grammatically least likely, would have the injured party relinquishing the murderer's wives and sons and presumably retaining the field and slave. Since, as Freydank (1970: 262) has noted, the object of *-asta ... parā tarna-*, whether expressed or not, seems otherwise always to be a person, a third possibility might be to relate *-an-* here to the LÚ.U$_{19}$.LÚ alone, i.e., the person given as compensation. In this case, the injured party would retain the field and the wives and children, but return the slave.

27. I.e. in the first case the original owner gets back his thieving servant, but in a condition of reduced value. In the latter case the original owner loses his slave entirely; see Freydank 1970: 260 and n. 21. For the blind in Hittite texts, see Arıkan 2006.

28. The traces preceding GAL seem to suggest a horizontal rather than a vertical, militating against É, as is often assumed, e.g., by von Schuler (1959: 447).

29. Von Schuler (1959: 447) suggested *na-aš-ma-*[*ad-du-z*]*a*, "to you(sg.)," which would indeed fit the available space and traces well, but the rest of the paragraph addresses its audience in the 2nd pl., suggesting, perhaps, that the 2nd sg. here might be unlikely.

30. The fact that AGRIG never occurs but once in the instructions (No. 2, §18″, 9′), as Singer has noted (1984: 107 and n. 58), would suggest that its restoration here, as assumed by von Schuler (1959: 447) and often repeated since, might be unlikely.

31. Among the indications that this paragraph is corrupt is the reflexive particle (*nu=z*a*=(s)ta*), which occurs with the phrase *-asta ... parā tarna-* only here. Cf. Catsanicos (1991: 14–15 and n. 1). The following *nu-wa-aš-šu* found in B_1 iii 6′ at this point should probably not be booked as a variant of *na-aš-šu*, *pace CHD* L–N, 405a, since (1) this is apparently the only attestation of such a writing, and (2) since there are several similar copying mistakes in this paragraph in the duplicate, as noted by Otten (1979: 275). The copying scribe presumably simply misread *na-* as *nu-wa-*, just as he wrote *tar-aš-ši-i* for *tar-na-i* in the following line, both misreadings being graphically quite understandable.

32. Perhaps ⌜LÚ⌝*ma-ni-ia-aḫ-ḫa-an-da-aš ŠA* is preferable, despite the lack of space between the signs and despite the resultant word order, as it would otherwise be difficult to explain the gemination and the final vowel.

33. The traces in the duplicate here do not seem amenable to *a*[*p-pé*]*-ez-*, as there appear to be more than two horizontals before the break and too little room for *pé*.

34. Perhaps either *ta-a-an* or -TA.ÀM; this ambiguity, and the fact that there is room for two further signs in the break, *pace* other treatments (e.g., Klinger 1996: 341), advise against restoration and interpretation.

35. It seems unlikely that DUB.X.KAM would have stood in the break, as it would only just fit the space, perhaps, and only if one chose to assume that the erased and/or damaged traces before the break represent the first portion of DUB, which does not seem overly likely.

36. Westbrook and Woodard (1990: 646–53) argue extensively for the meaning "to pursue," relating it to PIE **sek*w-; cf. Güterbock 1983: 78–80; *CHD* Š, 52–53.

37. At least some elements of this obstinate paragraph would seem to be corrupt (see e.g., n. 31), and the translation here attempts to find a balance between the literal and the interpretive. For the latest treatments, with references to older literature, see Dardano 2009: 5 and Marazzi 2012; for alternative readings, see Freydank 1970: 264–67.

38. As Riemschneider (1961: 28) noted, it may well be the case that LÚ*aras=sis* and LÚḪA.LA-*ŠU* are to be seen as one and the same person, which would imply that the administrator (*maniyaḫḫandas*) of 15′ would be the subject of the entire paragraph. Cf. now Marazzi (2012), who translates "(56)Wer angesichts (der Verletzung) dieser königlichen Vorschriften schweigen wird (57)und darüber hinaus – sei er (sc. derjenige, der die Sache nicht anzeigt) sein (d.h. desjenigen der die Vorschriften verletzt hat) gleichrangiger Kollege – (die Sache) verheimlicht, (58)und dieser (sc. derjenige, der die Vorschriften verletzt hat) ihm (sc. demjenigen, der die Sache verheimlicht hat) Schweigegeld gibt, (59)– sei er

(sc. derjenige, der die Sache nicht anzeigt) ein Mitarbeiter des Verwalters (sc. der die Vorschriften verletzt hat) – und er ihn (sc. denjenigen, der die Vorschriften verletzt hat) nicht (dem königlichen Gericht) überlässt, (60)so dass das vorgesehene gerichtliche Verfahren bez. der (Rechts)sache verhindert wird, (61)jedoch später die Sache aufgedeckt wird, (62) dann wird man beide für verantwortlich halten." It should be noted, however, that the translation fails to take account of (1) the 2nd sg. of *munnāsi* in 14′, translating "verheimlicht," (2) the gemination and final vowel of *maniyaḫḫandass=a* and (3) *nassu* in 13′ and 15′, which should indicate alternatives.

39. There is no apparent justification for reading this name Šaušga-ziti, as does Gordin 2010: 165.

40. For a recent study of the GIŠ.KIN-*TI*, which I have rather freely translated "labor bureau," cf. Gordin 2010 and Torri 2010.

No. 9. Tudḫaliya I's Decree on Penal and Administrative Reform

41. Beal's (1993: 32) [*ma-a-na-aš-ta* ...] (cf. *-asta* ... *karp-* in l. 12) leaves space for ca. 1–2 signs, certainly too little for *an-da-ma*, perhaps approximately enough for *-ma*. Giorgieri's (1995: 122) [*ma-a-an BE-LU* GAL EGIR-*aš an-tu*]- would be too long, though one could drop the GAL to reach approximately the right length. One would expect *-asta* (or *-kan*), though.

42. Giorgieri's (1995: 123) [*kiš-an*? *ḫa-an-da-an*? *ma-a-a*]*n*? is much too long for the available space.

43. The oft-read *ḫu*!*-ma-an* (e.g., Marazzi 2004: 317), even apart from the lack of plene writing, must be considered very unlikely. The sign before *-ma-an* is quite clearly a BI, before which a clear vertical, probably belonging to the preceding sign, can be seen. The traces before the vertical seem perhaps to be written over other sign traces and/or an erasure. They do not convince as A.Š]À.

44. Or *-wa*? Certainly no space for Y. Cohen's (2002: 137)]x-⸢*na*⸣-[*aš-š*]*i*, and the traces do not suggest Marazzi's (2004: 317) *ma*]-⸢*a*?*-na-wa*⸣, especially the *-a-*.

45. The writing *-u-wa-e-ni* for a 1st pl. pres., be it *ḫuwai-/ḫui-*, "to run," or some other verb, is surely errant. Neither do the traces of the first sign readily convince as a *ḫu-*, but suggest rather *ú-*, so that one suspects that the scribe may have bungled an intended *wemiyaweni*, adding it at the end of the line and forgetting to erase this first attempt. Alternatively, and perhaps more likely, the scribe may have intended to write *ú-wa-u-e-ni*, "we will come," probably in a phraseological or serial construction, whereby he simply inverted his *wa* and his *u*.

46. LÚMÁŠDA and LÚ.MEŠMÁŠDA are entirely excluded by the traces visible on the photos. Though perhaps a possibility, ⸤LÚ*ME-ŠE-DI*⸥ does not quite convince either. Further, LÚ.MEŠ is not the only possible reading of the first traces; one could opt, e.g., for ⸤*ni*-x x⸥. I suspect, though, that *IŠ*]*TU* may well serve as an instr. of accompaniment rather than spacially as an abl., as it is usually understood, yielding "[and] they *expel* [*him* alo]ng with (his) [...]-*persons*," whereby the persons in question might be the family of the culprit. In

fact, ^{LÚ}É-*ŠU* would fit at least most of the visible sign traces, but one would probably like to see LÚ^{MEŠ} É-*ŠU* or simply É-*ŠU* for such.

47. Clearly -*šu*, not -*ma*, as in *HW*^{2} A, 220b.

48. I have retained the clear *KI*-, reading Akk. *kīnu* (see *CAD* K, s.v. 3), rather than emending to *DI*-, despite the rarity of the word in the Hittite texts. In all previous treatments *DI*$^!$-*NAM* has been read and translated either as "law case" (or similar) or "payment/compensation" (or similar), or simply omitted. In fact, a translation such as Beal's (1993: 32; similarly *CHD* P, 290b), "He will compensate (for) the legal-case with his house," is quite acceptable contextually. Still, despite the common inversion of KI and DI, I would prefer not to emend the sign if avoidable. The index cards at the Akademie der Wissenschaften in Mainz reveal only two attestations of *kīnu*, both in Akkadian texts, i.e., KBo 1.23 obv. 7 (*ki-i-na*, *CTH* 170: Fragment of Correspondence with Egypt; Edel 1994: 166) and KUB 4.4 obv. 8′ (*CTH* 314: Trilingual Hymn to Iškur/Adad), read *ki*$^!$-*ni*$^!$ by Klinger (2010: 322), but ˌ*di*ˌ-*š*∘*i*$^?$ by Schwemer (2001: 194). My thanks to Silvin Košak, who kindly searched for the occurrences for me.

49. These traces seem quite amenable to the reading ˌ*a-a-ra-pát*ˌ, though the context remains somewhat uncertain. As Y. Cohen has pointed out (2002: 171–72 and n. 5), *āra* does not otherwise take enclitics, so that this would be exceptional. For the potential exception in VSNF 12.7 i 6′, see Cohen 2002: 171–72 and Groddek 2002b: 87. One would like to see a negation, but neither *na-a*[*t-ta*] nor ˌ*Ú-UL*ˌ would seem to fit the space and traces before or after ˌ*a-a-ra-pát*ˌ. If not negated, perhaps the clause is to be understood as a rhetorical question. As far as Marazzi's (2004: 318, 321) suggested *na*-x-x-x ⌜*kar*$^?$-*pí*$^?$⌝-[is concerned, the BI would be quite possible, but KAR does not seem amenable to the traces. I have avoided restoring the remainder of the paragraph after No. 12, §26″, as the two are clearly only largely parallel, not duplicate. See Introduction to No. 9 and n. 186.

50. The -*a*- was omitted in the edition, KUB 13.7.

51. For recent discussions of -*asta*/-*kan* ... *karp*- in judicial parlance, see, in addition to the dictionary treatments, Beal 1993: 32–34; Giorgieri 1995: 125–26; and Marazzi 2004: 307–12; the latter is followed here.

52. I.e., assuming …-*pí*=*man*; alternatively one could read …-*pí*=*ma*=*an*, i.e., "but […] him$^{(acc.)}$." The third possibility, an irrealis, though not impossible, seems less likely.

53. I.e., an attempt to render *appan wemiya*-, lit. "find/meet/reach behind."

54. The significance of the taking of the client's sacrificial meat is not clear. Perhaps bilking the victim of his last possessions, even his offerings intended for the gods, is implied. Marazzi (2004: 313) thinks of the suspension of religious duties or perhaps "alle misure prese per garantire il ripristino dei diritti dei soggetti che hanno subito il sopruso."

55. Or "he shall be in good standing (i.e., right) with regard to His Majesty"? Cf. e.g., *HW*^{2} A, 220a.

56. Lines 3′–7′ are written in a smaller script in a different hand, perhaps some time after the rest of the tablet had been written and had begun to dry, as they are also impressed more shallowly.

57. Possibly "The king himself [may not pardon him]; it is not permissible for him," or similar. For recent discussion, see Marazzi 2002: 80.

No. 10. Tudḫaliya I?'s Instructions and Oath Imposition for All the Men (*CTH* 259)

58. This reduplication may be one hint that at least §§9″–11″ were significantly reworked during the text's redactional history. Note also the sudden switch from 1st to 3rd person and back again mid-sentence in §9″, 12–15.

59. Cf. KUB 26.57 i 8′–13′ (No. 22.2), KUB 21.46 i 6–10 (No. 23), KUB 31.44 i 25–29 (No. 14.1), and KUB 26.24 i 16′–21′ (No. 14.3.A). One expects Tudḫaliya, Nikkalmadi, perhaps Arnuwanda, and "sons and grandsons" in ll. 3′–4′.

60. Giorgieri (1995: 141, 255) restores *linkten* at the end of 5′ (cf. *link*]*iskewani* in No. 22.2 i 11′) and [... *LI-IM* DINGIR^MEŠ^ *tu-li-ia ḫal-zi-ú-en*] here based on No 22.2 i 13′, which is surely not far from the mark. If [*ka-a-š*]*a* is indeed to be restored at the beginning of l. 6′, however, it would all but ensure that the first paragraph was spoken in the 1st person, in keeping with Rieken (2009).

61. [^d^LA]MMA also graphically possible.

62. So, rather than MUNUS.LUGAL ^d^A[N (e.g., Trémouille 1997: 24, n. 58), as there is a significant space between the two AN signs.

63. As noted by Groddek (2008a: 173 and n. 391), my copy in KBo 50 fails to number the traces in the column divider preserved on 1098/u. The]x-*mi* would seem to belong to the last or second to last line of a previous paragraph, the latter trace probably to l. 2′.

64. Also possible: ⸢*tar*?-*na*⸣-[

65. Or "you have brought." All 2nd person verbs and pronouns in this text are 2nd pl. unless otherwise indicated.

66. Von Schuler's (1956: 213) [*ma-a-an* ^LÚ^*ḫu-ia-an-d*(*a*)]-*a*[(*n*)] is excluded by the traces in A iv 8′.

67. The restoration is based on No. 7 (KUB 26.17 i 9′–10′), whereby a Sumerographic writing is perhaps preferable to Alp's (1947: 390) [... *i-ia-u-wa-an-zi*], which would require essentially the entire verb to be written in the column divider.

68. Or perhaps *QA-TAM*-<*MA*> ⸢*e*⸣-[*eš-du*]. The sign before the break can hardly be an *i*[*š*-; cf. e.g., *CHD* P, 298a, probably influenced by *iš-ša-at-tén* in l. 19.

69. Alp (1947: 390), followed, e.g., by *CHD* Š, 323a, has *t*[*uzzin*, but the traces suggest rather the head of a horizontal than a wedge.

70. The restoration would extend significantly into the column divider and must be considered quite uncertain. One could perhaps restore merely [*ma-aḫ-ḫa-an*] and translate "And [just like] (the command) of My Majesty you shall carry (his) out." Alp (1947: 390) restores *isḫiul apella QATAMMA*, emending *maḫḫan* before the break, but syntax allows it to follow as well; see *CHD* L–N, 110b, and cf. l. 25, where *maḫḫan* follows ^d^UTU-*ŠI tūwaz*.

71. Lit. "a protected work of the future"; see *CHD* P, 10a.

72. Though one would indeed like to see *n*[*a-at* here, the traces, *pace* del Monte 1975a: 128, are clearly *n*[*u*.

73. Both the writing here, which can only be understood as *tuekkass=a*, "and to the person(s)," and -*e*]*g-ga-aš-ša-aš* in D_2, 5′, which can only be *tuekkas=sas*, "of his person," "his own," would seem to be errant. For simply d.l. pl. one would expect *tuekkas*, while an enclitic pronoun should result in *tueggas=smi*. Conceivably *tuekkas=sas*, "his own," could have functioned as a general possessive, i.e., "his(your) own wives, your own sons, your own homes."

74. This is apparently the only attestation of a stem *kaenant-*, while there are many cases of *kaena-* and two of *kaenatar* in the d.l., *kaenanni*, so that one might consider emending here to *ka-e-na-an-ni*!(TI), or even *ka-e-na-aš*!*-ši*! (i.e., *kaenas=si*). If indeed *kaenanti*, it would of course be d.l. as opposed to the rest of the elements in the series, which stand in the gen., except for *ari=ssi*, also in the d.l. For the most recent discussions of Hittite kinship terms, see Puhvel 2009 and Pringle 2010.

75. NINDA is clearly defective, though this is not apparent from the copy.

76. Cf. *CHD* L–N, 169b, 426b; Rieken (1999a: 120–22), who maintains that *maniaḫḫiatti* is "bestimmt eine künstliche Fehlbildung."

77. LUGAL-*ia* *ŠA*! would seem to be corrupt, as there is no space between IA and ŠA, though there is no way to sensibly parse LUGAL-*ia-ša* in the context. Neu (1982a: 123) sought to understand LUGAL-*iyas=a* as a gen., i.e. "... Angesicht des Königs," but *menaḫḫanda* is not otherwise attested with a gen.; see also *HW*² Ḫ, 442a, "... bringt auch vor den König, euren Herrn...." Though dreadfully un-Akkadian, perhaps the scribe sought by means of *ŠA* to express the genitive relationship between the king and the addressees, for which one would naturally expect *ANA* LUGAL-*ia* *ANA BĒLĪ=KUNU*, i.e., "to the king, your lord." One might indeed consider emending *ŠA* to *A*!*-NA*!.

78. Presumably referring back to the troops, chariotry and frontier posts at the end of the previous paragraph; cf. *CHD* Š, 44a, 45a, where it is assumed that this neut. enclitic proves the existence of neut. *saklai-*.

79. Quite uncertain if in fact to be attributed to *kunna-*, "right; good," as assumed here; cf. *HED* K, 248.

80. Presumably either (1) an error for *zi-ia-an-du*, "may they cross"; (2) a singular attestation of the declension *ziyadu*, "let him cross," instead of expected *zau*; or, contextually unlikely, (3) the 3rd sg. imp. of otherwise med.-pass. *ze/iya-*, "to cook."

81. Alp's (1947: 396) 3rd sg. active *paḫsanuzi* is not attested, and the med.-pass. form is to be preferred.

82. Giorgieri (1995: 178–79 and n. 154) presents plausible argumentation for seeing *isḫiula* as a collective rather than emending to *iš-ḫi-ú-la-*<*aš*>.

No. 11. Instructions and Oath Impositions for the Successions of Tudḫaliya I and Tudḫaliya III (*CTH* 271)

83. KBo 31.81 (203/f) is often treated together with these fragments due to similar prosopography, but since its hand is clearly that of another scribe, it is not included here.

84. Klinger (1995: 96–99) has suggested dating these fragments to Tudḫaliya I. While Gurney (1979) and Haas (1985: 270 and n. 16), e.g., accept a coregency, Beal (1983: 119–22) and van den Hout (1991: 278, n. 14) reject the hypothesis.

85. Carruba (1977: 188) reads ^{m}A[rn]u[wanda, but this clearly fits neither the traces visible on the photos nor those copied in the edition.

86. Ḫimuili is here and below not written with a plene *-u-*, as assumed in some treatments, but with a form of *-mu-* with a trailing wedge that can be mistaken for an *-u*.

87. Certainly not *tá*[*k-*, as read by Carruba (1971: 91), but rather *k*[*u-*, with Giorgieri (1995: 118), perhaps *k*[*u-it-ki*.

88. The second sign is actually much more amenable to *-m*[*a-* than *-k*[*u-*; if in fact to be read *-k*[*u-*, then presumably from either *takku-*, the meaning of which is not known for certain, or *takkuwa-*, "enclose?" (*HEG* T/D, 52–53). If the latter, perhaps *ták-k*[*u-an*]*-zi*? Giorgieri (1995: 118) ventures a reading *ták-*⸢*ka*⸣?-[*aš*]?-⸢*zi*⸣, which cannot be excluded, though the inset element in the traces before the break would seem to be a horizontal rather than the wedge seen, e.g., in the KA at the end of l. 3′. Perhaps *ták-*<*ki*>*-i*[*š-iz/an*]*-zi* is the best solution.

89. Generally read ^{m}*Me-e-ša-m*[*u-wa*, but in light of *sumē/ās* in 12′, 13′, and 17′, this seems more likely. A reading *sumēs=as=m*[*u* would also be possible, but the first person does not seem to occur otherwise in this text. As this was the only attestation for Mēsamuwa, it should be struck from the known onomasticon.

90. Clearly *-zi*, and thus not *takkesta*, as in Melchert 1994: 134.

91. Certainly not *ḫ*[*ar*, as Carruba (1971: 91) reads, since the traces begin with two (or three) horizontals. More likely would be Giorgieri's (2005: 333) *a*[*p-pa-an-du ... ḫar-ni-in-kán-du*], or similar. As Winkels (1978: 93) has observed, this is the earliest of only four attestations of *NĪŠ* DINGIR-*LÌ* that seem clearly to refer not to the oath but to the oath deities as active agents (normally represented with *NĪŠ* DINGIR^{MEŠ}) and that cannot be chalked up to a late copyist.

92. Collation of the photos strongly suggests I rather than DUMU, as suggested as a possibility in *HEG* T/D, 390.

93. The semantic range of *takks-* is very broad (*EDHIL*, 813–14), and with insufficient context it is very difficult to determine what exactly the meaning is.

94. "You$^{\text{(pl.)}}$ protected" also possible.

95. Tischler (*HEG* T/D, 390) suggests reading]x-LUGAL, i.e., "sie setzen x-šarri in die Königsherrschaft ein." While this possibility should not be rejected out of hand—it would, e.g., eliminate the redundancy in "installing the king in kingship"—the sign traces before LUGAL do not suggest *-m*]*i-*, which would allow *Ta-aš-m*]*i-šarri*, the only known

prince from this period who might be a candidate. The suggestion in *HW*[2] Ḫ, 478a, to restore [*A-NA* T]I and translate "für das Leben des Königs setzt [man] in die Königsherrschaft ein" seems rather unlikely contextually and lacks parallels. Another possibility would be Giorgieri's (1995: 119) [ŠÀ.BA]L LUGAL, "[einen Nachkom]men des Königs."

96. Certainly not DUMU, as read by Carruba (1977: 184).

97. Clearly *-ma*, and thus not *appan*, as in Carruba 1977: 184; 2008: 113.

98. The horizontals of the UD[!](DI) are not as clear on the photos as they are in the copy, and when one compares with the clear horizontals in KI in lines 4′ and 7′, it seems doubtful that horizontals were intended here, so that many treatments (e.g., Otten 1987: 29; Taracha 2004: 636) emend to UD[!ḪI.A] and translate "in those days," yielding good sense in context. On the other hand, UD should take KAM, not [ḪI.A] (for an exception see KBo 19.38+, 42; Weeden 2011: 626), and "in those law cases" would yield a sensible result as well.

99. Carruba (1977: 184) restores [LÚ.MEŠ]*ḫant*]*izilis=a*, presumably because he felt that the traces before *-zi-* are more amenable to *-t*]*i-* than *-t*]*u-*, but since Kantuzili's name is spelled plene in A_1 r. col. 10′, it is likely to be spelled plene here and perhaps in the rest of the text as well, except maybe in A_4 r. col. 3′.

100. Carruba's (1977: 187) *ku-e*[*n-* seems unlikely in view of the traces. Perhaps *ku-i*[*n~* is to be preferred.

101. Clearly so, with Neu (1968: 136), not]-*zi*, as read by Carruba (1977: 187).

102. Or *ku-na-an-*[*zi*, "they will kill." It should be noted, contra what is claimed in much secondary literature (e.g., Freu 2007b: 33), that nowhere in this text is it stated that Muwā killed the queen; rather it repeatedly states that he will (or intends) to kill her.

103. Purely graphically *l*[*i-* and perhaps ˹*še-e*˺-[also possible. With Houwink ten Cate (1995–96: 61), maybe *uwat t*[*uwattu*, "mercy!" Giorgieri (1995: 121), following Carruba (1977: 190), assumes *t*[*u-li-ia*.

104. This treatment of these lines assumes that the edge of the tablet is reached with the suggested restorations, which, though not entirely certain, seems quite likely based on how these minimalist restorations align at left and on the appearance of the left break of the fragment.

105. Houwink ten Cate's (1995–96: 61) L[UGAL-*i* is excluded by the traces visible before the break.

106. Clearly *-ta*, not *-ša*, as in Carruba 1977: 190.

107. Among the conceivable restorations, [*an-d*]*a-ma* might be a bit long; [*ku-i*]*t-ma* might be preferable, though the traces would seem to suggest rather *-d*]*a-* than *-i*]*t*.

108. *CHD* Š, 204b, reads [LÚ.MEŠ]*ša-p*[*a-ša-al-li-e-eš*]. Pecchioli Daddi (2003b: 88, n. 46) opts for *ša-l*[*a-ašḫeš*.

109. In all treatments of which I am aware transliterated NIN[ḪI.A]-*Š*[*U* without question, though the sign traces are anything but incontrovertible. DAM could be read just as well, and *-Š*[*U-NU* can also not be excluded.

110. One could consider reading] *A-BI-IA pí-ip*-x[and translating "topple my father," but the attestations for *pippa-* in *CHD* P show no such usage.

111. Otten's (1990: 224) [*Ù A-N*]*A* is quite possible but hardly the lone possibility.

112. Otten (1990: 224, n. 8) is certainly correct when he states that "nach Verlauf der Bruchlinie" the reading ^{LÚ}*t*[*u-* is all but impossible. That said, one should not conclude too hastily how the line is to be understood. One cannot necessarily conclude, with Otten (p. 225), that "Anscheinend erhebt der Großkönig seinen ‚Bruder' … Tutḫalija zu neuer Würde," as one could just as easily assume, e.g., that ŠEŠ[^{MEŠ}-*ŠU* or other possibilities might be restored, including Houwink ten Cate's (1995–96: 66) PN or simply -*ŠU*.

113. If one allows the left edge of the column to be determined by the restorations [^{m}*Du-ut*]-*ḫa-li-ia-an* in 3′, [^{m}*Du*]-*ut-ḫa-li-ia-aš* in 7′, and [^{m}*Túl-pí*]-⌜d⌝10-*ub-aš-ša* in 9′ (cf. signs in ll. 4′ and 2′), it becomes clear than the most common restorations [*na*]-*an* in 4′, [*n*]*a-an-kán* in 5′, and [DUMU^{M}]^{EŠ}-*ŠU-* in 8′ would be significantly too short. Houwink ten Cate's (1995–96: 66) [*ma-a*]-*an* would fit the space in 4′ quite well. Either [ŠEŠ^{M}]^{EŠ}-*ŠU-* or, purely theoretically, [DUMU.DUMU^{M}]^{EŠ}-*ŠU-*, would fit nicely in 8′. Perhaps [*nam-m*]*a-an-kán* would be a possibility in 5′. [*nu-wa-aš-ma*]-⸤*ša-at*⸥ fits the space and traces in 10′ perfectly.

114. Traces exclude Houwink ten Cate's (1995–96: 66) *š*[*a-a-ak-k*]*u* and are not favorable to Giorgieri's (1995: 120) LUGA]L$^{?}$-, while the latter's -⌜*TI*⌝$^{?}$ would be a possibility.

115. Presumably either ŠEŠ (e.g., Giorgieri 1995: 120; Taracha 1997: 76; Dinçol 2001: 96; Fuscagni 2002: 289, n. 3; O. Soysal 2003: 50 and n. 34; Marizza 2007: 27) or DUMU (Otten 1990: 225 and n. 12; Klinger 1995: 96–97), the former of which would fit the space well enough (cf. n. 113). Klengel's (1999: 131 n. 205) statement, "Tuthaliya wird in KUB XXXVI 119 + … 8 als „Bruder" des Großkönigs bezeichnet," is incorrect.

116. As no hint of the right column edge is preserved, it is difficult to argue for or against the possibility that Mannini, known from KUB 45.47+ as another brother in this group, might have stood in the break as well; cf. Otten 1990: 225 and Marizza 2007: 25–27.

117. Houwink ten Cate (1995–96: 66) considers restoring [-*ta*] here, and one could similarly venture an [-*at*] at the end of the following line, but neither is strictly necessary; see van den Hout (2001: 174–75).

118. Gurney's (1977: 222–23) [*ták-šu-l*]*a-ša-at*, "a treaty of [loyalty]," falters on Watkins' Rule, i.e., one would not expect the subject pronoun -*at* in such a transitive sentence.

119. As indicated by Houwink ten Cate's (1995–96: 66) -*ir*$^{!}$, the traces are not overly convincing as -*ni-ir*; -*TÌ* is graphically and, in light of GAL$^{HI.A}$-*TÌ* a few signs later in the line, also contextually preferable. Perhaps ^{GIŠ}ŠÚ.A^{HI}]⸤^{A}-*TÌ* is the most likely restoration.

120. For Houwink ten Cate's (1995–96: 66) *k*[*u-*(*i*)]-*e*, in any case an uncommon form, there is insufficient space.

121. Often read *da*[*m-* and restored *da*[*m-me-eš-zi*, "shall not oppress," or similar, but a reading *šal-l*[*a-*, as seen already by Giorgieri (1995: 120), is graphically much more

convincing. Contextually similar are KBo 1.5 i 41–43 (Sunaššura Treaty; Schwemer 2005: 100).

122. Houwink ten Cate's (1995–96: 66)]-˻*ub*˼-*aš*-˻*ša*˼ is excluded by the traces.

123. There does not appear to be sufficient space for Carruba's (1977: 194) -*zi* in the break.

124. DUMU^{MEŠ}-*IA*, "my sons," naturally also possible, but this would not seem to fit the admittedly all but incomprehensible context.

No. 12. Instructions and Oath Imposition for Princes, Lords, and Military Officers (*CTH* 251)

125. All 2nd person verbs and pronouns in this text are 2nd pl. unless otherwise indicated.

126. The traces actually suggest rather -*V*]*ḫ*-*ḫa*, leading one to think of *laḫḫa*-, which, however, would be odd with *wida*-. Though not attested as such, could one think of "when I bring a military campaign (= war/battle) to them," or similar?

127. Traces exclude Oettinger's (1979 [2002]: 60) -*r*]*a*- (see already Giorgieri 1995: 98 n. 10), suggesting rather *n*]*a*-, -*š*]*a*- or -*t*]*a*-. Giorgieri (1995: 98, n. 10) considered *tarn*]*atta*, but cf. Neu (1968: 168 n. 1).

128. *CHD* Š, 252a, followed in *EDHIL*, 732, reads and restores [GIM-*an*(?)]=*ma*=*z*=*kan zaḫḫiy*[*awanzi ēpzi nu* LÚ.KÚ]R?-*aš* (or: [*tuzz*]*iaš*) and translates "[When it (i.e., the army) begins to join] battle(?), let it maul(?)/press(?) the first (rank) of [the enem]y? (or: of [the (opposing) arm]y)." The traces are, however, ill-suited to a KÚR, while the restoration with *tuzziyas* (11 signs) seems a fair bit too long for the gap. Perhaps *ap-p*]*é-ez*-˻*zi*˼-*aš ḫa-an-te*$_9$-*ez-zi* in i 77′ points in the right direction.

129. As noted by Giorgieri (1995: 98, n. 13), the restoration *ninink*]*iskanta* in *CHD* L–N, 439a, is problematic, as this would be med.-pass., while a transitive verb is expected.

130. The traces visible in the photographs make a perfectly good *n*]*i*-. Cf. *CHD* L–N, 440a: [o-]x-*ma mān* ERÍN.MEŠ-*an la*[*ḫḫa* o o o o-*k*]*i-iš-kán-ta* [*nu*] *ḫūmanza nuntarriē*[*ddu* o o o o *n*]*i*!-*ni-ik-du-ma-at*, "When they [...] the troops [for] a c[ampaign(?)], let everyone make haste. [...] Get moving (pl.)!" Dardano (2009: 5) restores *nu-un-tar-ri-e-e*[*d-du nu* ÉRIN^{MEŠ} *ni*]-*ni-ik-du-ma-at* in 18′ and *le*-˹*e*˺ [*ku-iš-ki nu* ^{LÚ}KÚR-*an a*]*r*-*ḫa* in 19′, translating "[e] ognuno si affret[ti.] Mobilita[te l'esercito. Nessuno] compia un atto di forza, nessuno rilasci [un nemico] e prenda una ricompensa. [Questo] sia posto [sotto giuramento]." The suggestion is quite attractive, its only weakness being too few signs in 18′, which is easily remedied by, e.g., a *nam-ma* rather than a *nu*. Neu (1968: 81, n. 6) assumes *ḫa*]*rnikdu*-, contextually less likely, but rightly noting that a 3rd sg. imp. with enclitic =*ma*=*at* would also be possible.

131. Assuming the restoration of the following line is correct, then that in *CHD* L–N 209a, [*nu* LÚ.KÚR-*an a*]*rḫa*, would be far too short here.

132. *Pace* Giorgieri (1995: 98), the MH date of the text as well as the space available would suggest *kat-ta-an* rather than GIM-*an*.

133. For this passage cf. No. 10, §7″. As noted by Groddek (2008a: 163, n. 355), the *Ú-UL* in the column divider belongs at the end of l. 25′, not here, as assumed in earlier treatments.

134. The traces before the break speak more readily for *m*[*a-* than Giorgieri's *t*[*e-* (1995: 99). Beal's (1992: 476 n. 1758) contextually attractive restoration, *ma*[*nikuwa*]*ntes* would be a fair bit too short, even after adding an *-in-*, i.e., *m*[*a-ni-in-ku-wa-a*]*n-te-eš*. Neither does *maninkuwan*(*t*)-, "near," seem to occur with *anda*; see *CHD* L–N, 171–74. The following ^{LÚ}KÚR$^{HI.A}$-*an* of dupl. B_2, 3′ is thus seen to be a sg. acc.; cf. Neu 1979: 415, n. 15.

135. Space is insufficient for Beal's (1992: 476) *nasma*; and since *ḫūwai* begs for a *-kan*, as in l. 31′ and, if the verb is restored correctly, in 21′, it should be added as well.

136. For the restoration, see ll. 19′–20′ and 32′; cf., e.g., Reichardt 1998: 28; Christiansen 2008: 268.

137. The restoration follows *CHD* L–N, 330b; Rizzi Mellini's (1979: 518) *ar*]*nuzzi*=, followed in most other treatments, would be far too short.

138. Cf. No. 10, §10″, 16.

139. Beal (1992: 131 n. 480), without the benefit of the dupl., restored ^{URU}*Kilimu*[*na walaḫ*]*ten nuza š*[*umenzan*] / [ERÍN.MEŠ-*KUN*]*U*.

140. Traces in B_4, 3′ almost certainly *-z*[*a*.

141. Space prohibits Haas's (1981: 646 and n. 31) KIN-*a*[*n-ma-wa l*]*e-e*, but other options seem equally unlikely. One would hardly want to read *k*]*e-e*, e.g., as KIN-*a*[*n* is surely acc. sg. comm. (cf. i 16′). If one opted for *aniyatte*[*n* rather than *aniyatten*[*i*, one would want to eliminate *lē* if interpreting the verb as an imp. (but cf. n. 142), but an alternate reading for]x-*e* is not immediately apparent; contextually it is equally difficult to read the verb as a pret. rather than the imp. Perhaps the scribe simply neglected to add either *-ma* or *-wa*. One might speculate that the scribe intended the errantly added *-wa* in 39′ to go here but misplaced it.

142. On the photos it seems that a trace of the head of a vertical is visible, thus *-e*[*n*, not *-n*[*i*, but it is difficult to imagine what one could read instead of *l*]*e-e* before the verb, so that *-n*[*i* still seems the better option. For the occasional *lē* with an imp., see *GrHL* §26.17.

143. In a text of this date one would expect *-az*, but space is very tight, so that *-za* seems much more likely.

144. For the restoration cf. i 55′ and 62′, the other two places in this text where *sumenzan* is found.

145. Though apparently a correction, the passage would seem to make more sense without the quotative particle, and the dupl. B_4, 7′ indeed omits it (see also n. 141). Christiansen (2008: 268) restores [*me-ma-aḫ-te-e*]*n* at the beginning of 39′, and while the traces following the break indeed fit an *-e*]*n* well, placing the curse formula in the mouths of the subordinates being addressed is, as far as I have been able to ascertain, unparalleled as

well as contextually unlikely. Perhaps rather *nu ki-iš-š*[*a-an*] / [*wa-aš-ta-at-te-e*]*n*, "and th[us yo]u [erred]"?

146. Morphologically equally possible, "you(pl.) mobilized."

147. The passage would seem to recall some sections of the Siege of Uršu Text (Beckman 1995) in its mocking tone toward military officers with regard to their incompetence during previous campaigns.

148. Mere *A-NA* (e.g., Groddek 2008a: 164) would be far too short for the space.

149. Space might be a bit tight for [*e-ez-za-az-z*]*i*, while it might be a bit long for Rizzi Mellini's (1979: 522) and Giorgieri's (1995: 100) [*e-ep-z*]*i*. For Haas's (1981: 646) "Wer aber sein Soldatenbrot [hat] und nicht beginnt zu handeln …," i.e., [*ḫar-z*]*i*, the space is far too long, and one would expect for such a translation also a *-ma*. A restoration [*Ú-UL ḫar-z*]*i* would be contextually satisfying and fill the space nicely; this assumes that the traces in B_3 5′, which do not allow *ḫ*[*ar-*, do not duplicate these signs but rather *Ú-U*[*L*] x-*ia-an-na*, further to the right.

150. Presumably either (1) an acc. with the conjunction or (2) an inf. II form, though the obvious candidates (*tiyanna* [ME-*ianna*, GAR-*ianna*], *piyanna* [SUM-*ianna*], *siyanna*) can be all but excluded, as the sumerographic writings would be both unexpected in a text of this date and would fit the space and/or traces poorly; the phonetic writings would be equally ill suited. Haas's (1981: 646 and n. 33) [KIN]-*iyanna*, i.e., the participle with a conjunction (*aniyann=a*), which provides good sense, would not fit the traces, nor would [*a-n*]*i-ia-an-na*.

151. Goedegebuure's (2003: 123) and Dardano's (2007: 235, n. 54) [*ku-u-ru-ur pa-ra-a*] and [*a*]*l-pu-e-eš-zi* are excluded by traces and space; see already Güterbock 1988: 169–70. There is, however, space for [*nu*] thereafter, rendering superfluous Christiansen's (2008: 268–69) considerations on the syntax.

152. Giorgieri's (1995: 101) restoration *d*[*u-ug-ga-ru-uš-ma-ša-at*] is indeed attractive, and it seems that traces of *-a-ru-* may even be visible on the photos. Whether the scribe was able to add the entire enclitic chain may be doubted, however, since the verb itself would reach to the end of the line and through the column divider, and since little space remains before the *-an* at the end of 47′ in the column divider, where one would perhaps have expected to see some traces continuing from here in 51′ if they had been there. Perhaps only *-uš-ma-aš* would suffice, despite the need for the subject pronoun in this intransitive sentence.

153. For discussion of the unexplained writing *du-ud-du-mi-ìš-ša*, which I have assumed to be linked with *duddumar*, "benevolence," along with the conjunction (i.e., *duddumiss=a*), see Starke 1990: 119–20; *HEG* T/D, 477.

154. Cf. i 36′, 37′, 57′: *ḫ*[*u-u-da-ak/aš*] fits the traces just as well if not better than *Q*[*A-TAM-MA*] and seems to provide better sense. Starke (1990: 119) opts for the likewise plausible *ḫ*[*u-u-ma-an*~, "alles Wohlwollen der Majestät."

155. Or perhaps ˻*ḫu-u*˼-x[.

156. Giorgieri's (1995: 101) *k*[*u-iš-š*]*a-at* is somewhat too long. A further possibility would be *m*[*a-a-n*]*a-*˹*at*˺.

157. Available space would seem to require more than Rizzi Mellini's (1979: 524) and Giorgieri's (2005: 330) *nu*.

158. Giorgieri's (2005: 330) ⸢^{URU}*Ḫa-at*⸣-*t*[*u-ša-an pa-aḫ-ḫa-a*]*š*$^{?!}$-*du*-[*ma*], "you protect" is what one might expect, but it does not seem amenable to the traces; cf. Haas (1981: 646 and n. 34), whose *pa-aḫ-aš-du-ma-a*]*t* at the end of the following line fits quite nicely; one would, however, expect gemination or a writing *pa-aḫ-ša-du-ma-a*]*t* (*CHD* P, 2–3).

159. Haas's (1981: 646) and Giorgieri's (2005: 330) *šu-me-eš* would be too short for the space; even *šu-me-e-eš* would likely leave space for a further sign.

160. Rizzi Mellini's (1979: 524) LUGAL-*w*]*a-aš* would leave space for about two signs, likely too much for the addition of merely *nu*, as in Giorgieri (2005: 331). Haas's (1981: 646) [^{d}UTU-*š*]*i-aš* would also be a bit short.

161. Though perhaps just a bit tight, *i-da-a-lu* might work at the end of 64′. The break at the beginning of 65′ would seem to be a bit long for *kuiski*.

162. Beal's (1983: 121) *ku*-[*in* does not fit the traces, as noted by Giorgieri (2005: 331); cf. Yakubovich 2005: 124.

163. Beal's (1983: 121) *na-an* (without brackets) and Giorgieri's (2005: 33) *nu-kán* are a bit too short, while *na-an-kán* (cf. KUB 36.90 obv. 15–18) or *a-pu-u-un* would likely be a bit too long.

164. Beal's (1983: 121) restoration (without brackets) fits the space and perhaps even the traces in the middle of the break remarkably well.

165. Beal (1983: 121) has *sakten*; *še-ek-* seems the more likely MH form and would fit nicely.

166. As *i-da-a-lu* alone would seem to be somewhat short for the break, something more must have stood here. For *-pat* with demonstratives, see *CHD* L–N sub *-pat* 12.d.5′. For earlier reconstructions of this paragraph, cf. Kümmel 1967: 44–45; Carruba 1977: 184–87; Haas 1981: 646; Beal 1983: 120.

167. For similar constructions, cf. *CHD* Š sub *-pat* B, 2.h.7′ (p. 149).

168. For the restoration cf. i 25′. The following sign is not quite the nicely formed *nu* implied in the edition and accepted, e.g., by Kümmel (1967: 44). It seems that the scribe may have begun his *mu-* here, then decided to place it further to the right, after which he neglected to erase the earlier traces. Cf. in ii 6′.

169. With *CHD* L–N, 287b, *pace* Haas 1981: 646: "[Wenn] man Soldaten für die Schlacht aufbietet, so soll er vom Hauptmann sein Soldatenbrot (und) sein Mehl erwarten." Unsettling, however, is the singular verb with an explicitly plural comm. subject that would not seem to lend itself to an interpretation as a collective or pl. tant.

170. The translation is a paraphrase. Cf. e.g., *CHD* Š, 238a, "Do you actually not know [the matter] of campaigning: that something concerning (it) has been transgressed?" Haas (1981: 646): "[den Vertr]ag des Kämpfens kennt ihr wohl, …," restoring [*iš-ḫi-u*$^{!}$]-*ul*, which would in fact fit the space nicely; a translation "[the oblig]ation to fight" might be a more suitable translation, however. See also Boley 1989: 269; 2000: 45.

171. Cf. Goedegebuure 2002/3: 22; *HEG* T/D, 87; Güterbock 1988: 169–70; Boley 1989: 182, 298.

172. Giorgieri's (1995: 102) suggestion of reading EL (*HZL* no. 307/7) is a possibility, but the sign is most easily read as LAM, making it congruent with acc. *kuinki* and eliminating the status constructus without a dependent noun.

173. For the uncertain reading, cf. Neu 1968: 130 n. 3; *CHD* L–N, 473b.

174. *Pace* Tjerkstra 1999: 35, n. 45 there is no need to interpret this form as an archaic gen. pl., since *kurur* is well enough attested as a comm. alongside its usual neut. form, for which see, e.g., *HED* K, 282.

175. I.e., assuming *paḫḫasdumat*, 2nd pl. imp. Parsing *paḫḫasdu=ma=at* would allow "But let him protect it/them!"

176. The available space would require the unexpected *-ia-*.

177. Two horizontals are clearly visible on the photo.

178. Cf. Rizzi Mellini's (1979: 530) *la-aḫ-ḫi-ia*?]-⸤*a*⸥*-u-wa-aš* and Neu's (1982a: 134) *me-mi-i*]*a-u-wa-aš*.

179. Clearly insufficient space for Rizzi Mellini's (1979: 532) *-kán*.

180. Cf. Y. Cohen's (2002: 141) *ku-in-*[*na*]*-aš-ta*.

181. The gap is far too long for BAD alone (cf. Giorgieri 1995: 106), as seen by Cotticelli-Kurras (1998: 113); for Akkadographic writings cf. i 72′ and iv 11–12. For this passage see also *CHD* P, 106b; Y. Cohen 2002: 141–42.

182. So, with Cotticelli-Kurras (1998: 113), rather than *ḫ*[*a*]*-ap-*, as in Neu 1974: 80 n. 151.

183. Or perhaps *kum*-x[? Or <LÚ>*TAP-PÍ-a*[*n*?

184. A reading L[ÚMÁŠD]A would seem to be too short by exactly the length of a MEŠ (cf. Pecchioli Daddi 2002a: 261, n. 3), which would in turn match the pl. verb in the following line.

185. Giorgieri's (1995: 107) otherwise attractive proposal of reading *da-aš-ša-mu-u*[*š li-in-g*]*a-uš* would seem to be a bit too long for the available space.

186. This passage is generally restored after No. 9, §2, 19–23 (e.g., most recently, Y. Cohen 2002: 140–43 and, more cautiously, Marazzi 2002: 80; 2004: 321; cf. Dardano 2004: 285), but since this text must be emended at several points to achieve the feat, it seems more prudent to accept that the passages are largely parallel but not duplicate and to avoid extensive restorations. Presumably the *-an* should be understood as a 3rd sg. acc. enclitic pron., not an acc. ending on LUGAL, for which one would expect LUGAL-*un*, i.e., *ḫassun*.

187. Where the quoted passage begins cannot be determined for certain. It definitely ends with "they made swear an oath," *pace* Pecchioli Daddi 2002a: 261 and n. 3, as made clear by the following lack of the quotative particle *-wa-*, otherwise consistently employed in this text. Where the second quoted speech passage at the end of the paragraph ends is equally uncertain.

188. Giorgieri's (1995: 107) *an-du-uḫ-ša-a*[*n* I-NA KUR ^{URU}*Ḫ*]*a-at-ti* is a good bit too long for the space. Omitting KUR might allow the restoration, though it would remain quite tight.

189. There would seem to be insufficient space for Giorgieri's (1995: 107) *me*-[*na-aḫ-ḫa-an-d*]*a-ma-aš-ši*.

190. The reconstruction of the position of the left edge of the tablet at this point is quite secure, both from projection from the edge preserved at ll. 27–31 and from the restoration of [^{m}*Mu-u-wa-at-t*]*a-al-li-iš* in l. 15. Giorgieri's (1995: 107) otherwise attractive suggestion [*e-eš-ḫa-na-aš u*]*t-tar* would seem to be somewhat too long, and further, one might like to see a conjunction. Houwink ten Cate's (1998: 44) [*iš-ḫa-na*(*-a*)*-aš-wa*? *u*]*t-tar*, based on comparison with KUB 11.1 iv 19′ (Telipinu Proclamation), would be much too long, while a version without the extra *-a-* and the superfluous *wa* might fit well enough, even if a bit tight. The topic of the paragraph, the oath taken by the author's father to Ḫuzziya, would seem to suggest itself, thus [*nu* NI-IŠ DINGIR-LÌ *u*]*t*?*-tar*, "the matter of the oath," which would fit the space quite well. *CHD* Š, sv., however, contains no attestations of *sarlai-*, normally "praise, exalt," with the meaning, "to raise (an issue)"; neither is *sarlai-* attested in the sense "raising to the throne," a question already discussed by de Martino (1991: 10 n. 39). Most if not all treatments seem to ignore the fact that *sarlai-* introduces quoted speech here, which only the translation "praised, acclaimed" would seem to require, and which renders Houwink ten Cate's suggestion (1998: 44), [*išduwāti*], "it became known," senseless. For further interpretations, see Freu 1996: 21; 2007a: 175; de Martino 1991: 10.

191. Rizzi Mellini's (1979: 534) widely accepted A-[NA A-BI ^{d}UTU]-ŠI*-ma-aš-ši* is far too long for the break. A-[NA ^{d}UTU]-ŠI*-ma-aš-ši* would fit well enough, though also a bit tight. I am unable to imagine how Freu (1995: 137) arrives at the translation "Muwatalli a tué Ḫuzziya mais au père du Soleil [n'a pas fait de mal(?)."

192. While Carruba (1977: 182) read SISKUR, Giorgieri (1995: 108) correctly reads GAZ-, considering the possibility of it being a sumerographic writing for *kunanza*, "killing." Perhaps more likely is a *ga*-stem in the abl., i.e.,]*gazz=a=wa=ssi*, for which, however, I can offer no sensible interpretation.

193. *HW*² Ḫ, 471a, suggests *nu=war=*⸢*an*⸣ ^{d}UTU-ŠI LUGAL-[*u*]-⸢*iz*⸣-*z*[*i-ia*?] / [*titta-nut*? *nu=war*]*=aš=kan* LUGAL-*u*-⸢*iz*⸣-[*zi-ia*? *a*?]*ki* ^{LÚ}ŠU.GI, "Ihn [setzte?] Meine Sonne in den königlichen Status [ein, und] er wird in der Königsherrsch[aft ster]ben? als ein alter Mann."

194. The first sign could just as well be L]I, the second perhaps TU[M, less likely D[U.

195. While the edition shows *-l*[*a-*, a rather clear *-a*[*k-* is visible on the photo.

196. Neither Giorgieri's (1995: 108) NUMUN^{MEŠ}[Š nor Rizzi Mellini's (1979: 536) *nu ut-ta*[*r* is entirely convincing.

197. One is reminded of the curse formula of earlier paragraphs, so that one is tempted to restore [*na-an ke-e* NI-IŠ DINGIR^{MEŠ}] *ap-p*[*a-an-du na-an* QA-DU DAM-ŠU DUMU^{MEŠ}-ŠU *ḫar-ni-in-kán-du*].

198. Literally "The f[ather of] My [Majesty], though, was with regard to him his oath," whereby the poss. pron. -*ŠU* surely relates to *nīš ili*, "oath," not to "deity" alone, with Houwink ten Cate (1998: 44). Cf., e.g., de Martino (1991: 10), "il giuramento del suo dio era ...."

199. Where the quoted passage begins and ends cannot be determined for certain. Assuming that Tudḫaliya I is indeed the author of the text, one might speculate—and it would be very speculative indeed—that §§33″–35″ (and perhaps §§36″–37″ as well) could provide an answer, however sketchy, to the question raised by the discovery that Tudḫaliya's father was named Kantuzilli, who apparently never reigned as king. Presumably §33″ refers to the royal blood (i.e., Ḫuzziya's) that peasants/commoners and/or high officials (among them Muwattalli) had shed. Perhaps §34″ can be understood as seeking to justify Kantuzzili's involvement in the murder of Muwattalli I, in that he (Kantuzzili) had been bound to him (Ḫuzziya) by oath and that all of Ḫattusa was behind him (Kantuzzili), calling for him to get rid of him (Muwattalli) and perhaps not to leave "a single one" of his accomplices. As for the question of kingship, however, §35″ might indicate that the men of Ḫattusa appealed to the gods to grant him (Tudḫaliya I) the kingship rather than an old man (Kantuzzili), and further, to confirm his (Tudḫaliya's) sons and grandsons in office as well. See also n. 190.

200. As there seems to be a space between *ḫa-az-zi* and Ú (cf. Giorgieri 1995: 109), it seems preferable to see in *ḫazzi* the 3rd sg. pres. act. of *ḫat(t)*- or *ḫazzi(ya)*-, "to pierce," otherwise written *ḫatzi* or *ḫazzi(a)zzi* in the -*mi* conjugation, *ḫatt(a)i* in the -*ḫi*; cf. *HW*[2] Ḫ, 483b, and Cotticelli-Kurras (2007a: 180), who would prefer to see a haplography.

201. It is difficult to imagine what *ḫūdantes* could be other than the pl. comm. participle from a verb *ḫūda*-, which should presumably be linked to *ḫūda*-, "readiness," and *ḫūdak*, "readily, quickly"; see already Rizzi Mellini (1979: 553). Naturally, one could think of emending to *ḫu-u-ma*!(DA)-[*a*]*n*?-*te*-*eš*, with Christiansen (2008: 272).

202. Again, one is tempted to restore (some variant of) *na-an ke-e* NI-IŠ DINGIR^{MEŠ} *ap-pa-an-d*]*u na*-[*an* QA-DU DAM-ŠU DUMU^{MEŠ}-ŠU *ḫar-ni-in-kán-du*. For an attempt to restore some of the deities in this paragraph, see D. Yoshida 1996: 30.

No. 13. Instructions of Arnuwanda I for the Mayor (of Ḫattusa) (*CTH* 257)

203. Reconstruction of A col. i according to the duplicates suggests that the numbering in the edition should be modified. There seem to be at least 9, probably 10, lines in the first paragraph rather than only 7; line numbers should be added between the edition's lines 1′ and 2′, between lines 5′ and 6′, and probably at the end of the paragraph.

204. ˻3˼ also possible, but elsewhere in this text these guards, if numbered, occur always in pairs.

205. Otten (1983a: 134), followed, e.g., by Singer (1998: 170) and Groddek (2008a: 168), restores M[AŠKIM and thus interprets the paragraph differently, but E[N.NU.UN is clearly to be preferred, though both would fit the traces, as this and the following paragraph

concern themselves exclusively with these guards, while MAŠKIM occurs first in ii 29′, where it is written with URU[KI].

206. There is one other occurrence of BÀD as a clear comm., i.e., *ku-u-un* BÀD-*an* in ABoT 60, 16′.

207. Groddek's (2008a: 166–67) reconstruction of ms. C fails to recognize that the left edge of the fragment is the left edge of the column.

208. All 2nd person verbs and pronouns in these texts, i.e., Nos. 13.1–4, are 2nd sg. except that in §14″, 7′ (cf. n. 226).

209. Singer (1998: 170) understands the phrase *Ḫattusi ser* as "over; in charge of Ḫattusa," and while this might appear to yield good sense in this particular passage, it does not seem to be attested as such elsewhere, nor would it seem that these two guards in particular are in charge of Ḫattusa in any more elevated a way than any of the other guards mentioned in the rest of the text; cf. usage also in §11″, 13′ and perhaps in §10″, 10′.

210. It has in recent years become perfectly clear that the upper city of Ḫattusa was extant already in MH times at the latest (e.g., Seeher 2006, 2008; Schachner 2011: 82–98). The present passage, however, *pace* de Martino (2007: 87), who bases his conclusions on Seeher 2006: 143, cannot serve as support for the new interpretation, as "upper" and "lower" here could just as well refer, e.g., to the lower city and the citadel, as was long assumed (e.g., Pierallini 2002: 628; Popko 2003a; cf. Miller 2005b: 287–88). Seeher's cautious note in fact suggests merely that the new dating of the upper city provides a further possibility for this passage.

211. Singer (1998: 171) prefers "the 'Silver Woods', which could refer to silver birches or similar trees."

212. Preferable to Otten's (1983a: 136) KÁ.GA]L, as it fits the traces better and since a further sign would seem to demand more space than is available. The *ḫaniya*-gate is attested with KÁ alone also in KUB 34.69+34.70 i 27′. See also n. 220.

213. On the scribal errors here and in ii 19′, as well as for scribal errors in general, see Cotticelli-Kurras 2007a: 186 and Rüster 1988: 300.

214. One possibility that would seem to fit the traces and space would be Á]G?-*ia*, "favorite," but this is very rare in Hittite texts and thus quite unlikely.

215. In light of §1, 10 one would like to see *ḫa-ad-da-an-ta-an* here, but only the apparently errant form *ḫa-ad-da-an* from §1, 10 would fit the space well, and the traces do not seem amenable even to this. Otten's (1964: 92, n. 9) *ḫa*-[*aš-šu-wa-an-zi* does not convince vis-à-vis the traces either.

216. Otten (1964: 92, n. 9) opted for *TÁ*]*Š-PUR*, which is a possibility, but above (§1, 10) the 2nd sg. imp. is employed in a similar context, so *Š*]*U-PUR* would perhaps be the better option. See also No 13.3, §4′, 21′.

217. It is presumably the son or servant who turns to the seal (in order to open it) rather than the seal itself turning, as implied in Otten's (1964: 92; 1983c: 51, with n. 35) translation, "sobald der Siegel sich dreht," though one would admittedly expect to see the subject resumed pronominally. Cf. Singer (1998: 171): "And when the seal on the gate 'turns' (i.e., 'is broken')."

218. There is certainly no room for Pecchioli Daddi's (1975: 102) *-la-*[*ša ku*]*-iš*.

219. Kammenhuber (1991: 153) assumes that the locution signifies "Getreidespeicher" in this case, but since guards are apparently to be stationed at (the temple of?) the Storm God of Zippalanda (l. 7′) as well, either option seems entirely possible; cf. n. 225.

220. For recent overviews on city gates and locks, see Miller 2011c; Hagenbuchner-Dresel 2007.

221. Imparati (1982: 248 and n. 84), followed by Starke (1996: 159 n. 82), argues that *ḪAZANNU* is to be equated with EN/*BĒL* [URU]*Ḫatti/Ḫattusa*, but this passage would seem to militate against the suggestion.

222. One would expect a sg. verb form here, but the traces do not allow *-i*]*a-*˻*iz*˼*-zi*, suggesting rather a pl. *-i*]*a-*˻*an*˼*-zi*, unless one could read *-i*]*a-ap/at-zi* or the like.

223. D iii 2′ shows a clear 5.

224. For what would appear to be the correct understanding of this passage, see Beal 1992: 258, n. 970; cf. Cotticelli-Kurras 1991: 49; 1992: 113.

225. Deities, of course, are indeed bathed, but to find these persons washing Ḫalki, the grain deity, in a pool seems odd. It may be that washing grain itself, here divinely determined, is to be avoided; cf. n. 219.

226. As this is the only 2nd pl. form in the text, one suspects it may be a mistake, especially in view of the writing of the signs over wayward traces.

227. For the reading of the number, cf. n. 232. The traces following the break would seem to be corrupt, and could conceivably represent a failed attempt either at [LÚ]*ḪA-* or *QA-TI*.

228. The signs are clearly A ŠA KUŠ; see note in *HZL* sub 161 and cf. [LÚ.MEŠ]A *ŠA* KUŠ.LÁ in No. 2, §13″, 21, and 26.

229. The restoration of *ḫu-*[*wa-a-i* seems quite obvious (see already Giorgadze 1987: 254), although, curiously, the verb is only rarely attested with *arḫa*, only three times as far as I could ascertain (*HBM* 63 rev. 22–23; *HBM* 64 obv. 9; KBo 39.28, 3′). None of these attestations are to be found in the standard dictionaries (*HED* H, 419–23; *HW* 78, 3. Erg. 16; *HHw* 63–64) as far as I was able to determine. Thanks are due to J. Hazenbos for the Maşat attestations.

230. The join would seem to clarify to some degree how the verb *samenu-* is to be understood (cf. *CHD* Š, 122), even if difficulties remain. The form in *-s*, if not simply a scribal mistake for expected 2nd sg. pres. *samenus/ti*, would suggest either a 2nd or a 3rd sg. pret. Actual elision of the final vowel seems unlikely; equally unexpected would be the intrusion of *-s* for *-t* into the 2nd sg. imp.; cf. the intrusion of *-t* into the 2nd sg. pret. for *-s* (*GrHL* §11.11 with n. 27). For the rare combination of *lē* with the imp., apparently only with the 3rd person and only in NH copies of OH originals, see *GrHL* §26.16–17.

231. Otten (1983a: 137; but cf. p. 136) assumes that the composition is not finished at this point, presumably because No. 13.2, also a tablet of obligations for the mayor, is marked as the second tablet. The final paragraph, however, likely represents a concluding admonition. It seems that one is thus forced to assume either that 13.1.E contained the

entire composition on this single tablet, which does not seem likely judging from its very large script, or that there were two such compositions, one spanning two tablets, the other only one. That said, the "2" of 13.2 iv 1′ is oddly formed, so that one might want to leave open the possibility that it represents a muddled "1."

232. Conceivably GIŠ-*pát*, "the aforementioned wood."

233. Or]x ≮*ip-pí-aš-ma-aš*? Puhvel (*HED* E/I, 377–78) books among his *ippi(y)a-/eppiya-* occurrences determined with GIŠ and with Ú as well as some provided with a *Glossenkeil.* Perhaps to be parsed *(p)ippi=(i)a=smas*, i.e., "and 1 *(p)ippi*$^{\text{(nom.)}}$ to/for them"; what one would do with the *-as* of *(p)ippas=ma=as* would remain a mystery; perhaps rather *(p)ippia(n)=smas*, "1 *(p)ippi*$^{\text{(acc.)}}$ to/for them"?

234. Neither *ḫuek-*, "to swear," nor *ḫuek-*, "to thresh," seem inclined to take the refl., and the verbal substantives do not appear to attest the writing *ḫu-e-eg-* (HW^2 Ḫ, 619–29), so that this form must remain a riddle for the time being.

235. Graphically no less likely would be U]N-*an*, i.e., "he shall not send a [...] man to/for the office of horse trainer," or *-i*]*a-an*.

236. The passage is almost certainly corrupt. The enclitic chain in 3.B, 6′, *na-aš-*[*š*]*i*/[*w*]*a-aš-kán* can hardly be parsed as is; what would seem to be a *mi-* in 3.C ii$^{?}$ 6 is written over several other elements; the *-ia-* in 3.B is ill formed; and the verb, if indeed to be read *miyaḫunteszi*, would not yield an immediately apparent sense in the admittedly fragmentary context, unless one should understand, "he shall not grow old in the courtyard (waiting for you to fulfill your duties)," which does not seem overly likely.

237. Ünal's (1993: 129) *la-a*[*ḫ-* is impossible in light of the traces. Perhaps ⌜BÀD⌝^{M}[^{EŠ}.

238. Ünal's (1993: 129) *le-e* is a misreading. Certainly not *tu-e-e*[*l*; possibly *tu-e-e*[*k*~, but not overly convincing as such; perhaps *tu-e-l*[*a-*.

239. Clearly *ŠA*, not *I-NA*, as read by Ünal (1993: 129).

240. Also possible would be ⌜BÀD⌝^{MEŠ}-*na-aš*; cf. l. 20′. Ünal's (1993: 129) DUB^{MEŠ} fits neither the sign traces nor the context.

241. Clearly so, i.e., an inf., as indicated also by the following imp., not *tal-za-a*[*ḫ-ḫa-an-z*]*i*, as read by Ünal (1993: 129).

242. "He let [...] be seen!" morphologically also possible.

243. As seen in the numerous notes to the transliteration, much of Ünal's (1992: 215–23; 1993: 129–36) translation and interpretation must be abandoned.

244. The *asusa*-gate was one of several city gates of Ḫattusa. For an overview of city gates at Ḫattusa see Miller 2011c.

245. Clearly *ḪA.LA.AB*, not *Ḫa-ad-du-*, *pace* Ünal (1993: 129), and presumably the same in 16′, though there too damaged to be certain.

246. Ünal's (1993: 129; 1996: 41, n. 55) alternative reading *ú-ul-te-eš-kán-zi* is entirely prohibited by the traces.

247. Ünal (1993: 129) restores only [*ma-a-an-z*]*a*, but there is room for nearly ten signs.

248. Clearly *pa*-, not *i*-, *pace* Ünal (1993: 130).

249. Though Ünal's (1993: 130) *ḫa-aḫ-ra-an-na-aš-ša* cannot be said to be impossible, there is a significant space between the *-aš* and the *ŠA*.

250. The well-attested mountain Tāḫa is quite clear, rendering Ünal's (1992: 216; 1993: 130) reading and interpretation of the passage obsolete.

251. I am unable to ascertain for certain what signs follow *le-e*, but *ka*-, *kam*- and *ša*- (i.e., for *kamars*- and *sakniya*, the latter of which is more likely to mean "anoint" according to *CHD* Š, 47) can be ruled out, rendering Ünal's (1992: 216; 1993: 130) "de[fecate" untenable. My best guess would be *ur*-x[, perhaps indicating a prohibition on burning.

252. There is certainly insufficient space to restore [URU*Ḫa-a*]*d-du-ša-kán* here, and the city is otherwise written with TU in this text; cf. Ünal 1992: 216; 1993: 130.

253. Restoration with Puhvel (1979: 303) and Ünal (1993: 130), as space is insufficient for the oft-restored [*nu-za*] (e.g., Košak 1993: 109; Hoffner 1997a: 202). Hoffner required it because of his assumed *ēsten* at the end of the line, but his restoration *naḫḫan*[*teš* (followed, without brackets, by Rose 2006: 337), is to be given up in favor of *na-aḫ-*˹*šar*˺-x[, however it is to be understood, perhaps *na-aḫ-šar-r*[*a-at-ta-an* in a clause such as those collected in *CHD* L–N, sub *naḫšaratt*-, 2, p. 344. Ünal's (1993: 130) *na-aḫ-ša-an-t*[*e-eš* is impossible in light of the traces.

254. For a clear overview of the long-debated lexeme *ḫass*-, "ash," previously understood as "king" (e.g., Hoffner 1973: 110), see Rieken 1999a: 19–23; Puhvel 1994.

255. For a thorough overview of *ḫusseli*, see Hoffner 1997a: 201–2, where for the verb here the equally possible *isḫuwandu* is restored; Ünal (1993: 130) restores *isḫuwatten* for the previous line as well.

256. Perhaps É DI[NGIR-*LÌ*], "temple," but certainly not É.G[AL-*LÌ*], ruling out Ünal's (1992: 216; 1993: 130) "palace" and his further considerations on p. 218.

257. Ünal's (1993: 130) [*šu-me-eš*]-*kán* is prohibited by space and traces.

258. URU*Ḫa-at-tu-ši* (cf. 9′) would fit the break quite well.

259. For this passage and a possible connection with the architecture of Ḫattusa, see Miller 2011b: 202–4; Schachner 2012a: 141.

260. On agriculture among the Hittites, see most recently Klengel 2006.

261. For "orchards," "Baumpflanzung," rather than "forests," see Oettinger 2002: 255.

262. "To sprinkle" assumes an inf. from *ḫurai-/huwarai*-, but it does not seem likely that the]x-*ra-u-wa-an-z*[*i*] in B—whereby the trace after the break could be -*i*]*n*,]-*ni* or]-*ir*—represents an inf. of the same verb. In any case, *pace* Ünal (1992: 216), there is no reason to think that the passage continues with the issue of sewage disposal.

263. For an overview of irrigation and water management among the Hittites, see Hoffner 1974: 22–24 and, from the archaeological perspective, Hüser 2007; Wittenberg and Schachner 2013.

No. 14. Loyalty Oath of Town Commanders to Arnuwanda I, Ašmunikkal, and Tudḫaliya (*CTH* 260)

264. The troop configuration of 14.2 and 14.3 may be more complex than this, however, as suggested by DUG]UD$^{?}$-*TÌ ŠA* KUR ^{URU}*KA.LA.AŠ.MA* in 2 i 1 and by [*Š*]*A*$^{?}$ ÉRIN$^{⌜\text{MEŠ}}$ ^{URU}*UN*$^{?⌝}$.*TA*.x[and ^{LÚ}DUGUD *ŠA* ÉRIN^{MEŠ} ^{URU}*ŠA*.x[in 3.A i 2 and 10′, respectively. RGTC 6, 85 and Beal (1992: 77) understand the juxtaposition of Kalasma in 2 i 1 and Ḫa/uranāssi in 2 ii 6 to indicate that Ḫa/uranāssi would have been located within the land of Kalasma. For a recent study of the geography of Ka/issiya and its environs, see Forlanini 2009: 58–59.

265. For a recent study of the prosopographical evidence, see Marizza 2007.

266. Equally possible: "[T]hus (says) the Overseer of the [C]lans: The Commanders of the troops of Kinnara (are the following): …" For a discussion of these "commanders" (^{LÚ}DUGUD) and their functions, see Beal 1992: 488–504; in the present volume the words "commanders" and "dignitaries" have been chosen to translate ^{LÚ}DUGUD for military and nonmilitary contexts, respectively.

267. There is a rather clear ŠI inserted above and between the PI and the AN, but omitted by von Schuler (1956: 224) and Giorgieri (1995: 213).

268. Von Schuler (1956: 224) and Giorgieri (1995: 213) read, graphically likewise possible, *Mar-ta*.

269. Von Schuler's (1956: 224) *Zi-*[*it*$^{??}$-*ḫ*]*a*$^{?}$-*ra* is ruled out by the traces.

270. For the placement of the largest fragment of KUB 26.24 at the bottom of col. i rather than iv, as in the edition, see Giorgieri 1995: 220.

271. The LÚ is entirely uncertain, as is the oddly shaped *ri*, while the *-na-* could perhaps also be an *-it-*. The traces normally read as URU are doubtful. At the end of the line von Schuler (1956: 225) read *ú-e-eš*, "we," seeing in it the beginning of the following sentence, but the traces do not convince as such. Giorgieri (1995: 214, n. 11), followed, e.g., by Groddek (2008a: sub No. 273), considered *ú-it*$^{?}$, "he came," the transliterations of which would yield "[…]-*azzi*, the man of the town of Ḫinariya, came to the troops of the land of Kinnara." The copy suggests perhaps *ú-šal-li*?, but while this would yield an Akkadian word, "flood plain; field," it would be difficult to make any sense of it. Another possible reading, the negation *Ú-UL*$^{!}$, would be equally mysterious. In any case, the third sign would seem to have been partly erased by the scribe. Moreover, while previous treatments have assumed that DINGIR^{MEŠ} should follow ^{URU}Kinnara of line 30 (or 31′), the parallel version suggests that there is no place for it there; for lack of a better alternative, one could feasibly assume that it might belong here at the end of 24, though no convincing interpretation of the line is apparent.

272. For the restoration, see Beal 1992: 46, n. 181.

273. Lorenz's (2010: 262) comments, according to which Giorgieri's (2005: 337) reading ⌜ITU-*mi*! ITU⌝-*m*[*i* at the end of 3.A i 21′ cannot be confirmed because the traces in 3.B$_1$ i 2′ do not support it, require revision. The traces in 3.B$_1$ i 2′ are to be read *li-in-k*]*u-u-wa-n*[*i* and therefore follow the end of 3.A i 21′. The signs in 3.A i 21′ are amenable to

˹*še-er* *ITU-*mi* ITU*˺-*m*[*i*, though they seem to be written over an erasure and/or unintended stray wedges.

274. Von Schuler's (1956: 228) -*r*[*a*?- does not fit the traces; cf. Giorgieri's (2005: 337) URU*Ḫar-t*[*a-a-na-ma-at*].

275. It seems unlikely that the suspect (or his messenger) is to be blinded before being brought to the king for investigation (cf. Hoffner 2002: 68), which could clearly lead to rampant vigilante justice, allowing essentially anyone to claim some impropriety on the part of another and to blind him (or his messenger) before having the king decide his guilt or innocence. Perhaps the suspect is to be blindfolded rather than actually blinded.

276. Space would seem to be prohibitively tight for Groddek's (2008a: sub Nr. 62) [DUMUMEŠ].

277. Cf. Puhvel's (1980: 69) "propitiate."

278. In which order the following poorly preserved passages should be placed is unclear.

No. 15. Instructions and Oath Imposition(s) of Arnuwanda I (*CTH* 275)

279. The only other possible attestation, *BE-EL* NA4KIŠI[B? in KBo 16.45 obv. 11, is likewise uncertain, though seemingly not unlikely.

280. Presumably to be parsed *kī iššaš*, though there is no space between -*i* and *iš*-.

No. 16. Decree of Queen Ašmunikkal concerning the "Royal Funerary Structure" (*CTH* 252)

281. Contra Rosi (1984: 126) the document is not sealed with the seal of Ašmunikkal.

282. Beal (1992: 435, n. 1630) lists a number of further decrees that exempt their recipients from various duties.

283. For discussion of this form and the reading -*ut*-, see most recently K. Yoshida 2008: 852 and n. 4.

284. Singer (2009b: 171) identifies the "stone-house" as a "single institution of the Royal Cemetery, which must have been a sizable complex situated somewhere in Hattusa or its vicinity," the "place where the bones of the deceased were brought after the cremation ceremony." This is surely essentially correct, but since it appears to have been at least partially a built (perhaps also partially hewn?) structure, the term "columbarium," in its most general sense of "a (stone)-built structure with niches or receptacles for the internment of the cremation remains," rather than "cemetery" or "burial ground," seems more appropriate; cf. similarly Groddek 2001. Still, because the more specific picture evoked in modern parlance by the term "columbarium" may well be misleading, the more general translation "royal funerary structure" has been preferred.

285. The *saḫḫan* and *luzzi*-levies were "obligation(s), service(s), or payment(s) due

from land tenants to the real owners of the land (palace, temple, community, or individuals)" (*CHD* Š, 2b; see also Haase 1996).

286. *Pace* Klinger (2001a: 73), who translates "Ein Hund bellt. Dort aber, wo er stehen bleibt und schweigt, gießt man aber Öl aus," an interpretation as a relative sentence is unwarranted. Neither is his translation of the following sentence with "Sie dürfen jenen (den Hund) aber nicht übersehen" convincing, as *apus* is unmistakably comm. nom. pl., the only conceivable alternative being a comm. acc. pl. Cf. *CHD* P, 125a–b, where both clauses are understood as conditional, despite no such marking, which, though possible, seems unlikely.

287. While the literal meaning of these sayings is clear, their figurative import and relevance have long remained a mystery. Groddek (2001: 215) and Dietrich and Loretz (2004) compare the passage concerning the barking dog with a verse from the Keret Epic from Ugarit, the latter translating (p. 259), "Wie Hunde jaulen wir laut in deinem Palast, wie Welpen in der Sakralgrube deines Totenheiligtums" (KTU 1.16 i 2–3). Collins (2002: 242) suggests that "the reference may be to zealous bureaucrats who 'bark' for payment of an obligation that they cannot collect from exempted persons, and so fall silent," while Klinger (2001a: 72) considers the possibility that "es sich doch um eine Art Orakel oder Vorzeichen handeln (dürfte), bei dem ein Hund verwendet wird, mit dessen Hilfe wohl ein Haus oder eine Familie der Stiftung von generellen Abgaben freigestellt wird," both of which seem perhaps rather too imaginative. It is also doubtful that the "Bewohner des Hauses … durch das Verhalten des Hundes bezeichnet wurde" (p. 73, n. 8a). Haas (1994: 242) suggests a "Stillegebot," while Giorgieri (pers. comm.) believes that it concerns "eine Vorschrift (wohl eine Reinheitsvorschrift), wenn ein Hund sich dem 'colombarium' nähert (*ari* 'comes, arrives' …). 'Die oben genannten' (*apuš*), d.h. diejenige, die sich nach dem vorhergehenden Paragraphen im 'colombarium' finden, müßen in keinem Falle herauskommen. Ich nehme mit *CHD*, P, 125a–b an, daß die vorhergehenden Sätze als hypothetisch zu verstehen sind: '(If) a dog barks, but he arrives there (i.e., at the colombarium), and (if) he is quiet, but oil is poured out (i.e., wohl ein Reinigungsritus), those must not come out!'"

288. Groddek (2001: 214), following Neu, is certainly correct in reading É.[NA_4]-*NI*-here in B rather than ⸢É *a*⸣-*ni*-, as did van den Hout (1990: 426), but thereafter one must read ⸢É.[NA_4?]-*NI*-*ia-az* A.⸤ŠÀ⸥ as opposed to their É.[NA_4]-*NI*-*ia-az-za*.

289. The planting of an *eya*-tree before a door or gate could apparently symbolize exemption from certain obligations (Christiansen 2006: 152–53) or the elimination of illness (Haas 2003: 292). There seems to be no reason to translate *parā … tarnai* as "Let no one sell them (as slaves)!" as does *CHD* L–N, 55b; cf. more convincingly *CHD* P, 125a–b, 295a.

290. Cf. Beckman (1986a: 17, n. 23): "Let them give (their daughters) for the purpose of brideship internally, to the men of the mausoleum (estate)! Let no one give out(side of the estate) a male or female youth for brideship or *antiyant*-ship!"

291. From this point on the translation is based on a rather maximalist attempt at transliteration of the severely burned and otherwise badly damaged B. It should thus be taken with due caution.

NO. 17. INSTRUCTIONS OF ARNUWANDA I FOR THE FRONTIER POST GOVERNORS (*CTH* 261.I)

292. Further fragments that exhibit similarities to various passage of this composition include KUB 40.72, KBo 52.7 (cf. §9), 243/v and Bo 69/80.

293. The Hurrian-Hittite parables translate Hurrian *ḫalzūḫla*, derived from Akk. *ḫalṣum*, with Hitt. *aurias isḫān* (KBo 32.14 i 33–34 // ii 33–34; Neu 1996: 133–34). Durand (1997: 120–21) has recently suggested that the basic meaning of *ḫalṣum* is "delimited (zone)," not "fortification," and that it is to be derived from *ḫarāṣum*, "retrancher d'un ensemble," rather than related to Hebrew *ḥālaṣ*, "équiper pour la guerre."

294. This results in a different paragraph numbering than that found in McMahon 1997: 221–25 or Pecchioli Daddi 2003a.

295. Three clues suggest that one must increase the line numbering of C_1 i by one: first, on the photos there would seem to be traces above the first line found in the edition (if I were forced to give a reading of these traces, I would suggest LUGAL.GA]L ⌜^{URU}*ḪA*⌝.*A*[*T.TI*], but this would be rather optimistic.); second, assuming that the text of C_1 was roughly parallel to A and B_1 at this point, there is no way that the entire text of A and B_1 up to *aurius* could fit in a single line before the *a-ú*]-*ri-uš* in C_1 i 2$^{!}$; third, the scribe also began writing at the top edge of C_1 ii.

296. Much would speak against restoring anything more than LUGAL.GAL here, e.g., LUGAL KUR ^{URU}*Ḫa-at-ti*, as does Pecchioli Daddi (2003a: 68). First, while enough space might conceivably be found for such in A i 1, it is difficult to imagine a reconstruction that would allow for it in B_1. Second, those few Arnuwanda I texts to which one might point as comparable (KUB 31.123+ i 1; KBo 5.7 obv. 1; KBo 16.27 i 21′; but cf. the NH copy KUB 23.64 i 1) show merely LUGAL.GAL. Further, Pecchioli Daddi's composite reconstruction, though yielding good sense as it stands, is actually entirely impossible as an actual restoration in A or B_1, while too little is preserved of C_1 to make any confident statement in this regard.

297. Restoring *a-ú-ri-ia-aš* alone here would yield a mere six signs as opposed to nine in the first line. A potential solution would be to restore *ma-a-an* as well, at least for B_1.

298. In A i 2 the traces are almost certainly not *MAD*-[, as read by Goetze (1960: 69), Beal (1992: 270, n. 1011), and Giorgieri (1995: 189 and n. 199); cf. von Schuler's (1957: 59) N[Í. Examination of the photos suggests that the most convincing reading would be ⌜*MA*⌝-*A*[*D*-.

299. The *ḫa-an-te-ez-zi-uš a-ú-ri-*˻*uš*˼ in B_1 i 2 can by no means fit in the space available in A i 2, and even an unlikely *a-ú-wa-ri-eš* (cf. *a-ú-wa-ri-e-eš* in A i 19, 31, 33), yielding LÚ^{MEŠ} *BE-EL* ⌜*MA*⌝-*A*[*D-GAL*$_9$*-TI a-ú-wa-ri-eš d*]*a-aš-*⌜*kán*⌝*-z*[*i* (or *ú-e-d*]*a-aš-*⌜*kán*⌝*-z*[*i*), would seem quite long. One possibility might be URU$^{\text{DIDLI.ḪI.A}}$, as in A i 4, where it is modified with *ḫantezziēs* BÀD$^{\text{ḪI.A}}$-*as*. Perhaps the most likely explanation is that this MH text left the object unexpressed, the scribe considering LÚ^{MEŠ} *BĒL MADGALTI* to be clear enough.

300. For thoughts on restoring the verb, see Pecchioli Daddi 2003a: 69, n. 101. As-

suming that *weda-* would be a leading possibility, it should be noted that nowhere else in this text does *weda-* take a local particle. The trace before *-aš-* would not seem to favor Fritzsche's (2010) otherwise reasonable *pa-aḫ-ḫa*]*-aš-kán-zi*. She restores in A $^{\text{LÚ.MEŠ}}$*BE-EL* ˹*MAD*˺-[*GAL*$_5$*-TI ku-i-*(˹*e*˺*-eš ḫa-an-te-ez-zi-uš a-ú-ri-*˹*uš*˺) *pa-aḫ-ḫa*]*-aš-kán-*˹*zi*˺, which yields the attractive translation "[Für] die *BĒL MAD*[*GALTI*, die] die vordersten Grenzposten dauerhaft [schütz]en…," but which is too long for the break between the two fragments at this point.

301. The sign in B_1 i 5 would appear to be a BÀD that the scribe neglected to complete with its trailing PA, thus UR]U$^?$˻$^{\text{ḪI.A}?}$˼ BÀ<D>.

302. It seems highly unlikely that Pecchioli Daddi's (2003a: 68) *paḫḫasnuwantes* would fit into the space available at the end of A i 4. In any case, the sense seems to be, "The [(forti)fi]ed frontier towns shall be [provided (with a) wa(tch)], and the w[(atch) shall be (wel)l] kept." Perhaps nothing need be restored after *ḫaliyaz*.

303. The traces in B_1 i 6 are SI]G$_5$-˻*in*˼, not (*paḫḫasnuwan*)*-t*]*e-eš*, as found in Pecchioli Daddi 2003a: 68.

304. In C_1 i 5$^!$ most likely ˹*uš-ket*$_9$*-tén*˺, though conceivably, even if less likely, ˹*uš-ka*$_4$*/ket*$_9$˺*-t*[*e-en*]; Pecchioli Daddi's (2003a: 70) ˻SIG$_5$$^?$*-aḫ*$^?$˼-[*ḫa-an* is out of the question, as are the previously suggested readings noted by her (n. 107).

305. Since A i 11 shows the 3rd sg. verb *weddu*, and since the space in the break in A i 10 might be a bit tight for ^{L}[($^{\text{Ú.MEŠ}}$EN.NU)].UN, I have restored ^{L}[(^{Ú}EN.NU)].UN rather than the $^{\text{LÚ.MEŠ}}$EN.NU.UN of C_1 i 9$^!$, though the numerical incongruity common in these mss. (cf. n. 312) may well have extended to this point as well.

306. The visible traces in C_1 i 14$^!$ would seem to suggest ˹*ḫar*$^?$*-zi*$^?$˺, even if certainty cannot be claimed. Further, some faint traces appear to follow ˹*ḫar*$^?$*-zi*$^?$˺, traces that seem to curve up into the column divider. Since one would expect a conjunction and a resumptive pronoun before *para wemiyanzi*, one might read ˹*na*$^{??}$*-at*$^{??}$˺ here, though one could hardly claim to be able to identify the signs as such based on the meager traces alone.

307. The traces in C_1 i 15$^!$ can hardly be read -˻*an*˼*-z*[*i*, as do Pecchioli Daddi (2003a: 74) and Beal (1992: 272, n. 1016), but rather almost certainly -˹*an-du*˺. This renders the reconstruction (especially) of A i 16 rather difficult, as one would expect a pres.-fut. predicate following *mān*, and only then the main clause ending with *wemiyandu*, for all of which there would seem to be precious little space available (cf. n. 313), i.e. "… and if [they do not find anything], (§7) then [they shall let] the cattle, the sheep (and) the workmen down from the town," as, e.g., in Singer 2009a: 44, "אן אם [לא] ימצו [דבר]."

308. Singer (2009a: 44) suggests "protected," "יש [להגן]."

309. C_1 i 5$^!$ "And you$^{\text{(pl.)}}$ shall observe (*usketten*) the watch well."

310. Surely so, with *CHD* L–N, 422b, rather than "district," as in *GrHL* §26.15.

311. The long-accepted meaning "sector; plot" for *kuranna* was called into question by Güterbock and van den Hout (1991: 45) on the basis of their reading of ˹*ku-ra-an*˺*-ni-it* in IBoT 1.36 i 8 (No. 4 in this volume) in a context suggesting that the object can be lifted, and thus perhaps a closing device, and in this they were followed by Prins (1997: 83–84). The reading there (No. 4, §1, 8 and n. 95), however, is highly uncertain and can hardly be

used to overrule the evidence here; cf. A i 30 and *ku-ra-an*]-⸢*nu*⸣-*uš* in C_1 i 8[!], whereby the -*m*]*u-uš* drawn in KUB 31.108 i 7 (i.e., 8[!]) is clearly to be read]-⸢*nu*⸣-*uš* based on the photos; cf. *HED* K, 214.

312. Ms. A certainly shows numerical incongruity in this paragraph; in fact, A often treats groups of persons as a pl. tant. taking singular verbs, pronouns, etc., while C_1 consistently uses the 3rd pl. See also n. 305.

313. This is the only attestation of *parā wemiya-*, lit. "find out/away/forth," and it would be only an assumption that it might mean the same as the English expression "find out," German "herausfinden." In the context I am inclined to think that "find forth," i.e., "search further," would be the best interpretation.

314. The numerical incongruity between subjects and verbs continues in this paragraph. Though such incongruity is certainly present in A (e.g., LÚ.MEŠNÍ.ZU ... *e-ep-du* in i 12), how much of the incongruity in this paragraph is due to restoring the verb forms from the duplicate, which often deviate from A in this regard, is impossible to establish.

315. C_2 (i.e., KUB 40.57) sets in at this point, and since its first line can be correlated with l. 16[!] of C_1 (i.e., KUB 31.108), I have continued the line numbering as such, the only change being that from the exclamation mark to the prime numbering, signaling uncertainty.

316. It is extremely unlikely that the text can be reconstructed so that the *nu* at the end of C_2 i 23′ can be placed immediately before the *namma* at the beginning of A i 23, as does Pecchioli Daddi (2003a: 78; cf. Beal 1992: 255, n. 966). If such were the case, then the entire first clause of A i 23 (i.e., *nam-ma* LÚ.MEŠNÍ.ZU-*TÌ* *ku-i-e-eš a-ú-w*[*a-ri-e-eš e-ep-per*) would have to be restored after *nu* in C_2 i 23′, which would require most of it to be written in the column divider. Rather, C_2 i 23′ probably ends with a short sentence (also omitted from A; see n. 334), such as "they shut the doors."

317. The sign at the end of C_2 i 29′ is quite clearly *lu*-[, suggesting *lu*[*staniyas*. The ⸢*A*⸣-*NA* GIŠKÁ.⸤GAL⸥[in D i 4′ may thus have duplicated A i 26, in which case some of the ensuing text in A would probably have been omitted in D; alternatively, ⸢*A*⸣-*NA* GIŠKÁ.⸤GAL⸥[in D i 4′ might be seen as a variant to *lu*[*staniyas* in C_2 i 29′.

318. As there seems to be too little space for the *nu*, and since it is very unlikely to have stood alone at the end of l. 30, one should reckon here either with an asyndetic construction without *nu*, an uncommon writing of *awariyes* such as [*nu a-w*]*a*-, or with *nu* and some additional element at the end of the preceding line.

319. Here begins C_3 (i.e., KUB 31.85), and since it seems that no line is fully lost, I have continued the line numbering from C_2, adding the double prime numbering to indicate uncertainty.

320. It may be doubted whether all of LÚ.MEŠKIN GU₄ UDU ANŠE.KUR.RAMEŠ ANŠE, partially preserved in C_3 i 33″ and G_1 i 7′, actually stood here in A. If so, it would have bled significantly into the column divider. Since the words in l. 31 are set with quite a bit of space between them, and since merely *QA-TAM-MA tar-na-an-du* was written in l. 32, it seems that the scribe hardly would have written far into the column divider in l. 31 if he had had so much space to work with in ll. 31–32. It also seems that the heads of two

horizontals, not just one, the upper pulled to the right, are visible at the end of l. 31, which would suggest *k*[*at-ta*, and thus a variant word order.

321. There is clearly no room in the break in A for the *nam-ma* of C_3 and H.

322. The sign is without a doubt EG[IR, not *a*[*p*-, as read by Goetze (1960: 70) and Pecchioli Daddi (2003a: 84).

323. On photos of D i 10′ the heads of two horizontals of -*d*[*u* are clearly visible, not a single broken horizontal, as drawn in the edition.

324. The sign in D i 11′ is clearly [*p*]*a*-, not [*š*]*a*-, as in Pecchioli Daddi 2003a: 86.

325. The signs in A can hardly be read]-⸤*ia-aš-ša*⸥ following C_3, as read by Goetze (1959: 69; 1960:71) and Pecchioli Daddi (2003a: 86). There is nowhere near enough room for -*aš-ša* following -*ia*-, and the heads of two verticals are clearly visible, as represented correctly in KUB 13.1 (though with far too much space). Moreover, as *ḫar*(*k*)- does occur with the reflexive, there seems to be no reason to reject a -*za* here.

326. At the beginning of the line in A there is no room for the *nam-ma-kán* of the duplicates, which might perhaps have fit at the end of the previous line, nor for [$^{\text{LÚ.MEŠ}}$NÍ.ZU]-*TÌ*, as assumed in other treatments. KASKAL$^{\text{ḪI.A}}$- fits nicely, with no room to spare. The *nam-ma-kán* of the duplicates would not appear to fit space and traces at the beginning of B_1 i 2′ either.

327. One cannot restore the end of A i 37, where KUB 13.1 and KUB 31.87 join, as Pecchioli Daddi does (2003a: 88), i.e., *a-ú-*⸤*ri*⸥*-ia-*⸤*aš*⸥ [...]. It must rather be read/restored *a-ú-*⸢*ri*⸣-[*ia-aš* $^{\text{LÚ.MEŠ}}$NÍ].⸢ZU⸣-*ia*[ ]. Further, when one places the missing signs between the two fragments, one sees that the pieces actually do not directly join, as suggested in Pecchioli Daddi's (2003a: 304) sketch, but that a ca. half-centimeter gap intervenes between them; cf. n. 330.

328. Goetze's (1960: 71) [ÉRIN^{MEŠ} *a-ú*]-*ri-ia-aš* is too long for the available space, which allows no more than [*a-ú-wa*]-.

329. Examination of the photos indeed leads one to suspect ⸤3⸥, as in the edition, and one should not emend such differences too hastily (cf. Pecchioli Daddi 2003a: 88), as this might, e.g., obscure changes from the MH to the NH period. B_1 i 4′ and D i 15′ show 2.

330. As is the case with l. 37 (cf. n. 327), a direct join between KUB 13.1 and KUB 31.87 here would yield far too little space for the signs expected. *Pace CHD* Š, 153b, it does not seem that the paragraph can be divided into two sentences. At approximately this point in D i 15′ there are traces of perhaps three further signs in the column divider, but I am unable to determine to what they correspond in B_1.

331. As Mouton (2008: 457) has noted, the signs in A i 39, in any case corrupt, actually look more like GIM-*an* than anything else. This, of course, would be rather unexpected in this MH ms., all the more so since GIM never appears in any of the mss. of this composition, young or old.

332. At this point the inexact edition of KUB 40.58 and Pecchioli Daddi's sketch (2003a: 312, i.e., her E) combine to form a misleading picture for D. First, there is no paragraph divider toward the end of KUB 40.58. The last traces on this fragment are in fact the heads of the two verticals of -*zi* in ⸤*ú*⸥*-wa-*⸤*an*⸥*-z*[*i* in l. 17′. This paragraph thus contains

lines 12′–17′, and the line count must be reduced by one from this point vis-à-vis that in Pecchioli Daddi's treatment. There are therefore 29 lines preserved of col. i.

333. C_2 i 18′: "They shall go." In the break Singer (2009a: 44) restores "a second watch," "של המשמרת השנייה."

334. The paragraph up to this point was (presumably inadvertently) omitted in A, and is taken from C_2 i 22′–23′. The other mss. set in only after this point, so that it is not known whether they retained the sentences or not.

335. C_2 i 27′, surely errantly, "lords."

336. C_3 and G_1, perhaps because their scribes found the omission of the object in A confusing, make the object explicit: "they shall release the workmen, the cattle, the sheep, the horses, (and) the donkeys down from the town."

337. C_3, D, and H all deviate from A to at least some degree (D seems perhaps to be a composite of both versions), but cannot be restored with any confidence (cf. Pecchioli Daddi 2003a: 84), while G_1, as far as is preserved, follows A, except for the oft-occurring deviation in pl. vs. sg.

338. The clause as usually translated, e.g., "Let the garrison which holds the posts be protected" (e.g., Goetze 1960: 71), is contextually odd. It is of course the troops that are there to protect the post, not themselves to be protected. And who would protect the troops? The villagers? In fact, the clause seems in a sense to resume the gist of the previous paragraph: "The scouts [s(hall tak)e up] the posts on the main road aga[in], (34)[and the tow]n shall (thereby) be protected." Further, the counter argumentation offered by Pecchioli Daddi (2003a: 87, n. 199) does not convince, in part because no "uso tecnico" is intended here, but rather the most basic semantic meaning of the verb, "to have; possess" and thus, "to be provided with."

339. B_1 i 2′ makes explicit the subject, "the scouts."

340. The 3 is abundantly clear on the photos, despite the two verticals in the edition.

341. Some four lines are missing from A i before picking up again here. If one inserts four lines of text (from B_1) between KUB 31.87 (Bo 2891) and KUB 40.55 (Bo 3707), one sees that the direct join in Pecchioli Daddi's (2003a: 304) sketch is not at all likely. Instead, KUB 40.55 should be set somewhat farther down, so that there is some minimal space between the fragments, or at best, so that the upper right corner of KUB 40.55 just touches the lower left of KUB 31.87. For the join with KBo 50.280a (1236/u) and an initial reading, see Kühne 1972: 255.

342. The available space would seem to require the restoration with *-wa-*, and while B_1 generally shows the writing without, there are three cases with: B_1 ii 42′, iii 60′, iv 22′.

343. Pecchioli Daddi's (2003a: 100) additional URU-*an ú-e-da-i nu* can by no means fit in the space available. That said, once one inserts *ḫu-u-da-a-ak* into the space, there is room left for about one further sign, and one might consider adding, e.g., *-pát*. Cf. *CHD* P, 8b.

344. Without the emendation the text reads EN KUR-*TI*, "Lord of the Land," attested elsewhere, but not in this composition.

345. The word is a hapax. Goetze (1959: 69) suggests either "installations" or "supplies" of the posts; cf. differently *GrHL* §22.24: "Let them keep *ḫurup*-ed and keep track of the fortified cities...." Singer (2009a: 46) suggests "fortifications/defense," "ההגנה."

346. For considerations on the structures described in the following paragraphs, along with a rather more optimistic reconstruction and translation, see recently Singer 2008: 253–56.

347. I have translated *gipessar* as "ell" and *sekan* as "hand," assuming ca. 50 cm for the former and ca. 5–8 cm for the latter, though these must be seen as mere approximations for present purposes. For thorough discussions, see van den Hout 1989–90; Singer 2008: 252.

348. While it seems likely that A, C_1, and D are duplicates in this paragraph, no one line is actually certainly the duplicate of any other. It is therefore not to be entirely excluded that a gap exists in the text at this point, and that C_1 and D pick up only at some juncture once A breaks off after i 75′. Since, however, there does seem to be a reasonable likelihood that the three mss. overlap here, no gap is assumed in this treatment. Further, it must be noted that the placement of the various elements from the different fragments in relation to each other is anything but certain.

349. One would, of course, like to be able to read *še-e*]*r ar-ḫa* here, after D ii 9′, but the traces are hardly amenable to such. *CHD* L–N, 186b, suggests *kat-ta-a*]*n*. Another option would be [UG]U, though not likely in this MH ms.

350. The sign is clearly defective and yields neither an *ar-* nor a convincing *pal-*. I am able to see no more than AN followed by one, probably two wedges, and I suspect that the surface is well-enough preserved so that these traces represent all that was originally here. Of course, the clear *ar-ḫa-ia-aš* in D ii 10′ leads one to prefer *ar*$^{!}$-. Cf. von Schuler 1957: 42, 53; Starke 1990: 257; *CHD* L–N, 186b; *CHD* P, 64a–b.

351. D ii 10′ shows a clear 3.

352. The traces in D ii 12′ clearly indicate *-kán*, too, with the remains of the heads of two horizontals, not wedges, as in the edition.

353. C_1 ii 10 seemingly "5."

354. The three mss. preserving this paragraph offer interesting differences, prompting Pecchioli Daddi (2003a: 108–15) to present them as variant paragraphs, though they may perhaps be expressing the same thing in slightly differing ways. Unfortunately, there is not enough preserved of the duplicates to warrant placing them side by side. The *a*]*n-da* 𒑱 *ka-ta-pé-en-ni-iš* in B_1 ii 5 (and *k*[*a-* in C_1 ii 12) may parallel *-kán ḫu-u-ta-nu-e-uš* in D ii 15′; *katapenni-* is a *hapax*, and it may simply be a variant on *ḫutanu*(*e*)- and/or its Luwian counterpart. The difference between *kattanda* in D ii 16′ and *š*]*e-er ar-ḫa* in B_1 ii 6, as well as between *sara* in D ii 21′ and *kat-t*[*a~* in C_1 ii 17, may be merely variation in counting from the top to the bottom vs. from the bottom up. The difference between *kuitman* in D ii 17′ and *maḫḫan* in B_1 ii 7 is a matter of nuance. The variance between *asandu* and *estu*, *zennai* and *zenna*]*nzi* among the various mss. is no more than the number variation that one encounters continually throughout the text (cf. n. 312). And *še-er ar-ḫa-ia-at-kán* in D ii 19′ vs. *n*]*a-aš-kán še-er ar-ḫa* in B_1 ii 9 is simply syntactical variation. Finally, while the

restoration in B$_1$ ii 10 is uncertain (*ú-e-d*]*a*$^?$*-an-da*$^{(?)}$*-ma-aš-kán*), it may be that it replaces the locution found in D ii 20′ with a syntax using the instrumental, e.g., "Even if it is not forced up by water."

355. For the restoration see D ii 28′.

356. The sign seems clearly to be an *-uš*, on the photo and in the edition, not *-iš*, as read by Pecchioli Daddi (2003a: 108). On *ḫūtanu*(*e*)-, cf. *HED* H, 416; *HHw*, 57; Haas and Wegner 1993: 56; *CLL*: 78; Miller 2005a: 10 (my comment there regarding the appearance of *ḫutanu-* and *da-* together should be ignored).

357. Though Bo 69/105+KBo 57.10 of D cannot be physically joined to KUB 31.86 (Bo 2417), as they are stored in different museums, a photo reconstruction would seem to suggest that hardly more than "1," at the very most "2," could fit here. B$_1$ ii 6 shows a clear 2. Restoring "*kat-ta* 1," as Pecchioli Daddi (2003a: 108) does, is out of the question.

358. The space available would seem to permit only this writing, as in 17′, not the longer, as in 18′, and there is certainly no space for Pecchioli Daddi's (2003a: 108) *gi-p*[*í-eš-šar pád*]*-da-an-te-eš*; see already Laroche 1957: 127.

359. Cf. D ii 19′; Pecchioli Daddi 2003a: 108 and n. 270.

360. Here in D is a seemingly clear writing of nom. sg. comm. *wetinants* with the *-ant* animating morpheme (other examples are found in KUB 7.41 ii 24, 33 // KBo 10.45+ ii 24, 33 and KBo 54.81, 8′), though one could argue that this is either an error for an abl. *wetinaz* or the result of dissimilation from it, especially since there is no explicit object in the sentence; cf. Rieken 1999a: 292; Melchert 1977: 324. Or should one in light of these difficulties assume a *t*-stem *wetinant-*, "builder$^?$," derived somehow from *wete-*, "to build"? In any case, Pecchioli Daddi's (2003a: 112, 279, there B$_3$) *e-eš-t*]*u an-da-ma-aš-kán* in B$_1$ ii 10 is unlikely, since there seems to be no space between *an-da* and the traces before it.

361. Rather clear are ˻*nu-u*˼-, with no space between them. In the ensuing break there is hardly room for anything other than *-wa* or a similarly short sign, and indeed *-wa* fits nicely. It would even seem that a hint of the (upper?) wedge of *-w*[*a*] may be visible.

362. The collation and interpretation by Košak (1993: 110) are surely correct; cf. Laroche 1957: 127, followed by Goetze 1959: 69; Haas-Wegner 1993: 56–57; Boysan-Dietrich 1987: 38–39.

363. This paragraph is fragmentarily preserved in B$_{1-2}$, C$_1$ and E, but apparently omitted from D. In B$_1$ the text of this additional paragraph breaks off after just two lines, while C$_1$ breaks off after six lines. I have reconstructed this section assuming that C$_1$ ii 22 (*a-š*[*a*$^?$-) is duplicated by B$_2$ ii 16′ ([*a*$^?$*-š*]*a*$^?$*-an-du*[), but this is anything but certain. And since this is the only relevant overlap in the paragraph, it is in fact quite uncertain how many lines the paragraph originally contained, and therefore equally uncertain whether the missing portion should be restricted to one paragraph only. The ensuing paragraph is thus provided with the prime numbering.

364. E ii 4′ shows BÀD$^{\text{ḪI.A}}$*-aš* ^{GIŠ}AB$^{\text{ḪI.A}}$*-uš*, "windows of fortifications," its scribe perhaps having misread *ŠA* BÀD.URU$^{\text{DIDLI.ḪI.A}}$ in D ii 23′; cf. Beal 1992: 427 and n. 1595.

On the other hand, it is now clear that at least some city gates, e.g., the northwestern gate at Kuşaklı/Sarissa, indeed had windows (Mielke 2006: 29).

365. Otten (1976: 95) suggested II$^{?}$ ^{GIŠ}*al-la-a-i*[*a*$^{?}$-, which is graphically possible, though the traces do not appear to necessarily suggest ^{GIŠ}; Pecchioli Daddi's (2003a: 114) ˻*wa-na*˼-*al-la-a*[*n* is out of the question. Cf. Boysan-Dietrich's (1987: 92) 2$^{?}$ ^{GIŠ}*al-la-a*[(*n*)] and Hoffner 1977: 152, ns. 3–4; 1978: 245. The traces in E ii 6′, where *a-* is omitted, would seem perhaps to support the suggestion that a space is to be assumed before the *al-*. The word *allān* would be a *hapax*, probably relating to thickness or height (cf. Luw. *āla/i-*?).

366. One would like to have seen a further *ēsdu* here, but perhaps the *ēsdu* of the previous clause, closely linked to this one, remains in force.

367. The traces in E ii 8′ do not suggest the expected URU, but rather -*r*]*i*, which led Pecchioli Daddi (2003a: 304) to suggest [*a-ú-r*]*i-an-ma*, for which there is insufficient space; see also Marazzi 1979: 79–81. The best solution may be [URU-*r*]*i-an* (i.e., *ḫappiriyan*; cf. KUB 8.4 i 7′; KUB 36.18a, 5′; KBo 34.110 obv. 7; IBoT 3.120 l. col. 3′; Bo 6351 i 5′), though this would also appear to be just slightly too long for the space.

368. The following lines seem to suggest this solution at the end of 28′ and the beginning of 29′, as there it is said that the worker will make "likewise" of stone (30′); and indeed, N[A$_4$ fits the traces in E ii 8′ exactly (certainly not *Š*[*A*, as in Pecchioli Daddi 2003a: 116), even a trace of the wedge being visible; and NA$_4$ also fits perfectly into the space available at the beginning of D ii 29′. While it thus seems likely enough that NA$_4$ is to be restored at the beginning of the line, the traces of what is probably phonetic complementation are more difficult to interpret. Based on *pé-r*]*a*$^{?}$*-an* NA$_4$*-aš ḫa-ak*$^{?}$-˹*ku*$^{?}$*-un*$^{?}$*-na*$^{?}$*-i*$^{?}$˺~[in G$_3$ ii 1′ alone it would seem that [NA$_4$-**a*]*š*$^{!}$* would be the best reading. The traces could perhaps be *a*]*n*, but are not overly convincing as such, since the horizontals of this scribe's ANs do not generally cut through his verticals, as would seem to be the case here. Pecchioli Daddi (2003a: 116, 294) restores [ZABA]R, i.e., [UD.KA.B]AR, but while the traces could indeed allow B]AR, there is by no means enough space available for [UD.KA.B]AR. As to why exactly a "coppersmith" should be required to construct a stone *ḫakkunnai*, one might suppose either that the installation also included metal elements, or that TABIRA is not necessarily always so specific, but could also mean "skilled craftsman" or the like.

369. E places *ḫakkunnai-* in the acc. ([*ḫa-a*]*k-ku-un-na-i-in*), while D either places it in the d.l. or treats it as a neut. G$_3$ ii 1′ shows]x-*an* NA$_4$*-aš ḫa-ak*$^{?}$-˹*ku*$^{?}$*-un-na*˺*-i*[*n*$^{?}$]. The traces preceding *-an* preclude TIBIR]A, suggesting rather R]A, or similar, allowing the suggested *pé-r*]*a-an*.

370. All 2nd person verbs and pronouns in this text are 2nd sg. (except in §32′, in quoted speech).

371. Often translated "moat" (e.g. Singer 2008: 255), but Akk. *ḫe/irītu*(*m*) can just as well mean "ditch, channel, canal," so that it is anything but certain that specifically "moat" should be understood here. On the contrary, it is more likely that structures relating to water supply, storage, and drainage are at issue. On the water-related architecture of Kuşakli/Sarissa, by far the most thoroughly studied case from Late Bronze Age Anatolia, see Hüser 2007, with comparisons to other Anatolian sites.

372. The sense of the clause is entirely unclear. The only other attestation of *sarā*

arnu-, lit. "bring/move up," is apparently that in KUB 36.90 obv. 5–6 (*HW*[2] A, 335a; Singer 2002: 106), in which it seems to be used to indicate the waking up of the Storm God. B_1 ii 10 shows "But he/it [...] with [wa]ter?" (*ú-e-t*]*a*?*-an-da-ma-aš-kán*).

373. This translation of *nūwa* (cf. n. 361) actually employs a usage that is not generally acknowledged for this temporal lexeme, i.e., in the sense "nonetheless, despite of which." Cf. *CHD* L–N, 468–70, where the examples under b, 2′ might be amenable to such an interpretation.

374. The considerations on these "trenches" by Haas and Wegner (1993: 56–57) and Singer (2008: 255–57) have become obsolete due to the joins with KBo 57.272 and Bo 69/105. On the Hittite, Hurrian, and Akkadian terms, see Trémouille 2002. On Hittite archaeological remains for water supply and drainage, see Hüser 2007; Wittenberg and Schachner 2013.

375. Lit. "Further the heads of the staircases of the posterns of the city-gates shall be doors (and) bolts of fortified cities." The suggested translation is anything but certain (cf. e.g., *HW*[2] Ḫ, 356, 494b; *CHD* L–N, 88a). In both D and E ii 3′–4′ (*nam-ma* KÁ.GAL-*TÌ lu-uš-ta-ni-e-eš* GIŠ*i-la-na-*[*aš* SAG.DUMEŠ*-uš*] / BÀDḪI.A*-aš* GIŠABḪI.A*-uš* GIŠIG*-an-te-eš ḫa-at-tal-wa-an-*[*te-eš a-ša-an-du*]) insufficient and/or too ambiguous morpho-syntactical information is given for one to be able to attain certainty about the relationships among the elements (similarly Beckman 1986b: 572), and several interpretations are possible. The significantly deviating mss. along with forms such as SAG.DUMEŠ*-uš* (certainly not acc. comm., as in *HW*[2] Ḫ, 345a; cf. p. 356), which cannot reflect the known word for "head," *ḫarsar/ḫarsan-* (n.), suggest that the ancient scribes may also have had their difficulties with the passage.

376. It seems that there is no conflict between the versions, as one can easily restore both mss. identically, i.e., D ii 26′–27′: *na-aš-ta* ˻*šu*˼*-u*[*ḫ-ḫa le-e*] ˻*wa-ar*˼*-*[*ḫ*]*u-i za-ap-pí-ia-at-ta-ri le-*˹*e*˺[ ]; and E ii 7′: [*na-aš-t*]*a šu-uḫ-ḫa le-e wa-ar-ḫu-u-i za-ap-pí-ia-*[*at-ta-ri le-e*]. See discussions in Pecchioli Daddi 2003a: 117, n. 308 and Prins 1997: 97.

377. Marazzi (1979: 79–81) suggests that the *ḫakkunnai-* might be the door socket, i.e., *Drehpfanne* or *Angelstein*, which may well be the case. Indeed, door sockets made of bronze are attested from Hittite sites (see refs. in Marazzi 1979: 81). Still, the more general translation "installation" is kept here, since these *ḫakkunnai-* are not provided with the determinative for bronze, even though a metalworker is to create them, and would seem to be made at least in part of stone. Moreover, in other contexts (see *HED* H, 10–11; *HW*[2] Ḫ, 15–16), *ḫakkunnai-* are given the DUG, "vessel," determinative and used, e.g., to pour libations of oil into a river.

378. While D shows *purutti=a=ssan*, employing *purut-*, "mud; mud brick; mud-brick structure," E (ii 12′: *pu-ru-ut-ti-*eš*-n*[*i*?*-ia-aš-ša-an*) and G_3 (ii 5′: *pu-ru-ut-t*]*e*?*-eš-ni-ia-aš-ša-an*) use the nominal abstract *puruttessar*, i.e., *puruttesni=a=san*. See discussion of forms in Rieken 1999a: 160–63.

379. G_3 ii 6′ shows an unexpected *-w*]*a*?*-an-zi*.

380. There is clearly no room at the beginning of D ii 41′ for the *ša-ra-a* of the duplicates, and the scribe presumably used UGU, which, however, appears nowhere else in any of these mss. Perhaps *še-er* would be a suitable alternative.

381. The emendation, originally suggested by Goetze (1959: 70) and adopted by Pecchioli Daddi (2003a: 124; there, however, *andurza=ša*, creating an otherwise nonexistent enclitic particle), is quite uncertain, but seems to be the best solution offered thus far. There is, in fact, no space between *an!durza* and *ŠA*, and if one were to insist on keeping them together, one might think of *andurza=as=a*, i.e., a 3rd pers. pron. (but referring to what?) and the conjunction, but such a writing would be quite unexpected.

382. It seems unlikely that the signs preserved in A ii 11′ would have stood here in the break, as they do not appear to fit the context well, and they would be too short for the available space. Curiously, what would fit exactly into the break is *na-ak-ki-iš*, which precedes *ḫarduppis* in D ii 46′, and it may be that *na-ak-ki-iš* once stood here, in which case it, along with *ḫarduppis*, should probably be viewed as the result of scribal confusion during the copying process.

383. Too much space is available for merely *-k*[*i ḫ*]*a-*, and *-pát* would seem to be a simple solution.

384. One might expect a verb for "supply" at this point, but no verb beginning with d/t yielding such is known to me.

385. D omits *nu saramnit katta zikkeddu.*

386. Cf. *CHD* P, 396b, "and let them not drive the livestock, horses, mules (and) donkeys to the (area of) wet mudbricks"; Boysan-Dietrich 1987: 14.

387. The position and function of "wood" in the sentence is syntactically ambiguous. One might also translate it "… Holz (und) Fackel …" (Otten 1971b: 8; Boysan-Dietrich 1987: 18) or "… fiaccole die legno …" (Pecchioli Daddi 2003a: 119). The verb is likewise ambiguous, allowing "take (in)to" or "place at/on/in." The *ANA* would seem to (slightly) favor the latter. Translating "in inner and outer tower(s)," as does Boysan-Dietrich (1987: 18; cf. Laroche 1957: 127), does not seem likely, as this would suggest a double wall around relatively unimportant frontier towns. Further, it is unlikely that guards, e.g., would not have been allowed to ascend a tower with the aid of a torch during the night. Perhaps affixing (the base of) a burning torch to a wooden tower—or a tower made to some extent of wood; see Naumann 1955: 255, n. 28—and letting it burn is being forbidden.

388. Lit. "from the front"; for abl. *ḫantaz*, see Rieken 1999a: 123; *HEG* A–K, 153; Szemerényi 1982: 232; Melchert 1977: 322.

389. Seemingly less likely, if one chooses to see in *-an-* a resumption of ^{LÚ}KÚR rather than an anticipation of URU, one might translate, "the town will […] him (i.e., the enemy) with this (wood)."

390. D iii 1–2 reads ⸢*ḫa*⸣*-a-ni-*⸢*iš-šu-wa-ar-ma-kán*⸣ *k*[*u-it*] ⸢*ku-ut-ta-az*⸣ *ka*[*t-ta*] / *ma-uš-ke-et-ta-ri*, pace *CHD* L–N, 213a–b.

391. The variant in C$_4$ ii 9′ should presumably be read *pár-ga-nu-uš-kán-d*[*u*], not as a med.-pass. form ending in *tari*, as assumed, e.g., by *CHD* P, 157b, 158a, thereby eliminating the only med.-pass. attestation for the verb. After this point D iii 4–11 continues with three deviating paragraphs (see translation in n. 400): $^{(4)}$*suḫḫaz katta IN*[*A* …]x.KAM UD.3.KAM *ser lē* $^{(\S 5)}$GIŠ-*ṢU=ia=kan* $^{\text{GIŠ?}}$*ḫar-*x[…]x x x x*-az* EGIR-[…] $^{(6)}$*lē ḫarapp*[*i-* …] x x[…] $^{(\S 7)}$URU*-r*[*i*]-x[…] $^{(8)}$*wet*[*enaza*$^{(?)}$…] (cf. B$_1$ ii 23′) $^{(9)}$*ŠA* MUŠEN[$^{\text{ḪI.A}}$…] (cf. B$_1$ ii

24′) ⁽¹⁰⁾*n=an*[…] ⁽¹¹⁾*kar*?-x[…]. The second sign in D iii 5 is clearly ZU, as read by von Schuler (1957: 45, n. 10), not AB, as read by Pecchioli Daddi (2003a: 130). In D iii ca. 39″ is preserved *n*]*a-a*[*t*, in 40″ perhaps] -*d*[*u*, and in 41″ maybe Ḫ]I.A *k*[*u*-.

392. DU$_{10}$ is present on the tablet, but was left out of the copy, as noted already by Goetze (1959: 70).

393. C$_4$ ii 17′–18′: "But [the birds in the pond]s in the district shall be well" (*ma-ni-ia-˻aḫ-ḫi-ia˼-at-ma-ká*[*n*] / *na-at* SIG$_5$-*an-t*[*e-eš* …] ⌜*a-ša-an*⌝-*du*), its scribe having read *at*-, "they," in the text from which he was copying instead of -*ia*-, "also," as well as *ma*, "but," instead of -*tá*(*k*)-, "your" (B$_1$ ii 24′), raising the question of which version might have stood in the original. Since the 2nd sg. is so uncommon in this text, it may be that C$_4$ preserves the better version, though the assumedly anticipatory -*at*- does seem a bit odd.

394. Photo shows clear TA rather than the ŠA in the edition.

395. For the suggestion of a Luwianized 3rd pres. pl. in -*za*, see Melchert 1994: 183.

396. A relatively clear wedge of the -*ni* can be seen on the photo, as opposed to the horizontal alone in the edition.

397. Since this writing, i.e., without DINGIR-*LÌ*, appears in B$_1$ ii 45′ and iii 21 as well, I would suggest that the scribe is employing an abbreviation, and that it should therefore not be emended as an error (*pace*, e.g., Mouton 2006: 130 sub 91, in a comparable case; cf. *CHD* Š, 191a; Taggar-Cohen 2006: 30–31; and most recently and extensively Weeden 2011: 146–48).

398. At this point KBo 50.280b joins KUB 31.88 (both A), their left edges aligning approximately. In Pecchioli Daddi's (2003a: 305) sketch, KBo 50.280b (1128/z) is placed to the left of its correct position vis-à-vis KUB 31.88. Fragment KUB 40.56 of A, which begins here, preserves cols. iii–iv rather than i–ii as indicated in the edition.

399. D iii 2 adds "monthly."

400. C$_4$ ii 9′ has "But they shall not raise the foundation stones"; cf. Boysan-Dietrich 1987: 41: "Die Fundamentmauern darf man nicht (zu) hoch führen." According to *CHD* Š, 116b, "It is possible that both versions are expressing the same requirements." After this point D iii 4–11 continues with a variant passage, becoming ever more fragmentary. Still legible are one line of the present paragraph, two of a second and the first six of a third: "Down from the roof […] beyond (lit. "above") day 3 shall no[t …]. § And the wood [and?] the *ḫar*...-wood […] shall n[o]t [be] separat[ed] from […] again. § In the town [… with?] wate[r? …] of bird[s(?) …] and him/it(acc.) […]." The last paragraph might perhaps be a version of §30′, if *wet*[*enaz* in iii 8 can be matched with the same in B$_1$ ii 23′, *ŠA* MUŠEN[ḪI.A in 9 with MUŠENḪI.A in B$_1$ ii 24′.

401. The *tarnu*-building is most often attested as a building in which ritual bathing takes place. Here the sense is clearly another, and "water installations" or "water building" seems fitting.

402. *CHD* Š, 169b, has "Let them patrol the water pipes…," that is, it understands this med.-pass. conjugation of *weḫ*- as transitive. However, while *weḫ*- certainly can mean "to patrol," there seems to be no other such case of a transitive usage (see, e.g., Neu 1968: 195–99). Moreover, while regularly inspecting the pipes makes good sense, "patrolling"

them is somewhat difficult to imagine. Neu (1968: 197) translates "die Kanäle ... sollen in Bewegung bleiben," which of course makes little sense. Against the translation suggested here might speak the fact that there exists a Hittite word for "flow," i.e., *ars-*. Presumably, if correct, the meaning "circulate" refers here to something more specific than simply "flowing."

403. Also possible, with *CHD* L–N, 80b, 168a, "the bird ponds."

404. Since the other three designations in the list are religious professions, it may perhaps be this usage of the Sumerogram that is to be preferred, rather than "old men; elders," as is usually translated; cf., however, the usage in B_1 iii 9 (§37′), clearly "elders"; see also Pecchioli Daddi 2003a: 135; McMahon 1997: 223b; Klengel 1965: 232.

405. The scribe employed the quoted speech particle only in the first clause, but the quotation presumably continues into the next paragraph.

406. Due to the surprising asserverative statement, *CHD* Š, 191b (also L–N, 401b), perhaps understandably, seeks to translate the phrase as a question, i.e., "And he should ask them: 'In this city, is some cult sanctuary of the Stormgod or some cult sanctuary of some other deity now neglected and/or is it ruined? Are the priests, 'mother-of-the-deity' priestesses and GUDU$_{12}$-priests not accounted for?'" *CHD* Š, 140b, in contrast, understands them as conditional, as does Karasu (2003: 224); *CHD* L–N, 461b, translates as indicatives, while *CHD* L–N, 336b, muddles the issue. Though translating as a question might seem attractive, *memau* means "speak," not "ask," for which one would expect *punuss-*, and the following paragraph makes clear that these statements are in fact to be understood as indicatives. Further, precisely this logical curiosity is no rarity in the Hittite texts; see e.g., No. 10, §15′, 8–11, or in Papanikri's Birth Ritual, §3 (*CTH* 476; KBo 5.1 i 14–17; Strauß 2006: 284–309).

407. It is actually not certain at what point the quoted speech ends. See Pecchioli Daddi 2003a: 137; McMahon 1997: 223b; *HED* K, 69; Karasu 2003: 224. In any case, C_4 iii 1–2 restructures the passage, continuing the quote from the previous paragraph thus: "You priests, mother-deity priestesses, (and) anointed ones shall keep it maintained!" Thereafter follows, presumably no longer as part of the quoted speech, "And they shall restore it."

408. Lit. "greatly established." Cf. *CHD* L–N, 247a–b, 344a, where undeclined forms of *mekki*, "greatly, much, in large numbers," are understood, presumably correctly, as adverbs. I suspect, however, that the sense of *CHD*'s "let respect for the Stormgod **particularly** be established" (p. 344a) would have been rendered by Hittite ^{d}10=*ma*=*san*=***pat***.

409. The first two lines of B_1 iii, which presumably should have contained the text found in A iii 8′–9′, were left blank, which in turn resulted in a rather awkward reworking of the ensuing lines in B_1.

410. B_1 iii 3 shows *pí-*ia*-an-du*, "they shall provide"; F_1 iii 12′ *pé-eš-kán-d*[*u*, "they shall provide regularly."

411. Pecchioli Daddi's (2003a: 144, 275) [*k*]*u-e-da-ni* is far too short for the break, and syntactical considerations suggest that *nu* should be included as well. Context and

traces would seem to allow either the relative pronoun, with Pecchioli Daddi, or the demonstrative, thus [*k*]*e*-.

412. In F_1 iii 16′ a wedge can be seen on the photo, yielding -*ni*, as opposed to the edition.

413. For a Luwianized 3rd pres. pl. in -*za*, see Melchert (1994: 183); cf. *kappuwanza*, above, in §32′, 32′.

414. MA in the edition (perhaps influenced by *MA-ḪAR* of 24), but I can see only the two expected horizontals on the photo.

415. As *iye*- in the first clause of 25 in an exactly parallel locution takes no refl. particle, perhaps the chain here is to be interpreted as a graphic variant for =*at*=*san* rather than =*at*=*z*=*san*, as in *CHD* Š, 129b, 152b; cf. *CHD* L–N, 426b.

416. The *le-e ku-iš*-[*ki* in D iv 13 is surely parallel to *le-e* at this point, despite the lack of *kuiski* here, not the *le-e ku-iš-ki* at the end of the line; and judging by space available in D iv 11, *le-e ku-iš-ki iye*/*azzi* is most likely to be restored there, too.

417. The traces in D iv 15 are probably to be read [*ka*]*t*-⸤*ti-ir*⸥-*r*[*a*, not ⸤*ku-it ḫa*⸥-[(*pace* Pecchioli Daddi 2003a: 154), which does not fit the traces.

418. A careful reconstruction of these lines in D suggests that the join KUB 31.86 (Bo 3063) with KUB 13.25 (Bo 3886) is also not direct (cf. nn. 327, 330, 341), as drawn in Pecchioli Daddi's (2003a: 313) sketch. KUB 13.25 must be moved slightly downwards and to the left. The first traces in KUB 13.25 are likely ⸢*ḫa*⸣-[*an-da-an*, which necessitates the restoration [*ku-it*] ⸢*ḫa*⸣-[*an-da-an* in KUB 31.86(+)KUB 13.25 iv 16′, and one can very likely read [*ka*]*t*-⸤*ti-ir*⸥-*r*[*a* in KUB 31.86(+)KUB 13.25 iv 15. The line numbering must therefore be increased by one from this point as opposed to Pecchioli Daddi's numbering; since the join can no longer be considered direct, I have continued from this point with prime numbering.

419. Syntactically "ancient" could just as well modify "town," but contextually it would seem to refer to the *ḫuwasi*-stele.

420. B_1 iii 1, "you(pl.)."

421. Thus Melchert 1985: 189.

422. There is no need to place the object in parenthesis (as does, e.g., McMahon 1997: 224b), as the sentence-initial enclitic chain must be parsed as *n*=*as*(<*an*)=*san*, and since, according to Watkin's Law (2004: 562–63), an enclitic pronoun in a transitive sentence refers to the object. Of interest is the assimilation here in iii 15 vs. the retention of *n* in iii 16.

423. For considerations on the meaning of the verb, obviously a form of punishment, see *CHD* Š, 52; Güterbock 1983: 79; Westbrook and Woodard 1990: 647–53.

424. Presumably in a more general sense than the core meaning "craftsmen," as assumed e.g., in *CHD* L/N, 344b, Š, 152b, 197a.

425. For discussion and various interpretations of this passage, cf. Symington 1991: 119; *CHD* Š, 16b–17a.

426. A similar clause is found in Mursili's Dictate to Tuppi-Teššub's Syrian Antago-

nists (*CTH* 63); see d'Alfonso 2005: 55; Miller 2007a: 137 and n. 39. For similar cases in the texts of the present volume, see Introduction, p. 44.

427. For a recent study of Hittite *maskan*-, "bribe," see Dardano 2009.

428. See discussion in Introduction, sub Envisioning the Setting, pp. 26–27.

429. Understood as an example of the occasional loss of *n* before *t* in *GrHL* §1.135. Cf. *CHD* Š, 71a, where the *n* is restored.

430. In the *Inhaltsübersicht* to KUB 31, sub 84, Otten writes, "gehört nach Forrer RHA I 153–54 Anm. 32 zu XIII 2; auch nach Photographie wahrscheinlich. Bei Kol. III ist die letzte Zeile von XIII 2 vielleicht gleich der ersten Zeile unseres Textes (-*i̯a* wäre XIII 2 noch in Spuren erhalten)." I can add merely that my examination of the photos and electronic join of the pieces only lends credence to Otten's observations. Still, since the fragments have apparently never been physically joined, as far as I know, and since no ms. is preserved at this point that would enable one to determine if the line (and paragraph) numbering is complete, I have opted to continue the line count from this point with prime numbering. Since, however, it seems all but certain that KUB 13.2 and KUB 31.84 belong to the same tablet, regardless of whether they join directly at this point or not, they both are labeled as B_1.

431. The trailing vertical, as intimated also in the edition, seems to have been superimposed by a more clearly impressed one, almost giving the impression of ZU rather than KU. The verb's meaning remains unclear, but appears often with *anda*, as here. For the form with -*u*-, cf. *ku-un-ku-uš-ke-nu-un* in KBo 20.82 ii 14; for further discussion, see *HHw*, 84 ("untersuchen, (an)schauen"); *HED* K, 248–50 ("condition, prepare, ready," for *anda kunk*-); Ünal 1991: 806 "(sich) putzen, pflegen, bereinigen, beseitigen, kämmen, striegeln"; Neumann 1973: 240; Neu 1968: 102 "aufrichten"; med.-pass., "sich aufrichten."

432. Traces would seem much more amenable to ^{GIŠ}]˹TIR˺ than Pecchioli Daddi's (2003a: 162) ^{GIŠ}KIRI$_6$.

433. On the photo a rather clear -*da* seems to suggest itself, as opposed to the -*uš* in the edition, which would, if correct, render untenable the otherwise reasonable suggestions by von Schuler (1957: 49), *Ú-SAL-LU*]-*uš*, "und die [Wiese] soll nicht abgeweidet werden," and Neu (1968: 200), GUD$^{\text{ḪI.A}}$]-*uš*, "Rinder sollst du darauf nicht weiden." As far as I know, *wesiya*- is otherwise not attested with *anda*, leaving perhaps a nom.-acc. neut. participle as a possibility.

434. The [*nam-ma* ^{GIŠ}KIRI$_6$] restored by Pecchioli Daddi (2003a: 162) would likely be ca. one long sign too short; cf. the sequence ^{GIŠ}TIR$^{\text{ḪI.A}}$ ^{GIŠ}MÚ^{SAR} ^{GIŠ}KIRI$_6$.GEŠTIN in B_1 ii 19′.

435. The line numbering in the edition of KBo 50.277 (C_1) is too high by one, and should be 9′, 10′–18′.

436. Obviously not to *ku(e)ra*-, known to be a Hittite word for (a type of) "field." In the light of *kuranna*, above (§§4–5, l. 10), probably to be translated "section, plot" (though in a different context), it may be that **kuranni* stands behind the Sumerogram here. Cf. *HED* K, 214, 216–17; *HEG* A–K, 608, 645; *EDHIL*, 486–87.

437. Certainly so, as seen, e.g., by Catsanicos 1994: 310, *pace* Oettinger 1979 (2002): 488, who read *da-a-lí-ia-mi*.

438. *Pace CHD* P, 263a and *EDHIL*, 947, which read *-aš ŠA*, there is clearly no space between *-aš* and *-ša*. On this paragraph, see also Marazzi 1979: 83–85; Neu 1968: 152, n. 2; Beal 1988: 283, §17.

439. *Pace CHD* P, 263a, the sign on the photo could just as well be a *ta-*, as far as I can judge. Cf. *CHD* Š, 162b.

440. McMahon (1997: 224b) translates "widow," but *wannummiya-*, as recognized by Pecchioli Daddi (2003a: 157), who translates "una donna sola," can refer to a woman without children or simply to an orphan. A *wannummiya-* woman is therefore a more general term than "widow."

441. D iv 24′: "he." Further, D omits the section with the troops from the various towns, replacing it with "The troops [of$^?$] the po[st ...] which are up in the town, ..." For discussion see Torri (2005: 396), who, however, assumes that the situation reflected in B_1 would have prevailed in the MH period, though the only MH ms., A, is not preserved at this point and it is entirely unclear whether B_1 or D would reflect the original MH situation.

442. Cf. usage in B_1 iii 63′, where clearly "stores; provisions" is intended for *isḫuessar*. Cf. *CHD* Š, 71a, 143b, "firewood"; *HED* A, 408; McMahon 1997: 224b; Pecchioli Daddi 2003a: 159.

443. For thorough discussion of these "land tenants" (LÚ ^{GIŠ}TUKUL), see Beal 1988.

444. Literally, "the eyes of the governor of the post shall be running over them all as well," whereby Goetze 1959: 70 is preferred to *CHD* Š, 70a, "let the provincial governor and everybody else watch (them)."

445. Clearly *AŠ-RA*, with von Schuler (1957: 50), not *pé-da*, as read by Pecchioli Daddi (2003a: 168 and n. 425), or N[AM.R]A, as read by Marazzi (1979: 84, n. 19).

446. It is not certain how many lines, if any, are lost between §48′ (B_1) and §49′ (A). According to a note in the edition of KUB 13.2 (B_1), "Es fehlen 3–4 Zeilen" at the top of col. iv, but if one copies several lines from elsewhere in B_1 and inserts them at the top of col. iv, one sees that probably more like 6 lines are missing, and this matches better the number of lines from the top of A iv that find no parallel in B_1; i.e., the first certain duplicate lines are A iv 10′ // B_1 iv 3′, for a difference of 7. Moreover, there seems to be no paragraph divider extending into the preserved column divider of B_1 rev., as one would expect judging from the ensuing paragraph dividers, so that it appears that no paragraph, and perhaps no single line, is entirely missing.

447. Certainly not *-T*]*I* as in Pecchioli Daddi 2003a: 172 and *CHD* L–N, 287a. A *-T*]*U*$_4$ would be graphically possible, but never occurs in this text.

448. *Pace* Pecchioli Daddi (2003a: 172, n. 446),]~⸤*ti*⸥*-ia-za* in E iv 2′ is clear on the photo as well as in the edition, however it is to be interpreted. B_1 iv 3′ shows KÙ.SI]G$_{17}$ *ŠA* ^{LÚ}KUŠ$_7$*-ia*.

449. *Pace* Pecchioli Daddi (2003a: 176–77), it must be regarded as extremely unlikely that [^{É}*ḫa*]*-le-en-tu-u-wa-ia-ták-kán* from E iv 6′ can be restored here. E omits this

entire paragraph, and one can hardly justify extracting the first word from the ensuing paragraph, which E does retain, and placing it here.

450. The trace at the end of A iv 16′ does not look like a paragraph divider; too little of it is left to know what it was, but it looks like the head of a vertical.

451. *HW*[2] Ḫ, 64b, has [*Ù ŠA*], but this is completely excluded by the available space; *ŠA* fills it quite exactly.

452. E, which begins with [[É]*ḫa*]-*le-en-tu-u-wa-ia-ták-kán* É.GAL[ḪI.][A in iv 6′, would seem to have simply changed the sentence's word order, beginning it with the subjects, while *maniyaḫḫi-* presumably followed (cf. n. 449). If so, [[É]*ḫa*]-*le-en-tu-u-wa-* would seem, pace Alp (1983: 12–13), to replace É[ḪI.A] *BE-LU-TI*/*TÌ* in A and B_1, in line with the likely interpretation of *ḫalentuwa-* as a palatial residence (see, e.g., Singer 1975: 84 and n. 76; Mora 1987: 555), not "der Hauptkultraum des Tempels," an interpretation to which *HW*[2] Ḫ, 20, unfortunately still adheres. Otherwise, E and F_1 essentially follow B_1 as far as can be ascertained.

453. Akk. *ēkallītī* would of course be "palace officials," but this occurrence is surely to be explained on the graphic level, presumably a confabulation of oft-occurring É.GAL-*LÌ* and É.GAL-*TÌ*.

454. E may well have omitted some portion of this section of the text, perhaps *na-aš-ma-za da-a-an ku-iš-ki ku-it-ki ḫar-zi*, since its (reconstructed) line 7′ would be much longer than the rest of its (reconstructed) lines if the clause had been included.

455. In F_1 iv 5′ *ḫa-ap*]-*pí-ra-a-an* is to be read, making my comment in KBo 53, IX, sub 255 superfluous.

456. Whether this should be connected with *walḫ-*, "to strike," or not remains uncertain; see most recently *EDHIL*, 947. Marazzi (1979: 82) suggests "Diejenigen, welche beim Felder Umbrechen (sind), auf sie achte in der Angelegenheit der Einrichtung/Urbarmachung (der betr. Felder)."

457. Cf. *CHD* L–N, 287a–b.

458. The reconstruction of this paragraph in Pecchioli Daddi 2003a: 172–75 must be rejected wholesale, as there is too much space available in both A and B_1.

459. A, "he must."

460. While the reading and interpretation follow Hoffner (1971: 33), neither are entirely convincing, and I wonder if one should not instead read KIN.ÉRIN-*aš* and translate, "and you shall tend to the winter (and) harvest work-troop," despite the fact that the only three (perhaps four, if one includes [LÚ.MEŠ]É]RIN.KIN(?) in KUB 26.9 iv 2′) attestations for the two signs in conjunction show ÉRIN[MEŠ] KIN (KBo 5.6 i 13; KUB 31.112, 4′; KUB 13.2 iv 6′, i.e., the present composition, B_1 iv 6′). ÉRIN would fit the traces at least as well as *-ši*, in my view better (Hoffner himself admitted to seeing the second wedge), and it would dispense with the odd, though not impossible, d.l. pronoun. As seen in B_1 iii 72′, EGIR-*an arḫut* governs the d.l. in this ms., and ÉRIN-*aš* would thus presumably be a d.l. pl., despite the lack of MEŠ.

461. Reflexive, not ablative, as in Pecchioli Daddi 2003a: 180, assuming "-" there instead of "=" is not merely a typo; cf. *namma=za* in duplicates.

462. B_1 iv 29′ and E iv 17′ show ḪA.LA-*za/az nu a-pu-u-un*.

463. The *IŠ-TU* that Pecchioli Daddi (2003a: 186) reads in B_1 iv 30′ should be read *ku*]-˻*iš-ki*˼[.

464. Only after publishing KBo 50 (see p. XI, sub 271) did I realize that KBo 50.271 is in fact duplicate, not just parallel, to these lines, and further, that it must belong to KBo 53.255. Fragment M iv 5′ shows a rather clear *a*]*r-ḫa ša-ar-ru-*[at this point, a rather puzzling piece of evidence, perhaps to be understood as "(and) [f(urther they are separat)ed]," even if the CV-VC- writing rather than CVC- for *sarra-* would be anomalous.

465. M iv 6′ shows a clear 6.

466. The sign is no normal ḪA. If it is nevertheless to be read ḪA, then its wedge is pulled much farther to the left that normal in this text. Otherwise, it could represent a fourth, rather tardy, wedge of *-eš-*.

467. The position of KBo 50.280a vis-à-vis KUB 13.1 is quite uncertain, the reconstruction of the paragraph equally so.

468. This occurrence of *appa tiya-* with the acc. is unique and may well be a scribal error, especially in light of the fact that much of the line is written over erased sign traces. Another possibility would be an acc. of relation, i.e., "stand back in relation to him," perhaps to be understood as "do not interfere with him," which would be contextually problematic if in fact "If a provincial governor has [taken something] from the serv[ants], you shall not interfere with him" is to be restored, as is usually assumed, on the basis of the ensuing paragraph. Perhaps the acc. of relation, "stand back in relation to him," might be understood rather as "you shall distance yourself from him"? See further discussion in Pecchioli Daddi 2003a: 181, n. 476; Hoffner 1971: 32 and n. 9.

469. I would be wary of restoring this paragraph on the basis of the preceding and following ones, since this paragraph in A was omitted and/or altered in the duplicates.

470. B_1 iv 27′: "Further, … of the plant of the garden and field."

471. E iv 16′: "They shall be densely planted."

472. Since E iv 17′ has ḪA.LA-*za nu a-pu-u-un* ḪA.LA *az-zi-*˹*zi*˺-[*kán-du*, while B_1 iv 29′ shows [*ku*?-*i*]*š* ḪA.LA-*az nu a-pu-*[*u-u*]*n* [*az-zi-zi*]-*kán-du*, it may well be that 3-*i*[*š*? here is simply an error for *ku-i*[*š*, in which case one should translate "And that portion which is for the *parzaḫanna*-cattle, [(they shall regularly eat that portion)]."

473. It is entirely uncertain how much text is lost between these last lines of A iv and the few lines of C_2 iv preserved before its colophon. Since C is a first tablet, upon which the entire text up to this point was thus likely contained, the gap is probably not great.

474. The 2nd sg. pronoun and the PN that I would like to read here are highly uncertain, but would be of great interest for the discussion of the initial *Sitz im Leben* and the ensuing development of the text.

475. Pecchioli Daddi (2003a: 192–93) restores "finita" in the break, but it seems quite clear that the composition does not come to an end at this point and that there must have been at least one further tablet. This is suggested both by D, which preserves the beginning of the colophon area after duplicating B_1 iii 35, and by A, which reaches the end

of iv with no colophon at all, perhaps in mid-sentence, having not yet reached this portion of text preserved in C.

No. 18. Instructions and Oath Imposition for Military Commanders (*CTH* 268)

476. Giorgieri's (1995: 243) *ḫa*-[*a-li-ia-at-tal-li-iš* $^{\text{LÚ.MEŠ}}$*a-ú-ri-ia-li-iš* $^{\text{LÚ.MEŠ}}$*u*]*š-ki-iš-ga-tal-li-iš-ša* fits the space tolerably well, even if perhaps just a touch long, as opposed to Otten's (1969: 15) *ḫāliyattalis* alone. Still, since one would have to emend $^{\text{<LÚ.MEŠ>}}$*ḫa*-[…, the restoration is not adopted here.

477. Traces on the photo would seem to suggest a vertical in addition to the traces seen in the copy.

478. All 2nd person verbs and pronouns in this text are 2nd pl.

479. Cf. Košak 1990: 81: "If some[where] on a campaign, [the enemies are rushing before] me, let the front protection be satisfactory, if [they are rushing behind] me, let the rear protection be satisfactory! § If they are rushing on my left and on my right, may I be adequately protected from the flanks!" And Giorgieri 1995: 240: "Se talv[olta] in una spedizione militare [il nemico] mi [viene addosso di fronte], la parte davanti (lett. il petto) sia 'tranquille'! § E se mi attacano da destra (e) da sinistra, io voglio essere 'tranquillo' ai fianchi!" Since *ḫuiyant*- generally refers to a person who is running away, i.e., a fugitive or a deserter, not a person who is attacking, this last phrase is presumably a call for loyal men to fill the gaps left by any who might flee from the king's side. The interpretation suggested here also assumes that *warsiyant*- is derived from *wars-/warsiya*-, "to wipe off, sweep away; make free; clear off," rather than *wars*-, "to calm down."

480. The restoration assumes that the tail of the wedge seen in the copy is to be ignored, as I can see no such trace on the photo.

481. As comparison with the beginning of the following line shows, there is almost certainly insufficient room for Košak's (1990: 79) and Giorgieri's (1995: 239) [*an-tu-uḫ-š*]*a-an* here.

482. Cf. Goedegebuure 2003: 267: "even if he (is) not your enemy, (so) that you do not march against him."

No. 19. Āšḫāpala's Oath regarding an Obligation to Supply Troops (*CTH* 270)

483. Cf. Otten 1960: 122: "Folgendermassen Ašḫapala, fer[ner ihr$^{?}$,] welche bei ihm (seid): Unter E[id soll euch$^{?}$] folgendermassen gel[egt sein:]."

484. Cf. somewhat differently Kassian, Korolëv, and Sidel'tsev 2002: 624–65.

No. 20. Instructions for Priests and Temple Personnel (*CTH* 264)

485. This, of course, is hardly unique to "polytheistic non-salvation religions," as implied by Beal (2002: 11): "In polytheistic non-salvation religions, the relationship between man and god often has a practical character, grounded in mutual benefits to both parties." Obviously, the "monotheistic" (or rather, henotheistic) salvation religions are very much a matter of mutual benefits to both parties, even if most modern versions do not often offer their deity benefits as concrete as food.

486. For a recent thorough discussion of the concept of purity in Hittite culture, see Christiansen 2013.

487. Also the elders of the city of Ura were to undergo a drinking ordeal from a silver rhyton; see Klengel 1965: 226–28; de Martino 1996: 73–79. For recent discussion of the connection with the biblical ordeal, e.g., in Num 5.27, see Giorgieri 2002: 300 and n. 55.

488. Collation of photos suggests that the damaged plene vowel should be read as an *-i-*, not *-e-*; cf. Schwemer (2009: 98), who would read *-⌜a⌝-*. For *isḫini-*, which occurs only in this text (also iii 62), and is assumed to mean "hair" or "beard," see Beal and Collins 1996: 314 n. 37; Oettinger 1985: 300.

489. Sturtevant and Bechtel's (1935: 148) [*ma-a-an* UL] is excluded by the traces before and after the break and is too long. One might expect an adjective for "impure," or similar.

490. Sturtevant and Bechtel (1935: 148), followed by Süel (1985: 22), have [ŠE$_{12}$-*nu-uš*]-*kán-zi* (i.e., **warsanuskanzi*), "propitiate," but *warsanu-* is never attested with *-ske-* or *-za*, and the space available is likely insufficient. Cf. *man=ma tuk* ANA DINGIR-LÌ ZI-*an warsanumini* in KUB 16.39 ii 16, 44, and here in iv 11. Held (1957: 37) suggests [*ša-ak*]-*kán-zi*, "Let any (persons) who know the will and character of the gods prepare them." Klinger (2001a: 74) suggests "versorgen," but without suggesting what should be restored.

491. Accusativus relationis/limitationis, with Neu (1968: 164–65 and n. 11), hence emendation of *-za* not necessary; cf. Kammenhuber 1964: 177; van Brock 1964: 139–41.

492. With Neu (1968: 164–65 and n. 12), who translates "deswegen" for *-at-*, i.e., presumably an accusativus relationis.

493. See *CHD* Š, 57b–58a.

494. The word is a *hapax*, and its meaning is derived from the context of this passage alone. See discussion and refs. in *HED* H, 89.

495. Though translated as a pl. due to the constraints of English, *kainas* is presumably gen. sg., though Kühne (1975: 202), Goetze (1950: 207), and McMahon (1997: 218) all translate it as an acc. pl., for which one would expect *-uš*, and, ideally, $^{\text{LÚ.MEŠ}}$. Puhvel (*HED* K, 12) similarly rejects the pl., opting for the nom. sg., but this ignores the fact that all these terms should probably be in the acc., thus *kainan*; Puhvel's interpretation thus assumes a semigrammatical list, which is a good possibility.

496. *CHD* P, 136b, suggests [DIB-*zi*]-*pát*, "or [they] only [seize] him," which would fit the traces tolerably well (one could even read D[IB-*z*]*i-pát*) and may be the best solution,

but one would expect *-an-zi*, against which the scribe would likely have had no qualms due to space considerations, as shown by his numerous forays into the column divider.

497. *Pace* Groddek (2008a: 185), *a-pé-e-da-ni-pát* in L must be placed at the end of l. 2′, not at the beginning of 3′, where there is insufficient space. Presumably the same would apply to *ša-an-aḫ-zi* and *mar-ri*, which Groddek places at the beginning of 5′ and 6′, respectively.

498. Since there is no gender in the Hittite language, since the Hittite temple personnel included male and female persons, and since the Hittite pantheon was populated with female as well as male gods, I would normally use s/he and him/her when the gender of the person or deity in question is not obvious from the context. It is clear, however, that the author of the present text had male temple personnel (e.g., i 36′–37′) and male deities (e.g., i 65′) in mind when composing his text, and I have therefore used the male pronoun throughout.

499. All 2nd person verbs and pronouns in this text are 2nd pl.

500. Thus the common translation (e.g., *HED* K, 109–10) of the word, which may well be correct, the basic meaning of which is "to cut off; separate"; but since the subject is clearly the personnel, not their hair (which is often understood to be the subject of the following sentence, i.e., *isḫīni-*, attested only here and below, iii 62, with dupl.), perhaps they are to be "cut off," "sequestered" for the period of their service? Cf. the insightful comments by Christiansen (2013: §2, n. 14), who suggests that it might have to do with their being "separated" from impurity.

501. Generally translated simply "When a slave stands before his master" (e.g., Sturtevant and Bechtel 1935: 149; Neu 1968: 9), but such translations ignore the *sarā*, which would seem to imply that the scribe envisioned the servant "standing up," perhaps from a bowing, kneeling or prostrate position. Cf. now *CHD* Š, 226a, "When a slave is standing ready (lit. upright) before his master."

502. The translation follows *CHD* Š, 57b. Cf. Klinger (2001a: 74): "Wenn er *bemüht* ist, wird er (der Herr) keinen Fehler an ihm finden."

503. Neu's (1968: 166, n. 4) interpretation, i.e., ZI-*an*<*-za*>*-ši-ma ta-ma-a-iš ku-iš-ki*, "ihm (ist) der Sinn aber ein anderer," seems less likely, if for no other reason than its need of the emendation.

504. That "either slave or slavewoman" should apply to the slave here is argued by Schwemer (2009: 101–2). The interpretation assumes, of course, that the clause was added as an afterthought, when the scribe was no longer cognizant of the DAM-*ŠU* toward the end of 30′. One might also argue that the list of family members who are to suffer with the offender is a rather stereotyped list, and that its scribe did not think of the fact that the servant would likely not have had servants himself.

505. The usage is singular and uncertain; cf. *CHD* P, 136b; Klinger 2001a: 75: "*gedroht*"; Christiansen 2013: §2, n. 17: "[er]greifen und es *publik machen*, ihm aber nichts antun?"

506. There is certainly no room for Reichardt's (1998: 98) *an*[*da=ši*.

507. Suel's (1985: 32) [*pár-ḫi-eš-ga*]*-aḫ-ḫu-ut* is much too long for the available

space. [*ki-ia-aḫ-ḫu-ut*] would fit the space nicely, is attested with *appan* in the meaning "im Nacken sitzen, bedrängen" (Neu 1968: 87), and sometimes takes *-san* or *-kan*. Cf. *CHD* Š, 223a, restoring [*iy*(*aḫḫut*)], "Go after him (the offender), O god, my lord! And may he defame/disgrace his house." Reichardt's (1998: 71) [*ḫarkand*]*u* would fit the context well, but ignores the]-*aḫḫut* preserved in H i 12′.

508. I.e., the bread, beer, and wine at issue beginning with 60′. Cf. Sturtevant and Bechtel 1935: 152, followed by Süel 1985: 34 and McMahon 1997: 218: [*nu ḫu-u-ma-a*]*n*, "everything"; Kühne 1975: 203, "[Ferner:]"; *CHD* P, 252a.

509. The latter phrase could just as well belong to the rhetorical question, with Reichardt 1998: 98.

510. This phrase is generally understood to indicate that the temple personnel are being warned against taking payment from those who deliver these provisions, e.g., Sturtevant and Bechtel (1935: 151): "and you, temple officials, accept pay from those who give it." However, anyone who would deliver such provisions to the temple personnel would hardly want to give them a payment along with the provisions, but would surely expect to receive a payment for their goods. Thus, both syntactically and contextually it seems that it is the temple officials who are responsible for delivering the provisions to the aforementioned festivals, and that they are being warned not to sell them instead of delivering them.

511. The *sarā tiyanda* is the "set up (things)," i.e., the provisions, as in l. 47′ immediately above, rendering Cotticelli-Kurras' (1991: 151) parenthetical addition superfluous.

512. Cf. below, iv 18–20, as well as *CHD* Š, 229b (and 236b), "you give half of half (var. by halves)"; and *HEG* T/D, 44, "(wenn) ihr es (Halb-)Teil für (Halb-)Teil (weg)gibt."

513. H, probably justifiably, omits.

514. Often restored [*na-at* I-NA] (e.g., *CHD* P, 252a), but from the context it is not necessarily self-explanatory whether "before," "after," "during," or "on the third day" is intended; further, one would certainly need a couple more signs than merely *na-at* I-NA to fill the available space.

515. Mistakenly written -ŠU-NU in each of the three occurrences in this line. Though an unconditioned scribal slip is naturally a possibility, the fact that it recurs might suggest that the scribe was copying from a text version formulated in the 3rd person, a type of variation seen in the several mss. of a number of other instructions as well (see, e.g., No. 17).

516. For considerations on how to restore the line, see Schwemer 2009: 98. The trace at the beginning of the copy of H i 16′ suggesting the head of a vertical, however, appears on the photos to suggest rather a hint of a wedge, which would presumably be the upper element of -*n*]*i*, though one would, if so, like to see a bit of the horizontal as well, which is not the case. Schwemer is certainly correct in his observation that there is no room for *le-e*, and I have therefore placed it at the end of the previous line.

517. Bread in C_1 ii 9 and beer and wine here would seem to refer to the bread, beer, and wine mentioned in A i 60′ and C_1 ii 6, if my restoration in the latter is correct.

518. All recent treatments have assumed a restoration with the verb *sarra-*, translating "The beer and wine is not to [cross] the threshold of the gods" (McMahon 1997: 218), or similar (Goetze 1950: 208, without the benefit of H, which provides the "beer and

wine"; similarly Kühne 1975: 203; Taggar-Cohen 2006: 47, 73, 97–98, 99; Süel 1985: 34–35; Schwemer 2009: 99, with *šarraškitta*). The verb *sarra-*, however, would not be expected to function as an intransitive verb with an inanimate subject (Goetze, McMahon), nor is it attested in the meaning "to cross" with any object other than "oath," or similar (see *CHD* Š, 236–38). Taggar-Cohen's translation avoids these pitfalls, but ignores the fact that the particle *-kan* is unexpected with the translation "to divide" (see *CHD* Š, 230–36), and is unlikely contextually, since the parallels dealing with the threshold (iii 5, 60) clearly indicate that the issue is one of not taking goods belonging to the gods outside of the limits of the temple precinct. The easiest solution is therefore to simply restore *pedatteni* or a similar verb.

519. H i 18′ either omits LUGAL-*aš-ša* or had a different word order.

520. The *-n*]*a* is quite clear, as Schwemer (2009: 99) has seen, excluding Sturtevant and Bechtel's (1935: 152) [*a-pa-a-š*]*a*. One might argue that one would expect *adanna akuwanna*, but the available space is far too short, even for [GU_7-*na* NAG-*n*]*a*.

521. Restoration, with Klinger 1992: 202, supported by *peḫutezzi* in C_1 ii 16.

522. The UN-*aš* would seem to be necessary to fill the available space, and *araḫzenas* is usually used adjectivally (*HED* A, 133–34), as in KUB 7.46 rev. 10 (*araḫzenas* UN-*as*), except in No. 2 iii 16: LÚ*a-ra-a-aḫ-zé-e-ni-ma*.

523. One would like to see the object expressed, but [*na-aš a-ku ku-i-ša-an ku-i*]*š* in C_1 ii 16 would likely be too long for the space available. The trace following the break, however, could just as well be an *-a*]*n* as an *-i*]*š*; collation of photos suggests that the hint of a wedge in the edition (KUB 13.5 ii 16) should be disregarded, and further, that a trace of a horizontal before the vertical is visible, allowing for [*na-aš a-ku ku-i-ša-a*]*n*. Cf. e.g., *HW*2 A, 242b.

524. Compared to the previous and following lines, the space here would seem too short for merely GAM-*an*, as in B_1 ii 5′.

525. Cf. A i 64′, 66′, where *tuel* and *apel* are written plene, which would fill the space here better.

526. The traces in C_1 ii 26 clearly suggest Ḫ]A.⌞LA⌟ rather than]-*at*, as read in other treatments (e.g., *CHD* P, 118a; Schwemer 2009: 99), while *a-pé-el* ZI-*aš* is provided now by M, 7′.

527. Considering A iv 49–50, 72–73, one might consider restoring *šu-me-el* ZI-*ni pé-eš-te-ni*, or similar, yielding "and you give it to yourselves." For another recent attempt at restoring and understanding this passage, though without the benefit of M, see Schwemer 2009: 99. C seems to have omitted the whole of A ii 17″.

528. For the restoration, cf. iv 48 and Schwemer 2009: 99.

529. In B_1 ii 13′ there does not appear to be enough space for NU, while in A there seems to be enough for NU and perhaps another sign or two.

530. *Pace* Hoffner (1996: 756), all three versions preserved at this point show -*KU-NU*; since apparently not one scribe saw fit to amend to -*ŠU-NU*, perhaps one should accept -*KU-NU*, despite the attendant difficulties with the following clause discussed by Hoffner, whether one emends or not. Incidentally, accepting the 2nd person would have the advan-

tage of eliminating the exception to Hoffner's rule concerning the refl. particle in nominal clauses (*GrHL*, §28.32–42).

531. Cf. *CHD* Š/2, 236b: "(You, your wives, your children, and your servants should eat and drink the god's leftovers on the day they are offered or at most over three days. But if a privileged foreigner visits someone, [(if he)] has the privilege of going up to the temple) and he is accustomed to crossing the gods' and the king's threshold, (let [(hi)]m [escort] him up. Let him eat and drink)."

532. For a further recent attempt at understanding these puzzling clauses, see Schwemer 2009: 102. Perhaps one could place the clause boundaries thus: NU.GÁL *ku-it-kán* DINGIR^{MEŠ}*-aš pár-ni an-da* / NU.GÁL *ku-it ku-it* / DINGIR-*LÌ-ni-ma-at e-eš-zi-pát* and translate, "Is not what is in the house of the gods; is not whatever (is there); is it not exclusively for the deity?" Obviously, NU.GÁL would be an unexpected writing in such rhetorical questions, for which one would presumably expect *UL* ... *eszi*. Floreano (2001: 221, n. 40) notes a number of passages in which priests were accused of stealing temple silver and gold.

533. For *-wa-at-* instead of expected *-wa-ra-at-* (in B_1 ii 28′ as well), see *GrHL*, §28.6.

534. Cf. *CHD* P, 125a, where *pedi* is unnecessarily emended to correspond with B_1 ii 31′; and *HED* H, 205–6, *HW*^{2} Ḫ, 385, for examples of adverbial use of *ḫarwasi*.

535. *Pace* Neu 1974: 82, n. 157, there is no need to excise the negation as a scribal error. The receiver of the royal gift is indeed to sell it, but openly before witnesses rather than secretly. The following phrase in 47″ (*QATAMMA=pat*) refers again to the forbidden private sale of the gift. It is also not correct (p. 26) that the receiver of gifts must bring them to the royal gate. Rather, he who catches him selling them clandestinely is supposed to bring the seller to the king's gate, i.e., to trial.

536. For the reading and interpretation, see Schwemer 2009: 99. Unfortunately, the last 2–3 cm of the last 8–9 lines of the paragraph, present when the copy of KUB 13.4 was made, is broken away in the photographs available to me.

537. Photos show a clear *Ù*. The edition misleadingly suggests **nu-uš**, causing all commentators but Goetze (1950: 209), judging from his translation, to opt for *nu-uš*<*-ma-aš*>.

538. Cf., e.g., *CHD* Š, 16a, "Let them seal it provisionally"; Neu's (1980c: 79) spatial interpretation, "vorn siegeln," is of course grammatically valid, but does not take into account the fact that it will be sealed again when the king arrives.

539. This recalls Tudḫaliya IV's promise not to switch festivals in his prayer: "I will not again interchange the spring and [autumn festivals]. [The festivals of spring] I shall perform only in the spring, [and the festivals of] autumn I shall perform only in the autumn" (KBo 12.58+ obv. 7–9; Singer 2002: 108).

540. McMahon's (1997: 219a and n. 10) translation mistakes *uwaya-*, "to cause pity," "jemandem Leid tun" (see Neu 1968: 185–87), for *aus-/uwa-*, "to see"; cf. Klinger (2001a: 77 and n. 64a), who translates "überreden," and *HEG* U, 171.

541. Süel's (1985: 54) ^{d}U[TU-*uš ša-ra-a nu-za ḫu-u-da-ak wa-ar-ap-*]*du*, based on iii 71–72, is far too long for the available space; see already Schwemer 2009: 100.

542. Lit. "taken" (not "gegeben," as in Klinger 2001a: 77), perhaps an error or aberrant writing for "set," *ti-ia-an-te-eš*. A iii 7 shows *da-an-te-eš*, D_1 iv 8′ *ta-a-an-te-eš*. Beal (1992: 253, 261) suggests "hired."

543. Süel (1985: 56), following Sturtevant and Bechtel 1935: 156, reads *a*[*n-d*]*a*, which is quite unlikely, as it would be far too long; *-kán*, on the other hand, fits the traces nicely, and *ses-* is well enough attested with *-kan*.

544. My tentative understanding of ll. 21–23 (see also ns. 548–50) differs from translations suggested thus far; cf. "If anyone has some (official) duty to perform in Hattusa, and (either) a priest (or) an "anointed" is to admit people who are accompanied by guards, he will admit those too" (Goetze 1950: 209); "Whatever rite (there is) for someone up in Ḫattuša: If someone normally admits a priest, an anointing priest, or guards, let him admit them only" (McMahon 1997: 219); similarly *CHD* P, 219b. The translations depend largely on what is restored at the end of l. 22, where Sturtevant and Bechtel (1935: 158) have *ku-i*[*š-ki*], Süel (1985: 58) *ku-i*[*š ku-i*]*š*. On the photos I am unable to see any traces that would indicate what Goetze drew in the edition, and that would suggest or allow an *-i*]*š*, and thus the *ku-i*[*š-ša-aš*] suggested here. This interpretation has the advantage of taking the nom. pl. comm. *ḫaliyattalles* at face value, whereas one would expect acc. *ḫalliyattallus*, e.g., for McMahon's translation. For *mān* alone, i.e., without the succeeding *mān*(s), in the sense of "whether … or …," cf. iii 48–49, below; *CHD* L–N, 158–59; Taggar-Cohen 2006: 57, 78; Beal 1992: 253; *HEG* T/D, 196.

545. Lit. "But further, (those) who are priests: he who shall be$^{\text{(imp.)}}$ of the gate of the temple, he must guard the temple." For considerations on the odd sentence structure and *ku-iš-ša* vs. *ku-iš* ŠA, see Schwemer 2009: 102–3.

546. Lit., "In whatever watch an offense occurs, he shall die," whereby the subject of the main clause has no antecedent in the dependent clause.

547. Lit. "he shall not turn/spin." While the import of this phrase is presumably similar to those in i 59′ (EGIR-*pa waḫnumar=si le ēszi*) and ii 51″ (*nu=smas* EGIR-*pa waḫnumar le=pat ēszi*), the lack of *appa*, the addition of *kan* and the med.-pass. give one pause. While at least the literal sense of the two former passages seems clear enough, "turning back," perhaps "revision," the precise sense of the present locution is not entirely certain; cf. Neu 1968: 197, "Ausflüchte machen; versuchen, sich aus der Affäre ziehen."

548. More literally, "But for whom (there is) some rite up in Ḫattusa, be he a priest, an anointed one (or) the watchmen, he w[ho] normally lets [them] in, he shall let only them in."

549. Lit. "If for anyone there is (the matter of) a guard," assuming that one should restore ^{LÚ}*ḫa-li-*⌈*ia-at*⌉*-tal-*[*la-aš*]. Schwemer (2009: 103–4) suggests restoring an otherwise unattested abstractum ^{LÚ}*ḫa-li-*⌈*ia-at*⌉*-tal-*[*la-tar*], "watch," "watch-duty." Also syntactically possible, with Klinger (2001a: 78), is "Wenn ein Wächter für irgendjemand dabei ist, dann muß er auch auf Wache gehen," which, however, would imply that the bodyguard of any high-ranking person who goes to the temple would have to serve guard duty there, which cannot be considered likely; similarly Cotticelli-Kurras 1991: 68.

550. The translation in *CHD* P, 226b, "If someone has an escort, he shall surely go into the courtyard," mistakes *ḫāli*, "watch," for *ḫila-*, "courtyard." Schwemer (2009: 103)

suggests "(Betreffs) der Regel, die für jemanden in Ḫattuša droben gilt: Wenn, wer auch immer es ist, seit jeher einen SANGA-Priester (oder) einen GUDU-Priester als *ḫaliyattalla*-Wachen einteilt (wörtl: "losläßt"), soll er (sie) auf jeden Fall auch weiterhin einteilen."

551. Perhaps equally likely, "and the temple personnel see those (enemies$^{?}$)," whereby the change from acc. sg. *-an* at the beginning of l. 28 to the acc. pl. *apūs* here would be only slightly disconcerting. In no case can *apūs* be taken as the acc. sg., as Beal (1992: 253) does.

552. Presumably to be read as such, with Neu 1968: 128 and Schwemer 2009: 100, though *namma* would largely overlap with *anda=ma* semantically and does not occur as such elsewhere in the text.

553. Süel's (1985: 60) restoration with [*ma-a-a*]*n* x[ ]-*tuh*-... is excluded by the traces; similarly Neu 1968: 129, n. 10. Might one think of *am*$^{!}$(TAḪ)-*me-ia-an-za*? Perhaps GIBIL$^{!}$~*ia-an-za*?

554. Cf. Neu 1968: 128–29 and n. 12; *CHD* L–N, 443b–45a.

555. Though traces are indeed visible here, as noted by Schwemer (2009: 100), they do not seem especially amenable to the suggested (e.g., Süel 1985: 62) *nam-ma*. [EGI]R-[*a*]*n* might be a possibility, though perhaps just slightly long.

556. For extensive discussion of *sannapi*, a *hapax*, see *CHD* Š, 158–59.

557. Schwemer (2009: 100) justifiably wonders if the sign trace should simply be ignored. *HED* A, 359, opts for *ma*.

558. Contra Haas (2004: 221), there is no reason to assume that this punishment has anything to do with a magical rite that is to be understood as a sort of rain dance, and neither are there any grounds to believe that it has any connection with the scene from the KI.LAM festival in which two entertainers sit naked in a bathtub while liquids are poured over them.

559. Klinger (2001a: 79) suggests "Der Sinn der Götter soll kein Fehl an euch finden."

560. Following *e-eš-du* in KUB 13.6 iii 14′ the copyist has assumed that only one empty line (i.e., 15′ in the copy) should be expected, but two lines (i.e., 15′–16′) should be assumed before *ša*]-*li-i*[*k*- in 17′$^{!}$, so that these last 3 lines of KUB 13.6 iii should be numbered 17′$^{!}$–19′$^{!}$.

561. Süel's (1985: 70) restoration, SA[L]-*i̤* [GAM-*an š*]*e*-[*e*]*š*-[*d*]*u*, does not fit the traces.

562. B seems likely to have omitted some of A iii 72–73.

563. Dupl. I, 6′ (see Lorenz 2010: 263) has *še-eš-z*]*i a-pu*-[*u-un-ma-kán*, providing a demonstrative for which there is no space here in A; neither is there space for what would seem to be a *-ma-* in B_1 iii 25′,]-⸢*ma*$^{?}$⸣-*ká*[*n*.

564. The locution *appan damass-* is unique. There are two cases of *appa damass-* in KUB 44.61 rev. 25′ (with *na-an*) (Burde 1974: 20–21) and No. 4 i 6 (*nu-za-kán*), neither of which seem to be of any help here.

565. Though I was unable to collate these signs in A, as the lower left corner of col.

iii is missing in the photos available to me, there is surely no reason to retain Sturtevant and Bechtel's (1935: 162) [*tá*]*k*-[*k*]*u* in A iii 82 in the light of the clear *na-an* in B_1 iii 31′ (i.e., FHL 100, 7′), as do Taggar-Cohen (2006: 63, 82, 105) and *CHD* Š, 157b; see already Schwemer 2009: 100.

566. For a suggested restoration, see Schwemer 2009: 100.

567. It seems that enough of the surface is preserved here to make unlikely Süel's (1985: 74) ZI-*ni*.

568. Cf. iv 39.

569. Cf. Melchert 1977: No. 126; *CHD* L–N, 422a.

570. Understanding the verb as *uwaya*-, "to cause pity," eliminates the need to emend -*ta*, "to you," to -*si* "to him," as Klinger (2001a: 79) is forced to do; see also n. 540, above, and Zeilfelder (2004: 665), who translates "er gekommen ist," taking *uwaitta* as the 3rd person pret. of *uwa*-, "to come," apparently ignoring -*ta*.

571. For the collation of -*ḫi*, see *CHD* L–N, 164a.

572. Generally read [KISLA]Ḫ^{MEŠ}-*aš* (e.g., Taggar-Cohen, 2006: 65; Klinger 2001a: 80), which does not fit the traces, and translated "threshing floor," which makes little sense in the context. ⌞ÉSAG⌟ fits the traces quite nicely, and this may have been what led Goetze (1950: 210) to translate "magazines."

573. The traces visible on the photograph suggest a perfectly good *uš*-; cf. *CHD* L–N, 286b.

574. While Goetze (1950: 210) and McMahon (1997: 221) understood -*smas* as a pl. acc., for which one would rather expect -*at*, it is clear that it serves here as a reflexive; cf. -*za* ... *anda peda*- below, iv 70, and in KUB 13.35+KBo 16.62 iv 20–21 (for which see *CHD* P, 297b).

575. Alternatively one could emend *šu-me-el-*<*ša*>*-ma-aš-kán* and translate, "they shall take all of your grain away from you."

576. Unless a scribal error is to be assumed, the form *tāisteni* can hardly be derived from *taya*-, "to steal" (as assumed by Goetze and McMahon, for which one would expect *taya(i)tteni*), from *da*-, "to take" (for which one expects *datteni*), or from *taistai*-, "to load" (for which one would expect *taista(i)tteni*), whereby one would not expect the allomorph -*steni* for the verbs of the *mi*-conjugation. It must therefore come from *dai*-, "to place," despite the unexpected *ta*-, as A. Kloekhorst (pers. comm.) kindly clarified for me. If so, perhaps one is to understand that the personnel is being warned against killing or otherwise disposing of and profiting from the valuable plough and threshing oxen, which are to be used for labor instead of sacrifice, and then presenting it (or what might remain of it or perhaps the proceeds from its sale) to the deities as if it had somehow died by accident or disappeared in some other way. Support for this interpretation can perhaps be seen in the similarly formulated iv 75, where *tarnummen* is found rather than *taisteni*.

577. Contra other translations, the repeated "or" can hardly belong to the quoted speech itself, but must rather belong to the background narrative.

578. In previous treatments this locution here and in §§18′ and 19′ has not been fur-

ther discussed, and the translations imply, "if it (i.e., the crime) does not become known." It seems unlikely, however, that the writer would be requiring a person who has committed a crime that has not been discovered to voluntarily turn himself in. Further, if the thief would come forward and proclaim his guilt, then there would be no need for the drink ordeal, intended to distinguish the guilty from the innocent, which follows explicitly in §§18′ and 19′, implicitly here in §17′. Therefore it seems more likely that the drink ordeal in the presence of the deity is to be conducted if and when it has not yet been discovered *who* has committed the crime, the aim of the ordeal being to identify the culprit (cf. Pecchioli Daddi 2004: 455–56; van den Hout 2003b: 129). See now similarly, Schwemer 2009: 104.

579. On Akk. *ḫakkurrāte*, see Hoffner (2004a), who suggests "umbilical cord."

580. For a "milk" rather than a "cup" festival, see Güterbock 1967: 141–42; *CHD* Š, 202.

581. As Schwemer (2009: 105) points out, only the relative sentence is explicit, the self-curse remaining implicit, as is often the case, e.g., in the treaties. For the full formulation, see e.g., below, ll. 71–77.

582. Generally translated "the rhyton of the god of life" (*BIBRÛ* DINGIR-*LI* ZI-*TI*), e.g., by McMahon (1997: 221) and Marazzi (2010: 207–8), but it seems more likely that ZI is used here as it is throughout the rest of the text in reference to the essence, spirit, or self of the deity; see already Giorgieri 2002: 319 and n. 54 and cf. in a similar vein Klinger 2001a: 81.

583. Despite *nasma=wa=nnas=an* in the following line, this is presumably to be accepted as is and parsed *nu=war=an=nas=an*; for discussion and attestations of the doubled acc. enclitic pronoun before and after an enclitic d.l. personal pronoun, see Christiansen 2006: 102; *GrHL*, §30.19; Sidel'tsev 2010, 2011a, 2011b, in press a, in press b. Reichardt's (1998: 10) *nu=war=an=nas=san* must be considered unlikely, *inter alia*, because *pai-* would not be expected to take *-san*.

584. B_1 iv 34′ provides the expected ≮*zu-u-wa-aš*.

NOTES TO CHAPTER THREE

NO. 21. INSTRUCTIONS FOR SUPERVISORS (*CTH* 266)

1. Presumably to be understood as LÚ^{MEŠ}=(*s*)*mas*, as comparison with *parnas*=(*s*)*mas* in l. 10′ suggests.

2. Merely *nu* would seem somewhat too short to fill the gap, but none of the parallel clauses suggests that anything else should be added.

3. Presumably potential *man=asta* (cf. iii$^?$ 16′), as there seems to be too little space for [*ma-a-n*]*a-*, whereby the writing *-aš-da* would be extremely rare, if not unique.

4. One would expect either [$^{\text{LÚ.MEŠ}}$]*ḫattalwalles*, "guards of the gate," or [^{GIŠ}] *ḫattalwallas*, gen., "(men of) the door-bolt," i.e., "guards of the gate."

5. Riemschneider (1965: 337–38) and Beal (1988: 284) assume É-*ia*, but the gen. would likely be expressed either with É-*TI* or É-*aš*.

6. *GrHL*, 247, translates the verb as a 3rd sg. pres., but the *memi* in l. 18′ suggests that *isḫāi* here and *ḫalzāi* in 17′ are likely to be taken as 2nd sg. imp. forms as well.

No. 22. Instructions of Suppiluliuma I for the Military and a Corresponding Oath (*CTH* 253)

7. One would expect *ku-i*[*š*, of course, but the traces do not seem to suggest such.

8. Sidel'tsev (2008: 690) reasonably suggests *paḫḫsnutten*, "you shall protect."

9. Exactly where the quoted speech begins and ends can no longer be ascertained.

10. Perhaps either *tuz*]*zis*, "the entire army" (Laroche 1957: 125), or *ḫantezzis appez*]*zis*, "everyone, of highest and lowest (rank)" (del Monte 1975a: 134, n. 21).

11. Or perhaps *ka*[*t-ta*], as restored by Laroche (1957: 125) and others?

12. Or perhaps *tuliya*, "to assembly," with Giorgieri (1995: 255).

13. For the restoration of this paragraph cf. KUB 21.46 i 6–10 (No. 23), KUB 31.44 i 25–29 (No. 14.1); KUB 26.24 i 16′–21′ (No. 14.3.A); KUB 26.11 i 1′–6′ (No. 10).

14. Parallel passages would suggest [^{d}UTU *ŠA-ME-E* ^{d}UTU ^{URU}*A.RI.I*]*N.NA* / [^{d}10 *ŠA-ME-E* ^{d}10 ^{URU}*ḪA.AT.TI* $^{GUD/d}$*Š*]*E.*⸤*E*⸣*.RI* / [$^{GUD/d}$*ḪUR.RI* …, or similar (e.g., Giorgieri 1995: 255).

15. Freu (2007b: 209) opts for "aux princesses," which would be unprecedented as far as I am aware.

No. 23. Oath of the Men of Ḫattusa to Ḫattusili III and Pudu-Ḫepa (*CTH* 254)

16. If indeed an -*in*-, then a very long one.

17. For an attempt at more extensive restorations of this paragraph, based largely on No. 22 (KUB 26.57 i 1′–7′), cf. Giorgieri (1995: 254–58, 261–67).

18. For the reconstruction of the paragraph cf. No. 14 (1 i 25–30, 3.A i 16′–21′); No. 22 (KUB 26.57 i 8′–13′); Giorgieri (1995: 254–58, 261–67).

No. 24. Instructions for Priests and Diviners (*CTH* 275)

19. Certainly not *iš-ḫi-ú-u*[*l*], as read by Haas (1970: 130).

20. Also possible would be *pí*[*d-da-iš-ke-ez-zi*], "And the daily bread which His Majesty b[rings] for the deity."

NO. 25. INSTRUCTIONS FOR THE UKU.UŠ-TROOPS (*CTH* 267)

21. Cf. the writings with *-ket₉-* vs. *-ke-et-* in ll. 6′ and 7′, the phonetic writing *tuzit* in 11′ and the variation between *-teni* and *-tani* in 10′, 12′, and 16′, all far too little for any certainty.

22. Though often translated "heavily armed soldiers," Beal (1992: 51–52 and n. 197) shows clearly that this is no more than a guess and that it remains unclear what subgroup of soldiers they would have been.

23. Cf., e.g., *ḫu-up-pí-da-nu-e-eš* PA$_5$$^{HI.A}$-*ša* in No. 17 B iii 58′ and Beal's (1992: 44, n. 172) comments.

24. Beal's (1992: 43, n. 172) PA$_5$.ḪI.[A-*š*]*a* can be excluded on the basis of the photos.

25. Clearly so rather than Beal's (1992: 43, n. 172) *kuitki*.

26. Beal's (1992: 43, n. 172) and Rosi's (1984: 113) UKU.UŠ is an error, as UŠ is seen neither in the copy nor on the photos.

27. Or]^{MEŠ}-*ša*, or even]^{MEŠ} *ŠA*.

28. Or, in light of the following "but now," perhaps "You$^{(pl.)}$ indeed [...]-ed."

NO. 26. TUDḪALIYA IV'S INSTRUCTIONS AND LOYALTY OATH IMPOSITION FOR LORDS, PRINCES, AND COURTIERS (*CTH* 255.1)

29. A *-ma-* is also possible.

30. Von Schuler's (1957: 23) [*a-wa-an* GAM] and alternative suggestion [*IŠ-TU* MUNUS.LUGAL] would both be far too long for the available space, as would even the considerably shorter [*ŠA* MUNUS.LUGA]L, for which cf. §24″, 16.

31. Since a 3rd sg. verb here would normally refer anaphorically to "some brother" or "some lord" in the preceding clause, one might want to read *ša-ak-ti₄*(DI), "you know." This, however, would be extremely unusual graphically and would introduce an odd, though not entirely unprecedented, switch from the 2nd sg. to 3rd sg. *memai* in the following clause.

32. Other treatments have not emended *-smas*, but comparison with §3′, 20′–21′ and §7′, 39′ show that the (enclitic pronoun functioning as the) reflexive is to be expected.

33. All 2nd person verbs and pronouns in this text are 2nd plural unless otherwise indicated.

34. An "if" must occasionally be added to the translation, as its previous occurrence remains in force, even when the scribes often do not bother to repeat it in every clause.

35. For this sentence as a rhetorical question, see Otten 1957–58: 389; Melchert 1985: 186; cf. Goedegebuure 2003: 237. The passage is thoroughly misunderstood by Held (1957: 35).

36. Cf. *CHD* Š, 24a, "... someone 'holds' (i.e., entertains) with another an evil (plan) against ...."

37. Cf. *CHD* P, 152b, "But in opposition to the oath ... he does not tell (it)."

38. The translation of *apadda=ia* as "this too" in *CHD* L–N, 65b, suggests that the editors have understood it as the dem. pron. *apat* with a doubly expressed "and," but this must be considered unlikely. Cf. *GrHL* §8.9 and 154, n. 7.

39. There are several ways one could restore the ends of these lines, e.g., with a 2nd pl. imp. at the end of 4′ and 5′ and a 3rd d.l. sg. rather than 2nd at the end of 6′; cf. Goedegebuure 2003: 192, 324–25, where, incidentally, the *-ta* at the end of 6′ is assumed to be preserved instead of restored.

40. For the restorations of *-kan*, cf. iii 11–12 (though there with the acc.).

41. The IN is either damaged or partly erased or both, allowing the alternative reading *-te-ni*, favored, e.g., by Starke (1996: 176), Goedegebuure (2003: 184, 192, 311), and del Monte (1980: 114). Since the 2nd pl. pres. is always written *-te-ni* in this text, the 2nd pl. pret. (and imp.) always with *-tén*, the scribe was clearly thinking of the former at least as far as his *-te*.

42. Because of the many uncertainties involved, I have not made extensive restorations in the main treatment, but I suspect that something like the following would have been present: (37′)*na[m?-ma-i]a-za* UN-*an* *ŠA MA-ME-TI* *le-e k[i?-iš?]-⸢tu?⸣-[ma?-ri?]* (38′)*a[n-na-za n]am-ma* *PA-NI A-BI* ^{d}UTU-*ŠI* *ku-it* *N[I-ÌŠ]* DINGIR-*LÌ* GAM] (39′)*t[i-ia-a]t-tén nu-za* EN LUGAL 1-*aš* 1-*e-da-[ni]* (40′)*l[i-in-ga-nu-uš]-ke-et ki-nu-un-˻ma˼-a[t?-kán?]* (iii 1)*le-⸢e⸣ [šar-ri-ia-zi k]u?-⸢iš?⸣-k[i?]* (2)*ku-i[š-m]a-at* DÙ-*zi na-at* GAM-*an* *N[I-ÌŠ]* DINGIR-*LÌ* GAR-*ru*], "An[d furth]er, you shall not p[ledge alle]gi[ance] (to anyone else). [Mo]reover, because you fo[rmerly] s[wor]e an [oat]h before the father of My Majesty, and he s[wore] each of you in as one lord of the king; now, then, no on[e shall transgress it. Wh]oev[er] does it, though, then it [shall be placed] under the o[ath]." The restoration at the beginning of 37′ seems quite likely, even if what seems like the head of a vertical on the photo does not seem to be placed where one would expect. *kistumari* at the end of the line is a reasonable assumption when one compares the following paragraph, though the 2nd pres. pl. is otherwise not attested (cf. Starke 1996: 164, n. 104, *le-e [k]u-[iš-ki]* D[Ù-*zi*]); some traces on the edge would fit a *-tu-* rather well, but nothing further is visible. Though speculative, *annaz* fits the space, traces, and context very well. At the end of 38′ the signs would bleed significantly over the edge, where no clear traces are now visible. Quite likely is *tiyatten*, as it fits the space, traces, and context very well, while 1-*edani* is essentially certain. Less certain is *linganusket*, since it would fit the space tolerably well, though perhaps a touch short, and since the traces before the break would seem either to point toward something else or to an early form of *li-*, which one would not expect in such a late text that is presumably not dependent on an earlier version. The restorations of the end of 40′ and of iii 1 are entirely speculative.

43. Reichardt's (1998: 26) faulty translation stems from a transliteration that omits *Ú-UL*.

44. *Pace CHD* L–N, 166a, *ḫantezi aurius* is surely to be translated as such, not "... in the first place ... border points ..."; cf., e.g., *HED* A, 232–34; *HW*² Ḫ, 177a. *Pace* Klinger (1998: 107), it is clear that this passage demonstrates that Azzi, the Kaska, and Lukka were independent of and not on especially good terms with Ḫatti at this time.

45. For varying interpretations of *arrusa*, cf. *HW*² A, 355, "Verrat," *HED* A, 182–83, "secession"; *GrHL*, §26.7, "defect"; *CHD* P, 40a; Š, 166b.

46. Presumably "you" is intended (see, e.g., Starke 1996: 165, n. 108), but the scribe confused this curse formula with those, such as at the end of the previous paragraph, which are formulated in the third person and therefore correctly end with "for him."

47. Intended is, it seems, "and he (the runaway) divulges the matter (of his fall and escape) to (one of) you, and he acclaims you, though he (the runaway) denigrates My Majesty." Lit. "And he places that one to the right, though he places My Majesty to the left," employing the left=bad, right=good symbolic common in so many cultures, including the Hittite. Cf. Goedegebuure 2003: 274 and Starke 1996: 165, n. 108, with different interpretations.

48. The parenthetical additions are an attempt to render comprehensible these indicative past tense clauses, lit. "Further, that which you have done (or are doing; see n. 41): You have united all the rebel lands into one, and you have made the enemy lands strong, but you have made the lands of Ḫattusa weak." For further recent attempts, see Starke 1996: 176 and n. 153; d'Alfonso 2006a: 345.

49. Neu (1968: 96) restored -[*ik-ki*] here, and in fact one can see traces of what might have been an -*ik*- on photos of the edge (see also Starke 1996: 164, n. 105), while the -*ki* would have been on the curve onto the obv., which is not visible on the photos available to me.

50. Possibilities would be (1) ŠÀ.BAL.BAL, to which the traces on the edge are quite amenable, but this seems to be attested only in royal genealogies, without ḪI.A, while in this text NUMUN is always used; and (2) perhaps ŠÀ É.LUGAL (with a free-standing gen.) in some fashion; cf. KUB 21.19+ i 20, KUB 14.7 i 16′ (*CTH* 383, Prayer of Ḫattusili III and Pudu-Ḫepa to the Sun Goddess of Arinna; Sürenhagen 1981: 88, 90; Singer 2002: 98). Starke's (1996: 164, n. 106) reading fails for lack of space and the final traces, which do not seem amenable to -*di*.

51. Photos show a clear -*ki* as opposed to the -*di* in the copy.

52. The -*ra*- is perfectly clear on the photos (see already Starke 1996: 164, n. 106), though inexplicably neglected by the copyists of both KUB 26.12 and KUB 21.42. The -*aš*, on the other hand is not at all clear, but could have been obliterated by the damage right behind -*ra*-, which, however, is too small to cover an -*at*, which would allow "It (the situation) has become bad."

53. This has hitherto been read *maniyaḫ* and assumed to be a 2nd sg. imp., and indeed the copy shows nothing more than -*ia-aḫ* on the edge. The following traces have presumably been ignored because they collide with the last two signs of *wa-at-ku-wa-an-za* of ii 23′. While it is admittedly rather difficult to extricate one sign from the other, it is clear that not all the traces at this point can be attributed to -*an-za*. And if one examines all traces superfluous to the -*an-za*, one sees a nearly complete -*zi*.

54. Though it is difficult to be certain, the traces would seem more amenable to LUGAL-*i* than to ᵈUTU-*ŠI*, assumed, e.g., by *CHD* Š, 63a.

55. The break is far too short for von Schuler's (1957: 27) [*na-an ku-iš-k*]*i* or the

[*na-an ta-ma-i*]*š* found in *CHD* P, 372b and Š, 63a. The restoration here would provide all the expected elements of the sentence, but might also be just a touch too long, so that one might prefer [*ku-iš-k*]*i* alone, which would fit well, as would *ta-ma-iš* alone. Cf. i 3′, 6′.

56. The traces would also allow, e.g., *m*[*a-a-a*]*n-kán*, with von Schuler (1957: 27), or *n*[*am-m*]*a-kán*.

57. For *lala-/memiya- walḫnu-*, see Hoffner 1997b: 195–96.

58. Lit. "But to whomever he says it he does not denounce him, …."

59. For conflicting views on the meaning of *mu'irtu*, cf. *CAD* M/II, 180 and *CHD* L–N, 167a; Š, 4b–5a, "population, people, subjects"; *AHw*, 669a, "Untergebene(r)?"; *HHw*, 320, "Verwalter."

60. Presumably the lord or prince.

61. Or perhaps "You are called good, …"? Cf. Neu 1968: 36; Kühne and Otten 1971: 43; *CHD* L–N, 167a, where a close parallel from the treaty with Šaušgamuwa can be found. The reading *maniyaḫzi* (see above, n. 53) hardly solves the difficulties with this challenging passage, leaving unclear who is the subject and who is the object. An alternative translation would be, "but he is delivering His Majesty to perdition," but who exactly would be affecting the king this way would remain unclear, and it would not result in the negative assessment of the king which the addressees are to shun. A further possibility would perhaps be, "But My Majesty is delivering (him) to perdition," which could yield the negative with regard to the king, but neither alternative would seem amenable to the obvious parallel from the treaty. Naturally, any of the clauses could be understood as a rhetorical question as well. Thus, e.g., "Can you call yourself good, while His Majesty is administering poorly?"

62. The enclitic pronoun in 22 must assumedly resume *kuinki*, the "someone" who the king had promoted or favored. This is perhaps a mental slip on the part of the scribe, as presumably the addressee of the passage is being warned against calling the good deed of the king his own, for which one would expect *-at-* or *apāt*, not against calling the person who is promoted his own goodness, which would be quite difficult to understand. If not, then one would presumably have to translate, "and you call him your own good (doing)," whereby *assul-* is otherwise not attested in such usage. Cf., e.g., Starke 1996: 165, n. 109.

63. For the corrections, see, *inter alia*, Kammenhuber 1965: 189–90; Carruba 1964: 408, n. 2; Goetze 1959: 68a–b; *CHD* P, 126a.

64. The scribes were certainly having their difficulties with this passage. Fortunately, C becomes available at this point, though it too seems to show some confusion. First, it is clear that the scribe of A inadvertently omitted *memai* at the end of 13, assured by its inclusion in C i 3. Perhaps the fact that his *tameda* ends right at the beginning of *memai* in iii 11 played a role in the slip. Second, the conjunction and enclitic seem to have been confused as well, as shown at least by the *-at* written over or with other sign traces. Conceivably one could simply read *na-at*! and translate "but he twists the words of the king, and he <(tells)> them to someone else," but these appear to be two different transgressions and would better be connected with "or." See also the following footnote.

65. One could perhaps translate "or he speaks of the king's person in order to di-

vulge" (similarly Starke 1996: 171; Zeilfelder 2001b: 403–4), but this would be a very odd construction. In C i 4 one finds *pa-ra*]-⸢*a*⸣ *me-mi-ia-wa-an-*⸢*zi*[!] *e*[!]⸣*-ep-z*[*i*], whereby the rather common scribal error of writing *-an-še* rather than *-an-zi* is seen. The phrase is clearly preferable to *memiyawanzi memai*. Interestingly, the scribe of A seems to have erased *e-ep-zi* at the beginning of 15, as the sign traces still visible are quite amenable to such, and replaced it with *me-ma-i*.

66. The photos show an obvious -TU_4 rather than the clear -TI in the copy.

67. Generally emended to *ša-ku-wa-aš-ša-ra-*<*aš*> and related to the MUNUS.LUGAL (e.g., *CHD* Š, 62a), i.e., "born of a 'full' Great Queen," which is perhaps possible. However, while one might well qualify the Great King's wives according to various grades, one would hardly qualify the "Great Queen" as "full; entirely legitimate" vis-à-vis "not full; not entirely legitimate"; and further, the elliptical parallel passages (e.g., above, §§4′, 5′, 9″) would seem to suggest that it should relate to the brothers, in which case one would expect *ša-ku-wa-aš-ša-re-eš*. See also n. 73.

68. Von Schuler's (1957: 28) [*i-i*]*a-an* is a fair bit too long, and one sees no sign of a broken final vertical.

69. Cf. l. 44, below.

70. Both von Schuler's (1957: 29) [*tu-ek-k*]*i-i*, followed, e.g., in *CHD* Š, 101b, and Goetze's [*ša-aš-t*]*a-i* (cf. Kammenhuber 1965: 191, n. 50) are disallowed by the traces; the latter is also rather daring in light of the vastly more common NÍ.TE^{MEŠ}-ŠÚ just three lines later. (Goetze's [1933: 264] comment in his treatment of the Annals of Mursili is presumably based on this passage.) This text otherwise uses NÍ.TE (A iv 14) or NÍ.TE^{MEŠ}-ŠÚ (A iv 37, B iv 5′), while in No. 27 NÍ.TE-ŠU is found (No. 27, A iii 23, B ii 3′, C i 7′). NÍ.TE-*i* alone here would be too short (cf. van den Hout 1998: 2, n. 5), and TEs in this text have the wedges, not the horizontals. The traces exclude Š]Ú, leaving perhaps [NÍ.TE-Š]U-*i* as the most likely restoration. That said, the reading -Š]U is also less than entirely satisfactory, as one would expect to see traces of another horizontal or two.

71. Tischler's (*HEG* T/D, 382) [*ḫa-an*]*-da* and Goetze's (1959: 68b) [IGI-*an*]*-da*, followed, e.g., by *CHD* L–N, 198b, are far too short. Perhaps [*a-pé-e*]*-da*, "for that reason; to that end."

72. There is no room for Goedegebuure's (2003: 263) *nu* here.

73. Lit. "Brothers of My Majesty who are full of the queen born afterwards" (see also n. 67). Extant treatments tend to ignore *awan katta* (e.g., *CHD* Š, 62a; *HED* H, 214; *HW*[2] Ḫ, 466b; *GrHL*, §16.73). As J. Hazenbos has kindly pointed out to me, however, the preverb is presumably to be understood as temporal rather than local, as in i 19′, 36′ and iv 19; cf. also iv 25. D'Alfonso's (2006a: 337) transliteration and translation require several emendations.

74. Unless *kuēl* and *linganuzi*, both sg., treat the brothers as a collective, one must assume that the passage envisions a third party, whose oath is imposed upon the addressees for the brothers. Cf. similarly in i 16′–17′.

75. The lines of this paragraph up until this point would seem to cut the flow of the clauses before and after them.

76. The passage is certainly corrupt. The emendations suggested here represent one possible way out of the mess. For other recent attempts to elucidate the text, see Starke 1996: 166, n. 113; Dardano 2005: 111.

77. For *I*[!]-*DE* instead of *tardi*, see Otten (1957–58: 389). As *sakk-* does not seem to be otherwise attested with *awan katta*, one suspects that *awan katta* here may be a further scribal error, probably conditioned by the several cases of such in the surrounding clauses. For two attestations of *sakk-* with *kattan*, see *CHD* Š, 28a, "to foresee"; cf. *HEG* T/D, 141, "im geheimen kennt."

78. Or "some prince, a brother of the king."

79. For discussion of *tisḫantes*, see *HEG* T/D, 381–82. Here in A there is a significant space between the *-ḫa* and the *-an*, while there is less space in B iv 3′, in which manuscript the spacing between words in general is minimal.

80. With, e.g., van den Hout (1998: 2, n. 5) and Klinger (2001b: 284, n. 35), this treatment understands the body or person of the king in this and related passages in a literal sense, and therefore rejects Starke's interpretation (1996: 172), according to which it would represent the Hittite state embodied in the king.

81. On the basis of this passage a meaning "to defect, commit treason" has been assumed for *ḫarpiya-* (*HW*[2] Ḫ, 336a sub III; *EDHIL*, 311; cf. *HED* H, 176), which otherwise means "to heap up, accumulate; assemble; support/join (someone)." The meaning "to defect," however, depends entirely on the restoration of the end of l. 45 here, where one could just as easily restore, e.g., *tamēdani*, "to another," or *šumē/āš*, "to you." (In fact, the traces visible on the photographs at the end of B iv 14′ might allow a reading *š*[*u*-, but this would have to be collated on the original.) Thus, instead of "[(Schon) früher?] (46) bin ich in [gut]er Gesinnung nicht abtrünnig geworden, und [auch in Zukunft?] (47) werde ich nicht abtrünnig werden" (*HW*[2] Ḫ, 336a sub III), one could, e.g., translate "I have not (ever) supported [another/you] in comradery, [but/and] I will not support the [king/you] (now)," or the like. Melchert's (2010) recent assumption that the word originally included the nuance "separate oneself from something" in addition to "join something else" does not convince. In the two cases (p. 180) said to include the separative element, the simple "join something else" seems entirely sufficient.

82. Von Schuler's (1957: 29) and Goetze's (1959: 69) ḪUL-*lu* is far too long for the space available. At the end of B iv 17′ the traces would allow or suggest a *š*[*A*, which would fit the space and context, as far as preserved, well enough.

83. For the restoration, cf. ii 8′–9′.

84. Since each line here seems to finish sensibly with the preserved signs, and since the traces to the right seem to begin at least a new clause, it seems likely that the text of the left edge was divided into two columns, for which cf., e.g., KUB 5.1.

85. Or "(If) the king has sen[t] you out …," parsing LUGAL=*(s)mas*.

No. 27. Tudḫaliya IV's Instructions and Oath Imposition for Courtiers (*CTH* 255.2)

86. It is not necessarily the case that the passage is speaking of the king's own women, i.e., his harem (see already Starke 1996: 167, n. 114). The focus of these paragraphs seems not to be keeping men away from the king's women so that any children born of them are guaranteed to be his own, but rather nipping in the bud any relationship to a woman who might serve as an inside, clandestine source from which a LÚ SAG might obtain privileged information. This one might conclude from the stipulation "i]f anyone (of you) has known any one (of them), (33)[(b)u]t he does not [(now)] break it off with [he]r …"; i.e., it is not necessarily a problem if a LÚ SAG has up until his acceptance into the inner workings of the royal administration had a palace woman as a lover, as long as he breaks it off at that point. This does not sound like a stipulation concerning a harem.

87. Peled (in press), who maintains that the LÚ^{MEŠ} SAG would have been eunuchs, admits that the eunuchs would have been sexually active, referring to the possibility that they might have had their testicles removed but not their penises. Even apart from the entirely ad hoc nature of the speculation and the complete lack of any evidence for such a claim, it seems unlikely in the extreme that men castrated in this way would be entrusted with securing the exclusiveness of the harem, as Peled suggests, if they nonetheless had to be prevented with texts such as the present one from having sexual relations with the women of the harem.

88. The traces appear to suggest, purely graphically, AN DI/KI LU LA/AT/ŠU/I[A] or similar, and the only sense I can make out of such a string is *AN-DI-LU-IA/ŠU*, which would yield, "You are men of my/his protection." But since no such thing is attested at Boğazköy as far as I know, I have avoided restoring or translating as such. One might think of *linkiyas/isḫiulas* UN^{MEŠ}-*uš*, i.e., "men of the oath/obligation(s)," but it is difficult to see such in the visible traces. Nor do the traces seem to be amenable to a negation such as that at the beginning of No. 26, §2′. Goetze's (1959: 66a) *an-na-ú-l*[*e-eš*], followed, e.g., by del Monte (1988: 518) and Pecchioli Daddi (2006: 123), can in my view be excluded by the traces, *pace* Starke (1996: 168 and n. 117).

89. There is no space for anything between -*uš* and *A*-; cf. *CHD* L–N, 429a; P, 129a, where ŠEŠ is restored, and Goetze's (1959: 66a) [DUMU *A*]-*BI*.

90. Literally "to you at hand" (with Starke 1996: 168), often translated "in your hands," which would imply a situation presumably not intended; but cf. B ii 4′.

91. All 2nd person verbs and pronouns in this text are 2nd pl. unless otherwise indicated.

92. Literally "And his fathers to him are many," i.e., "and he has many fathers." Von Schuler's (1957: 9) solution to this obviously unexpected locution, followed, e.g., by van den Hout (1995: 101–2) and *CHD* Š, 323a (differently *CHD* L–N, 245b, 429a), was "und sie (scil. die Majestät) (hat) viele Vorfahren(?)," which remains a possibility. The translation here assumes either a scribal mistake or a collective usage for the clearly sg. -*ŠU* and sg. -*ssi*, relating them to the many brothers rather than to the king. Translations that restore

ŠEŠ or DUMU must be abandoned (see n. 89), e.g., Bryce 2005: 300; del Monte 1988: 518; Giorgieri and Mora 1996: 57.

93. Bryce's (2005: 300) translation of these lines, "and someone approaches another person," leaving out the preceding clause, must be emended.

94. With Rost (1956: 332–33) and Otten (1957–58: 388a): "Wen (wollen) wir uns nun (als Herrscher) aufnehmen? (Ist) denn nicht auch jener für uns ein Sohn unseres Herrn?" Followed by Cotticelli-Kurras (1991: 103). Cf. von Schuler (1957: 9), "Wen sonst nehmen wir uns (als Herrscher) auf? Jener (ist für) uns keineswegs der Sohn unseres Herrn"; Goetze (1959: 66a), "He whom we actually select for us, needs not even be a son of our lord," followed by Bryce (2005: 300); *CHD* P, 39a, "the one whom we are taking up is not a son of our lord."

95. Though the copy shows rather clearly ⸢ŠA⸣ EN x x[, on the photo is visible a damaged but nevertheless perfectly clear ⸢*ta-me-e-da*⸣-[*ni*.

96. Certainly not *N*[*I*-.

97. One would like to see a -*r*[*a*- or perhaps -*r*[*i*- here, but the traces do not really suggest such.

98. For this passage cf. *CHD* L–N, 282a, P, 7b, where the emendation is surely premature in light of the state of preservation.

99. The traces exclude von Schuler's (1957: 10) [*ḫa*?]-; see Otten (1957–58: 388).

100. Since no other occurrence of *parā mema*- in this text takes a local particle, I assume that one must parse *lē=war=an=za=an* (with, e.g., Goedegebuure 2003: 332) rather than *=z=(š)an*, as in *CHD* P, 350b.

101. UD-*za* would be too short for the space; cf. UD.KAM-*za* in iii 22, iv 35.

102. One can be quite confident about the reconstruction of the line numbering up to this point, due above all to the availability of the duplicates, which end with this paragraph.

103. Perhaps "deception, subterfuge; insult"; cf. *HEG* A–K, 618.

104. Lit. "I make him a witness before (me)." Cf. iv 15.

105. Cf. §2, 7.

106. Cf. §17″, 59′.

107. Von Schuler's (1957: 12) [*nu-uš-ma-aš*?] would be ca. 2 signs too short for the space, [*šu-um-ma-aš*] ca. 1–2 signs too short, therefore [*nu šu-um-ma-aš*], [*šu-um-ma-aš-ma*] or Starke's (1996: 165, n. 111) [*na-aš-ma-aš-ma-aš*] seem more likely. Cf. iii 32, 45 and 61.

108. For the restoration, as well as the writing with the added -*i*- vis-à-vis von Schuler (1957: 12), necessary also to fill the space, cf. iii 34.

109. The -*kán* is suggested by the space and by the previous line, in which -*kán* likewise occurs with *waḫnu*-.

110. Since von Schuler's (1957: 12) restoration of *nu* alone leaves space for 2–3 signs, one should presumably restore according to No. 26, A i 10′ or 18′, and since *nu-uš-ma-aš* would perhaps be somewhat too long, *nu-uš-ši* is probably the best solution. Alter-

natively, since this paragraph is exceptionally placed in the 2nd sg., one could consider [*nu-ut-ta*].

111. Rather than Goetze's (1959: 67b) pres. *isdamaszi*, one would, analogue to A iii 18 and No. 26, A iv 27 and in view of *karū* before the break, expect a pret.; see Starke 1996: 166, n. 133.

112. The traces suggest either *e-* or *mar-*, the latter leading one to suspect a derivation either from *markiya-*, "disapprove" or, perhaps less likely, of *marsa-*, "profane"; cf. A ii 17, iv 24, No. 26, A iv 36.

113. Though the copy shows an unequivocal EN, the photos reveal a rather clear UN (see already Otten 1957–58: 388). The trace thereafter could perhaps be a MEŠ, but is not overly convincing as such.

114. Purely graphically, the first sign could just as well be a corrupted E as a muddled KAR.

115. While the copy suggests ⸢*da-aš*⸣-*k*[*e-*, on the photos can be seen clear ⸢*uš-ke*⸣-*e*[*t*$^?$, whereby only the -*e*[*t* must remain uncertain.

116. Photo shows clear *n*[*u*.

117. Presumably the words of the messenger.

118. Lit. "runners before," but not to be taken literally, *pace* Cotticelli-Kurras 1991: 144. In Hittite imagery one who "runs before," often a deity, is one who supports, protects, leads, guides, and defends a person or persons. See e.g., *CHD* P, 300.

119. Lit. "If the day of his father, the day of his mother, for someone is long." Clearly an indication of a long life, not that the end of one's life is near, *pace* Cotticelli Kurras 2007b: 143b.

120. Lit. "has already turned to the day."

121. Starke (1996: 165, n. 111) suggests ⸤1⸥-[*an-kán*]. Kings of Ḫattusa also advised kings of other lands with whom they maintained diplomatic relations to be wary of their messengers who might twist the words of the Great King, warning them to make certain that a messenger's spoken words matched those sent along with him on a tablet, e.g., in the Sunaššura-Treaty (KBo 1.5 iv 32–39; Schwemer 2005: 105)

122. *Pace GrHL* §1.66, the sign here is KU, not MA, probably conditioned by the many nearby *kui-* derivatives, so that at least this occurrence can be struck from the list of problematic *e* > *ae* attestations; see similarly Rieken (1999a: 244, n. 1140); *EDHIL*, 270.

123. Clearly -*mu*, not -*aš-še*, *pace* Dardano 2002: 344.

124. Lit. "you build out a bridge for it."

125. Lit. "On this day for which regulation I was not present, it is no crime for me." The syntax has led to the suggestion that *saklai-* also entails the meaning "work, Dienst, servizio," but this does not seem to be necessary. Cf. *CHD* Š, 45a, "'For what rule on this day I was not present, it is not a sin for me' (i.e., I am not accountable for a rule made on a day when I was not present)." *HW*^{2} A, 198–99 "An diesem Tag – zu welchem Brauch ich nicht gestanden habe, das (ist) mir keine Sünde," whereby it is not clear that the same meaning for Hittite *ar-* should be assumed as for the German "zu etwas stehen;" Otten

1983b: 434, "Heute bin ich nicht zu irgendeinem Dienst angetreten"; and Otten 1957–58: 388b; Giorgieri 1995: 168, "In questo giorno non sono stato (pre)posto ad alcun servizio, e di ciò (*scil.* non aver rivelato una macchinazione ai danni del re) non ho colpa!" Similarly del Monte 1988: 518; Starke 1996: 169 and n. 127.

126. Cf. *CHD* L–N, 153a, "If you hear from someone an evil word (i.e., slander) or something unfavorable concerning My Majesty."

127. "You swore the oath as one" is equally possible.

128. Del Monte's (1988: 518) assumption that these brothers are kings of equal rank, i.e., the other Great Kings of Egypt, Assyria, etc., is unlikely in view of how the brothers are discussed in the rest of the text.

129. Perhaps half or step brothers; cf. *CHD* P, 129a, whereby the comparison with [ŠEŠ] ⸢*A*⸣-*BI*^{MEŠ} in i 9 must be dropped; see there and n. 89. See also Starke 1996: 165–66, n. 111.

130. In B iv 5 the copyist has errantly copied *-an* instead of clear *-aš m*[*e-* on the photo; see already Otten 1957–58: 388b.

131. With Starke 1996: 167, n. 114 and Hawkins 2002: 223. The copy would suggest rather *ku-w*[*a-*, but may be somewhat optimistic in light of what can be seen in the photographs. The primary difficulty of reading *ku-w*[*a-*, of course, is that the enclitic chain would therefore be separated from the first element of the sentence, which would be highly unexpected. The restoration does fit the space very well, assuming that indeed *INA* rather than *I-NA* stood here, as in the duplicate, which would otherwise have been completely unexpected.

132. The *-du* is written over traces amenable to *-zi*, although, if so, placed too close to the *-eš-*; and indeed an indicative would perhaps have made better sense than the imp.

133. Hawkins' (2002: 223) additional *INA* would probably be too long for the space.

134. Both von Schuler's (1957: 16) and Otten's (1957–58: 389) restorations, (*EL-LU nu-za-*)[*kán*] and (*EL-LU nu-za*[*-a*])*n*$^{?}$, respectively, are considerably too short for the available space. The verb *sak-* does not take *-kan* in general, never in this text, and the traces after the break are almost certainly *-a*]*n*. As it is unlikely that the enclitic chain after *nu-za* can be extended far enough to fill the space, *mān* or GIM-*an* would seem to do so well enough and to fit the context at the same time.

135. Von Schuler's restoration (1957: 16), (*ki-nu-un-n*)*a-kán*, is far too short. The traces in B might allow *-n*[*a-* but favor *-m*[*a-*; either would fit with the restoration given here. The combination *-kan* ... *appa*(*n*) *katta kars-* seems to take either a direct object alone (e.g., in KUB 41.21 iv 10–14; *HED* K, 101) or, when dealing with persons who are to keep their distance from other persons, with a direct object and the reflexive (e.g., KUB 26.18 obv. 9′–12′; Otten 1988: 8 and n. 29; Giorgieri 1995: 277; van den Hout 1995: 101). Since this text regularly shows *-an-za-an* for the 3rd sg. acc. with the reflexive, and since the traces before *-kán* would seem to exclude *z*]*a-*, the suggested solution, which fills the space nicely, seems not unlikely.

136. It is difficult to imagine what one should read here other than *-š*[*i*. The only other attestations of both direct and indirect objects with *isdamass-* known to me are KUB

14.1 obv. 24 (*HED* E/I, 452) and above, A iii 47–49. Hawkins' (2002: 223) *na-an-ši-kán* alone would be too short.

137. Hawkins' (2002: 223) [*na-at iš-du-wa-r*]*i* is certainly a possibility, but in contrast to a number of other instructions, this verb is never found in these loyalty oaths of Tudḫaliya IV, for which *istamas-* or *sak-* is preferred.

138. Von Schuler's (1957: 16) (*A-NA* [SAL-*TI ŠA*?]) would be far too short, and even with the additional É the space is not quite satisfactorily filled; perhaps the longer -*TÌ* would be enough.

139. The -*kán* is required by *ḫantī tiya-* and by the space (cf. e.g., *CHD* L–N, 94b), for which *ma-a-na-kán* would be a bit short. Another option might be *na-aš-ma-kán*, but the conditional seems more amenable to the context.

140. As *ti-ia-zi* would be a fair bit too short for the gap, a form such as *ti-i-ia-zi* or *ti-ia-az-zi* might have stood in the break, though none of the other forms in these texts would have suggested such.

141. Lit., "Out behind the lordship of My Majesty, it wishes another man for the lordship."

142. The word is attested only here. From the present context a meaning "embarrassing," "confidential" (e.g., *CHD* P, 225b), or the like, has been assumed.

143. Compared to [*ku-e-da-n*]*i-ik-ki* in the following line, [*na-aš-m*]*a* here would seem a bit short; [*ma-a-an-m*]*a* would be somewhat better.

144. As von Schuler (1957: 16) realized, *an*]-*da* alone would be too short. Other possibilities would be [*kat-ta-an*]-*da*, but this would likely have been written [GAM-*an*]-*da*, which would likewise be too short; [*me-na-aḫ-ḫa-an*]-*da*, which would be too long; [IGI-*an*]-*da*, which would be too short; [*ta-me-e*]-*da*, which would probably be a bit too long and would yield an unexpected meaning. The nuance with *appanda* would perhaps be coming upon a person from behind, i.e., unexpectedly; hence, by chance? The only other examples of *appanda ... aus-*, however, are found with -*kan* (*HW*^{2} A, 616b, but cf. 588, "Geklärt ist dabei bereits, daß *appa, appan, appanda* keine Ortspart. bedingen").

145. Lit. "performs the turning up of the *seknu*-garment," a common gesture of disdain, insult and curse among the Hittites; see Melchert 1983: 141–45; *CHD* P, 270b-271a; cf. *CHD* L–N, 67b.

146. For this important city, see most recently Lebrun 2001: 328–30 and in the introduction, sub Political History.

No. 28. Suppiluliu/ama II's Instructions and Oath Imposition for the Men of Ḫattusa (*CTH* 256)

147. Thus the writing of the name of this late Hittite king in i 5, as opposed to Suppiluliuma in iv 18′.

148. Meriggi (1962: 93) saw in iii 9′, "the obligations concerning the ancestors," a fitting title for the composition. There seems to be no basis for Singer's (2009b: 184) state-

ment, according to which "the other partner to this unique treaty are the dead" (see also n. 153). The contractual arrangement or imposition of obligations relates to those persons who are responsible for the funerary institutions, not the dead.

149. Or perhaps "[... A]nd [h]e, as far as the oath is concerned...." Giorgieri's (1995: 293, n. 7) *ki-i-*[*ia ut-ta*]*r* would seem to be excluded by the space available.

150. Imperatives morphologically also possible.

151. All 2nd person verbs and pronouns in this text are 2nd pl.

152. Traces do not suggest ^{d}1[0.

153. Giorgieri (1995: 296) and Singer (2009b: 184), following Meriggi, restore *l*[*i-in-ik-tén*], which should not be excluded, though swearing an oath to the ancestors would, as far as I am aware, be unique, and one should, if indeed to be restored as such, surely speak of swearing an oath with regard to (the obligations concerning) the ancestors.

154. In light of *ku-wa-ta-i* in KBo 4.14 iii 42, one might consider the possibility that *ku-wa-at-tén* could be a 2nd pl. pret. or imp. from *kuwa*(*ya*)-, "to fear." Emending *ku-wa-*<*ia*>*-at-tén* (cf. iv 1′) would be a further possibility. Cf. Giorgieri 1995: 313.

155. There appears to be no space between the first visible traces and *-ti-*.

156. Singer (2009b: 185) suggests that this paragraph "must have provided some sort of historiosophical explanation for the decline of Hatti as being the revenge of the dead for their negligence and humiliation," but this would seem to eke somewhat more from the fragmentary passage than is warranted.

Notes to the Sources

1. Fragments of a single letter but assigned a subscripted number can only with varying degrees of confidence be regarded as belonging to a single tablet, and usually their line numbering in the transcriptions is independent of the associated pieces. See Silvin Košak's online concordance (http://www.hethport.uni-wuerzburg.de/hetkonk/) for further information on the tablets' find spots, bibliography, and more.

2. IBoT 4.5 (see pp. XIII, XXV) is frequently listed as an indirect join to KUB 13.3 (e.g., *Konkordanz*), but if this tiny fragment can be attributed to any composition, then it should presumably be placed with *CTH* 264, as Pecchioli Daddi (2004: 452 and n. 7; 2005a: 282–83 and n. 27; 2005b: 602, n. 26) has repeatedly noted. Taggar-Cohen (2006: 39, 93) argues against this classification, but—without wanting to plead for the attribution—her arguments do not convince. Groddek (2007: 3–4) would simply place it among the innumerable festival fragments (*CTH* 670).

3. With Pecchioli Daddi (2004: 452 and nn. 9–12), there seems to be no concrete reason to include KUB 40.45 among these text fragments (cf. *Konkordanz*). Kühne (1972: 255), the first to associate the two, merely pointed out some similarities.

4. KBo 30.187 is often considered part of this composition (e.g., *Konkordanz*), though it is too fragmentary to be at all certain. Groddek (2002a: 256–57), e.g., would attribute it to

CTH 763. It does not duplicate any preserved passage of IBoT 1.36, so would presumably have belonged to a further tablet if it does belong to the text.

5. For excellent photos of KUB 13.7 I am indebted to Elena Devecchi.

6. It is assumed that KUB 34.40 represents the obv., KUB 34.41 the rev.

7. KBo 52.6 (cf. *Konkordanz*) and KBo 19.93 (cf. Carruba 1988: 210–11) are not included in this volume as part of the *CTH* 271 compositions, since (1) they are NH copies, whereas all other extant ms. are MH; (2) they stem from the Temple I complex, while all other fragments come from rooms 2–5 of Building A on the Büyükkale or nearby; (3) and since none of the identifying features seen in the other fragments are found in them.

8. Nothing would prohibit 1.B and 1.C from belonging to the same tablet, and their hands would seem to suggest such.

9. The hands of 1.D and 2 are quite similar, so that they might perhaps represent tablets 1 and 2 of the series. The fact that they were found together (note excavation numbers 245/p and 246/p) in Building K of the citadel (see *Konkordanz*) naturally fits the suggestion nicely.

10. The join assumed by Otten (1983a) of KUB 26.9+340/z (the latter now KBo 50.262) is incorrect. KBo 50.262 could conceivably belong to the same tablet as KBo 50.261+Bo 4468, but so little of the fragments is preserved that it is difficult to be certain.

11. 3.A and 3.C show a very similar hand and may well belong to the same tablet, and what little of 4.B is preserved would seem to suggest that it might show the same hand as well. If the former assumption is indeed correct, then 3.A, B, and C would likely all be part of the same composition. If the latter is correct as well, then all fragments of 3 and 4 might well belong together.

12. Though 3.B (930/z+Bo 4468) and 3.C (Bo 3977) are listed as duplicates to 3.A (Bo 2749+Bo 4007) in the *Konkordanz* (Version 1.75, sub *CTH* 257), they in fact are only parallel to some degree, above all 3.A, 12′–27′ and 3.C, 1–15. Both are concerned, e.g., with workers (3.A, 12′, 19′; 3.C, 11), the courtyard (3.A, 13′; 3.C, 3, 6), the work projects (3.A, 20′, 22′, 24′, 25′; 3.C, 8) of the king (3.A, 14′, 23′; 3.C, 4), the office of horse trainer (3.A, 15′; 3.C, 1), doing royal work in one's own home (3.A, 16′, 19′, 24′; 3.C, 9), and carpenters (3.A, 23′; 3.C, 8, 11). They are clearly not duplicates, however, and the differences between them, i.e., 3.A addressing its addressee directly in the 2nd sg., 3.C in the 3rd person, may perhaps be of greater interest than their similarities. 3.B. and 3.C would seem to be more inclined to preserve older graphic forms, such as *pí-i-e-ez-zi* (3.B, 11′; 3.C, 1) and *pí-i-e-eš-ke-ed-du* (3.B, 3′, 5′; 3.C, 4), *pace* Kammenhuber (1970a: 63). The fragmentary condition of both prohibits more far-reaching conclusions, but they do seem to provide a glimpse of redactional history.

13. Houwink ten Cate (1983: 164) refers to KBo 13.53 iii 7′–25′ where 13.58 is intended.

14. Further fragments that could well belong to this set of compositions include KBo 50.99, which shows the same strikingly slanted hand as do the 3.B fragments, KBo 50.146, and KBo 50.263.

15. Although two of the joins long assumed to be direct are actually indirect, i.e.,

KUB 13.1(+)KUB 31.87 and KUB 31.87(+)KUB 40.55 (cf. n. 16), in both cases with only minimal space between them, it nonetheless seems so very likely that all of these MH pieces belong to a single tablet that I have avoided assigning subscripted numbers to them. Indeed, after ascertaining this by my own means, I saw that Laroche (1957: 126) had already requested of M. Çiğ to clarify this question, and that she had responded that "Die Nummern Bo 2362, Bo 2891+2988 keinen eigentlichen Join bilden, wobei sie doch eine Zusammengehörigkeit aufweisen."

16. Though KUB 13.25 does not join KUB 31.86 directly, as previously assumed (cf. n. 15), the unique handwriting in both would seem to constitute sufficient reason for regarding them as assuredly belonging to the same tablet, and hence no subscripted numbers have been assigned.

17. The script of F_1 is strikingly similar to that of F_2. They both have NAM with a ḪU; KÁN with inset verticals under and/or to the left of the upper horizontal; NA with two wedges inline; PI with the upper horizontal pulled to the right.

18. KBo 22.44 may belong to B, and if so, could even join KUB 13.2 directly, though there may well be a few millimeters of space between them. (As KUB 13.2 is stored in Istanbul, KBo 22.44 in Ankara, the possibility cannot be checked.) If it does not join B, then it might belong to E; cf., among other considerations, the find spots for KBo 22.44 and KBo 60.11 (before Magazin 10 of the Temple I complex), both show a "grauer gebrannter Ton" (http://www.hethport.uni-wuerzburg.de/hetkonk/), and the fact, for what it's worth, that both (Bo 69/381 and 69/350) appear on the same photo (Phb 2308) at the Akademie der Wissenschaften, Mainz. Among the signs on the two fragments there seem to be no decisive indicators for or against the attribution. (Incidentally, KBo 22.42, booked in the *Konkordanz*, Vers. 1.3, does not belong to *CTH* 261. The error can be traced to a typo in Houwink ten Cate 1983: 166, where KBo 22.42 appears instead of KBo 22.44.)

19. Naturally, the attribution of the small fragments B_2, F_{1-2}, and G_{1-3} to their respective tablets must be regarded as highly tentative.

20. The arrangement here maintains the traditional sigla, including Schwemer's (2009: 98) most recent updates, though much of it is almost certainly wrong, primarily as regards B and C. While it is admittedly terribly difficult to ascertain to which tablets various small fragments might belong, it seems quite likely, first, that B_2 (KUB 31.120+KBo 50.276b) and B_3 (KBo 50.276a) do not belong to B_1 (KUB 13.6+13.17+13.19+FHL 100) at all. Further, it seems unlikely that KUB 31.92 joins KBo 50.283, which together have been regarded as C_2. The latter, KBo 50.283, would seem rather to belong to B (KUB 13.6++). How the remainder of the fragments is to be distributed must remain uncertain, but it seems worth considering the possibility that B_2 (KUB 31.120+KBo 50.276b), B_3 (KBo 50.276a), F_1 (KUB 31.94) and F_2 (*HT* 28) might belong to a single tablet (As none of these fragments duplicate $C_{1(+)3}$—i.e., KUB 13.5(+)KUB 31.92—and since the scripts of all these pieces show some similarities, the possibility exists that they might all belong to C.); that M (Bo 8054) might belong with D_2 (KUB 26.31), which, incidentally, was assumed by Hulin (1970: 155) to belong with D_1 (AnSt 20) on the most tenuous of grounds, so that its attribution must remain entirely conventional; and that J (KBo 50.274) and K (KBo 57.11) might well belong to a single tablet. Finally, Pecchioli Daddi (2004: 452) may well

be right in her suggestion that IBoT 4.5 belongs here as well, but too little of the fragment remains to allow any certainty.

21. KUB 26.55 and KBo 50.122 are ascribed to *CTH* 255 in the *Konkordanz* as well, but since these cannot at present be sensibly integrated into the texts as a whole, they have been ignored here.

22. It would seem likely that 2.C and 2.D belong to the same tablet, whereby they are probably to be dated as sjh. rather than jh., as in the *Konkordanz*.

23. Houwink ten Cate's discussion (2007: 200–203) relates to KUB 23.1++, not KUB 26.1++, as found on p. 200.

References

Akdoğan, R. 2013. "Zu einigen unveröffentlichten Bo-Tafeln." *AoF* 40.

Alp, S. 1947. "Hitit kıralı IV.(?) Tuthaliya'nın askerî fermanı./Military Instructions of the Hittite King Tuthaliya IV.(?)" *Belleten* 11: 383–414.

———. 1983. *Beiträge zur Erforschung des hethitischen Tempels. Kultanlagen im Lichte der Keilschrifttexte. Neue Deutungen.* Ankara: Türk Tarih Kurumu Basımevi.

———. 1991. *Hethitische Briefe aus Maşat-Höyük.* Ankara: Türk Tarih Kurumu Basımevi.

Alster, B. 1974. *The Instructions of Suruppak. A Sumerian Proverb Collection.* Mesopotamia: Copenhagen Studies in Assyriology 2. Copenhagen: Akademisk Forlag.

———. 2005. *Wisdom of Ancient Sumer.* Bethesda, MD: CDL.

Altman, A. 2003. "Who Took the Oath on the Vassal Treaty: Only the Vassal King or also the Suzerain? – The Hittite Evidence." *ZABR* 9: 178–84.

———. 2009. "Tracing the Earliest Recorded Concepts of International Law. (4) The Near East in the Late Bronze Age (1600–1200 BCE)." *Journal of the History of International Law* 11: 125-86.

———. 2010. "How Many Treaty Traditions Existed in the Ancient Near East?" Pp. 17–36 in Pax Hethitica*: Studies on the Hittites and Their Neighbours in Honour of Itamar Singer*, edited by Y. Cohen, A. Gilan, and J. L. Miller. StBoT 51. Wiesbaden: Harrassowitz.

Archi, A. 1979. "L'humanité des Hittites." Pp. 37–48 in *Florilegium Anatolicum: Mélanges offerts à Emmanuel Laroche*, edited by E. Akurgal, F. Josephson, and E. Laroche. Paris: Boccard.

———. 2007. "The Cult of the Royal Ancestors at Hattusa and the Syrian Practices." Pp. 49–55 in *VITA: Festschrift in Honor of Belkıs Dinçol and Ali Dinçol*, edited by M. Alparslan, M. Doğan-Alparslan, and H. Peker. Istanbul: Ege Yayinlari.

———. 2008. "Le 'leggi ittite' e il diritto processuale." Pp. 273–92 in *I diritti nel mondo cuneiforme (Mesopotamia e regioni adiacenti, ca. 2500–500 a.C.)*, edited by M. Liverani and C. Mora. Pavia: IUSS.

———. 2010. "When Did the Hittites Begin to Write in Hittite?" Pp. 37–46 in Pax Hethitica*: Studies on the Hittites and Their Neighbours in Honour of Itamar Singer*, edited by Y. Cohen, A. Gilan, and J. L. Miller. StBoT 51. Wiesbaden: Harrassowitz.

Arıkan, Y. 2003. "Hitit Çivi Yazılı Kaynaklarında ^{LÚ}*zilipuriịatalla-* Görevlisi." *ArAn* 6: 1–26.

———. 2004. "Hitit Çiviyazılı Belgelerinde Geçen LÚ*akuttara*- Görevlisi Üzerine Bir Araştırma." *ArAn* 7: 24–43.
———. 2006. "The Blind in Hittite Documents." *AoF* 33: 144–54.
Balza, M. E. 2008. "I trattati ittiti: sigillatura, testimoni, collacazione." Pp. 387–418 in *I diritti nel mondo cuneiforme (Mesopotamia e regioni adiacenti, ca. 2500–500 a.C.)*, edited by M. Liverani and C. Mora. Pavia: IUSS.
Balza, M. E. and Mora, C. 2012. "'And I Built this Everlasting Peak for Him'. The Two Scribal Traditions of the Hittites and the NA4*ḫekur* SAG.UŠ." *AoF* 38: 213–25.
Bányai, M. 2010. "Ist Urḫi-Tešup der König von Zulapa?" *Anatolica* 36: 1–16.
Beal, R. H. 1983. "Studies in Hittite History." *JCS* 35: 115–26.
———. 1988. "The GIŠTUKUL-institution in Second Millennium Ḫatti." *AoF* 15: 269–305.
———. 1992. *The Organisation of the Hittite Military*. THeth 20. Heidelberg: Carl Winter.
———. 1993. "Kurunta of Tarḫuntašša and the Imperial Hittite Mausoleum." *AnSt* 43: 29–39.
———. 2002. "Gleanings from Hittite Oracle Questions on Religion, Society, Psychology and Decision Making." Pp. 11–37 in *Silva Anatolica. Anatolian Studies Presented to Maciej Popko on the Occasion of His 65th Birthday*, edited by P. Taracha. Warsaw: Agade.
Beal, R. H. and Collins, B. J. 1996. "Hittite *pankur*, A New Suggestion." *AoF* 23: 308–15.
Beckman, G. 1982. "The Hittite Assembly." *JAOS* 102: 435–42.
———. 1983. *Hittite Birth Rituals*. StBoT 29. Wiesbaden: Harrassowitz.
———. 1986a. "Inheritance and Royal Succession among the Hittites." Pp. 13–31 in *Kaniššuwar: A Tribute to Hans G. Güterbock on His Seventy-Fifth Birthday, May 27, 1983*, edited by H. A. Hoffner, Jr. and G. M. Beckman. AS 23. Chicago: The Oriental Institute of the University of Chicago.
———. 1986b. Review of Hoffmann 1984. *JAOS* 106: 570–72.
———. 1991. Review of J. Friedrich and A. Kammenhuber, *HW*², Lief. 9–10. *BiOr* 48: 210–15.
———. 1995. "The Siege of Uršu Text (CTH 7) and Old Hittite Historiography." *JCS* 47: 23–34.
———. 1996. *Texts from the Vicinity of Emar in the Collection of Jonathan Rosen.* HANE/M 2. Padova: Sargon.
———. 1999. *Hittite Diplomatic Texts.* 2nd ed. WAW 7. Atlanta: Society of Biblical Literature.
———. 2000. "Hittite Chronology." *Akkadica* 119–120: 19–32.
———. 2002. "'My Sun-God'. Reflections of Mesopotamian Conceptions of Kingship among the Hittites." *Melammu Symposia* 3: 37–43.
———. 2006. "Hittite Treaties and the Development of the Cuneiform Treaty Tradition." Pp. 279–301 in *Die deuteronomistischen Geschichtswerke. Redaktions- und Religionsgeschichtliche Perspektiven zur „Deuteronomismus"-Diskussion in Tora und Vorderen Propheten*, edited by M. Witte et al. Berlin: de Gruyter.
Bemporad, A. 2009. "I Ḫabiru nella documentazione ittita." *SMEA* 51: 71–93.
Bin-Nun, S. R. 1975. *The Tawananna in the Hittite Kingdom*. THeth 5. Heidelberg: Carl Winter.

Bittel, K. 1950/51. “Bemerkungen zu dem auf Büyükkale (Boğazköy) entdeckten hethitischen Siegeldepot.” *Jahrbuch für kleinasiatische Forschungen* 1: 164–73.

Black, J. A. et al. 1998. “The Instructions of Shuruppag.” *The Electronic Text Corpus of Sumerian Literature*. Online: http://etcsl.orinst.ox.ac.uk/section5/tr561.htm.

Boese, J. 2008. “‚Ḫarbašipak‘, ‚Tiptakzi‘ und die Chronologie der älteren Kassitenzeit.” *ZA* 98: 201–10.

Boley, J. 1984. *The Hittite* hark-*Construction*. IBS 44. Innsbruck: Institut fur Sprachwissenschaft der Universität Innsbruck.

———. 1989. *The Sentence Particles and the Place Words in Old and Middle Hittite*. IBS 60. Innsbruck: Institut fur Sprachwissenschaft der Universität Innsbruck.

———. 1992. “The ‘Local’ Sentences Particles in Hittite.” Pp. 1–31 in *Per una grammatica ittita*, edited by O. Carruba. StMed 7. Pavia: Gianni Iuculano.

———. 2000. *Dynamics of Transformation in Hittite. The Hittite Particles* -kan, -asta *and* -san. IBS 97. Innsbruck: Institut fur Sprachwissenschaft der Universität Innsbruck.

———. 2004. “The Storyteller’s Art in Old Hittite: The Use of Sentence Connectives and Discourse Particles.” *RAnt* 1: 67–110.

———. 2005. “Riflessioni sulla logica e sul modo di pensare antichi.” *RAnt* 2: 41–60.

Boorn, G. P. F. van den. 1988. *The Duties of the Vizier: Civil Administration in the Early New Kingdom*. New York: Taylor & Francis.

Bossert, H. Th. 1944. *Ein hethitisches Königssiegel. Neue Beiträge zur Geschichte und Entzifferung der hethitischen Hieroglyphenschrift*. Istanbuler Forschungen 18. Berlin: Wasmuth.

Boysan-Dietrich, N. 1987. *Das hethitische Lehmhaus aus der Sicht der Keilschriftquellen*. THeth 12. Heidelberg: Carl Winter.

Brinkman, J. A. 1990. “Political Covenants, Treaties, and Loyalty Oaths in Babylonia and between Assyria and Babylonia.” Pp. 81–111 in *I trattati nel mondo antico: forma, ideologia, funzione*, edited by L. Canfora, M. Liverani, and C. Zaccagnini. Rome: L’Erma di Bretschneider.

Brock, N. van. 1964. “Les thèmes verbaux à redoublement du Hittite et le verbe indoeuropéen.” *RHA* 22/75: 119–65.

Bryce, T. R. 2002. *Life and Society in the Hittite World*. Oxford: Oxford University Press.

———. 2005. *The Kingdom of the Hittites*. (New Edition). Oxford: Oxford University Press.

———. 2007. “The Secession of Tarḫuntašša.” Pp. 117–29 in *Tabularia Hethaeorum: Hethitologische Beiträge Silvin Košak zum 65. Geburtstag*, edited by D. Groddek and M. Zorman. DBH 25. Wiesbaden: Harrassowitz.

Burde, C. 1974. *Hethitische medizinische Texte*. StBoT 19. Wiesbaden: Harrassowitz.

Cambi, V. 2007. *Tempo e aspetto in ittito, con particolare riferimento al suffisso -ske/a-*. Alessandria: Editioni dell’Orso.

Cammarosano, M. 2006. *Il decreto antico-ittita di Pimpira*. Eothen 14. Firenze: LoGisma.

Carruba, O. 1964. “Hethitisch *-(a)sta*, *-(a)pa* und die anderen ‚Ortsbezugspartikeln‘.” *OrNS* 33: 405–36.

———. 1971. “Hattusili II.” *SMEA* 14: 75–94.

———. 1977. “Beiträge zur mittelhethitischen Geschichte, I. Die Tuthalijas und die Arnuwandas II. Die sogenannten ‚Protocoles de succession dynastique' I.–II." *SMEA* 18: 137–95.

———. 1988. "Stato e società nel Medio Regno eteo." Pp. 195–224 in *Stato, Economia, Lavoro nel Vicino Oriente antico. Atti del convegno promosso dal Seminario di orientalistica dell'Istituto Gramsci Toscano*, edited by A. Zanardo. Milano: Franco Angeli Libri.

———. 1990. "Muwattalli I." Pp. 297–300 and 539–54 in: *X. Türk Tarih Kongresi, Ankara: 22–26 Eylül 1986*. Ankara: Türk Tarih Kurumu Basımevi.

———. 2008. *Annali Etei del Medio Regno*. StMed 18. Pavia: Gianni Iuculano.

Catsanicos, J. 1991. *Recherches sur le vocabulaire de la faute*. Cahiers de *NABU* 2. Paris: Sepoa.

———. 1994. "La mise à jour du système de transcription des textes hittites." *IF* 99: 301–35.

Charpin, D. 2010. "Un Nouveau 'Protocole de Serment' de Mari." Pp. 49–75 in *Opening the Tablet Box. Near Eastern Studies in Honor of Benjamin R. Foster*, edited by S. Melville and A. Slotsky. Culture and History of the Ancient Near East 42. Leiden: Brill.

Christiansen, B. 2006. *Die Ritualtradition der Ambazzi: Eine philologische Bearbeitung und entstehungsgeschichtliche Analyse der Ritualtexte CTH 391, CTH 429 und CTH 463*. StBoT 48. Wiesbaden: Harrassowitz.

———. 2008. *Schicksalsbestimmende Kommunikation: Sprachliche, gesellschaftliche und theologische Aspekte hethitischer Fluch-, Segens- und Eidesformeln*. PhD dissertation, Freie Universität Berlin.

———. 2013. "Reinheitsvorstellungen und Entsühnungsriten der Hethiter und ihr möglicher Einfluss auf die biblische Überlieferung." Pp. 131–53 in *Anatolien und die Welt der hebräischen Bibel*, edited by M. Hutter. Themenheft *Biblische Notizen*. Freiburg: Herder.

Christiansen, B. and Devecchi, E. 2013. "Die hethitischen Vasallenverträge und die biblische Bundeskonzeption." Pp. 65–87 in *Anatolien und die Welt der hebräischen Bibel*, edited by M. Hutter. Themenheft *Biblische Notizen*. Freiburg: Herder.

Civil, M. 1994. *The Farmer's Instructions: A Sumerian Agricultural Manual*. AuOr Supplementa 5. Barcelona: Editorial AUSA.

Cohen, C. 1997. "Hippiatric Texts." Pp. 361–62 in *The Context of Scripture*. Vol. 1. *Canonical Compositions from the Biblical World*, edited by W.W. Hallo. Leiden: Brill.

Cohen, Y. 2002. *Taboos and Prohibitions in Hittite Society: A Study of the Hittite Expression* natta āra *('not permitted')*. THeth 24. Heidelberg: Carl Winter.

———. 2013. *Wisdom from the Late Bronze Age*. WAW 34. Atlanta: Society of Biblical Literature.

Collins, B. J. 1997. "Rituals." Pp. 160–77 in *The Context of Scripture*. Vol. 1. *Canonical Compositions from the Biblical World*, edited by W. W. Hallo. Leiden: Brill.

———. 2002. "Animals in Hittite Literature." Pp. 237–50 in *A History of the Animal World in the Ancient Near East*, edited by B. J. Collins. HdO I/64. Leiden: Brill.

———. 2007. *The Hittites and Their World*. Atlanta: Society of Biblical Literature.

Cotticelli-Kurras, P. 1991. *Das hethitische Verbum 'sein': Syntaktische Untersuchungen.* THeth 18. Heidelberg: Carl Winter.

———. 1992. "Die hethitischen Nominalsätze." Pp. 99–135 in *Per una grammatica ittita*, edited by O. Carruba. StMed 7. Pavia: Gianni Iuculano.

———. 1998. "Eine lexikalische Untersuchung, Annelies Kammenhuber gewidmet." Pp. 109–18 in *Acts of the IIIrd International Congress of Hittitology, Çorum, September 16–22, 1996*, edited by S. Alp and A. Süel. Ankara.

———. 2007a. "Versuch einer Fehlertypologie in der hethitischen Keilschrift." Pp. 175–202 in *Tabularia Hethaeorum: Hethitologische Beiträge Silvin Košak zum 65. Geburtstag*, edited by D. Groddek and M. Zorman. DBH 25. Wiesbaden: Harrassowitz.

———. 2007b. "Die Rhetorik als Schnittstelle zwischen Lexikon und Syntax: Das Hendiadyoin in den hethitischen Texten." Pp. 137–46 in *VITA: Festschrift in Honor of Belkıs Dinçol and Ali Dinçol*, edited by M. Alparslan, M. Doğan-Alparslan, and H. Peker. Istanbul: Ege Yayınları.

d'Alfonso L. 2005. *Le procedure giudiziarie ittite in Siria (XIII sec. a.C.).* StMed 17. Pavia: Italian University Press.

———. 2006a. "Alcune riflessioni preliminari sulla formulazione degli ordini e dei divieti nella normativa per gli ufficiali dello stato ittita." Pp. 331–47 in *L'ufficio e il documento. I luoghi, i modi, gli strumenti dell'amministrazione in Egitto e nel Vicino Oriente antico. Atti della giornate di studio degli Egittologi e degli Orientalisti italiani, Milano - Pavia, 17–19 febbraio 2005*, edited by C. Mora and P. Piacentini. Milano: Cisalpino.

———. 2006b. "Die hethitische Vertragstradition in Syrien (14.–12. Jh. v.Chr)." Pp. 303–29 in *Die deuteronomistischen Geschichtswerke. Redaktions- und religionsgeschichtliche Perspektiven zur „Deuteronomismus"-Diskussion in Tora und Vorderen Propheten*, edited by M. Witte et al. Berlin: de Gruyter.

———. 2007. "The Treaty between Talmi-Teššub King of Karkemiš and Šuppilulii̯ama, Great King of Ḫatti." Pp. 203–20 in *Tabularia Hethaeorum: Hethitologische Beiträge Silvin Košak zum 65. Geburtstag*, edited by D. Groddek and M. Zorman. DBH 25. Wiesbaden: Harrassowitz.

———. 2008. "Le fonti normative del secondo millennio a.C. Confronto tra le culture della Mesopotamia e l'Anatolia ittita." Pp. 325–59 in *I diritti nel mondo cuneiforme (Mesopotamia e regioni adiacenti, ca. 2500–500 a.C.)*, edited by M. Liverani and C. Mora. Pavia: IUSS.

Dardano, P. 1997. *L'aneddoto e il racconto in età antico-hittita: la cosiddetta "Cronaca di Palazzo."* Biblioteca di Ricerche Linguistiche e Filologiche 43. Rome: Casa Editrice "Il Calamo."

———. 2002. "'La main est coupable', 'le sang devient abondant': sur quelques expressions avec des noms de parties et d'éléments du corps humain dans la littérature juridico-politique de l'Ancien et du Moyen Royaume hittite." *OrNS* 71: 333–92.

———. 2004. Review of Y. Cohen 2002. *OrNS* 73: 280–85.

———. 2005. "I costrutti perifrastici con il verbo *ḫar*(*k*)- dell'ittito : stato della questione e prospettive di metodo." *OrNS* 74: 93–113.

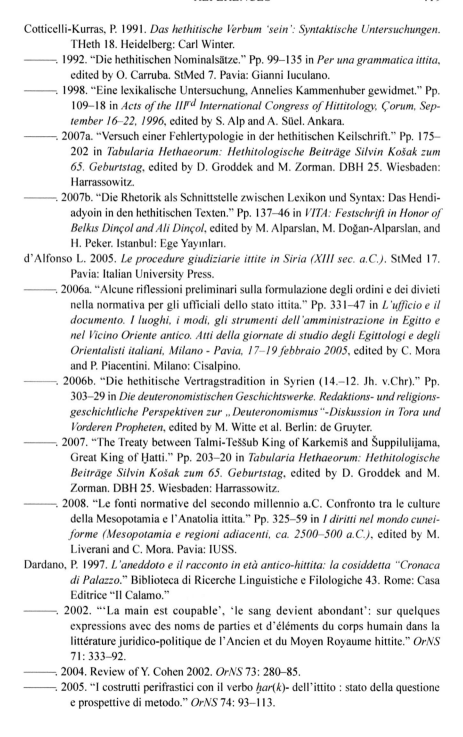

———. 2006. *Die hethitischen Tontafelkataloge aus Ḫattuša (CTH 276–282)*. StBoT 47. Wiesbaden: Harrassowitz.

———. 2007. "In margine al sistema di Caland: su alcuni aggettivi primari in *-*.nt*- dell'anatolico." Pp. 221–46 in *Tabularia Hethaeorum: Hethitologische Beiträge Silvin Košak zum 65. Geburtstag*, edited by D. Groddek and M. Zorman. DBH 25. Wiesbaden: Harrassowitz.

———. 2009. "Per l'etimo dell'ittito *maškan-*." *RAnt* 6: 3–12.

———. 2011. "Erzählte Vergangenheit und kulturelles Gedächtnis im hethitischen Schrifttum: Die so genannte Palastchronik." Pp. 63–81 in *Hethitische Literatur: Überlieferungsprozesse, Textstrukturen, Ausdrucksformen und Nachwirken. Akten des Symposiums vom 18. bis 20. Februar 2010 in Bonn*, edited by M. Hutter und S. Braunsar-Hutter. AOAT 391. Münster: Ugarit-Verlag.

Devecchi, E. 2012. "Treaties and Edicts in the Hittite World." Pp. 637–45 in *Organization, Representation, and Symbols of Power in the Ancient Near East. Proceedings of the 54th Rencontre Assyriologique Internationale at Würzburg 20–25 July 2008*, edited by G. Wilhelm. Winona Lake, IN: Eisenbrauns.

Dietrich, M. and Keydana, G. 1991. "Der Dialog zwischen Šūpē-amēli und seinem 'Vater'. Die Tradition babylonischer Weisheitssprüche im Westen." *UF* 23: 33–74.

Dietrich, M. and Loretz, O. 2004. "Hunde im *ap* des königlichen ‚Mausoleums' nach dem ugaritischen Keret-Epos." Pp. 253–62 in *Šarnikzel. Hethitologische Studien zum Gedenken an Emil Orgetorix Forrer (19.02.1894–10.01.1986)*, edited by D. Groddek and S. Rößle. DBH 10. Dresden: Technische Universität Dresden.

Dinçol, A. M. 2001. "Ein interessanter Siegelabdruck aus Boğazköy und die damit verknüpften historischen Fragen." Pp. 89–97 in *Akten des IV. Internationalen Kongresses für Hethitologie Würzburg, 4.–8. Oktober 1999*, edited by G. Wilhelm. StBoT 45. Wiesbaden: Harrassowitz.

Durand, J.-M. 1988. *Archives épistolaires de Mari I/1*. ARM 26. Paris: Éditions Recherche sur les Civilisations.

———. 1991. "Précurseurs syriens aux protocoles néo-assyriens." Pp. 13–71 in *Marchands, diplomates et empereurs: Études sur la civilisation mésopotamienne offertes à Paul Garelli*, edited by D. Charpin and F. Joannès. Paris: Éditions Recherche sur les Civilisations.

———. 1997. *Le documents épistolaires du palais de Mari*. LAPO 16/1. Paris: CERF.

Ebeling, E. 1951. *Bruchstücke einer mittelassyrischen Vorschriftensammlung für die Akklimatisierung und Tranierung von Wagenpferden*. Berlin: Akademie.

Edel, E. 1994. *Die ägyptisch-hethitische Korrespondenz aus Boghazköi in babylonischer und hethitischer Sprache*. Band I. *Umschriften und Übersetzungen*. Abhandlungen der Rheinisch-Westfälischen Akademie der Wissenschaften 77. Opladen: Westdeutscher Verlag.

Eidem, J. 2011a. *The Royal Archives from Tell Leilan*. PIHANS 117. Leiden: Nederlands Instituut voor het Nabije Oosten.

———. 2011b. "Staatsvertrag (treaty). A. 3.–2. Jahrtausend." *RlA* 13: 38–40.

Fadhil, F. 1983. *Studien zur Topographie und Prosopographie der Provinzstädte des Königreichs Arrapḫe*. Baghdader Forschungen 6. Mainz: von Zabern.

Feder, Y. 2010. "The Mechanics of Retribution in Hittite, Mesopotamian and Ancient Israelite Sources." *JANER* 10: 119–57.

Floreano, E. 2001. "The Role of Silver in the Domestic Economic System of the Hittite Empire." *AoF* 28: 209–35.

Forlanini, M. 2005. "Hattušili II. - Geschöpf der Forscher oder vergessener König?" *AoF* 32: 230–45.

———. 2009. "On the Middle Kızılırmak, II." Pp. 39–67 in *Central-North Anatolia in the Hittite Period: New Perspectives in Light of Recent Research. Acts of the International Conference Held at the University of Florence (7–9 February 2007)*, edited by F. Pecchioli Daddi, G. Torri, and C. Corti. StAs 5. Rome: Herder.

Fortson, B. W. 1998. "A New Study of Hittite *-wa(r)*." *JCS* 50: 21–34.

Foster, B. R. 2005. *Before the Muses. An Anthology of Akkadian Literature*. 3rd ed. Bethesda, MD: CDL.

Freu, J. 1987. "Problemes de chronologie et de geographie hittites: Madduwatta et les debuts de l'empire." *Hethitica* 8: 123–75.

———. 1995. "De l'ancien royaume au nouvel empire. Les temps obscurs de la monarchie hittite." Pp. 133–48 in *Atti del II Congresso Internazionale di Hittitologia*, edited by O. Carruba, M. Giorgieri, and C. Mora. StMed 9. Pavia: Gianni Iuculano.

———. 1996. "La 'révolution dynastique' du Grand Roi de Hatti Tuthaliya I." *Hethitica* 13: 17–38.

———. 2004. "Le grand roi Tutḫaliya, fils de Kantuzzili." Pp. 271–304 in *Antiquus Oriens: Mélanges offerts au Professeur René Lebrun*, vol. 1, edited by M. Mazoyer and O. Casabonne. Paris: Kubaba.

———. 2005. "Des Grand Rois de Tarḫuntašša aux Grand Rois de Tabal." *RAnt* 2: 399–417.

———. 2007a. "Télipinu et l'Ancien Royaume de Ḫatti." Pp. 29–186 in *Des origines à la fin de l'Ancien Royaume Hittite: Les Hittites et leur histoire*, by J. Freu and M. Mazoyer. Paris: L'Harmattan.

———. 2007b. "L'affirmation du nouvel empire hittite (c. 1465–1319 av. J.C.)." Pp. 1–311 in *Les débuts du nouvel empire hittite: Les Hittites et leur histoire*, by J. Freu and M. Mazoyer. Paris: l'Harmattan.

Freydank, H. 1970. "Zu *parā tarna-* und der Deutung von KUB XIII 9+." *ArOr* 38: 257–68.

Friedrich, J. 1928/29 "Reinheitsvorschriften für den hethitischen König." *MAOG* 4: 46–58.

Fritzsche, E. 2010. "Die Aufgaben des *BĒL MADGALTI* nach CTH 261 und nach den Maşat-Briefen." Hausarbeit, Institut für Altorientalistik, Freie Universität Berlin.

———. 2011. "GA.KIN.AG *EMṢU* im Hethitischen." *AoF* 38: 15–62.

Fuscagni, F. 2002. "Walanni e due nuove possibili sequenze di regine ittite." Pp. 289–97 in *Anatolia Antica: Studi in memoria di Fiorella Imparati*, edited by S. de Martino and F. Pecchioli Daddi. Eothen 11. Firenze: LoGisma.

García Ramón, J. L. 2007. "Zur Entstehung und Semantik der hethitischen Supinumperiphrase." *SMEA* 49: 281–92.

Genz, H. and Mielke, D. P., eds. 2011. *Insights into Hittite History and Archaeology.* Colloquia Antiqua 2. Leuven: Peeters.

Gilan, A. 2007. "Bread, Wine and Partridges – A Note on the Palace Anecdotes (CTH 8)." Pp. 521–34 in *Tabularia Hethaeorum: Hethitologische Beiträge Silvin Košak zum 65. Geburtstag*, edited by D. Groddek and M. Zorman. DBH 25. Wiesbaden: Harrassowitz.

———. 2009. *Historische Erzählungen aus der althethitischen Zeit – Versuch einer Klassifizierung.* PhD dissertation, Universität Leipzig.

Giorgadze, G. G. 1987. "Two Forms of Non-Slave Labour in Hittite Society." Pp. 251–55 in *Labor in the Ancient Near East*, edited by M.A. Powell. AOS 68. New Haven: Eisenbrauns.

Giorgieri, M. 1995. *I testi ittiti di giuramento.* Tesi di dottorato. Firenze.

———. 2001. "Aspetti magico-religiosi del giuramento presso gli Ittiti e i Greci." Pp. 421–40 in *La questione delle influenze vicino-orientali sulla religione greca*, edited by S. Ribichini, M. Rocchi, and P. Xella. Rome: Consiglio nazionale delle ricerche.

———. 2002. "Birra, acqua ed olio: paralleli siriani e neo-assiri ad un giuramento ittita." Pp. 299–320 in *Anatolia Antica: Studi in memoria di Fiorella Imparati*, edited by S. de Martino and F. Pecchioli Daddi. Eothen 11. Firenze: LoGisma.

———. 2005. "Zu den Treueiden mittelhethitischer Zeit." *AoF* 32: 322–46.

———. 2008. "Verschwörungen und Intrigen am hethitischen Hof: zu den Konflikten innerhalb der hethitischen Elite anhand der historisch-juristischen Quellen." Pp. 351–75 in *Ḫattuša – Boğazköy: Das Hethiterreich im Spannungsfeld des Alten Orients. 6. Internationales Colloquium der Deutschen Orient-Gesellschaft, 22.–24. März 2006, Würzburg*, edited by G. Wilhelm. Wiesbaden: Harrassowitz.

Giorgieri, M. and Mora, C. 1996. *Aspetti della regalità ittita nel XIII secolo a.C.* Biblioteca di Athenaeum 32. Como: Edizioni New Press.

———. 2010. "Kingship in Ḫatti during the 13th Century: Forms of Rule and Struggles for Power before the Fall of the Empire." Pp. 136–57 in Pax Hethitica*: Studies on the Hittites and Their Neighbours in Honour of Itamar Singer*, edited by Y. Cohen, A. Gilan, and J. L. Miller. StBoT 51. Wiesbaden: Harrassowitz.

Glocker, J. 2009. "Zwei weitere Textbruchstücke zu der hethitischen „Eidesleistung eines Schreibers" CTH 124." *AoF* 36: 146–58.

Goedegebuure, P. M. 2002/3. "The Hittite 3rd Person/Distal Demonstrative *aši* (*uni*, *eni* etc.)." *Die Sprache* 43: 1–32.

———. 2003. *Reference, Deixis and Focus in Hittite.* PhD dissertation, University of Amsterdam.

———. 2006a. "A New Proposal for the Reading of the Hittite Numeral '1': *sia-*." Pp. 165–88 in *The Life and Times of Ḫattušili III and Tutḫaliya IV. Proceedings of a Symposium Held in Honour of J. de Roos, 12–13 December 2003, Leiden*, edited by Th.P.J. van den Hout. PIHANS 103. Leiden: Nederlands Instituut voor het Nabije Oosten.

———. 2006b. "The Bilingual Testament of Hattusili I." Pp. 222–28 in *The Ancient Near East. Historical Sources in Translation*, edited by M.W. Chavalas. Malden, MA: Blackwell.

———. 2010. "The Alignment of Hattian: An Active Language with an Ergative Base." Pp. 949–81 in *Language in the Ancient Near East: Proceedings of the 53e Rencontre Assyriologiquie Internationale I/1*. Edited by L. Kogan et al. Babel und Bibel 4/1 = Orientalia et Classica: Papers of the Institute of Oriental and Classical Studies 30/1. Winona Lake, IN: Eisenbrauns.

Goetze, A. 1933. *Annalen des Muršiliš*. Mitteilungen der Vorderasiatisch-Aegyptischen Gesellschaft 38. Leipzig: J. C. Hinrichs.

———. 1938. *The Hittite Ritual of Tunnawi*. AOS 14. New Haven: American Oriental Society.

———. 1950. "Hittite Instructions." Pp. 207–11 in *Ancient Near Eastern Texts Relating to the Old Testament*, edited by J. B. Pritchard. Princeton: Princeton University Press.

———. 1959. Review of von Schuler 1957. *JCS* 13: 65–70.

———. 1960. "The Beginning of the Hittite Instructions for the Commander of the Border Guards." *JCS* 14: 69–73.

González Salazar, J. M. 1994. "Tiliura, un ejemplo de la política fronteriza durante el imperio hitita (CTH 89)." *AuOr* 12: 159–76.

———. 1999. "El papel de los funcionarios periféricos en la administración hitita (I). El caso del *BĒL MADGALTI* o *auriyaš išḫa-*." *Gerión* 17: 105–27.

Goodnick Westenholz, J. 2012. "The Body and the Mind in Mesopotamian Traditions." Pp. 459–77 in *Menschenbilder und Körperkonzepte im Alten Israel, in Ägypten und im Alten Orient*, edited by A. Berlejung, J. Dietrich, and J. F. Quack. Orientalische Religionen in der Antike 9. Tübingen: Mohr Siebeck.

Gordin, Sh. 2008. *Scribal Families of Hattuša in the 13th Century BCE. A Prosopographic Study*. M.A. thesis, Tel Aviv University.

———. 2010. "Scriptoria in Late Empire Period Ḫattusa: The Case of the É GIŠ.KIN.TI." Pp. 158–77 in Pax Hethitica*: Studies on the Hittites and Their Neighbours in Honour of Itamar Singer*, edited by Y. Cohen, A. Gilan, and J. L. Miller. StBoT 51. Wiesbaden: Harrassowitz.

Groddek, D. 2001. "‚Mausoleum' (É.NA_4) und ‚Totentempel' (^{É}*ḫištā*) im Hethitischen." *UF* 33: 213–18.

———. 2002a. *Hethitische Texte in Transkription: KBo 30*. DBH 2. Wiesbaden: Harrassowitz.

———. 2002b. "Eine Reinigungsritual für Muršili II. anläßlich seiner Thronbesteigung." *Hethitica* 15: 81–92.

———. 2007. *Hethitische Texte in Transkription: IBoT 4*. DBH 23. Wiesbaden: Harrassowitz.

———. 2008a. *Hethitische Texte in Transkription: KBo 50*. DBH 28. Wiesbaden: Harrassowitz.

———. 2008b. *Hethitische Texte in Transkription: KBo 22*. DBH 24. Wiesbaden: Harrassowitz.

Gurney, O. R. 1979. "The Anointing of Tudhaliya." Pp. 213–33 in *Studia Mediterranea Piero Meriggi dicata*, edited by O. Carruba. StMed 1. Pavia: Aurora.

Güterbock, H. G. 1967. "Lexicographical Notes III." *RHA* 25/81: 141–50.

———. 1983. "Noch einmal die Formel *parnaššea šuwaizzi*." *OrNS* 52: 73–80.

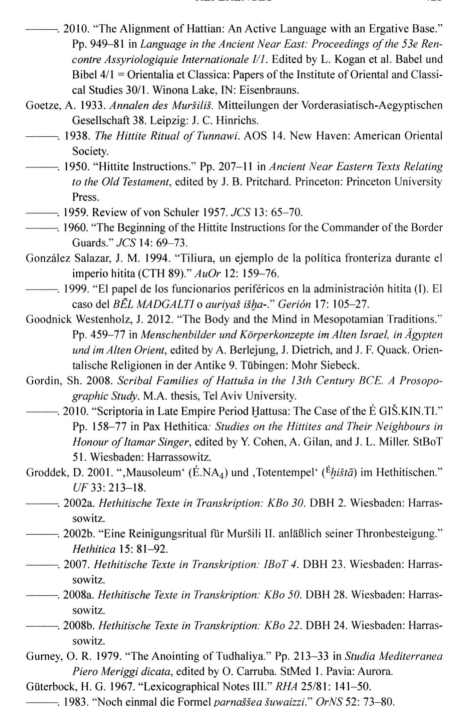

———. 1988. "Bilingual Moon Omens from Boğazköy." Pp. 161–74 in *A Scientific Humanist: Studies in Memory of Abraham Sachs*, edited by E. Leichty, M. J. de Ellis, and P. Gerardi. Philadelphia: University Museum.

Güterbock, H.G. and van den Hout, Th. P. J. 1991. *The Hittite Instructions for the Royal Bodyguard*. AS 24. Chicago: The Oriental Institute of the University of Chicago.

Haas, V. 1970. *Der Kult von Nerik. Ein Beitrag zur hethitischen Religionsgeschichte*. Studia Pohl 4. Rome: Pontificum institutum biblicum.

———. 1981. Review of *Studia Mediterranea Piero Meriggi dicata*, edited by O. Carruba. StMed 1. Pavia: Aurora, 1979. *BiOr* 38: 642–46.

———. 1982. *Hethitische Berggötter und hurritische Steindämonen: Riten, Kulte und Mythen*. Kulturgeschichte der Antiken Welt 10. Mainz: Zabern.

———. 1985. "Betrachtungen zur Dynastie von Ḫattuša im Mittleren Reich (ca. 1450–1380)." *AoF* 22: 269–77.

———. 1994. *Geschichte der hethitischen Religion*. HdO I/15. Leiden: Brill.

———. 2003. *Materia magica et medica hethitica. Ein Beitrag zur Heilkunde im Alten Orient*. Berlin: de Gruyter.

———. 2004. "Rituell-magische Aspekte in der althethitischen Strafvollstreckung." Pp. 213–26 in *Offizielle Religion, lokale Kulte und individuelle Religiosität. Akten des religionsgeschichtlichen Symposiums „Kleinasien und angrenzende Gebiete vom Beginn des 2. bis zur Mitte des 1. Jahrhunderts v. Chr." (Bonn, 20.–22. Februar 2003)*, edited by M. Hutter and S. Hutter-Braunsar. AOAT 318. Münster: Ugarit-Verlag.

———. 2006. *Die hethitische Literatur*. Berlin: de Gruyter.

———. 2007. "Zwei Verfluchungen im hethitischen Schrifttum und in der Ilias." *JANER* 7: 1–6.

———. 2008. *Hethitische Orakel, Vorzeichen und Abwehrstrategien: Ein Beitrag zur hethitischen Kulturgeschichte*. Berlin: de Gruyter.

Haas, V. and Wegner, I. 1993. "Baugrube und Fundament." *IstMitt* 43: 53–58.

Haase, R. 1965. "Zum hethitischen Prozessrecht." *ZA* 57: 249–57.

———. 1984. *Texte zum hethitischen Recht. Eine Auswahl*. Wiesbaden: Ludwig Reichert.

———. 1996. "Anmerkungen zum sogenannten Lehensrecht der Hethiter." *ZABR* 2: 135–39.

———. 2003. "The Hittite Kingdom." Pp. 619–56 in *A History of Ancient Near Eastern Law*, edited by R. Westbrook. HdO I/72. Leiden: Brill.

Hagen, F. 2012. *An Ancient Egyptian Literary Text in Context: The Instruction of Ptahhotep*. Orientalia Lovaniensia Analecta 218. Leuven: Peeters.

Hagenbuchner-Dresel, A. 2004. "Die Fortbewegungsmittel des hethitischen Königspaares im Kult." Pp. 361–72 in *Šarnikzel. Hethitologische Studien zum Gedenken an Emil Orgetorix Forrer (19.02.1894–10.01.1986)*, edited by D. Groddek and S. Rößle. DBH 10. Dresden: Technische Universität Dresden.

———. 2007. "Verschlußsysteme bei den Hethitern." Pp. 353–65 in *Tabularia Hethaeorum: Hethitologische Beiträge Silvin Košak zum 65. Geburtstag*, edited by D. Groddek and M. Zorman. DBH 25. Wiesbaden: Harrassowitz.

———. 2010a. "Fluch (*ḫurtai-*) und Verfluchen (*ḫu(wa)rt-*) in der hethitischen Gesellschaft." Pp. 155–74 in *Festschrift für Gernot Wilhelm anläßlich seines 65. Geburtstages am 28. Januar 2010*, edited by J. C. Fincke. Dresden: Islet.

———. 2010b. "Segen und Fluch. B. Bei den Hethitern." *RlA* 12: 348–50.

Hawkins, J. D. 2002. "Eunuchs among the Hittites." Pp. 217–33 in *Sex and Gender in the Ancient Near East. Proceedings of the 47th Rencontre Assyriologique Internationale, Helsinki, July 2–6, 2001*, edited by S. Parpola and R. M. Whiting. Helsinki: Eisenbrauns.

———. 2011. "The Seals and the Dynasty." Pp. 85–102 in *Die Siegel der Grosskönige und Grossköniginnen auf Tonbullen aus dem Nişantepe-Archiv in Hattusa*, edited by S. Herbordt et al. Boğazköy-Ḫattuša 23. Mainz: von Zabern.

Hazenbos, J. 2003. *The Organization of the Anatolian Local Cults during the Thirteenth Century B.C. An Appraisal of the Hittite Cult Inventories.* CM 21. Leiden: Brill/Styx.

Heimpel, W. 2003. *Letters to the King of Mari.* MesCiv 12. Winona Lake, IN: Eisenbrauns.

Held, W. H., Jr. 1957. *The Hittite Relative Sentence*. Language dissertation No. 55. Baltimore: Linguistic Society of America.

Herbordt, S. 2005. *Die Prinzen- und Beamtensiegel der hethitischen Großreichszeit auf Tonbullen aus dem Nişantepe-Archiv in Hattusa*. Boğazköy-Ḫattuša 19. Mainz: von Zabern.

Herbordt, S. Bawanypeck, D., and Hawkins, J. D. 2011. *Die Siegel der Grosskönige und Grossköniginnen auf Tonbullen aus dem Nişantepe-Archiv in Hattusa.* Boğazköy-Ḫattuša 23. Mainz: von Zabern.

Hoffmann, I. 1984. *Der Erlaß Telipinus*. THeth 11. Heidelberg: Carl Winter.

Hoffner, H. A., Jr. 1971. "Hittite *ega-* and *egan-*." *JCS* 24: 31–36.

———. 1973. "The Hittite Particle *-PAT*." Pp. 99–117 in *Festschrift Heinrich Otten*, edited by E. Neu and C. Rüster. Wiesbaden: Harrassowitz.

———. 1974. *Alimenta Hethaeorum. Food Production in Hittite Asia Minor*. AOS 55. New Haven, Connecticut: American Oriental Society.

———. 1976. Review of H. Otten and C. Rüster, *KBo* 22. *BiOr* 33: 335–37.

———. 1977. "Studies in Hittite Vocabulary, Syntax, and Style." *JCS* 29: 151–56.

———. 1978. Review of J. Friedrich and A. Kammenhuber, *HW*^{2}. *BiOr* 35: 242–46.

———. 1986. "Studies in Hittite Grammar." Pp. 83–94 in *Kaniššuwar: A Tribute to Hans G. Güterbock on His Seventy-Fifth Birthday*, edited by H. A. Hoffner, Jr. and G. M. Beckman. AS 23. Chicago: Oriental Institute of the University of Chicago.

———. 1992. "Studies in the Hittite Particles, II: On Some Uses of *-kan*." Pp. 137–51 in *Per una grammatica ittita*, edited by O. Carruba. StMed 7. Pavia: Gianni Iuculano.

———. 1995. "Legal and Social Institutions of Hittite Anatolia." *CANE* 1: 555–69.

———. 1996. Review of J. Boley, The Hittite Particle *-z/-za*. In *BiOr* 53: 750–61.

———. 1997a. *The Laws of the Hittites*. DMOA 23. Leiden: Brill.

———. 1997b. "On the Hittite Use of Sumerian BAL in the Expression BAL-*nu-*." *ArAn* 3: 191–97.

———. 1998. "From the Disciplines of a Dictionary Editor." *JCS* 50: 35–44.

———. 2002. "The Treatment and Long-Term Use of Persons Captured in Battle according to the Maşat Texts." Pp. 61–72 in *Recent Developments in Hittite Archaeology and History. Papers in Memory of Hans G. Güterbock*, edited by K. A. Yener and H. A. Hoffner, Jr. Winona Lake, IN: Eisenbrauns.

———. 2004a. "Placenta, Colostrum and Meconium in Hittite." Pp. 337–58 in *Antiquus Oriens: Mélanges offerts au Professeur René Lebrun* (Vol. I), edited by M. Mazoyer and O. Casabonne. Paris: Kubaba.

———. 2004b. Review of Bryce 2002. *JNES* 63: 305–7.

———. 2007a. "On Higher Numbers in Hittite." *SMEA* 49: 377–85.

———. 2007b. "Asyndeton in Hittite." Pp. 385–99 in *Tabularia Hethaeorum: Hethitologische Beiträge Silvin Košak zum 65. Geburtstag*, edited by D. Groddek and M. Zorman. DBH 25. Wiesbaden: Harrassowitz.

———. 2009. *Letters from the Hittite Kingdom.* WAW 15. Atlanta: Society of Biblical Literature.

Hout, Th. P. J. van den. 1989/90. "Maße und Gewichte. Bei den Hethitern." *RlA* 7: 517–27.

———. 1990. Review of A. Archi, *KUB* 57. *BiOr* 47: 423–32.

———. 1991. "Hethitische Thronbesteigungsorakel und die Inauguration Tudḫalijas IV." *ZA* 81: 274–300.

———. 1994. "Death as a Privilege: The Hittite Royal Funerary Ritual." Pp. 37–76 in *Hidden Futures: Death and Immortality in Ancient Egypt, Anatolia, the Classical, Biblical and Arabic-Islamic World*, edited by J. M. Bremer, Th. P. J. van den Hout, and R. Peters. Amsterdam: Amsterdam University Press.

———. 1995. *Der Ulmitešub-Vertrag. Eine prosopographische Untersuchung.* StBoT 38. Wiesbaden: Harrassowitz.

———. 1997. "Biography and Autobiography." Pp. 194–204 in *The Context of Scripture.* Vol. 1. *Canonical Compositions from the Biblical World*, edited by W. W. Hallo. Leiden: Brill.

———. 1998. *The Purity of Kingship: An Edition of CTH 569 and Related Hittite Oracle Inquiries of Tutḫaliya IV.* DMOA 25. Leiden: Brill.

———. 2001. "Neuter Plural Subjects and Nominal Predicates in Anatolian." Pp. 167–92 in *Anatolisch und Indogermanisch / Anatolico e Indoeuropeo - Akten des Kolloquiums der Indogermanischen Gesellschaft, Pavia, 22.–25. September 1998*, edited by O. Carruba and W. Meid. IBS 100. Innsbruck: Institut für Sprachen und Literaturen der Universität Innsbruck.

———. 2002. "Tombs and Memorials: The (Divine) Stone-House and Ḫegur Reconsidered." Pp. 73–91 in *Recent Developments in Hittite Archaeology and History. Papers in Memory of Hans G. Güterbock*, edited by K. A. Yener and H. A. Hoffner. Winona Lake, IN: Eisenbrauns.

———. 2003a. "Studies in the Hittite Phraseological Construction I: Its Syntactic and Semantic Properties." Pp. 177–203 in *Hittite Studies in Honor of Harry A. Hoffner Jr. on the Occasion of His 65th Birthday*, edited by G. M. Beckman, R. H. Beal, and G. McMahon. Winona Lake, IN: Eisenbrauns.

———. 2003b. "Ordal (Ordeal). B. Bei den Hethitern." *RlA* 10: 129–30.

———. 2006. "Institutions, Vernaculars, Publics: The Case of Second-Millennium Anatolia." Pp. 217–56 in *Margins of Writing, Origins of Cultures*, edited by S. L.

Sanders. Oriental Institute Seminars 2. Chicago: The Oriental Institute of the University of chicago.

———. 2008. "A Classified Past: Classification of Knowledge in the Hittite Empire." Pp. 211–19 in *Proceedings of the 51st Rencontre Assyriologique Internationale Held at the Oriental Institute of the University of Chicago, July 18–22, 2005*, edited by R. D. Biggs, J. Myers and M. T. Roth. Studies in Ancient Oriental Civilization 62. Chicago: The Oriental Institute of the University of Chicago.

———. 2009a. "A Century of Hittite Text Dating and the Origins of the Hittite Cuneiform Script." *IL* 32: 11–35.

———. 2009b. "Reflections on the Origins and Development of the Hittite Tablet Collections in Hattuša and Their Consequences for the Rise of Hittite Literacy." Pp. 71–96 in *Central-North Anatolia in the Hittite Period: New Perspectives in Light of Recent Research. Acts of the International Conference Held at the University of Florence (7–9 February 2007)*, edited by F. Pecchioli Daddi, G. Torri and C. Corti. StAs 5. Rome: Herder.

———. 2010. "^{LÚ}DUB.SAR.GIŠ = 'Clerk'?" *OrNS* 79: 255–67.

Houwink ten Cate, P. H. J. 1983. "Instructies voor hittitische Functionarissen." Pp. 160–81 in *Schrijvend Verleden. Documenten uit het oude Nabije Oosten vertaald en toegelicht*, edited by K. R. Veenhof. Leiden: Ex Oriente Lux.

———. 1995–96 "The Genealogy of Mursilis II. The Difference between a Legalistic and a Genealogical Approach to the Descent of Suppiluliumas I." *JEOL* 34: 51–72.

———. 1998. "An Alternative Date for the Sunassuras Treaty (KBo 1.5)." *AoF* 25: 34–53.

———. 2007. "The Hittite Usage of the Concepts of 'Great Kingship', the Mutual Guarantee of Royal Succession, the Personal Unswerving Loyalty of the Vassal to His Lord and the 'Chain of Command' in Vassal Treaties from the 13th Century B.C.E." Pp. 191–207 in *Das geistige Erfassen der Welt im Alten Orient. Sprache, Religion, Kultur und Gesellschaft*, edited by C. Wilcke. Wiesbaden: Harrassowitz.

Hrozný, F. 1920. *Über die Völker und Sprachen des alten Chatti-Landes*. BoSt 5/3: 25–48.

Hulin, P. 1970. "A New Duplicate Fragment of the Hittite Instructions to Temple Officials." *AnSt* 20: 155–57.

Hutter, M. 2009. "Weisheit und „Weisheitsliteratur" im hethitischen Kleinasien." *Caucasian and Near Eastern Studies* 13 (Giorgi Melikishvili memorial volume): 63–76.

———. 2011. "„Annalen", „Gebete", „Erzählungen", „Ritualtexte" und anderes. Wie haben die Hethiter ihre Literatur kategorisiert?" Pp. 111–34 in *Was sind Genres? Nicht-abendländische Kategorisierungen von Gattungen*, edited by S. Conermann and A. el Hawary. Narratio Aliena? Studien des Bonner Zentrums für Transkulturelle Narratologie 1, Berlin: EB Verlag.

Hüser, A. 2007. *Hethitische Anlagen zur Wasserversorgung und Entsorgung*. Kuşaklı-Sarissa 3. Rahden: Leidorf.

Imparati, F. 1974. "Una concessione di terre da parte di Tudhaliya IV." *RHA* 32: 5–209.

———. 1982. "Aspects de l'organisation de l'état hittite dans les documents juridiques et administratifs." *JESHO* 25: 225–67.

———. 1991. "Autorità centrale e istituzioni collegiali nel regno ittita." Pp. 161–81 in *Esercizio del potere e prassi della consultazione. Atti dell'VIII colloquio internazionale romanistico-canonistico (10–12 maggio 1990)*, edited by A. Ciani and G. Diurni. Roma: Libreria editrice vaticana. Reprinted as: Pp. 369–88 in *Studi sulla società e sulla religione degli Ittiti*, edited by G. Pugliese Carratelli and S. de Martino. Eothen 12. Firenze: LoGisma.

———. 1999. "Die Organisation des hethitischen Staates." Pp. 320–87 in *Geschichte des Hethitischen Reiches*, by H. Klengel. HdO I/34. Leiden: Brill.

Jackson, S. A. 2008. *A Comparison of Ancient Near Eastern Law Collections Prior to the First Millennium BC.* Giorgias dissertations 35, Near Eastern Series 10. Piscataway, NJ: Giorgias.

Jakob-Rost, L. 1966. "Beiträge zum hethitischen Hofzeremoniell (IBoT I 36)." *MIO* 11: 165–225.

Jankowska, N. B. 1969. "Communal Self-government and the King of the State of Arrapḫa." *JESHO* 12: 231–82.

———. 1981. "Life of the Military Élite in Arrapḫe." SCCNH 1: 195–200.

Jin Jie 1994. *A Complete Retrograde Glossary of the Hittite Language*. Uitgaven van het Nederlands Historisch-Archaeologisch Instituut te Istanbul 71. Leiden: Nederlands Historisch-Archaeologisch Instituut te Istanbul.

Kammenhuber, A. 1961. *Hippologia Hethitica.* Wiesbaden: Harrassowitz.

———. 1964. "Die hethitischen Vorstellungen von Seele und Leib, Herz und Leibesinnerem, Kopf und Person. I. Teil." *ZA* 56: 150–212.

———. 1965. "Die hethitischen Vorstellungen von Seele und Leib, Herz und Leibesinnerem, Kopf und Person. 2. Teil." *ZA* 57: 177–222.

———. 1970a. "Die erste Computer-Analyse des Hethitischen." *MSS* 28: 51–69.

———. 1970b. "Keilschrifttexte aus Bogazköi (KBo XVI)." *OrNS* 39: 547–67.

———. 1972. "Keilschrifttexte aus Boğazköy (KUB XL)." *OrNS* 41: 432–45.

———. 1976. *Orakelpraxis, Träume und Vorzeichenschau bei den Hethitern.* THeth 7. Heidelberg: Carl Winter.

———. 1991. "Die hethitische Getreidegottheit Ḫalki/Nisaba." Pp. 143–60 in *Near Eastern Studies Dedicated to H.I.H. Prince Takahito Mikasa on the Occasion of His Seventy-fifth Birthday*, edited by M. Mori. *BMECCJ* 5. Wiesbaden: Harrassowitz.

Kapełuś, M. 2007. "La «maison (le palais) des ancêtres» et les tombeaux des rois hittites." *RAnt* 4: 221–29.

Karasu, C. 2003. "Why Did the Hittites Have a Thousand Deities?" Pp. 221–35 in *Hittite Studies in Honor of Harry A. Hoffner Jr. on the Occasion of His 65th Birthday*, edited by G. M. Beckman, R. H. Beal, and G. McMahon. Winona Lake, IN: Eisenbrauns.

Kassian, A. S., Korolëv, A. A., and Sidel'tsev, A. V. 2002. *Hittite Funerary Ritual* šalliš waštaiš. AOAT 288. Münster: Ugarit-Verlag.

Klengel, H. 1965. "Die Rolle der „Ältesten" (LÚ^{MEŠ} ŠU.GI) im Kleinasien der Hethiterzeit." *ZA* 57: 223–36.

———. 1999. *Geschichte des Hethitischen Reiches.* HdO I/34. Leiden: Brill.

———. 2006. "Studien zur hethitischen Wirtschaft, 2: Feld- und Gartenbau." *AoF* 33: 3–21.

Klinger, J. 1988. "Überlegungen zu den Anfängen des Mitanni-Staates." Pp. 27–42 in *Hurriter und Hurritisch*, edited by V. Haas. Xenia 21. Konstanz: Universitätsverlag Konstanz.

———. 1992. "Fremde und Außenseiter in Ḫatti." Pp. 187–212 in *Außenseiter und Randgruppen*, edited by V. Haas. Xenia 32. Konstanz: Universitätsverlag Konstanz.

———. 1993. "Zu einigen hattischen Ausrufen in hethitischen Festritualen." *SMEA* 32: 91–110.

———. 1995. "Das Corpus der Maşat-Briefe und seine Beziehungen zu den Texten aus Ḫattuša." *ZA* 85: 74–108.

———. 1996. *Untersuchungen zur Rekonstruktion der hattischen Kultschicht.* StBoT 37. Wiesbaden: Harrassowitz.

———. 1998. "Zur Historizität einiger hethitischer Omina." *AoF* 25: 104–11.

———. 2000. "Zur Geschichte des hethitischen Reiches." *OLZ* 95: 5–13.

———. 2001a. "Hethitische Texte." TUAT Erg.: 61–81.

———. 2001b. "Historiographie als Paradigma: Die Quellen zur hethitischen Geschichte und ihre Deutung." Pp. 272–91 in *Akten des IV. Internationalen Kongresses für Hethitologie Würzburg, 4.–8. Oktober 1999*, edited by G. Wilhelm. StBoT 45. Wiesbaden: Harrassowitz.

———. 2002. "Die hethitisch-kaškäische Geschichte bis zum Beginn der Großreichszeit." Pp. 437–51 in *Anatolia Antica: Studi in memoria di Fiorella Imparati*, edited by S. de Martino and F. Pecchioli Daddi. Eothen 11. Firenze: LoGisma.

———. 2005a. "Das Korpus der Kaškäer-Texte." *AoF* 32: 347–59.

———. 2005b. "Hattisch." Pp. 128–34 in *Sprachen des Alten Orients*. Edited by M. P. Streck. Darmstadt: Wissenschaftliche Buchgesellschaft.

———. 2007. *Die Hethiter: Geschichte – Gesellschaft – Kultur.* München: Beck.

———. 2010. "Literarische sumerische Texte aus den hethitischen Archiven aus paläographischer Sicht – Teil II." *AoF* 37: 306–40.

Klinger, J. and Neu, E. 1990. "War die erste Computer-Analyse des Hethitischen verfehlt?" *Hethitica* 10: 135–60.

Kloekhorst, A. 2010. "Initial Stops in Hittite (with an excursus on the spelling of stops in Alalaḫ Akkadian)." *ZA* 100: 197–241.

Koch, C. 2008. *Vertrag, Treueid und Bund: Studien zur Rezeption des altorientalischen Vertragsrechts im Deuteronomium und zur Ausbildung der Bundestheologie im Alten Testament.* Beihefte zur Zeitschrift für die Alttestamentliche Wissenschaft 383. Berlin: de Gruyter.

Korošec, V. 1931. *Hethitische Staatsverträge. Ein Beitrag zu ihrer juristischen Wertung.* Leipzig: Zentralantiquariat der Deutschen Demokratischen Republik.

———. 1974. "Einiges zur inneren Struktur hethitischer Tempel nach der Instruktion für Tempelleute (KUB XIII, 4)." Pp. 165–74 in *Anatolian Studies Presented to Hans Gustav Güterbock on the Occasion of His 65th Birthday*, edited by K. Bittel, et al. Uitgaven van het Nederlands Historisch-Archaeologisch Instituut te Istanbul 35. Istanbul: Nederlands Historisch-Archaeologisch Institut in het Nabije Oosten.

Košak, S. 1980. "Dating of Hittite Texts: A Test." *AnSt* 30: 31–39.

———. 1988a. "Ein hethitischer Königserlaß über eine gesellschaftliche und wirtschaftliche Reform." Pp. 195–202 in *Documentum Asiae minoris antiquae: Festschrift für Heinrich Otten zum 75. Geburtstag*, edited by E. Neu and C. Rüster, Wiesbaden: Harrassowitz.

———. 1988b. Review of A. Archi, *KUB* 57. *ZA* 78: 309–14.

———. 1990. "Night and Day, in War and in Peace." *JAC* 5: 77–86.

———. 1993. "Die Stadtwerke von Hattuša." *Linguistica* 33: 107–12.

Kühne, C. 1972. "Bemerkungen zu den kürzlich edierten hethitischen Texten." *ZA* 62: 236–61.

———. 1975. "Hethitische Texte: IV. Eine Dienstanweisung." Pp. 200–204 in *Religionsgeschichtliches Textbuch zum Alten Testament*, edited by W. Beyerlin. Göttingen: Vandenhoeck & Ruprecht.

Kühne, C. and Otten, H. 1971. *Der Šaušgamuwa-Vertrag*. StBoT 16. Wiesbaden: Harrassowitz.

Kümmel, H. M. 1967. *Ersatzrituale für den hethitischen König*. StBoT 3. Wiesbaden: Harrassowitz.

Lambert, W. 1960. *Babylonian Wisdom Literature*. Oxford: Clarendon.

Laroche, E. 1953. "Šuppiluliuma II." *RA* 47: 70–78.

———. 1957. Review of E. von Schuler 1957. *RHA* 15/61: 123–28.

———. 1973. "Fleuve et ordalie en Asie Mineure hittite." Pp. 179–89 in *Festschrift Heinrich Otten, 27. Dezember 1973*, edited by E. Neu and C. Rüster. Wiesbaden: Harrassowitz.

Lauinger, J. 2012. "Esarhaddon's Succession Treaty at Tell Tayinat: Text and Commentary." *JCS* 64: 87–123.

Lebrun, R. 2001. "Propos concernant Urukina, Ussa et Uda." Pp. 326–32 in *Akten des IV. Internationalen Kongresses für Hethitologie, Würzburg, 4.–8. Oktober 1999*, edited by G. Wilhelm. StBoT 45. Wiesbaden: Harrassowitz.

Lenzi, A. 2008. *Secrecy and the Gods. Secret Knowledge in Ancient Mesopotamia and Biblical Israel.* State Archives of Assyria Studies 19. Helsinki: Neo-Assyrian Text Corpus Project.

Lichtheim, M. 1973. *Ancient Egyptian Literature: A Book of Readings*, vol. 1. Berkeley: University of California Press.

———. 1996. "Didactic Literature." Pp. 243–62 in *Ancient Egyptian Literature: History & Forms*, edited by A. Loprieno. Leiden: Brill.

Liverani, M. 2001. *International Relations in the Ancient Near East, 1600–1100 BC.* Studies in Diplomacy and International Relations. New York (u.a.): Palgrave Macmillan.

———. 2004. *Myth and Politics in Ancient Near Eastern Historiography*. Ithaca, NY: Cornell University Press.

Loretz, O. 2001. "Der ugaritische architektonische Begriff *ḫšt*, „Totenheiligtum"." *UF* 33: 377–85.

Lorenz, J. 2010. "Fragmente hethitischer Verträge und Instruktionen." *ZA* 100: 257–63.

Maidman, M. P. 2010. *Nuzi Texts and Their Uses as Historical Evidence.* WAW 18. Atlanta: Society of Biblical Literature.

Malul, M. 1990. *The Comparative Method in Ancient Near Eastern and Biblical Legal Studies*. AOAT 227. Kevelaer: Butzon & Bercker.

Marazzi, M. 1979. "Zwei Randbemerkungen zu den *Bēl Madgalti*-Instruktionen." *VO* 2: 79–86.

———. 1988. "Note in margine all'editto reale KBo XXII 1." Pp. 119–29 in *Studi di storia e di filologia anatolica dedicati a Giovanni Pugliese Carratelli*, edited by F. Imparati. Eothen 1. Firenze: Elite edizioni librarie italiane estere.

———. 1994. "Tarife und Gewichte in einem althethitischen Königserlaß." *OrNS* 63: 88–92.

———. 2000. "Sigilli e tavolette di legno: le fonti letterarie e le testimonianze sfragistiche nell'Anatolia hittita." Pp. 79–102 in *Administrative Documents in the Aegean and Their Near Eastern Counterparts: Proceedings of the International Colloquium, Naples, February 29–March 2, 1996*, edited by M. Perna. Torino: Paravia scriptorium.

———. 2002. "Richtig/Gerecht e il suo opposto in lingua hittita." *Annali del Dipartimento di Studi del Mondo Classico e del Mediterraneo Antico, Sezione linguistica* 24: 73–84.

———. 2004. "'Depistare' il re nell'adempimento della giustizia: il verbo *kar(a)p-/karpija-* e il testo di 'giuramento' KUB XIII 7." Pp. 307–24 in *Centro Mediterraneo Preclassico. Studi e ricerche I*, edited by M. Marazzi. Napoli: Università degli Studi Suor Orsola Benincasa.

———. 2007. "Gli editti reali hittiti: definizione del genere e delimitazione del corpus." Pp. 487–502 in *Tabularia Hethaeorum: Hethitologische Beiträge Silvin Košak zum 65. Geburtstag*, edited by D. Groddek and M. Zorman. DBH 25. Wiesbaden: Harrassowitz.

———. 2010. "Pratiche ordaliche nell'Anatolia hittita. Pp. 197–230 in ana turri gimilli: *studi dedicati al Padre Werner R. Mayer, S.J. da amici e allievi*, edited by M.G. Biga and M. Liverani. Vicino Oriente, Quaderno 5. Rome. Università degli Studi di Roma «La Sapienza».

———. 2013. "Königserlass (Tutḫaliya I/II) (CTH 258.1)" in the online *Konkordanz* at hethiter.net/: CTH 258.1 (INTR 2012-07-16).

Marazzi, M. and Gzella, H. 2003. "Bemerkungen zu SAG.DU-*ZU waš*- und *wašše*- in CTH 258 und HG §198/*84." *SMEA* 45: 71–78.

Marizza, M. 2007. *Dignitari ittiti del tempo di Tuthaliya I/II, Arnuwanda I, Tuthaliya III*. Eothen 15. Firenze: LoGisma.

———. 2009. *Lettere ittite di re e dignitari*. Brescia: Paideia.

de Martino, S. 1991. "Himuili, Kantuzili e la presa del potere da parte di Tuthaliya." Pp. 5–21 in *Quattro studi ittiti*, edited by F. Imparati. Eothen 4. Firenze: Elite edizioni librarie italiane estere.

———. 1996. *L'Anatolia occidentale nel Medio Regno ittita*. Eothen 5. Firenze: Il vantaggio.

———. 2007. "Ḫattuša, la capitale del regno ittita: nuovi dati sull'edificazione della «città alta»." Pp. 77–91 in *Le capitali del vicino oriente antico: regalità e culto, monumentalità e amministrazione. Atti del convegno internazionale Milano, 18 gennaio 2006*. Milano: Ares.

———. 2010. "Some Questions on the Political History and Chronology of the Early Hittite Empire." *AoF* 37: 186–97.

de Martino, S. and Devecchi, E. 2012. "Death Penalty in the Hittite Documentation." Pp. 191–201 in *Strafe und Strafrecht in den Antiken Welten: Unter Berücksichtigung von Todesstrafe, Hinrichtung und peinlicher Befragung*, edited by R. Rollinger, M. Lang, and H. Barta. Philippikia, Marburger altertumskundliche Abhandlungen 51. Wiesbaden: Harrassowitz.

de Martino, S. and Imparati, F. 1998. "Sifting through the Edicts and Proclamations of the Hittite Kings." Pp. 391–400 in *Acts of the III*^rd^ *International Congress of Hittitology, Çorum, September 16–22, 1996*, edited by S. Alp and A. Süel. Ankara.

Mazoyer, M. 2007. "Remarques sur «la maison du dieu»." *RAnt* 4: 249–57.

McMahon, G. 1997. "Instructions." Pp. 217–30 in *The Context of Scripture*. Vol. 1. *Canonical Compositions from the Biblical World*, edited by W.W. Hallo. Leiden: Brill.

Melchert, H. C. 1977. *Ablative and Instrumental in Hittite*. PhD dissertation, Harvard University, Cambridge, MA.

———. 1980. "The Use of IKU in Hittite Texts." *JCS* 32: 50–56.

———. 1983. "Pudenda hethitica." *JCS* 35: 137–45.

———. 1984. *Studies in Hittite Historical Phonology*. *ZvS* Ergänzungsheft 32. Göttingen: Vandenhoeck & Ruprecht.

———. 1985. "Hittite *imma* and Latin *immō*." *ZvS* 98: 184–205.

———. 1994. *Anatolian Historical Phonology*. Leiden Studies in Indo-European 3. Amsterdam-Atlanta: Rodopi.

———. 1996. Review of Güterbock and van den Hout 1991. *JNES* 55: 134–35.

———. 2003. *The Luwians*. HdO I/68. Leiden: Brill.

———. 2008. "Middle Hittite Revisited." *SMEA* 50: 525–31.

———. 2010. "Hittite *ḫarp(p)-* and Derivatives." Pp. 179–88 in *Investigationes Anatolicae: Gedenkschrift für Erich Neu*, edited by J. Klinger, E. Rieken and C. Rüster. StBoT 52. Wiesbaden: Harrassowitz.

Meriggi, P. 1962. "Über einige hethitische Fragmente historischen Inhaltes." *WZKM* 58: 66–110.

Michel, C. 2001. *Correspondance des marchands de Kanish au début du II*[e] *millénaire avant J.-C.* LAPO 19. Paris: Cerf.

———. 2003. *Old Assyrian Bibliography of Cuneiform Texts, Bullae, Seals and the Results of the Excavations at Aššur, Kültepe/Kaniš, Acemhöyük, Alişar and Boğazköy*. Old Assyrian Archives, Studies 1. Leiden: Nederlands Instituut voor het Nabije Oosten. (updates in *AfO* 51, 2006, 436–49 and *AfO* 52, 2011, 396–417)

Mielke, D. P. 2006. "Abschluss der Grabungen am Nordwest-Tor." *MDOG* 138: 26–33.

Milgrom, J. 1970. "The Shared Custody of the Tabernacle and a Hittite Analogy." *JAOS* 90: 204–9.

———. 1976. "The Concept of Maʿal in the Bible and the Ancient Near East." *JAOS* 96: 236–47.

Miller, J. L. 2004. *Studies in the Origins, Development and Interpretation of the Kizzuwatna Rituals*. StBoT 46. Wiesbaden: Harrassowitz.

———. 2005a. "A Join to the Hittite Atramḫasi Myth (KUB 8.63+1718/u)." *NABU* 2005/1: 10.

———. 2005b. Review of *Hittite Studies in Honor of Harry A. Hoffner Jr. on the Occasion of His 65th Birthday*, edited by G. Beckman, R. Beal, and G. McMahon, Winona Lake, IN: Eisenbrauns, 2003. *JAOS* 125: 283–88.

———. 2007a. "Mursili II's Dictate to Tuppi-Teššub's Syrian Antagonists." *KASKAL* 4: 121–52.

———. 2007b. "Joins and Duplicates among the Boğazköy Tablets (11–20)." *ZA* 97: 125–32.

———. 2007c. "Joins and Duplicates among the Boğazköy Tablets (21–30)." *ZA* 97: 133–41.

———. 2008. "Joins and Duplicates among the Boğazköy Tablets (31–45)." *ZA* 98: 117–37.

———. 2009a. "Ša/inaḫu(i)t(ta)." *RlA* 12: 4–6.

———. 2009b. Review of Christiansen 2006. *ZA* 99: 153–57.

———. 2010. "Practice and Perception of Black Magic among the Hittites." *AoF* 37: 167–85.

———. 2011a. "Diverse Remarks on the Hittite Instructions." *Colloquium Anatolicum / Anadolu sohbetleri* 10: 1–20.

———. 2011b. "Die hethitischen Dienstanweisungen: zwischen normativer Vorschrift und Traditionsliteratur." Pp. 193–205 in *Hethitische Literatur: Überlieferungsprozesse, Textstrukturen, Ausdrucksformen und Nachwirken. Akten des Symposiums vom 18. bis 20. Februar 2010 in Bonn*, edited by M. Hutter und S. Braunsar-Hutter. AOAT 391. Münster: Ugarit-Verlag.

———. 2011c. "Stadttor. B. Philologisch. Bei den Hethitern." *RlA* 13: 88–91.

del Monte, G. F. 1975a. "Le «istruzioni militari di Tutḫalija»." *Studi Classici e Orientali* 24: 127–40.

———. 1975b. "Le fame dei morti." *Annali dell'Istituto Orientale di Napoli* 35: 319–46.

———. 1980. "Traduzione e interferenza nei trattati siro-hittiti." *VO* 3: 103–19.

———. 1988. "Dal giuramento di fedeltà degli eunuchi a Tudkhaliya IV." Pp. 518–19 in *Antico Oriente: storia società economia*, edited by M. Liverani. Roma-Bari: Laterza.

———. 2003. *Antologia della letteratura ittita.* Pisa: Servizio Editoriale, Universitario di Pisa.

Mora, C. 1987. "Su alcuni termini architettonici ittiti." *Athenaeum. Studi Periodici di Letteratura e Storia dell'Antichità, Nuova Serie* 65: 552–59.

———. 2004. "'Overseers' and 'Lords' of the Land in the Hittite Administration." Pp. 477–86 in *Šarnikzel. Hethitologische Studien zum Gedenken an Emil Orgetorix Forrer (19.02.1894–10.01.1986)*, edited by D. Groddek and S. Rößle. DBH 10. Dresden: Technische Universität Dresden.

———. 2007. "I testi ittiti di inventario e gli 'archivi' di cretule. Alcune osservazioni e riflessioni." Pp. 535–50 in *Tabularia Hethaeorum: Hethitologische Beiträge Silvin Košak zum 65. Geburtstag*, edited by D. Groddek and M. Zorman. DBH 25. Wiesbaden: Harrassowitz.

———. 2008. "La 'Parola del re'. Testi ittiti a carattere politico-giuridico e politicoamministrativo: editti e istruzioni." Pp. 293–323 in *I diritti nel mondo cuneiforme (Mesopotamia e regioni adiacenti, ca. 2500–500 a.C.)*, edited by M. Liverani and C. Mora. Pavia: IUSS.

———. 2010a. "Seals and Sealings of Karkamiš, Part III: The Evidence from the Nişantepe-Archives, the Digraphic Seals and the Title EUNUCHUS$_2$." Pp. 170–81 in Ipamati kistamati pari tumatimis: *Luwian and Hittite Studies presented to J. David Hawkins on the Occasion of His 70th Birthday*, edited by I. Singer. Tel Aviv: Emery and Claire Yass Publications in Archaeology, Institute of Archaeology, Tel Aviv University.

———. 2010b. Review of Herbordt 2005. *OrNS* 79: 92–97.

Mora, C. and Balza, M. E. 2010. "Importanza politica ed economica di alcune istituzioni religiose e funerarie nell'impero ittita (Attualità degli studi di Fiorella Imparati)." *SMEA* 52: 253–64.

Mora, C. and Giorgieri, M. 2004. *Le lettere tra i re ittiti e i re assiri ritrovate a Ḫattuša.* HANE/M 7. Padova: Sargon.

Mouton, A. 2006. Review of Miller 2004. *BiOr* 63: 129–33.

———. 2008. Review of Pecchioli Daddi 2003a. *BiOr* 65: 456–59.

Müller, M. 1968. *Die Erlässe und Instruktionen aus dem Lande Arrapḫa. Ein Beitrag zur Rechtsgeschichte des Alten Vorderen Orients.* PhD dissertation, Leipzig.

———. 1971. "Sozial- und wirtschaftspolitische Rechtserlässe im Lande Arrapḫa." Pp. 53–60 in *Beiträge zur sozialen Struktur des Alten Vorderasien*, edited by H. Klengel. Berlin: Akademie.

Naumann, R. 1955. *Architektur Kleinasiens von ihren Anfängen bis zum Ende der hethitischen Zeit.* Tübingen: Ernst Wasmuth.

Neu, E. 1968. *Interpretation der hethitischen mediopassiven Verbalformen.* StBoT 5. Wiesbaden: Harrassowitz.

———. 1974. *Der Anitta-Text.* StBoT 18. Wiesbaden: Harrassowitz.

———. 1979. "Hethitisch *kurur* und *taksul* in syntaktischer Sicht." Pp. 407–27 in *Studia Mediterranea Piero Meriggi dicata*, edited by O. Carruba. StMed 1. Pavia: Aurora.

———. 1980a. *Studien zum endungslosen „Lokativ" des Hethitischen.* IBS, Vorträge und Kleinere Schriften 23. Innsbruck: Institut für Sprachwissenschaft der Universität.

———. 1980b. "Akkad. ^{LÚ}*MU-RI-DI* = hethit. ^{LÚ}*damšatallaš*." *RO* 41: 83–87.

———. 1980c. "Die hethitischen Verben des Kaufens und Verkaufens." *WdO* 11: 76–89.

———. 1982a. "Studie über den Gebrauch von Genetivformen auf -*u̯as* des hethitischen Verbalstubstantivs -*u̯ar*. Pp. 116–48 in *Investigationes philologicae et comparativae: Gedenkschrift für Heinz Kronasser*, edited by E. Neu. Wiesbaden: Harrassowitz.

———. 1982b. "Hethitisch /r/ im Wortauslaut." Pp. 205–25 in *Serta Indogermanica. Festschrift für Günter Neumann zum 60. Geburtstag*, edited by J. Tischler. IBS 40. Innsbruck: Institut für Sprachwissenschaft der Universität Innsbruck.

———. 1983. *Glossar zu den althethitischen Ritualtexten.* StBoT 26. Wiesbaden: Harrassowitz.

———. 1984. Review of *Florilegium Anatolicum: Mélanges offerts à Emmanuel Laroche*, edited by E. Akurgal. Paris: Boccard, 1979. *AfO* 31: 97–100.

———. 1996. *Das hurritische Epos der Freilassung 1: Untersuchungen zu einem hurritisch-hethitischen Textensemble aus Ḫattuša*. StBoT 32. Wiesbaden: Harrassowitz.

Neu, E. and Rüster, C. 1975. *Hethitische Keilschrift-Paläographie 2 (14.–13. Jh. v. Chr.)*. StBoT 21. Wiesbaden: Harrassowitz.

Neumann, G. 1973. Review of *StBoT* 14, 15, 16, 17, 20. *IF* 78: 239–47.

Oettinger, N. 1976. *Die militärischen Eide der Hethiter*. StBoT 22. Wiesbaden. Harrassowitz.

———. 1979 (2002). *Die Stammbildung des hethitischen Verbums. Nachdruck mit einer kurzen Revision der hethitischen Verbalklassen*. DBH 7. Dresden: Technische Universität Dresden.

———. 1985. "Thematische Verbalklassen des Hethitischen: Umlaut und Ablaut bei Themavokal." Pp. 296–312 in *Grammatische Kategorien: Funktion und Geschichte. Akten der VII. Fachtagung der Indogermanischen Gesellschaft, Berlin, 20.–25. Februar 1983*, edited by B. Schlerath and V. Rittner. Wiesbaden: Reichert.

———. 2002. "Hethitisch *warhuizna*- „Wald, heiliger Hain" und *tiyessar* „Baumpflanzung" (mit einer Bemerkung zu dt. *Wald*, engl. *wold*)." Pp. 253–60 in *Silva Anatolica. Anatolian Studies Presented to Maciej Popko on the Occasion of His 65th Birthday*, edited by P. Taracha. Warsaw: Agade.

Oppenheim, L. et al. 1970. *Glass and Glassmaking in Ancient Mesopotamia: An Edition of the Cuneiform Texts which Contain Instructions for Glassmakers with a Catalogue of Surviving Objects*. Corning, New York: Corning Museum of Glass.

Otten, H. 1952. "Beiträge zum hethitischen Lexikon." *ZA* 50: 230–36.

———. 1953a. *Zur grammatikalischen und lexikalischen Bestimmung des Luvischen. Untersuchung der luvili-Texte*. Institut für Orientforschung, Veröffentlichung 19. Berlin: Akademie.

———. 1953b. *Luvische Texte in Umschrift*. Institut für Orientforschung, Veröffentlichung 17. Berlin: Akademie.

———. 1957. "Zwei althethitische Belege zu den Ḫapiru (SA.GAZ)." *ZA* 52: 216–23.

———. 1957–58 "Bemerkungen zu den hethitischen Instruktionen für die $^{LÚ.MEŠ}$SAG." *AfO* 18: 387–90.

———. 1958. *Hethitische Totenrituale*. Institut für Orientforschung, Veröffentlichung 37. Berlin: Deutsche Akademie der Wissenschaften zu Berlin.

———. 1963. "Neue Quellen zum Ausklang des Hethitischen Reiches." *MDOG* 94: 1–23.

———. 1964. "Aufgaben eines Bürgermeisters in Ḫattuša." *Baghdader Mitteilungen* 3: 91–95.

———. 1969. *Sprachliche Stellung und Datierung des Madduwatta-Textes*. StBoT 11. Wiesbaden: Harrassowitz.

———. 1971a. *Ein hethitisches Festritual (KBo XIX 128)*. StBoT 13. Wiesbaden: Harrassowitz.

———. 1971b. *Materialien zum hethitischen Lexikon*. StBoT 15. Wiesbaden. Harrassowitz.

———. 1973. *Eine althethitische Erzählung um die Stadt Zalpa.* StBoT 17. Wiesbaden: Harrassowitz.

———. 1974. "Die Schenkungsurkunde KUB XIII 8 - Eine junge Kopie." Pp. 245–51 in *Anatolian Studies Presented to Hans Gustav Güterbock*, edited by K. Bittel et al. Istanbul: Nederland Historisch-Archaeologisch Institut.

———. 1976. "Bemerkungen zum Hethitischen Wörterbuch." *ZA* 66: 89–104.

———. 1979. "Original oder Abschrift — zur Datierung von CTH 258." Pp. 273–76 in *Florilegium Anatolicum: Mélanges offerts à Emmanuel Laroche*. Paris: Boccard.

———. 1983a. "Der Anfang der *ḪAZANNU*-Instruktion." *OrNS* 52: 133–42.

———. 1983b. "„Brücken" im hethitischen Schrifttum." Pp. 433–34 in *Beiträge zur Altertumskunde Kleinasiens: Festschrift für Kurt Bittel,* edited by M. Boehmer and H. Hauptmann. Mainz: von Zabern.

———. 1983c. "Zur frühen Stadtgeschichte von Ḫattuša nach den inschriftlichen Quellen." *IstMitt* 33: 40–52.

———. 1987. *Das hethitische Königshaus im 15. Jahrhundert v. Chr. Zum Neufund einiger Landschenkungsurkunden in Boğazköy*. Sonderabdruck aus dem Anzeiger der phil.-hist. Klasse der Österreichischen Akademie der Wissenschaften, 123, Jahrgang 1986, So. 2. Wien: Österreichische Akademie der Wissenschaften.

———. 1988. *Die Bronzetafel aus Boğazköy. Ein Staatsvertrag mit Tutḫalijas IV.* StBoT Beiheft 1. Wiesbaden: Harrassowitz.

———. 1990. "Bemerkungen zur Überlieferung einiger hethitischer Texte." *ZA* 80: 223–27.

Otten, H. and Rüster, C. 1977. "Textanschlüsse und Duplikate von Boğazköy-Tafeln (41–50)." *ZA* 67: 53–63.

———. 1978. "Textanschlüsse und Duplikate von Boğazköy-Tafeln (51–60)." *ZA* 68: 150–59.

Otten, H. and Souček, V. 1965. *Das Gelübde der Königin Puduḫepa an die Göttin Lelwani.* StBoT 1. Wiesbaden. Harrassowitz.

Parkinson, R. B. 1999. *The Tale of Sinuhe and Other Ancient Egyptian Poems*. Oxford World's Classics. New York: Oxford University Press.

Parpola, S. 2003. "International Law in the First Millennium." Pp. 1047–66 in *A History of Ancient Near Eastern Law*, edited by R. Westbrook. HdO I/72. Leiden: Brill.

———. 2011. "Staatsvertrag (treaty). B. Neuassyrisch." *RlA* 13: 40–45.

Parpola, S. and Watanabe, K. 1988. *Neo Assyrian Treaties and Loyalty Oaths.* State Archives of Assyria 2. Helsinki: Neo-Assyrian Text Corpus Project.

Paulus, S. in press "Ordal statt Eid – Das Beweisverfahren in mittelbabylonischer Zeit." Lebendige Rechtsgeschichte. Wiesbaden: Philippika.

Pecchioli Daddi, F. 1975. "Il *ḪAZAN(N)U* nei testi di Hattusa" *Oriens Antiquus* 14: 93–136.

———. 1979. "A proposito di KBo XVI 24(+)25." *Atti della Accademia Nazionale dei Lincei, Rendiconti: Classe di Scienze morali, storiche e filologiche* 34: 51–55.

———. 1982. *Mestieri, professioni e dignità nell'Anatolia ittita.* Incunabula Graeca 79. Rome: Edizioni dell'Ateneo.

———. 1994. "Il re, il padre del re, il nonno del re." *Orientis Antiqui Miscellanea* 1: 75–91.

———. 1996. Review of Güterbock and van den Hout 1991. *BiOr* 53: 139–44.

———. 2002a. "A 'New' Instruction from Arnuwanda I." Pp. 261–68 in *Silva Anatolica. Anatolian Studies Presented to Maciej Popko on the Occasion of His 65th Birthday*, edited by P. Taracha. Warsaw: Agade.

———. 2002b. "Testi politico-amministrativi: formazione, tipologia, attribuzione." *SMEA* 44: 330–32.

———. 2003a. *Il vincolo per i governatori di provincia*. StMed 13. Pavia: Italian University Press.

———. 2003b. "Le cariche d'oro." Pp. 83–92 in *Hittite Studies in Honor of Harry A. Hoffner Jr. on the Occasion of His 65th Birthday*, edited by G. M. Beckman, R. H. Beal, and G. McMahon. Winona Lake, IN: Eisenbrauns.

———. 2004. "Palace Servants and Their Obligations." *OrNS* 73: 451–68.

———. 2005a. "Die mittelhethitischen *išḫiul*-Texte." *AoF* 32: 280–90.

———. 2005b. "Classification and New Edition of Politico-Administrative Texts." Pp. 599–611 in *Acts of the Vth International Congress of Hittitology, Çorum, September 02–08, 2002*, edited by A. Süel. Ankara: Balkan Cilt Evi.

———. 2006. "The System of Government at the Time of Tutḫaliya IV." Pp. 117–30 in *The Life and Times of Ḫattušili III and Tutḫaliya IV. Proceedings of a Symposium Held in Honour of J. de Roos, 12–13 December 2003*, edited by Th. P. J. van den Hout. PIHANS 103. Leiden: Nederlands Instituut voor het Nabije Oosten.

Peled, I. in press. "Eunuchs in Hatti and Assyria: A Reassessment." In *Proceedings of the 56th Rencontre Assyriologique Internationale, Barcelona, July 26–30, 2010*.

Pierallini, S. 2002. "Luoghi di culto sulla cittadella di Ḫattuša." Pp. 627–35 in *Anatolia Antica: Studi in memoria di Fiorella Imparati*, edited by S. de Martino and F. Pecchioli Daddi. Eothen 11. Firenze: LoGisma.

Polvani, A. M. 1988. *La terminologia dei minerali nei testi ittiti*. Eothen 3. Firenze: LoGisma.

Popko, M. 1994. *Zippalanda: Ein Kultzentrum im hethitischen Kleinasien*. THeth 21. Heidelberg: Carl Winter.

———. 2003a. "Zur Topographie von Ḫattuša: Tempel auf Büyükkale." Pp. 315–23 in *Hittite Studies in Honor of Harry A. Hoffner Jr. on the Occasion of His 65th Birthday*, edited by G. M. Beckman, R. H. Beal, and G. McMahon. Winona Lake, IN: Eisenbrauns.

———. 2003b. "Zum hethitischen Schutzgott der Lanze." *JANER* 3: 93–97.

———. 2005. "Einige Bemerkungen zum alt- und mittelhethitischen Duktus." *RO* 58: 9–13.

Pringle, J. 2010. "Further Comments on a Hittite Kinship Term." Pp. 193–98 in Ipamati kistamati pari tumatimis: *Luwian and Hittite Studies presented to J. David Hawkins on the Occasion of His 70th Birthday*, edited by I. Singer. Tel Aviv: Emery and Claire Yass Publications in Archaeology, Institute of Archaeology, Tel Aviv University.

Prins, A. 1997. *Hittite Neuter Singular - Neuter Plural: Some Evidence for a Connection.* Leiden: CNWS.

Pruzsinszky, R. 2009. *Mesopotamian Chronology of the 2nd Millennium B.C. An Introduction to the Textual Evidence and Related Chronological Issues.* Wien: Österreichische Akademie der Wissenschaften.

Puhvel, J. 1979. "Some Hittite Etymologies." Pp. 297–304 in *Florilegium Anatolicum: Mélanges offerts à Emmanuel Laroche.* Paris: Boccard.

———. 1980. "On the Origin and Congeners of Hittite *aššu-* 'good'." *ZvS* 94: 65–70.

———. 1994. "Ash and Soap in Hittite." Pp. 215–18 in *Iranian and Indo-European Studies. Memorial Volume of Oktar Klíma*, edited by P. Vavroušek, Prague.

———. 2004. "Secrecy in Hittite: *munnai-* vs. *sanna-*." *IL* 27: 101–4.

———. 2009. "Hittite *pankur*: Return to Common Sense." *AJNES* 4: 56–62.

Quack, J. F. 1994. *Die Lehren des Ani: ein neuägyptischer Weisheitstext in seinem kulturellen Umfeld.* OBO 141. Freiburg: Vandenhoeck & Ruprecht.

Redford, D. B. 1995. "Ancient Egyptian Literature: An Overview." *CANE* 4: 2223–41.

Reichardt, K. M. 1998. *Linguistic Structures of Hittite and Luvian Curse Formulae.* PhD dissertation, University of North Carolina, Chapel Hill.

Rieken, E. 1999a. *Untersuchungen zur nominalen Stammbildung des Hethitischen.* StBoT 44. Wiesbaden: Harrassowitz.

———. 1999b. "Zur Verwendung der Konjunktion *ta* in den hethitischen Texten." *MSS* 59: 63–88.

———. 2009. "Hethitisch *kaša, kašma, kašat(t)a*: Drei verkannte deiktische Partikeln." Pp. 265–73 in *Pragmatische Kategorien. Form, Funktion und Diachronie. Akten der Arbeitstagung der Indogermanischen Gesellschaft, Marburg, 24.–26. September 2007*, edited by E. Rieken and P. Widmer. Wiesbaden: Harrassowitz.

Riemschneider, K. K. 1958. "Die hethitischen Landschenkungsurkunden." *MIO* 6: 321–81.

———. 1961. Review of *Festschrift Johannes Friedrich zum 65. Geburtstag am 27. August 1958 gewidmet*, edited by R. von Kienle et al. Heidelberg: Carl Winter, 1959. *BiOr* 18: 23–29.

———. 1965. "Zum Lehnwesen bei den Hethitern." *ArOr* 33: 333–40.

Rizzi Mellini, A. M. 1979. "Un' istruzione etea di interesse storico: KBo XVI 24 + 25." Pp. 509–53 in *Studia Mediterranea Piero Meriggi dicata*, edited by O. Carruba. StMed 1. Pavia: Aurora.

Rollinger, R. 2004. "Die Verschriftlichung von Normen: Einflüsse und Elemente orientalischer Kulturtechnik in den homerischen Epen, dargestellt am Beispiel des Vertragswesens." Pp. 369–425 in *Griechische Archaik und der Orient: Interne und externe Impulse*, edited by R. Rollinger and Chr. Ulf. Berlin: Akademie.

Römer, W. H. Ph. 1990. "Rat des Schuruppag." TUAT III/1: 48–67.

Rose, S. R. 2006. *The Hittite -hi/-mi Conjugations: Evidence for an Early Indo-European Voice Opposition.* IBS 121. Innsbruck: Innsbrucker Beiträge zur Sprachwissenschaft.

Rosi, S. 1984. "Il ruolo delle «Truppe» UKU.UŠ nell'organizzazione militare ittita." *SMEA* 24: 109–29.

Rost, L. 1956. "Die ausserhalb von Boğazköy gefundenen hethitischen Briefe." *MIO* 4: 328–50.

Roth, M. T. 1995. *Law Collections from Mesopotamia and Asia Minor.* WAW 6. Atlanta: Society of Biblical Literature.

Rüster, C. 1988. "Materialien zu einer Fehlertypologie der hethitischen Texte." Pp. 295–306 in *Documentum Asiae minoris antiquae: Festschrift für Heinrich Otten zum 75. Geburtstag*, edited by E. Neu and C. Rüster. Wiesbaden: Harrassowitz.

Rüster, C. and Wilhelm, G. 2012. *Landschenkungsurkunden hethitischer Könige*. StBoT Beiheft 4. Wiesbaden: Harrassowitz.

Sallaberger, W. 2010. "Skepsis gegenüber väterlicher Weisheit: zum altbabylonischen Dialog zwischen Vater und Sohn." Pp. 303–17 in *Your Praise Is Sweet. A Memorial Volume for Jeremy Black from Students, Colleagues and Friends*, edited by H. D. Baker, E. Robson, and G. Zólyomi. London: British Institute for the Study of Iraq.

Schachner, A. 2011. *Hattuscha. Auf der Suche nach dem sagenhaften Großreich der Hethiter*. München: C. H. Beck.

———. 2012a. "Gedanken zur Datierung, Entwicklung und Funktion der hethitischen Kunst." *AoF* 39: 130–66.

———. 2012b. "Die Funktionen des Palastes der hethitischen Großkönige in Boğazköy-Hattuša." Pp. 81–96 in *Orte der Herrschaft: Charakteristika von antiken Machtzentren*, edited by F. Arnold et al. Rahden: Leidorf.

von Schuler, E. 1956. "Die Würdenträgereide des Arnuwanda." *OrNS* 25: 209–40.

———. 1957. *Hethitische Dienstanweisungen für höhere Hof- und Staatsbeamte. Ein Beitrag zum antiken Recht Kleinasiens*. *AfO* Beiheft 10. Graz: Biblio-Verlag.

———. 1959. "Hethitische Königserlässe als Quellen der Rechtsfindung und ihr Verhältnis zum kodifizierten Recht." Pp. 435–72 in *Festschrift Johannes Friedrich zum 65. Geburtstag am 27. August 1958 gewidmet*, edited by R. von Kienle et al. Heidelberg: Carl Winter.

———. 1964. "Staatsverträge und Dokumente hethitischen Rechts." Pp. 34–53 in *Neuere Hethiterforschung*, edited by G. Walser. *Historia* 7. Wiesbaden: Franz Steiner.

———. 1965a. *Die Kaškäer: Ein Beitrag zur Ethnographie des alten Kleinasien*. Untersuchungen zur Assyriologie und vorderasiatischen Archäologie 3. Berlin: de Gruyter.

———. 1965b. "Sonderformen hethitischer Staatsverträge." *Jahrbuch für kleinasiatische Forschungen / Anadolu Araştirmalari* 2 (Fs. H. Bossert): 445–64.

———. 1976–80 "Instruktionen, Hethiter." *RlA* 5: 114–17.

———. 1982. "Vorschriften für Diener des Königs." TUAT I/1: 124–25.

Schuol, M. 2004. *Hethitische Kultmusik. Eine Untersuchung der Instrumental- und Vokalmusik anhand hethitischer Ritualtexte und von archäologischen Zeugnissen.* Orient-Archäologie 14. Rahden: Leidorf.

Schwemer, D. 2001. *Wettergottgestalten: Die Wettergottgestalten Mesopotamiens und Nordsyriens im Zeitalter der Keilschriftkulturen: Materialien und Studien nach den schriftlichen Quellen.* Wiesbaden: Harrassowitz.

———. 2005. "Der Vertrag zwischen Tutḫalija von Ḫatti and Šunaššura von Kizzuwatna." TUATNF 2:97–106.

———. 2009. Review of Taggar-Cohen 2006. *OrNS* 78: 96–105.

Seeher, J. 2006. "Ḫattuša – Tutḫalija-Stadt? Argumente für eine Revision der Chronologie der hethitischen Hauptstadt." Pp. 131–46 in *The Life and Times of Ḫattušili III and Tutḫaliya IV. Proceedings of a Symposium Held in Honour of J. de Roos, 12–13 December 2003, Leiden*, edited by Th. P. J. van den Hout. PIHANS 103. Leiden: Nederlands Instituut voor het Nabije Oosten.

———. 2008. "Abschied von Gewusstem: Die Ausgrabungen in Ḫattuša am Beginn des 21. Jahrhunderts." Pp. 1–13 in *Ḫattuša – Boğazköy: Das Hethiterreich im Spannungsfeld des Alten Orients. 6. Internationales Colloquium der Deutschen Orient-Gesellschaft, 22.–24. März 2006, Würzburg*, edited by G. Wilhelm. Wiesbaden: Harrassowitz.

Seminara, S. 2000. "Le Istruzioni di Šūpê-amēlī. Vecchio e nuovo a confronto nella "sapienza" siriana del Tardo Bronzo." *UF* 32: 487–529.

Sidel'tsev, A.V. 2008. "Middle Hittite *-ške*-forms in Benedictions and Curses." *SMEA* 50: 681–704.

———. 2010. "Proleptic Pronouns in Middle Hittite." Pp. 211–48 in *Proceedings of the 53e Rencontre Assyriologique Internationale.* Vol. I. Part 1. *Language in the Ancient Near East*, edited by L. Kogan et al. Babel und Bibel 4. Winona Lake, IN: Eisenbrauns.

———. 2011a. "Clitic Doubling: A New Syntactic Category in Hittite." *AoF* 38: 81–91.

———. 2011b. "Hittite Parallels for Balkan Sprachbund Clitic Doubling." *Zbornik Matice Srpske za filologiju i lingvistiku* 54: 9–26.

———. in press a. "Hittite Clitic Doubling as an Innovative Category: Its Origin." In *Proceedings of the 57th Rencontre Assyriologique Internationale, Rome, 4–8 July 2011*, edited by A. Archi et al.

———. in press b. "The Origin of Hittite Right Dislocations." In *Proceedings of the 8th International Congress of Hittitology, Warsaw, September 5–9, 2011*, edited by P. Taracha.

Singer, I. 1975. "Hittite *ḫilammar* and Hieroglyphic Luwian **ḫilana*." *ZA* 65: 69–103.

———. 1983. *The Hittite KI.LAM Festival. Part One*. StBoT 27. Wiesbaden: Harrassowitz.

———. 1984. "The AGRIG in the Hittite Texts." *AnSt* 34: 97–127.

———. 1998. "The Mayor of Ḫattuša and His Duties." Pp. 169–76 in *Capital Cities: Urban Planning and Spiritual Dimensions*, edited by J. Westenholz. Jerusalem: Bible Lands Museum.

———. 2001a. "The Treaties between Karkamiš and Hatti." Pp. 635–41 in *Akten des IV. Internationalen Kongresses für Hethitologie, Würzburg, 4.–8. Oktober 1999*, edited by G. Wilhelm. StBoT 45. Wiesbaden: Harrassowitz.

———. 2001b. "The Fate of Hattusa during the Period of Tarhuntassa's Supremacy." Pp. 395–403 in *Kulturgeschichten. Altorientalistische Studien für Volkert Haas zum 65. Geburtstag*, edited by T. Richter, D. Prechel, and J. Klinger. Saarbrücken: Saarbrücker Druckerei und Verlag.

———. 2002. *Hittite Prayers*. WAW 11. Atlanta: Society of Biblical Literature.

———. 2005. "On Luwians and Hittites." *BiOr* 62: 430–51.

———. 2006. "The Urḫi-Teššub Affair in the Hittite-Egyptian Correspondence." Pp.

27–38 in *The Life and Times of Ḫattušili III and Tutḫaliya IV. Proceedings of a Symposium Held in Honour of J. de Roos, 12–13 December 2003, Leiden*, edited by Th.P.J. van den Hout. PIHANS 103. Leiden: Nederlands Instituut voor het Nabije Oosten.

———. 2008. "On Siege Warfare in Hittite Texts." Pp. 250–65 in *Treasures on Camels' Humps: Historical and Literary Studies from the Ancient Near East Presented to Israel Eph'al*, edited by M. Cogan and D. Kahn. Jerusalem: Hebrew Univ. Magnes Press.

———. 2009a. *The Hittites and Their Civilization*. Biblical Encyclopedia Library 26. Jerusalem: Mosad Bialik. (Hebrew)

———. 2009b. "'In Hattuša the Royal House Declined.' Royal Mortuary Cult in 13th Century Hatti." Pp. 169–91 in *Central-North Anatolia in the Hittite Period: New Perspectives in Light of Recent Research. Acts of the International Conference Held at the University of Florence (7–9 February 2007)*, edited by F. Pecchioli Daddi, G. Torri, and C. Corti. StAs 5. Rome: Herder.

———. 2011. "Between Scepticism and Credulity: In Defence of Hittite Historiography." Pp. 731–66 in *The Calm before the Storm. Selected Writings of Itamar Singer on the End of the Late Bronze Age in Anatolia and the Levant*. WAW Supplements 1. Atlanta: Society of Biblical Literature.

von Soden, W. 1990. "Ratschläge und Warnungen." TUAT III/1: 163–69.

Soldt, W. H. van. 2003. "Ordal. A. Mesopotamien." *RlA* 10: 124–29.

Soysal, O. 2003. "Kantuzzili in Siegelinschriften." *BiOr* 60: 41–56.

———. 2004. *Hattischer Wortschatz in hethitischer Textüberlieferung*. HdO I/74. Leiden: Brill.

———. 2005. "On the Origin of the Royal Title *tabarna / labarna*." *Anatolica* 31: 189–209.

———. 2006. Review Y. Cohen 2002. *JNES* 65: 129–34.

Soysal, Y. 2001. "Hitit din ve sosyal hayatında $^{\text{LÚ/MUNUS}}$Ú.ḪÚB 'sağır'." Pp. 652–69 in *Akten des IV. Internationalen Kongresses für Hethitologie Würzburg, 4.–8. Oktober 1999*, edited by G. Wilhelm. StBoT 45. Wiesbaden: Harrassowitz.

Starke, F. 1977. *Die Funktionen der dimensionalen Kasus und Adverbien im Althethitischen*. StBoT 23. Wiesbaden: Harrassowitz.

———. 1985. *Die keilschrift-luwischen Texte in Umschrift*. StBoT 30. Wiesbaden: Harrassowitz.

———. 1990. *Untersuchung zur Stammbildung des keilschrift-luwischen Nomens*. StBoT 31. Wiesbaden: Harrassowitz.

———. 1995a. *Ausbildung und Training von Streitwagenpferden: Ein hippologisch orientierte Interpretation des Kikkuli-Textes*. StBoT 41. Wiesbaden: Harrassowitz.

———. 1995b. "Zur urkundlichen Charakterisierung neuassyrischer Treueide anhand einschlägiger hethitischer Texte des 13. Jh." *ZABR* 1: 70–82.

———. 1996. "Zur „Regierung" des hethitischen Staates." *ZABR* 2: 140–82.

———. 1997. "Troia im Kontext des historisch-politischen und sprachlichen Umfeldes Kleinasiens im 2. Jahrtausend." *Studia Troica* 7: 447–87.

———. 2002. "Die Verfassung des hethitischen Reiches." Pp. 316–17 in *Die Hethiter und ihr Reich. Das Volk der 1000 Götter. Katalog der Ausstellung, Bonn 18. Januar–28. April 2002*, edited by H. Willinghöfer. Bonn: Theiss.

Stivala, G. 2003. *I canti corali hattici*. Tesi di dottorato. Università degli Studi di Firenze.

Strauß, R. 2006. *Reinigungsrituale aus Kizzuwatna*. Berlin: de Gruyter.

Streck, M. P. 2006. "Sibilants in the Old Babylonian Texts of Hammurapi and of the Governors in Qaṭṭunān." Pp. 215–51 in *The Akkadian Language in Its Semitic Context*, edited by G. Deutscher and N. J. C. Kouwenberg. PIHANS 106. Leiden: Nederlands Instituut voor het Nabije Oosten.

———. 2009. Review of *CAD* Vols. 18, T (2006), and 19, Ṭ (2006). *ZA* 99: 135–40.

Sturtevant, E. H. 1934. "A Hittite Text on the Duties of Priests and Temple Servants." *JAOS* 54: 363–406.

Sturtevant, E. H. and Bechtel, G. 1935. *A Hittite Chrestomathy*. Philadelphia: Linguistic Society of America.

Süel, A. 1985. *Hitit Kaynaklarında Tapınak Görevlileri ile Ilgili Bir Direktif Metni*. Ankara: Ankara Üniversitesi dil ve Tarih-Coğrafya Fakültesi Yayınları.

Sürenhagen, D. 1981. "Zwei Gebete Ḫattušilis und der Puduḫepa. Textliche und literaturhistorische Untersuchungen." *AoF* 8: 83–168.

———. 2001. "Dimensionen sakralen Königtums im hethitischen Staat: Einige Bemerkungen zum Forschungsstand." Pp. 403–10 in Lux orientis: *Archäologie zwischen Asien und Europa. Festschrift für Harald Hauptmann zum 65. Geburtstag*, edited by D. Sürenhagen, R. M. Boehmer, and J. Maran. Rahden: Leidorf.

Symington, D. 1991. "Late Bronze Age Writing-boards and Their Uses: Textual Evidence from Anatolia and Syria." *AnSt* 41: 111–23.

Szemerényi, O. 1982. "Anatolica II (8–10)." Pp. 215–34 in *Investigationes Philologicae et Comparativae: Gedenkschrift für Heinz Kronasser*, edited by E. Neu. Wiesbaden: Harrassowitz.

Tadmor, H. 1982. "Treaty and Oath in the Ancient Near East: A Historian's Approach." Pp. 127–52 in *Humanizing America's Iconic Book: Society of Biblical Literature Centennial Addresses 1980*, edited by G. M. Tucker and D. A. Knight. Chico, California: Scholars Press.

Taggar-Cohen, A. 2006. *Hittite Priesthood*. THeth 26. Heidelberg: Carl Winter.

———. 2011a. "Biblical *Covenant* and Hittite *išḫiul* reexamined." *Vetus Testamentum* 61: 461–88.

———. 2011b. "Covenant Priesthood: Cross-cultural Legal and Religious Aspects of Biblical and Hittite Priesthood." Pp. 11–24 in *Levites and Priests in History and Tradition*, edited by M. A. Leuchter and J. M. Hutton. Atlanta: Society of Biblical Literature.

Taracha, P. 1995. "Zum Stand der hattischen Studien: Mögliches und Unmögliches in der Erforschung des Hattischen." Pp. 351–58 in *Atti del II Congresso Internazionale di Hittitologia*, edited by O. Carruba, M. Giorgieri, and C. Mora. StMed 9. Pavia: Iuculano.

———. 1997. "Zu den Tutḫalija-Annalen (CTH 142)." *WdO* 28: 74–84.

———. 2004. "On the Dynasty of the Hittite Empire." Pp. 631–38 in *Šarnikzel. Hethitologische Studien zum Gedenken an Emil Orgetorix Forrer (19.02.1894–*

10.01.1986), edited by D. Groddek and S. Rößle. DBH 10. Dresden: Technische Universität Dresden.

———. 2009. *Religions of Second Millennium Anatolia.* DBH 27. Wiesbaden: Harrassowitz.

———. 2010. Review of Taggar-Cohen 2006. *BiOr* 67: 158–62.

Tigay, J. H. 1993. "On Evaluating Claims of Literary Borrowing." Pp. 250–55 in *The Tablet and the Scroll. Near Eastern Studies in Honor of William W. Hallo*, edited by M. R. Cohen et al. Bethesda: CDL.

Tjerkstra, F. A. 1999. *Principles of the Relation between Local Adverb, Verb and Sentence Particle in Hittite*. CM 15. Groningen: Styx.

Torri, G. 2005. "Militärische Feldzüge nach Ostanatolien in der mittelhethitischen Zeit." *AoF* 32: 386–400.

———. 2007. "Subject Shifting in Hittite Magical Rituals." Pp. 671–80 in Tabularia Hethaeorum: *Hethitologische Beiträge Silvin Košak zum 65. Geburtstag*, edited by D. Groddek and M. Zorman. DBH 25. Wiesbaden: Harrassowitz.

———. 2008. "Der Kult der königlichen Statuen in den hethitischen keilschriftlichen Quellen." Pp. 173–90 in *Fest und Eid: Instrumente der Herrschaftssicherung im Alten Orient*, edited by D. Prechel. Würzburg: Ergon.

———. 2010. "The Scribal School of the Lower City of Hattuša and the Beginning of the Career of Anuwanza, Court Dignitary and Lord of Nerik. Pp. 383–96 in ana turri gimilli: *studi dedicati al Padre Werner R. Mayer, S.J. da amici e allievi*, edited by M.G. Biga and M. Liverani. Vicino Oriente, Quaderno 5. Rome. Università degli Studi di Roma «La Sapienza».

———. 2011. "The Phrase *ṬUPPU* ^{URU}*Ḫatti* in Colophons from Ḫattuša and the Work of the Scribe Ḫanikkuili." *AoF* 38: 135–44.

Trémouille, M.-C. 1997. ^{d}*Hebat, une divinité syro-anatolienne.* Eothen 7. Firenze: LoGisma.

———. 2002. "Hittite *ḫutanu*, Hourrite *ḫirīti*, Akkadien *ḪIRĪTUM*." *SMEA* 44: 145–49.

Ünal, A. 1991. "Hethitische Hymnen und Gebete." TUAT II/6: 791–817.

———. 1992. "Ritual Purity versus Physical Impurity in Hittite Anatolia: Public Health and Structures for Sanitation according to Cuneiform Texts and Archaeological Remains." Pp. 208–23 in *Uluslararası 1. Hititoloji Kongresi Bildirileri (19–21 Temmuz 1990)* Çorum: Uluslararası Corum Hitit Festivali Komitesi Başkanlığı.

———. 1993. "Ritual Purity versus Physical Impurity in Hittite Anatolia. Public Health and Structures for Sanitation according to Cuneiform Texts and Archaeological Remains." Pp. 119–39 in *Essays in Anatolian Archaeology*, edited by T. Mikasa. *BMECCJ* 7. Wiesbaden: Harrassowitz.

———. 1996. *The Hittite Ritual of Ḫantitaššu from the City of Hurma against Troublesome Years*. Ankara: Turkish Historical Society Printing House.

Veenhof, K. R. 1995. "Kanesh: An Assyrian Colony in Anatolia." *CANE* 2: 859–71.

Veenhof, K. R. and Eidem, J. 2008. *Mesopotamia: The Old Assyrian Period.* OBO 160/5. Fribourg: Academic Press.

Vieyra, M. 1970. "Les textes hittites." Pp. 159–566 in *Les religions du Proche-Orient asiatique. Textes babyloniens, ougaritiques, hittites*, edited by R. Labat et al. Paris: Fayard.

Waal, W. 2011. "They Wrote on Wood. The Case for a Hieroglyphic Scribal Tradition on Wooden Writing Boards in Hittite Anatolia." *AnSt* 61: 21–34.

———. 2012. "Writing in Anatolia: The Origins of the Anatolian Hieroglyphs and the Introduction(s) of the Cuneiform Script." *AoF* 39: 287–315.

Watanabe, K. 1989. "Mit Gottessiegeln versehene hethitische „Staatsverträge"." *Acta Sumerologica* 11: 260–76.

Watkins, C. 1982. "Notes on the Plural Formations of the Hittite Neuters." Pp. 250–62 in *Investigationes Philologicae et Comparativae: Gedenkschrift für Heinz Kronasser*, edited by E. Neu. Wiesbaden: Harrassowitz.

———. 2004. "Hittite." Pp. 551–75 in *The Cambridge Encyclopedia of the World's Ancient Languages*, edited by R. D. Woodard. Cambridge: Cambridge University Press.

Weeden, M. 2011. *Hittite Logograms and Hittite Scholarship*. StBoT 54. Wiesbaden: Harrassowitz.

Weeks, N. 2004. *Admonition and Curse: The Ancient Near Eastern Treaty / Covenant Forms as a Problem in Inter-Cultural Relationships*. Journal for the Study of the Old Testament Supplement Series 407. London: T&T Clark.

Weidner, E. F. 1923. *Politische Dokumente aus Kleinasien: Die Staatsverträge in akkadischer Sprache aus dem Archiv von Boghazköi*. BoSt 8–9. Leipzig: J. C. Hinrichs.

———. 1954–56 "Hof- und Harems-Erlasse assyrischer Könige aus dem 2. Jahrtausend v. Chr." *AfO* 17: 257–93.

Westbrook, R. and Woodard, R. D. 1990. "The Edict of Tudḫaliya IV." *JAOS* 110: 641–59.

Wilhelm, G. 1978. Review of Oettinger 1976. *Kratylos* 23: 95–98.

———. 1988. "Zur ersten Zeile des Šunaššura-Vertrages." Pp. 359–70 in *Documentum Asiae minoris antiquae: Festschrift für Heinrich Otten zum 75. Geburtstag*, edited by E. Neu and C. Rüster. Wiesbaden: Harrassowitz.

———. 1999. "Reinheit und Heiligkeit. Zur Vorstellungswelt altanatolischer Ritualistik." Pp. 198–217 in *Levitikus als Buch*. Bonner biblische Beiträge 119, edited by H.-J. Fabry and H.-W. Jüngling, Berlin – Bodenheim: Philo.

———. 2001. "Epische Texte. Das hurritisch-hethitische „Lied der Freilassung"." TUAT Erg.: 82–91.

———. 2005. "Zur Datierung der älteren hethitischen Landschenkungsurkunden." *AoF* 32: 272–79.

———. 2011. "Staatsvertrag. C. Bei den Hethitern." *RlA* 13: 45–49.

Wilson, J. A. 1969. "Egyptian Instructions." Pp. 412–25 in *Ancient Near Eastern Texts Relating to the Old Testament*, edited by J.B. Pritchard. Princeton: Princeton University Press.

Winkels, H. 1978. *Das zweite Pestgebet des Mursili. KUB XIV 8 und Duplikate*. PhD dissertation, Universität Hamburg.

Wittenberg, H. and Schachner, A. 2013. "The Ponds of Hattusa: Early Groundwater Management in the Hittite Kingdom." *Water Science & Technology: Water Supply* 13: 692–98.

Yakubovich, I. S. 2005. "Were Hittite Kings Divinely Anointed? A Palaic Invocation to the Sun-god and Its Significance for Hittite Religion." *JANER* 5: 107–37.

———. 2008. "Hittite-Luvian Bilingualism and the Development of Anatolian Hieroglyphs." Pp. 9–36 in *Acta Linguistica Petropolitana*. Transactions of the Institute for Linguistic Studies, 4/1. St. Petersburg: Nauka.

———. 2009. *Sociolinguistics of the Luwian Language*. Leiden: Brill.

Yoshida, D. 1987. *Die Syntax des althethitischen substantivischen Genitivs*. THeth 13. Heidelberg: Carl Winter.

———. 1996. *Untersuchungen zu den Sonnengottheiten bei den Hethitern*. THeth 22. Heidelberg: Carl Winter.

Yoshida, K. 2008. "Another Archaic Linguistic Feature in Hittite." *SMEA* 50: 851–59.

Zaccagnini, C. 1979. *The Rural Landscape of the Land of Arrapḫe*. Quaderni die Geografia Storica 1. Rome: Università di Roma, Istituto di Studi del Vicino Oriente.

———. 1990. "The Forms of Alliance and Subjugation in the Near East of the Late Bronze Age." Pp. 37–79 in *I trattati nel mondo antico: forma, ideologia, funzione*, edited by L. Canfora, M. Liverani, and C. Zaccagnini. Rome: L'Erma di Bretschneider.

Zeilfelder, S. 2001a. *Archaismus und Ausgliederung: Studien zur sprachlichen Stellung des Hethitischen*. Heidelberg: Carl Winter.

———. 2001b. "Zum Ausdruck der Finalität im Hethitischen." Pp. 395–410 in *Anatolisch und Indogermanisch / Anatolico e Indoeuropeo - Akten des Kolloquiums der Indogermanischen Gesellschaft, Pavia, 22.–25. September 1998*, edited by O. Carruba and W. Meid. IBS 100. Innsbruck: Institut für Sprachen und Literaturen der Universität Innsbruck.

———. 2004. "Topik, Fokus und rechter Satzrand im Hethitischen." Pp. 655–66 in *Šarnikzel. Hethitologische Studien zum Gedenken an Emil Orgetorix Forrer (19.02.1894–10.01.1986)*, edited by D. Groddek and S. Rößle. DBH 10. Dresden: Technische Universität Dresden.

Index

Divine Names

10 (s. Storm God)
30 (s. Moon God)
Adad (s. Storm God)
Alalu, 310–11
Anu, 310–11
Askasepa, 146–47
Ea, 146–47, 310–11
Ereškigal, 310–11
Ḫalki, 184–85, 365(225)
Ḫallāra, 310–11
Ḫantitassu, 310–11
Ḫat-…, 146–47
Ḫattaka, 310–11
Ḫazzi, 310–11
Ḫebat, 146–47, 310–11
Ḫebat-Šarruma, 310–11
Ḫurri, 240–41, 272–73, 398(14)
IŠKUR (s. Storm God)
Ištar/Šaušga, 146–47, 202–3, 310–11, 346(12)
Iyarri, 146–47, 200–201
Kulitta, 310–11, 346(12)
LAMMA (s. Tutelary Deity)
Lelwani, 310–11
Mammi, 310–11
Moon God, 94–95, 310–11
Namni, 310–11
Napsara, 310–11
Narā, 310–11
Ninatta, 310–11, 346(12)
Patron Deity (s. Tutelary Deity)
Pirwa, 310–11
Protective Deity (s. Tutelary Deity)
Storm God, 63, 146–47, 184–85, 195, 200–205, 226–27, 240–41, 277–79, 308–11, 351(48), 365(219), 379(372), 398(14), 410(152)
Sun Deity, 80–81, 326(31), 393(541)
Sun God of Heaven, 147, 241, 398(14)
Sun Goddess of Arinna, 146–47, 180–81, 195, 200–203, 240–41, 272–73, 398(14), 401(50)
Šaušga (s. Ištar/Šaušga)
Šēri, 240–41, 272–73, 398(14)
Taruppasani, 63, 308–11
Telipinu, 146–47
Tutelary Deity, 146–47, 180–81, 202–3, 240–41, 310–11 264–65, 351(61)
UTU (s. Sun Deity/God/Goddess)
War God, 146–47, 240–41, 310–11
Zababa (s. War God)
Zitḫariya, 146–47, 310–11

Personal Names

Agip-taššenni, 68
Alexander (the Great), 327(45)
Aliḫḫini, 58, 65, 138–39
Amen-em-opet, 66
AN.ŠUR-LÚ, 58, 138–39
Andulu, 196–97
Angulli, 57, 65, 96–97
Ani, 66
Anuwanza, 57, 65, 96, 97
Apa/ittī, 196–97
Apassiya, 198–99
Arnili, 17, 79, 82–83, 334(49)
Arnuwanda I, 3, 5, 11–12, 14, 18–23, 25, 33, 35, 38, 40, 49, 51, 53–54, 59–61, 66, 78–79, 129, 144, 155, 168, 182–83, 194–95, 198–201, 204–8, 212, 216–17, 242, 325(22–24), 332(28), 352(59), 354(85), 371(296)
Ašmu-^{d}NIN.GAL (s. Ašmunikkal)
Asarhaddons (s. Aššur-aḫḫē-iddina)
Āsḫapāla, 6, 10, 23–24, 41, 62, 195–97, 242–43, 324(14), 388(483)
Ashurbanipal (s. Aššur-bāni-apli)
Ašmunikkal, 3, 10, 11, 25, 40, 51, 53–54, 60–61, 155, 194, 198–99, 204–5, 208–9, 369(281)
Aššur-aḫḫ*ē*-iddina, 70, 328(58–59)
Aššur-bāni-apli, 70
Aššur-rēša-iši, 69
Atakkal, 68
Attā, 196–97
Cesar, 327(45)
Duda, 58, 65, 142–43
Dutḫaliya (s. Tudḫaliya)
Eḫeya, 19–20
Esarhhadon (s. Aššur-aḫḫē-iddina)
GIŠ.GI-PÌRIG, 57, 65, 96–97
GIŠ.KIRI$_6$.NU, 58, 138–39
^{GIŠ}GIDRU.DINGIR-*LÌ* (s. Ḫattusili III)
Ḫakku, 196–97
Ḫalwaziti, 58, 65, 142–43
Ḫāmmi, 196–97
Hardjedef, 66
Ḫattusili I, 17, 73, 78
Ḫattusili II (cf. Ḫattusili), xii, 154
Ḫattusili III, 3–4, 10–11, 21–22, 42, 54–55, 62–65, 209, 274–75, 277, 283–85, 295–97, 308–9, 329(1), 332(26), 401(50)
Ḫattusili (cf. Ḫattusili II), 155, 162–63
Ḫimuili, 34, 52–53, 127, 154, 156–61, 328(52)
Ḫittal-, 196–97
Ḫuitta, 196–97
Ḫummili, 52, 126–27
Ḫurmel, 74–75
Ḫuttaziti, 196–97
Ḫuzziya II, 53, 168, 178–79, 362(190–91), 363(199)
Isputaḫsu, 19–20, 71
Kantūzili, xii, 34, 51, 53, 127, 154–61, 164–68, 245, 328(52), 355(99), 363(199)
Karana, 69
Keret, 370(287)
Kūkku, 74–75
Kuruntiya (s. also Ulmi-Teššub), xii, 3–4, 54–55, 65, 195, 283, 297
Lalantiwasḫa, 53, 166–67
Maḫḫuzi, 58, 65, 142–43
Mameta, 196–97
Mannanni, 196–97
Marakkui, 198–99
Marta, 368(268)
Massanuzzi, 283
Masturi, 283
Mauiri, 57, 96–97
Meri-ka-re, 66
Mēsamuwa, 354(89)
Mita, 11
Mursili I, 12, 50, 73, 75, 78, 122
Mursili II, 54, 145, 284–85, 297, 327(42), 383(426), 403(70)
Mursili III (s. also, Urḫi-Teššub), 283, 295–96
Mušteya, 68
Mušu-Ḫepa, 53, 164–65
Muttalli, 52, 126–27
Muwā, 53, 74–75, 158–59, 355(102)

Muwattalli I, 21, 52–53, 127, 154, 158, 168, 178–79, 362(190–91), 363(199)
Muwattalli II, xii, 54–55, 283–85, 296–97
Nāna, 198–99
Nāni, 196–99
Nāwiniya, 196–97
Nikkalmadi, 352(59)
Ninna, 198–99
NIR.GÁL (s. Muwattalli II)
Nunnu, 74–75
Pabba, 196–97
Pa/illiya, 19–20, 71
Pallullu, 196–97
Papanikri's, 382(406)
Pariyawatra, 51, 53, 155, 164–65
Pilliya (s. Pa/illiya)
Pimpira, 12, 45, 75
Pissā, 196–97
Ptahhotep, 66
Pudu-Ḫepa, 42, 54, 62–63, 274–75, 295, 401(50)
Sakkapi, 57, 65, 96–97, 335(63)
Sarka, 74–75
Sarpa, 196–97
S/Tātīli, 196–97
S/Tatīya, 196–97
Sennacherib (s. Sîn-aḫḫē-erība)
Sîn-aḫḫē-erība, 328(59)
Sinaḫḫuwa, 78
Sûmu-ḫadû, 69
Sunaššura, 71, 357(121), 407(121)
Suppiluliuma I, xii, 13, 29, 53–54, 64, 154, 270–73, 296–97, 308–9, 329(1), 332(26)
Suppiluliu/ama II, 23, 37, 55, 63–64, 308–9, 312–13, 323(4), 409(147)
Šaušgamuwa, 23, 283
Šaušgaziti, 350(39)
Šuruppak, 12, 66
T/Sātīli, 196–97
T/Satīya, 196–97
Tadu-Ḫepa, 29, 54, 271–73
Taḫurwaili, 19–20
Tarmi-Tilla, 68
Tās, 74–75, 330(14)
Tašmi-šarri, 354(95)
Tašuḫḫe, 67
Telipinu, 16–17, 19–21, 34, 53, 71, 79, 155
Tiglatpileser I (s. Tukultī-apil-Ešarra)
Tudḫaliya I, xii, 4, 12, 14, 16, 18–23, 33–34, 39–40, 43–44, 52–53, 57–59, 71, 79, 122, 127, 129, 134–37, 140, 142–44, 152–54, 156, 168, 198, 202, 325(22), 332(28), 337(88), 352(59), 354(84), 363(199)
Tudḫaliya III, xii, 3, 5, 11, 23, 25, 34, 40, 53–54, 60, 63, 65, 71, 135, 144, 154–55, 164–65, 194, 198–201, 203–5, 271, 356(112–13)
Tudḫaliya IV, 3, 5, 11, 21–23, 26, 36, 54–55, 63–64, 135, 144, 195, 212, 282–83, 294–97, 308–9, 312–13, 323(4), 335(63), 393(539), 409(137)
Tudḫaliya the Younger, xii, 53
Tukultī-apil-Ešarra I, 69, 71
Tulpi-Teššub, 51, 53, 145, 155, 164–65, 356(113), 357(122), 383(426)
Tuttu, 196–97
Tūtuili, 198–99
Ubariya, 78
Ulmi-Teššub (s. also Kuruntiya), 4
Ura-…, 236–37
Urḫi-Teššub (s. also Mursili III), 4, 22, 54–55, 283, 295
Uza, 57, 96–97
Wattassu, 195
Zar/ldumman(n)i, 25, 195–97
Zidanta I, 52
Zid/tant/za II, 19–20, 52, 71, 126–27
Zimrī-Līm, 69–70
Zitanza (s. Zid/tant/za II)
Ziudsura, 66
Ziwiniya, 196–97
Zuliya, 17, 79, 82–85, 198–99, 334(49)
Zūru, 74–75
Zuwā, 58, 138–39
x-at$^?$ta, 196–97
x-riya, 196–97
x-riyassarma, 196–97
x-šarri, 354(95)
-azzi, 368(271)
-iariya, 196–97
-iyanna, 196–97
-lulu, 198–99

Geographical Names

Aleppo (s. Ḫalab)
Amqa, 327(42)
Amurru, 23, 283
Ankara, 1
Ankuwa, 310–11
Antakya, 328(58)
Arinna, 122–23, 146–47, 180–1, 195, 200–203, 240, 272–73, 398(14), 401(50)
Arrapḫe, 67
Arsāsa, 196–97
Arziya, 310–11
Ar-x-s/tama, 196–97
Aššur, 66
Āssuwa, 43, 53, 57–58, 135–37
Assyria, 65, 69–70, 408(128)
Atarrawanna, 196–97
A/Za?tarziya, 196–97
Azzi, 54, 286–87, 400(44)
Babylon, xii
Boğazkale/Boğazköy, 1
Dawiniya (s. T/Dawiniya)
Durmitta (s. T/Durmitta)
Egypt, 408(128)
Gaggab/paḫa (s. K/Gaggab/paha)
Ganin-… (s. K/Ganin-…)
Garaḫna (s. K/Garahna)
G/Kaska (s. K/Gaska)
G/Ta-x-wiya, 196–97
Ḫa-…, 146–47
Ḫa/ur(ra)nassi, 194, 200–205, 368(264)
Ḫa/ursuwanda, 196–97
Ḫa/urta-…, 200–201
Ḫa/urtāna, 196–97
Ḫaḫḫa, 116–19
Ḫalab, 190–92, 240–41, 366(245)
Ḫara-…, 196–97
Ḫarḫarna, 122–23
Ḫartāna, 369(274)
Ḫatti, *passim*
Ḫattusa, *passim*
Ḫimmuwa, 22, 54, 230–31
Ḫin(n)ariya, 204–5, 368(271)
Ḫissaspa, 310–11
Ḫūḫuli, 196–97
Ḫur(ra)nassi (s. Ḫa/ur(ra)nassi)
Ḫurma, 310–11
Ḫursuwanda (s. Ḫa/ursuwanda)
Ḫurta-… (s. Ḫa/urta-…), 200–201
Ḫurtāna (s. Ḫa/urtāna), 196–97
Ḫutarna~…, 198–99
Ḫūwarra, 204–5
Iḫuwalli-…, 196–97
Ilios (s. also Troy and Wilusiya), 53
Isarwissa, 196–97
Ismerig(g)a, 3, 25, 144, 195
Isuwa, 22, 54, 230–31
Ka/issiya, 194–201, 230, 368(264)
K/Gaggab/paha, 196–97
Kakarpa, 198–99
Kalasma, 195, 368(264)
Kaneš, 335(65)
K/Ganin-…, 196–97
K/Garahna, 202–3, 310–11
Karkamiš, 54–55, 324(13)
Kasiya, 22, 54, 231
K/Gaska, 114–15, 145, 150–51, 212, 286–87, 400(44)
Kayseri, 335(65)
Kazzilu-…, 198–99
Kilimuna, 170–71, 358(139)
Kinnara, 60, 194–95, 198–201, 204–5, 368(266, 271)
Kipazziya, 196–97
Kissiya (s. Ka/issiya)
Kuizna, 196–97
Kuīzzana, 195
Kültepe, 335(65)
Kūluppa, 74–75
Kummaḫa, 114–15
Kuşaklı (s. Sarissa)
Leilan, Tell, 329(60)
Liḫs/zina, 240–41, 310–11
Lukka, 54, 286–87, 400(44)
Ma?-…, 196–97
Makarwasiyanda, 196–97
Mall?ittama, 196–97
Mallitaskuriya, 196–97
Malliwatta, 196–97

Mari, 69, 328(59)
Maşat Höyük (s. Tapikka),
Me/Siku-x, 204–5
Mittani, 54
Nerik(ka), 63, 308–9, 146–47, 202–3, 240–41, 277–79
Nesa (s. Kaneš)
Nineveh, 310–11
Ninniwa, 196–97
Nuzi, 67–68
Paḫḫuwa, 11
Pitte/iyarig(g)a, 202–3, 240–41, 310–11
Pukkissuwa, 198–99
Rubicon River, 327(45)
Sa-…., 196–97, 368(264)
Saiztawa, 196–97
Samūḫa, 146–47, 202–3
San(a)ḫuitta, 17, 78, 82–83, 332(26, 28)
Sappa, 196–97
Saressiya, 310–11
Sarissa, 240–41, 378(364, 371)
Sāsana, 196–97, 243
Seḫa River, 283
Si/Meku-x, 204–5
Sure/ista, 17, 84–85
Syria, 72
T/Ga-x-wiya, 196–97
Tagarama, 22, 54, 230–31
Tāḫa, Mt., 192–93, 367(250)
Taḫaramma, 196–97
Takkisa, 196–97
Tapapaḫsu, 242–43
Tapapanuwa, 242–43
Tapikka, 25, 52, 195, 212, 365(229)
Tarḫuntassa, xii, 3–4, 54–55, 65, 195, 283, 297
Taruisa, 53
T/Dawiniya, 310–11
Ta'yinat, Tell, 328(58)
Tiliura, 11
Tīsama, 310–11
Tiyassilta, 242–43
Troy (s. also Ilios and Wilusiya), 53
Tuarpā, 196–97
Tunna, 310–11
T/Durmitta, 310–11
Ugarit, 65–66, 370(287)
Ukkueriya, 198–99
Un$^{?}$ta-, 195, 368(264)
Ura, 11, 389(487)
Uršu, 359(147)
Ūssa, 54, 63, 297, 306–7
Wastisa, 198–99
Wilusiya (s. also Ilios and Troy), 53
Wisaspura, 196–97
Za/A$^{?}$tarziya, 196–97
Zāzza, 196–97
Zinip~…, 196–97
Zip$^{?}$-, 198–99
Zippala(n)d/ta, 63, 146–47, 184–85, 240–1, 308–9, 365(219)
Zitḫara, 368(269)
Zittissa, 198–99
Ziwasra, 196–97
…-sa, 198–99

CPSIA information can be obtained at www.ICGtesting.com
Printed in the USA
BVOW03s2049211013

334084BV00002BA/2/P